W9-BKX-905

Also by Kevin Brownlow

The Parade's Gone By . . .
How It Happened Here

THE WAR THE WEST AND THE WILDERNESS

THE WAR THE WEST AND THE WILDERNESS

KEVIN BROWNLOW

Alfred A. Knopf • New York • 1979

THIS IS A BORZOI BOOK
PUBLISHED BY ALFRED A. KNOPF, INC.

 Published in the United States by Alfred A. Knopf, Inc., New York. Distributed by Random House, Inc., New York.

Since this page cannot legibly accommodate all acknowledgments for illustrations, they appear on pages xi–xii.

Library of Congress Cataloging in Publication Data
Brownlow, Kevin.
The war, the West, and the wilderness.
"Sources of the films": p.
Includes bibliographical references and index.
1. Moving-pictures—United States—History.
2. Silent films—History and criticism.
3. European War, 1914–1918, in motion pictures.
4. Western films—History and criticism.
5. Moving-pictures, Documentary—United States—History.
I. Title.
PN1993.5.U6B76 791.43'0973 78–54934
ISBN 0–394–48921–7

Manufactured in the United States of America

First Edition

FRONT ENDPAPER: *Cowboys round up cattle in the Mojave Desert for* The Wind *(1928). Victor Seastrom (center) directing.*

BACK ENDPAPER: Trader Horn *on location in Africa.*

To Merian C. Cooper and Ernest B. Schoedsack

CONTENTS

ACKNOWLEDGMENTS

I owe my fascination with historical authenticity to Andrew Mollo, with whom I have been in partnership, as a film-maker, for many years. This book is a direct result of his influence, although any errors are *my* responsibility! The book has depended upon an unlimited supply of generosity from a great many individuals and organizations: Russell Merritt generously gave me the benefit of his researches and saved me from some dire mistakes. David Bradley put his vast collection of films, books, and knowledge at my disposal, enabling me to see some of the rarest material, as did James Card, formerly of George Eastman House, and William K. Everson, doyen of silent-film historians. David Shepard shared my fascination with documentary, found many of them, and has given me a great deal of help. William Coleman has guided me in my investigation into William Cody. Frank Holland's storehouse of knowledge has been of immense assistance. Without Vicky Wilson, the editor, the book would never have appeared. And special thanks to my wife, Virginia, for inestimable help and encouragement.

The list is long, but I have tried to make it complete. If I have omitted a name, I apologize. To everyone . . . thank you:

Academy of Motion Picture Arts and Sciences
Teddy Adcock
John E. Allen
Norman Alley
American Film Institute
H. J. P. Arnold
Anthony Arthur
John Baxter
Jim Belson
Spencer Berger
Bob Birchard
Jeremy Boulton
Eileen Bowser
David Bradley
British Film Institute
Virginia Brownlow
J. M. Burgoyne-Johnson
John Caesar
James Card
Harry Carey, Jr.
Anthony Cassa
William Coleman
W. Jack Coogan
Dorothy Jordan Cooper
Mary Corliss
Clive Coultass
Sue Craig
Bob Cushman
Bob Davies
Brenda Davies
William Dorward
Allan Dwan
George Eastman House
John Edwards
Bernard Eisenschitz
Eldon K. Everett
William K. Everson
Raye Farr
Films in Review
Anne Fleming
Robert Florey
David Francis
Joan Franks
Annie Gibbs
David Gill
Gillian Hartnoll
Mamoun Hassan
Moya Hassan
Frank Holland
Margaret Holland
Imperial War Museum
Jeremy Isaacs
Philip Jenkinson

Dick and Pauline Jobson
Neal T. Jones
Kathy Karr
Lawrence Karr
Paul Killiam
Barry King
John Kobal
Howard Lamar
Bert Langdon
Betty Leese
Library of Congress
Jack Lodge
Jim Lucas
Tom Luddy
Sue McConachy
Teri C. McLuhan
Karl Malkames
Holly McNeely
David Meeker
Russell Merritt
Lt. Col. George J. Mitchell, Jr.
Paul Mix
Becky Mlynarczyk
William Murphy
Museum of Modern Art
National Archives
National Film Archive
Captain Noel
Mrs. Noel
Linda Olson
Marylea O'Reilly
Barry O'Riordan
Robert Parrish
Lisa Pontecorvo
George Pratt
Charles Phillips Reilly
Julie Richardson
David Robinson
Joseph Rosa
Sam Rubin
Markku Salmi
Richard Schickel
Ruth Rose Schoedsack
Harold Schuster
Sloane Shelton
David and Kim Shepard
Mildred Simpson
Michael Sissons
Anthony Slide
Jack Spears
Paul Spehr
Charlotte Staub
Sun Valley Center
Liz Sutherland
Thames Television
David Thaxton
John Thayer
King Vidor
Alexander Walker
Marc Wanamaker
J. P. Ward
Derek Ware
Tom Webster
Herman Weinberg
Janice Weiss
Chris Wicking
Jim Wilde
Vicky Wilson
Mike Wooller

And my gratitude to all those who gave me interviews:

Lucien Andriot
Dorothy Arzner
B. R. Brookes-Carrington
Karl Brown
Douglas Burden
Yakima Canutt
Olive Carey
Charles Clarke
Iron Eyes Cody
Dorothy Jordan Cooper
Merian C. Cooper
Allan Dwan
Robert Florey
George Folsey
Ted French
Lillian Gish
Henry Hathaway
Joseph Henabery
Errol Hinds
R. Lee Hough
Al Hoxie
Lucien Hubbard
Mrs. Buck Jones
Leona Kelly
Henry King
Emery Kolb
Jesse Lasky, Jr.
Rowland V. Lee
Bessie Love
Colonel Tim McCoy
Teri C. McLuhan
Enid Markey
Sam Marx
Lewis Milestone
Victor Milner
Captain Noel

L. William O'Connell
Harvey Parry
Harry Perry
Hal Roach
Alfred Santell
Ernest B. Schoedsack
Ruth Rose Schoedsack
Harold Schuster
P. J. Smith
George Stevens
Valerie von Stroheim
Eddie Sutherland
Blanche Sweet
Phil Tannura
Lowell Thomas
V. Tourjansky
Stella Court Treatt
King Vidor
Raoul Walsh
Gilbert Warrenton
John Wayne
Grant Whytock
Irvin Willat
Lois Wilson

If you spot mistakes, I would be very grateful if you would write to me, in care of the publishers, so that I can correct them in any subsequent editions. Thank you!

—Kevin Brownlow

Illustration Credits

Academy of Motion Picture Arts and Sciences: pages 35 (top), 42, 79, 151 (bottom), 251 (top), and 549 (top).
Norman Alley: pages 225 (middle and bottom), 226, 228, 231 (top), and 234 (bottom).
Bob Birchard Collection: pages 298 (bottom), 310–11, and 315 (top).
Brown Brothers: pages 14–15.
Kevin Brownlow Collection: pages 10 (bottom), 17, 19, 23, 26, 29, 34, 44, 56, 58, 67, 71 (bottom), 75 (right), 83, 85, 88–9, 93, 94–5, 97, 100, 105, 107, 109, 110, 114, 117 (top right and bottom), 142, 150 (bottom), 163, 165 (bottom), 170, 173, 174–5, 180, 185 (bottom), 212, 215, 218, 220, 236 (bottom), 241 (top), 242 (bottom), 258 (top), 263, 266 (bottom), 272 (bottom), 282, 291 (bottom), 298 (top), 306 (bottom), 308, 315 (bottom), 318 (top), 328, 333 (top), 336 (bottom), 347, 352–3, 370, 387, 393 (top), 404 (top), 413, 414, 416, 419, 435 (bottom), 439, 451, 477 (top), 493, 517, 518, 519, 520, 521, 524, 527, 528, 530, 533, 535, 536 (bottom), 540, 541, 549 (bottom), 552 (bottom), 561, and back endpaper.
Buffalo Bill Memorial Museum: pages 225 (top), 231 (bottom), and 234 (top).
Yakima Canutt: pages 355 and 356.
Harry Carey, Jr.: pages 292–3, 297, and 300.
Charles Clarke: pages 486 and 489.
Iron Eyes Cody: page 332.
George Eastman House Collection: pages 251 (bottom), 259 (top), and 379 (bottom).
Flaherty Study Center: pages 472 (top), 479, and 513 (top).
Errol Hinds: pages 509, 513 (bottom), 514, and 567.
Al Hoxie: page 294 (top right and left).
Imperial War Museum, London: page 63.
Mrs. Buck Jones: pages 319 (top) and 322.
John Kobal Collection: pages xiv, 7 (bottom), 39, 133, 136, 138 (bottom), 179, 190, 192, 199, 201 (bottom), 216 (bottom), 246, 274, 291 (top), 382 (top), 498, 563, and 565.
Emery Kolb: pages 400 and 422–3.
Jesse Lasky, Jr.: page 241 (bottom).
Bessie Love: page 364 (bottom).
Teri C. McLuhan: pages 339, 340–1, and 342.
George Mitchell Collection: pages ii–iii, 7 (top), 10 (top), 200 (bottom), 216 (top), 238–9, 246 (top), 272 (top), 303 (bottom), 333 (bottom), 389 (bottom), 393 (bottom), 397 (bottom), and 407.

Museum of Modern Art / Film Stills Archive: front endpaper and pages 31 (bottom), 35 (bottom), 69, 71 (top), 91, 118, 138 (top), 146–7, 159, 168–9, 183, 197, 200 (top), 203, 204, 207, 209, 246 (bottom), 247, 262, 285, 294 (bottom left and right), 304, 313, 316 (right), 349, 359, 360–1, 362, 364 (top), 367, 385, 394–5, 412, 417, 428 (bottom), 432 (bottom), 435 (top), 465, 467, 472 (bottom), 477 (bottom), 494, 496, 500–1, 505, 506, and 536.

National Archives, Washington, D.C.: pages xviii, 106, 113, 120–1, 123, 124, 127, and 128.

National Film Archive, London: pages 5, 50, 57, 75 (left), 150 (top), 154 (top), 195, 201 (top), 242 (top), 269, 303 (top), 306 (top), 316 (left), 318 (bottom), 325, 346, 382 (bottom), 389 (top), 409, 508, 543, 544, 547, 552 (top), and 557.

Captain J. B. L. Noel: pages 452, 457, 460, and 463.

L. William O'Connell: pages 31 (top), 117 (top left), 165 (top), and 166.

Harry Perry: pages 319 (bottom) and 336 (top).

Paul Popper Ltd.: pages 427, 428 (top), 431, and 432 (top).

Harold Schuster: page 397 (top).

Science Museum, London: page 49.

David Shepard: page 483.

Smithsonian Institution: page 326.

Thames Television: page 154 (bottom).

Lowell Thomas: pages 442, 445, and 448.

Marc Wanamaker Bison Archives: pages 151 (top), 160, 185 (top), 236 (top), 254, 255, 258 (bottom), 259 (bottom), 266 (top), 369, 371, 375, 377, 378, 379 (top), 398, and 404 (bottom).

Western History Collections, University of Oklahoma Library: pages 276, 279, and 288.

Grant Whytock: page 491.

INTRODUCTION

We are sitting on a celluloid time bomb. The explosive force of a single can of unstable nitrate, we are told, carries the impact of a hand grenade. Virtually all silent film was photographed and printed on this lethal substance. As film archives struggle to transfer their vast nitrate holdings to a safety base, regulations are tightened. Fire departments have declared the casual storage of nitrate illegal. Even so experienced a company as MGM is forbidden to remove more than six cans at a time from its vaults in Culver City. Small wonder that old films are incinerated in ever-increasing numbers.

The nitrate danger may have been over-rated, but because there *is* a danger, the destruction of these films seems sensible to practically everyone. This is a serious matter, for the films being junked are not simply ephemeral entertainment—which would be bad enough. They represent the history of our century, a history that was often captured on celluloid at great risk.

Private collectors and archives struggle to protect what they consider important, but so many films are shrouded in obscurity that their importance to posterity can only be guessed at. A wrong guess, and more precious history hits the junk pile. Entertainment films have been the subject of much analysis and documentation. But what about the films of fact? Often without credits, these obscure documentaries put researchers in a quandary. So few of them have lived up to the high ideals laid down by the followers of Robert Flaherty that historians have dealt with them as severely as the film industry itself, consigning a whole epoch to oblivion. Collectors ignore them. Very few archives preserve them. But so violently does our way of life alter that films once considered dull, dismissed as "educational," can be transformed by the passage of time into priceless relics that recapture our past in an astonishingly vivid manner. And documentary film-making has never been confined to the factual film; it exists in many story films, which, at their best, can present history as faithfully as any newsreel, with the added advantage of emotional involvement.

This book is a journey of discovery through archives, private collections, and stock-shot libraries in search of history on film. I began it with an idea—a theory—and very little more. The idea was simple; I was excited by the documentary aspects of certain silent feature films: *Hearts of the World,* shot in France during World War I, *Isn't Life Wonderful?,* shot in Germany during the collapse of the 1920s, *The Covered Wagon,* with its matchless re-creation of pioneer days, and *Grass,* the amazing record of the migration of a Persian tribe. I guessed that there must be other films with this enthralling alchemy of history and motion picture history. Early Westerns, for instance—were they not much closer to the frontier era? Surely they must have reflected it more accurately than Westerns of later vintage? I found more substantiation for this theory than I could ever have thought possible . . . including a film made in 1908 in a real Western town, featuring a real outlaw, and directed

This portrait of Theodore Roosevelt was part of Paramount's publicity for The Rough Riders (1927). *Roosevelt's impact on the early motion picture was particularly strong.* The Covered Wagon *was dedicated to him.*

by a real frontier marshal. My amazement may seem naive to those veterans of the motion picture industry who knew it all the time, but I am convinced that this collision of history and film history represents more than esoteric filmography. Silent films are becoming more and more widely used—for education as well as entertainment. And it is education, in the widest sense of the word, that will ensure their survival.

Quite outside the area of film appreciation, thousands of people throughout the United States and Europe devote their spare time to the study of a single subject—a subject they find of obsessive interest. Military history, Western history, and the history of exploration are, I believe, the three most popular. These elements also happen to occur most frequently in the American cinema, yet few of the military buffs, the Western enthusiasts, or the students of exploration have considered the value of film in their work. I have structured this book as a triptych to unite these subjects—surprising myself by the coincidence of name and title that results—and I offer *The War, the West, and the Wilderness* to these dedicated historians, hoping it will convey to them some of the excitement, fascination, and enjoyment that so much of their work has given me.

The Roosevelt Connection

In the realm of the silent drama, D. W. Griffith is proclaimed the guiding force, almost the patron saint. Was there a man whose spirit so affected the factual film? I submit there was. Not a film-maker, not even a regular film-goer, but a man whose spirit and example imprinted themselves indelibly upon the minds of the prewar generation: Theodore Roosevelt.

Roosevelt provides a sturdy link between the three sections of this book. His experience as soldier, cowboy, and explorer overshadowed even his years in the White House, giving him a charisma enjoyed by very few politicians. He was the youngest President ever at forty-two. As soon as he was free from the burden of office, he embarked on a hunting safari in Africa. What an impact this had on the factual film! Not only did it inspire Colonel Selig to fake a record of Roosevelt's travels, it popularized the safari for wealthy Americans and led to several important expedition films. But Roosevelt was not only a hunter, he was a conservationist. The very word "conservation" came into common use at this time, and became one of the key issues of the Roosevelt years. It was Roosevelt who created the National Parks. For many years, he expounded Progressivism and social reform, but in later years, Preparedness replaced them in his scale of priorities. This single-minded dedication to national defense led to one of the top-grossing films of the war years, *The Battle Cry of Peace*.

Roosevelt was as responsible as his friends Frederic Remington and Owen Wister for glamorizing the Old West. His sense of showmanship and his heroic image of himself inevitably invited parody. *Terrible Teddy, the Grizzly King*, made by Edwin S. Porter in 1901, showed T. R. firing a rifle into a tree and felling a cat—a domestic cat. Two men who shadow his every move wear placards proclaiming them to be "My Press Agent" and "My Photographer." Among the more inventive parodies was a pioneer cartoon series, *Colonel Heeza Liar*, which took the country by storm and ran for five years, initiating mass popularity for the animated cartoon.

His self-assertive showmanship echoed that of Buffalo Bill Cody, and when Roosevelt formed the 1st Volunteer Cavalry Regiment of cowboys to fight in Cuba, he called them Rough Riders, borrowing the name from Cody's show. (Colonel Cody took back not just the name, but the men themselves, under special arrangement with the government.) Paramount Pictures celebrated this colorful legion with an epic production in 1927, a tribute to the memory of Roosevelt, *The Rough Riders.*

Roosevelt was as much the father of the factual film as the Lumière brothers, for he created a market for the documentary.

In 1910 the film industry saluted Roosevelt's concern for its activities with an article entitled "Theodore Roosevelt—The Picture Man." He lent his name, and often his presence, to films that he considered worthy of his support, such as the 1915 *Spirit of Audubon.* His endorsement was sought as earnestly as an Academy Award. Just before he died, a biographical film was mounted with his cooperation, entitled *The Fighting Roosevelts.* It appeared in 1919, after a war that greatly changed the former President. Newsreels show him urging hostilities before the war and sadly watching the return of troops after it. He suffered greatly, losing a son (Quentin) and ultimately his health. He died in 1919, and such was the affection for Roosevelt, expressed throughout America, that the title of the film was changed from *The Fighting Roosevelts* to *Our Teddy.*

Attitudes have changed violently and this affection is seldom in evidence today; historians have bruised Roosevelt's reputation, charging him with imprinting the worst traits of naked aggression into the American ethos. But admiration and affection were what he inspired in the decades dealt with in this book, and, as a film accurately reflects its time, so, I hope, will the following chapters.

THE WAR
THE WEST
AND THE
WILDERNESS

1

THE WAR

"The peculiar fact for screen history is that the vast experience of the war contributed nothing whatever to the art of the motion picture."

—Terry Ramsaye,
A Million and One Nights

Opposite Page: *Privates Gordon Eikelberry and Charles Painter relax after a day's shooting in the trenches.* (*Signal Corps photograph*)

The motion picture came of age during World War I. Although President Wilson preached neutrality, the industry preferred the charismatic belligerence of his dedicated opponent Theodore Roosevelt, which found a fervent response at the box office.

The propaganda films cast a dark shadow across the cinema's history; they aroused hatred from the audience and disapproval from the White House. Nevertheless, by the time the conflict was over, the film had become a social force. It had grown out of the stage of mild diversion and into an era when life without it was unthinkable.

More than any general or politician, it was a motion picture star who raised morale. Charlie Chaplin was a true war hero, for his films did nothing but good. Other players, too, were held in high regard. Jean Cocteau recalled his surprise at finding in a ruined French village a cellar where people huddled together to watch Pearl White in an episode of *The Exploits of Elaine*.

During the war, military and civilian censors tried to chloroform history. Scenes that might have deflected recruits or assisted spies were destroyed, and with them went a great deal of irreplaceable historical evidence. Yet Great War footage survives in such vast quantities that, like the war itself, no one could hope to see it all. The dramatic films of the time tend to be overlooked because of their lack of documentary data, and yet many of them were packed with it. The newsreels, of course, are the most valuable, and yet they seem strange to modern audiences. In fiction films, silence was often an advantage, persuading the spectator to become creatively involved through his imagination. But in newsreels and factual films, the lack of sound serves no aesthetic function. A vital dimension seems to be missing when a shell explosion wafts across the screen, as silent as a dust cloud. And the fact that cameras were cranked at speeds that varied according to light conditions leads to unfortunate and near-comic results when old newsreels are shown on modern projectors.

They need to be looked at with new eyes. To bring these vitally important historical documents alive, and to relate the factual footage to the fictional, and thus to the attitudes of the time, is the object of this section.

THE BALKANS

The half century of peace in Europe that was shattered in August 1914 seems to have been something of a myth. In October 1912, first Montenegro, then Bulgaria, Serbia, and Greece declared war on Turkey. The prize was Macedonia, and the recently formed Balkan League expected to tear it into sections and divide it among themselves. The Turks, preoccupied with rebellion and invasion on other fronts, gave way. The members of the Balkan League traditionally loathed one another, and quarrels developed over who was to have what. In June 1913, the Bulgarians attacked the Serbs and the Greeks, and the Second Balkan War broke out.

Jessica Borthwick, twenty-two years old, spent a full year in the Balkans, taking motion pictures of the war. Asked why she undertook such a hazardous expedition,[1] she explained it, modestly, as curiosity. Her father, General Borthwick, had been employed by the Bulgarians in the 1880s to reorganize and command the army in Eastern Rumelia. She discovered that being General Borthwick's daughter often helped her to overcome what might have proved insurmountable difficulties. Her experience with a motion picture camera was negligible, and she received three days of instruction from camera manufacturer Arthur Newman before leaving for the front. Her account is full of references to bits falling off her camera, and to the frequent loss of equipment:

"The difficulties of taking cinematograph pictures on the battlefield, especially when you are alone and unaided by any assistant, are, as you can imagine, tremendous. The use of a tripod is a particular embarrassment. Things happen so quickly in time of war that, unless one can be ready with one's camera at a few seconds' notice, the episode one wishes to record will probably be over. During the Serbian war in Macedonia, my tripod was smashed by a shell, and although the camera was intact, the film . . . got hopelessly jumbled up and had to be cut away from the mechanism. . . .

"Another great difficulty was the want of a dark room. One day, while taking films in the Rhodope Mountains, I came to a strange village of wooden huts inhabited by a nomadic race called Vlaques. Something went wrong with my camera, and I tried to make the people understand that I wanted some place which would serve as a dark room. It was impossible to get them to grasp what I meant, however, until eventually I found a man making rugs out of sheeps' wool. After much persuasion, I induced him to cover me up with his rugs, and in this unusual and very stuffy 'dark room' I managed to open my camera in safety. Having no film box with me at the moment, I wrapped the negative up in pieces of paper and stowed it away in my pocket, carrying it thus for fifteen days until I returned to Sofia. Occupied with other matters, I forgot the film and handed my coat to a servant who, being of an inquisitive nature, unwrapped the negative, and finding it uninteresting, put it back in the pocket without the paper, afterwards hanging up the coat to air in the sun. Subsequently I developed the film—and found it one of the best I had.

"The want of a technical dictionary, combined with the natives' ignorance of photography, brought about several rather amusing situations. On one occasion, in

The image of the tough, self-reliant front-line cameraman is belied in the case of Jessica Borthwick, who covered the Second Balkan War at the age of twenty-two.

Adrianople, I lost a screw from my tripod. There were shops of most other kinds, but no ironmongers, and at last, in despair, I tried to explain to an officer what I wanted in dumb show, not knowing the word for 'screw.' Having followed my actions for some moments with apparent intelligence, he suddenly hailed a cab and bundled me hastily in. We drove right across the city, until eventually we entered some massive gates and drew up—inside the prison. However, I turned the misconception to advantage by securing some excellent snapshots and having some very interesting talks with the prisoners. One convict—a German of considerable education—invited me to go and see him hanged the next morning. I saw two executions in that prison.

"During the cholera rage in Adrianople, everything connected with that terrible disease was painted black. The carts in which the dead bodies were carried away were black, for example, as were the coffins in which cholera victims were buried. While the scourge was at its height, I went down into the gipsy quarter to take a film. The people in this part of the city had never seen a camera before, and when they saw me pointing my black box at various objects they thought I was operating some wonderful new instrument for combating the disease which was destroying them. Quickly surrounding me, they came and knelt upon the ground, kissing my feet and clothing, and begging with dreadful pathos that I should cure them. It was a task as sad as it was difficult to explain that their hopes were mistaken, and that I was impotent to help them. . . .

"With regard to the future, I shall leave England in June next for the Arctic regions, where I want to start a colony for the cure of consumption and other diseases. This is the dream of my life. The great open spaces of the North are God's sanatorium, and I believe that, when once their possibilities are known, their value will be recognised. I have been in the Arctic regions before. Yes, I shall take two or three cameras with me, including Mr. Newman's wonderful new hand cinematograph camera. When shall I return? That I cannot say. Perhaps at the end of a year—perhaps never."

PROPAGANDA

A decade before Sarajevo, a European power had lost a war to an Asiatic country because, it was thought, too little attention had been paid to propaganda. The Russian middle classes, its merchants and businessmen, had little to gain from a war with Japan, and without their support, the war effort foundered.

In 1914 the British recognized the need for propaganda, but found the necessity for it somewhat embarrassing. It was therefore developed in conditions of near secrecy. Charles F. G. Masterman, a member of the cabinet, set up his propaganda bureau in Wellington House, Buckingham Gate, London, home of the Insurance Commission. Instead of providing news stories—the job of the Press Bureau—Wellington House concentrated on the production, translation, and distribution of books, pamphlets, and speeches, and the placing of extracts and articles in the world's newspapers and magazines.[1]

The British began the war with an ideal propaganda platform. The German invasion of Belgium was in violation of a treaty, for which the Chancellor, Theobald von Bethmann-Hollweg, apologized: "We were compelled to override the just protests of the Luxembourg and Belgian governments. The wrong—I speak openly—that we are committing we will endeavour to make good as soon as our military goal has been reached."

In the Belgian campaign, the Germans remembered the *franc-tireurs* of the Franco-Prussian War, and were ruthless in dealing with suspected partisans. Every civilian shot or hanged provided the strongest possible anti-German propaganda. The atrocity stories were embellished until journalistic reports became the word-picture equivalents of Hieronymus Bosch paintings. Artists, many of them working for Wellington House, offset the lack of photographic evidence with pictures so horrifying that their publishers, in peacetime, would have risked prosecution.

That the propaganda people should have placed so much emphasis on tales of simple barbarism, when weapons of indescribable ferocity were being used by both sides, now seems ironic. But in a situation of unimaginable horror, familiar horror had to be aroused. The German word *Schrecklichkeit* was translated as "frightfulness" and applied only to the behavior of its originators. As the stories of rape and mutilation proliferated, the Germans became a race apart. The Kaiser might have been a cousin of King George, but he was sired by the devil as far as British propaganda was concerned. The Germans lost their status as Europeans; embodying the most terrifying traits of ancient savagery, they became Huns.

Propaganda apart, it is hard to convey the ingenuousness of the motion picture audiences of 1914. Scientific miracles had appeared at such breakneck speed that the public abandoned its skepticism, and named such phenomena "white magic." Ordinary people accepted that pictures moved, just as we now accept that rockets reach the moon, without the slightest idea how. They knew all about trick pictures, such as photographs of ghosts, yet they believed that the camera could not lie, and that the photographic image represented undistorted reality.

It was therefore a shock when the War Office placed a virtual ban on war correspondents, photographers, and moving picture cameramen. All news was to be filtered through the Press Bureau. The attitude of the authorities appears to have

Propaganda posters fueled the movies, and vice versa; a scene from The Unpardonable Sin *(1918) with Blanche Sweet, directed by Marshall Neilan.*

Charlie Chaplin parodies the propaganda image of the Frightful Hun in his Shoulder Arms *(1918). Despite the impeccable uniform, he still manages to give his boots the insouciant tilt of the tramp.*

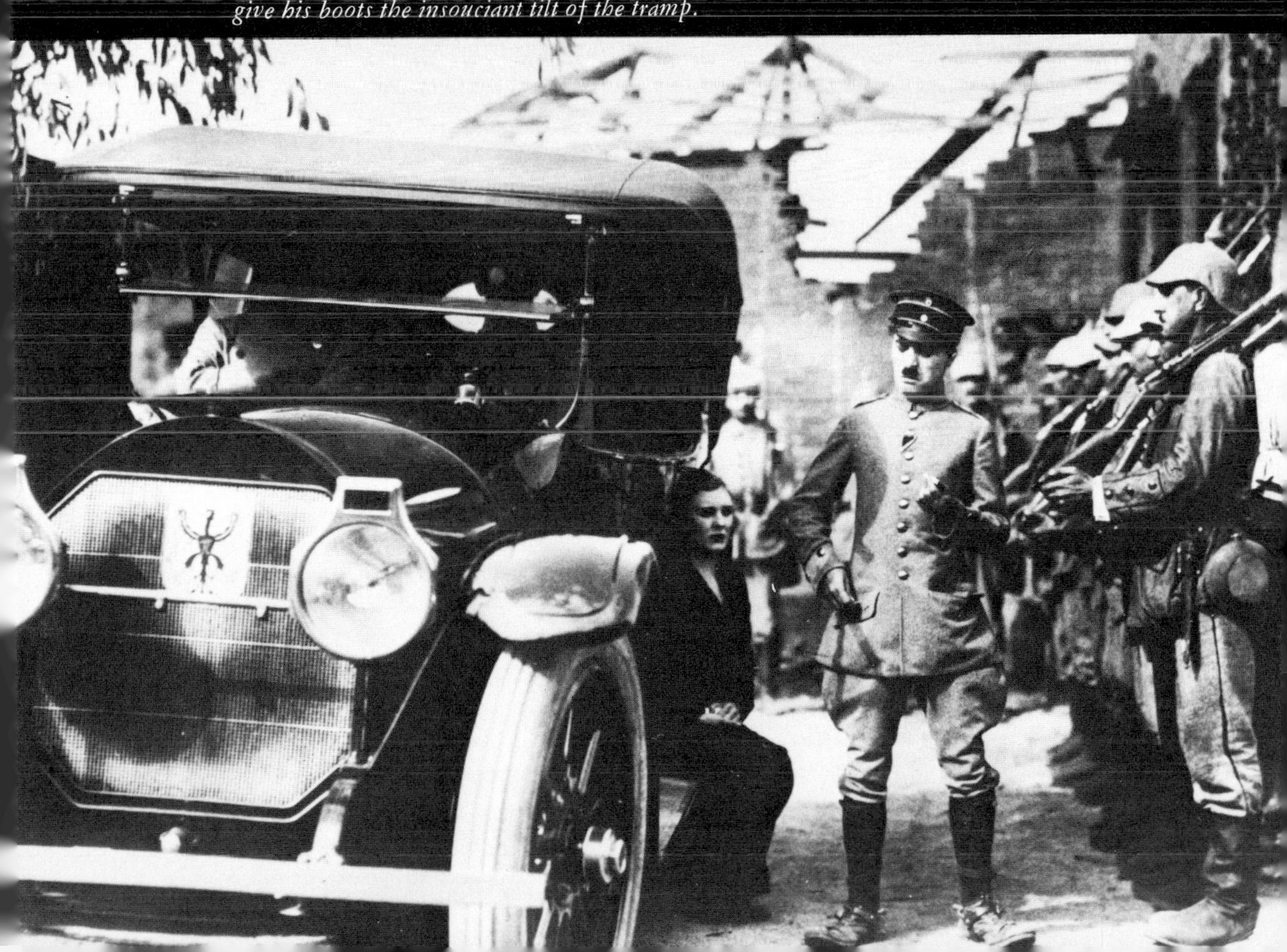

been defensive, the fear of espionage obliterating all other considerations. The cinematograph had been praised by the army for its value in target practice (cameras recorded the effects of gunfire, and a machine was invented that provided moving pictures for riflemen to fire at), but they thought of it simply as a sophisticated toy. A handful of operators were assigned to the War Office, but those without permits were roughly dealt with when they tried to beat the ban.

The penalty for being caught taking photographs at the front was the firing squad. One optimistic young American cameraman, unnamed in contemporary reports but probably Donald Thompson, set out from Paris on a bicycle, with his apparatus slung over his shoulder. On the second day out, cycling nearer and nearer to the sound of gunfire, he found himself surrounded by soldiers. He was immediately taken before the local German command, but the officers merely laughed at his impudence, calling it "American brass." They ordered him away. Next morning he had set up his machine, and was just starting to turn the crank when his camera was knocked over and he was dragged in front of some French officers. During an interrogation, soldiers who spoke German rattled some phrases at him in the hope of taking him by surprise. But the young American was simply bewildered. He was held, and treated, as a spy, until the officers realized he was just a crazy American and he was released, together with his camera. But he was told that no one, not even French correspondents, was allowed within thirty miles of a battle.

The American *Moving Picture World* considered the ban nothing less than a loss to civilization.[2] Theodore Roosevelt declared that this attitude was losing Britain support in the United States. Newspapers were prejudiced, wrote Stephen Bush: "The only real and incorruptible neutral in the war is not the type but the film." Take the alleged German atrocities in Belgium, he said. A committee of prominent Belgians was coming to America to lay evidence of these outrages before the President. If they had a motion picture, the whole question could be proved with finality. "If the reports are false or greatly exaggerated, it would be enough to disprove them by showing the actual conditions in the cities and villages where the wanton destruction is claimed to have occurred. At any rate, the camera would render a service to humanity by giving a true and honest account of things."

Not only did the ban affect the taking of news film, it also prevented exhibitors from showing pictures in any way connected with the current war. Hoping it would all be over by Christmas, renters dug out war films about South Africa and India, and dreamed up new patriotic slogans.

BELGIUM

"In Belgium, the cinema is a thing of the past," wrote Evan Strong. "The cinemas have been converted into hospitals. I was first struck in Brussels by a huge red cross on one closed cinema and, inquisitive, asked if this sort of thing were general. The reply was that all cinemas were being held in reserve for Red Cross work, but that, oh, irony! the German-owned cinemas would be appropriated for this purpose first."[1]

For days, anyone with a camera was threatened with death. Most correspondents gloomily admitted that the chances for photography were zero.

"The authorities put the ban on photography, the mob made it impossible," wrote Strong. "The camera was the badge of a spy, and the mob would tear a suspect limb from limb if the guards did not arrest him first. A friend of mine was arrested twelve times in one day—and he had left his apparatus at home!"

The Germans had just occupied Brussels (on 20 August) when Gaumont cameraman Bertram Brookes-Carrington arrived in Belgium. "You never knew if you were going to run across a German or not," he recalled. "They thought I was a civilian—a Belgian. They wouldn't have thought I was British, otherwise I wouldn't be here. If I saw anything interesting, I took it perfectly openly. No good trying to hide. Try and hide and you arouse suspicion at once."[2]

Nevertheless, Brookes-Carrington narrowly escaped death when he wandered into an area where only Flemish was spoken. He was immediately taken for a spy, and the locals were on the point of hanging him from a lamppost when an officer arrived, who spoke both French and Flemish, and everyone became apologetic.

Even today Brookes-Carrington has no doubts that such spies existed, in considerable numbers. A lot of Belgians, he declared, were pro-German. At one village, it was found that the housewives were signaling to the Germans by the way in which they hung their washing on the lines. Then there was his own grim experience with a spy.

"I was instrumental once in getting a Belgian killed. He was definitely spying for the Germans. He was a sort of freelance cameraman, and he'd come through from the German lines—being a German-speaking Belgian—and meet me. I'd collect a can of negative from him, and give him a fresh roll. He couldn't get film, since the Gevaert factory had been smashed by the Jerries. I took his film home as well as my own. After two or three meetings like that, I thought to myself, 'I don't like it. If he's doing this for us, he may be doing the same for them.' There was a general furtiveness on his part. He didn't seem quite straight. Then I began to put two and two together, and I decided it wasn't worthwhile giving information back to the Jerries for a few feet of picture. So I got him watched. I gave a tip to one or two of the officers I came across. He was shot eventually. Perhaps he didn't deserve it. But there you are, war is war."

Britain's famous animal and bird photographer Cherry Kearton was another of the select handful permitted to make moving pictures in Belgium. He operated the Aeroscope, a portable compressed-air camera with gyroscopic attachment, invented by Kasimir de Proszynski and marketed by Kearton, which weighed only fourteen pounds including 320 feet of film. With this machine hidden under his raincoat he was able to capture intimate shots of refugees and street scenes during hostilities. His one-reel film *War-Stricken Louvain* was released in America in September 1914, and German sympathizers requested the National Board of Censorship to suppress it. Synopses indicate that Kearton's predilection for animals led to an emphasis on scenes of dogs (drawing machine guns), cavalry horses, and carrier pigeons.

"I tried to get pictures of shells exploding while the battle of Alost was on," Captain Kearton told the London *Daily News*,[3] but it was next to useless, for they hardly show on the film. In the trenches, too, it is useless, and rather brutal it

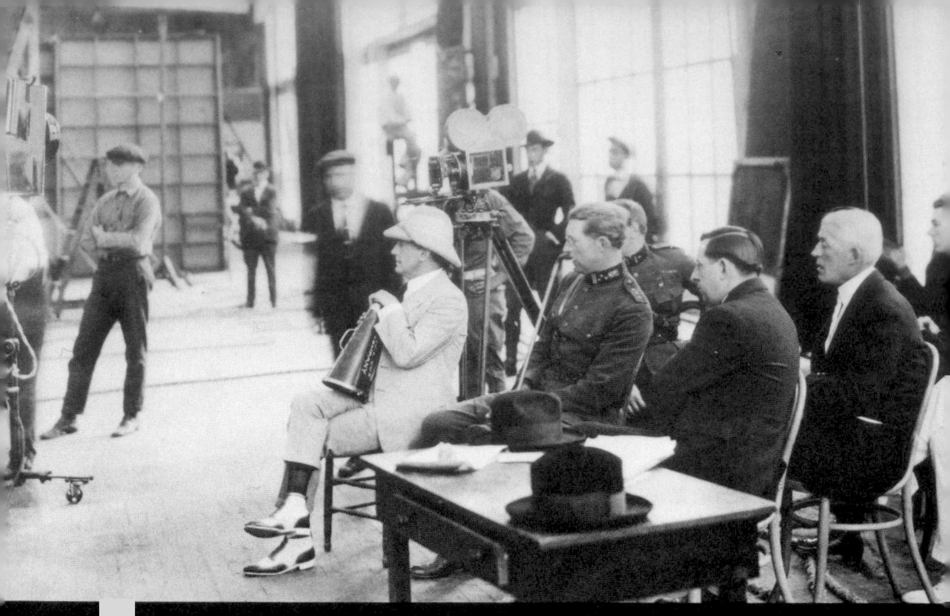

King Albert of the Belgians visits the American Film Company at Santa Barbara. George L. Cox in topee; white-haired William Worthington, right.

A firing squad or a lynching awaited cameramen in Belgium. J. M. Downie, of Universal Animated Weekly, wisely made friends with members of the French cavalry. The camera is a Debrie. (Copied from Moving Picture World.)

seems to me—to try to get pictures. By the time I had finished trying to get pictures of shells exploding among the houses I saw it was time to get out; so I started down the street with a Belgian. One thing was interesting; a dog and a cat followed us, and as the shells burst the dog went dodging about, but the cat never turned a hair. . . . When the war is over, I know a nice quiet place in Central Africa, and I'm going back. This job is too difficult, and it is not very satisfactory working a cinematograph when you would rather work a mitrailleuse [machine gun]."

The Chicago *Daily Tribune* succeeded in a brilliant coup when they signed a special deal with the Belgian government to permit Edwin Weigle to take pictures, the profits from which would go to the Belgian Red Cross. Weigle, who published a sixty-page booklet on his experiences, was able to announce at the end of 1914 that his film on the fall of Antwerp (*On the Belgian Battlefield*) had made $20,543 for the Belgian Red Cross.

J. M. Downie, of the Trans-Atlantic Film Company, the English end of Universal, was another of the successful cameramen who managed to beat the ban. His success was due as much to his personality as to circumstances. "Mr. Downie enjoys a wide circle of friends among the Belgian and French armies. He was not only allowed to move pretty much as he pleased, but some of the army officers assisted him at times, in moving his camera and securing passage through restricted districts."[4] Downie, a young Scotsman, stayed in the besieged city of Antwerp until a few hours before the German occupation.

Donald Thompson had sailed to Europe as a representative of a Montreal paper, but once in the war zone he defected to the Chicago *Tribune* and anyone else who would pay him. He became briefly notorious in trade circles in England when two Belgians initiated a court case against him. Thompson had been commissioned by these two men to shoot front-line action pictures. As soon as he had undertaken the assignment, his camera was seized. He managed to hang on to his film—five thousand feet—and conveniently disappeared. The King's Bench Division in London fined Thompson in his absence the sum of £146, 10s plus costs.[5] Nevertheless, Thompson was to become an important maverick cameraman in various wars and revolutions.

A spectacular scoop was secured by an intrepid Eclair cameraman, Monsieur Bizeul, who deliberately concealed himself in an empty house to film German troops entering Ghent. The fact that he risked being shot as a spy makes his achievement doubly impressive. Bizeul explained:

"During the night of Sunday, all the allied troops left Ghent, and it was officially announced that the Germans were going to enter in possession of the town on the following morning. This did not prevent us from enjoying a good night's rest at the Hotel Gaud, where I was staying. On Monday morning at about 8 A.M. a small patrol of German dragoons and cyclists arrived at the Town Hall, took down the Belgian flag, and hoisted the German standard in its place. This patrol announced to the burgomaster that General von Bessler would arrive at the Town Hall at 11 A.M. I made my arrangements and with great difficulty obtained a room on the second floor of a cafe facing the Town Hall. There I ensconced myself, with my camera carefully hidden, the lens alone passing through a slightly opened window, and I went to dinner, awaiting events.

"About three o'clock the Germans began to march past, and continued to do so until a quarter past four, the procession consisting of a squadron of Dragoons and Death's Head Hussars, followed by about a regiment of infantry, with their convoys, and then the artillery. . . .

"Having taken my film, I heaved a sigh of satisfaction, but this was not all. I must get out of Ghent, not by any means an easy matter. One way only was open to me for getting to England—namely, through Holland."[6]

Bizeul obtained a milk-cart, in which he concealed his films, persuaded a Flemish-speaking guide to accompany him, and suitably disguised in eight days' growth of beard and some old clothes, he set out for Holland. Sentries searched them en route, but they were primarily concerned with weapons. At Mendonck, Bizeul changed over to a dog-cart and acted the part of a refugee. "Without turning a hair, I passed over the Selzaete Bridge, which was guarded by half a score of German sentinels. I then crossed the frontier into Holland, and reached London, thankful to have succeeded in getting away with my films."

H. A. Sanders, the original *Pathé Gazette* cameraman, entered the dining room of his hotel in Ghent just as somebody cried out "The Germans are in the Hotel de Ville!" Panic broke out. Sanders, in possession of British papers and a Pathé camera, had to make a rapid decision. The attitude of the German authorities toward cinematographers without permits had not yet been ascertained. And, said Sanders, he wasn't going to be the first to find out. Accompanied by a *Daily Sketch* reporter and two Belgian soldiers who jumped aboard the car and refused to leave it for love, money, or threats, Sanders and his driver raced out of Ghent. On the hood of the car fluttered a Union Jack, a cause for concern when they encountered a German cycle patrol.

"Again flight was the only thing to be done in the circumstances," wrote Sanders, "and our chauffeur, who was in as great a state of panic as a man could be, dashed by with the total disregard for brakes, ditches or humanity that only fear can engender. Immediately we had put a safe distance between us, I jumped out, took off the Union Jack and jettisoned all our souvenirs, including a German rifle, into the canal. When the Belgians, who were standing near, saw these trophies they thought we were the real thing and implored us not to shoot.

"We passed company after company of troops. They were the retreating army, but we didn't know they were until some hours after. At Ostend, we found the whole population had been warned of the approach of the Germans. I saw there scenes so pitiful and of such great pathos that I cannot give any adequate idea of them."[7]

Brookes-Carrington found thousands of Belgians trying to get aboard four or five ships. "They were screaming, shouting and jostling. I thought to myself, 'this will show the people of England exactly what's happening here.' I selected an elevated position, put the camera and tripod up and started shooting. I got booed and sworn at—God knows what—until I managed to explain that the reason for taking them was to show the people of England what *they* were suffering, and to ensure them a good welcome. I got out of it that way, but they didn't like it.

"I got away from Ostend in a rowing boat and was picked up outside the harbour by an American steamer carrying grain. She anchored off Dover. They put me in a ship's boat and rowed me ashore. I landed on the beach, with my camera and a very small tripod in a big Gladstone bag, said goodbye to the chaps, walked into town to the station and came back to Victoria. And nobody said a word to me. I could have been a spy as easily as anything. That was one of the most extraordinary things I encountered in the entire war."

Despite the ban on war photographers, despite the paucity of graphic pictures of the campaign, the Universal Film Manufacturing Company announced in September 1914 that it would send a team of eight cameramen to the front. Their London representative, John D. Tippett, pleaded with them to think again about the operation, as it meant a man's life to take pictures in the war zone.

"You have no conception of conditions across that channel," he wrote, "absolutely no conception. I do not care what the American papers print, it is just twice as terrible."[8]

Anything shown in America, declared Tippett, was a fake. He explained how, even if a man were permitted to set up his machine at the front, the enemy would assume he was operating a newfangled gun and would shell him.

"You received a subject from me a short time ago of some prisoners at Bruges. Well, that cost me altogether between $700 and $800, for I have had two men in Belgium from the very first, and good men, too. They were half of the time in jail and finally managed to leave there the other day, with the loss of a lot of film and I think a camera as well. I understand some officers have given orders to kill every English correspondent, and many of them have made a practice of killing any person caught with a camera, irrespective of who he is. The story has never been told as to what has happened during the last few weeks in Belgium, and men from America, and people from other neutral governments, have disappeared and will never be heard of again."

AMERICAN CAMERAMEN WITH THE GERMANS

The Allies sacrificed an enormous propaganda victory by their extended ban on war correspondents. They drove the cameramen from neutral America into the arms of the Central Powers, whose own ban was soon relaxed. It is a tragedy for history that no one interviewed these cameramen in any depth when they were still active. If any are still alive, they live in the deepest obscurity, and despite attempts to trace them with the help of camera guilds and union locals, I have had no success. However, I did come across a fragmentary account of Albert K. Dawson's work in the Galician campaign in a little-known book called *The Cameraman* by Francis A. Collins.[1] Dawson went to Europe in November 1914 for the American Correspondent Film Company (two of whose organizers were later imprisoned for their allegedly pro-German activity).

"I had spent ten days," Dawson told Collins, "in travelling from the Carpathians to join the forces bombarding Przemysl. My army pass permitted me to ride on any means of conveyance as long as there was room. Sometimes I travelled by train, but most of the distance was covered tediously in army wagons. My tent

ASTORIA
Kapitän Kleinschmidts
Polarjagden
ASTORIA

As the first troops leave for the front in 1914, they pass pitchmen advertising Captain Kleinschmidt's Polar Hunt. *So successful was this film that Kleinschmidt became the only American cameraman permitted to travel with the Austrian General Staff. He was arrested upon his return to the United States.*

was finally pitched with the artillery shelling Przemysl. It was hardly a tent but rather a very crude shelter made with barrel hoops covered with blankets, but it kept the worst of the weather off for a couple of weeks.

"The range was about four miles so that our camp was continuously under fire. I was able to make moving pictures of the men bringing up the great siege guns, the work of setting them up, and the actual bombardment. Some of the guns were only a few feet from my tent and the shock of the reports was deafening. Like all the soldiers, I had to go about with my ears stuffed with cotton. This lasted for days until the forts of Przemysl fell and we rushed forward to find that the great fortifications of steel and solid masonry had been turned upside down by the bombardment."

Dawson apparently preferred the front line to working among refugees. Women and children, he told Collins, crowded about his camera, begging him to protect them from shellfire until he could stand their entreaties no longer and asked permission to go to the rear.

When the four-reel *The Battle of Przemysl* was shown in America, its advertising exploited the antipathy that existed then for the old Russia: "Smashing the armies of the Tsar!" wrote *Moving Picture World*. "To a degree, of course, the picture tends to glorify the prowess of the Teutonic allies. It could not be otherwise, for Cameraman A. K. Dawson was one of them during the campaign in Galicia. But an audience which is totally out of sympathy with the motives behind the armies of the Kaiser and Archduke Frederick may overlook the political significance and marvel at scenes which so graphically suggest human suffering and military resourcefulness. Cameraman Dawson frequently risked his life in the making of this picture and for a crowning achievement photographed an actual battle—the capture of a town. It seems safe to suppose that these scenes in the concluding reel have never been equalled."[2]

The full film has been lost, and all that remains of the unusual sequence referred to in the review is a frame enlargement (reproduced opposite). It looks suspiciously like a specially staged scene, for the camera is in a position commanding an excellent view of the assault, and the explosion appears to be simulated. Dawson, however, claims that he anticipated the charge and set up his camera in the shelter of a heavy stone wall. After several hours of waiting, the advance occurred, and Dawson captured his unique footage. Before he could return to safety, the Russians defending the fortress found the range. The wall collapsed, and stone and dust and shrapnel rained about him. Dawson says he grabbed his camera and outran the soldiers in the retreat.

Przemysl first appeared in the headlines in 1914, when a garrison of 120,000 Austrians was isolated in the town, guarded by one of the most modern and heavily armed fortresses in Europe. Its strategic importance included a railway junction linking Cracow, Lemberg (Lvov), and the middle Vistula. The Russians bombarded Przemysl for six months before the town surrendered on 22 March 1915, a large number of its inhabitants having died of hunger.

During the siege, the main motion picture operator was George Ercole, half Irish and half French, who was employed by Pathé Frères. He won renown for filming a Russian cavalry charge, which, in the early days of the war, was regarded as the finest achievement of a front-line cameraman. When the Austrians began shelling the Galician town of Tarnow, about eighty miles from Przemysl, Ercole rushed over to film it. A shell exploded near him, wrecked his camera, and some of the fragments buried themselves in Ercole's shoulder. Newspapers declared he continued cranking until he dropped unconscious by his machine. He was mentioned in dispatches, and later decorated by the Czar with the St. George's Cross.

John Allen Everets, an American, accompanied the German armies in the East and, like Dawson, covered the recapture of Przemysl for the American Correspondent Film Company. His account in *Motion Picture Magazine*[3] is one of the most vivid and convincing by a cameraman.

He traveled by wagon train. The wagons, he said, were similar to prairie schooners, but smaller, and drawn by a pair of sturdy little horses to whom a monument should be erected after the war. The front was running away from his camera at twenty kilometers a day. Exchanging the wagons for a fast army auto, Everets found himself subjected to shellfire, before he reached the Corps *Kommando,* where he was received with "the greatest courtesy" by General Martine.

"I could hardly sleep that night. At two o'clock I woke up and looked out. The rain poured down, so I decided to go back and sleep. Bang! The earth shook and I awoke with a start. It was five-thirty and the play had begun. I got on my way as quickly as I could get a wagon.

"They were beginning to speed up, and I got some real pictures. The earth trembled. Leaves and branches were blown off by the pressure. Brick walls fell

American cameraman A. K. Dawson, with an entire army at his control, films Austrian troops storming Przemysl—the simulated explosion suggests this was re-enacted shortly after the actual event. The propaganda value of such motion pictures led to the imprisonment of his employers when America entered the war. (*Copied from* The Cameraman)

apart; the air was full of noise. Soon the pieces, further forward, began to join the concert. I had no time to lose. I had to press further forward where I could see the shells fall. . . .

"My way wound up a hill. I noticed another noise, much more unpleasant than any I had heard, and coming from the shells which were thrown toward us. Boom! Boom! Two shells struck the road ahead of us. You could hear the devils coming through the air but you never knew where they were going to strike until it might be too late. Two more landed to the right of us. Every moment I expected to be hurled into the air, but at length I reached the field batteries in safety. Here the din was increased by the constant firing of fifty guns. I found an officer and succeeded in making him understand where I wanted to go. He just pointed ahead and said 'Up the hill.'

" 'Up the hill' seemed a million miles off, and impossible to reach without being hit by the Russians, but I decided that having come so far I must go on. . . . There was little to see. The mortar batteries behind me made such a noise at every shot that I thought my ears should burst. Further forward, the field batteries had raised their more feminine voices. Occasionally, a shell would come uncomfortably close, making me wince. A look at the driver, who calmly disregarded everything except his horses, made me feel ashamed to show I was afraid. At last we arrived at a clump of trees in safety, where a reserve ammunition train was standing. An officer came forward and eyed me with suspicion. 'What business had I there?' 'Where was I going?'

"I showed him my permit and explained that I desired to go where I could see the fortifications. 'You must leave the wagon here,' he ordered. 'The road further up is under fire and you will be better off walking.'

"Extremely consoling, I thought him, and at the moment I wished I had never seen the front. He gave me two men to help carry the apparatus and we started. . . . The two soldiers did not come along fast enough to suit me, and it seemed an eternity before we reached the crest of the first hill."

Here, Everets found himself in a wooded valley away from the point where he wanted to be. He caught a glimpse of the village of Krazizyn, within easy reach of the Russian batteries, where the peasants were still working in the fields, oblivious of the artillery duel. The camera team came under direct fire again, and took refuge in the woods. Finally, they came to an eight-cornered earthwork, which turned out to be the observation post for the concentration of Skoda mortars.

"A glance at the nature of my post showed me that it was impossible to use my camera tripod. The only places permitting the exposure of the camera were apertures dug in the dirt wall for observation purposes. I built a crude stand of logs, and set my camera upon it, bringing the lens as close as possible to the narrow little window. The pictures were all made from Oberstleutnant Rittner's observation-hole, from which he had been watching the breaking of the Austrian shells on the outer works of Przemysl. This gave me a clear, unobstructed view. For three hours I heard nothing but the ear-splitting yelps of shells, but I had a chance to make dandy pictures, and ground away until I had 'shot' a thousand feet of good Kodak film."

Everets said that he was hardly afraid at all when actually filming; in fact, he never realized the danger he had been in until Przemysl had fallen, and he had

Capturing The Kaiser

DONE BY AN AMERICAN NEWSPAPER MAN. HIS MAJESTY WAS NOT ONLY CAPTURED, BUT CANNED.

By Harry C. Carr

Durborough set up his machine about thirty feet away from the Kaiser's car and began grinding away for dear life.

LEFT: *W. H. Durborough in action with the German Army. At a military review Durborough took pictures of the Kaiser without permission—causing gasps from the assembled officers. (Copied from* Photoplay)
RIGHT: *Captain Kleinschmidt poses in Austrian officer's uniform and aviator's helmet. This photograph, from* Moving Picture World, *did not help Kleinschmidt's case at the time of his arrest. He sold some of his front-line footage to D. W. Griffith for* Hearts of the World.

visited the wrecked fortress. "Horrible sights. The dead lay in heaps. The men had tried to get their guns away, but had been caught in a rain of iron that had torn craters twenty metres wide in the landscape and scattered death everywhere."

Harry Carr, of the Los Angeles *Times*, and already a motion picture scenario writer,* watched the Austrian assault of another fortress, Novogeorgievsk, during his travels with German troops. He was one of a party of fifteen correspondents in the charge of two German staff officers, "who fussed over us like a couple of old hens with a brood of ducklings." Warsaw had just fallen to the Germans, and the correspondents were rushed out to see the final stages. For several days they watched the Austrian howitzers pounding the fortress; then one morning an agitated orderly woke them to say that the fortress had fallen (19 August 1915), and they were to start at once for the scene. Carr wrote:

"I never believed they intended us to see it, but we accidentally bumped into the most majestic of military ceremonies—a Kaiser review. The troops which had taken part in the battle were assembling on the battlefield when we got there. It was a splendid picture. The fortress was on fire against the sky. Down one road filed a long procession of Russian prisoners marching to the rear. Down another road trundled the big guns that had driven the Tsar out of Poland. In the middle

* Later D. W. Griffith's press agent.

of a great hollow square of troops stood the War Lord, leaning on a little cane, addressing his soldiers. Behind him were his Field Marshals, von Hindenburg, von Baseler, von Falkenhayn, and his sons Prince Eitel Fritz and Prince Joachim.

"W. H. Durborough, a cameraman from one of the on-the-spot press associations, begged our officer to let him slip between the files and shoot a picture. The worthy captain looked as though he was going to faint at the suggestion.

" 'Aw, just for a minute' pleaded Durborough, pathetically, but the captain had turned from him to a correspondent who had lit a cigar. 'One does not smoke at a Kaiser review,' he said, in a thunderous stage whisper.

"Finally, the ceremony came to a close. 'Adieu, Comrades!' cried the Kaiser. 'Adieu, Majesty!' they shouted back. The ranks fell back; the square opened. The Kaiser strode back to his auto and climbed in. Spying Dr. Sven Hedin,* the famous Swedish explorer, in the crowd, the Emperor beckoned him to the car. This was more than Durborough could stand. He suddenly broke away and we saw him running full tilt across the cleared space that the awe of the soldiers had left around His Majesty. Our captain was too much overcome to follow. To the frozen horror of the whole German army, Durborough set up his machine about thirty feet away from the Kaiser's car and began grinding away for dear life.

"The Kaiser looked up and took in the whole situation with his quick, comprehending eyes. He laughed and lit a cigarette, talking a little while longer, we believe, to give the plucky Yankee boy a chance.

"Finally, the Emperor and Dr. Hedin shook hands; the chauffeur of the car threw in the hop, and the Imperial auto started with a leap.

"As it went by, Durborough took off his hat and said with honest sociability, 'Much obliged!' The Kaiser straightened up and one gauntleted hand rose to the visor of his helmet in salute to the American boy who had the nerve to snap an Emperor without asking permission."[4]

The Arctic explorer and pioneer film-maker Captain Kleinschmidt wrote from the Austrian front line to *Moving Picture World,*[5] which expressed amazement at the idea of a plain American traveling with the Austrian General Staff.

Kleinschmidt's letter explained how he had brought off this coup. "Upon my arrival at the Great Headquarters of the Austrian Army, I was invited by the Crown Prince to give a lecture on my last Arctic Expedition and show my moving pictures to the officers of the General Staff. This lecture gave me the magic key that unlocked all doors and gave me privileges and opportunities to accomplish things."

Kleinschmidt wrote of Austrian hospitality, and "the Austrian readiness to help and favour you" and compared it to the hospitality he encountered among the prospectors in their cabins and on the trail to Alaska. The Austrians might not have fought any battles for the benefit of the camera, but they were willing to go to great lengths to be helpful to Kleinschmidt.

"Last week, while I was in the foremost trenches, and took pictures of the Russian trenches only 300 yards away, a whole battery was ordered to cover the Russian trenches with shrapnel to enable me to take pictures of the exploding bombs. Troops of cavalry have been alarmed for me, fliers have taken me up to

---

* Hedin appears as "a friend of Germany" in many Nazi newsreels (Clive Coultass). He also made a remarkable travel film, released in 1929: *Through the Death Deserts of Asia.*

take pictures from above; in fact, everything has been done for me that could possibly be done, even the huge mortars that destroyed the forts of Antwerp, Liege and Namur were ordered to be set in action for me, although even one shot costs a pretty sum of money."

So enthusiastic was Kleinschmidt about his material that he said he could stay with the work throughout the war, scarcely duplicating a scene, since a fresh aspect appeared every day.

"A modern battlefield really shows little or nothing, and the real scenes are diametrically opposed to the usual 'posed' battle scenes with which our public has been regaled so much. In real life, a man who has been hit by a bullet does not throw up his hands and rifle and then fall in a theatrical fashion and roll a few times over. When he lies in the trenches and is hit he barely lurches a few inches forward or quietly turns over on his side."

The real picture might not be as dramatic as the fake picture, said the captain, but he felt that the grimness of the genuine scene would grip the audience far more strongly than the fake. One could see better animal pictures taken in a zoo than he had taken at such risk in the wilderness, but the public appreciated the difference.

The reviewers singled out one scene, which went some way to prove Kleinschmidt's point. "The camera was evidently in a protected position in the trench," wrote Peter Milne in *Motion Picture News,*[6] "and consequently it has been able to catch the soldiers dropping one by one, wounded and sometimes killed."

One of the main problems of the roving cameraman in front-line areas was obtaining raw stock. "Films," Kleinschmidt said, "are a rare article here. The Eastman films have been out of the market for four months, and I have had much trouble obtaining the German Agfa material. The life of a camera is short; the strain is something terrible. The jolting over littered streets, on horseback or jumping ditches and kicking around barbed wire entanglements loosens every screw and breaks the bolts. When you ride with an Uhlan regiment, all young horses that shy at every shell and trench, and you succeed in getting out your camera at the psychological moment only to find it a pitiful ruin, you begin to realise the meaning of the phrase 'swearing like a trooper.' I have an Aeroscope, worked with compressed air instead of a crank. It is a delicate and fine apparatus—whenever it works. I took some nice pictures from an aeroplane with it, but most of the time it has the habits and propensities of the automobile of twenty years ago."

Kleinschmidt traveled later in 1915 to the Italian front and upon his return to America presented the film under the title *War on Three Fronts.* The profits, he announced, would go directly to the German-Austro-Hungarian Relief Association, not perhaps the most tactful proposal in late 1916. Nevertheless, his film was marketed by Lewis J. Selznick, although as America entered the war, *Moving Picture World* considered that any exhibitor who displayed the subject "would be buying a riot."[7]

Captain Kleinschmidt was arrested on 24 November 1917, not on the charge of distributing enemy propaganda—a charge that could have been leveled against Selznick—but on the rather more feeble count of possessing a loaded revolver. *Moving Picture World* did nothing to help its old friend, declaring "the sub-titles and the accompanying lecture by Captain Kleinschmidt were of the sort to please the most pronounced pro-German and pro-Austrian."[8]

D. W. Griffith returned from the battlefields of France without the vital German footage he needed, and he purchased Kleinschmidt's film for $16,000.[9] The hard-won action footage seemed destined for a degree of immortality in *Hearts of the World*, but Griffith was advised not to touch it, for fear of besmirching his reputation. Nevertheless, he used one or two shots. The rest of the material, a priceless record, vanished into oblivion.

NEUTRALITY

The war in Europe took the United States completely by surprise. President Wilson requested audiences in movie theaters not to show support for one side or the other.* "The war," he said, "is one with which we have nothing to do, whose causes cannot touch us."[1]

"If it is true that no war pictures may be shown in London," wrote Stephen Bush to *The Bioscope,* "you have particular reason to congratulate yourselves. The market here has been flooded with so-called war pictures which are nothing more or less than badly executed dupes of old and scratched positives that have been culled from weekly animated gazettes and pictures of manoeuvres. The curious part of it all is the hunger with which even this poor stuff is swallowed by the public. Even the simplest mind and the poorest pair of eyes must see that the pictures are wretched dupes, the scenes are all blurred, indistinct and weak, but they seem to hold the attention of the populace."[2]

Despite the heat wave that had swept over much of the country during August, motion picture theaters were doing greatly improved business in 1914. By sheer coincidence, a George Kleine import called *When War Threatens* was in release at the outbreak of war. Within a month virtually all New York theaters were running some kind of war picture—*War Is Hell, With Serb and Austrian, The Battle of Waterloo, The Tyranny of the Mad Czar,* and *The War of Wars* ("the Franco-German invasion of 1914—the kickiest two-hour show ever").

Examining the trade papers of the time, one is struck not by concern or alarm about the war, but by the callous glee with which exhibitors and producers greeted this threat to rival concerns. "So far as this company is concerned," said Lewis J. Selznick, "the turmoil in Europe would not be at all for the worse."[3]

But when making pictures about the war, producers were cautious. The President's policy of neutrality kept open Central European markets in theory, even if the British blockade was gradually closing them in practice. Besides, it was felt that modern war could not last more than a few months. A feature film of quality required time, and although Universal's short *Be Neutral* was allegedly rushed out in forty-eight hours to support the presidential plea,[4] a more elaborate production demanded eight to twelve weeks from scenario to release. By that time the war in Europe might be stale news.

---

* By 1916 movie theaters were sometimes wrecked by fights between, for example, the Austrian and Italian communities.

The gleeful callousness of this advertisement typifies the attitude of certain producers in America to the European war. (From Moving Picture World*)*

The most tragic and ironic release of 1914 was *Lay Down Your Arms,* a Danish-made production of Baroness Bertha von Suttner's novel on the horrors of militarism.* It had been intended to form part of the program at the Peace Convocation to be held in Vienna during the summer of 1914. Desperate for war movies, New York exhibitors ran it anyway.

TERROR WEAPONS

The Vitagraph Corporation of America, one of the most prosperous of the early studios, was controlled by a triumvirate: Albert E. Smith, J. Stuart Blackton, and William T. Rock. All three were British born, and although immensely loyal to America, they were convinced that her role lay in fighting alongside the Allies in the cause of Civilization. Vitagraph became an unsolicited output of Wellington House. Later in the war Blackton embarked on a series of films based on the novels of Sir Gilbert Parker. Parker was Director of Propaganda at Wellington House, with responsibility for America, and when he visited America he stayed with Blackton and issued highly complimentary statements about Blackton's work.

Warfare in the Skies was an early example of Vitagraph's "frighten-them-to-death" pictures—so early that it was completed before the war began. Nevertheless, it featured the bombardment of America from the air. When this picture was released, in August 1914, the *War Illustrated* noted that none of the sensational expectations of the destructive action of aircraft had yet been fulfilled. "The bombs dropped by German airmen have ruined a few peaceful buildings in Belgium, but when launched at troops in action, they have done less harm than a shell from a quick-firer."[1]

Before the appearance of the tank, the armored car was presented as a weapon of uncanny power. In a three-reel British drama made by Clarendon in 1915, *Under the German Yoke,* a Belgian family is saved from execution by the arrival of British armored cars. "The way they rush through the valley, firing right and left," said the *Kinematograph Weekly,* "is particularly effective, and shows in a realistic manner the deadliness and power of these modern moving fortresses."[2]

The Zeppelin, a vast, cigar-shaped airship which bombed England in night raids, was more effective as a terror weapon, although the damage caused by the bombs was not very great. Even with the help of searchlights, it was out of the question to film the Zeppelins at night, and so a 335-foot film entitled *The Strafer Strafed* was produced by Percy Smith in 1916:

"First of all we are shown the giant Baby Killer embarking at dusk on its murderous mission. It arrives over London. The slender searchlights nervously probe the inky darkness, and the airship suddenly flashes into view, like a steel-bright bolt caught in their long, straight fingers. As it eludes their grasp again, a diamond shower of shrapnel bursts around it. Anon, like some prodigious flying-fish it spawns its fiery eggs into the night beneath. And then comes the turn of the Zep-

* *Die Waffen nieder!* (1889), published as *Lay Down Your Arms* (London, 1892).

pelin-killer, whose deed of immortal heroism has aroused the whole world to wonder. The new St. George strikes the new aerial dragon with his flaming dart. A point of light gleams in the heavens. It glows like a monstrous star, growing bigger and fiercer each moment, until the whole sky seems ablaze and the overhanging mist is drenched with the blood-red reflection. Subsequently, by the cold light of dawn, we inspect the ruins. Nothing is left of the vast night-bird but a few grey bones."[3]

All of which was a profound tribute to Smith's ingenuity, for Smith, later famous for his *Secrets of Nature,* made the film at his home in Southgate using a toy Zeppelin, some cotton wool, and a trail of smoke.

The weapon of war that held especial terror for people in the United States was not so much the aeroplane nor the Zeppelin, with its then limited range, but the submarine. It represented the most disturbing development of modern science. Travel abroad became hazardous, even for citizens of neutral countries. Invasion by massed submarines did not seem impossible.* The U-boat, silent and invisible, preyed on the nerves like the first signs of a plague.

The submarine scare reached epidemic proportions with the sinking of the *Lusitania* in May 1915. In his brilliant and disturbing book *Lusitania,* Colin Simpson proves that the ship was loaded with so much war material that she thoroughly justified the German allegation of "a floating arsenal." America's neutrality was heavily weighted in favor of the Allies, for German liners were interned in New York harbor as "auxiliary cruisers" while very few British passenger ships left the United States without war materials. The U-20 fired one torpedo at the *Lusitania,* which was not enough to sink her. Following the initial impact, a second, far more devastating explosion occurred, which ripped the hull from stem to stern. The ship sank in eighteen minutes, with the loss of 1,198 lives. The implication Simpson draws from the Admiralty's behavior over the incident was that the *Lusitania* was deliberately sacrificed to bring America into the war.

Among the passengers were several closely connected with motion pictures. Edgar Hounsell, of Midland Exclusive Films, Birmingham, described his experience[4] for *Kinematograph Weekly:* Hounsell and his associate Edward Barry were finishing lunch when they heard the dull thud, followed by a loud explosion.

"Immediately she was struck, the ship listed over. All the plates and dishes and glasses rolled off the table. The women started to scream and there was a general rush to the upper deck. Had they made for their state rooms and put on their life-belts I feel sure a great many more lives would have been saved."

Hounsell waited until the rush was over, then went for his life-belt. He reached the upper deck too late for any lifeboat. As the ship went down, some of the men started to sing "Tipperary."

"She was torpedoed at 2.10 and my watch stopped at half-past two—about the time I got into the water. I had lighted a cigarette and as I could not swim, I thought

---

* The *Deutschland,* a commercial submarine carrying dyestuffs, visited America in July 1916, proving that U-boats were capable of crossing the Atlantic. Marcus Loew telegraphed a $3,000 offer to Captain Paul Koenig for a three-day vaudeville appearance (New York *Times,* 12 July 1916, p. 9:5). The submarine's arrival was filmed for issue 57 of the *Selig Tribune.*

A survivor of the Lusitania, *actress Rita Jolivet restaged the tragedy for he*
usband's propaganda film Lest We Forget (*1918*).

Sinking of the Veritania, *with Mary Pickford and Bobby Gordon* (*center*)
rom The Little American (*1917*). *Placing America's sweetheart in this situa*
tion made the loss of the Lusitania *all the more vivid to audiences of the tim*

there was not much chance for me. As the ship was going down, I thought I would get clear of the suction, so I jumped off the stern, but the suction pulled me against the side of the vessel and seemed to pin me there. I could not get away, and was dragged down with her, but as she sank bow first, she also turned on one side. This seemed to release me, for though I went down I was not held by the boat. The pressure of the water hurt me, and I had a buzzing sound in my ears. Suddenly, I shot up to the surface again and at such a rate that I rose right out of the water. A second but weaker suction drew me under again, and when I once more came up, I could see no sign of the *Lusitania*."

The sea was covered with wreckage, and Hounsell clung to a piece of timber for an hour. An upturned collapsible boat floated past, and the men on top of it hauled him up. A trawler came to the rescue at six p.m.

Among Edgar Hounsell's luggage on the *Lusitania* were prints of several films, including *Ireland a Nation,* the nationalist film that had caused a furor in New York.

Justus Miles Forman, novelist and author of several motion pictures, was drowned, as was a former president of the World Film Corporation. Charles Frohman, the impresario who had staged the plays of J. M. Barrie, also lost his life. Frohman had recently affiliated himself with Famous Players. The French actress Rita Jolivet was rescued. "Mlle Jolivet gave such a vivid account of her experiences to a prominent producer," said *The Bioscope,* "that it was decided to film the incident, not as a propaganda film, but as a realistic topical drama."[5]

The prominent producer behind the affair was Mlle Jolivet's husband, Count Giuseppe de Cippico, and the director and scenario writer was Leonce Perret, a pioneer with a reputation on both sides of the Atlantic. With such a sure-fire idea, it seems strange that they should have waited for three years; *Lest We Forget* was not released until 1918. By then, the *Lusitania* had been referred to in countless war films, had been the subject of a Mack Sennett comedy and a Winsor McCay cartoon; Kapitän-Leutnant Schwieger of the U-20 had been dead a year, and the *Lusitania*'s captain had been torpedoed for a second time.

Despite *The Bioscope*'s account, the disaster had such a traumatic effect on Mlle Jolivet that for a long time afterward she was unable to talk about it. Eventually, in mid-1917, she began work for the producers, Count de Cippico and J. L. Kempner, who spent $250,000 on the picture, twice as much as an ordinary feature. Lucien Andriot photographed the film, which took six months to make. The water scenes were postponed when cold weather caused one of the actors to be seized with violent cramps—an indication of how so many of the original victims died. Since the war was on and soldiers were no longer freely available for motion picture work, director Perret was at his wits' end to find enough competent riders to play German lancers. A cowpuncher called Texas Cooper agreed to play the captain of the troop, to corral a platoon of exhibition riders, and to charge through the little French village of Rose-sur-Meuse, constructed on the Watson farm in Westchester County.

Rogers Lytton, of the Vitagraph Company, was excused from duty at the military training camp of Plattsburg to play the role of the Baron von Bergen, enamoured of Rita, who begs her not to travel on the *Lusitania.* The picture extended the story to include scenes unacceptable in peacetime; at the end of the film, despite the baron's considerate warning, she ties his head to the bedrail and chokes him to death. "But after the wonderful *Lusitania* scenes," said *The Bioscope*, "most of the incidents savour of anti-climax."[6]

The sinking of the *Lusitania* was so brilliantly reconstructed that reviewers were unanimous in their praise. "A stupendous work," said *The Bioscope*. "Never was there so realistic a reproduction of a great disaster at sea. The producer of these scenes is a genius; it is all real, a real monster liner, with tier upon tier of deck, real boats, real gear, hundreds of supernumeraries, each of whom is a genuine performer. The effect is electric, thrilling, wonderful, enough by itself to make the fortune of the film."[7]

So powerful was this film as propaganda that when Rita Jolivet appeared in person at Waterbury, Connecticut, she sold $258,000 worth of Liberty Bonds. And when it was shown in Geneva, Switzerland, after the war, the German consul protested so vehemently that the *Lusitania* scenes were cut.

To harness the disaster for propaganda was one thing; to re-create the catastrophe on film, without the resources of a studio, was quite another. But cartoons and drawings had played an enormous part in the Allied propaganda campaign. The Central Powers acknowledged their impact. Therefore an animated cartoon film of the *Lusitania* was commissioned.

Winsor McCay, pioneer film cartoonist, produced *The Sinking of the Lusitania* in 1918. The one-reeler consisted of 25,000 drawings, which took twenty-two months to complete and eight days to photograph. Animation at this period was in its formative stage and generally appears quite crude. Certainly the liner, when she appears, is unsteady; the upper decks wobble due to fractionally incorrect registration. But the conception is dynamic and imaginative, and McCay achieves remarkable effects: two fish, swimming placidly along, suddenly dart out of the way of an approaching torpedo. The conning tower of U-20 glides remorselessly toward the camera, its black shape increasing in size—an innovation in perspective usually attributed to the Disney films of later years.

The titles are Standard Propaganda-film Inflammatory: "Germany, which had already benumbed the world with its wholesale killing, then sent its instrument of crime to perform a more treacherous and cowardly offense." . . . "Germany, once a great and powerful nation, had done a dastardly deed in a dastardly way." . . . "The babe that clung to his mother's breast cried out to the world to avenge the most violent cruelty ever carried out on an innocent and unsuspecting nation."

In a short film packed with effective moments, two remain in the memory: the uncanny twisting of the smoke from the four funnels, suggestive in its weird writhing of the appalling destruction below decks; and the final shot of a young mother, in the long dress of the period, holding her baby above her head as she sinks below the waves. This is one of the most potent propaganda images of all the war films,* and it is bolstered by the title:

The man who fired the shot was decorated by the Kaiser.
AND THEY TELL US NOT TO HATE THE HUN!

---

* A strikingly similar image is used by Fred Spear for a poster showing a drowning mother and child and the legend "ENLIST!"

A frame enlargement from Fernfahrt von U-35; *crossing the name of his latest victim from the pages of Lloyd's Shipping Register is Kapitän-Leutnant Lothar von Arnauld de la Perière (left.)*

The sinking marked a turning point in American public opinion. Its appearance in so many American war films—from *Civilization* to *The Kaiser—The Beast of Berlin*—and the controversy that exists to this day demonstrates how a single, symbolic act, once dramatized, can carry far stronger impact than a massive battle with hundreds of thousands of casualties. While it failed to bring America into the war in 1915, it provided a widespread revulsion against the submarine campaign and smoothed the way for the declaration of war in 1917 after repeated sinkings by U-boats.

While a vessel carrying a serial called *Secret of the Submarine* was itself torpedoed off Ireland (the film was rescued, although the fate of the crew was not divulged), the most extraordinary film on submarine warfare was *Fernfahrt von U-35* (*The Distant Voyage of the U-35*). The commander of the U-35 was Kapitän-Leutnant Lothar von Arnauld de la Perière, the son of a French officer captured in the Franco-Prussian War who chose to remain in Germany. De la Perière commanded his first U-boat in 1915, and by the end of the war had sunk 194 ships—453,216 gross tons. This achievement, a record for the war, gave him the kind of reputation on the sea that Richthofen enjoyed in the air. As the Germans filmed Richthofen's squadron, so they installed an official cameraman on the U-35.

Fernfahrt von U-35 is devoted mainly to the last moments of Allied shipping in the Mediterranean, and it contains some sobering shots. In one of them, the camera is set up on the conning tower, looking forward, as a torpedo is fired directly amidships at an ore-carrying ship, S.S. *Maplewood.* The torpedo splashes into the water, churns a white path to the squat merchantman, which erupts with a tall pillar of smoke and water and sinks in less than two minutes. The S.S. *Parkgate* is badly holed after a running fight, and the crew abandons her in lifeboats. A destruction party from the submarine rows across in a small boat, opens safety valves, and places explosive charges in the hold. The submarine's guns fire at the ship to help her on her way. She collapses into the water and, in what the titles claim to be the most remarkable shot ever taken of a ship sinking,* her boilers explode at the moment she sinks beneath the surface.

The schooner *Miss Morris,* bound for Genoa with a cargo of turtles, is lovingly photographed against the light. Then the crew is taken off, together with some of the cargo, and she is sunk under full sail; the camera grinds until the sea is completely calm again. De la Perière calls for Lloyd's Shipping Register, and he sits on the conning tower, surrounded by his smiling officers, places the book on his knees, and ceremoniously draws a line through the name of the vessel he has just sunk.

The material filmed aboard the submarine was so striking it was released in England in 1919 as *The Log of the U-35* and in the United States via Hearst News. The Americans were told that the film had been taken "for the exclusive entertainment of the Kaiser."[8]

Lothar von Arnauld de la Perière commanded the *Emden* between the wars, and in World War II, as a vice-admiral, he was shot down over France and killed on 24 February 1941.

THE BATTLE CRY OF PEACE

Theodore Roosevelt used his powerful influence to ensure the success of one important American film—one that espoused his own passionate cause of preparedness, *The Battle Cry of Peace.* His part in the production was never publicly admitted, and only the unpublished autobiography of J. Stuart Blackton details his involvement.[1]

J. Stuart Blackton was, with Sigmund Lubin, the first of the motion picture millionaires to live in the style now inescapably identified with movie moguls. His share of Vitagraph's profits was so vast that he was able to build Harborwood in Oyster Bay, Long Island, at a cost of $300,000. This Italianate mansion was flanked by the homes of Theodore Roosevelt on one side and Louis Tiffany on the other. Blackton's consuming desire for social recognition was probably due, as Lloyd Morris observed, to the contempt for his source of wealth that prevailed among the upper classes. His appointment as Commodore of the Atlantic Yacht Club led him to adopt that quasi-naval rank, in the style of Commodore Vanderbilt, perhaps to match those titles assumed by his colleagues Colonel Rock and Captain Smith. In the circles in which Blackton now moved, intervention on the side of the Allies was a foregone conclusion, and America's lack of preparedness was a constant topic. If the Allies won, America's interests were safe.

* A distinction that must be given to the sequence of the Austro-Hungarian battleship *Szent Istvan* sinking in the Adriatic, 10 June 1918, with its crew swarming desperately over the hull as the vast ship slowly keels over and disappears. (It appears in the compilation film *Forgotten Men* as the *Blücher.*)

J. Stuart Blackton uses the trenches dug on the Lasky ranch for Hearts of the World *for another war film,* Missing *(1918). L. William O'Connell at camera (far left). James Young directed under Blackton's supervision.*

Hudson Maxim with his brother's invention, the Maxim machine gun, which he called "the greatest life-saving instrument ever invented." From The Battle Cry of Peace *(1915).*

At the home of Hudson Maxim, one evening, Blackton was given a copy of Maxim's book *Defenseless America* (published by Hearst's International Library), which revealed the pitiful state of America's armed forces; the mobile army of the richest country in the world was only twice the size of the New York City Police Department. Blackton decided at once to turn the idea into an epic film. It would be the standard-bearer of preparedness propaganda, to convince Congress and the country of the peril at hand.

Maxim was given a prominent role, playing himself, and issuing graphic warnings of the horrors to come. At this time, Maxim was associated with the E. I. Dupont de Nemours Company, which had received a grant of a million dollars from England to expand the plant capacity of its explosives division. Among the explosives manufactured by Dupont was the Maxim-Schuphauss powder, invented by Maxim—the first smokeless powder to be produced in the United States. He also invented a high explosive for use in torpedoes. Maxim's brother, Sir Hiram Stevens Maxim, was the inventor of the machine gun that bears his name. (*Defenseless America* paid tribute to it with the fractured logic of the preparedness campaign: "The quick-firing gun is the greatest life-saving instrument ever invented.")

Blackton was deeply impressed by the evangelistic aspect of Maxim's book; he also saw a heaven-sent opportunity to garner some of the praise lavished on Griffith, and to cap the financial success of *The Birth of a Nation* with an even more profitable sensation. With the inspired title *The Battle Cry of Peace* he set out to show America what life would be like when the invaders came.

But Vitagraph's other directors, Smith and Rock, objected. Fearing that Washington, with its strict observance of neutrality, would clamp down and stop the exhibition of the picture, they forced Blackton to arrange the financing himself and to use the Vitagraph studio facilities only on a rental basis. (They later relented, and joined Blackton's venture.) In a concentrated burst of activity, Blackton wrote the scenario in three days and nights, and then read it to Roosevelt. Roosevelt was exultant. A few days later, he arranged a gathering of immensely influential people—the mayor of New York, Admiral Dewey, Major General Leonard Wood, Elihu Root, president of the War College in Washington, Brigadier General Cornelius Vanderbilt, of the National Guard—and each expounded on the deficiencies of the defense system. "Put *that* in your picture" barked Roosevelt, after each discourse. The last to speak was venerable Dr. Lyman Abbott, editor of *Outlook:* "I cannot think that all war is wrong. If I did I should not want to look upon a Bunker Hill monument—it would be a monument to our shame! I should never want to speak the name of Gettysburg. I should want to bury in the grave of oblivion the names of Washington and Grant." This comment from the church was a benediction on the production. "Get every word of that in your picture," ordered Roosevelt. "Drive it home to the peace-at-any-price *creatures!*"

LIKE SO MANY APPARENTLY original ideas, *Battle Cry* had a solid ancestry. As early as 1906, Pathé filmed German soldiers marching down the rue de la Paix in Paris. The company drove up early in the morning, staged the scene, and rushed away as the police arrived, for the Franco-Prussian War was still fresh in the memory.

England's vulnerable insularity made her obsessed with the danger of invasion;

literature expressing this fear dated back to the 1870s and that same Franco-Prussian War. Inspired by H. G. Wells's novel of 1908, *The War in the Air,* Charles Urban's *The Battle in the Clouds* (1909) depicted invasion by airship squadrons. In 1906, William le Queux (himself a British agent in World War I) wrote a story called "The Invasion of 1910" about the cruelty of the "Nordener" army as it swept across the English countryside. The 1914 film version depicted the executions of resisters at Beccles, and the last stand of the British Army at Maldon in Essex, where their central position was defended by trenches and barbed-wire entanglements, swept by machine-gun fire. Most films about the Great War featured these elements, but the *Invasion of Britain* was completed by Gaumont *before* the war had broken out. It had been submitted to the British Board of Film Censors with a futuristic title, *The Raid of 1915,* and had been rejected as offensive to a foreign power—precisely the fate Vitagraph feared for *Battle Cry.* With the declaration of war, it was released, with alterations, as *If England Were Invaded.*

When *Battle Cry* was released in England, Blackton's title was changed to *An American's Home,* in deference to a celebrated prewar stage play, *An Englishman's Home* by Guy du Maurier, which had been filmed by J. B. McDowell's British and Colonial Kinematograph Company in 1914.* *An Englishman's Home* described what happened to Mr. Brown and his family when the Germans arrived; the high spot of the drama occurred when Mr. Brown, exasperated by the behavior of the invaders, exclaims "I'll go and fetch a policeman!"

The idea of witnessing one's worst nightmare taking shape on the screen has always been irresistibly compelling. *The Battle Cry of Peace* did tremendous business, grossing more than a million dollars. It was estimated that over fifty million people saw it. In England it ran in the open air, night after night, in Trafalgar Square, as a recruiting aid.

Battle Cry made a special appeal to the women in the audience, and Blackton used a quotation that became a pivotal element in Griffith's later *Intolerance:* "'The hand that rocks the cradle rules the world." The film involved a modern story, and two allegorical sequences. In the opening scene Hudson Maxim delivers a lecture at Carnegie Hall, emphasizing the defenseless condition of the United States. A young banker, John Harrison (Charles Richman), impressed by Maxim's words, determines to do all he can for preparedness. His fiancée, however, Virginia Vandergriff (Norma Talmadge), is the daughter of a millionaire, T. Septimus Vandergriff, who firmly believes America must have peace at any price. Harrison tries to show Vandergriff the consequences of his belief—that he is risking not only his country but his fortune and even the lives and happiness of his wife and children. Vandergriff remains unmoved.

A close friend of the millionaire is a foreigner, a peace propagandist called Emanon. (Anxious to avoid an identifiable foreign name, Blackton settled for No Name, spelled backwards.) Emanon is a spy, the head of a band of conspirators plotting the invasion of America, whose agents are behind the peace movements and whose lobbyists exert heavy influence against army and navy appropriations.

Vandergriff is delivering a speech at a huge peace rally when a shell crashes through the wall of the building. Enemy battleships bombard New York. The

* McDowell was soon to become one of the top British front-line cameramen (see p. 59).

Massacre of American workers in Battle Cry of Peace.

J. Stuart Blackton took pains to design a uniform that would offend no foreign nation. But these invaders in Battle Cry of Peace *fulfill to the letter the propaganda image of the Hun.*

"Peace at any price"—the Roosevelt vision depicted by Blackton in Battle Cry of Peace.

Battle Cry of Peace: *American civilians rounded up by the invader.*

downtown district is devastated by shells and by bombs from aeroplanes. Harrison's mother and sister are killed. Vandergriff is shot in the street. Harrison himself is bayonetted as he tries to protect his fiancée. Virginia's mother, to avoid disgrace at the hands of the enemy, kills her two daughters and herself.

Following the dramatic section came two allegorical scenes: Columbia crushed, bleeding, trampled by a merciless foe; and Columbia proud, commanding, and supreme—"Columbia as she should be."

THEODORE ROOSEVELT'S SUPPORT brought an unprecedented degree of cooperation. Major General Wood, commander of the army in the East and Roosevelt's closest friend, arranged for 2,500 marines to be placed at Blackton's disposal, entirely without charge; all he had to do was feed them. Elsie Janis entertained the troops, as she was later to do so memorably in France.

Blackton had to tread very carefully in his depiction of the invading army, for the Germans were still represented diplomatically in America—Count Bernstorff had not yet departed—and a protest at high level could cause embarrassment for everyone concerned with the project. "I designed a special uniform, unlike any other worn," said Blackton. "I defy anyone to find in it the slightest resemblance to the uniform of any power. I spent a great deal of time in designing the helmet, and it is absolutely original."[2] The helmet, he revealed later, was merely a derby hat with the front brim removed.

What was not original was the behavior of the invaders. They were shown committing many of the acts attributed to the Germans in Belgium. They sported Kaiser Wilhelm mustaches. Although essentially comic-opera soldiers, they set the style for the American film presentation of the Hun for the duration.

The film has always been acknowledged as the work of Commodore Blackton, yet he was not the director. Wilfred North, an Englishman, a Vitagraph actor (and a former cowboy), was credited as director, with Blackton supervising the production.

"Blackton really *did* supervise it," James Morrison told Anthony Slide. "There wasn't an important scene that he wasn't on. Wilfred North held the thing together, and he didn't fall in esteem by doing so. It was just a case, when Blackton came in to direct a scene, of having God in on it."

After more than sixty years, it is impossible to judge the quality of the film. Only half a reel of out-takes survives, at George Eastman House. The reel opens with a scene of panic-stricken evacuation, civilians dashing through smoke-filled streets, which is as striking as an impressionist painting, and some dynamic shots of automobiles struggling across a bridge. The single glimpse of a studio scene, with Norma Talmadge, is so well shot that one can safely assume *Battle Cry* was a handsome film to look at. (The cameraman credited on the slate board is Frank Tyrell.)

A significant part of the exploitation consisted of the speeches that accompanied the film. Captain Jack Crawford, the poet scout, Indian fighter, and Civil War veteran, who appeared in the film with veterans from the Grant Post of the Grand Army of the Republic (G.A.R.), came on at the opening and declared his abhorrence for the song "I Didn't Raise My Boy To Be a Soldier." He told of his own four wounds and how his father, severely wounded, had been nursed back to health by his mother, who then sent him back to fight.

J. Stuart Blackton used the opening as an opportunity to declare his loyalty to the United States. "When I realized the great importance of this propaganda and what it meant to the United States and realized also that I had never been naturalized I hurried down and took my oath of allegiance to this country. And I hope that through no act of mine will it ever be said that my citizenship has in it anything of the hyphenated variety" (Applause).[3]

An editorial in *The New Republic* described the film as being nauseating without being properly effective. The method used was the artful provocation of fear. "It fails of its own violence, like an overdose of poison."[4]

The publicity campaign dismayed the pacifists. The preparedness advocates had the advantage of support from police forces, and the appearance of police reservists to handle crowds at showings of *Battle Cry* turned ordinary screenings into newsworthy events. Particular attention was focused on Detroit, headquarters of the Ford Motor Company. Henry Ford had declared that he would burn his factory rather than produce cars for war purposes and was sponsoring a Peace Ship for Europe, in the hope of getting the troops out of the trenches by Christmas. As *Battle Cry* opened, a huge publicity campaign was climaxed by the appearance of an aircraft that circled the city and dropped "bombs" upon streets, parks, homes—and the Ford factories. Upon these paper bombs was printed: "This might have been a real bomb. Prepare. *The Battle Cry of Peace* at the Broadway Strand Theater shows us what might happen if we don't prepare."[5]

Henry Ford replied in a full-page manifesto entitled *Humanity—and Sanity,* which he ran in no fewer than 250 newspapers. "For months," the manifesto declared, "the people of the United States have had fear pounded into their brains by magazines, newspapers and motion pictures. No enemy has been pointed out. All the wild cry for the spending of billions, the piling up of armament and the saddling of the country with a military caste has been based on nothing but *fiction.*"[6]

According to Ford, the Dardanelles had shown how the greatest battle fleet in history had failed to effect an invasion, and a general was quoted: "The placing of an army on American soil is the last thing any European government would attempt."

"Have you seen that awful moving picture *The Battle Cry of Peace*? Did you shake with fear and tremble for your country's safety? Did you know that others were shaking at the same time, but with laughter at your fear, and with joy at the fat contracts your fear might bring them?"

The manifesto did not resort to innuendo. It openly accused Hudson Maxim of using the picture to advertise his wares and playing on public fears to make a market for his goods. It quoted from a stock report of the Maxim Munitions Corporation, founded in November 1915. This offer of stock had brought about resignations from a committee formed to urge the preparedness program upon Congress. One of the committee had called Maxim's action "treasonable."

Maxim answered the accusations with a bland declaration of innocence: "*Defenseless America* was written during the month of February 1915, before I had any idea whatsoever of becoming financially involved in any munitions corporation."[7] Vitagraph filed suit for a million dollars. "The printed statement that munitions manufacturers were back of [*Battle Cry*] prejudiced many people and damaged business of theatres in many cities," they complained.[8] This allegation was not true. Vitagraph, as Blackton later admitted, was thrilled beyond words with the full-page newspaper publicity, paid for by Henry Ford at rates between $500 and $5,000. And Roosevelt willingly threw himself into the anti-Ford campaign: "Blackton's film has done more for the Allied cause than twenty battalions of soldiers," he declared. All the fuss kept the picture before the public—and did Vitagraph a power of good. A year later the company was awarded judgment of the million they asked for, but the judgment was purely technical. It was the result of Ford's attorney filing a demurrer to the suit, which was accepted by the court as an admission by the defendant that the complaint was justified. With Henry Ford transformed into a super-patriot, and the Ford factories mobilizing for war, Vitagraph obligingly dropped the case.

Blackton told a group of students in 1929 that the film was deliberate propaganda to embroil the United States in the war. As he had remarked to a party of Australian naval cadets visiting Vitagraph in December 1915: "I am neutral only in this respect—that I don't care which one of the Allies wins."[9]

Yet when America entered the war, some preachments in *Battle Cry* proved embarrassing. In his anxiety to alarm Americans into action, Blackton had overplayed the horrors of war. The proprietor of a Pittsburgh theater was jailed because the handbills he had used to advertise the picture were calculated to prevent enlistment.

All prints of *Battle Cry* were recalled, re-edited, and retitled. The picture became *The Battle Cry of War,* and another picture of that title, intended as a sequel, became *Womanhood, Glory of the Nation.* Blackton declared that Vitagraph was with the government body and soul: "While the changing of all the prints will be costly, we consider it our patriotic duty to make the change."[10] But the object of the exercise had been achieved: America was in the war, and Vitagraph's trade figures were the envy of the industry.

THE CHAPLIN CRAZE

If Charlie Chaplin had done what was expected of him and answered his country's call to the colors in August 1914, the chances of his surviving the war would have been slight. Chaplin would have been a footnote in film history. Having arrived at Mack Sennett's Keystone Company in December 1913, he was already experiencing his first rush of popularity, although trade press reviews still referred to him as Chapman or Chaplain. But his pictures were made under the influence of Sennett. His own genius had yet to emerge, and would therefore not have been missed.

As he grew more famous, the decision to stay in California must have become increasingly hard. Englishmen of military age who remained out of uniform received white feathers; propaganda portrayed them as the lowest form of human life, and many young men joined up because they could not bear such humiliation from friends and family. Chaplin not only received white feathers, but also threatening letters and public attacks in the papers.

Between takes on The Bond, *a Liberty Bond short* (1918). *Charlie Chaplin, Sydney Chaplin, Henry Bergman.*

The fact that as Chaplin became the best-loved personality of the war, he also became one of the richest, gave him a certain respite. The British government cared no more for his artistry than for that of the thousands of other actors, writers, poets, and painters who served at the front. But he was a willing source of finance for the British government as a contributor to war funds.[1] For as long as they could use him in this way, they left him alone.

His apparent lack of patriotism created bad feeling in England. Some of this resentment was undoubtedly whipped up by people with financial reasons for discrediting him. Nevertheless, to those who had lost sons, husbands, and fathers, Chaplin's apparent invulnerability suggested the inevitable gap between the privileged and themselves. The combination of affection and resentment expressed itself in a soldiers' song, a parody of *Redwing:*

> The moon shines bright on Charlie Chaplin,
> His boots are cracking,
> For want of blacking,
> And his little baggy trousers
> They want mending
> Before we send him
> To the Dardanelles.[2]

Alistair Cooke says that Chaplin's reaction when he first heard the song was undiluted fear: "I really thought they were coming to get me. It scared the daylights out of me."[3]

"Had he gone to the front," wrote William Dodgson Bowman, "the British Army would have gained a recruit of indifferent physique and doubtful value; but it would have lost one of the few cheering influences that relieved the misery and wretchedness of those nightmare days."[4]

When Chaplin signed his celebrated contract with Mutual in 1916, the lengthy document included an element of war risk. Mutual insisted that Chaplin should not leave the United States within the life of the contract without the permission of the corporation. One can safely assume that a sizable slice of that $670,000 per year went to the British government, for such a clause would not have been legally binding without their assurances. Mutual also insured Chaplin's life for $250,000.

The clause created an outcry in the British press, and criticism flared again when Chaplin signed his First National contract for $1 million plus a bonus upon signature of $15,000. On this occasion, the trade press hailed Chaplin as a national asset and suggested that if Chaplin's joining up would put an end to the terrible sacrifice of war, only then should he be enlisted.[5]

But by now the United States was in the war, and the campaign against Chaplin became more vindictive. According to Raoul Sobel and David Francis, he went to a recruiting office and was rejected by army doctors for being underweight.[6] Once this was announced, the campaign abated. His brother collected the signatures of influential men to justify his remaining out of uniform. But as a British citizen, it was the British Army that expected him to enlist; a correspondent in England received a letter from Chaplin, explaining the situation.

"I only wish that I could join the English army and fight for my mother country. But I have received so many letters from soldiers at the front, as well as civilians, asking me to continue making pictures that I have come to the conclusion that my work lies right here in Los Angeles. At the same time, if my country thinks it needs me in the trenches more than the soldiers need my pictures, I am ready to go."[7]

In 1918 a treaty was finalized between Great Britain and the United States permitting the drafting of British subjects resident in America. Films were not yet a vital industry, and about two hundred motion picture people in Los Angeles were affected by the treaty; Chaplin was one of them.[8] The London *Times*[9] carried the news that Chaplin had been drafted, and had waived his rights to exemption. A few days later came a report that Chaplin would abandon his British nationality and join the U.S. Army in July—"a national calamity," said *The Bioscope*.[10] "I feel as though I only want liberty to make three more pictures, and then I'll be gladly going 'over there,' " said Chaplin. "But I've put a lot of money into my studio; I've assumed a lot of obligations, the future must be provided for, and I actually need the money that will come from three more pictures. I'm in the Southern California draft under the new treaty with England."

July came and went, and although Chaplin was in khaki, it was for his new comedy, *Shoulder Arms*. In September, announced the *Times,* Chaplin would come to England to take part in propaganda film production; but the improvement in the war made such a plan superfluous.

The appearance of a cut-out figure of Charlie at the entrance to a theater was enough to fill the seats. A detachment of the Highland Light Infantry, on the eve of their departure, captured one of these figures and carried it off as a souvenir to the trenches. These life-size models were popular with the troops, who would stand them on the parapet during an attack. The appearance of a crudely painted tramp, with baggy trousers and a bowler hat, must have bewildered the Germans, who had no idea who he was. To add to the confusion, British officers with a sense of humor would cultivate Chaplin mustaches, and in prison camps, every hut had its Chaplin impersonator.

Chaplin's very familiarity was of value in rehabilitating shell-shocked soldiers. Dr. Lewis Coleman Hall, with the U.S. Army in France, was attached to a neurological unit, and he asked Chaplin to help him in his work by sending some autographed pictures. "Please write your name on the photos," he wrote, "the idea being that nearly everyone has seen you in pictures. I will show your picture to a poor fellow and it may arrest his mind for a second. He may say 'Do you know Charlie?' and then begins the first ray of hope that the boy's mind can be saved." Chaplin sent the pictures, and declared that the letter would always rank among his most treasured possessions.[11]

Once America entered the war, Chaplin's motion picture activities were curtailed by his energetic campaigning for Liberty Bonds. After one three-week stint, he collapsed with exhaustion. But for the Liberty Loan and the Red Cross he brought in staggering amounts; one lady donated $20,000 to the Red Cross merely to sit next to Chaplin at a gala dinner.

Apart from his well-known films, Chaplin made a number of short comedies, some of which remain to be unearthed. Early in 1918 he made a five-hundred-foot film for wounded British soldiers in which he appeared with Harry Lauder, each comedian playing in the other's style. The same year, to boost the Fourth Liberty Loan, Chaplin made a one-reeler called *The Bond,* which was rediscovered not long ago and is available on 16 mm. It is a charming fragment of Chaplin whimsy, which illustrates the bond of friendship, the bond of love, the bond of marriage, and "most important of all—The Liberty Bond." The purpose of the Liberty Bond is explained in a triptych tableau; Charlie appears in the middle, hands a bag of money to Uncle Sam on the left, who passes Charlie a scroll and gives the money to a figure on the right called Industry. A soldier materializes, and Industry presents him with a rifle. The soldier thanks Uncle Sam and marches off. Charlie is so impressed he digs deeper in his pockets and produces another bag. After the same routine, a sailor is presented with a rifle. Charlie shakes Uncle Sam and Industry by the hand before sneaking up to the maddened Kaiser and thumping him on his helmet with a huge hammer labeled "LIBERTY BONDS." With his foot on his supine victim like a big game hunter, Charlie tells the audience to buy their bonds right away, cheers and waves and smiles delightedly as the scene fades.

Chaplin filed suit against several companies and individuals who pirated his work. Henry "Pathé" Lehrman, who had been Chaplin's first director, and who was profoundly jealous of him, nurtured a replacement called Billy Ritchie, a former member of the Karno troupe. His films enjoyed some success, and one of them led to a remarkable incident.

A Chicago motorcycle policeman named Robert Beck, an English subject, returned to enlist a few weeks after the outbreak of war. Sent to Belgium as a motorcycle dispatch rider, he was shot off his machine by a sniper at Dixmude. As a result of his injuries, he became deaf and dumb and was confined to a hospital for

On location for Shoulder Arms; *Chaplin is seated right of center, on chair. Albert Austin, far left; Syd Chaplin, with mustache; Alf Reeves, straw hat; Rollie Totheroh, cameraman, in white eyeshade.*

wounded soldiers near Liverpool. Manager Pearson of the local cinema, the Aintree Palace, invited all the soldiers who felt well enough to come to a free show. Corporal Beck sat in silence with his comrades until the final item—a Billy Ritchie film called *The Fatal Note.* Ritchie's main stunt in this picture was to suspend several policemen on a forceful jet of water. Beck became convulsed with laughter, and suddenly realized that the mysterious sound he heard was his own voice. Such a miraculous recovery would normally have meant little more than a swift return to the trenches. But Beck was a decorated veteran of the African wars, and he was able to return to Chicago.[12]

Chaplin's *Shoulder Arms* is the only film from the entire period to be remembered with unqualified admiration. Chaplin was warned that it was a dangerous project, and Cecil B. DeMille suggested he delay the release because of its "bad taste." Made toward the end of the war, the film came out just before the armistice,* after which advertisements announced "*Shoulder Arms* has come at the right time. People can laugh at it without any guilty feeling now."[13]

There was criticism of the sequence that began with the title "Poor France" and showed a shattered building and a weeping French girl (Edna Purviance). "The setting undoubtedly had great possibilities for comedy elements," wrote Frances Taylor Patterson in *Cinema Craftsmanship,*[14] "but the writer should not

---

* It opened at the Strand Theater, New York, on 20 October 1918, with Broncho Billy's *Shootin' Mad.* Pat Sullivan had released a cartoon a couple of months earlier called *How Charlie Captured the Kaiser.*

have emphasized the real distress that lay behind it by calling attention deliberately to 'Poor France.' " (Miss Patterson considered that *Shoulder Arms* would not appeal nearly so much to audiences of the far future when military matters had been more or less forgotten.)

Chaplin planned the film as a five-reeler (it was released in three reels), and a domestic sequence at the beginning was discarded. In the original ending, which historians Bardeche and Brassilach claim was banned and which Chaplin says was never shot,[15] the Allies organize a banquet for Charlie. M. Poincare makes a speech, and when Charlie rises to reply, King George creeps up and sneaks a button as a souvenir. More surprising, perhaps, was the fact that in some countries, the capture of the Kaiser was removed.

The public reaction to *Shoulder Arms* was, on at least one occasion, so violent that considerably more than box-office records were shattered. "Six doors torn from their hinges, seven lobby frames trampled to bits, a ticket box crushed beyond repair, a cast iron effigy of Charlie Chaplin battered to pieces, a special detail of policemen so badly bruised and manhandled that two bottles of Omega Oil were used . . . are the outstanding features of two cyclonic days experienced by the manager of the Star Theatre, Elgin, Ill., when he played *Shoulder Arms*."[16]

The same mass adulation greeted Chaplin on his European tour in 1921. He was mobbed in London and in Paris. But his films were not yet generally released in Germany, and in Berlin he was ignored. Just one man, a former prisoner who had seen the films in captivity, recognized him, rushed over to him in a cafe, and kissed him.

CINEMAS AT THE FRONT LINE

After being in the front line for weeks at a time, troops were taken a few kilometers behind the line for a six-day rest, ready to go into action again at a moment's notice. Here they were allocated billets, perhaps an old farm, or a house half-destroyed by shellfire. In such conditions, one would imagine the cinema to have been a nostalgic dream, as far from reality as the local pub. Yet cinemas were a regular feature of life at the front from August 1915. Initiated by wealthy citizens of France to entertain French troops, they were converted from any building within easy access of the front lines that was still upright. When a show was announced, it was a foregone conclusion that it would be packed. By mid-1916, there were twenty cinemas within the British sector.

"Just fancy for a moment," wrote Sergeant C. G. Lilley. "You enter an old barn almost falling to pieces, with all the openings blocked up with sacks or anything that comes to hand that will exclude the light. The floor covered with empty petrol boxes, with pieces of old wood, all sizes and thicknesses, to take the place of tip-up seats. Outside, you will see perhaps 300 men all lined up, and our capacity is 200, but they all manage to get in somehow. Once in they manage to make themselves comfortable. Then the show commences. Here you have 300 happy smiling faces, without a thought for what may happen tomorrow. If the Trade could only

The original text reads: "To this haven come tired fighting men of the Allied Armies after their weary vigil in the trenches. Here is peace and sanctuary from the fray. No messengers of death can enter here.

"The once fair city of Verdun is a scene of desolation and ruin, tenanted only by military patrols. Far under the surface, however, the daily life of the city goes on with its stores and homes and its moving picture theatre, a marvel of engineering accomplishment."

Subterranean Cinema

90 Feet Under Shell-Torn Verdun

To this haven come tired fighting men of the Allied Armies after their weary vigil in the trenches. Here is peace and sanctuary from the fray. No messengers of death can enter here.

The once fair city of Verdun is a scene of desolation and ruin, tenanted only by military patrols. Far under the surface, however, the daily life of the city goes on with its stores and homes and its moving picture theatre, a marvel of engineering accomplishment.

D. W. Griffith outside a front-line cinema in France.

see one of these shows in progress they would send us more films than we could use. That is our one drawback—lack of films."[1]

Sergeant Lilley's current program included the American serial *The Million Dollar Mystery,* featuring Florence La Badie and James Cruze. "There is every prospect of it being the rage of France," he wrote. "I think it is more talked about here than the war."

At first the films were rented at great expense from Paris, and machines were set up and operated by men who had been projectionists in civilian life. One officer, on leave in London, acquired from the Hepworth Company the gift of sixteen thousand feet of film and he brought it back with him. This was such a success that returning officers who had contacts in the trade made a point of bringing back fresh film in their luggage.

"To present 'drama' to men fresh from the trenches seems at first an exquisitely superfluous operation," said *Kinematograph Weekly,* "and the thought of such men growing excited over the immature warfare between the sheriff's posse and the horse stealers has an appealing incongruity."[2]

The front-line cinemas were very vulnerable. A Scottish soldier reported that he was sitting in one when the Germans began firing at the area and the whole place began to shake. "The peculiar part is that the pictures go on as if nothing had happened."[3]

One American observer saw motion pictures run in an old dugout that held fifty men. "Those ragged, dirty fellows, caked with mud and covered with vermin, did not want to look at the pictures that well-intentioned folks thought they would be interested in, but were eagerly enthusiastic over scenes of city streets of Paris, London, New York. You see, they had got in a state of mind where none of them believed they would ever see a city street again, and a city street with well dressed crowds walking about. Love plots didn't seem to interest them much, but a comedy —I mean regular slapstick stuff—started them shouting with glee."[4]

The front-line cinema circuit began by accident. "Somewhere in England," said *Moving Picture World,* "a film show was shipped to somewhere. It landed in Plugstreet [Ploegsteert] and the Tommies found it. The good show wasn't going to waste, not while there was a man who could put it on. A man was found—the show enjoyed."[5] Harry Wood, then managing director of the Gaumont Company in London, was given the rank of lieutenant by the War Office, and attached to the British Expedition Forces Canteens.

As the front-line circuit spread, the professionalism increased. Men who had worked in cinemas in England declared that they were seeing pictures as bright and as crisp as in their own theaters. Premises could be converted rapidly. A projector would be installed on a table, while the operator stood on another table set up alongside. A projection box would be made of a canvas screen, with the operating ports cut in the appropriate spots. Jokes were made about the fire risk and the terrible danger to the troops. Outside the hut an electrical generating plant was set up, sheltered by tarpaulin.

Gradually, the circuit expanded. The old barns were turned into first-class halls, the planks and petrol tins were replaced with tip-up seats (some of them made by German prisoners), and the old rainstorm prints, which renters sent to the troops instead of the incinerator, were replaced by top-quality prints of the latest releases.* Lieutenant Wood and Sergeant Major Cross were in charge of this main circuit, although other cinemas were operated independently. One independent cinema boasted an orchestra of eight, as well as a Boyd piano.

Inevitably, as the front line bulged and receded, some of these cinemas were captured. During the great German push of 1918, an operator lost his projector and all his films. He returned on leave in such a state of dismay that a concert was arranged in his home town, Grantham, to raise money to replace the equipment.

American pictures were most in demand; Nestors, Jokers, Victors, 101 Bisons, Vitagraphs, and Keystones were the most prominent. Chaplins were run until the prints were shredded.

The fascination with pictures expressed itself in everyday speech. Trenches were called "Picture house tea rooms" by British troops, who referred to machine guns as "cinema cameras," and instead of being ordered to open fire, they were told to "turn the crank." An offensive was a show, and Lewis Jacobs mentions dugouts labeled Vitagraph Village and Keystone Kottage. "The pictures" was a euphemism for the operating theater.

Bennett Molter, an assistant director from Metro, who had worked in California with James Young Deer and Francis Ford, went to war as an aviator to gain first-hand knowledge, which he intended to use in the production of war films. The front-line cinemas were a particular joy to him, as he explained in a letter to Robert Huntington, at the New York Metro studio. "Can you beat it? Last night I had the pleasure of seeing the 'M' in Metro tumble around, and the stars take their places, and then the Drews in *At the Count of Ten.* Sidney Drew got many laughs. Believe me, Bob, it was a real treat for me to see the old faces again, to imagine big Bob Kurrle at the crank, Eddie Shulter running around back of the set, and maybe you looking on. It took me back to Sixty-First street for an hour or so. And all the time the picture was on, we could hear the 'boom, boom' of the cannonading."[6]

Molter explained that the troops loved the Westerns, but he felt "a real picture"—a dramatic feature—might fall flat: "they don't want to have to think." In conversation with the lieutenant in charge of the cinema, Molter learned that he paid $24 a week for this service, and his overhead for petrol and so on was about the same, but he took in from 750 to 1,000 francs a week, with the profits helping to finance other shows at various parts of the front.

In 1917 the chairman of the Cinematograph Trade Council, A. E. Newbould, and the secretary, Frank Fowell, visited the front lines. The invitation was evidence of the authorities' changing attitude toward the moving picture, a change stimulated not only by the success of *The Battle of the Somme,* the first of the official films, but by the proof that the existence of a cinema near a French town substantially reduced the figures for drunkenness and crime.

Newbould, a Boer War veteran, was all too conscious of the inferior status of his trade. "I was not unprepared," he wrote, "for a certain amount of patronage towards the cinema. It is not that I am lacking in pride for what the cinema has done, but after all, it *is* an amusement industry, and I was going out in the middle of a bloody war."[7]

---

* Renters complained of difficulty in getting prints back from France.

He expected to be received with coolness, but he found the officers keenly interested in the cinema, more anxious to talk about it than he was. All agreed how incalculable had been the value of these entertainments during the long winter months. "I found the cinema was regarded as a really serious moral factor in the successful prosecution of the war."

By this time, Lieutenant Wood had control of over a hundred and fifty cinemas. Programs changed twice a week, and the admission charge of thirty centimes—six cents (NCOs and officers paid more)—went to the British Expeditionary Forces' Canteen Cinema Supply.

"Everywhere I went I was continually being reminded of moving pictures. Even in the most wretched ruins of what were once carefully tended towns and villages, my eye was caught by the hand-painted notice–often crudely lettered–'To the Cinema.' I came across the cinemas, apparently flimsy structures of wood and sheet iron, or wood and canvas, just behind our lines. I saw the fragments of one such theatre which had 'copped it.' In time, one came to realise that apart from the drab, sordid monotony of man-killing, the cinema took first place in the soldier's mind."

The internee camps did rather less well for entertainment. Civilians of German or Central European nationality were interned at Knockaloe Aliens' Camp on the Isle of Man; Hall Caine wrote a book about this camp, *The Woman of Knockaloe,* which was filmed in 1927 as *Barbed Wire* (see page 211).

W. Schlesinger, who ran the camp cinema, complained that none of the renters in London would provide him with prints. He was perfectly prepared to pay the full price, and he expected no favors, but never could he extract a reply to his requests. The trade press chided their readers, pointing out that their opposite numbers in Germany put up no barriers for the internee camp entertainment at Ruhleben.

But the exhibitors who had sent their worst prints to the troops had nothing to spare for enemy aliens.

BRITAIN PREPARED

From the moment of its formation, Wellington House tried to impress upon the War Office and the Admiralty the vital importance of cinematograph propaganda, but not until the autumn of 1915 were "the difficulties overcome"—to quote the official phrase. Operators were then sent to photograph the Grand Fleet, the Royal Flying Corps, and the training of troops. The material was combined with footage supplied by Messrs. Vickers, the armament manufacturers, linked with titles, and released as *Britain Prepared.*

As a film, *Britain Prepared* is unusual, if not unique, in the history of propaganda films. It is absolutely honest. It sets out to show a nation preparing for war (while the war is on, for there was little preparation beforehand) and it does so with an artless pride that is quite disarming. Nowhere is there an attempt to falsify a situation, or to suggest that the British are somehow superior to any other form of life. Each branch of the service, together with munitions factories and shipbuilding yards, is illustrated with a sober simplicity to which no one, not even a German sympathizer, could object. Seen today, this sort of documentary, showing scenes that have become tediously familiar over the past sixty years, is more likely to send an audience to sleep than into a patriotic fervor. But it is easy to understand its impact at the time. For each image, however mundane, represented an important step forward for the British cinema; at last the government had accepted the power of the new medium.

English audiences were surprised at the monumental scale of the industrial and military enterprise they were involved in, and they were also moved and excited by the glimpses of a life hitherto forbidden to public scrutiny. If the slow traveling shots along the tremendous hulls of warships are awe-inspiring today (the horizon of Scapa Flow is so thick with capital ships one unjustly suspects a process shot!) then the effect in 1916 must have been pulverizing. And one is given a glimpse into the kind of war the authorities had expected to fight, with the sequences of motorcycle battalions, racing from one rapid assault to another, like the German Army in their *Blitzkrieg* of twenty-five years later.

American audiences would not have realized that the entire film was shot in Britain, and would have imagined the maneuvers on Salisbury Plain to have been the real thing in France, despite the frankness of such titles as "The turf clods being thrown represent bombs." A Royal Flying Corps bombing raid on a farmhouse is shown at embarrassing length; all the bombs miss and, being merely smoke bombs, inflict no damage whatever. The cheapest product from American studios portrayed war as more devastating and terrifying than this picture, but then *Britain Prepared,* true to its title, devotes itself purely to the build-up, and not a shot is fired in anger. The most sobering thought one carries away from *Britain Prepared* is that the vast majority of the soldiers, seen exuberantly fighting mock battles in 1915, would have been dead or wounded by 1918.

The picture reached audiences from high society in Paris to ordinary Russian soldiers on the Eastern Front. This latter feat was accomplished by Captain Bromhead, a well-known figure of the trade, who, with his assistant Private Greengrass, carried this "celluloid national anthem" to Russia. "Yesterday, I went to England for three hours!" wrote one Russian newspaperman.[1] "It cost me 5 kopeks on tram no. 9. And yet there are people who abuse the cinematograph! Yesterday, at any rate, the cinema rose to the occasion, and I am very grateful to it. It made it possible for me to peep as it were through a chink in a wall and see what is being done in England—what a colossal effort is being made by our loyal ally. Even in that conventional presentation (the cinema is not always wholly truthful) we felt the concentrated cheerfulness of a nation, alien to war by its very nature, but plunging as one man into hard collective toil. What impressed me most was the mobilisation of industry."

Captain Bromhead's shows were received with rapturous delight by audiences often consisting of as many as six thousand troops. The power was supplied by searchlight dynamos—although the Russians eventually became so pressed, with all the searchlights in action, that shows had to be canceled. These pictures were frequently accompanied by gunfire, and one show was visible from the Austrian lines; the Austrians obligingly held their fire until the very end—when "God Save the

Britain Prepared (*1915*), *frame enlargement. The Grand Fleet in action.*

King" was played—and even then they shelled another part of the line.*

Britain Prepared was received with enthusiasm wherever it was shown. Even the Germans went on record with a testimonial in the *Rheinisch-Westphälische Zeitung:* "We must admit, a more clever advertisement could hardly be made by the English Ministry of War for its Army and Fleet, and for its services in the war in general. This speculation on the sensibilities of the cinema visitor will not fail of its object. Strongly recommended for imitation."[2]

THE PICTURE WAS DIRECTED, edited, and titled by Charles Urban. Urban was an American, although he was a leading figure in the English film trade. He did not use his full name, which was tactful, since it was Charles von Urban. Born in the Scioto River region of Ohio in 1867, he spent his boyhood in Cincinnati and Detroit. The trade press claimed that his work in producing the Bioscope projectors, and making them available to lecturers with Edison films, brought motion pictures "out of the big city and to the people." He went to London in 1896 on an eight-month trial to handle the Edison agency, and there he became a naturalized British subject. If he did not invent Kinemacolor, an honor that must go to his partner

* Third Report, Imperial War Museum, London, p. 104. Bromhead showed British propaganda films during the Russian Revolution, according to British agent R. Bruce Lockhart, who reported that they seemed merely to increase the number of deserters. "It was not Bromhead's fault. He was a splendid fellow, who realized the futility of showing war pictures to men whose sole thought was peace. Still, he had his duty to do. Films were part of the Whitehall scheme for the regeneration of Russia, and shown they had to be." Quoted in Wenden, *Birth of the Movies* (London: Macdonald, 1975), p. 135.

Charles Urban in action with Kinemacolor camera aboard a German liner before the war.

French cameraman hurries out of range of J. B. McDowell's camera as he photographs an injured prisoner in December 1916.

George Albert Smith, Urban was the one who energetically promoted it.

Never greatly interested in fiction films, Urban became associated with the British government over a motion picture record of gun and ammunition tests at Whale Island, and this led to his classic coup—the Kinemacolor film of the Delhi Durbar, 1911. Urban was greatly enamored of high society and bought a sizable country estate, where he raised orchids and roses. Upon this estate was a large aviary, and here Percy Smith (later responsible for *The Strafer Strafed*) shot many of the Kinemacolor films of bird life.

Before the war Urban ran the Warwick Trading Company,* and his sumptuously produced catalogue was full of war films, from the Russo-Japanese War to the war in the Balkans; the stills accompanying the titles suggest that the quality of these films was unusually high. Urban even marketed a film called *The Invasion of England,* a jocular item that took advantage of a visit by the Bulgarian Army. The official ban on photography in 1914 offended everything Urban stood for. He campaigned vociferously for the production of propaganda films, and in 1915 became chairman of the Cinema Committee, a subcommittee of the British Government Propaganda Committee (known as the British Topical Committee for War Films).

"We had been trying to convince the Admiralty for eighteen months that pictures of the fleet at work should be taken," Urban told the New York *Times,* "when finally I succeeded in getting First Lord of the Admiralty Balfour and Sir Henry Jackson to come to my office to see some of my pictures. The next day I received an order to be at Euston Station with three cameramen, ready to start for an unknown destination somewhere in the north of Scotland."[3]

Urban joined the fleet on 5 October 1915, and the filming at first went smoothly. "But the commander of HMS *Queen Elizabeth* began forming the habit of putting his hand before the lens when the men were taking scenes where there was any shore background and of catching the men by the arm, so they could not crank."

Urban was beside himself with anger, but there was a limit to what one could say to a high-ranking officer.

He received a placating letter from Sir Gilbert Parker, in charge of propaganda for America at Wellington House. "I am sure your own tact and happy manner and capacity for interesting others in your work will give you all that you want in the end. Keep a good heart."[4]

Urban was summoned to the flagship of the Grand Fleet to meet Admiral Jellicoe himself. The film-maker was in awe of the admiral—"when you caught his eye you realized that here was a *man*"—and was relieved to be given a courteous explanation. Apparently an innocent snapshot taken of the admiral had been loaned to a newspaperman and had ended up in a London illustrated paper. The shore topography unmistakably showed the location of the flagship, and Jellicoe had been forced to abandon the harbor. He added, however, that he had implicit confidence in Urban and his team, and hereafter they would not be molested.

While they were on the gigantic *Queen Elizabeth,* Urban was particularly

* He then became chairman of Kineto, Ltd.

eager to secure good shots of the firing of broadside salvos by her fifteen-inch guns. But he underestimated the impact of these enormous guns. At the first blast the concussion lifted the tripod several inches from the deck and froze the operator's hand at the crucial moment. Urban was able to transfer to a destroyer, and photographed impressive broadsides in black and white and color.

Wellington House was pleased with Urban's work. "If we had only had permission to arrange this six or seven months ago," wrote Charles Masterman on 5 January 1916, "I believe we could have shown places like Bulgaria pictures of the British fleet and they would never have gone over to the enemy." In the same letter he emphasized that for his own purposes he wanted the Vickers munitions film shown in America, more than in any other country. "I am told today on competent authority that the Americans believe that we are making no munitions at all, but merely buying ammunition from them. It would be well if they were disillusioned on this subject."

Urban was deeply offended by the studied indifference of most American film men to *Britain Prepared*. "I would not trust myself to express my opinion of the film crowd on this side in cold type," he wrote from New York to Wellington House.[5] Those who did not want to offend Urban called the picture "too classy," implying that it would be above the head of their average patron. Others thought the stuff was lousy and said so. "It has no punch. If it showed troopers being blown to pieces, it would go all right."

In New York, motion picture theaters were open to the public from eleven in the morning until midnight, and in the entire city Urban could find no theater available for a press screening. He had to settle for a hall owned by Wurlitzer, the organ people. According to the official invitation, the film was presented "to show what America will be obliged to do in the Event of Foreign Complications." The reviews next morning were most encouraging, but they were followed by total silence. A syndicate of British sympathizers came to the rescue and set up the Patriot Film Corporation of New York. The general manager (a position later held by Al Lichtman) was William J. Robinson, who had lived in America for thirty years but was still a citizen of the Crown. He introduced Charles Urban to President Wilson and masterminded special screenings for foreign embassies, the Senate, Congress, and other prominent people.

On 15 May 1915, under the sponsorship of the National Press Club, a gala opening was held at the Belasco Theater in Washington, D.C. The title was now *How Britain Prepared*. The National Press Club was so violently beset with criticism and threats of resignation that the club's president was obliged to defend himself in a speech before the audience. The pro-German press denounced the picture as a fake; the elaborate factory scenes had, they alleged, been taken in America.

As Masterman had predicted, the politicians were particularly struck by the munitions factory scenes shot at Messrs. Vickers. They were amazed by the fact that thirty thousand women were employed at making munitions. A member of the House of Representatives wrote, "I realize that this is what the women of America may be called upon to do in the event of war involving the U.S. To avoid such calamitous conditions, we should do everything practicable to insure against the war, and the best method is to build up a great navy for the defense of the nation."

Assistant Secretary of the Navy Franklin D. Roosevelt's letter was a sharp backhander to his own government: "These pictures will undoubtedly carry the lesson that while an enormous amount of work has been done by England since the war began, all this would have been very greatly simplified if there had been more adequate preparation for it before hostilities commenced."

The New York opening, at the Lyceum Theater on 29 May 1916, was an occasion of great emotion. One of the key points of the film was a scene of King George V reviewing forty thousand troops, who were going to relieve their comrades at the front. A title identified them as Irish. A few weeks earlier the Easter Rising in Dublin had been crushed by the British Army, and while popular feeling was still generally pro-Ally, it was anti-British. To Urban's surprise and relief, the scene received violent applause, and when the orchestra swung into "Tipperary" a voice took up the refrain. It belonged to Mary Garden, the celebrated opera star, who was in one of the boxes. Soon the whole audience was singing with her. At Ford's Opera House, Baltimore, two officers from the German submarine *Deutschland* attended *How Britain Prepared* and took notes.

By the time Urban was ready to return to London in June, the film had been shown in Boston and booked for Chicago. The Mexican alert caused a substantial increase in bookings. The film's future seemed assured. He was therefore astonished to learn that *How Britain Prepared* had been a financial disaster. Opposition from German-American interests and from isolationists had combined with exhibitor resistance to force the Patriot Film Corporation to fold with a loss of £20,000.

Furthermore, 1916 was the worst year in the history of the business. July broke all records for excessive heat, and an epidemic of infantile paralysis severely affected the picture business, forcing many theaters to close permanently.

With an unfairness characteristic of the time, the English press attacked Urban for his failure to put over the country's message. Certain newspapers made the spine-chilling accusation that because of Urban's film the chances of America entering the war had actually been lessened.

William Robinson explained to the *Kinomatograph Weekly* that there was nothing more Urban could have done for the British cause, for one simple reason. Practically all the theater owners were German, Polish, or Russian Jews. British propaganda in America had cast suspicion on all Jews, declaring that their primary loyalty was to the fatherland.

Urban tried again with the first of the official films, *The Battle of the Somme,* and Hearst's International Film Corporation offered to distribute it. Robinson was about to conclude the deal when he was told that the Hearst papers were subsidized by the German government, and the company intended to acquire the film merely to suppress it. Robinson believed the rumor, and canceled the deal. It took the intervention of financiers as powerful as William K. Vanderbilt and J. P. Morgan (represented by H. P. Davison) before the *Somme* could open in New York.

"I realised," said Urban, "knowing a good deal about the American film business, that we could not put out the *Somme* as it was originally arranged here, so I re-edited it, combining it with *Britain Prepared* and American field ambulance sections, put in subtitles suitable for American audiences, eliminating what we should call British patriotism, and converting the whole picture into a strong serial story of fourteen reels, running through seven weeks' exhibition at each theatre."[6]

The serial came in three main parts presented by Official War Pictures: *Jellicoe's Grand Fleet, Kitchener's Great Army,* and *The Battle of the Somme,* supported by *The Munitions Makers* and *The Destruction of a Zeppelin in England.* The General Film Corporation handled distribution, and in April 1917 Pathé took over from them. The advertising assumed a vigorous new look, and sandwiched in with other attractions, the *Somme* reached sixteen thousand theaters. Urban re-edited the other official films, too, but was furious when the Strand Theater in New York did some re-editing of their own, remaking the main title and claiming that fourteen cameramen had filmed the production, four of whom had lost their lives.*

Urban pointed out that this kind of distortion cast doubts upon his integrity, and upon the government he represented. Two cameramen had been involved [Malins and McDowell], and both were still active. The re-editing was also unacceptable. The Strand Theater manager apologized for the factual error but declared that the film was totally unsuitable for his patrons in its original form. Despite all such irritations, Urban claimed that by the end of 1917, sixty-five million people had seen the *Somme.* Patriot had initiated a profit-sharing scheme with the exhibitor. Vanderbilt and Morgan insisted that profits should now be shared with war relief, and £47,000 was made for the American Ambulance Corps alone.

Urban remained in America, exploiting the subsequent official films, directing British propaganda work in America, and editing *Official War Review.* One of his less publicized activities was a Kinemacolor film on venereal disease, which was compulsory viewing for troops in France. His loyalty to his adopted country must have known some pressure, but none more intense than when William Jury, of Jury's Imperial Pictures, Ltd., received a knighthood. Jury was responsible for distributing the official films in England, hardly such a challenging job as the one that faced Urban.

Urban wrote: "Sir William Jury got his knighthood on the strength of distributing the films in England which were produced and edited by Charles Urban."† This statement may be subjective, but it expresses justifiable resentment. If honors were to be handed out to anyone for the official films, however, surely the cameramen, the men who took the risks, deserved more than the Order of the British Empire?

British propaganda was completely reorganized in December 1916, when the energetic Lloyd George became Prime Minister, and the confidential activities of Wellington House were superseded by the Department of Information, under the command of Lieutenant Colonel John Buchan. A well-known novelist (his most famous book was *The Thirty-Nine Steps*), Buchan had spent the summer of 1916 observing the war on the Western Front. He soon ran into trouble in his new job, and Sir Edward Carson temporarily took over to smooth out the difficulties. The original British Topical Committee was superseded by the War Office Cinematograph Committee, with Lord Beaverbrook as chairman. So much criticism of the failings of British propaganda had been voiced in the press that Lloyd George abolished the Department of Information in February 1918 and created the Ministry

---

* It was standard practice for the Strand to re-edit films (George Pratt).

† Handwritten on Urban scrapbook, Science Museum, London.

of Information. Control was given to Lord Beaverbrook, chief critic. Sir William Jury was appointed Director of Cinematography at the ministry, and with these appointments Wellington House was finally closed.

THE FRONT-LINE CAMERAMAN

Despite the ban on photography, despite the fierce penalties, a handful of maverick cameramen from America bluffed their way to the front lines, determined to capture history in the making. They risked a soldier's death, they risked execution as spies, and they supplied no explanation for their exemplary behavior. To catalogue the obstacles they overcame would invite incredulity. Consider simply their equipment: the infantryman carried a pack weighing seventy pounds as well as his rifle. The motion picture cameraman was saddled with equipment that could weigh more than a hundred pounds, and none of these mavericks employed assistants. They were often obliged to carry their camera, tripod, stills camera, and ancillary equipment on ten-mile marches. Yet they stuck to their job, and after their initial tour of Europe, they returned again and again, seeking further war and revolution when the Great War ended.

Donald Thompson caught his enthusiasm for motion pictures when he covered the Baltimore Democratic Convention of 1912 at the age of twenty-three. He added a motion picture camera to his still-picture equipment and free-lanced for a while, finding himself in Canada at the outbreak of war. He secured permission to film the Canadian contingent and later traveled to France on a freighter as a Canadian correspondent. It is generally acknowledged that no film was shot at the retreat from Mons, but Donald Thompson was there, under fire for seven days and nights, and taking what *Moving Picture World* described as "some of the most remarkable pictures of the entire war."[1] In London he acted as correspondent for the New York *World* and later joined the Belgian Army. Upon his return to the United States, he claimed to have worked with the British, French, Belgians, Germans, Turks, Russians, Serbians, and Bulgarians, tactfully complimenting all the combatants on their bravery and skill in war. His pictures were snapped up by the Paramount News Service, and when he returned to the front lines late in 1915, he represented not only Paramount but *Leslie's Weekly*. His material was edited into a picture released in December 1915, called *Somewhere in France*. Thompson was wounded at Verdun, and as a result of his work he was made an official cinematographer for the French government. The French were able to scrutinize his material, and they seized seventy percent of it, pretending he would get it back after the war. This must have dismayed Thompson more than his wound, but his comments about the French were also censored. He described a lost scene to *Moving Picture World:* "One of the most impressive incidents is the complete obliteration of a portion of a trench and a number of soldiers by a shell. The men are seen hurling hand grenades in the direction of the enemy. The next instant the shell strikes squarely in the centre of their ranks, the air is filled with flying debris, and nothing remains but a gaping hole in the ground."[2]

J. B. McDowell, who was decorated for his courage as a front-line cameraman, with Moy Bastie camera.

German officers regard the camera with disdain. (Photo: J. B. McDowell)

German soldiers regard the camera with amusement—for the old soldier it was

LEFT: *Merl La Voy (right), after flight over Paris in military biplane. (Copied from* Picture Play)
RIGHT: *When Donald Thompson filmed at the front with Russian forces, he was ordered to wear a Russian uniform. (Copied from* Motion Picture Magazine)

Another American cameraman, D. J. Dwyer, also made use of the Canadians. Frustrated by red tape and the War Office ban, he enlisted in the Canadian Expeditionary Force and succeeded in reaching Europe as an official photographer. The problem, once he had secured his pictures, was how to get back. An apoplectic letter from the army completes the story: "Dwyer was beyond all control and discipline. He defied the military authorities in the most open and flagrant way. By some means which I have never been able to ascertain, he eluded the Military Authorities and the Naval Authorities and got away." Dwyer, "elusive as an eel," was struck off the strength of the CEF, but the letter added: "no price could have been too high for the riddance of Dwyer."[3]

Merl La Voy, a young cameraman from Chicago, began his career as dangerously as he meant to pursue it—by attempting to climb Mount McKinley in Alaska. In 1910 he failed; in 1912 he succeeded. He was financed by prominent Chicago businessmen, all of them French sympathizers, and was equipped with letters from the American government. La Voy traveled to France in 1915 and managed to stay twenty-two months, with authority from the American Relief Clearing House. Attached to the First Aid Corps, La Voy had a green pass, which meant "leave him alone." As an adventurer, he was bound to appeal to the American legionnaires of the Lafayette Escadrille, who took him up in an aircraft to photograph reserve encampments behind Verdun. In his film *Heroic France,* he featured such star aviators as Raoul Lufberry and Kissin Rockwell (who was killed in September 1916).

In 1917 La Voy accompanied the American Red Cross mission to Serbia, the result of that expedition being *Serbia Victorious.* In 1918 he joined Burton Holmes, the pioneer of travelogues, on a tour of the European battlefields. After a period on the staff of the Red Cross, La Voy became a newsreel cameraman for Pathé News.

THE BRITISH OFFICIAL KINEMATOGRAPHERS were no less courageous, but they were supported by assistants, motorcars, and army rations. Appointed by the British Topical Committee, which covered all expenses without any government subsidy, they were paid one pound per day. They wore the uniform of war correspondents, which consisted of British Army officer's uniform without insignia. Some of the Official Kinematographers, such as the two star operators, Geoffrey Malins and J. B. McDowell, were commissioned, and wore their rank badges.*

To the ordinary soldier, the camera was a welcome diversion. The cameraman was regarded with considerable respect, since many soldiers had seen the kind of risks he took. A soldier at the Somme was P. J. (Jack) Smith, later a newsreel cameraman himself: "Certainly I saw cameramen from time to time, but I never saw one with a tripod in the trenches. The troops would probably curse it for getting in the way. The cameramen that I saw always used an Aeroscope, as this was the only automatic camera that could be hand-held, and it was very compact. The camera operator used to set the camera on top of the trench parapet in the dark, cover it with sandbags and turf, leaving only the lens showing, having pumped it up beforehand by means of a triple-pump. He would leave it until daylight and watch for action—shells bursting, troops going over the top, etc., and release the mechanism by remote control, at the same time watching through a periscope. Some of these cameramen went over the top with the rest of us, starting the camera as they went, perhaps running off the whole magazine without stopping. They had guts, did those chaps."[4]

The exploits of Geoffrey Malins gained considerable circulation in the newspapers, and wild stories developed about the kind of shots he obtained. These were given substance by Malins himself, in his book *How I Filmed the War.* The censor was undoubtedly responsible for destroying the more horrific scenes, but the material surviving in the Imperial War Museum offers little evidence that any Official Kinematographer secured astounding action footage. Most of it is very plain coverage of troop movements, artillery barrages, and behind-the-lines activity. Because of the scarcity of telephoto lenses the shots have a kind of proscenium effect, a detachment due to the distance between the camera and the subject. This treatment results in some magnificent landscapes and some impressive portraits. But it does not make for dynamism.

The zoom lens has given the modern cameraman a godlike ubiquity; the Official Kinematographers were generally limited to one ordinary lens—a 50 mm—the equivalent of the lens issued with most snapshot cameras. It is the lens that professional still photographers today always carry with them, but hardly ever use. It shows too much, they say, yet not enough. Long-focus lenses were not permitted at the front—although they were used furtively—and cameramen were forbidden to film aircraft closer than forty yards.

The cinema was such a novel form of expression that few of the Official Kinematographers knew how to use it to its best advantage. The great works of Griffith began to appear during the war, but the culmination of the Griffith technique, the editorial innovations of Abel Gance and the Russians, all lay in the future.

---

* In France the operators performed their duties under the supervision of Captain F. C. Faunthorpe, Military Director of Kinematograph Operations for the Western Front, and Dr. Distin Maddick, Director of Kinematograph Operations for the War Office.

The Official Kinematographers approached their work like still photographers with a very special item of equipment. Movement was everything. If the subject was static, then the camera must move. An outstanding feature of all the war coverage is the endless panorama. Having struggled to set his machine up, the operator felt obliged to show as much as he could from one vantage point. Cranking the camera with his right hand, he would crank the pan handle on the tripod with his left, an ambidextrous feat requiring a great deal of practice. The camera would slowly circle the area, giving columns of troops and empty fields equal prominence. With the circle almost complete, the cameraman would stop cranking and enter the scene in his notebook. When his material reached England, no editing in the creative sense was necessary. If his scene was passed by the censor, and if it was considered suitable for the public, a title was stuck on the front and it became a sequence.

Soldiers always talked of the sounds of war, and how potential death could be ascertained by an almost musical distinction between several kinds of whine. The lack of sound robs the shots of any sense of threat. The enemy could not be seen, but he was heard almost incessantly. Without the sounds, the terrible explosions seem little more than harmless plumes of smoke, as attractive as a fountain. The tiny figures, crouching low, dodging the machine-gun bullets, seem ridiculous, for one can neither see the bullets nor hear the machine guns, and on modern projectors, the soldiers' desperate zigzagging reminds audiences of the Keystone Cops.

Homer Croy in *How Motion Pictures Are Made*[5] refers to the death of a cameraman, operating an automatic camera, during the Battle of Verdun, and how the camera continued to photograph after the cameraman had been killed. This remarkable incident was confirmed by Bela Belazs.[6] The piece of film was used in a French compilation, *Pour la Paix du Monde,* which was dedicated to the six French cameramen killed in active service. "One shot darkens and the camera wobbles. It is like an eye glazing in death. The director [Colonel Piquard of Les Gueules Cassées] did not cut out this 'spoilt' bit—for it showed where the camera was overturned and the cameraman killed while the automatic mechanism ran on. In another [shot] we see the cameraman dying for the sake of his picture."[7]

One of the few compilations to do justice to the work of the front-line cameraman was the BBC's *Great War* series of 1964. With the addition of sound, stretch-printed so that the movement appeared more acceptable, the newsreels came alive. Sound effects, which would have crippled a silent fiction film, here restored the drama and the tension. Television audiences who might not have accepted the newsreels in their original form were profoundly moved when they saw them in this new context. The impact, which had evaporated over the years, was fully restored, and the series led to an enormous resurgence of interest in the period.

But the BBC series highlighted a problem that has disturbed historians: the arbitrary use of film as historical evidence. No historian would include in an account of 1914 an incident he knows very well occurred in 1918. Yet this happens constantly in motion picture compilation work. So far, no historical compilation has been entirely free from such distortion.

In the CBS *World War One* TV series, in an episode entitled "Clash of the Generals," French cavalry are showing riding past the Arc de Triomphe. The commentary would have us believe that this footage was taken just before the declaration of war. But the shot is on panchromatic stock, and obviously belongs to the

1930s. German soldiers "attacking a Belgian fort in 1914" are wearing model-1916 steel helmets. This haphazard use of news footage has a definite purpose—to ensure the greatest possible fluidity in the editing. If the makers of the film were to stick rigidly to shots of the event, they would end up with considerable lengths of black spacing.

More heinous than confusion of newsreels is the use of feature material as if it were news film. This occurs almost always in battle scenes, and *The Great War* series committed the sin frequently. The producers argued that without such footage they would have no battles. The habit has a long pedigree. *The World War as Seen Through German Spectacles,* a 1927 compilation of German material, made by UFA as *Der Weltkrieg,* contained fifty percent reconstruction—scenes that have cropped up in dozens of "newsreel" compilations since.

Future generations will accept such distortions at face value, for the difference will not be as apparent to their eyes as it is to ours.

THE ARRIVAL OF THE FRENCH official war films, which were instituted in April 1915, brought the British public out of the darkness—to a degree. The first in the series consisted almost entirely of the comings and goings of generals and ministers, alternating with a march past, a parade, or a mobilization scene. It was not a very exciting beginning, but the trade press found it reassuring that Lord Kitchener, Sir John French, and Marshal Joffre had bodily form after all. "The most informal conversation in the street or on the steps of the French war office between these worthies somehow imparts a confidence that the cause of the Allies is in competent hands and that all is well."[8]

When the front line at last appeared on British screens, reviewers referred to "the curiously constructed trenches" and urged that the films should be given a place in a national museum for their immense importance as historical records. It was apparent, even to those unfamiliar with front-line newsreels, that "a careful editor" had taken the trouble to eliminate all that might be "painful and gruesome."[9]

The first of the British official war films, *The Battle of the Somme* (1916), had a traumatic effect on people in Britain, not because it contained horrific scenes, but simply because the majority of civilians had only the vaguest conception of modern war. Those who were there remember screams from the audience. People had seen pictures in the magazines and the topicals of the elements of the *Somme* —the guns, the troop movements, the trenches, and the explosions—but never had a film shown in Britain contained the full range of permissible war scenes; jammed together, one amazing spectacle upon another, it was a revelation that inspired the highest praise.

James Douglas, writing in *The Star,* captures exactly that sense of wonder and horror that gripped the audiences of the time. "Somebody in the War Office or at G.H.Q. has at last realised that the war film is the only substitute for invasion. Somebody has grasped the power of the moving picture to carry the war on to British soil. We see the Manchesters on the eve of battle standing in a circle round a chaplain in a white surplice . . . We see a General sitting like a bronze man on a bronze charger addressing Lancashire fusiliers . . . Then comes the grim prelude —shell-fire . . . Fantastic smoke-shapes, strangely slow in the melting. Dark upheavals. And under them we know that German soldiers are hidden in the creases and wrinkles of the soil. We see the monstrous howitzer with its fifteen-inch mouth, its recoil, the shaking of its mounting, the tremor of its branches. It looks like a live thing. . . .

"We see helmeted soldiers fixing their bayonets and being passed round the corner of a trench like a football crowd going through a turnstile. We see a vast mine exploding. We see a row of soldiers standing with fixed bayonets in a trench waiting for the signal to scramble over the parapet. Suddenly an officer is seen on the parapet with a gallant gesture of leadership. He is not there alone for a second. The whole line lifts and goes simultaneously. All but two. One on the right. One on the left. They slip back very quietly. They lie against the sloping face of the trench. They lie upright with their faces to the clay and the enemy. The man on the right does not move a limb. The man on the left moves his arms a little and then is at rest.

"Is it right to let us see brave men dying? Yes. Is it a sacrilege? No. These pictures are good for us. The dead on the battlefield, the drivers of the gun-teams steering the wheels clear of the corpses, the demented German prisoners, the kindly British soldiers showering cigarettes upon their captives, the mangled heap of anguish on the stretcher . . . these vilenesses are war. War is the enemy and Germany is its patentee, its idolator, its worshipper. It is our task to beat the German sword into a ploughshare so that the nations may learn war no more."[10]

The trade was immensely gratified that films were being taken seriously at last. Yet some exhibitors were disturbed. In Hammersmith the manager of the Broadway displayed a slide which, instead of announcing the *Somme,* declared his intention not to show it: "This is a Place of Amusement, not a Chamber of Horrors."[11]

To the *Evening Standard,* the theater's manager, W. Jefferson Woods, explained that the decision was a matter of feeling and taste. " 'If we were showing it, people said they were not coming.'

" 'But why not show it, thousands are seeing it.'

" 'I don't think it is suitable for those who have lost relatives. I think it is harrowing and distressing.'

" 'But it is historical.'

" 'I was at the Trade Show, and one man gave a shriek and said, "Let me out. I feel so bad. I have just lost a brother." '

" 'But the public can stand seeing what the boys go through.'

" 'The papers are full of it every morning. We see for ourselves the wounded walking about our streets . . . and another point,' " added Woods, " 'in the film you see stretcher after stretcher coming in with wounded Germans. I think it is likely to create pity for the brutes. It is possible for people to say "Poor devils!" It is likely to create pity for the enemy.' "[12]

The picture was squeezed for every last drop of its propaganda value. A letter was published in a fan magazine, purporting to be from Adelaide Archer, a munitions worker: "As I saw the great piles of munitions I at once realised how much Tommy depends on us for help. *How* many hundreds of precious lives you and I might save by working our very best all the time. Tommy doesn't grumble and worry about Bank Holidays or Sundays off—no, he works and 'rests' . . . week in, week out—and always with a smile and a song."[13]

THE FAMOUS "OVER THE TOP" SCENE FROM *The Battle of the Somme*, ACTUALLY FILMED AT A TRENCH-MORTAR BATTERY SCHOOL.

Stage one.

Stage two.

Stage three. Had this scene been real, the cameraman would have been in as much danger as the troops.

As the picture reached the provinces, observers noted that audiences were not nearly as shocked as had been expected. Instead, they were gratified by the realism. They felt that war films of the past had shown only the "glory" of war—the Somme pictures showed what war really meant. The film was banned in British Columbia, however, in case it discouraged recruiting.

The film can be seen today at the Imperial War Museum in London, in exactly the form in which it was released. It is hard to believe that this film attracted so much controversy. Lengthy scenes photographed at or near the front (by Geoffrey Malins, with some scenes from J. B. McDowell) are linked with subtitles that, in the manner of primitive dramas, account for two or three episodes:

—Industrious French peasants continue their activities just outside the firing line.
—Care of artillery horses.
—The Mascot of the Royal Field Artillery caught in France.

Although mention is made of events that occurred offscreen ("Twenty minutes after these pictures were taken, these men came under heavy machine-gun fire"), the film tells nothing of the cost in lives, beyond a few shots of corpses, which, while undoubtedly unique for the time, are not very eloquent. The film conveys no sense of the discomfort and terror of life in the trenches. It all looks amiably shambolic. Being an official war film, it is hardly likely to hint at the devastating casualty figures; the first day on the Somme was the worst day in the history of any army—57,470 officers and men killed, two for every yard of the British front. No one seeing the film could guess that this was the bloodiest defeat in England's history.

Malins has an eye for mass movement, as in a battle painting, with squadrons of troops on the move half a mile from the camera. But he has none for intimate and telling detail, and those that do occur happen accidentally in a corner of frame. A bemused German prisoner bumps into a British soldier with an injured arm—and the soldier uses his arm to give the man a vicious shove. It happens in a mass shot, and one only notices it on a second or third viewing.

Occasionally, a scene appears that is beautiful or bizarre. Like a Millet painting, two French peasant women, bent low, their faces obscured by white caps, work a field, while the wind blows through the crops, and away in the distance, like a swarm of locusts, hover thousands of soldiers, making camp. Four stretcher-bearers tramp along an empty road at the top of a ridge. They pause, and rest their charge, and we suddenly notice that behind them, on the plain, is the front line, with the zigzag trenches, the furious shellfire proving that the bombardment is at its height.

What is so curious about the film is that it gives the impression of being an outsider's film. It shows everything from a distance—both figuratively and literally. And there is very little action.

This would not be surprising were it not for the existence of a book written by Lieutenant Geoffrey Malins, *How I Filmed the War,*[14] which includes detailed descriptions of the Somme, and how he secured film of a major attack. "What a picture it was! They went over as one man. I could see while I was exposing that numbers were shot down before they reached the top of the parapet; others just the other side. They went across the ground in swarms, and marvel upon marvel, still smoking cigarettes. One man actually stopped in the middle of No Man's Land to light up again."

The only remotely similar scene included in the film is the one of soldiers going over the top, described by James Douglas in *The Star.* The shot has appeared in almost every compilation film about the First World War. The staff at the Imperial War Museum have doubted its authenticity, but have been unable to pin down their suspicions. The shot lacks that indefinable air of reality, but it is hard to say why until you determine the position of the camera. For the first shot—of the men in the trench—the camera should have been low in the trench, sheltering from the fire. It is not. It is almost as high as the soldiers themselves. The following shot shows troops walking toward the enemy, crossing barbed wire of ankle height, and two men falling somewhat unconvincingly near the camera. The camera is at ground level, and in order to have taken this shot, the cameraman would have had to operate fully exposed to the enemy fire that has just killed the men in the trench.

"Early in '17, I was in Roclincourt close to St. Paul, where there was a trench-mortar battery school," said Bertram Brookes-Carrington. "I was having a cup of coffee, when a chap passing by saw my camera and tripod. 'Excuse me,' he said, 'do you know Lieutenant Malins?' I said yes. 'I wonder how his pictures came out. He did a lot here at the battery school. I was one of the blokes that fell down dead in the trench.' " Little else in the *Somme* is faked, and for such a scene to be reconstructed suggests that censorship demanded it.

But Geoffrey Malins's book is so packed with preposterous exaggeration that his real achievements suffer by comparison with his imaginative exploits. He paints a picture of himself as a John Buchan hero, beset by petrifying danger, yet laughingly grinding his camera in the very teeth of the Hun. Despite the tight restrictions on photography in Belgium, Malins breezes up to the front line, grabs his shots at terrifying risk, and returns to admiring gazes and such remarks as "Ah, you English. You are *extraordinaire.*" Although born in Boston, Lincolnshire, Malins was not English, but Irish, and that, together with his natural boastfulness and his flair as a showman, may help to account for his outrageous book. It depicts Malins being blown up at least twice per chapter, being shot at every time he erects his tripod, and narrowly escaping death in virtually every paragraph. He recounts his adventures in a breathless shout:

"Snipers seemed to be in every tree. Bullets whistled down like acorns in the autumn breeze, but the French suddenly formed a semi-circle and pushed right into the wood, driving the enemy from their perches in the trees or shooting them as they scrambled down. Through the wood I plunged, utterly ignoring every danger, both from friend or foe, in the thrill of that wonderful 'drive.' Luck, however, was with me. Neither the French nor the Germans seemed to see me, and we all suddenly came out of the wood at the far side, and I then managed to get a splendid picture of the end of the pursuit when the French, wild with excitement, plunged madly down the hill in chase of the last remnants of the sniping band."

Malins's Münchhausen style obscures his enormously important contribution to the films of the war. And it infuriated the authorities. A newspaper article prompted a memo to Beaverbrook: "Can anything be done to make this fellow hold his tongue?" His book, written in 1916 as *Adventures of a War Film Artist,* ran into such resistance that it failed to appear until 1920. Brigadier General Charteris of the General Staff wrote in 1917 about its many exaggerations: "It gives the impression that the author was under no supervision and went about as he liked, ordering officers about, frequently drawing the enemy's fire and being a public nuisance. As a matter of fact, this operator, until the arrival of McDowell late in June, was almost invariably accompanied by an officer." The general commented on the numerous inaccuracies, which the officer in charge of the cinematographers vouched for, and added, "I think it is regrettable that the author, who has undoubtedly displayed courage and undergone risk and discomfort on occasions, should not have confined himself more nearly to the truth."[15]

In contrast to Malins, most newsreel cameramen—especially those from England—are known for their noncommunicative nature. This was particularly true of the Official Kinematographers; although only one was alive when I was researching this book, I talked to the widows of several of the others. They all said the same thing: "Oh, he never talked about it." "He never told me anything." "He never mentioned the war."

I met the last survivor of the British front-line cameramen at Glebelands, the film industry home in Berkshire. He was alert and active, although in his eighties, and was as helpful as he could be. But even *he* was remarkably uncommunicative. Bertram Brookes-Carrington had been a cinematic adventurer of the first order; besides being a war correspondent, he made pictures in Africa, worked with Mr. and Mrs. Martin Johnson, and accompanied several expeditions. Yet when asked to relate these adventures, British reticence ruled. He shrugged, wrinkled his large nose, and stared at the ceiling, acting for all the world as though he'd spent his life drinking civil service tea. It was a struggle to get him to tell of his war experiences, but at least, when he did come out with something, the account was straightforward and unadorned.

"After my work in Belgium, I did a few bits and pieces at the Gaumont studio, then back to France again. I didn't get much more of France, though, until 1917. The Battle of Arras was going on all the time, so I got mixed up in that for about six months.

"I never saw the stuff I shot until I got home. They only sent reports if it was no good. I was lucky in the early part of the war, when I got back fairly frequently—three months away, one month back. Later on, I didn't see my stuff at all. It was out and published and forgotten. The footage released for showing to the general public was not more than about ten percent of the total footage we took. The War Office used to see to that.

"You carried perhaps twelve hundred feet as a rule. Sometimes you were lucky if you got, oh, fifty feet. Other times you could get rid of a magazine-full—four hundred feet at one go. First of all, loaned by Gaumont to the War Office, I used a Debrie. Later on, when I was an Official Kinematographer and in uniform, I was using a Moy. Of course the Moy wasn't as efficient as the Debrie. You were hard up for f2 lenses in those days. I only had one, as early as that. Lenses were mostly f3.5.

"Matters would have been a great deal easier out there if we'd had a really efficient hand camera. The Aeroscope was a good camera if it was looked after, but there weren't enough of them. As a matter of fact, I was with the Warwick Trading Company when we built the first one. Kasimir de Proszynski, the inventor,

Having caught this still picture of a shell explosion, J. B. McDowell set up his motion picture camera and secured a famous shot of a direct hit on an artillery train.

came across with his designs and patents and we built the first one there in Charing Cross Road.

"Hand cranking came naturally. Purely automatic, even under shellfire. Sixteen frames a second, two turns a second—and then you've got a tripod head with a tilting handle and a panorama handle that you've got to run in either direction at different speeds. That was no trouble to me at all. But if I'd had an Aeroscope on that job, or some similar type of camera, I could have done far better. It was mobility that was lacking. You couldn't take a really satisfactory picture without a hefty great tripod. Sometimes you felt like throwing it away.

"In the ordinary course of events, without a special assignment, you started the day by getting up at daybreak. Then you'd go to the mess, have your breakfast, and see the colonel in charge. Colonel Faunthorpe was there then. He'd say, 'Well, there's not much doing today. Just scout around and see what you can find.' Or else —'There might be a bit of a show at So-and-so. Go up there.' You went out, and if there was anything worth shooting, you just shot it; if there wasn't, you came back without anything at all. And as soon as you got back, the war correspondents, who had been sitting back there all the time, would come up to the cameramen wanting stories. Quite a number of them used to do that, including some very well-known names.

"I didn't get so much in the trenches. Two or three days at a stretch now and again. Usually, it was before something was coming off, like when they opened up during the battle for Arras. I had to make for a place called Orange Hill, at least that was our name for it. I stayed in the trenches overnight and took up a position on that hill, and at daybreak we opened up a terrific offensive. It was estimated that several thousand guns went off at once, stretched over a semi-perimeter for miles. Lovely sound.

"One place I'll never forget was Bullecourt. About five or six weeks previously, about three thousand cavalrymen were carved up there, and they were lying there still. I filmed some of it, but it wouldn't have been shown. The War Office would have seen to that.

"One of the most gruesome sights was close to the crossroads, as you went in to Arras. There was a field where there had been quite a carve up, and the bodies had been somewhat hastily buried. The main highway ran just past this little sector and every now and again, due to the sinking of the soil, you'd see arms and legs sticking up. It wasn't a very pleasant sight.

"I remember when we took the Messines Wytschaete Ridge, I wanted some shots so I walked along the top. I was carrying the camera; I had an orderly carrying the tripod. All of a sudden, Jerry started shelling the top of the ridge. I said, 'Hell, he knows it's empty. What the blazes is he shelling for?' And then I thought, 'Oh, perhaps he thinks this is a rangefinder outfit. So he's shelling *me.*'

"It didn't take long to slip on the other side, and then he doesn't know where you are—whether you've retraced your steps and gone back, or whether you're waiting perfectly still for the shelling to stop.

"I've been afraid several times in my life, but if you've got a camera in your hands and you know there's a picture to be got, you just get it, and you forget all about fear.

"Captain McDowell was in the front line one night, and they were going over the top the next morning. There was a shell hole between the two lines; the ground was sloping up slightly towards the Germans so that their lip of the shell hole was higher than ours. He crept up and got into that shell hole with a camera and tripod. He could look down at our chaps coming out of the trenches. When you're taking a picture, you don't care what's happening at all. The picture's all you think about. He got so enthused that he jumped out of the shell hole and shot them going into the Jerry trenches as well. He got the M.C. for that.

"I never had any doubt that we were going to win. Things might have been going badly now and then, but how could the British Empire lose?

"Funnily enough, I finished the war as an American officer. They made me a very good offer—it was equivalent to twice as much as I had been getting with the Gaumont Company, and the war looked as though it might last forever in '18. I joined the Photographic Section of the Signal Corps; we had a unit almost entirely on its own. There was Adrian Gil-Spear [scenario editor from the Goldwyn Studios], Paul Foster, and a chap who had been secretary to Jack London. We formed our own little bunch and we spent most of our time doing scenics in Britain, showing what the American boys had been seeing. We did a series called *Beautiful Britain.*

"But the incidents of those days have become like those little snapshot books you used to flick over. You become blasé to it. Your memories become . . . I won't say dulled . . . I can't think of the word I want. Funny, I can't think of an English word to describe it."[16]

A child plays among the ruins of war—on the deserted set of Civilization. *Inceville, 1916.*

PACIFISM

When British producers first felt the impact of their American rivals, they were at a loss to know how to deal with them. No one could deny the superiority of their product, or the massive popularity of their stars. Certain individuals therefore chose to ignore the pro-Allied content of American films, and to foment a whispered campaign. It had no basis, even in rumor; it was a crude and desperate attempt to discredit business rivals, and it was centered solely upon the names of prominent American producers.

English renters and manufacturers noted that the American film industry was ruled by Central Europeans: Selig, Kleine, Laemmle, Kessel, Thanhouser, Baumann, Lubin, and Zukor must be German, Austrian, or Hungarian, therefore it was obvious that their attempt to capture the British market was a plot originated in Berlin.

It sounds preposterous, but it was no more ridiculous than the campaign that led to the resignation of the First Sea Lord, Prince Louis Battenberg. ("Blood is said to be thicker than water," wrote Horatio Bottomley,[1] "and we doubt whether all the water in the North Sea could obliterate the blood ties between the Battenbergs and the Hohenzollerns when it came to a life and death struggle between Germany and ourselves.")

American correspondents in England responded laconically, referring to "thrilling accounts of how in the backwoods of Brooklyn, German agents were sending films to this country under well-known American trademarks."[2]

Stephen Bush of the *Moving Picture World* answered the charges with the assurance that all the American producers supported the Allies.[3] He was a trifle over-emphatic in claiming that they were all true-blue Americans, with never a German among them. But it was true that the personal loyalties of the American producers, when they ran contrary to their business interests, were never permitted to interfere. The Universal Film Manufacturing Company, headed by Carl Laemmle from Laupheim, South Württemberg, produced some of the most heinous anti-German pictures; but when the war was over, Laemmle was the first in the industry to campaign for money and food for starving Germany.

Equating pacifism with treachery, the English trade would have welcomed an antiwar film from one of these producers. But they were to be denied that satisfaction. The most highly regarded pacifist film was directed by an Anglo-Irishman, Herbert Brenon, and produced by a Russian, Lewis J. Selznick. Adapted from a one-act play, *War Brides* starred the Russian actress Nazimova; it was set in a mythical kingdom where the prime function of women was to produce children to stoke the fires of war. Critic Alan Dale said it aroused his extreme enthusiasm: "It is certainly the very finest picture that I have ever seen, and I make no exceptions. You can have all the 'big' films, and the million-dollar productions, and the terrific things that are announced with the flourish of trumpets, but you can leave me *War Brides.*" The film's enormous success at the end of 1916 conflicts with the theory that the public rejected D. W. Griffith's *Intolerance* purely on the basis of its pacifist message. *War Brides* was not even officially withdrawn when the United States entered the war.*

Before April 1917 American films about the war were shaped with the Allied market in mind, but with pacifists, pro-Germans, and preparedness-mongers among the domestic audience, manufacturers were obliged to appeal to as many groups as possible. *Shell 43,* a Thomas Ince production, did its best to smile in every direction. The hero was introduced as an American journalist, then as a German secret service agent, and later as an English lieutenant who falls for the daughter of a German baroness. At the climax, he directs artillery to an area of strategic importance, which he himself is occupying, and blows himself to bits.[4]

Like many American films, *Shell 43* proved unsatisfactory propaganda once it arrived in England. "It is difficult for the British public to accept a spy as a figure of romance," said *The Bioscope,* "and perhaps for this reason, the film seems a little lacking in sympathy. The hero is compelled to cheat and lie to his friends in his country's cause and the slight love interest is, unfortunately, on the enemy side. This might be acceptable in a neutral country, but we imagine it may be detrimental to its interest in the opinion of a British audience."[5]

To save import charges on shipping film, which was subject to taxation as

---

* Nazimova had already appeared in the play *War Brides* on the vaudeville circuit. For the fate of *War Brides* in wartime America, see James R. Mock, *Censorship 1917* (Princeton University Press, 1941), p. 175, and "Nazimova" in Jack Spears, *Civil War on the Screen and Other Essays* (New York: A. S. Barnes, 1977).

Without visiting the front, no one could imagine what warfare looked like in 1916. The battle scenes of Civilization, *though well produced, were rooted in the Civil War and the Franco-Prussian War of 1870.*

Edward G. Robinson was a bit player in Arms and the Woman *(1916)—he is on the right in a peaked hat. Made when America was still neutral, the film had an overtly pacifist message that was cut for export while the story's industrial saboteurs were firmly identified as Austrian.* *(See p. 72.)*

well as to duty on arrival in England, titles were reduced to a few frames. It was little trouble to set up special titles, change the original wording, and transform "neutral" American films into fervent pro-Ally propaganda. The effect of this operation was to persuade audiences that America was considerably more outspoken in her sympathies for Britain and her distrust of the Central Powers than was, in fact, the case.

Arms and the Woman (1916) was a Pathé–Gold Rooster drama about the manufacture of munitions for the Allies. Written by Ouida Bergere and directed by George Fitzmaurice, it featured Mary Nash as Rozika, a Hungarian girl who emigrates to the United States with her brother. Rozika gets a job as a singer in a New York dive. During a brawl, her brother kills a man and has to go into hiding. An anarchist brotherhood gives him shelter. Rozika sings in the streets, but her companion ill-treats her and steals her money. She escapes, and attracts the attention of David Fravoe (Lumsden Hare), the owner of a big steel factory that has been turned over to the manufacture of war material. Married to him, Rozika achieves success in opera. Her brother, however, becomes involved in a plot to destroy the munitions factory. Rozika warns her husband, but too late to prevent the destruction of the works. After wounding Fravoe with a revolver shot, Rozika's brother dies in the fire he himself has started.

This film could not possibly have been shown in England in its original form. The Hungarians were enemies of Britain, and so Rozika became Lucia, an Italian girl who lived under Austrian rule, which was so abhorrent to her that she was forced to emigrate. Her brother became a young Austrian, Karl, who is in love with Lucia, and emigrates on the same boat. Even the name Fravoe was removed and replaced by the undeniably Anglo-Saxon Trevor. The original version had a pacifist element, which was cut out; Rozika is horrified by the instruments of death and destruction manufactured by her husband, and a quarrel breaks out. As the flames destroy the factory, the husband remarks: "It is better so."

Arms and the Woman included several documentary sequences, which would be fascinating today, if only the film had been preserved: on board the emigrant ship; in the New York slums ("almost unnecessarily sordid in detail," said one review[6]); and in a munitions factory, showing the manufacture of big guns. It was also notable for an appearance of Edward G. Robinson in a small part.

THE MOST PRETENTIOUS AMERICAN pacifist film emerged from the studio of Thomas H. Ince. It was scarcely an ideal subject for Ince, for he was a fervently patriotic individual, to whom the whole notion of pacifism was anathema. But anxious to ingratiate himself with the government, he made this contribution to Wilson's peace platform.

So expert had the company become at staging violence—from earthquake through riot to Armageddon—that a film opposing the whole idea of war must have seemed blasphemous. Known at first simply as "Ince's Big Picture" and then as *He Who Returned,* the film mirrored the allegorical approach of Blackton; it envisaged the Second Coming as the only event powerful enough to bring the war to an end. The final release title was *Civilization,* and Ince hoped it would do for him what *The Birth of a Nation* had done for Griffith.

Civilization is credited in practically all the history books as being directed by Thomas Ince. Every mention of the picture at the time was accompanied by Ince's name. This obscured the fact that a number of directors worked on various sections—Raymond West was responsible for most of it; Jay Hunt, Reginald Barker, J. Parker Read, Walter Edwards, and David Hartford directed other sections. Cameramen included O. M. Gove, Joseph August, Clyde de Vinna, Dal Clawson, Irvin Willat, Charles Kaufman, and J. D. Jennings.

A cutting room fire, so severe that it destroyed the work print of *Civilization,* caused Ince to start editing again from scratch. He placed Irvin Willat in charge. "This was a big job for a little kid," said Willat (he was then in his twenties). "I brought out my idea of adding pictures to subtitles. Painted backgrounds so that the title wasn't just lettering. In addition, I made a prologue and epilogue for the story. The first was war—a view over the valley with a cannon and the army below, fire and explosions. The epilogue was the valley at peace, with a dove resting on a broken cannon, a shepherd and sheep. They turned out very successfully, but there was still something missing.

"In the battle scenes we had stock shots bought from the government; shots of battleships and artillery firing. They were very few and far between, so I tried another idea. I enlarged explosions and used them several times to heighten the effect. I would take an explosion which was some way off, and bring it up close. I made an optical printer to do this which was a simple thing, just like enlarging anywhere. Surely, the grain was enlarged, but in the heat of battle it wasn't too important. What they wanted was action."[7]

The premiere of *Civilization* was held at the Triangle Majestic Theater in Los Angeles on 17 April 1916. It was a success with the audience. David Hamburger, millionaire department store owner, wrote to Ince: "I really believe that if it could have been brought to the attention of President Wilson before the serious aspect of the U-boat controversy, he would have hesitated a long time before taking serious steps in the matter."

However, Ince and his colleagues were not pleased with the business that the picture was doing on the West Coast. Willat says that he suggested they take the high points from another picture, *The Purple Cross,* made, thanks to Ince's characteristic economy, with the same leading players and the same costumes as in *Civilization.* It was about a submarine and could tie in effectively with the submarine in the main picture.

The new version of *Civilization* opened at the Criterion Theater in New York on 2 June 1916. Only one mishap marred the opening; five reels at a time had been mounted on large spools—and the projectionist started with the wrong spool. To reload took time. "I still remember that moment and how I sunk into my seat," said Willat. "But we got it back together and ran it and we had some very good reports. It was not the equivalent of one of Griffith's pictures, but with all the effects we put into it, I was very proud."

Willat was now in an invidious position as Ince's fair-haired boy. He was given charge of several departments, among his responsibilities being that of rescuing unreleasable pictures. Ince put them on the shelf, and it was up to Willat to take them off. He used his device of illustrated titles and sometimes shot additional scenes.

"I don't think I failed on any of them. But there was one tough one he handed me. It was the remains of *The Purple Cross.* He had a lot of money in it, and I had to change it enough so he could use it."

Willat turned the submarine into a Zeppelin and, with the aid of miniatures, came up with another pacifist picture—*Zeppelin's Last Raid,* which he both directed and photographed. Said *Moving Picture World,* which gave the director's credit to Ince: "Made as a companion picture to *Civilization* as a protest against war, this intensely absorbing story deals with the ending of the war through the growth and establishment of democracy as the German people throw off the Prussian yoke of militarism and again take their places in the sun. It is however more of a story than a propaganda, with intimate studies of the little-known Zeppelin type of air raider." The magazine added: "If you have seen the earlier form of this picture, it is well to remember that a rearrangement of the story has entirely altered its earlier pacifist tone."[8]

Perhaps it is worth pausing here to determine the degree of commitment to the pacifist cause of the man so responsible for these two pictures—Irvin Willat.

I had just started work on this book when Willat came to London. Since he was responsible, after *Zeppelin's Last Raid,* for the most virulent anti-German propaganda of such films as *Behind the Door,* in which a U-boat commander was skinned alive, I was intrigued to know whose side he was on when he first heard of the European war.

"When the war started?" he said. "I was on the German side. Most All-Americans were."

"Why were you on the German side?"

"I don't know. We've had good experience in America with the Germans. God knows, I shouldn't; they were pretty rough on the Poles. My father, who was Polish, didn't like the Germans. You've given me a problem there. I can't remember."

"What were your feelings about *Civilization*—a pacifist film?"

"I had a problem to solve, and the problem to me was more important than the propaganda. I was young. For a director I was about the youngest in the business."

"What was the feeling at the Ince studio?"

"I don't think they gave a damn. They wanted to make pictures sell. I don't remember any propaganda being brought in, or any resentment of the Germans, or anything else. We had a job to do, and we wanted to do it. A few years later I might have given it some thought. But you've got to realize this was an important move for me—to be able to handle these pictures."

"Did you read a newspaper every day?"

"No. When I started on a picture, nothing came in between. I ate it, slept it, and worked it. There was nothing on my mind but 'get that picture out.' Money was involved. I had to get it out the best I could for the least money. Because if you don't make a profit, there's no use to make it."

According to William Cochrane, press representative of the Democratic National Committee, *Civilization* played a considerable role in Wilson's victory in 1916.[9]

Seeing these old pictures again, one can usually find some quality in them, however horrendous the propaganda. *Civilization,* however, has practically nothing to commend it, and its undeniable impact on audiences of the time now seems

LEFT: *Thomas H. Ince and President Woodrow Wilson. Ince's* Civilization *played a considerable role in Wilson's re-election in 1916, according to the Democratic National Committee's press representative, but Wilson was no enthusiast for motion pictures generally.*
RIGHT: *Irvin Willat, who saved Ince's pacifist epic, sided with the Germans.*

baffling.* The best of Ince's pictures were fresh, simple stories, made with conviction and beauty. *Civilization* is a pretentious, disconnected, highly theatrical fable, as simple-minded as the most earnest Victorian morality play, and not even in its big set pieces does it convince for more than half a dozen shots at a time. The acting is wooden, and the film presents the view of war of those who have never seen it.

The picture opens with scenes laid in the countryside of the Kingdom of Wredpryd. Rumors of war bring Luther Rolfe (J. Frank Burke), an ardent follower of Christ and an advocate of universal peace, to plead for peace in the Senate. Count Ferdinand (Howard Hickman) is an inventor in the service of the king (Herschel Mayall); the count's submarine is about to bring him fame and riches. His fiancée (Enid Markey) is a pacifist, who vigorously disapproves of his work.

The king, persuaded by his ministers, agrees to war. The decision is a popular one, and when Luther Rolfe protests, the crowd attacks him. "After nineteen centuries of Christian spirit," says a title, "its mockery is laid bare in the sight of men thirsty for blood." Following a decisive battle, the king's army is thrown back, demoralized. Count Ferdinand's fiancée is shown evidence of an unseen army of women, striving to bring peace.

Aboard his submarine, Count Ferdinand is ordered to torpedo a liner carrying a full cargo of war materials: "Passengers used as blind. Disregard sentiment." In his imagination he sees the panic and bloodshed his action would cause. "Stop!" he cries. "Not a single torpedo against women and children!" The crew tries to overpower the count, but he releases a torrent of water into the submarine. Half-submerged, the submarine blows up.

The count is rescued, at the point of death. The king insists that he should live,

* This opinion is not shared by such critics as Clyde Jeavons and Tom Milne, who admire the picture.

but the count's soul descends to the infernal regions where, in his agony, he is confronted by the figure of Christ. He is told: "In thy earthly body will I return and with thy voice plead for peace."

The count awakens after the doctors have despaired of his life. The king takes this as a sign of his own divine power. Ferdinand sets out to preach the gospel of peace, but the war has reached its height and his words infuriate the crowds. Imperial troops arrest him on a charge of inciting riot, and at a court martial he is condemned to death. In his cell the count suffers a relapse. The king is informed of his death, and he is later confronted by the spirit of Christ, who shows him the terrible harvest of war.

New recruits for the cause of peace join the invasion of the capital—women sweep toward the palace, pleading for the war to end. The king, shocked into sanity by the visions, repents and signs the peace petition. "During my reign," he announces, "it is my command that my subjects enjoy peace and goodwill." The blare of the war bugle dies away, families are reunited, and the country is at peace once more.

A plausible explanation for the popularity of *Civilization* was provided by Richard Griffith,[10] who said that the regimentation of women and Christ's reappearance on earth were two themes that expressed the wishes of millions who wanted the war to end but saw no hope more practical than the miracle of divine intervention or an equally miraculous uprising by the mothers of the race.

And one cannot deny the film's impact at the time. Thomas Ince claimed to have received 1,427 letters within a period of four weeks, and he published one of them as an advertisement in *Moving Picture World:*

> For one who has been through the Gehenna of Nations in France, and for the millions who *remain,* as I went, to lay down my life for the defence of my country and my loved ones, I thank you, sir, with a simple soldier's prayer that your wonderful picture *Civilization* may waken your own great race to the Demoniac madness of modern war. What you in your screen sermon have depicted—vivid, remorseless and truly horrible as it is—is but the *least* part of the Saturnalia of war.
>
> Picture the stench of your comrades rotting in death by your side as you are bespattered by the hot blood of the freshly butchered in all the blistering heat and volcanic thunder of shrieking shells and belching guns! Then, in the black and deadlier silence of night, while you lie half-buried in muddy, bloody slime hour after hour waiting for hell's fire to burst out from earth and sky again, to feel the maggots, that are devouring in their millions the men you have lived and fought by, crawling over your own living carcass, as your brain reels in delirium at the sights and sounds you hear and see. . . . Then the thoughts of home, of the anguish of loved ones, their lack of your support—helpless women, hungry babes—Oh God! You can't think of it!
>
> No! Not even you, whose vision seems to have been made prophetic, clear and pure with the power of a great God-given purpose. I can write no more. I can think of no more that I dare write. . . .
>
> Yours for "Civilization"
>
> A Plain British Soldier Formerly of 2nd Wrcs. Batt., RFA[11]

No more extraordinary document has ever been used to publicize a film; it remains a powerful tribute to a far from powerful film.

Griffith's *Intolerance,* which opened in September 1916, confused, alarmed, and almost physically assaulted the audience, offering no solution to man's inhumanity to man, but more than three hours of graphic illustration. The failure of *Intolerance* and the success of *Civilization* was yet another illustration of how audiences preferred being diverted to being disturbed. It was a further victory for hokum.

The film was prepared for the British market, following its successful American run. The great American pacifist film was announced as *Civilization, What Every True Briton Is Fighting For.* Away went the introductory subtitle: "Can we call ourselves civilized when we shut our eyes against the command of the Prince of Peace—'Love thy Neighbor as thyself'?"

Luther Rolfe was spared any change of name—his own sounded German enough—but he was transformed into a socialist. Since the king had been costumed in a Prussian helmet, it was a simple matter for the subtitles to refer to him as the emperor. The similarity of the fictitious country Wredpryd to Germany caused this British version to run into trouble. How could Christ—hardly ever shown on the screen in England—appear to British audiences in the guise of a German officer? The emphasis was hurriedly altered; Count Ferdinand's body returned to earth merely *animated* by the Spirit of Christ, to spread the gospel of peace. The story then continued satisfactorily for the British authorities, for the gospel was preached only to the Germans, who promptly set about killing the count.

To ensure the film's acceptance in Britain, additional scenes were photographed. "The recruiting scenes outside an imaginary Whitehall," wrote the reviewer of *The Bioscope,* "admirable in their stage management, have an exuberance which is quite unlike the phlegmatic calm of a British crowd, while the enthusiastic young recruit who is introduced as a contrast to the enemy conscripts is so frankly American that his adoration of the late Lord Kitchener's portrait strikes an incongruous note."[12]

The Bioscope considered it dangerous that the film should arouse a desire for peace among women. "We cannot think that it is the time to advocate any measures which might relax the determination of the British public to prosecute the war to its final conclusion, and even the extremely beautiful concluding scenes, where the happy villagers welcome back their husbands, sons and sweethearts . . . lose something of their effect from the fact that the returning soldiers belong to that army for which at the present moment any excessive sentimentality would only be a sign of weakness."[13]

The film enjoyed a great financial success in Britain, and although its complete transformation from a pacifist plea to a call to arms did not prevent it being banned in Spain,* the changes proved highly appropriate. For just two months after its English opening, America entered the war.

---

* Sweden banned it, too: The "enemy" too closely resembled the Germans for any neutral nation.

THE GERMANS IN AMERICA

The independence of the United States was achieved with the defeat of the British Army. She fought the British again, as an ally of the French, in 1812. American patriotism was rooted in the Revolutionary War, yet the nation overwhelmingly supported Britain and her Allies in the Great War.

Historians have stressed the common language, the emotional ties evoked by Britain's past, and the debt owed to the country of Lafayette. In fact, the United States was so economically dependent upon the Allies she could not possibly have risked a German victory. After the disastrous slump following the outbreak of war in Europe, Allied orders caused trade figures to jump spectacularly; they increased from $825 million in 1914 to $3,214 million in 1916. Thanks largely to the British blockade, trade with the Central Powers dropped from $169 million in 1914 to a mere million in 1916.[1]

Those who ran the picture business would have been obliged to support the Allies, whatever the national economy dictated. For Great Britain was the film clearinghouse of the world. During 1916, despite the wretched conditions in Europe, United States manufacturers exported more film than at any time since the birth of the industry—$10 million worth. Of the total footage—224,518,880 feet—the majority went to, and through, England. The war might have lost England her supremacy as the world's film distributor, but even when the United States won that title, London remained America's most lucrative overseas market.

With virtually every American film about the war favoring the Allies, the discomfiture of those German-Americans who supported the Central Powers was understandable. In the wave of anti-German feeling following the sinking of the *Lusitania,* they became known as hyphenated citizens. Some newspapers held them responsible for their compatriots' every excess.

The German community defended itself vigorously, but as far as motion pictures were concerned, their efforts yielded small results. It took the combined efforts of several German-American organizations, the American Independence Union, *and* the German consul to have the anti-German posters for a war film removed from a San Francisco theater—and they succeeded only because the posters gave the address of Canadian recruiting stations.[2]

A similar attack was initiated against a film called *The Ordeal.* In the Franco-Prussian War, a young prisoner's refusal to reveal the whereabouts of his regiment causes his mother, sister, and sweetheart to be shot by the Prussians before his eyes. Adapted from the poem "The Ballad of Splendid Silence" by E. Nesbitt, better known for her children's books, the propaganda message—"his country stood before his loved ones"—was plain. *The Ordeal* was running at one of the biggest motion picture houses in New York early in 1915, when the License Commissioner served notice on the owner of the theater that he would be deprived of his license unless he took the picture off at once. The reason given was that the film violated the spirit of the President's proclamation of neutrality.

The Ordeal was produced by the Life Photo Play Film Corporation, which took this case of suppression of free speech to court. The German-Americans persuaded a fragile young girl to testify that the brutal general depicted in *The Ordeal* was

The ill-fated Robert Goldstein, right, on the set of Spirit of '76, *the film that was to land him in jail. Adda Gleason, left. Behind Goldstein is Chief Dark Cloud.*

British officers encourage the torture of Americans by Indians in one of the controversial scenes from Robert Goldstein's epic, Spirit of '76 (1917).

"an unfair characterization and a misrepresentation of the German army."

But such histrionics were unlikely to impress a court troubled by the *Lusitania.* Judge Whitaker, of the Supreme Court, took the unprecedented step of issuing an injunction against the License Commissioner, restraining him from interfering with the exhibition. He considered that the Board of Censors feared the disapproval of foreigners. "The court cannot give official sanction to the grouping of American citizens into different classes, shaping its decrees accordingly."[3]

To certain agencies of British intelligence in America, "German" and "Jewish" were virtually synonymous, and demanded equal surveillance.[4] In the case of Robert Goldstein, a Jew of German origin, such surveillance was unnecessary, for he advertised his allegiance with a motion picture.

The Goldstein Theatrical Costuming Company had supplied the costumes for *The Birth of a Nation.* When Griffith ran into financial difficulties, Goldstein accepted a percentage in lieu of payment. His $4,500 investment made him a stockholder of the Epoch Producing Company and brought such an enormous return that he set himself up as a producer, determined to create a picture even more controversial.

With *The Spirit of '76,* written by Goldstein and his partner George L. Hutchin, a promoter of the Portland Rose Festival, Goldstein did for the redcoats what Griffith had done for the renegade Negro. He depicted them in exactly the way the British were currently presenting the Germans. As a climax, he showed them indulging in the slaughter and rapine of the infamous Wyoming Valley Massacre. To complete the irony, he cast Howard Gaye, an Englishman last seen as Jesus Christ in *Intolerance.* He obtained from Griffith a promise that he would not make a film of the Revolutionary War for five years, and Griffith's assistant George Siegmann was slated to direct, although Frank Montgomery took over.

Goldstein had his bombshell ready to surprise the public when a setback occurred. The United States joined the war with Great Britain. "This film has been in production for over a year," announced Goldstein, in an optimistic advertisement, "and is now happily completed at this time to rouse the patriotism of the country."

Some freedom of speech survived in wartime America, for Goldstein's picture opened in Chicago in the summer of 1917. It caused a flutter of anxiety among the city fathers before it was suppressed by Major Funkhouser, the autocratic police censor, whose decision was supported by Judge Kavanaugh. Funkhouser objected to the violence in the picture. Goldstein protested that every incident was founded on recognized authority, and the city might as well remove history textbooks from public schools. The stockholders of the Continental Producing Company, which was responsible for the film, took out an injunction against Funkhouser, and after a two-week trial in the Superior Court of Cook County, Illinois, it was decided that the major had been wrong to suppress the picture. Funkhouser allowed it to be shown once two thousand feet had been cut. Chicago critics called it "a costume triumph" and none of them saw anything anti-British in it.

Despite this victory, Goldstein left Chicago with a deficit of $35,000. Later in the year, he was fortunate enough to secure a booking at Clune's Auditorium in Los Angeles, the prestigious showplace where *The Clansman* (*The Birth of a Nation*) had had its memorable premiere. Goldstein gave assurance to the tune of $2,000 that the performances would not be interfered with by the police or federal authorities. The police advised him to show the film privately to a representative of the government, but Goldstein refused, showing it only reluctantly to a group of Los Angeles citizens. Having carefully removed all the doubtful material, Goldstein was not surprised when the committee approved most of the picture—although some scenes were still regarded as objectionable. The committee recommended that these scenes be removed before the public opening. Far from removing anything, Goldstein restored all the horrors, and *The Spirit of '76* opened at Clune's on 27 November 1917, advertised as "A Startling Historical Superdrama." The picture was seized under Title XI of the Espionage Act by the American Protective League, and Goldstein forfeited his $2,000 on Thanksgiving night, 29 November.

Goldstein complained that he had never touched the picture and that there was obviously a conspiracy against him. Next day he was arrested. He had no money and none of his stockholders appeared to bail him out. He made approaches through legal channels for the return of his film, but in a case that became famous, *United States v. Motion Picture Film The Spirit of '76,* Judge Bledsoe denied his motion. Earl Rogers (father of film writer Adela Rogers St. Johns) was Goldstein's defense attorney. He told the court that Goldstein had lived all his life in California, and he was satisfied that there was no suspicion of pro-Germanism attached to his activities. Judge Bledsoe acknowledged that no evidence existed to prove that German money had financed the production, although it later turned out that the majority of stockholders were German. He objected to the Wyoming Valley Massacre, in which a British soldier was shown impaling a baby on his bayonet and whirling it around his head. On the stand Goldstein admitted restoring these scenes, but insisted they were necessary "to put pep in the show." Declared Judge Bledsoe: "This is no time, whatever may be the excuse, for the exploitation of those things that may have the tendency of sowing dissension among our people, and of creating animosity between us and our allies."[5] Any such attempt, he added, was a violation of the espionage law. He ordered that the film be seized.

The verdict on Goldstein was cruelly delayed. Facing bankruptcy, Goldstein said that he was being made "a goat"; the wealthy men who backed him were as guilty as he. Four months after his arrest, Goldstein's new defense attorney, Ryckman, reproached Judge Bledsoe for his bias against his client, who was still in jail. A verdict of guilty was returned before District Judge Bean, but sentence could not be passed until Judge Bledsoe's return. Goldstein sweated it out in the county jail, facing a maximum of twenty-two years and a fine of $11,000. Judge Bledsoe gave him ten years in the federal penitentiary at McNeil's Island on two counts of inciting mutiny among the armed forces, together with a fine of $5,000 on the first count and a further two years on the second. Reporters noticed that poor Goldstein shook visibly as the judge lashed him for his unpatriotic conduct. Judge Bledsoe now declared that the film was one of the most potent German propagandas of which he had any knowledge.

Goldstein was refused a new trial. He appealed, but Circuit Judge Hunt affirmed the finding of the lower court. Judge Hunt agreed that the picture might well have shown truthfully what happened during the Revolutionary War, but the treatment of it, in the current war, might have resulted in disloyalty or insubordination among the military forces. In 1919 President Wilson commuted Goldstein's sentence to three years, and the fine was remitted. After serving less than two years, Goldstein was released and in 1921 tried to recover some of his costs by reissuing *Spirit of '76* through a company called All-American. "Oh propaganda," said *Photoplay,* "what crimes are committed in thy name. *The Spirit of '76* was first designed as German propaganda. But the Germans, after seeing the film, evidently disowned it. So now it is called Irish propaganda. Whatever its political significance, it resembles nothing so much as a fourteen-reel Ben Turpin comedy without the talented Ben. If this is a specimen of the real Spirit of '76, how did we ever manage to win the Revolution?"[6]

The picture no longer exists in its original form, and archivists regard it as a lost film. But several reels can be found in the archives of John E. Allen of Park Ridge, New Jersey. The scenes are out of order, and with the majority of the atrocities removed, the picture loses much of its fascination. Nevertheless, it is capably and sometimes lavishly mounted. The film is oddly similar to Griffith's *America* (1924), particularly in its treatment of the British officer Walter Butler, who, in both pictures, is seen as an arch-fiend. Much of *Spirit of '76* is shot like a Film D'Art, and titles like "Your foul lies have aroused my wrath" do not help. The main impression the picture imparts is of the enormous amount of money Goldstein sank into it.

After *Spirit of '76* Goldstein returned to obscurity, and nothing is known for certain of his fate. Jane Novak, who played in the film, told Anthony Slide that she last met Goldstein when he was living in Berlin in 1924. As a Jew, he could hardly have chosen a more unsuitable country in which to settle. His sense of timing provides a final element of tragicomedy to the whole affair.

GERMANY'S SIDE OF THE WAR

Factual films about Germany's point of view were highly successful and were widely shown in prewar America. *Germany on the Firing Line* (1916) was said to have been put together from the best material shot by 106 cameramen, which was a tribute to Wilbur H. Durborough, who photographed most of it. It was presented in major cities under the auspices of such newspapers as the New York *Globe,* the Pittsburgh *Press,* and the Minneapolis *Tribune.* Exhibitors staged elaborate publicity stunts for the picture, some of which would have landed them in jail a year later. In Kansas City a vast wooden replica of a forty-two-centimeter gun was mounted on an automobile and driven through the streets, manned by "German" troops. Once inside the theater, patrons were shown to their seats by young ladies dressed in German uniform.

Edwin F. Weigle, who had filmed the fall of Antwerp for the Chicago *Tribune,* returned to Europe, and while staying with relatives in Germany, succeeded in producing a film called *Germany in Wartime* (1915). More of Weigle's footage, together with material shot by such cameramen as Donald Thompson, was edited into *The German Side of the War* (1915), which was a huge success.* "The

* Half the proceeds were pledged to a common fund for the relief of blind and crippled soldiers (New York *Times,* 21 September 1915, p. 11).

The famous statue of General Hindenburg in Berlin, photographed after the armistice; Ernest B. Schoedsack, foreground.

lines extended for four blocks," wrote Terry Ramsaye.[1] "Ticket scalpers, unable to renew their supply from the box office, went down the long lines selling strip soda checks to the unsuspecting."

German Official War Films, Inc., released *Germany and Its Armies Today* early in 1917. Besides the usual quota of parades and investitures, the film contained some effective propaganda: "Even a pro-Ally audience will enjoy the beautiful sarcasm of the title 'Pitiful victim of English food blockade' which accompanies a picture of a 'cop' fatter than Broadway's finest in the old days of Tammany."[2]

Berlin was shown in the third year of war, with public works improvement being carried on as though no war existed. Patriotic citizens were shown hammering gold and silver nails, purchased to aid the war fund, into a colossal wooden statue of General Paul von Hindenburg. At the race track it was apparent that women predominated, although the film was careful to show a representative selection of men. A rare contrast to the views of apparently normal community life were shots of women working with picks and shovels on railway repairs. Since the very word "occupation" summoned up images of execution and oppression, the Germans included scenes of the occupation of Lille, showing the feeding of the poor from the state commissary. The first prisoners from the Rumanian campaign were shown worshipping in a mosque especially constructed for them by German soldiers.

At the start of the war, the German High Command, like its Allied counterpart, banned all attempts to take pictures of the army in action. They suggested that cameramen take the lead from the illustrated magazines and concentrate on harmless marching shots, military wagon trains, and portraits of soldiers. But the Germans were quicker than the Allies to realize what they were missing. A mere twenty days after the outbreak of war, says Fritz Terveen, film people were admonished for allowing the cinema to miss "the small, rivetting and extraordinarily characteristic traits of a seriously disturbed time."[3] A living war journal was demanded, and plans were put forward for a war-panorama cinema, similar to the emperor battle panoramas, to show live pictures and landscapes familiar to the public from war reports.

The German military authorities shared the Allied opinion of the moving picture: they considered it ideal for target practice. They gave it no serious thought as a method of propaganda, and the credit for the organization of news weeklies must go to Oskar Messter. He joined the press department of the General Staff in September 1914, and began releasing material shot by official cameramen in newsreels known as *Messter-Woche*. Messter retained his official position, while organizing his own firm to cope with the new situation.

"From now on," announced Messter in October 1914, "pictures of battle areas may be shot only with the express permission of the High Command. Our operators are at the scene of the fighting, with the necessary permits, and we will show regularly the pictures they shoot there." The same month the first of these officially sanctioned front-line weekly newsreels were released, containing scenes of destruction caused by the Russian Army.

Messter was not the only newsreel producer, but his unique experience as a film pioneer and his position on the Acting General Staff gave him dominance. For small companies, red tape and censorship were a constant burden, and the trade press drew attention to the importance of the news film on their behalf: "This is a duty to posterity, for whom we can never get enough documents of this world war."

As the newsreel became a familiar part of their lives, the public began to suspect the difference between what was genuine and what was not. A large part of an audience at any film show was likely to consist of soldiers, and to add conviction to front-line footage, newsreels sometimes showed the reports and telegrams from cameramen:

> JUST BACK FROM FRONT SENT DAY BEFORE YESTERDAY FILMS TAKEN IN FRONT-LINE TRENCHES UNDER SHRAPNEL FIRE FURTHER FILMS AND REPORT TODAY FROEHLICH

The cameraman served among the troops in the capacity of a civilian war correspondent. He had to arrange his own accommodation and take care of himself generally, responsibilities which added greatly to the burdens of the job. He was treated by the soldiers as a rather troublesome guest and tended to be informed of troop movements only at the last minute. As Fritz Terveen put it, "There was still a long way to go to the slogan of the last war 'Propaganda saves blood.' "

Nevertheless, by 1915 the production and distribution of films had been placed under state control in Germany. Subsidies meant that German films cost much less than Allied ones and were seen more frequently in neutral countries. In 1916 Deulig (Deutsche Lichtspiel Gesellschaft) was organized to promote the German image, and an attempt was made to ban foreign films. Nordisk overcame the ban, to the dismay of local producers, who thought their main rival had at last been ousted.

The same year the Austrians were first among the Central Powers to entrust

German naval cameraman aboard a torpedo boat.

moving picture coverage to the army. Soldiers, they realized, could take pictures no one else could achieve. In 1917 the Picture and Film Board (BUFA—Bild und Filmamt) was founded in Germany, responsible not only for producing instructional films and newsreels but also for maintaining front-line cinemas. BUFA followed the Austrian example.

When the United States entered the conflict, the Germans realized their film industry was far too puny to withstand such an assault. General Ludendorff, deciding that the propaganda film was vital to the war effort, consolidated the disparate elements of the industry into UFA (Universal Film A.G.), headed by the munitions king, Krupp, and other bankers and industrialists.

Wrote Ludendorff in a letter of 4 July 1917: "the war has demonstrated the superiority of the photograph and film as a means of information and persuasion. Unfortunately, our enemies have used their great advantage over us in this field so thoroughly that they have inflicted a great deal of damage. Nor will films lose their significance during the rest of this war as a means of political and military persuasion. For this reason it is of the utmost importance for a successful conclusion to the war that films should be made to work with the greatest possible effect wherever any German persuasion might still have any effect."[4]

BUFA was absorbed by UFA at the end of 1918; surviving defeat, revolution, and conversion to private ownership, UFA eventually became a significant threat to the film industries of the former Allied nations. Once the war was over, the fresh talent released from the trenches revitalized UFA, and in the manic-depressive atmosphere of postwar Germany, led to such astonishing works of art as *The Cabinet of Dr. Caligari, Siegfried, Variety,* and *Metropolis.*

FRANZ SELDTE WAS MINISTER OF LABOR under Hitler.* He was president of the Stahlhelm, the right-wing veterans' organization, and had been a machine-gun officer at the front. Serious wounds kept him from further active service, and he was attached to BUFA. The Germans now organized their newsreel crews on Austrian lines as military units, with officers in command. Seldte, with an arm missing, could never have operated a camera. But as a film-unit commander, he became a director.

I am indebted to Clive Coultass of the Imperial War Museum for the information that Seldte had written a book of his experiences. Published in English by Hutchinsons in the 1930s under the title *Through a Lens Darkly,* Seldte's book is as much a tribute to his own courage as Malins's *How I Filmed the War.* He writes of himself in the third person—as Stahl—but the book is acknowledged by the publishers to be his own adventures.

Before the war Seldte had regarded films as inferior; he was prejudiced against them as being "superficial," as doing harm to the legitimate theater, and as having a flattening effect on the minds of the public. Paradoxically, he landed in the film department, where he quickly realized the cinema's potential. And when he saw the Allied pictures and those he had obtained himself, and felt their tremendous propaganda effect, he was seized by an enormous enthusiasm for his work. Apart from news pictures, BUFA produced an occasional story film, on such themes as war loans, and this brought Seldte in contact with film producers from the major studios, "some of whom," Seldte says ominously, "were Jews."

During a visit to Holland, Seldte was distressed to see the extent to which Allied propaganda had succeeded in convincing this neutral people that Belgium's fate might well be theirs. He countered their alarm with characteristic sang-froid: "We won't waste words on stories of children's hands cut off and violated women. I dare say you remember how the English and French press raged over the Congo atrocities of the inhuman Belgians—the same Belgium which is now held up as a crucified martyr against us Germans."†

As a former front-line officer, Seldte was filled with admiration for the nerve and resourcefulness of the film units: "It was no joke to work a camera in places where an old front soldier would instinctively take cover or go at the enemy." On the Italian front he was gratified to find the value of film units appreciated by men instructed to give every cooperation. Some stills men were attached to the film unit, and Seldte further improved relations by sending photographs to the troops.

The "director" of a film unit, as an officer, was expected to offer the kind of leadership that few directors could manage; Seldte had to guide his men through shellfire so intense that "hot gas vapour swept over them, splinters screamed and showers of stones rained down heavily on their helmets."

He came to the conclusion that when a man is not actually fighting, he feels the effects of battle in his bones: "Perhaps having to observe and photograph is even more of a strain on the nerves." But he makes it clear that this is the life he loves—"Battle, father of all things!"—and he regards the filming of prisoners,

---

* Seldte served throughout the Third Reich, and died in the prison of Fürth, Bavaria, on 1 April 1947.

† The Belgian Congo revelations of 1904 were the work of Roger Casement.

guns, and supply dumps as a trifle demeaning. He reminds himself that in neutral countries the deepest impression was made by films showing that the Germans could capture in a few days more matériel than the British could manage in months. Yet Seldte was convinced that if the British and Germans fought side by side, they could rule the world.

Most revealing are the references to the American propaganda films. In Switzerland, Seldte talks to a BUFA agent, who reports that a film showing there is having a distressing effect on women and "the weaker brethren."

"Oh, that must be the amazing American performance, *The Fall of a Nation,*" replies Seldte. "I know the sentimental slush. A nation turned beast attacks free America, torturing women and cutting off children's hands. Of course, America wins in the end and the glittering bayonets of the troops of freedom are turned into sheaves of palms. The very word 'America' fills me with dumb fury. They've invented a new doctrine over there; America for the Americans. All right, then. But in that case what are the Americans doing in Europe? And all that damned hypocrisy about world peace, freedom and justice from the very fellows who wiped out the whole gifted race of Indians with powder and lead and spirits so they could settle in their nest themselves."

MEXICO

Except for an occasional film like *Juarez* or *Viva Zapata,* it has seldom been the intention of the motion picture industry to take Mexico seriously. Depicted on the screen as a comic-opera land of violence and *mañana,* filled with gap-toothed peons, oily villains, and dusky señoritas, Mexico's reputation rests on revolution.

Yet the motion picture has never acknowledged the role it played in the revolution. One journalist[1] has gone so far as to call it "The War Waged to Make a Movie"—an understandable exaggeration, for the motion picture had never before been drawn so close to politics. And while it had frequently recorded history, film had hardly been considered as a means of changing history's course.

The revolution that broke out on 20 November 1910 was not simply another rebellion to add to an endless list. Previous conflicts had been fought between potential rulers. The revolution that toppled the dictatorship of Porfirio Díaz was a popular uprising—the first time in Mexican history that the people had demanded their part in running the country.

The leadership of the revolution came not from the officer class, or from dissident ministers, but from the common people, from men like Pascal Orozco and Pancho Villa—although its nominal leader, Francisco I. Madero, was a man of the land-owning class. The success of the uprising exceeded even Madero's expectations, and on the day he was installed as President, the largest crowds Mexico City had ever seen appeared on the streets to cheer him.

The American ambassador, Henry Lane Wilson, was an important figure in Madero's downfall. Despite instructions from President Taft to remain impartial, he loathed Madero and lent his support to his opponent, Victoriano Huerta. After

Pancho Villa after the fall of Ojinaga, a battle he delayed for the benefit of the motion picture cameras. Note the overstamp: "Copyright, 1914 Mutual Film Corporation."

a ten-day bombardment of the National Palace, Madero was seized, his resignation forced from him, and on 22 February 1913, he was murdered by Huerta's men.

Huerta was recognized by the major European powers, and it seemed that the revolution was at last over. But Madero's killing inflamed the country once again. The new administration of Woodrow Wilson refused to recognize Huerta, despite Ambassador Wilson's assurances that he would protect American interests; the ambassador was recalled and his resignation followed.

Now began "Carranza's rebellion," the struggle between isolated rebel commanders—Carranza, Villa, Zapata, Obregón—and Huerta's Federal Army. And it was during this period that Pancho Villa began his unlikely connection with motion pictures.

Under the Díaz regime, most of Mexican industry and much of her land had passed into foreign hands. William Randolph Hearst and his family owned millions of dollars' worth of oil, mining, timber, and chicle holdings in Mexico; the family property has been described as "about the size of Maryland and Delaware combined." Villa's irregulars had looted Hearst's ranch at Chihuahua and commandeered sixty thousand head of cattle, which were distributed to the peons. Whoever ran the country, no regime could be as congenial to Hearst as that of Díaz; under his regime American investment had reached a figure of $1 billion, forty percent of her total foreign investment. Hearst instructed his newspaper editors to launch a full-scale attack upon Mexico, representing her as a potential enemy of the United States and urging the government to send in troops to restore order. When the European war broke out, Hearst preached peace. But Mexico, he declared, was an ally of Japan, and recalling a speech by Admiral Yashiro, in which he referred to the "quiescent volcanoes" of each country, which might soon erupt and make the world "tremble at their fury," Hearst announced that the two countries planned a massive invasion of the United States. He went so far as to finance an elaborate serial, *Patria,* in which this unholy alliance is defeated by Irene Castle, as a member of a munitions family called the Channings, but based on the Dupont de Nemours. Since Japan was an ally of Great Britain, President Wilson was forced to intervene personally in an attempt to have the serial banned. Hearst modified it but kept it in circulation.

Hearst's picture editor, Edgar Hatrick, had experimented with a newsreel in 1911, but the scheme went little further than a 1913 short about the inauguration of the President. In early 1914, however, rumors that Hearst was extending his news empire into the motion picture theaters came as bad news not only for rival business interests but for the government itself. Although Wilson, before becoming President, had tried to crush the Madero regime, he was totally opposed to Huerta, whom he considered a "murderer" and a "usurper." America had no alternative but to support Carranza and the rebels, or Constitutionalists.

In Kalem's* 1911 production *A Prisoner of Mexico,* the revolution was portrayed as a struggle for freedom along the lines of the Revolutionary War. It declared that the Americans who were fighting for the Mexicans and who had been dismissed as "malcontents" and "soldiers of fortune" were actually patriots, ready to die so that Mexico "might take her place proudly among the real republics, the

---

* Also in 1911, Kalem had released a documentary, *Juarez After the Siege* (*Moving Picture World* 10 June 1911, p. 1304).

William Randolph Hearst's serial Patria *(1916–17) aroused presidential wrath with its depiction of America's "true enemy," an unholy alliance between Mexico and Japan. Photographs like this one, showing Irene Castle in a sort of Royal Flying Corps uniform, suggest that there were plenty of concessions to Allied sympathizers.*

leaders of the world." *A Prisoner of Mexico* is an early example of a motion picture romanticizing a political figure, for it was "General Madero" who rode, at the head of his cavalry, to the rescue of the hero and heroine.

With Madero gone, and Huerta increasingly dependent on support from Europe, particularly Germany, Wall Street foresaw further great losses to its investments. Winifred Johnston alleges that Lord Cowdray, head of British oil interests, was behind Huerta's rise to power, for Huerta was a former Díaz man. And the Royal Navy secured its oil from Mexico. "Wall Street," wrote Johnston, "reached out for all available means to mobilize public opinion."[2]

An ideal opportunity was offered by Villa himself. After his capture of Juarez, he approached the moving picture men covering the event and offered the companies they represented a deal. He would allow cameramen to accompany him on his campaigns, he would provide horses, food, and escorts, if they would agree to give him a fifty-fifty share of the profits of the films. The cameramen wired the offer to their head offices in the East. None of them acted except the Mutual Film Corporation, the company whose enterprising president, Harry Aitken, had signed Griffith and would shortly produce *The Birth of a Nation.* Mutual, which was backed by the Wall Street banking partnership of Kuhn, Loeb, sent an emissary, Frank M. Thayer, with lawyer Gunther Lessing, to meet Villa. In one of the most curious and remarkable deals in film history, Pancho Villa signed an exclusive $25,000 contract with the Mutual Film Corporation. The most important clause in the contract stated that General Villa must not allow any other moving picture men on the field during his battles.

The Hearst newsreel, as expected, appeared the following month, as the Hearst-Selig News Pictorial. Its first installment was dated 28 February 1914,[3] and in each issue, Mexican war scenes predominated.* As expected, its editorial tone re-

---

* Filmed by such cameramen as E. A. Wallace. In August 1914 the Hearst-Selig News Pictorial announced close-ups of General Villa (*Moving Picture World,* 8 August 1914, p. 836). Hearst secured these scenes through "arrangements" with cameramen employed by other organizations.

flected that of the newspapers: "the way to impress the Mexicans is to REPRESS the Mexicans." But the area around General Villa was now safely in the hands of Mutual.

When the New York *Times* called Harry Aitken at 1 a.m. on 7 January 1914 about the highly secret negotiations with Villa, Aitken was astounded: "How on earth did the *Times* hear about that? I did not want the story to get out yet. But it is true. I am the partner of Gen. Villa, and it has been worrying me a lot all day. How would you feel to be a partner of a man engaged in killing people?"[4]

According to Aitken, the leader of the Mutual expedition was an Italian cameraman who had covered the Balkan wars and had bullets in his body to prove it. Aitken further declared that a special camera had been designed that could be operated under fire, with the machine exposed, and the cameraman in a concealed position. It had been agreed with Villa that if no satisfactory motion pictures were made during the battles, Villa would stage one especially for the cameras.

This historic contract had an immediate effect on history. General Villa delayed the attack on Ojinaga to allow the motion picture men to reach Presidio and cross the rebel lines.[5] The Federals took advantage of this unexpected breathing spell to bring across millions of cartridges from the American side—unofficial aid, since a U.S. government arms embargo was in force. They laid in food stocks for a lengthy siege and shot some more rebel prisoners. And General Mancilla took the opportunity of deserting, offering himself to the Americans for asylum, the first high-ranking Federal to do so. Then, with the Mutual cameramen in position, the battle resumed.*

The New York *Times* pointed out that if Villa hoped for a monopoly of Mexican war films, he was liable to be disappointed. An enterprising cameraman had been active throughout the siege of Ojinaga and had made many action films on both the rebel and the Federal sides. Charles Pryor had been arrested, had had his camera smashed by a shell, and had been escorted to the American side by the Federals. "His films are now being developed."[6]

Inside Ojinaga, by an unfortunate mishap, was one of the Mutual cameramen who had been in Mexico before the contract was signed. Charles Rosher, an Englishman, was placed incommunicado until he was brought before General Salvador Mercado. "He noticed the tiny Masonic pin I wore in my buttonhole. He gave me the Masonic greeting; he was a Mason, too! Turned out that . . . Huerta was this general's brother-in-law. . . . Well, I was entertained royally in Ojinaga."[7]

After a desperate resistance, prolonged until only a few rounds of ammunition remained, the Federals crossed the Rio Grande and surrendered to General Pershing.†

Harry Aitken was somewhat embarrassed when he presented the film of the

---

* One of the casualties was the elderly Ambrose Bierce, who, fascinated by Villa, had followed his campaign and disappeared during the battle for Ojinaga.

† Mexican troops interned by the United States at Eagle Pass took part in battle scenes for *Under Fire in Mexico* (1914), directed by Otis Thayer for the Colorado Motion Picture Company. And Colonel Zack Miller of the 101 Ranch bought the entire equipment of the defeated army, used some of it in his show, and sold the rest back to Huerta.

Battle of Ojinaga at Mutual's headquarters in New York on 22 January. Despite General Villa's delaying tactics, there was no battle. As the New York *Times* reported it, "The 'movies' showed General Villa leading his army to battle at Ojinaga in the dusk of the evening. He wore a broad smile. Another film showed him leading his forces away from the battlefield the next morning. He was still smiling."[8]

But an unexpected incident gave Aitken's picture dramatic coverage. Francisco Madero, father of the murdered President, was present in an invited audience. Among the officers who rode beside General Villa was one Madero recognized. He jumped from his seat: " 'Raul,' he exclaimed. 'My son, Raul. I did not know that he was fighting.' "[9]

Alfonso Madero, a brother of the President, tried to calm his father, and explained that everyone else in the family knew, that it was one of the worries they had hoped to spare him. The old man could not watch any more. He left the projection theater, and paced up and down in the hall outside, waiting for his son to join him.

As the screening came to an end, Aitken promised the pressmen that General Villa would do better by Mutual at the Battle of Torreón.

H. N. Dean, who had gone to Mexico with Charles Rosher, was the first of the Mutual cameramen to describe their collective experience. "We slept, ate and worked under fire constantly during the last fifteen days of the campaign. The desert dust bothered us terribly. Martin for five days was helpless from mountain fever; and for thirty hours at one stretch we were without food after a previous twelve day diet of tortillas. Our cameras, of course, offered the finest sort of target

During his captivity by Federal troops, Charles Rosher, center, in soft cap, had this souvenir picture taken of himself, with General Mercado in pickelhaube, and staff (some Mexican uniforms were modeled on the Prussian).

Charles Rosher films the camp followers of General Villa.

for Federal marksmen. In order to get good pictures we were obliged to set up on some sort of elevation, and the Federal range-finders seemed to pick us out almost instantly. Federal gunners, up on Cerro Grande, a mountain to the south of Torreón, watched us set up our cameras on an outlying 'dobe house and sniped at us with Mausers and shells. We got the picture, and as soon as we left the roof, the firing ceased. We soon got to know what to do under fire. When we hear a sound like the ripping of coarse cotton cloth, sometimes preceded and sometimes followed by a shrill whine about our heads, we immediately throw ourselves flat in the desert sand, no matter whether the *mezquito* barbs were sharp or not. That whine meant a machine gun was trying to connect."[10]

Villa's example spread. In July 1914 General Obregón, commander of the western division of the Constitutionalist Army, signed a contract with Byron S. Butcher for exclusive motion picture rights to *his* branch of the rebel army. Butcher had been with the army for four years.[11] General Obregón was fascinated by motion pictures, and in 1917 paid an official visit to Universal City.

In his book *Film Folk,* Rob Wagner interviewed an unnamed American cameraman who served not with Villa, but with the Federals:

"The big battle stuff is almost impossible to get, and the best war pictures taken in Mexico have been faked. Mexican generals are more vain than actors, and are most eager to go bowling down to posterity in the movies. In order to perpetuate their heroics, they would re-ride a battle after it was over, with the dead still lying on the ground. This method was perfectly safe and it gave me a chance to get some swell close-ups. A lot of the historical film in the archives of the Mexican government was made in this way.

"My greatest difficulty was in getting and keeping an assistant. A movie outfit is a fierce bunch of stuff to pack over a desert country, and though there were lots of Mexicans available, they would not stick. So, often I would have to load the whole darned equipment aboard a burro, like a mountain gun, and go out after the war stuff alone.

"There were lots of American soldiers of fortune, but they were invariably looking for trouble and thought packing a camera much too slow. I had one Iowa chap for three days, who finally quit me for some excitement 'over there.' He found it, all right. For two days later, when I was pulling into Veracruz, I saw seven ghastly creatures hanging by their necks to a telegraph pole, and who should be among them but my little Yankee camera boy.

"Street fighting is the easiest to film, for if you can get a good location on a side street, you have the protection of all the intervening buildings from artillery and rifle fire, while you occasionally get a chance to shoot a few feet of swell film. I got some great stuff in Mexico City a few days before Madero was killed. One fellow, not twenty feet from my camera, had his head shot off. But do you know—the darn censors would never let us show the picture in the States? What do you suppose they send us to war for?"[12]

L. M. Burrud, another of the Mutual cameramen, reaped the benefits of the exclusive arrangement with Villa. He was provided with a special boxcar whenever the troops traveled by rail. When the roads were good enough, he was assigned a fast automobile and on mountain trails was supplied with fresh mounts. His adventures, as described in *The Cameraman,*[13] read very much like the kind of sensa-

L. M. Burrud poses with his Indian bodyguards (stripped for pictorial impact, one suspects).

The walls of a jail, splashed with VIVA VILLA, *house a condemned prisoner, whom Charles Rosher is obliged to film.*

tional story made up under newsreel men's by-lines by the publicity department in later years. But hyperbole or no, Burrud was there and played an important part in filming Villa's campaign.

He brought back a shot of street fighting that particularly impressed the author of *The Cameraman:*

"Several soldiers are shown running with fixed bayonets directly towards the camera—one is actually falling forward—and so close to the camera that the strained expression of their faces is vividly shown.

" 'A closeup like that,' Burrud explained, 'could scarcely be planned. The most daring photographer would not venture so far in. I happened to be down the street with my camera set up in the shelter of a wall when the charge came. It was too good to miss. When I saw them coming, I swung my camera round, and it happened that I could operate it with only one arm exposed to a chance shot. I took that chance.' "

Not one of the Mutual cameramen, in any of their accounts, referred to the specially built cameras which could be operated from concealed positions. The first Mutual release, called, simply *Mexican War Pictures,* came out in February 1914 and contained no battle scenes whatever. *Moving Picture World*'s reviewer, W. Stephen Bush, found the scenes deeply depressing. "After viewing the Greek-Bulgarian war pictures, I could not believe that anything lower might exist in the scale of civilized warfare, but these Mexican pictures have added a new, though not a bright leaf to history."

By a curious coincidence, four cameramen, who were to become the most celebrated and sought-after in their field, were present in this war: Charles Rosher, later cameraman for Mary Pickford; Fritz Arno Wagner,* who became one of the leading German cameramen; Victor Milner; and Gilbert Warrenton, who filmed *The Cat and the Canary.*

Wagner, working for Pathé, sent a letter from Mexico to *Moving Picture World* in July 1914, which stripped the glamour from the news cameraman's life. "For a couple of days I had nothing to eat and was forced to drink from the mud puddles of the road. The consequence was, when I reached Saltillo, I was sick, deadly sick, and became little more than skin and bones. I am not afraid, whatever may happen, but I never thought I would come out alive from this trip.

"I have seen four big battles. On each occasion I was threatened with arrest from the Federal general if I took any pictures. He also threatened on one occasion when he caught me turning the crank to smash the camera. He would have done so, too, but for the fact that the rebels came pretty close just then and he had to take it on the run to save his hide.

"At Lagruna, the battle became a rout and the disorganization of the Federal forces was complete. Napoleon's retreat from Moscow was but a disaster on a larger scale. I had saved my film and camera (60 lbs.) and went on foot with this load through the desert for 25 miles. . . .

"For five nights I lay on the stones without a blanket, with my films for a pillow, and my camera in my arm. I was afraid to take more than broken naps for fear my camera would be stolen. As it was, when I finally got back to Mexico City

---

* He later worked for the American Correspondent Film Company (see p. 13).

after breaking jail I had left only a shirt, trousers, coat and a pair of shoes. I tried hard to save my films, but I guess I am lucky at that. Those that I brought with me I had in my pockets. The rest made fine kindling for the campfires of the rebels."

Wagner got another camera from the Pathé agent in Mexico City and set off again. But this time Huerta's secret service men shadowed him. Eventually, Huerta himself told Wagner to develop the films (under supervision) and to project them:

"He censored the films, and had me cut out all the parts unfavorable to the Federals, and then ordered the 'Salon Rojo' to show them as advertising for his troops. Huerta was much pleased with the show, otherwise I would have lost the films. I saw my chance, and decided to beat it before another storm broke. I told the Chief of Police that Huerta had OK'd the films, and it was all right for me to go to Veracruz. The Chief was very decent and gave me his card, which I used as a passport. I hid myself in a freight car and finally got to Veracruz OK.

"When Victor Miller, your cameraman, arrived with a new outfit for me, for the first time in weeks I was able to eat with an appetite and sleep as a man should sleep."[14]

VICTOR MILNER'S INVOLVEMENT in Mexico was such a footnote to his long and distinguished career as a Hollywood cameraman that he seldom thought it worth mentioning. Very little is known about it, perhaps because at that time he called himself Victor Miller. As soon as I realized that Miller and Milner were one and the same, I wrote to him in Hollywood. Shortly afterward, I heard that Victor Milner had died. I was therefore astonished, two months later, to receive a long and informative letter, forwarded by his son, Colonel Victor Milner, Jr., who added: "I have taken up these notes of Dad's where he left off. While he was getting them ready for you he was taken ill and went to the hospital where he died suddenly. I hope they are not too late and that they will be of some use to you."

Milner said that his great coup as a newsreel cameraman had occurred at Veracruz. A minor incident, involving the arrest of some U.S. sailors by Federal troops, blew up into an international drama. Admiral Mayo demanded that the Federal officer responsible should be punished and that the American flag should be hoisted and saluted with twenty-one guns. Huerta's refusal angered President Wilson, who, that same year of 1914, was to win such respect with his views against war. "I have no enthusiasm for war," he said, "but I have an enthusiasm for the dignity of the United States." Veracruz was shelled, and the port invaded by American marines. British and German warships were in the area to protect their countries' oil interests. Nineteen Americans were killed, and an unknown number of Mexicans; the two countries were brought almost to the point of open war.[15] Carranza opposed Veracruz, and only Villa remained pro-American. Wilson therefore supported him. Villa, meanwhile, had turned against Carranza.

Milner said that at the time he understood some Mexican bandits had taken over the city, threatening American oil interests, and that an expeditionary force had been sent in to help the Mexican government restore order. A telegram told him to travel to Galveston, Texas, where a U.S. Navy ship would take him to Veracruz.

"When I arrived in Galveston, I went to get my orders at the local telegraph

WEEK ENDING MARCH 20, 1915 527 PICTURES AND THE PICTUREGOER

The Tragedy in the Life of General Villa

Adapted from the Film by IVAN PATRICK GORE.

"CURSE this place!" Lieutenant Paolo of the Federal Army grumbled as he leaned against the door of his quarters and looked out over the dry Mexican plain which stretched away as far as the eye could see toward the distant foothills. "What a hole to be quartered in! One might just as well be in one's grave."

His companion laughed lazily. "Come, my friend, things are not so bad as all that. I'm afraid last night's festivities are to blame for making you so discontented to-day. Cards, women, wine—what more can a soldier want?"

Paolo scowled without taking the trouble to agree or contradict him; then his eyes fell upon the figure of a woman who limped towards them. "So—who have we here?"

"Villa's sister ——"

They watched the cripple as she hastened past; then the younger man

this hole these three months without knowing that such red lips were near at hand!"

entered and shut the door behind them.

"Don't be frightened, little one," Paolo laughed, enjoying her evident fear, "we mean no harm."

"My brother is out, Senor," Juanita gasped, more than ever terrified at the expression in his bloodshot eyes, "and I do not know when he will return."

"Our visit is not to him, but to you, little one. Come, a bottle of wine, a few kisses, and ——"

"Steady!" his friend cried, "remember, Paolo, there are two of us."

"Bah! we won't quarrel, but ——" with another laugh, which sent poor little Juanita still further back into her corner, Paolo drew a pair of dice from his pocket and threw them into the air. "Come, we will toss to see who stays to keep the little one company."

Hugging her doll as though she fancied it gave her some measure of protection, Juanita watched the dice

Raoul Walsh as the young Villa in The Life of Villa.

Both scenes are reconstructions from The Life of Villa *(1915) but are used as newsreels to this day. (Copied from* Pictures and Picturegoer*)*

office but found that they had not yet arrived. I went to the local hotel and at the bar there, I met several of my friendly competitors who were also awaiting transportation to Veracruz. I was really crestfallen when I learned that they were leaving late that night and they had already been given their authority to go down on the destroyers. That night, after they had departed, I went back to the telegraph office and though my orders hadn't arrived, the lady who ran it told me that if I hurried, I could catch a freighter that was leaving for Veracruz any minute. I arrived at the dock after they had already dropped the stern lines, so I threw my camera and suitcase up on the bow and got on by the skin of my teeth. The mate and I made a little arrangement, and I was able to use his stateroom for the trip. On arrival at Veracruz, I found that the Navy ships had beaten us in by several hours. On getting ashore, I further found that my friends had not gotten any of the action relative to the marines storming the Post Office, which was the last stronghold of the bandits.

"After the heckling they had given me at Galveston, when they left me on the dock, I wasn't too anxious to sit around and drink and mourn with them at the bar over their bad luck. So I looked over the town. While doing this, I ran across an Army officer friend of mine from the States and told him my story. He was in the public relations business and was anxious to get some good publicity for the Navy and Marines. He got together with the local commanders and they staged the greatest replay of the storming of the Post Office you could imagine. I am told it was far better than the real thing. . . . The pictures were a newsreel sensation and were shown as scoops in all the theaters before any of us got back to the States. To this day, I don't think anyone in the States was aware that they were a replay, and the shots were staged."[16]

Jack London went to Veracruz as a war correspondent to write a scenario for a major Hobart Bosworth Mexican war film, which, sadly, was never made. However, the Veracruz incident inspired a Lubin film, *The Insurrection.** The invasion and bombardment were justified in this film by the revelation of secret Mexican plans to attack the fleet; it also hinted at an end to American benevolence to the rebels, since the villains this time were not Federals but Constitutionalists.

The Mutual Film Corporation made news once again when Harry Aitken returned from Juarez in March 1914 with yet another contract with General Villa.† This agreement was for a feature film, *The Life of General Francisco Villa,* to be directed by D. W. Griffith, with General Villa in the leading role. Selected to play Villa as a young man was Raoul Walsh, later one of Hollywood's most successful directors. He was given responsibility for securing background footage. According to Walsh:

"We paid Villa $500 gold a month to photograph him, his battles and his executions. I had been associated with a lot of Mexicans across the border when I lived in Del Rio.

---

* Lubin's actor-director Romaine Fielding made a series of pictures about the Mexican war. He worked near the border.

† "I found him," said Aitken, "a very different man from the uncouth bandit he has been painted in this country. He is a serious, dignified man who conducts the affairs of his army in a systematic and orderly manner, which would do credit to a much older and more experienced military man" (New York *Times,* 11 March 1914, p. 2).

"Villa liked pictures, and he liked the gold, but I had a terrible time. Day after day, I would try to take shots of him coming toward the camera. We'd set up at the head of the street and he'd hit that horse with a whip and his spurs and go by at ninety miles an hour. I don't know how many times we said *'Despacio, despacio*—slow—Señor, please!'

"I used to get him to put off his executions. He used to have them at four or five in the morning, when there was no light. I got him to put them off until seven or eight. I'd line the cameramen up, and they'd put these fellows against the wall and then they'd shoot them. Fellows on this side with rocks in their hands would run in, open the guys' mouths, and knock the gold teeth out. The fellows on the other side would run in and take the shoes and boots off them. Later on, they made the picture, but D. W. Griffith didn't direct it—he was busy on something else. Christy Cabanne directed it, and I played Villa as a young man.

"Of all the people I've seen executed—not one of them ever wanted to be blindfolded, not one of them gave a damn. Some of them stood up there and cursed, you know, but no cowards—no falling down or anything like that.

"We got some of Villa's battles, but they weren't too spectacular. When we came back we had to invent some of them.[17]

The film was released under a confusing range of titles, not only *The Life of General Villa* but also *The Tragedy in the Career of General Villa* and *The Tragic Early Life of General Villa. Moving Picture World* described vivid action scenes, showing the rebels advancing under fire, in the actuality section of the film. The dramatic section concentrated on the story of Villa's sister, raped by a Federal officer. Villa (whose real name was Doroteo Arango) killed the officer and took to the hills as an outlaw. When the revolution broke out, he linked his bandit army with the rebels, and the film envisioned his final victory over the Federal Army and his proclamation as President of the Republic of Mexico.

IN 1915, WILSON FINALLY RECOGNIZED Carranza, and turned against Villa. The violent change in the American attitude toward the rebels was reflected in such pictures as *Love Thief* (1916), which centered around the attack on Columbus, New Mexico, by Villa. The attack itself had been reminiscent of a scene from a movie, and no one was sure why it had taken place. James Gerard, U.S. ambassador in Berlin, telegraphed: "Am sure Villa's attacks are made in Germany."[18] Actually, Villa was trying desperately to force American intervention, in the hope that they would take on the army of the Carranza government, which was rapidly defeating him. President Wilson, still isolated from the war in Europe, mobilized his troops. An expeditionary force was entrusted to the command of General Pershing, who, as a young lieutenant, had had experience in northern Mexico pursuing the Apache chief Geronimo. Pershing's aide was First Lieutenant George Patton, the famous general of World War II.

Hi Sibley reported that a regiment of movie men had occupied Columbus, jamming the tiny Hoover Hotel, since the largest hotel had been burned to the ground by Villa, and causing a desperate run on the food supply. "The desert is alive with them. . . . If a motor train is sighted on the horizon there is a stampede of tripods and leather puttees; if a cavalry horse stands up on its hind legs there is a fusillade of rapid-fire film exposures shot at him."[19]

The Eagle Film Company went so far as to take out an advertisement: "We have received from W. Kendall Evans some 4,000 ft. of scenes of activities with the United States troops along the Mexican border. After putting it on the screen we are not satisfied with its 'amusement value.' As a matter of fact, nothing of a sensational character has as yet happened in Mexico, nothing to thrill an audience —nothing to make either of us a reputation. We have been too long in the business to try to fool the public with mediocre pictures. We would rather lose all the money we have spent in sending Mr. Evans to Mexico than to release to you anything that is not creditable and worth while."[20]

The punitive expedition was poorly prepared, but it made up for its lack of equipment with enthusiasm. Many people looked upon it as a rehearsal for Europe. One of the soldiers was Merian C. Cooper, later to win fame for his films *Grass, Chang,* and *King Kong:* "I don't know how many times I crossed the Rio Grande—a fellow named Willard Murphy and myself. We were determined that the two of us were going to get Villa. We never saw Villa or anyone else, but we had the best quail shooting."[21]

The motion picture coverage of the punitive expedition when it finally moved into Mexico was of an unusually high standard. Much of it was included in the episode on Mexico in the CBS *World War One* television series, and the long shots of the cavalry against the evening sky suggested something from a John Ford film.

The expedition never caught up with Villa, although on one occasion they thought they had and reported that Villa had been killed.* In order to identify the body beyond any shadow of doubt, the army selected the man who was more familiar with Villa's face than any other American—Mutual cameraman L. M. Burrud. Accompanied by Mexican officers, acting as bodyguards, Burrud visited Chihuahua.

"The appearance of the American photographer and his camera started a violent demonstration. He was pelted with decayed vegetables and other missiles, and hooted through the streets. . . . Burrud improved the perilous opportunity by securing some very spirited scenes, barely escaping from the mob with his life and his films. As all the world knows, he was able to decide that the dead man was not Villa."[22]

Unsuccessful as the punitive expedition was, it was a godsend to motion picture melodramas. Three episodes of *Liberty,* a Universal serial of 1916, directed by Jacques Jaccard, concentrated on a clash between American and Mexican troops.

Gilbert Warrenton, another of the news cameramen associated with the Mexican war who later became a leading Hollywood cinematographer, did a spell for Universal News Weekly at the border. Universal told him it would be a vacation. Warrenton went down to Columbus with Beverly Griffith, only to find the other news weeklies in occupation; in particular, Hearst's man, Tracy Mathewson. The army had imposed a strict censorship, and Warrenton, despite his proper credentials, was refused permission to shoot anything. He managed to find an old gentleman with one leg who had lain on the floor and shot half a dozen bandits as they tried to enter his house, and this made a good item. But it merely encouraged Uni-

* Lieutenant Patton shot one of Villa's lieutenants (General Cardenas) and two other Mexicans with his pistol (George J. Mitchell).

versal's editor to demand more. Faced by the army ban, Warrenton got a job as a truck driver and used his truck as a hide to photograph the maneuvering of army transports. The army heard about this, told him it was very unethical ("That's News Weekly, Sir!"), and demanded the film. Warrenton pulled the old newsreelman's trick of handing over the magazine containing the unexposed film. The exposed material he canned up and sent in.

When General Calles, a future President of Mexico, came to a conference with General Obregón at night, Warrenton and Griffith startled their competitors by setting up the camera in the pitch dark and, as Calles appeared, setting off magnesium flares. Warrenton also accompanied Calles on an orphan-gathering trip, which resulted in a public relations special. On a railroad journey to Chihuahua, he experienced civil war conditions firsthand; with no supplies, troops shot cattle from the train and dragged the meat aboard. Upon arrival at Chihuahua City, Warrenton was arrested at gunpoint by cavalrymen. But with that special brand of newsreelman's blarney, he talked the soldiers out of murdering him and into providing an enthusiastic guard, which escorted him to the nearest hotel. He used the same powers of persuasion to borrow an officer's roadster and to race into Mexico ahead of the cavalry on a bandit-chasing operation, when the army had banned photography.

Tracy Mathewson, the Hearst cameraman, had an enviable reputation for scoops, but, as he himself admitted, he never managed to film any action: "For three years, I chased up and down the border, trying to get a moving picture of a fight. I lugged my heavy pack through alkali and cactus, across rivers and mountain ranges, in pursuit of 'action,' which is a by-word with the movies no less than with the army. And I always missed it. I was at Norias just six hours after that gallant little band of eight cavalrymen and five citizens had held off and finally whipped a band of eighty-five Mexican bandits. . . . I got into Columbus the night after Pancho Villa and his renegades raided that town. I went in with the First Punitive Expedition under General Pershing, actually joining the army for the chance to get some real 'action.' I was allowed to go no further than Casas Grandes with my camera, and, of course, the expedition put off all its fighting until I had returned."[23]

The Hearst publicity men made up for this inglorious but perfectly standard situation by inventing action for him. The story appeared under Mathewson's byline, but even he must have squirmed when he read it, for the ghost writer clearly had no experience with a camera:

"Out over the edge of the arroyo we scrambled. I jumped over with my camera and tripod. I jammed the steel claws into the sand and rocks just as the rifles began to spit. 'Please God, let me get it!' I cried. Then I turned the handle and began the greatest picture ever filmed.

"One of my tripod bearers smiled at my shouting and as he smiled he clutched his hands to his abdomen and fell forward, kicking. I snatched up my camera—how feathery light it was—and went forward with our rifles. I timed my cursing to the turn of the handle and it was very smooth.

" 'Action!' I cried. 'This is what I've wanted. Give 'em hell, boys. Wipe out the blinkety blank dashed greasers!'

"I was in the midst of it. I learned the whistle of a bullet. They tore up little jets of sand all around me. All the time I turned the crank. One greaser made a rush

Charles Rosher with a military ambulance.

for my camera. As he swung his gun, someone shot over my shoulder. 'It's action!' I shouted.

" 'Next time, let go that handle and duck,' called Sgt. Noyes. 'They think that thing is a machine gun, I guess.'

" 'To hell with them!' I cried. 'Let 'em come and die in front of my camera. It's action!' "

This account, appearing in the popular magazine *Photoplay,* might have led to an invasion of theaters running the Hearst newsreels were it not for the final paragraph:

"Then somewhere out of that tangle of guns a bullet cuts its way. 'Zz-zing!' I heard it whistle. The splinters cut my face as it hit the camera. It ripped the side open and smashed the little wooden magazine. I sprang crazily to stop it with my hands. But out of the box uncoiled the precious film. Stretching and glistening in the sun, it fell and died. I stood and watched it dumbly.

"Some time later, they found me sprawled face downward under the tripod. They thought I had been killed, until they heard me sob. And then they knew it was only my heart was broken."[24]

MEXICO RETURNED TO THE FOREFRONT of world politics in 1917, when a telegram from the German Minister for Foreign Affairs, Alfred Zimmermann, to the German ambassador to Mexico was decoded: "We intend to begin on the first of February unrestricted submarine warfare. We shall endeavour in spite of this to keep the United States of America neutral. In the event of this not succeeding, we make Mexico a proposal of alliance on the following basis: make war together, make peace together, generous financial support and an understanding on our part that Mexico is to reconquer her lost territory in Texas, New Mexico and Arizona."[25]

As if to confirm Hearst's direst predictions, Japan was to be invited by Mexico to join in the plot. The telegram was at first considered a forgery, but when its authenticity was established, it helped to propel the United States toward war. Hostilities were declared on 6 April 1917.

Douglas Fairbanks at a Liberty Bond rally

THE UNITED STATES DECLARES WAR

In so many films about World War I, the declaration of war by the United States is portrayed with a feverish montage of flags and bands, marching troops and ecstatic civilians. According to the history books, the American people entered the war with a discernible lack of enthusiasm: "Millions of Americans were bewildered by the suddenness with which war had followed the peace mandate of November 1916 and they had no clear idea why the country was fighting. In areas where German-Americans or Irish-Americans or peace-minded Scandinavians were dominant, the war was greeted with indifference or sullen hostility."[1]

Curiously, the trade press paid little attention to the declaration of war, the first reference being a forecast by F. Collins of McClure Pictures: "The war will in no way harm the motion picture, and indications are that business actually will be benefited by present conditions."[2]

The prophecy was confounded almost at once, when an unexpected slump hit the theaters, due to the sudden increase in the cost of living and the preparation for military service. Theaters near cantonments enjoyed a boom, thanks not only to the troops but to their relatives, who poured in to visit the soldiers and to see how they lived. But elsewhere the atmosphere was depressingly bleak. Explanations formed a catalogue of war conditions: Young men have joined the army, young women have joined the Red Cross or taken government jobs. . . . Other women are absorbed in war work. . . . Taxes are too high. . . . People are curtailing their pleasures to invest in Liberty Bonds, War Savings Stamps. Distributors and exhibitors, who had fought a war tax *before* the war, now faced the war tax surcharge on top of all their other woes.

On the other hand, the motion picture publicity machine welcomed the war as a refreshing change. Tired gimmicks acquired a new urgency and nobility of purpose. In peacetime a photograph of an actress posing for a painter would have vanished into the wastebasket of every editor in the country. But in 1917 a picture of Pearl White posing for Howard Chandler Christy's recruiting poster "Did You Think *I'd* Stay at Home?" made the front page. A prominent actor like Francis X. Bushman merely had to lend his name to a tobacco fund for soldiers, and newspapers poured forth paragraphs of praise.

Better than good reviews were good war angles. Publicity men used the war as a peg upon which to hang their star's latest model of patriotic selflessness:

The departure of so many men for France left jobs open for women; one was Dorothy Dunn of the Universal Animated Weekly. (*From* Moving Picture World)

"Among the busiest knitters in the Fox colony is little June Caprice," reported *Motion Picture Magazine* in June 1918, "who has filled in her time between scenes by turning out a heap of socks, wristlets, mufflers and scarves which have found their comforting way to the army camps."

More serious were the attempts by individual stars, such as Norma Talmadge, to start Red Cross circles, or, as in the case of Enid Bennett, Sylvia Breamer, and Olive Thomas, to form a nurses' class. The Motion Picture War Service Association, headed by Cecil B. DeMille, Lois Weber, Douglas Fairbanks, Charlie Chaplin, and William S. Hart, arranged for stars to appear at benefits and entertainments. This organization was formed one Sunday afternoon at a mass meeting, and inside forty-five minutes, $32,000 was raised for a hospital fund. The Red Cross organized a big tea shop in Los Angeles, which was packed every Wednesday evening, when some famous star was guest of honor. Picture people staged vaudeville shows there, and D. W. Griffith built them a theater.

But by far the most significant contribution to the war effort made by the motion picture colony was its participation in the Liberty Loan drives. Chaplin, Fairbanks, Hart, and Pickford proved to be the greatest bond salesmen of all, taking part in whirlwind tours, yelling themselves hoarse to vast crowds, only a fraction of whom could ever hope to hear them, and doing impromptu stunts for the newsreel cameras.*

Addressing a bond rally at the corner of Fifth Avenue and 42nd Street, Douglas Fairbanks spotted a wealthy-looking lady in a passing automobile. He leaped from his platform, raced in front of the car, and forced it to a halt. He pleaded with the woman for a contribution. With the eyes of the crowd upon her, klaxons blaring, and a famous star seducing the very money from her purse, the lady gave way, and Fairbanks returned to the platform with a check for $1,000.[3]

Although megaphones were available, the human voice could only take so much strenuous activity. Fairbanks's voice eventually gave way and he fell back on pantomime. "When he couldn't make himself heard, he waved his arms, pranced about the stage and made unmistakable signs urging everybody to buy a bond."[4]

In a ten-day tour in 1918, William S. Hart addressed rallies in nineteen cities and sold two million dollars' worth of bonds.[5] Hart was frequently mobbed, his clothing torn, his red neckerchief ripped to shreds for souvenirs. Said Hart: "Anytime I'm wanted to go to war, I'm ready. I've seen wars and I've seen Liberty Loan Drives. Give me war."[6]

Besides her bond campaigns, Mary Pickford acted as godmother to six hundred soldiers in the Artillery Corps—they appeared in *Johanna Enlists*—and one hundred forty-four in the Aviation Corps. She made dozens of personal appearances for war charities and involved herself in a Red Cross fund-raising scheme, requesting a day's pay from every contributor and writing a personal letter of thanks. On top of this, she accepted the position of superintendent of the studio salvage department of the Red Cross, presenting them with two ambulances.†

---

* Treasury Secretary William Gibbs McAdoo, Wilson's son-in-law, became involved with the formation of United Artists as a direct result of the bond campaigns.

† At the end of the war, the Ambulance Fund was underspent—Mary Pickford suggested the balance form the basis of a motion picture relief fund.

The Claws of the Hun (*1918*). *Thomas H. Ince on platform, facing camera, with two officers of the Signal Corps, awaiting a troop train of the 40th (Sunshine) Division at the Parade Ground, Camp Kearny, California. Twenty-eight thousand troops were used.*

Photographed on location with D. W. Griffith's Romance of Happy Valley *(1918) by Madison Lacy, who comments: "One of the drivers brought us news of the first American victory in the war, hence the cheers for the camera." D. W. Griffith, second from left, foreground; Billy Bitzer, extreme right.*

Lasky Home Guard on parade at the Lasky ranch.

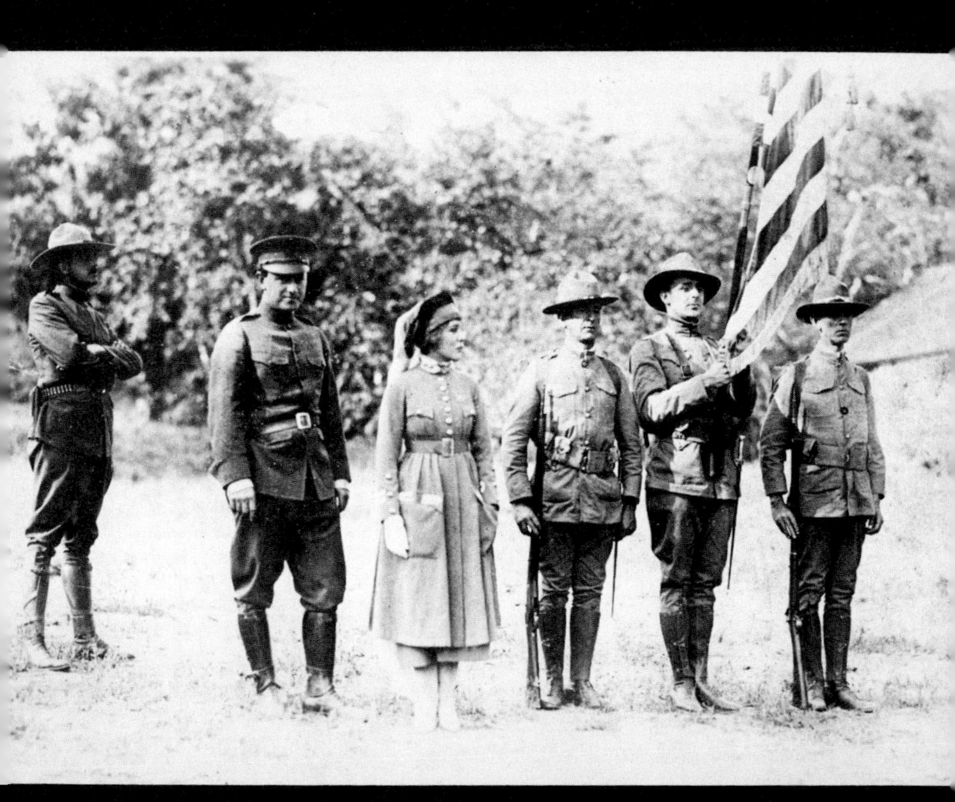

The Lasky Home Guard: left to right, Lieutenant Henry Woodward, Captain Cecil B. DeMille, Mary Pickford, Dave Archer, Wallace Reid (with standard presented by Miss Pickford), and James S. Stembridge.

The fourth Liberty Loan drive was launched by Mary Pickford smashing a bottle of California wine over a replica of a tank. "Do we owe our boys over there anything?" she cried. Before anyone could answer, she replied through her megaphone, "You bet we do!" With Miss Pickford's energetic patriotism reaching right down to their pocketbooks, the audience responded with enthusiasm; a special autographed souvenir of stars' photographs was auctioned for $50,000. Robert Z. Leonard and Ray Hanford presented a tableau, *The Soldier and the Kaiser,* in which the soldier was shown choking the wind out of Blustering Bill. Mr. and Mrs. Francis Ford and their son contributed with a tableau called *18 to 45,* in which father and mother offered their boy upon the altar of his country.

Behind the bond drives was Frank Wilson, director of publicity of the Liberty Loan Executive Committee. Wilson and the Treasury Department were responsible not only for the posters and the campaigns, but also for the special bond films made by the leading stars. Russell Merritt feels Wilson's department should take much of the blame usually attributed to George Creel for the fanning of hatred and hysteria with war posters and slacker films. On the other hand, Wilson was the government's champion of the movies, and after the war joined the staff of D. W. Griffith.

Wilson was also behind the scheme of the Four Minute Men, who toured theaters selling Liberty Bonds. One of their hard-sell techniques was to pick out a serviceman from the audience and demand, "Who will buy a hundred-dollar Liberty Bond for him?" So all-pervading was the military atmosphere that for a while saluting replaced the handshake as the standard greeting around the studios.

And then there was the Home Guard.

The Lasky Home Guard was more a target for funny stories than for the bullets of saboteurs. The studio announced that the corps, formed by Cecil B. DeMille and Jesse Lasky two weeks after war was declared, would be equipped, uniformed, and armed entirely at their expense. Skeptics were therefore delighted when the studio soldiers appeared on parade in civilian clothes, with property department rifles and brooms.

Several studios had organized home guards, which had been formed into the 51st Company, but when the Lasky Home Guard was promoted to battalion status by order of the Adjutant General of the state of California, it was able to recruit employees of other studios. The colors were presented by Mary Pickford and carried by Color Sergeant Wallace Reid. Under the command of Cecil B. DeMille, who was made a captain for the purpose (his brother, William de Mille, was only a top sergeant), the outfit included a band, a signal unit, two machine-gun sections, and a field ambulance "of the latest approved design." Henry Woodward, who had served in the Philippine constabulary, was chief drillmaster, and claimed that the full detachment could be mobilized and armed one hour after the sounding of the alarm. The Home Guard consisted of men who were not eligible for the first draft, or men having families who were dependent upon them. Able-bodied, unmarried men enlisted in the Naval Reserve or the Coast Artillery Federal Reserve.

Cecil B. DeMille claimed, in his autobiography,[7] that of the one hundred and five men who went into the regular army after their rudimentary training in the Lasky Home Guard, every one became a commissioned or noncommissioned officer.

The Lasky people had many preparedness enthusiasts among their employees. Company 17 of the Coast Artillery Federal Reserve had been formed before the United States entered the war and consisted almost entirely of picture people. Commanded by Captain Theodore Duncan and Lieutenant Walter Long, both of Lasky, with Tom Forman a corporal and Ernest Shields a sergeant, Company 17 was called into the service of the government in August 1917.

Ordered to operate a gun, the motion picture soldiers discarded the army instructions as "too technical." The following dialogue was overheard: "Raise your foreground—pan right two turns—Props!" A dummy shell was placed in the breech. "Smoke pot!" A powder bag was handed over. "Camera!" The breechblock was slammed, and the company stepped aside. "Action!" The lanyard was pulled and the mythical shell sped seaward.[8]

THE CREEL COMMITTEE

When a government decree of 1916 prohibited cameramen from following the armed forces of the United States, the editors of all the news weeklies swooped on Washington and barnstormed the government into changing its mind. The industry hoped this lesson would be remembered by the Committee on Public Information, the official propaganda organization, which was established on 14 April 1917. After all, the committee was described as "the world's greatest adventure in advertising," and began with an inestimable advantage—it could benefit from everyone else's mistakes. One of its first acts was to prohibit cameramen from following the armed forces of the United States.

Of course, the decision was forced on the CPI by the army, which insisted that only men in uniform could photograph in military sectors. A Photographic Section of the Signal Corps was duly announced, but when the CPI investigated, they found the section to be a hope rather than a fact. The committee made a rapid survey of photographers, and a number of Hollywood professionals—newsreel men and still photographers—were hastily drafted.

The routine was straightforward: "The negatives taken in France and the United States by the uniformed photographers of the Signal Corps were delivered, undeveloped, to the Chief of Staff for transmission to the War College Division. The material was 'combed' and such part as was decided to be proper for public exhibition was then turned over to the CPI in the form of duplicate negatives."[1]

Such a procedure sounds impressive. But shorn of its official language, what this statement means is that the production of propaganda films in the United States was left entirely to chance. The success of each segment of each film depended upon the enterprise and skill of the Signal Corps cameramen, yet those cameramen were not supplied with any overall directive. The CPI missed a tremendous and historic opportunity by failing to send directors to work alongside the cameramen in France. *Moving Picture World* sensed the lack of direction in the official films: "Commandeer Griffith and other good ones and let them plan the war narrative consecutively. Audiences get tired of marching troops and dreary landscapes. Give them the thrilling fact-story instead."[2]

The CPI was not convinced of the superiority of motion pictures as a propa-

George Creel. (*Signal Corps photo*)

ganda force, so the question of American superiority in this field was purely academic. The chairman of the CPI was George Creel: a reporter on the Kansas City *Star,* Creel first came into contact with the creative side of film-making after his appointment as Denver's police commissioner. Otis B. Thayer, a former Selig man in Colorado, persuaded him to write the scenario for a serious sociological film, *Saved by the Juvenile Court.* Thayer skipped the state, owing a lot of money, and the film was appropriated by the owner of the studio Thayer had rented. He changed the title to suit Creel's current drive against the red-light district, and screened it as *Denver's Underworld.* The drama was garnished with footage shot at the Cheyenne rodeo.[3]

Creel could hardly blame the entire industry for this isolated, if archetypal, experience. But the incident summed up the way men in authority expected the picture business to behave. From President Wilson down, most of them were saddled with distrust. As a result, the industry was not closely involved with the government war film effort. Protested the trade press: "With the exception of J. E. Brulatour, chairman of the National Cinema Commission, not an important man in the industry enjoys any authoritative connection with the vast Government motion picture work."[4] The distrust was mutual. Exhibitors didn't want the official films. Anything that smacked of government sponsorship was doubtful box office, to say the least. Russell Merritt has discovered letters from Creel to William Brady, head of the National Association of the Motion Picture Industry, asking if the industry would distribute the CPI's films. Brady, not even bothering to consult any of his colleagues, gave him a resounding "No."

When the CPI gave the task of distribution to the Red Cross, and exhibition to the YMCA and the Knights of Columbus, the industry was furious. For these

Industries that are winning the war

AGRICULTURE, steel, oil, transportation—all indispensable weapons. But there is another weapon to be fittingly grouped with them—a weapon of the heart—*motion pictures!*

Fittingly grouped with them, too, on their own basis of volume of business done and amount of capital invested, *as well as* on the basis of performing the indispensable duty of keeping up the national heart.

It is common knowledge that *the* quality of all others that America has brought to the Allies is buoyant morale, lightness of heart—and it is common knowledge from coast to coast that it is *Paramount* and *Artcraft* Pictures that have been adopted by the whole nation as the romantic fuel of its cheery temper.

Paramount and Artcraft Pictures have actually accomplished the magnificent destiny of raising the screen to the importance of a first-grade *weapon of victory.*

In thousands upon thousands of American communities the great Paramount and Artcraft Pictures, aflame with the purpose of victory, have shaped the public morale—the stuff of which victory is made—to a steely resoluteness!

No wonder the President has expressed his appreciation of the war-value of motion pictures!

The men and women of vision behind Paramount and Artcraft give their word to the nation that the weapon they wield shall always be kept polished and bright—

—bright with the shine "of *foremost* stars, *superbly* directed, in *clean* motion pictures."

Paramount and Artcraft Motion Pictures

"FOREMOST STARS, SUPERBLY DIRECTED, IN CLEAN MOTION PICTURES"

Look for the trade-marks as the sure way of identifying *Paramount* and *Artcraft* Pictures—and the theatres that show them

FAMOUS PLAYERS-LASKY CORPORATION
ADOLPH ZUKOR *Pres.* JESSE L. LASKY *Vice Pres.* CECIL B. DE MILLE *Director General*
NEW YORK

The industry combats government prejudice: inspired propaganda for Paramount, printed in Photoplay, *1918. The President's "appreciation" was mere window dressing; his private disapproval of the Hate-the-Hun films was profound.*

organizations not only controlled the government films but, as their buildings at camps and cantonments were the only places where pictures could be shown, they controlled the regular entertainment pictures as well.

"In the name of common sense," asked *Moving Picture World* in January 1918, "why start the Red Cross in the picture business? It would be much more reasonable to ask them to operate a chain of grocery stores."[5]

The government's aims—to give the soldiers decent films and to give the Red Cross its percentage—were praiseworthy, said the trade press, but their methods were wasteful and ineffective. Several members of the industry, notably Pat Powers, of Universal, had tried to work out plans to distribute the latest releases free to the troops, but the CPI had been uncooperative. The War Department, on the other hand, had appointed powerful clothing manufacturers to the Supply Board and permitted them to award multimillion-dollar contracts to one another's companies, but as far as motion pictures were concerned, the authorities were stern and unbending puritans.

"The YMCA has the monopoly of showing all the junk it can beg or buy at junk prices, and that is the best the soldiers are allowed to see. But at the Atlanta prison all of the very latest productions are shown to the various malefactors confined there."[6]

As the industry predicted, distribution quickly became an enormous headache for the CPI, and Charles Hart was brought in to sort it all out. If the CPI was anxious to add insult to injury, then the appointment of Hart fulfilled this purpose. "I knew nothing about films," admitted Hart, "but I was chosen for the post because I obviously had an independent attitude, and not being commercially interested in films, could not be accused of having an axe to grind."[7]

The industry did not agree with Hart; they felt his axe had been ground to a fine point of prejudice in favor of his former employer, the widely distrusted William Randolph Hearst. Hearst's allegedly pro-German leanings shadowed all his government activities. He had had cameramen with the German Army and his newsreels were banned in both England and Canada. Actually, Hearst was more of an isolationist than a German sympathizer; he felt that allowing America to bleed on behalf of Europe was criminal folly. Nevertheless, Theodore Roosevelt branded him as "one of the efficient allies for Germany on this side of the water,"[8] and that was enough. When the CPI banned *The Yanks Are Coming* (see p. 205), Robert Cochrane, of Universal, charged that the committee was Hearst-controlled, because so many of its employees had worked for the Hearst empire. By 1918 even Hearst's newsreel chief, Edgar Hatrick, was filming the battlefields for Creel. But this was just another example of the industry's petulance, and few took the charges seriously. The CPI defended itself against the Hearst label by making public the background of its employees, and Charles Hart survived.

The industry was also alarmed about Hart's Division of Films, imagining it would establish its own system of distribution and eventually supersede regular commercial channels, for Hart had been successful in combating the restrictive practices of the picture business. But the fear proved groundless. Hart felt that as soon as hostilities ended, the government film structure should be dismantled. As a political weapon wielded by the wrong side, the motion picture would be seriously destructive. "It is a very much more powerful agent than the Press," he said.[9]

Another figure of importance in the CPI was Jules Brulatour. Associated with William Brady in the World Film Corporation, he had been behind the making of Sir Gilbert Parker's *The Seats of the Mighty* in 1914, in which stage star Blanche Bates had "capitulated" to the screen. Miss Bates was, in domestic life, Mrs. George Creel.

Brulatour, aristocratic, Louisiana-born, and a shrewd entrepreneur, welcomed his role as chairman of the National Cinema Commission, which had responsibility for distribution to neutral countries. He contacted all the major corporations that used motion pictures, and asked them not only for money but for permission to make prints of their films. Realizing the advertising potential, the companies were only too glad to help. Henry Ford handed over a great many films and thousands of dollars. The Bureau of Parks and the Department of Agriculture were both pioneers of the documentary, and films from these government departments joined pictures from the U.S. Steel Corporation, Waterman's Pen Company, and International Harvester in a gigantic conglomeration of short subjects. Brulatour was far-sighted in his choice of activity for the war effort. Having acquired the positives on loan, it was his task to organize the manufacture of duplicate negatives and prints in sufficient numbers for worldwide distribution. And Brulatour was the agent for Eastman Kodak raw stock.

George Creel was especially concerned with the problem of the neutral countries. Not that the neutrals objected to American films. Far from it: they lapped them up. Anything American was welcome—particularly if it featured Norma Talmadge or Charlie Chaplin. U.S. films were so popular that the Germans had been doing excellent business, using them to fill theaters, while running their own propaganda material as support.

Everyone loved American pictures—until they saw the government films. The reaction was highly embarrassing to the CPI. Creel secured a ruling that every application for a license—without which no film could be exported—had to be endorsed by the CPI. He then followed the example of the Germans, and included his "educational matter" in every shipment of entertainment films. If any foreign exhibitor refused CPI propaganda, he was denied the films he really wanted. By 1917 American films were the only reliable and consistent source of popular entertainment, and to have the supply cut off was like being plunged into eternal darkness.

THE CPI'S NEWSREEL, the *Official War Review,* consumed much of the Signal Corps material not already incorporated into the CPI's big features, *Pershing's Crusaders, America's Answer,* and *Under Four Flags.* The regular news weeklies got whatever was left. The most successful of the CPI features was *America's Answer.** According to Creel, it broke all records for the number of theaters and the sheer range of its distribution. Released in Europe as *America's Answer to the Hun,* the film has lost the breathless relevance that caused Ray Hall, production manager for the Division of Films, to write: "I never saw greater response to any calculated effort at arousing enthusiasm than I witnessed while watching a first-

* The original main title was spelled out in gigantic letters by hundreds of soldiers, an idea repeated with ironic effect in Abel Gance's antiwar film *J'accuse* (1919).

LEFT: *Signal Corps cameraman L. William O'Connell was assigned to film a parade on New York's Fifth Avenue and to pan with the soldiers as they passed—but to linger long enough to photograph William Randolph Hearst and guest congressmen, Hearst supposedly being pro-German.*
RIGHT: *Douglas Fairbanks slugs Bull Montana for a Liberty Bond short of 1918, directed by Joseph Henabery*

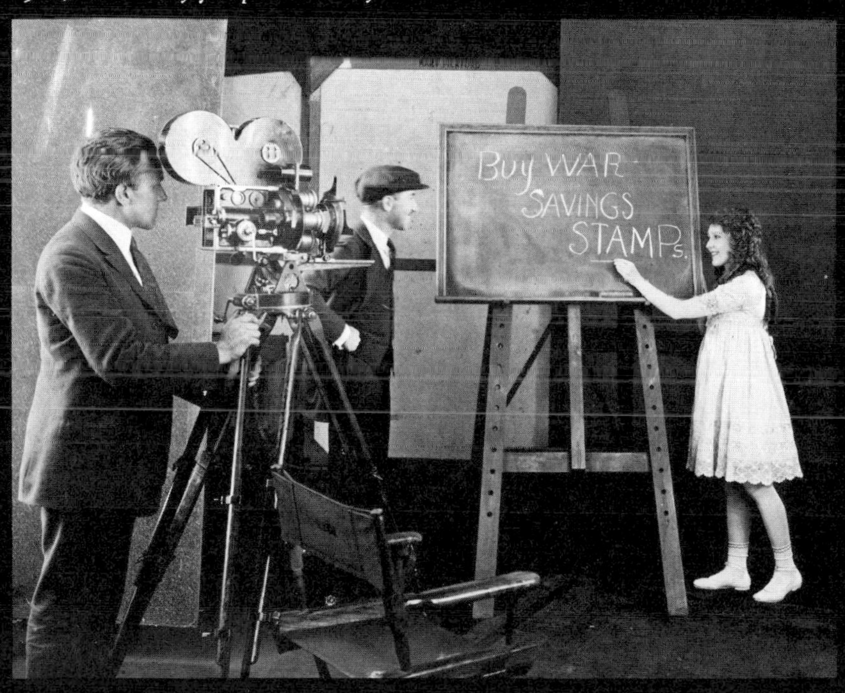

To aid the Victory Loan, Sidney Franklin, center, directs Mary Pickford in a propaganda coda to The Hoodlum *(1919). Charles Rosher at camera.*

A surprisingly dismal image from the propaganda film entitled America's Answer *(1918).*

night audience in New York."[10] Now it seems dry and predictable, punctuated by titles of extravagant patriotism. Since the CPI consisted of so many journalists and advertising men, words meant more than pictures and the titles are given unusual prominence.

"The time has come," says the introductory title, "when it is America's high privilege to spend her blood upon the fields of battle already hallowed by the sacrifices of her Allies' stalwart sons. Determined to exercise this privilege, America has called ten million men for military service. Of these, over 1 million are now in Europe, eager to emulate the heroic deeds of their brothers-in-arms."

Such a devastating statement of intent demands complementary images suggestive of heroism and sacrifice. In *America's Answer* the titles (by Kenneth Benton) exist in a vacuum, unsupported by the visuals, which remain, for the most part, plain and straightforward, rugged and honest. This title is followed, for instance, by a scene of a gun crew firing a French 75 mm. A few shots later, a small group of doughboys is shown miserably picking their way through a gigantic pile of old boots, salvaging them for refugees. The inevitable scenes of troops on the move are given emotional punch by such titles as "Through the quaint villages of France, American infantrymen are hurrying every day to swell the ranks of Humanity's defenders." A little group of children has been edged to the roadside by the cameraman, and rather self-consciously they wave: "Surely the sanctity of our cause is brought home to these new soldiers by this pathetic group of the orphans of France, waving brave little hands to their new friends."

Amused by the titles, intrigued by the antiquity of the equipment, a modern audience can sense none of the manipulative power that the film once had. It gave a very misleading picture. Vital sections of America's industry had failed to catch up with the war; shipbuilding fell so far behind schedule that the first vessel from the largest government shipyard was not delivered until the war was over. Factories produced heavy guns in sufficient quantities too late for the front lines. American aviators flew British and French planes, and soldiers fired French artillery.[11] Other areas of industry exceeded their targets, and thousands of new millionaires were created.[12] Yet *America's Answer* conveyed the impression of total victory on the industrial front.

"Perhaps some of the most rousing pictures are those which show the constant succession of gigantic liners transporting the troops under the escort of British and American warships," said *The Bioscope*.[13] "Another fact which must impress itself most deeply in the mind is the vast scope of the engineering organisation, the construction of railways, docks, munition plant and food storage, being alone sufficient to fill one with profound admiration for the mighty powers of our American cousins."

Sponsored in France by the steel and munitions trust, the Comité des Forges, the film carried such impact that the head of Renault said it meant for him "the postponement of any possible strike for six months."[14]

THE SIGNAL CORPS

With the formation of the Photographic Section of the Signal Corps, film history overlaps political history to a remarkable extent. Like every other branch of the service, the Signal Corps was unprepared for the gigantic undertaking in Europe. Founded on 10 June 1861 by Major Albert Myer, it was concerned exclusively with army communications; its insignia was crossed signal flags. Although photography was used during the Civil War, it played no significant part in Signal Corps activities and the army had made little use of the motion picture camera beyond a 1907 short of the Wright brothers' flight at Fort Myer. On 21 July 1917 the Corps was given the task of recording every stage of the American role in the war.

This decision was just another burden to the Signal Corps. Experience in the Mexican campaign had convinced the army that aviation would be used mainly for artillery spotting and reconnaissance; the Signal Corps had therefore become America's air force (until June 1918).

Although the Photographic Section was established and equipped according to instructions at its school at Columbia University, and although it was subject to military regulations and discipline, it found itself becoming less and less military. As more young men were drafted from the studios of New York and California, the outfit acquired its own, distinctly anarchic atmosphere. Motion picture men were accustomed to high salaries, and although they were used to working extremely hard, they were also used to a comfortable life.

Their attitude surprised and annoyed the military men, although it greatly impressed some of the new recruits. Ernest B. Schoedsack recalled one of these recruits—a man always in trouble with his puttees: "We were lined up one day and asked our salaries in civilian life. There was a director there called Alan Crosland. '$300 a week!' he called out. In those days that was a tremendous sum. Privates were paid $30 a month. 'Getting fresh, huh?' said the officer, and put him on the

coal pile. Well, this amount impressed the fellow who couldn't wrap his puttees, and after the war he got into the business at the cutting end of it. His name was Lewis Milestone."[1]

The Signal Corps was caught in the crossfire of changing policies. The army preferred to assign men to jobs for which they had no training, so they had nothing to unlearn before doing it the army way. But still photographers and motion picture cameramen could not be created overnight like transport drivers. Men could be taught the combination of optics, chemistry, and artistry, but there was no guarantee they would learn it. After some initial disasters, and at the request of the Creel committee, professionals were hurriedly drafted. Nevertheless, the army missed some splendid opportunities; Karl Brown, who had been assistant to the great G. W. Bitzer, was drafted into the Machine-gun Corps to look after mules.

So eager was the army to draft Irvin Willat that they arrested him on the set of *False Faces*—only to assign him to the Ambulance Corps:*

"I told them I had spent my life in the motion picture business—at least make me a cameraman. But it was no good. We were all set to go to Russia. At the last moment, thanks to Don Bell of Bell and Howell, and my brother 'Doc' Willat, who did some maneuvering, I was transferred from Camp Kearny to Columbia University. I was to learn photography. I met a lot of boys there I had known in the picture business. The instructor turned out to be an assistant cameraman, and the first day I gave him an awful hard time. I'd say, 'If I may . . . isn't it true that . . . ?' And he'd say, 'Oh, I think you're right.' No sooner was class over than he went to see the captain.

"I knew the captain. He'd been a cameraman in New York. He called me in. 'Irvin, you know the situation we're in. We got the best men we could, and some of them aren't too good. We aren't supposed to teach you. We're supposed to teach people who don't know anything about it. You're embarrassing the instructor very much and the class doesn't know what it's all about. I'm going to have to ask you not to go to class.'

"The captain promised me a commission when I got to Europe. I asked him why not now? 'I've got all these lieutenants who are supposed to know how to make still pictures or motion pictures,' he said. 'They don't know the front end of a camera from the back. They're political appointees. There's nothing I can do about it, and I wouldn't send them anywhere.'

"So they sent me to New Jersey, and I had to run all the film that came in from the French front, and report on it."[2]

Ernest Schoedsack was a sergeant in the National Guard (Corps of Engineers) when war broke out. He applied for the new Photographic Section, and thanks to his experience as a second cameraman with Mack Sennett (he worked on *The Submarine Pirate*) he was accepted. But someone made a clerical error and he was transferred to the wrong outfit—an air photographic unit in Oklahoma.

The army discovered the mistake and Schoedsack was transferred to Columbia University. In order to get into the Signal Corps, Schoedsack had had to drop to the

---

* Willat was charged with falsifying his draft exemption card, and threatened with jail (*Variety*, 26 April 1918).

A Signal Corps cameraman films a soldier shaving while a comrade holds a mirror. The scene was filmed, but from this posed shot you'd think the camera was aimed at the fields. Between Toul and Nanteuil, 29 June 1918. (Signal Corps photo)

The Chinese built the Western railroads and also served on the Western Front. Here, Chinese laborers inspect a Signal Corps Debrie camera. (Signal Corps photo)

American cameramen Sergeant Morris and Private Persse going into the battle on a British tank, between Villeret and Bellicourt. (Signal Corps photo)

level of private. Nevertheless, he was made an instructor—"I taught them how to put a camera on a tripod"—and eventually was ordered to leave for France.

"We finally reached Paris, and were taken off to Vincennes," said Schoedsack. "The Signal Corps occupied the Pathé château, and they had laboratory and cutting rooms on the fourth floor of the Pathé factory. The other floors were being used as a gas mask factory.

"The gentleman in command was a very nice old bloke. He had been an optometrist up in Oakland. He was a reservist in the National Guard, and they had to give him a job someplace. So, optometrist pertaining to lenses, lenses to photography—voilà! The only officer remotely connected with the picture business was Al Kaufman [Famous Players–Lasky studio manager], a very friendly fellow who was Adolph Zukor's son-in-law. The other three executive officers were characters they had no use for anywhere else. The general idea was to stay in Paris and have fun.

"I complained a lot, and agitated a lot, and finally they said, 'You want to go to the front? All right, you can go to the front.' A cameraman [Harris Thorpe, who had been with Douglas Fairbanks's company in Hollywood] pulled out of the combat area and I got my chance. I wanted a light camera. Oh, no. They gave me this damn great Bell and Howell and this great trunk. It weighed a hundred pounds. They needed the light cameras, the Debries, down in Paris, I guess, where all the action was.

"I had no directive, no passes, no nothing. They didn't even give me a gas mask or a helmet, although I did get a .45 and some ammunition. I got a truck down to the combat zone, but an MP stopped me because I had no gas mask or helmet. There were some fresh graves by the side of the road, and one of them had a gas mask and helmet. The helmet was kind of bashed in on one side, and I remember the name inside was Kelly. Anyway, that got me into the combat area.

"There was hardly any activity in the daytime. All the barraging and banging around was at night. Photographically, there was very little you could do."[3]

A PHOTOGRAPHIC UNIT, CONSISTING of one motion picture cameraman, sometimes an assistant, and one stills man, was assigned to each division. Altogether, there were thirty-eight of these units, which also accompanied the sea transport service, the Red Cross, the Services of Supply, and even the Salvation Army. Some units were fortunate enough to have a truck of their own, equipped with a darkroom. A water tank on the roof of the truck provided running water, and it was refilled from village wells or roadside pools with a hand pump. These photographic flying squads were often of immense strategic value. Still pictures taken from the air were pieced together to form mosaic maps, and these could give an infinite number of details for pinpointing enemy positions: fresh tracks in grass, newly dug earth, felled trees, clouds of dust. . . . The Hyper-Tele-Stereoscopy system, developed during the war, provided pictures in three dimensions, so that camouflage emplacements could be picked out from the surrounding trees.*

---

* Another wartime development was the wide-angle lens, invented by Henri Chretien in 1917 for tank drivers. This lens eventually formed the basis of Cinemascope.

The mobile darkrooms were equipped with bottles of what cameramen called their "eyewash," imported from Paris and used to soothe not so much the ocular nerve as the throbbing head. Food was seldom a problem, since a man equipped to take pictures could always get privilege rations from soldiers in the cookhouse, especially when they wanted snapshots to send home.

One Signal Corps achievement of this period has gone unnoticed, although it was perhaps the most extraordinary technical development of the war as far as motion pictures are concerned. A group of officers, physics professors in civilian life, invented a form of sound-on-film. Artillery spotting by sound ranging had been a haphazard operation; observers armed with stopwatches were stationed along the front, and whenever they heard the report of an enemy gun they pressed the button and sent their timings to a central station. This method proved inaccurate. The alternative was most sophisticated. Five-gallon gasoline cans were fitted up as microphones, connected to a motion picture camera, which recorded the sound waves —six tracks, one above the other, on regular 35 mm. film. Considering this took place a full decade before the public introduction of sound film, it is strange so little is known about it. *Stars and Stripes*[4] credits the invention to Lieutenant Colonel Augustus Trowbridge, Major Theodore Lyman, and Captain Charles B. Bazzoni, under the control of Colonel R. G. Alexander of the Topographical Section of the General Staff.*

Many Signal Corps photographic men, of course, never made it to France. A young soldier who had worked at the World Film Laboratory before being drafted won his first trade-paper publicity with his Signal Corps activities: "Joe Sternberg has been stationed at Columbia University, where he will be engaged in important work connected with the preparation of a film which will be used as an aid in training recruits. This film will show the molding of a citizen into a soldier, from his induction into the army to his advent on the field of battle, and will include the first steps in training, such as learning to salute, the manual of arms, etc. up to bayonet practice and bombing."[5]

Lewis Milestone's job was to assist cameraman Lucien Andriot—"All my work consisted of lugging the camera for him"—as he photographed operations for the Medical Corps. "It took me quite a while before I learned to control my dizziness." Milestone was based in Washington, where his unit also made short films instructing troops on posture and how to keep the teeth clean.

Another future director, George Marshall, had been a first lieutenant in the Coast Artillery in the National Guard, and for once his military experience paid off. At two in the afternoon of the day he volunteered, he was in uniform with a full sergeant's stripes and the command of 191 men. At first he was attached to the regular Signal Corps, laying cable lines in France; then he was transferred to the Photographic Section.

"Well, it sounded good after the mud and slop we were bathing in—my God, I'd never seen so much mud in my life," said Marshall. "But the Photographic Section! It was the most slipshod outfit you could possibly imagine. Later on, I began

---

* I have since learned that the recording apparatus was invented by Dr. Lucien Bull, of the Institut Marey, near Paris.

Harris Thorpe, cameraman for Douglas Fairbanks in civilian life, filming for the Signal Corps in a reserve trench, 1918. (Signal Corps photo)

to understand the reason for the laxity. They would be assigned to such-and-such a division. It wasn't like a hard and fast military encampment. They would go to the front and stay as long as that division stayed, and they'd come back to this big château. And there would be a big celebration, and then another assignment.

"I was still a first sergeant and I was so annoyed when I walked in there to see the barracks, and to see the way they were living. I raised hell for about two weeks. I had them up at six in the morning for reveille. I told them if they didn't appear, I'd give them clean-up duties. They'd never had this before, except the men who had been with other outfits.

" 'I can't stand this dirty, sloppy attitude,' I said. And then I slipped into discard with the rest. It was useless. You couldn't beat them down. I had all these characters, like those fabulous New York cameramen from Hearst News; they'd never taken orders in their life. I remember one of them coming out on parade with his shirt-tail sticking out. I said, 'You can clean up the barracks this morning.' He wanted to shoot me. 'Don't tell *me* what to do!' he said.

"We made up newsreels to send back home. We'd take a piece of film from here and a piece from there—they had no connection with each other whatsoever. We'd make up a big bombing episode, showing people carrying bodies which had been photographed fifty miles away. We were doing things pretty much on our own. They were screaming for film, but there was nobody to make decisions as to

Lieutenant McDonald filming impacts of German artillery on 8th Field Artillery (1st Division) positions at Exermont, 5 October 1918. (Signal Corps photo)

what sort of film they wanted. So we gave them that film on venereal disease, *Fit to Fight.** We used part of that one and mixed it with a second one and called it *Fit to Go Home*. We had no real producer. Al Kaufman was out there, and he got to be a captain. I used to razz him about it: 'Captain? Huh!' That was the kind of group where you'd say 'Captain? Huh!' God, it was really a hell of an outfit."[6]

Casualties among Signal Corps photographic personnel were remarkably low. Army records list only one fatality, First Lieutenant Edwin Ralph Estes, who was killed near Sedan just four days before the armistice. The plates from his camera recorded the last moments of his life. Reginald Lyons, Vitagraph cameraman, was gassed three times, lost the sight of an eye, and spent eleven months in hospital. Faxon Dean, whose father had covered the Mexican revolution for Mutual, was injured in a plane wreck.

Perhaps the most remarkable experience of any of the Signal Corps combat cameramen was told to me by a veteran who refused to allow me to mention his name—he wanted no intimation of heroics. The description sounded authentic, but I could scarcely believe the scene he claimed to have photographed. Without any proof, it was just a fascinating story. But while I was ploughing through Signal Corps material in the Imperial War Museum in London, I came upon the very shots he referred to. On the opening frame was the trace of a number, scratched on the negative. I copied it down and sent it to William Murphy, of the Audio-Visual Division

---

* Written and directed by Edward H. Griffith at Metro, featuring Ray McKee (1918).

at the National Archives in Washington. He searched through the old filing system and came up with all the relevant information—which film it had come from, and, most important, who had photographed it. The surname matched. I present the story, regretting the anonymity, just as it was told to me.

"The Germans were pulling back from the Vesle, where it had been very tight. I got the camera slung on my back and staggered on down the road. My assistant and I had about ninety pounds apiece. We arrive at the Vesle River, and shells are still flying about and there are a lot of dead around. The Vesle didn't turn out to be much, but right up beyond was the cliff where the Germans had been dug in for so long. I'll never forget struggling straight up that cliff on a hot summer evening, with a Fokker diving around. No sign of a fight. The shelling had died down. When we got to the top, it was dark. Some infantrymen were digging in for the night, so we climbed in with them.

"The next morning was the start of the greatest day I'd ever had. It was an early, gray morning. Nothing to see. We wandered down the road, dragging the stuff, and we came to a tiny village. A company of troops were sitting in a ditch, ready to carry on the advance. They're very unhappy—they haven't made contact with the enemy. Just then a squadron of French cavalry appeared—the last mounted troops I ever saw in action. They spread out across the plain, and each bush they came across, they rammed their lances into it. They were out to make contact. All of a sudden, bang! A shell goes off right near us. One of the Frenchmen goes down. They drag him away, put him on another horse and leave his own horse kicking. They'd made contact. Bang! Another. That's the way the Germans did it. They had lots of artillery, and as they pulled back they always left a gun or two to cover their retreat. Ahead of us were some woods and a lot of old barbed wire that must have been up for four years. We made for that and came across a little shelled dugout that faced the wrong way. The row subsided, and we expected Jerry to come out of the woods and try to take us, but he wasn't playing it that way. In our youthful fervor, we had advanced four or five kilometers ahead of the advancing infantry.

"I set up the camera on the road, and I'm just focusing it when a .77 opens up from the other side of a wooded ravine. I have never heard such a sound in my life. I don't think it missed me by much more than a foot or two. I could feel the hot wind as it went by. I dashed back into the dugout.

" 'Now I'm in a quandary,' I said. 'If I stay here, I'll get a good picture, but it'll be a massacre.' So I sent this corporal back with a note to warn the boys. He never did get to them. I don't know where he went.

"About noon they opened up. Not at me, but a little to the side. And here comes the whole bunch—all spread out—in broad daylight. And bang, bang, bang. All I had to do was take pictures of them. They dived into some dugouts and wire, yelling and crying out. But there was nothing I could do. The last ten feet I got was a fellow, festooned with canteens, running back. He simply disappeared in a cloud of smoke.*

"That night, a very welcome sound; a French battery had moved up, and was whamming at the Germans, just across the strip of wood. I could hear the gun

---

* This shot does not appear in the film I saw.

go off and then the shell pass over. Right on top of me. Next morning, early, a runner comes up. I've been reported up there, and I was to turn round and come back. Well, I was going back for film anyhow. And that was the end of that. But when they gave me my discharge papers, next to Record of Combat they put 'none.' "

THE PROPAGANDA FILMS

With America firmly in the war, producers might be forgiven for thinking that anything in the way of anti-German propaganda would be eagerly welcomed by the government. But President Wilson was not an enthusiast for the motion picture, and far from commending the "Hate-the-Hun" pictures, he privately deplored the medieval bloodlust of such films. His government gave the industry little encouragement, and classed motion pictures as nonessentials.

Theodore Roosevelt's energetic opposition to Wilson's policies gave the industry an ideal alternative leader and a perfect advance guard. His antagonism served to detonate any official land mines and acted as a precedent for the industry's own belligerence.

An enormous number of these propaganda films were made, but they were not all the patriotic box-office successes the circumstances might suggest. The industry, both in production and exhibition, was in a depression. Part of the problem lay with the nature of movie-going in wartime. The Treasury Department exhorted everyone to give to the Liberty Loans until it hurt, and this, as well as other government campaigns, created a climate which was not conducive to good business. In desperation, publicists tried to convey the impression that to miss the latest war film was tantamount to treachery. They did so to combat the sentiment fostered, albeit unwittingly, by the government campaigns, that it was unpatriotic to attend moving picture shows. The sentiment swept the country in what William Brady, head of the industry's wartime committee, called "a hysterical wave." "We do not believe," he wrote to George Creel, "that it is the policy of the government to destroy the greatest means of personal contact and information between it and the people."[1]

The self-indulgence of enjoying a film, the cost of running a theater, and the high salaries paid to the artists seemed inconsistent with the sacrifices demanded by a wartime economy. The situation reached a climax in May 1918, by which time thirty-two of the ninety-three Los Angeles theaters had been forced to close, thanks to poor attendance. War tax had put up the cost of admission, and even children, such an important part of any theater's business, had been deterred by their teachers' instructions to save their money for War Savings Stamps.

Brady sent urgent telegrams to Creel and William McAdoo, pleading for relief in terms which must have caused some wry smiles in Washington. Brady pointed to the wartime achievements of the industry—the fifty thousand Four Minute Men and the estimated $100 million raised for the war loans at movie theaters. The CPI's factual films had run into resistance from the industry—exhibitors had declared they were uninteresting to their audiences. Now Brady was obliged to backtrack, and to offer the services of the industry for the spreading of government propaganda. It was as a result of this campaign, and not the Hate-the-Hun films, that the picture business was at last declared a vital industry in August 1918.

Fresh propaganda poured into the theaters like poison gas. The Hate-the-Hun films were often undisguised incitements to race hatred, more extreme than anything in *The Birth of a Nation.* The idea of the Germans as a separate race was quickly established, for the movies borrowed heavily from the British propaganda model, causing profound anguish to a vast number of Americans of German origin.

In the absence of clearly defined war aims, it was left to the film-makers to select them from the simplistic catalogue of melodrama. Echoing Roosevelt, they whipped up the very kind of fervent nationalism the United States was trying to defeat. Their films, and the slightly more subdued war plays, came in for a barrage of criticism from the upper echelons of the press. Said *The Nation:* "These war melodramas that are becoming 'yellow' drama, without dramatic value, without depth, 'full of sound and fury signifying nothing' do not properly express our national spirit."[2] The sight of Americans behaving with the patriotic hysteria of Germans was offensive to large numbers of the middle class, including many of those in government. President Wilson consistently refused to appear in these films, or to endorse them, and the newsreel men had a hard job persuading him to pose for their cameras.

The government's factual films hammered the message of self-sacrifice, and showed the noble contributions of others. Audiences preferred propaganda about themselves. The films they went to see suggested that individuals determine the course of history. It was ordinary men and women, as portrayed by well-known players, who caused vast armies to be defeated, spy rings to be exposed, armadas to be destroyed at sea. This was how the movies depicted democracy. Most audiences were aware of the lurid exaggerations, but they loved the actors and actresses who convinced them that it was they, the ordinary members of the public, who held history in their hands. They felt pleasurably excited by the way the war films sometimes managed to sidestep censorship, showing the enemy committing acts which no peacetime film dared suggest. And they welcomed this encouragement to channel a whole spectrum of frustration and aggression into hatred of the Hun.

Thus the ordinary American entertainment film became the showcase for the war. The foreign-born producers turned out films that were more patriotic than the United States government itself; perhaps they felt obliged to over-react to counter any suspicion of pacifism or pro-Germanism.* Such films were often vicious and grotesque absurdities, but they caused dismay among the German High Command, and they helped to make the moving picture the most influential medium in the land.

As the war began for the United States, a remedy for the box-office malaise was a most unusual Mary Pickford film, *The Little American.* The story was planned, in Roosevelt style, to belittle the idea of neutrality, and it would have caused immense

---

* Carl Laemmle had given financial support to Henry Ford's Peace Ship. His company, Universal, made the most violently anti-German films, such as *The Kaiser—The Beast of Berlin.*

concern in government circles had it appeared before the declaration of war. But with the good luck characteristic of its director, Cecil B. DeMille, it was ready to go into production on 13 April 1917. In contrast to his "age-old call to a modern crusade," *Joan the Woman,* which had been only passably profitable,* *The Little American* caught the Hun campaign at its height and seemed set to make a fortune.

Everything about the film was carefully calculated. The subtitles were designed to attract storms of applause. Even the names of the characters were of a nationalistic nature. The girl, representative of all that is good in America (and played by the most popular actress in the world), is called Angela. The German-American diplomat who loves her and who is brutalized by the military machine is called Karl von Austreim (Jack Holt), suggesting that as an Austrian aristocrat he is not entirely to blame for Germany's misdeeds. The rival for Angela's hand, Count Jules de Destin, of the French Embassy, is equally aristocratic, his name positively mystical, but he is presented, oddly enough, somewhat unsympathetically by Raymond Hatton. He is decadent, a bit of a lounge lizard, slightly comic.

At the outbreak of war, the two men return to fight for their respective countries, and Angela, summoned to France by a dying aunt, decides to go too. She sails on the *Veritania*—and her unassailable neutrality is violated by a torpedo.

Angela is rescued, and reaches France to find her aunt dead and her château in a battle sector. She assumes responsibility for the place. Among the retreating French soldiers is de Destin, who conceals a telephone and leaves a soldier, posing as a butler, to act as artillery spotter. "I need hardly tell you," he says, "that it is death if the telephone is discovered."

"They wouldn't dare touch an American!" declares Angela, producing her flag.

That night the Germans attack the château, kill the soldier, and in the dark, one of them drunkenly attempts to rape Angela. When the light is restored, the officer freezes in horror. It is Karl. Angela pleads for the safety of the women in the house. Karl answers that he cannot give orders to his superior officers. "Somewhere in this house," says Angela, "must be a man who is something more than a splendidly-drilled beast!"

The house becomes divisional headquarters. Ancient statues are used to break up furniture for firewood. Priceless paintings are torn down and used to protect equipment. A squad shoots civilians in the courtyard. An old woman begs Angela, as an American, to stop the executions. She is powerless. But when a German heavy gun is set up on the grounds she relays the information over the telephone. The gun receives a direct hit, and the German general (Hobart Bosworth) realizes that someone is giving the position away and orders a search. Karl locates a tell-tale wire and bursts in on Angela. She says, "Make them think you've captured me. It's the only way."

At the court martial, Angela declares that she was neutral until she saw German soldiers destroying women and old men. "Then I stopped being neutral and became a human being."

She is told that by violating neutrality, she has forfeited her rights as an

---

* Partly because Geraldine Farrar, the star, had been associating with the German Crown Prince, causing nationwide agitation, which had already damaged *Carmen* at the box office.

Cecil B. DeMille's vision of modern war. From The Little American.

The Little American *company: Mary Pickford, center, with* [illegible] *B. DeMille to the lef*[illegible] *Ian Hay, who served as technical adviser. In* [illegible]*e as Captain Ian Hay Beith, he was an able representative for British intelligence. Hobart*

American. She is to be shot as a spy. And Karl, his complicity revealed, is to be shot for treason. The two are led outside and the firing squad takes aim. But the French have the range and shells blast the house and eliminate the firing squad. Angela and Karl are stunned, but they manage to struggle through an inferno of shells, away from the château, to a burned church where they take temporary shelter.

Next morning they are rescued by French soldiers, among them de Destin. Angela begs him to save Karl, and de Destin agrees. Karl is sent to a prisoner-of-war camp, but Angela is permitted a U.S. visa for him in recognition of her extraordinary service to France. They kiss through the wire of the compound. Fade to the Statue of Liberty. The end.

Despite the high quality of the production, the picture was a box-office failure; for many Pickford fans, the violence of the film was too much of a contrast to her regular productions, and there was a public outcry over the last scene. A substitute ending showed Angela returning home to await de Destin, even though he had been presented as a buffoon. Any alternative was preferable to that final, lingering shot of America's Sweetheart kissing a Hun through the wire of a prison camp.

WAR FILMS WERE TURNED OUT in astonishing numbers. A summary of them by Jack Spears was spread across two issues of *Films in Review* (May 1966 and June–July 1966);* it makes a fascinating and alarming study. As Spears pointed out there, one of the first propaganda objectives was directing public opinion against men who evaded the draft—Christy Cabanne's *The Slacker,* for example, in which a man's failure to do his duty was set against a kaleidoscope of patriotic events in American history. Children were used in these pictures to shame their fathers and brothers into enlisting. One of these, *Bud's Recruit,* was directed by King Vidor, later responsible for the war masterpiece *The Big Parade.* The Judge Brown story featured a boy named Bud (Wallis Brennan), who organizes his pals into a military unit and drills them regularly. Bud's elder brother Reggie (Robert Gordon) is a slacker who attends pacifist meetings with his mother, much to Bud's disgust. Bud disguises himself in a mustache and glasses, and goes down to the recruiting station, where he fills in an application in Reggie's name. "This results in an awakening of Reggie's manhood and also raises him in his sweetheart's estimation."[3]

The motion picture must take a large part of the responsibility for the campaign launched against German culture in the United States during World War I. Changing the name of sauerkraut to Liberty Cabbage was simply a comical aspect of a ferocious situation. Newspapers opposed to the war had their supplies cut off and were forced out of business. Vigilantes invaded farmhouses, coerced farmers to buy bonds, and if they failed to produce the prescribed amount, stained their homes with yellow paint. German-Americans were accused of crimes ranging from germ warfare to the introduction of ground glass into Red Cross bandages. Public figures were frequently responsible for these assertions, and motion pictures dramatized them convincingly. If your child had died of infantile paralysis, a disease

---

* Also published in book form as *Hollywood: the Golden Era* (New York: A. S. Barnes, 1971).

movies told you had been spread by Germans, it was hardly surprising that you turned to violence. Socialists and pacifists were to all intents and purposes Germans. In Butte, Montana, a crippled IWW leader, Frank Little, was dragged from bed by a band of masked men and hanged from a railway trestle. Democracy was interned for the duration.

Mob violence was advocated in Raoul Walsh's *The Prussian Cur* (1918). In an episode that aroused a great deal of comment, a German agent is shown visiting a Western town to persuade a German-born American to take part in aircraft sabotage. Outraged by the suggestion, the German-American throws the spy out of his house and has him arrested. No sooner is the spy safely in jail, however, than a crowd of pro-Germans appears on the streets in a rescue attempt. They storm the jail and batter down the doors. At this point (and one should remember that Raoul Walsh was a Griffith assistant on *The Birth of a Nation*) a squadron of horsemen appear, in the cloaks and cowls of the Ku Klux Klan, and sweeping into the mob, bring the riot to a swift close. These "loyal Americans," as a subtitle describes them, surround the pro-Germans and force them to kiss the American flag, before escorting them into the jailhouse.

"Thus in an American city, 'loyal Americans' are pictured in disguise, while pro-Germans work in the open," said *Moving Picture World*, "the exploiting of mob for mob being a direct incentive to flouting President Wilson's express wishes."[4]

MY FOUR YEARS IN GERMANY

Adapted from the book by James W. Gerard, American ambassador to Germany, *My Four Years in Germany* is of immense value historically, for Gerard himself worked on it. He helped director William Nigh (who himself plays a small part) to cast the picture, spending weeks finding faces resembling the Men of Blood in Germany.

"Fact, not fiction!" wrote Fred Dangerfield. "Constantly, during the private exhibition, these words were thrown upon the screen, and not without reason either, for it seems almost incredible that this peep behind the scenes of German militarism is an actual record of history and not the fantastic story of some crazy and imaginary kingdom. In his book, James W. Gerard gave a graphic idea of the things he saw in Kaiserdom; but the picturization of these records and reminiscences has a power which could be equalled in no other medium of expression."[1]

The emphasis on "fact" caused some members of the public to imagine they were watching newsreels of prison camp brutalities. POWs and civilians were shown scrambling for scraps of bread, being attacked by guard dogs, and being repatriated "the Hindenburg way"—through mass executions. Relatives of prisoners of war and interned British civilians were deeply upset by these scenes.

Long considered lost, the film was recently rediscovered. It is valuable as a depiction of the mental attitude of 1918—as such it is a frightening document—but as a film it belongs to the school of primitive propaganda. The Kaiser is played so broadly that, with his mustache, his leer, and his energetic eyebrows, he calls up

memories of Groucho Marx rather than fears of the devil. The German General Staff are presented as congenital idiots. Bethmann-Hollweg (played by an actor called Carl Dane, who, as Karl Dane, played in the great antiwar film *The Big Parade* in 1925, and who repeated his role as Chancellor in *To Hell with the Kaiser*) spends his time playing with toys. In one of the film's few inventive moments, the shot wipes halfway across the screen to show the Chancellor and his toys on one side, and various atrocities on the other. Admiral Tirpitz has a special desk; it opens up to reveal a basin of water, where he floats miniature battleships. Exactly what use these are to him is never explained; the director never permits him to proceed beyond the stage of rubbing his hands with glee. How blinkered by chauvinism were the reviewers of 1918! "The mistake has not been made of caricaturing the German officials."[2]

Gerard's contract stipulated that the film could not be cut or changed without his consent, and he clearly had enormous influence over the picture, for it groans with a surfeit of titles, many of them direct quotations from the book. Diplomatic activity—even in prewar Germany—was not noted for visual excitement, and visits, functions, and interviews scarcely encourage dynamic cinema. The Zabern affair, with cavalry charging civilians, provides some action, but most of the picture is presented claustrophobically in interiors.

One of the leading Germans is a socialist, who is outraged by this attack on civilians: "To hell with militarism!" he cries. But when war is declared, patriotism gets the better of his political judgment and he shouts, "Gott strafe England! There are no parties now. The Reichstag is united!"* As a humble sentry, he is

* In actuality this remark was made by the Kaiser.

forced to witness the roundup of all able-bodied women and the execution of useless ones. When he can stand the slaughter no longer, he is shot by his own side. "Oh Germany," he gasps, dying. "If only I had given my life to make you a republic!"

The simple-mindedness of the film is beyond belief, although, in fairness, equally stupid films were made in World War II. "Find me an excuse for war," demands the Kaiser. War comes, and the Kaiser is told, "The more the merrier—we have had millions of field gray uniforms made and stored for over a year." Ambassador Gerard was struck by the sight of the Kaiser sitting at his work table astride a vaulting horse. "FACT NOT FICTION" screams the title, as if the use of such an unusual item of furniture were evidence of a criminal mind.

The internment camps are the most interesting feature of the film. One inmate points at another, who is pirouetting around the compound. "See him? He was a well-known banker before the war." Other inmates shout at an American observer: "You're no American. If you were, you'd get us out of here!" British soldiers are penned together with Russians, who suffer from typhus; the disease spreads, and an American doctor asks why the Russians are not isolated. "They're Allies. Let them get acquainted."

The atrocities committed in this film, such as the mass execution of civilians, were actually carried out by the Nazis in World War II. When the charges were made, they were greeted by disbelief. We have films like *My Four Years in Germany* to thank for that.

The level to which popular entertainment had sunk during the war was illustrated by the last scene in *My Four Years in Germany,* which showed an American soldier indulging in slaughter with the devotion displayed on the college football field. As he rams his bayonet into one German after another, he cries exultantly, "I promised Dad I'd get six!"

The casual viciousness spread like the flu in 1918. In Cleveland a press show of *My Four Years in Germany* was enlivened by hanging the Kaiser in effigy. The pressmen were so carried away that the occasion developed into a riot, and mounted policemen rode out to clear the crowds. In Indiana the picture made more money than *The Birth of a Nation.* A theater in Massillon, Ohio, reported sabotage when electric wires were cut during an afternoon performance.

The reaction everywhere was ecstatic. "Show these pictures to the American people," said a senator, "and you will wipe Germanism from the earth."[3] President Wilson confided to another ambassador, however, that he was dismayed by the film. *My Four Years in Germany* must have seemed a savage moment of truth for this man who had been led so far from his ideals of peace and nobility.

The horrors were too much for Chicago's police censor, Major Metellus Lucullus Cicero Funkhouser, who brought about his long-awaited downfall by daring to touch this picture. No one had accused him of anti-German attitudes when he suppressed Goldstein's *Spirit of '76,* but when he laid his hands on Griffith's *Hearts of the World,* Morris Gest cabled the President. Funkhouser cut two scenes—a German stabbing a wounded Frenchman with a bayonet on the battlefield, and German officers "forcing their unwelcome attentions upon French girls in a dugout." Gest accused Funkhouser of German sympathies; the major said he was born in St. Louis, produced documentary evidence of his American an-

The Eagle's Eye (1918). *Original caption read: "Heinrich von Lertz and Baroness Verbrecht watch Dr. Wolf prepare a paste culture of infantile paralysis germs preparatory to feeding thousands of houseflies by permitting them to walk through the paste."*

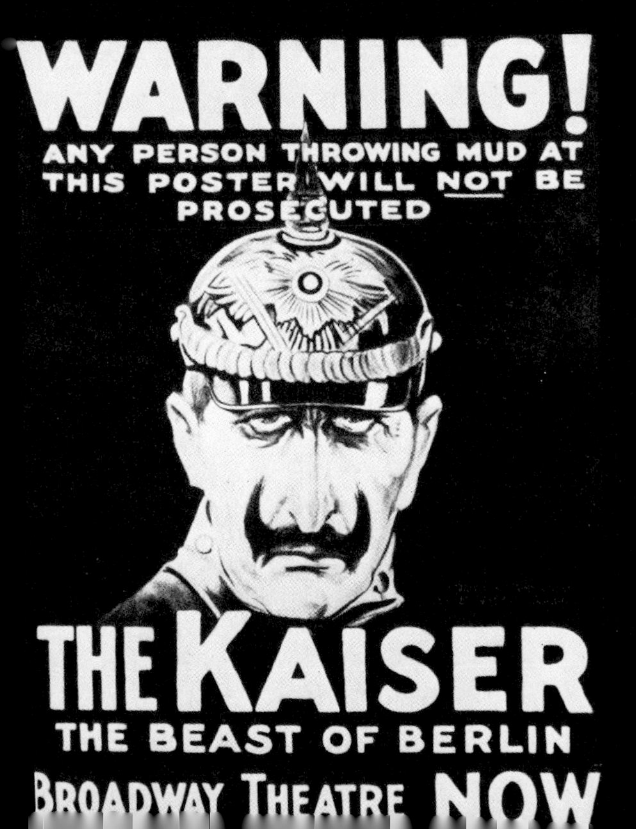

cestors back to 1700, and slapped a libel suit on *Exhibitors Trade Review* for criticizing his policy. He said he did not cut the whole bayonetting scene, but only the section showing blood gushing from the wound. In the dugout scene he removed only the part showing a girl writhing on the ground after receiving brutal treatment from a German officer. His decision was not arbitrary, as most people assumed, but was supported by the majority of his censor board.

He survived as censor for a few months, until he removed seven scenes and titles from *My Four Years in Germany*. J. D. Williams, head of First National, acting on behalf of Warner Brothers, who had produced the picture, sent a cable to George Creel. Pressure was brought upon Chicago city officials through the personal representation of Ambassador Gerard, and Funkhouser was replaced. The first action of his replacement, William Luthardt, was to restore the cut sections. They amounted in all to thirty-two feet. A massive campaign was then launched to pulverize poor Funkhouser, and he was suspended in 1918, not because of his censor activities but because of the way he ran the Morals Department. Phone-tapping charges were laid against him, and it was alleged that under his command, "large sums of money were spent by vice investigators in buying wine in disorderly places."[4] A five-week trial found him guilty, and he was drummed out of the police force with ignominy.

With the United States ambassador to Germany proving an immensely popular draw, the German ambassador to the U.S., Count Bernstorff, was made the subject of a serial, *The Eagle's Eye,* written by the recently retired chief of the U.S. Secret Service, William J. Flynn. The scenario was adapted from Flynn's story by Courtney Ryley Cooper. Among all the films of its time, this would be one of the most fascinating to see again, for it reconstructs many actual incidents, and among the characters portrayed were the German naval attaché, Captain Boy-Ed,* and the military attaché, Captain Franz von Papen, later associated with the Nazi Party and for a brief period Vice-Chancellor of Germany.

Von Papen was heartily loathed in America; he epitomized the suave, monocled Prussian officer soon to be portrayed by Erich von Stroheim. His attitudes were antediluvian; he liked to say in public that he was unable to understand how Americans had made the transition from walking on four legs to two, and that probably there was more money to be made by walking that way.[5]

The Eagle's Eye settled America's score with von Papen. The film accused him of arranging all the details of munitions explosions—and even of poisoning the mules on transports—in such a way that his superior, Count Bernstorff, was in no way compromised.

As von Papen was detested, so Count Bernstorff was admired. *The Eagle's Eye* showed him as a social lion in Washington, witty and compassionate on the one hand, a martyr to his country's indiscretions—and fomenting chaos and destruction under cover of his social success.

Episode one had the staff of the Imperial Embassy planning the destruction

---

* The first issue of the *Selig Tribune* newsreel showed Captain Boy-Ed aboard ship, recalled to Germany at the request of President Wilson. Before his expulsion, Boy-Ed proved very helpful to William Randolph Hearst, arranging for his cameraman Nelson Edwards to film exclusive material of the German fleet on the Kiel Canal.

of railroad bridges and foodstuffs, which is no more than von Papen admitted in his memoirs. More intriguing were the episodes on the Strike Breeders: how Bernstorff and Franz von Rintelen set their spies to work among the longshoremen, exaggerating grievances and promoting discontent.

The most fascinating episode was number seven, which reconstructed, exactly as it happened, an incident as outlandish and comic as anything a scenario writer could dream up. On 24 July 1915 an unfortunate German Privy Councillor in New York, Dr. Heinrich Albert, dozed off on his train. He woke up just in time to recognize his station and jump out. In his haste he left behind a brown portfolio. A messenger boy tried to run after him, but the train pulled away. The boy sat down, fully intending to hand it in at the next station. But out of curiosity, he sneaked a look inside. He saw enough to realize the importance of the contents and handed the portfolio to the authorities. The front page of the New York *World* began a nightmare for Dr. Albert and Count Bernstorff.

Von Papen wrote home to his wife, and even that intimate document was not safe from the Secret Service; it turned up in the London *Times:*

"We have great need of being bucked up, as they say here. Since Sunday a new storm has been raging against us. Unfortunately, they stole a fat portfolio from our good Albert in the Elevated (English Secret Service, of course), of which the principal contents have been published. Unfortunately, there were some very important things from my report among them."[6]

Among the revelations were the plans of the Central Powers to establish a lecture and moving picture bureau in the United States, ostensibly impartial, but actually under the control of the German government. Super-patriots like Burr McIntosh, actor, author, and coal mine magnate, and naval expert and artist Henry Reuterdahl were to be subverted without their knowing it, and their fervent Americanism used to alert the country to the danger of Japan and England.[7]

The Eagle's Eye was directed by Theodore Wharton at his studio in Ithaca, New York. When an explosion occurred at the Ithaca Electric Light and Power Company, German agents were thought to be responsible. The current was restored after a day, but the plant was forced to operate on reduced power, not enough to provide the town with heat and light, run the streetcar system, and light the studio. So Wharton switched his schedule and operated at night, and the authorities shut down the streetcar system.

ONE OF VON PAPEN'S SPIES in person—Captain Horst von der Goltz—was featured in *The Prussian Cur* (1918), a picture based on his revelations of the German spy system in America. Von der Goltz joined the United States Army at the time of the Madero uprising in Mexico. He later deserted to the Mexican revolutionaries, aligning himself with Pancho Villa and leaving his service only when summoned to Washington to act as a spy for von Papen. The Germans decided to strike against the Welland Canal in Canada and to von der Goltz fell the duty of leading the expedition to blow it up. The raid was a failure, and von der Goltz fled to England on a forged passport, in the name of Bridgeman Taylor. When von Papen was expelled from America, papers found on him by British officials implicated von der Goltz in acts of espionage against England; he was arrested and imprisoned in the Tower of London. For fifteen months he faced the death penalty but was eventually released to travel to the United States to give evidence in a spy trial. Convinced that von Papen had betrayed him, von der Goltz turned informer on his former comrades, providing a complete exposure of Berlin's secret methods. One of his rewards was this screen appearance.

THE WARTIME OUTPUT of the American film industry might appear to be a plethora of Kaiser parodies, sinking *Lusitanias*, and narrowly averted rapes by lustful Huns. Fortunately, there were many films considerably more intelligent than these melodramas would suggest.

Mary Pickford's *Johanna Enlists* (1918) depicted with wry humor how the war affected the lives of people in the most isolated communities. Adapted by Frances Marion from a Rupert Hughes story, it was directed by William Desmond Taylor, soon to rejoin the British Army.

The film opens with Mary Pickford sitting on the sun porch of a ramshackle farmhouse. "Three hundred and sixty-five days of maddening monotony" says a subtitle. Mary puts her hand into an old sock, ready to do some darning, but the sock is beyond repair. Inside the house her family is eating. The old grandfather picks up his soup plate and sucks greedily. Mary winces. Close-up of a bullfrog. Mary frowns. Close-up of a turkey, gobbling. Mary turns away in disgust. A donkey brays. Mary clutches her ears. Her rate of rocking increases. Her mother calls from the window, "Stop that infernal see-sawing."

"Can't I have no fun, mother?" wails Mary. "I'm just sittin' here, wishin' I was dead."

The mother grimaces. "Dead? You been dead from the neck up ever since you were born."

Furious, Mary hurls the darning basket at her family and rushes down the path, away from the house and into a wood. "Oh Lord," she says. "You promised often to come to our help. Now is Your chance." She raises her eyes to heaven. "Send me a beau!"

Cut to a close-up of a soldier blowing a bugle. Down the road stretches a long column of mounted troops with field artillery. The dust rises and the sun breaks through the trees in shafts of glimmering light. Mary Pickford breaks into a smile of deep contentment.

ERICH VON STROHEIM

No one embodied the quintessence of Prussian evil more powerfully than Erich von Stroheim, whose rise to fame was a direct, and ironic, result of the war. The propaganda people must have been pleasantly surprised to discover that the boldest figment of their collective imagination actually existed, and was only too anxious to project whatever vileness scenarists had in store for him.

Having worked at everything from shoveling mud to peddling flypaper, Stroheim was hired as an extra at Reliance-Majestic, where D. W. Griffith was chief director. What brought him to prominence was his passion for detail. Sitting on

Erich von Stroheim instructs Norman Kerry in the correct Austrian military salute. Merry-Go-Round *(1922). William Daniels at camera.*

the extra benches he saw an actor incorrectly dressed for his role as Alving in Ibsen's *Ghosts,* and Stroheim took the liberty of pointing this out. The actor was John Emerson, from the New York stage. Emerson later withdrew from the role and began work as director on a film of *Old Heidelberg* (1915). He hired Stroheim as his assistant and art director, and gave him the role of Lutz—his first important part.

When the United States entered the war, Stroheim was an obvious choice for directors eager for the latest thing in salivating Teutons. He displayed a curious mixture of contempt and delight for these roles. "The plot of *Sylvia of the Secret Service* had something to do with the Germans blowing up an ammunition dump," wrote Arthur Miller. "Von went to New York to research the names of the different explosives to be painted on cases stored at such a place. Between his appearance, and the sort of questions he was asking, it was no time at all before he was in the clink. The studio, of course, immediately went to his rescue and he was released. I am convinced, though, that the clever von Stroheim pulled the whole thing off for its publicity value."[1]

Anita Loos, who later married John Emerson, recalled that in a war film her husband directed in New York, von Stroheim played a German officer: "It was a hazard for von Stroheim, with his Prussian looks and mannerisms, even to appear in public. But when not needed on the set, Von, dressed in the Prussian uniform of the movie villain, would stalk over to the Plaza Hotel, engage one of the fiacres stationed there, and ride arrogantly through Central Park."[2] Such behavior positively invited abuse; certain actors at the Ship Cafe in Venice, California, hurled bread rolls and hissed him when he went there with his fiancée. Valerie von Stroheim remembered that the rolls hit her rather than him, and on armistice night, the crowd pelted them both with gravel.

It was a bizarre situation for von Stroheim, since technically he was a deserter. When the United States entered the war, he was still an Austrian subject.

Austria had conscription, and having ignored the call to arms in 1914, he faced a profound conflict of loyalties.

The truth about Stroheim's origins is hard to determine. The records of the United States Department of Justice, Immigration and Naturalization Service reveal that Stroheim arrived in New York from Bremen on the *Prince Friedrich Wilhelm* on 26 November 1909, giving his name as Erich Oswald Hans Carl Maria von Stroheim. He later claimed that his family name was von Nordenwall, that his father was a colonel in the Sixth Dragoons, his mother lady-in-waiting to Elizabeth, Empress of Austria-Hungary. Years later his passion for accuracy obliged him to recant, for Elizabeth, Empress of Austria, had been assassinated in 1896. He adjusted his father's rank from colonel of dragoons to a major in an infantry regiment, blaming the error on "certain journalists."

A certain journalist named Denis Marion went to the trouble of tracing his birth certificate. It proclaimed him the son of a merchant, a maker of felt hats, Benno Stroheim from Gleiwitz, and Johanna, née Bondy, from Prague; his birth was registered with the Register Office of the Jewish community of Vienna on 29 September 1885. Thomas Quinn Curtiss, in his biography of Stroheim,[3] challenges the authenticity of this birth certificate and suggests that it was a forgery, perpetrated by the Nazis to discredit the man who had himself so often discredited the German officer on the screen. But why, having forged it, did they not exploit it?

For his military experience, Stroheim claimed to have graduated as a second lieutenant from cadet school and to have been sent to the War College, where he passed the rigorous examination "sub auspices imperatoris," which carried with it the award by the Emperor of a diamond ring on which the royal initials were carved. He served during the annexation of Bosnia-Herzegovina, when he was wounded and decorated with the Franz Josef Cross and the annexation medal. He was then transferred to the Imperial Palace Guard at Vienna.

History does not record any military action during the annexation in which Stroheim could have been wounded. While he was undoubtedly a cadet, and a photograph exists to prove it, the names von Nordenwall or von Stroheim do not appear in the 1908 rank lists of the Austro-Hungarian Army.

"Neither his origin, nor the would-be term of service were taken at the time for gospel truth," wrote a relative, François Bondy. "There were too many people alive who knew his family in Vienna; even today there are close relatives between Vienna and Nice. The legend of the aristocrat has always been, in the truest sense, an 'open secret.' At his church burial [he was a practicing Catholic], the cross of the Legion of Honor, which was conferred upon him a few months before he died, was carried behind the coffin and many remarked this was, in fact, the only distinction which had been conferred on the man who had worn every conceivable medal."[4]

Herman Weinberg, who has written a great deal about von Stroheim, had extensive correspondence with Denis Marion and considers the birth certificate genuine. "I think it makes Stroheim all the more fascinating, a character right out of Rabelais, and I would be disappointed to learn that, as Curtiss stubbornly insists, he was, indeed, what he said he was. I think he would lose an incredible dimension."[5]

Von Stroheim's achievements are the important thing—his background is intriguing only for the light it casts upon his work and his attitudes. Nevertheless, it *is* intriguing, and while von Stroheim was one of the towering geniuses of the silent screen as director, his passion remained for the Vienna of his youth, for the army and the aristocracy. Was he reliving his past—or was he creating for himself an experience he had always longed for and from which he had been excluded?

GRIFFITH

The center of Ypres by 1917 has been so heavily shelled that the cathedral-like Cloth Hall has been blasted to a slender Islamic minaret. The other buildings, too, have been knocked into such extraordinarily delicate fingers of stone that there seems no way for them to remain vertical. Into this chilling scene steps a tall, jaunty figure in a smart tweed suit of English cut, a bow tie—and a tin hat. It is David Wark Griffith, recorded by a British official cameraman on his tour of the front.

The sight of this elegant figure touring the scenes of the battle is like something out of H. G. Wells's *Time Machine*. Griffith, dressed for a grouse shoot, appears to be on a thoroughly pleasant afternoon outing in the midst of the bloodiest war in history. A group of French soldiers ambles past the camera, some of them turning round to give a surly glance at the lens; Mr. Griffith follows them into the picture. The camera pans as he inspects a half-completed trench. French soldiers are sweating away with shovels. Griffith peers down, grins, makes a little digging gesture, and wanders out of shot. Next, he visits a heavily shelled concrete dugout. He stumbles over the rubble, awkward in his polished shoes, descends into a crater, and disappears into the dugout. Moments later he reappears to signal to the cameraman to cut.

All the scenes have been carefully posed, and at the start of each shot, the participants wait for a moment before jerking into action, as though instructed by a director. Everyone plays the game but Griffith. As the party files through a reserve trench, they all duck their heads. Griffith, however, remains imperiously upright, spoiling a subtitle's illusion that the enemy is but sixty yards away.

This trip to the front in May 1917 was a result of Griffith's agreement to make a propaganda film for the British. It is perhaps ironic that Griffith should have traveled to England, ostensibly to attend the premiere of his great pacifist film *Intolerance,* but actually to make a film to promote the Allied cause. I owe to Russell Merritt the startling information that Griffith had already been approached by the British government *before* he left for England. Griffith's own version has always been accepted as the truth: that he happened to be in England when a meeting of "the gifted men of Britain"—Barrie, Wells, Shaw, Bennett, Galsworthy, Chesterton—decided the most effective medium for the Allied nations was not a book or a play but "a drama of humanity, photographed in the battle area."

The new chairman of the War Office Cinematograph Committee was Lord Beaverbrook, and he had already instilled a more vigorous attitude to film-making among the Official Kinematographers. The idea of inviting Griffith to make a propaganda film was undoubtedly his, and the much-publicized meeting of the authors and playwrights probably a way of deflecting criticism from the fact that the "great director" was not British.

Griffith had left Triangle in March 1917, and a big special was part of his new contract with Adolph Zukor. By coincidence, one of the financiers of Triangle, and formerly of Mutual, was Otto Kahn, of Kuhn, Loeb and Company, who now moved to back Zukor. Otto Kahn was a close friend of Lord Beaverbrook, and despite being of German extraction, he was a naturalized British citizen who fervently supported the British war effort.

The New York *Times* leaked the news that Griffith's plan was to make a motion picture history of the war—on a commission from the Allies that would take him to all the fronts—that would eventually be placed in the archives.[1] This may have been a smoke screen for Beaverbrook's true intention; he seems to have had a massive propaganda epic on the lines of *The Birth of a Nation* in mind.

The offer from the British government came at a moment when history had inspired Griffith with a sense of adventure. "In one way, this is indeed a great day to be alive," he told reporters upon his arrival in Britain. "In another terrible. It is terrible when you see the things *you* must see and feel the things *you* must feel. It is the most terrific moment in the history of the world. We used to wish that we could have experienced the days of Caesar and Napoleon. And now incomparably greater times are taking place around us all."[2]

A special tour of the war zone was arranged for Griffith; he crossed the Channel in a Royal Navy destroyer and made a preliminary inspection of the front. Upon his return to England, he began to set up the production,* and cabled to California for Lillian and Dorothy Gish, Robert Harron, and Billy Bitzer.

In London the company stayed at the Savoy Hotel. Billy Bitzer picked up film from Kodak—during an air raid—and then bumped into Lowell Thomas, who was on a similar mission (see pp. 443–4). Thomas explained how hard it was to get film, and Bitzer told him to use his name. Thus the Griffith picture replenished the supplies of the Lowell Thomas operation, and when the two men met again, at a Press Association dinner at the Savoy, Thomas confirmed that the film was still coming through.

The Gishes and Bobby Harron had raced up to the roof of the Savoy during the raid, and had seen the German planes returning, the pilots waving at the watchers on the roof. Lillian Gish suggested they go out to see the damage, and they discovered that a school in Whitechapel had received a direct hit. "Children and teachers were the victims," wrote Bitzer. "When you hear the moans of the dying and see their mangled bodies, you realize what it is all about. We thought by getting to work immediately we might forget this scene. But we never did."[3]

Griffith, as a Southerner, was fascinated by the aristocracy of England. For a film concerned with the triumph of democracy, *Hearts of the World* was to have had a surprising amount of footage devoted to society beauties. But Griffith planned another film, *Women and the War,* to show how the idle rich had thrown them-

---

* Ernest Palmer, cameraman for George Loane Tucker, did much of this work for Griffith, on behalf of Bitzer, arranging for a part of Twickenham Studios to be allocated to the production.

D. W. Griffith, in tweed suit, at Cassel in France with British war correspondents, who are distinguished from regular officers by the lack of insignia. Second from right is Philip Gibbs of the Daily Telegraph *and* Daily Chronicle.

selves energetically behind the war effort. Dowager Queen Alexandra made an appearance and among the extras were such friends of Beaverbrook's as Lady Lavery, Elizabeth Asquith, the Countess of Massarene, Princess Monaco, and Lady Diana Manners. The scenes were shot at Lady Ripon's estate at Coombe Hill, Kingston, and the Army and Navy Hospital. Griffith sported his finest clothes; Bitzer was astounded at the gap between the classes, and wondered at the complacency of the working class in their support of the aristocracy. The material was eventually used in *The Great Love*.

Griffith was given facilities to film on Salisbury Plain, the British Army's central maneuver area, and at Witley and Blackdown, near Aldershot. Official receipts refer to vast numbers of troops and explosives—some of which blew up by accident in storage and were the subject of an army enquiry. According to Griffith, he was also given the opportunity to return to France, with his cast. A somewhat confusing impression of the film's production has grown up around this fact. Historians have stated that *Hearts of the World* was actually made at the front.

"The front" refers specifically to the battle area; the opposing trenches that zigzagged six hundred miles from the English Channel to Switzerland were known as the front lines. The only member of the company permitted to visit the front was Griffith himself, as the Ypres reels testify. Not even his cameraman, Billy Bitzer, was allowed near the place, although he flew to Le Bourget and filmed scenes in Montreuil. The fact that his full name was Johann Gottlob Wilhelm Bitzer didn't help, but the army refused to allow photographs to be taken in the war zone except by official cameramen. Griffith was assigned an Official Kinematographer at Ypres, Frank Bassill.

When he returned to France in October 1917, Griffith was based in Paris, and assigned a cameraman from the Section Cinématographique of the French Army. A great deal of conflicting information has been written about the adventure. Did anyone accompany Griffith? According to Lillian Gish, she, her sister and her mother, and Bobby Harron went over; the French trip was hair-raising, and "over the months" the Gish family became highly nervous and lost weight. But Griffith was only in France for a matter of two weeks. Mrs. Gish suffered a serious case of shell shock—was this due to the bombardment in France or to the concussion of the air defense guns situated next to the Savoy Hotel in London? The main location was the village of Ham, near St. Quentin, on the River Somme; Griffith stated that by a strange and unpleasant coincidence, the first scenes of the second act were taken in the village of Ham, "which has only recently fallen again into the hands of the German invader."[4] Yet just a handful of shots in the surviving versions were taken in France, and only one of them shows a member of the cast (Lillian Gish entering a devastated house).* Billy Bitzer states categorically, "While it is true many scenes were taken at the battle front by cameramen, I did not go there, and neither did any other member of the company, with the exception of Mr. Griffith."[5] (However, the Bitzer book is very inaccurate.)

Griffith later made a statement that, appearing out of context, makes him seem an obsessive, single-minded, and callous man: "Viewed as a drama, the war is in some ways disappointing." Single-minded Griffith may have been, but

---

* The shot appears only in the British Film Institute version (see Sources of the Films).

he was not callous. The quote comes from a *Photoplay* interview with his old friend Harry Carr, war correspondent and future Griffith press agent, and it goes on to say that everything he saw—troop trains moving away to the front, wives parting from husbands they were never to see again—precisely fitted his imagination. "All these things were so exactly as we had been putting them in the pictures for years and years that I found myself absently wondering who was staging the scene."[6] The front lines were lacking in visual impact. "Everyone is hidden away in ditches. As you look out over No-Man's Land, there is literally nothing that meets the eye but an aching desolation of nothingness. At first you are horribly disappointed. There is nothing but filth and dirt and the most soul-sickening smells. The soldiers are standing sometimes almost to their hips in ice-cold mud.

"It is too colossal to be dramatic. No one can describe it. You might as well try to describe the ocean or the milky way. A very great writer could describe Waterloo. But who could describe the advance of Haig? No one saw it. No one saw a thousandth part of it."

Griffith's disappointment with the war reflected his inability to capture any more than a fleeting impression of it. By this point, artillery bombardments and mortar shelling occurred intermittently around the clock, but the kind of action Griffith hoped for—"the dash and thrill of wars of other days"—tended to take place at night.

This is pure conjecture, but so much mystery surrounds the film that I feel obliged to make a few assumptions. Once Griffith had realized the difficulty of shooting at the front, he abandoned interest in it. His remarks to Carr suggest that he was justifying to himself his work of reconstruction—the real thing, after all, had proved indistinguishable from his inspired guesswork. There was no respect for documentary per se in those days, therefore why should he not reconstruct all the action scenes at his leisure, when he could lavish his customary care on each scene?

The reason advanced by Griffith for returning to France was to make use of the devastation; yet Russell Merritt has found evidence that the War Office offered Griffith the kind of ruins he needed in England. So why the second trip to France?

If it was for authentic backgrounds, why did they not appear more often in the final film? Only a few brief shots were taken in France. A cable from Griffith to Zukor refers to $5,000 paid to the French for "facilities," which may explain why Griffith did not shoot the entire film on the locations described in the story. I put forward the suggestion that the trip to France with the cast was the equivalent of the trip round the trenches; the idea of it gave the film a reputation for authenticity, and a veracity and dignity beyond all other war films. This is supported by the elaborate fiction given out by Griffith and his press agents,* for example in a New York *Times* interview of 14 April 1918, which asserts that Bitzer, George Siegmann, George Fawcett, and the child, Ben Alexander, went to France, which they did not, and which describes the company sheltering from bombard-

---

* Advertisements emphasized "Miles of Artillery—the March of Legions—Squadrons of Airplanes—Fleets of Zeppelins—the Destruction of Cities—the Charge of the Tanks" and claimed the film's biggest scene had been taken from Vimy Ridge, showing two battle fronts with a million soldiers. None of this is borne out by the film.

The prologue to Hearts of the World (1918) *showed D. W. Griffith with British Prime Minister Lloyd George at Number 10 Downing Street. The scene was filmed as Griffith said goodbye.*

D. W. Griffith being introduced to the Dowager Queen Alexandra at the Army and Navy Hospital, Coombe Hill, near Wendover, England, 1917.

D. W. Griffith in France for Hearts of the World. *The gas alarm consists of four shell cases which, when struck with the wooden hammer, resound like a gong. For the photographer, Griffith obligingly reaches inside the gas-mask case he wears over his shoulder.*

D. W. Griffith at the front in a British trench. The original caption said "50 yards from the German trenches."

ment for four hours in a cellar and becoming the target of an air raid. Lillian Gish, in her book *The Movies, Mr. Griffith and Me,* gives as definitive an account of the trip as we are likely to have; she talks of shells falling "close enough to make us nervous."[7]

The major action scenes were shot in California, at the Lasky ranch (these trenches were used again for J. Stuart Blackton's *Missing*). Seymour Stern mentions a site, too, near the Balboa-Laguna coastal highway. To show the German Army, Griffith purchased the footage of Captain Kleinschmidt at considerable expense—$16,000—only to be warned by Albert Bamzhaf, his personal representative, not to use it "on account of possible legal complications and injury to your prestige."[8] Banzhaf offered some alternative German material from a short-subject producer in New York, which indicates how little the War Office was involved by the end of production, for they had access to unlimited captured film.

Hearts of the World is a surprising film to result from a British government commission. It opens with titles that were expressive of Griffith's attitude to war but somewhat out of keeping with government propaganda: "God help the nation that begins another war of conquest or meddling!" "Brass bands and clanging sabers make very fine music. But let us remember—there is another side to war." "After all, does war ever settle any question? The South was ruined. Thousands of lives were sacrificed—but did the Civil War settle the Black and White question?"

Hearts of the World is primarily a love story. The war is shown mainly as it affects civilians. There are no politics in the picture at all; George Siegmann is seen as a prewar German tourist, taking an unusual interest in village architecture, and the German militarists are seen planning "a dastardly plot against France and civilization." But there is no further elaboration. During the occupation of the village, individual Germans are shown behaving brutally. Lillian Gish, who later regretted her part in this film, found the evil Huns rather absurd. "Whenever a German came near me," she said, "he beat me or kicked me."[9]

Three versions of the film were prepared originally—American, British, and French—together with revised editions for the armistice. In the peacetime version, the Germans' behavior improved. One soldier, whipping Lillian Gish, is restrained by another, who says, "War has made cruel beasts of most of us, but not all of us, Thank God." The nationalities of the principals were changed to suit the country of release, and the English cut the final sequence of the victorious Americans returning home "after freeing the world from Autocracy and the horrors of war—we hope for ever and ever."

William K. Everson called *Hearts of the World* a thinly disguised reworking of *The Birth of a Nation,* and that is the film the official documents continually refer to, using it as a precedent because of its high standards of production as well as its enormously successful method of distribution. Clearly Beaverbrook hoped for a second *Birth of a Nation* and arranged for British war charities to receive sixty percent of the net receipts from the United Kingdom and British Colonies release.

In program notes prepared for the royal command performance at Windsor Castle, Griffith wrote that the incident of the boy crossing into enemy territory followed exactly the experience of a young officer in the French Army, "save that his hiding place was a cellar instead of an upper room." Griffith added: "It is not a matter of extreme difficulty in quiet sectors to get into the enemy's trench and back areas. The great difficulty is in returning to one's own lines." Most of the events have a factual basis; even the "Dungeons of Lust" were based on recently discovered dugouts under a farm, which the Germans ran as a bordello. Nevertheless, nothing separates the attitudes of today from those of 1918 more vividly than one reviewer's reaction to Bobby Harron's leveling a pistol at Lillian Gish's head as the Germans smash down the door: "Mr. Griffith is entirely justified in using so old an expedient as the man about to kill the woman he loves; in such a situation it is the right thing to do."[10]

It is this lurid melodrama that acts as a barrier for modern audiences. George Siegmann's attempt to rape Lillian Gish seems somewhat less important today than the mass slaughter raging outside. While Siegmann's behavior would have aroused audiences of 1918 to a pitch of patriotic fury—and we must always remember that people reacted to films in those days far more intensely than we do today—sixty years later audiences are merely amused. But *look* at the scene. It is actually very cleverly directed. It begins as a game; Siegmann sees his opportunity, locks the door, and has a bit of fun with the girl. He leans back in a chair and traps her tiny figure with his legs. At this point, Siegmann plays the scene amusingly, and his jack-booted horseplay fits his character. He is transformed to door-battering fury not by his inability to rape Miss Gish, but by the more serious matter of enemy infiltration. Bobby Harron, a French soldier in German uniform, has penetrated the building, an officer has been killed, and Siegmann's desperation is thus dramatically legitimate.

Mrs. Woodrow Wilson, according to Russell Merritt, was horrified by the scenes of German brutality, and she conveyed her feelings, which undoubtedly coincided with those of her husband, directly to Griffith. He sent a lengthy telegram: "Spent a sleepless night and troubled day, trying to think why the play has made such an effect on you." He blamed his excesses on the fact that the public was "a very stolid, hard animal to move or impress. We must hit hard to touch them." Nevertheless, he agreed to eliminate a couple of scenes so that his film would "hit the masses" but would not offend "the refined and sensitive spirits such as yourself. Otherwise I shall be a very disappointed, broken individual, for my hopes and my work and prayers have been so bound up in this that, unless it is pleasing in your household, I feel that everything has been in vain."[11] Mrs. Wilson's criticism evidently led to the reshooting of the scene in which the German soldier whipped Lillian Gish.

Griffith must have been particularly hurt by Mrs. Wilson's reaction since he despised the pro-war propaganda pictures and was aiming at a much more elevated kind of film. Melodrama apart, the picture has some admirable scenes. Griffith never falls into the trap of romanticizing war. There are no false heroics, and the horrors of war are shown as powerfully as possible. "War's gift to the common people" declares a title before scenes of panic and evacuation in the village. Lillian Gish's old father refuses to leave his home. A shell explodes on the house. When Miss Gish rushes back to search for him, Griffith makes us flinch, even today, with a brief flash of the old man's body—blown in half. And the audience has to share Lillian Gish's agony at the death of her mother—a most moving performance—and her delirious state when she celebrates what should have been her wedding

Hearts of the World. *Dorothy Gish and Noel Coward (right) stand in a street at Stanton village, which, despite the Cotswold stone and seventeenth-century English style of architecture, is intended to represent a French village.*

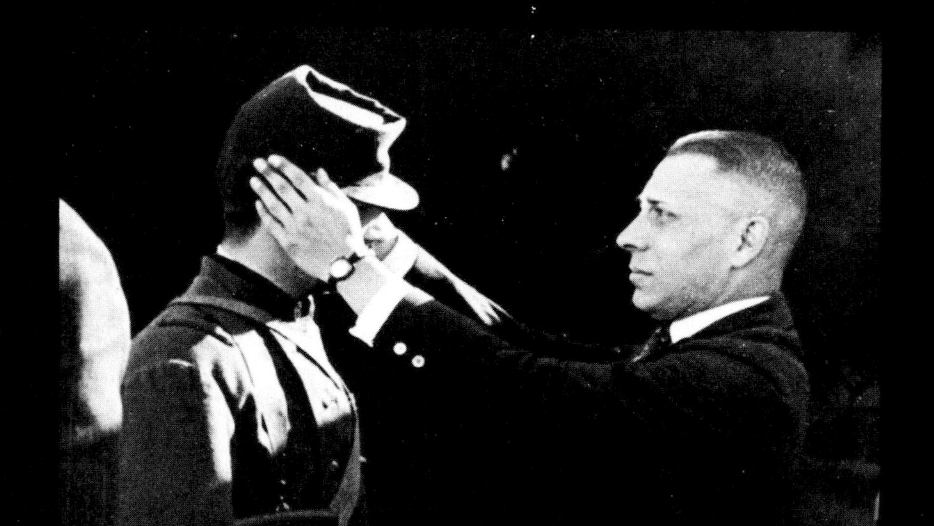

night. She finds out where Bobby Harron's company has been fighting, and by the light of the moon, she runs out to join him. When she finds him, he is apparently dead. Wrapping herself in her wedding dress against the cold, she gently presses her body against his and joins him in sleep.

It is the sense of authenticity that makes the film so compelling, and yet there is very little that is authentic. The village is compounded of parts of Stanton, near Broadway, Worcestershire, and Shere, in Surrey, together with back-lot construction in Hollywood (on the old *Intolerance* set). The close-combat scenes resemble Gettsysburg more than Verdun. Worse still, the child, Benny Alexander, remains the same age throughout the entire four years of war. But for much of the film, it takes an expert to distinguish the reconstruction from the actuality material. Griffith included documentary scenes that are now beyond price. Almost shyly, he begins the film with a title begging the audience's indulgence for his unusual prologue. "It has no possible interest except to vouch for the rather unusual event of an American producer being allowed to take pictures on an actual battlefield." Griffith is shown in the trench at Cambrin, and at Number 10 Downing Street; Lloyd George shakes Griffith's hand, wishing him "great success for his picture." (He was actually saying goodbye on the day Griffith left for the United States!) "Apologies and thanks," says a title. "The picture follows."

As war approaches, a reconstructed scene of the House of Commons on 3 August is followed by one of the French Chamber of Deputies on 4 August, featuring René Viviani. At Downing Street, Asquith, Grey, Churchill, and Lloyd George watch the clock ticking away the last seconds of peace. Frozen, as if in a painting, this last scene is so convincing that its reality is assumed, as part of the British government's cooperation. But it was shot in the studio.

The battle scenes are impressive, but they were even better in Universal's imitation, *Heart of Humanity* (1919). A common factor of both films was the presence, as actor and technical adviser, of Erich von Stroheim. He had been promised the part of the brutal German, named von Strohm in his honor, and was extremely upset when Siegmann took over the role. He played Siegmann's adjutant and claimed that he acted as military adviser on the scenes shot in California. Lillian Gish disputes this claim—"he couldn't have been an adviser to that war any more than any other actor—however they all helped Griffith in any way they could." Who but von Stroheim would have added those details to the German uniforms, such as sword knots, which create such a sense of conviction? And a photograph, recently discovered for Thames Television's *Hollywood* series, proves his participation beyond doubt.*

Hearts of the World justified Lord Beaverbrook's faith by serving as a powerful recruiting agent. In one city in California, according to Griffith, nine hundred recruits attributed their enlistment to seeing the film. But it could never have persuaded them that war was rewarding or romantic. Griffith may have been a showman; he may have dragged in hoary situations to improve the box-office returns, rather than the story, and he may have fabricated wild tales to make his film sell. But there can be no doubt that at heart he was a man of integrity.

---

* Curt Rehfeld, a former sergeant in the German Army in Africa, also served as an adviser. See pp. 202–3.

THE BRITISH NATIONAL FILM

D. W. Griffith's experience in wartime Europe has caught the imagination of film historians, but it is not generally known that at virtually the same time, another well-known American director was invited to make an equally spectacular film for the British government. Like Griffith, Herbert Brenon had recently completed an important pacifist film—*War Brides*. Brenon was born in Dublin, went to America at sixteen, and entered the picture business via the theater and, somewhat unusually, after managing a movie theater in Johnstown, Pennsylvania. Following his production of *Neptune's Daughter* and the astoundingly spectacular *Daughter of the Gods,* Brenon's standing among picture people in America rivaled that of Griffith and DeMille. In 1913 he had made *Ivanhoe* at Chepstow Castle, and his working methods were the subject of admiring articles in the English trade papers.

His great government film—the British National War Film—was the worst-kept secret of the war. Everyone in the industry knew that it was extremely expensive, that Hall Caine had written the story,* and that Matheson Lang, Marie Lohr, and Ellen Terry had donated their services. But the production dragged on and on, through the spring and summer of 1918, with no end in sight. A studio fire in June destroyed some of the negative, and reshooting added weeks to the schedule. Rival producers, anticipating that Brenon's film would outclass anything they might make, anxiously scanned newspaper reports, and tried to guess what it was about. Even Griffith expressed anxiety at Brenon seeing *Hearts of the World* before its release, and stealing ideas.

Anyone concerned with films knows how chaotic crowd scenes can be. But Brenon seemed to handle this mammoth epic with cool assurance, and every report made some reference to his personal magnetism. Such confidence made the English film people envious and uneasy. America had snatched most of their markets. Would Brenon's presence prove a Trojan horse?

One of the cast, Captain Arthur Applin, wrote a vivid account of Brenon's handling of crowd scenes—how this solitary figure with a megaphone, dwarfed by the massive Town Hall at Chester, coaxed and cajoled emotion from an embarrassed and shy crowd of women. Brenon addressed them as though at a birth of a revolution: "Women of Chester! Women of England!" Applin continued:

"Some of the women laughed. 'Silence!' roared Brenon through his megaphone. 'Listen to me, listen to every word I say.' He explained that the scenes about to be photographed had actually happened in Belgium, and might one day be enacted in England; 'scenes of bloodshed, violence, rape, murder.'

"Women in the crowd laughed.

"Brenon stopped. He looked at them. 'You *are* all Englishwomen? Have none of you fathers or sons or husbands dying for you at the Front, fighting to avenge those foul deeds committed in France and Belgium, to save you and your children from a like fate? Answer me! Don't laugh—answer me!'

"Now two scores of voices raised protestingly: 'Yes. Yes!'

---

* Hall Caine had accepted Lloyd George's invitation to become Controller of Cinema Propaganda with the Committee of War Aims in October 1917.

" 'Then listen! The Germans have landed in England, advanced on Chester, captured it.' Two women giggled. Brenon stopped, singled them out, pointing at them, shaming them to silence with six brief words.

" 'The Germans have taken all you women and put you in munition factories to manufacture ammunition which will be used to kill your men, the men who are fighting for you. Will you do it?'

"No response. But no laughter now. The crowd stirs nervously, anxiously.

" 'Answer me. Tell me, if this happened, would you make munitions for the Germans to kill your men? Answer!'

" 'No! No!'

"Brenon paused. The sweat was standing on his forehead. He looked up at the sky. The clouds were drifting away and the sun struggling through.

" 'Cameras ready,' he said. To the women he appealed again. His voice filled the square like a bugle call.

" 'I want you all, when Miss Marie Lohr, who has come up from her theatre in London especially to play this scene with you, puts that question to you, to answer with your hearts as well as with your lips. Would you make munitions for the Germans to kill your sons, your husbands, your lovers? Would you do this, you women of Chester? Wouldn't you rather *die* first?'

"He got it then. Crescendo. The phlegmatic British crowd of self-conscious women caught fire, forgot it was a mob and found it was a Soul. The Soul of an Empire.

"The effect of Miss Lohr's speech was electric. The women no longer acted. They began to live. The war was brought vividly to them as no casualty list, however hard it hit their homes, could bring it home to them.

"Again, the producer was on the steps, megaphone to his lips. 'Now follow Miss Lohr through the streets, pick up your banners and march to the castle.'

"Hardly a British crowd that now surged wildly through the quiet old Chester streets. These women might have stepped out of the French Revolution.

"Ahead of them a motor car with Brenon and his assistants, exposing reel after reel, making pictures—and history."[1]

Perhaps the only Allied unit dismayed by the armistice was Herbert Brenon's. To the immense satisfaction of British producers, Brenon was obliged to abandon the project. Having allegedly spent £70,000, he had to acknowledge that further expenditure was pointless.

"I found the British fearfully handicapped by an undramatic, phlegmatic temperament and a bad photographic climate," said Brenon.[2]

The setbacks and delays were not all Brenon's fault, although his self-regard aroused hostility. George Pearson remembered a shock he received from a large notice at Brenon's studio: "SILENCE—As the Church is to the Devout Worshipper, so is the Studio to the Sincere Artist."[3]

The unedited footage from the abandoned production ran into many thousands of feet. All that survives in the National Film Archive is 978 feet: "In a country cottage, a mother receives news that her eldest son has been killed—just as the youngest leaves for the front." So runs the Archive Catalogue entry.*

---

* The Ministry of Information wanted the footage preserved, but the government ordered

No crowd scenes. None of the bravura episodes which were to astound the industry. Herbert Brenon sailed for America in December 1918, and the material for *The Invasion of Britain* (or *Victory and Peace*) he left behind as just another government embarrassment. But somehow, after the expenditure on the war, £70,000 with nothing to show for it didn't seem so bad. The guns of the Western Front spent more than that in a day.

PEACE

In October 1918, General Ludendorff had opened negotiations with President Wilson on the basis of his Fourteen Points. The terms were offered to "the true representatives of the German people" but not to the military autocrats responsible for the war. A result of this proviso was the German revolution, which forced the Kaiser to abdicate and flee to neutral Holland and which brought about the November armistice.

Wilson should have been the hero of the hour. Instead, he entered the most critical period of his career: the battle for a just peace, and the foundation of the League of Nations.

Theodore Roosevelt represented the opinions of a formidable number of men in politics when he said, "Mr. Wilson and his Fourteen Points and his four supplementary points and his five complementary points and all his utterances every which way have ceased to have any shadow of right to be accepted as expressive of the will of the American people."[1] Once again, Roosevelt's virulence acted as an all-clear signal to the picture business.

The industry's concept of politics was presented through a haze of melodrama, and in melodrama, sins are expurgated through revenge. As the war drew to a close, a flood of revenge pictures swept the theaters, in direct conflict with President Wilson's desire for "a peace among equals." Wilson instructed the Creel Committee to try to stop the atrocity pictures because they made the job of securing a just peace yet more hazardous.

"We had nearly finished *The Unpardonable Sin,*" said Blanche Sweet, "when we received a letter from the government: 'Cut down on the German atrocities.' That told us the war was over. Two days later, the big headlines appeared."[2]

Wilson traveled to Paris to head the American Peace Delegation. He proved to be a skillful negotiator, and despite the stubbornness of the French leader, Clemenceau, he maneuvered the conference to the point of accepting the League of Nations as an integral part of the Treaty. But the Republicans in the United States, led by Senator Henry Cabot Lodge, a close friend of Roosevelt, sabotaged his efforts and forced him to abandon many of his cherished principles. He returned with a pact which Robert LaFollette said "would chill the heart of the

---

its destruction, for reasons unknown, in 1938, says Clive Coultass. Only this reel survives, preserved for the appearance of Ellen Terry. At a later date the MOI files on film propaganda were also junked.

Lieutenant Victor Fleming, Signal Corps, serving with the Presidential Peace Party, 1919; the camera is a Bell and Howell. Fleming had photographed many of Douglas Fairbanks's pictures and soon graduated to director. He eventually made two of America's best-known pictures, The Wizard of Oz *and* Gone With the Wind.

The cartoon on the ambulance is a clue to the driver's identity: Walt Disney, in France, shortly after the armistice.

world." Wilson undertook a tour of the nation to spread the message of the League, but it proved ineffective politically, and disastrous personally; he collapsed with a stroke which left him paralyzed. The League was now without a leader.

Yet a certain degree of enthusiasm had greeted the League in the United States, and Wilson found his message particularly welcome in California. Only a handful of Hollywood films, however, reflected his ideas: Frank Borzage's *Whom the Gods Would Destroy* (1919) was said to have been based on League of Nations principles, probably to give this expensive war film some much-needed topicality. André Beranger made a League film, *Uncle Sam of Freedom Ridge* (1920), but only as a two-reeler. Frank Wilson tried to get Douglas Fairbanks to make a short in which he would wallop opponents of Wilson as he had done the Kaiser, to make the point that to interfere with President Wilson's plans was equal to interference with Pershing's. Fairbanks did not make such a film, but despite his reverence for Theodore Roosevelt, his first United Artists release, *His Majesty the American,* reflected the Fourteen Points—amidst some high-spirited entertainment. Fairbanks's photographer, Victor Fleming, had accompanied Wilson's party as a Signal Corps cameraman.

Blame for America's eventual rejection of the League has been attributed partly to the flood of vengeance pictures, which confused the public. Like most propaganda films, the "Hang-the-Kaiser" pictures reflected extremes of public opinion; they did not create them. They acted, too, as a grisly but useful catharsis. For those fed up with Wilson's moralizing, Warner Brothers' *The Kaiser's Finish* (1918) demanded the public execution of the Kaiser by hanging in Times Square, but had him slaughtered by an illegitimate son. *Why America Will Win* (1918) destroyed the Kaiser with a lightning bolt. *America Must Conquer* (*King of the Huns*) (1918) wanted German militarists put in front of a firing squad—those spared were to be sterilized. *Daughter of Destiny* (1918) called for the extermination of all members of the Kaiser's family.[3]

Ambassador Gerard, after his immense success with *My Four Years in Germany,* had hopes of running for the presidency, and he cooperated with Warner Brothers and William Nigh on a sequel, *Beware,* in which the Kaiser was subjected to a war-crimes trial. Conceived, like most of these vengeance pictures, while the war was still on, it was overtaken by events; from a serial, *If I Tried Germany,* it was cut to feature length and released in June 1919. Gerard wanted to destroy the last vestige of German tradition and culture, including the German language; he accused the German people of insanity and warned, "They are already preparing." The film failed dismally.*

It was hardly surprising that when President Wilson, who had issued commendations to many industries for their part in the war effort, was asked by William Brady to do the same for the picture business, he declined to do so.

SMILES FILMS

In splendid contrast to the Kill-the-Kaiser epics was the Smiles Film scheme, an inspired and compassionate use of the motion picture to annihilate some of the loneliness of the boys in France. Closely associated with the idea was Rowland V. Lee, a former actor at the Thomas Ince studio, and later a prominent director.

Lee had had an extraordinary war. He had been offered a commission with Theodore Roosevelt's expeditionary force, which never materialized, and next tried to join the American Ambulance Corps, but discovered that the entrance fee was $250, plus the steamship fare and the cost of the uniform. Finally, he was drafted in the normal way, and at Officers' Training Camp he became a celebrity when they showed a picture he had made for Ince—*They're Off,* with Enid Bennett. After training with a Signal Corps unit in France, Lee was sent to the front with the Australians. He suffered from gas and from dysentery, and in that state went over the top.

"Going over the top is like the first night on stage—only it's much worse. You have butterflies, no question about that, but when they say 'go' you're off. I only got 100 yards when I was blown up. The rest of the guys in my squad were all knocked out; I never saw any of them again."[1]

After a spell in the hospital, Lee went back into action again at Brabant. An officer jumped into Lee's trench, directly onto the bayonet of Lee's rifle. He was severely wounded, and as he was being lifted away in a stretcher, he said, "Lee, you'll never get out of this. Never, never!"

---

* For an excellent survey of this and other Hang-the-Kaiser films, see Charles Reed Mitchell, *Journal of Popular Film,* IV, 1975, no. 4, p. 275.

Lee then fought in the Battle of St. Mihiel. Following the armistice, he found himself in Paris:

"I was assigned to the Committee on Public Information, and I met Roy Howard [United Press manager]—the man who was reported to have sent out the False Armistice message [7 November 1918]. I thought it the better part of diplomacy not to bring up the subject. Howard was full of personality and charm. He asked me if I knew Tom Ince, and when I replied that he gave me my start in pictures, his interest increased.

" 'Well, Tom Ince came up with a wonderful idea that we went right after. He proposed that the government finance a program of making motion pictures of families all over the country who have men overseas, then ship these films to France and see that they are shown to the men. Ince called them "Smiles Films" and we've kept the title.'

"Distribution was the headache, and Howard wanted me to take complete charge of Smiles Films to see that they got around to the right units. 'I'm not really a distributor,' I told him, 'but I do know how it's done. I'll be happy to see what I can do.'

"For days I saturated myself with Paris, then I returned to Luxembourg, where I was heartily greeted by Lieutenant Wilson, who had just been released from the hospital after his bayonet wound. 'Lee,' he said, 'you're going to find this hard to believe. After being stuck I remember saying to you that you'd never get out of it. Then I passed out, was operated on and remained unconscious for some time. When I came out of it I was lying on my back, looking up at the ceiling, and I saw a great big picture of you smiling and laughing. I was sure you'd been killed and that I was dead too. I called out your name and a nurse asked what was the matter. When I told her, she pointed to a motion picture machine which was projecting movies for the wounded on the ceiling. And you, Lee, were in the movie called *They're Off*.' "

Smiles Films were distributed under the auspices of Homer Croy's Overseas Weekly organization, a branch of the YMCA. (The idea had first been used in the 1911 Tripoli campaign by the Italians.) "At YMCA headquarters, I met Miss Ludlow, in charge of the distribution of the Smiles Films. She showed me a storeroom stacked to the ceiling with reels of film. We started work on a large map of France and the occupied territory of Germany. We put the names of hundreds of outfits on small flags, stuck them in the maps and prepared lists for the courier who would deliver them in person. In less than a week we were swamped with requests for the films and additional couriers were pressed into service. We got many notes telling of the joy the soldiers got out of seeing their home folks. Our principal problem was that the units liked to keep the films and show and reshow them, and they wouldn't send them back. I covered France, Belgium and our occupied area in Germany. Countless times I would stand by the projection machines, or in the audience watching the faces of the men as they recognized families or friends. Many of those who passed in front of the local cameras carried signs saying such things as 'Hello, Eddie,' or 'We love you, Chuck.' New babies that their fathers had never seen were held up for inspection. The men would talk back as though their families were actually there. 'Hello, Mom and Dad, you look great.' Many men cried openly. These Smiles Films were great morale builders and always found emotional audiences.

Front-line veteran Rowland V. Lee, wearing his own uniform, gas mask, helmet, and web belt, plays in Dangerous Days. *Reginald Barker directs. The story was by Mary Roberts Rinehart, novelist and war correspondent.*

"One afternoon I stood in the projection booth of a large theater at Coblenz, American Occupation Headquarters. The operator was running some films made by the Germans during the war. They had a remarkable film taken from a submarine showing the torpedoing and sinking of American ships. It was fascinating but gave me a sickening feeling. I decided to confiscate these films and have them shipped to America as a historical record. The operator, an American, left and I piled the German film cans in a corner and covered them with newspapers. When I returned that night they had disappeared. Someone had stolen them. I was mad as hell.*

"At the YMCA headquarters, however, the stock room of Smiles Films was almost empty. Almost all the films were in circulation and the stack of grateful letters proved the venture was bearing fruit. This so pleased Roy Howard that he put all of the Committee's propaganda and other films under my control."[2]

---

* A German-born Knights of Columbus secretary, P. H. Mackzum, took the film, and it was included in Hearst News No. 64, advertised as "the biggest scoop ever scored by any news picture organization since the cinema was invented" (*Moving Picture World,* 22 November 1919, p. 445; *ibid.,* 6 December 1919, p. 585). It was released in England as *The Log of the U-35* (see p. 29).

THE RUSSIAN INTERVENTION

The Russians had withdrawn from the war in December 1917, following the October Revolution. In that same month the White armies counterattacked, and the civil war began. Under the treaty of Brest-Litovsk, the Ukraine was occupied by the Germans. The Committee on Public Information representatives inside revolutionary Russia had a hard time under these circumstances arousing enthusiasm for America. It was difficult to use normal channels for anything, let alone motion pictures, and the CPI had to run the same reels over and over again. Thousands of fresh reels were packed up and sent off, but they got no further than the Russian frontier. When Bolshevik hostility toward the United States became apparent, the CPI changed its base of operations from Moscow and Petrograd to Archangel and Vladivostok. Japanese forces had landed at Vladivostok in December 1917, and with their help and that of a Czech army consisting of former prisoners of war, Admiral Alexander Kolchak had set up a White government at Omsk.* The British and French arrived in mid-1918, followed by the Americans in September, and the Allied Expeditionary Force, with a total of 300,000 men, carried out sporadic operations against the Bolsheviks until October 1919. The campaign was a disaster, and was noted for its chaos and its mutinies.

The Photographic Section of the Signal Corps became involved in the American Expeditionary Force for Siberia by special order on 26 August 1918. Five men were selected—Sergeant Beardsley, Sergeant Hemmer, Corporal Ostrom, and Privates O'Connell and Tannura. Two of them were motion picture men—L. William O'Connell and Philip Tannura, both veterans of the picture business.

O'Connell had worked for J. Stuart Blackton. When Blackton heard that he was acting as instructor at Columbia University, he tried to get him released so they could work together again. Despite innumerable letters, he never received any response. This was unusual behavior for the army; Blackton was making a propaganda film in New York, *The Common Cause,* and would normally have been given what he asked for. The explanation, O'Connell discovered, was a simple one—but he didn't learn it until the expedition was over.

The five men had been selected by Captain Howard Price Kingsmore. Since there were no officers among the five, Captain Kingsmore requested that Private O'Connell be commissioned; every captain had to have a lieutenant.

Arriving at Vladivostok was a bleak experience. During the Russo-Japanese War the Russians had built brick barracks at the foot of Golden Horn Bay. The Americans disembarked and found quarters among these deserted buildings.

Photographic activities ranged from such chores as covering the endless military parades in Vladivostok to recording U.S. personnel in distant locations. Admiral Kolchak's reputation for mass executions of Bolsheviks had reached a high level of notoriety. O'Connell was assigned to seek out and photograph whatever he could of Kolchak's activities at Khabarovsk, north of Vladivostok. "Being

---

* Carl von Hoffman, Russian-born Signal Corps cameraman, filmed Kolchak's unsuccessful assault on the Bolsheviks. All but 2,500 feet were destroyed during Red attacks (*Moving Picture World,* 31 July 1920, p. 899).

British sailors parade in Vladivostok in 1918. (Signal Corps photo; L. William O'Connell)

Captain Kingsmore's photographic expedition, Vladivostok, 1918. L. William O'Connell, second from left; Phil Tannura, third from right.

L. William O'Connell in buffalo coat, with Bell and Howell camera, Russia, 1919. These buffalo coats, reminiscent of the cavalry in the Indian wars, were standard winter issue for the U.S. Army.

L. William O'Connell and his "location droshky" in Russia.

an officer, I rated a private compartment on the Trans-Siberian railroad, but for a while I rode on the engine with the engineer and fireman. In their best Russian pantomime, they tried to explain how the Bolsheviks had murdered so many people at each spot we passed. Nobody paid the railroad people. We'd have to get out and load the firewood, which was put alongside the railroad by the natives. Then we'd go on to the next town. The Trans-Siberian railroad was built for military purposes, and didn't serve any of the villages along the way. They were all way off in the distance. Once in a while, there'd be a station with a restaurant where you'd get out and have some food. That's where I was one evening, just at sunset, having a nice bowl of hot soup when someone said that the armistice had been declared. I didn't know what the word meant.

"I went to Kolchak's headquarters early in the morning, only to be stopped at the door by soldiers with fixed bayonets. The wailing wives in an ante-room told me, with gestures, that fourteen of their menfolk had been shot that morning. For no reason at all, I cooked up a mock charge of Cossacks toward my camera; I set up low, and they charged me at full speed, spears drawn, shouting and screaming.

"While in Khabarovsk, I witnessed the Mercy Train being shuttled on its way to the rail terminal. Refugees had been locked in freight cars; they were suffering from typhus, and it was pitiful to see their hands reaching out through the gratings, begging for food. None of the villages would accept them. They would just hook on an engine and take them to the next stop. That's the way they kept going until they all died or finally got to Vladivostok. The Whites supplied another train—all white coaches—and the Americans sent over underclothes, pajamas and so on for these people. When they got to Vladivostok, they had to go through a typhus bath like a car wash."[1]

On the way back to the United States, O'Connell and Kingsmore shared a cabin. It was then that Kingsmore confided that all the letters from J. Stuart Blackton, requesting O'Connell's release, had come to his desk in Washington. He let none of them through. He decided that anyone who was so much in demand *must* be good—and he had to be on Kingsmore's expedition.

Kingsmore had been decorated by Admiral Kolchak with the Order of St. George, and the moment he returned he was hired by Fox News as a cameraman. Later he was told that although honorably discharged with the rank of captain, he would be commissioned a major in the Reserve Corps in recognition of his services in obtaining remarkable motion pictures in the heart of Russia.

PHIL TANNURA, A YOUNG SIGNAL CORPS cameraman, was selected for the Russian expedition because he had photographed one of the most successful war films, *The Unbeliever* (1918).

"First thing I know, I'm on my way from New York to San Francisco. We stopped there for about a month. And from there we went to Japan, and so to Vladivostok. We landed in Vladivostok in November. In Vladivostok we shot nothing but parades—diplomats meeting with the Chinese generals and admirals. We confiscated quite a few of the Russian barracks for our troops; they were cold, but they were good, clean barracks. There was an incident that happened; here we were feeding the Russians in the daytime, and at nighttime they surrounded the

Christabel Pankhurst, daughter of the Suffragette leader, with Yasha Bochkareva, the commander of the Women's Battalion of Death. A scene from Donald Thompson's German Curse in Russia *(1918). General Bochkareva*

had disguised herself as a man and fought so valiantly that Kerensky had decorated her. She persuaded him to form the Women's Battalion. Christabel Pankhurst was studying the fight of Russian women against Germany.

Phil Tannura, with a Bell and Howell, Siberia, 1919.

Phil Tannura films a Chinese admiral and general aboard the Chinese cruiser Hai Yung, *Vladivostok, May 1919.*

camp and killed thirty-four out of eighty-four men. Most of the rest were wounded. And these were the same people that we were feeding. I never got pictures of that because it happened fifty or sixty miles out of Vladivostok.

"We used to get all kinds of notices that the Reds were going to attack us. What we'd do is to set up machine guns at every window, and I would be alongside of a machine gun with the camera. Nobody ever showed up. But we never knew who the Reds were.

"Kingsmore and I went into the interior with the first Red Cross train that was allowed to go through. We went from town to town and fed the people. We went as far as the Ural Mountains and we couldn't go any further; that was where the Czechs were holding a battle line. They were fighting the Reds, and we weren't fighting anybody. The only thing I think *we* were doing there was keeping the Japs from taking over the country! We had to look after the Baldwin Locomotive Works; that was the big American investment. And the only reason why they sent us over there.

"That was really an exciting trip. They had blown up most of the tunnels that went around Lake Baikal and they built a trestle on a frozen part of the lake. You could see the train bobbing up and down on the ice. It was the darndest thing you ever saw. I was taking some pictures on a flatcar, and it was so cold the film just crumbled into pieces.

"In Omsk we got into the middle of the revolution. We were living on the train, in converted freight cars. Around six o'clock, shooting started up on both sides of the train, and everybody was ordered underneath. They figured it was safer there. Well, of course, I got under there with my camera, figuring I'd get something. But we never saw anybody. They were shooting right across, and they punctured the water tank in the dining car. But nothing ever came into view.

"We came to a prison in Omsk, and we said we'd like to shoot some pictures of the prisoners there. They were all political prisoners. They brought thirteen of them out and I noticed some soldiers on the side with guns. I asked what the soldiers were for. 'Well,' they said, 'you wanted to shoot them.'

" 'No,' I said, 'we just want to shoot some pictures of them. You can kill 'em tomorrow. But I don't want any prisoners shot for the camera.'

"When you saw the prisoners after they stopped marching them—it was pitiful. Especially the prisoners that were fighting the White Guard. We went to the hospitals and saw these people, and they were really bad. But you've got to give them credit; here it was, forty or fifty below zero, and they were fighting for their rights. They were a bad crowd, the Czar's bunch. The people deserved to have a revolution. We had one of the Czar's officers on the train with us and the way he treated some of the Russians was terrible. 'You're the reason they're having a revolution,' I told him.

"We went to the house [at Ekaterinburg] where they killed the Czar and his family. We couldn't find out whether they had actually been killed or not. We photographed all the rooms. They had ripped out part of the wall with the bullet holes in it. They said they had killed them off and drowned a couple of them in a well, but we never got any proof of it.

"Nobody objected to being photographed. Maybe once or twice when I was photographing a bread line; some of the natives didn't like the idea of being photographed when they were getting food. But I always had a bodyguard with me, because we traveled around in a motorcycle and sidecar.

"I had to get a special order from Washington before they'd let me out, because nobody in Vladivostok could give me orders to do anything. When I asked for a release, they said, 'You'll have to get your orders from Washington.' Eventually, they sent word that if I would train somebody I could get out. So I trained somebody and I got out in a little over a year."[2]

THE DEPARTURE OF THE WAR FILM

Film historians have often suggested that as soon as the ink was dry on the armistice agreement, war pictures vanished from the screen. But quite apart from the vengeance films, the familiar shot-and-shell pictures were as prolific as ever, most of them having gone into production in the spring and summer of 1918. Publicity men had their talents stretched to breaking point. Some pictures like *The Unpardonable Sin* and *Heart of Humanity* (both 1919) did well, but the public avoided most war films in favor of fresh subjects. War pictures were as inappropriate in the postwar atmosphere as khaki—yet both remained for reasons of necessity. The influenza epidemic of 1918 had cost the industry around $40 million; thus it was vital to sell whatever films were available.

The plummeting returns of war films puzzled producers, for they knew that after the Civil War, plays about the war continued in popularity for thirty years.* The exchanges, however, reported a complete lack of demand for war films, or for films with even a flavor of war, and blamed a boycott by exhibitors. Films had to be labeled "NOT a war film" and radically altered to cope with the change in conditions. Now that it had happened, *The Great Victory* was revised, and some scenes inserted showing President Wilson sailing for the Peace Conference. Raoul Walsh's *18–45* (the ages covered by the draft) was retitled *Every Mother's Son,* and changes were made to the story, although the scene of an American family burning German literature and sheet music at the outbreak of war remained, a grim reminder that the melodramatic extremism of these films would be re-enacted in reality less than twenty years later.

Two of the box-office hits of 1919 were concerned with the war. Henry King's *Twenty Three and a Half Hours Leave* referred to the furlough granted troops before they left for France. But it was no harrowing tear-jerker; it was light comedy, an affectionate portrayal by a great director, with the emphasis on small human touches. *Photoplay* considered that the story, by Mary Roberts Rinehart (a novelist who had covered the war), had been transferred to celluloid with perfection.

Behind the Door was its very antithesis. Directed by Irvin Willat from a story by Gouverneur Morris, it was the most outspoken of all the vengeance films. The impact it created was far more powerful than the routine "Hang-the-Kaiser" dramas; it told a story of a German-American, the hyphenated citizen, villain in almost every other war film. The audience was forced not only to sympathize with the man but to identify with him as he cut himself adrift from his past in a scene of Jacobean horror.

Hobart Bosworth played Oscar Krug, a skipper, who returns to his native Maine after many years' service in the Merchant Marine. He is no longer young. He is also German-American, and there is no one to give him a welcome upon his return. Krug falls in love with Alice Morse (Jane Novak). When the United States enters the war, Krug is set upon by the townspeople and forced to fight for his life. He weds Alice, joins the navy, and is given a command. Alice accompanies her husband aboard ship as a Red Cross nurse. On the first voyage the ship is torpedoed by a German submarine, and Krug and Alice drift in a lifeboat for days before another submarine is sighted. The commander, Brandt (Wallace Beery), takes Alice aboard but refuses to rescue Krug. Finally picked up by an American

* Charles Reed Mitchell, however, quotes *Variety* to suggest that after the Civil War eighty productions became valueless (*Journal of Popular Film,* IV, 1975, no. 4, p. 278).

Hobart Bosworth, his hands covered with blood, holds the razor that he has used to take the ultimate revenge on the U-boat commander. From Behind the Door *(1919), directed by Irvin Willat.*

ship, Krug is given another command. His one and only object now is to exact vengeance from the man who seized his wife.

One day his ship disables a U-boat, which is afterwards sunk, and he captures the commander, none other than Brandt. To convey a contemporary impression of the climactic scenes, one needs the memory of someone who saw the film at the time. George Stevens, the distinguished director of *Shane* and *Giant,* recalled that it was extraordinarily sadistic but remarkable as a drama:

"The sailors are about to throw the German captain into irons, but Bosworth says, 'No, I'll talk to the fellow.' He shuts the door of the cabin. Fred Kohler, his second-in-command, and the other members of the crew don't like this. They'd like to be in on it. Bosworth locks the door, and says, in German, 'I'll fix you some coffee.'

A scene that anticipates von Stroheim: German officers relax in Rex Ingram's Four Horsemen of the Apocalypse (1921). *Most of the scene survives in MGM's studio print, but seems to have been censored in the release prints.*

" 'Ja,' says Brandt. 'It's nice to hear your own language spoken by your captor.' And so they have some coffee, and they have some schnapps. Bosworth says, 'Well, it's great to be in the war, but it's over for you. You've done your duty. You must feel pretty good about it. Maybe you had some fun on these submarines at some time or other?'

"Well, they get around to some more schnapps, and finally the captain brings up the incident. 'There was this one time that was pretty good. There was this girl . . . when I finished with her I gave her to the crew. And when she died I shoved her out through the torpedo tube.' Now this is pretty wild stuff. But against that, Willat played the crew. 'We were right in the first place,' they said. 'What's he doing with that son of a bitch in there? Didn't he send out for more schnapps? What are they plotting?' The conspiracy grows. They've condemned Krug—they're about ready to get him and put him in irons because too much time has passed. And then comes the confrontation. They finally knock on the door. Kohler is their spokesman: 'Captain,' he says. 'We'd like to talk to you.' And old Bosworth was very restrained in the picture with Willat. 'What about?'

" 'About Brandt.'

" 'What about Brandt? That son of a bitch—I've skinned him alive behind that door.'* He pushes the door open and the shadow of the guy hanging on the door, just skinned alive, is visible. What happened after that I don't remember. I was under the seat somewhere at that point. This picture pleased the majority of people very much at the time."[1]

ALTHOUGH VIOLENCE ON THE screen returned from the front to its prewar domain of prairie and city street, films dealing with the contemporary scene could hardly avoid some reference to the war. The process of democracy had been greatly advanced by the experience of battle, these films insisted, although only Griffith suggested it had broken down racial prejudice, in *The Greatest Thing in Life* (1919). According to Lillian Gish: "The story ended in a shell hole with bombs bursting nearby. The snob is with a dying black man who in his delirium thinks the white man is his mother. He takes him in his arms and when he asks his 'Mammy' to kiss the pain away, the white man kisses him full on the lips—and holds it."[2]

The plight of the returning soldier was not shown as a national calamity until the facts were fully known, years later. In Roosevelt style, the post-armistice films endeavored to show the front line as a proving ground for character. In 1919 William S. Hart appeared in *The Cradle of Courage,* directed by Lambert Hillyer, as a burglar taught by the war to fight clean. "Go straight," writes his girl. "The stripes on your sleeve are better than the ones you get in jail." He becomes a policeman, pitched against friend and family. Henry King's *This Hero Business* took a more urbane view; William Russell, war hero, returns from France laden with decorations. By trying to evade adulation, he performs still more heroics.

No notice was taken of a little picture called *The Lost Battalion* (1919), directed by Burton King, yet it represented one of the few attempts at reconstructed documentary. "For the first time in the history of the world," said the opening

---

* The actual title was "I swore I would skin him alive, but he died on me—damn him!"

title, "you are to look upon a motion picture re-enacted by those who live again the historic events for which a grateful nation commended them. Every person, map, letter and document, when shown as such, is the original. The U.S. Signal Corps collaborated in photographing here and abroad, including the resting place of those who sleep forever where they fell in the place that will be known in history as 'The Pocket.' From Major General Alexander, Colonel Whittlesey, and Major McMurtry, to the the last private, all appear before you without compensation. We honorably proclaim our motives—may we prove worthy.—Edward A. MacManus."*

Major General Robert Alexander, commander of the 77th Division, was given the courtesy title of supervisor of the production. He made an inspection of the location, with Colonel Whittlesey—a location selected by regimental engineers as conforming in almost every respect to the actual site in the Argonne. Whittlesey chose men who had distinguished themselves in the siege to play in the picture.

The film introduces the main characters of the story: in the ghetto a Jewish boy kisses his parents farewell . . . a wealthy employer tries to use his influence to ensure a soft life at camp for his son . . . a criminal, wanted by the police, takes the place of a man who fails to report. The recruits pour into Yaphank, Long Island, to form New York's own 77th Division.

When the 77th Division arrived in France to complete its final training with the British, the snows were melting. On 26 September 1918 the stage was set for taking the Argonne forest. At a signal, trees were torn down to open firing lanes—and the drive was on. During the second day, the Germans attacked on four sides. Cut off and surrounded, the 1st Battalion of the 308th Infantry settled down to a siege. After a few days, the pangs of hunger and of thirst began.

Intercut with this sequence, we see the girls back home at a movie show, watching a news weekly of their boys in France, relaxing before the great drive. This experiment in time greatly enhances the siege scenes.

While the Lost Battalion contains two German-Americans, there is another, Leutnant Heinrich Prinz, "born in Germany, resident of Spokane, Washington, for six years, and now the scourge of the Lost Battalion." He demands surrender. Whittlesey replies with a note that became famous: "Go to hell." With twenty-four runners lost, the beleaguered troops place their hopes on a carrier pigeon, Cher Ami. "In his flight through storm and bullets, Cher Ami lost a leg and an eye, but the message gets through to headquarters." (The real pigeon was used in the film.)

Aeroplanes are sent over to drop supplies, but the food falls with agonizing regularity out of reach of the besieged men. Leutnant Prinz keeps the Americans pinned down with ceaseless sniping. A stagnant water hole promises relief, but each soldier who crawls down for a drink pays with his life.

"At nine p.m., Oct. 7, 123 hours from the moment of entering the Pocket, the Battalion was once again in touch with the Division, and another chapter of heroism was included in American history." The picture ends with a triumphant parade

---

* MacManus was former head of Hearst's International Film Service and instigator of the serial *Patria*.

through New York, and a view of the cemetery where the dead of the Lost Battalion were buried.

When the film was shown in Hartford, Connecticut, many of the survivors were in the audience. "These veterans sometimes twitted each other on their respective appearances in the film," said *Moving Picture World*.[3] The survivors who appeared in the picture included Colonel Whittlesey, Major George McMurtry, Captain William Cullen, Private Jack Hershkowitz, Corporal P. Cepaglia, Sergeant Herman J. Bergasse, Private J. J. Munson, Private J. W. Rosson, and Private Abraham Krotoshinisky.

The atmosphere might have been stronger with an entirely nonprofessional cast. Few of the details seem wrong, although the Germans wear helmets of a most peculiar shape, and the battle scenes are thin in the surviving print (at the Library of Congress) because the close-combat footage was cut out and used as newsreel in a 1933 compilation, *The Big Drive*. It is therefore hard to judge the central section. There seems little attempt to bring the characters to life during the siege, and there are no long shots to establish the position of the besieged troops in relation to the Germans. Nonetheless, *The Lost Battalion* is an honest attempt to re-create history and it deserves more than the obscurity in which it has spent the last half-century.

With the Huns being replaced by Bolsheviks, routine war films were almost extinct by 1920, so much so that when Reginald Barker's *Dangerous Days* was released, *Photoplay* found it quite nostalgic. "The thrills have been reduced to pleasantly reminiscent titillations by the element of time. Seeing the picture is a little like picking up a war-time copy of Philadelphia's favorite weekly and rereading the introduction to a story we recall as having stirred us profoundly a long time ago."[4]

Featured in *Dangerous Days* was Rowland V. Lee, who wore the uniform and equipment he had brought back from France. "My aunt saw the film. In a scene before we left for France, she said, 'I didn't like the way you played it. You looked as if you'd already been to war.' " Not long after this picture was released, Lee abandoned acting and became a director.

Despite the lack of interest in war movies, the box-office sensation of 1921 was an epic with the background of war. It had been delayed so that its release would coincide with the dedication of the grave of the Unknown Soldier at Arlington National Cemetery. *The Four Horsemen of the Apocalypse,* from the novel by Vicente Blasco-Ibáñez, was scripted by June Mathis (responsible for *To Hell with the Kaiser*), and directed by one of the most extraordinary talents in Hollywood, a young Irishman named Rex Ingram.

Ingram was twenty-nine when he made *The Four Horsemen.* He had joined the Royal Flying Corps in Canada in 1917, and was commissioned a second lieutenant. He returned to Universal after the war to get back his old job, for he was already an established director.

In a 1953 interview, Erich von Stroheim explained: "In 1919, I was directing a scene in *The Devil's Passkey,* the second picture I made, and I saw a man standing on the sidelines in a khaki officer's overcoat, no hat and really good-looking. I mean, good-looking isn't the word. He looked like a Greek god. He stared provokingly at me and it made me nervous. I didn't know who the hell he was and my position was a very cool one. People thought I was German, and you can im-

Rudolph Valentino as Julio Desnoyers in The Four Horsemen of the Apocalypse.

agine that people who had just lost some dear relative in Flanders didn't like me very much. Aside from that, I had just appeared in Austrian uniform in my first picture, *Blind Husbands,* which didn't help to promote love or goodwill. Well, I called my assistant, Eddy Sowders, and said, 'Who is this guy?' He said, 'That's Rex Ingram.' I said, 'Who's Rex Ingram?' He said, 'He used to be the white-haired boy around here, a great director. . . .' I said, 'What does he want?' He said, 'I don't know, but I'll go over and ask him.' So he went over, and Rex Ingram said, 'What is that son of a bitch doing here? He's got my job.' He had been a director before the war, and he went to fight for his country, and when he came back there was no job for him. They told him, 'Sorry, it's filled.' And the one that had apparently filled his vacancy was I.

"I went over and introduced myself, not clicking my heels as usually, but kind

Rex Ingram (left) and his friend Erich von Stroheim.

of friendly so that I wouldn't be too prominent. And we started talking. He said, 'Well, you know, it's very difficult for a man who comes back. Now I'm through the war, I have no money, and I've no civilian clothes. It's kind of tough to see the ex-enemy having my job.'

"I said, 'Well now, look, I mean I didn't take your job. I didn't know you. But I do believe the company did wrong in not giving you a job aside from mine.' Then I, of course, as usual, had a bottle of some sort of whisky—Scotch—and I offered him a drink and we had two, we had three, and after about ten or twelve we were very palsy-walsy. And he proved himself a great friend in many ways. He even gave me a pair of trench boots that didn't quite fit him and which I wore going into Death Valley on *Greed*."[5]

Collaborating with a cameraman of genius, John Seitz, and a great editor, Grant Whytock, Rex Ingram made of *The Four Horsemen* a saga that went beyond the melodrama of the script. He advanced film technique with creative and effective lighting and a fluid use of bold close-ups, a contribution that may not have been new but was handled with immense skill and was a lot more significant than it sounds. And he paid as much attention as his friend von Stroheim to authenticity.

Affectionate care is evident throughout the picture. Ingram even insisted on correct 1914 period costumes for civilians, a flourish that few of the other war films bothered with. To ensure the accuracy of the military scenes, Ingram had the benefit of advice from Colonel Starret Ford, who later became his production manager. One of the assistants was Curt Rehfeld, a former German soldier who, despite the disability of an artificial leg, was one of the most energetic and efficient men on the Metro lot. He taught the American soldiers and extras to behave like German troops, and his capacity for organization so impressed June Mathis and the studio head, Richard Rowland, that when they moved to First National they made him a director, giving him the benefit of another June Mathis script.

In spite of all the care, *Photoplay*[6] published an attack on the accuracy of *The Four Horsemen:* "Why did Ingram not spend an infinitesimal fraction of the million to engage a French non-com to find out what the French soldier wears? Why did some of the German soldiers wear dress-overcoats with their field uniforms?"

A furious reply from Eugene Touyet insisted that this correspondent was entirely wrong: "Very careful to surround himself with the required technical talent, Mr. Ingram engaged precisely a French Non-Com (myself). As such, I lived nearly three years in the trenches and was decorated with the Croix de Guerre. Needless to say, I must know something about the uniforms worn by the French, Allied and foreign armies."[7] Ingram also used Jacques d'Auray and former Signal Corps cameraman Paul Ivano as advisers.

The picture was exceptionally expensive, and although Ingram was supported by Metro's backer, Marcus Loew, he was taking a huge gamble by starring a relative unknown, Rudolph Valentino. "Through Marcus Loew's pockets rode the Four Horsemen" was a Hollywood quip of the time. The picture made a star of Valentino, and a star director of Ingram. The gross reached three million.

The German press protested angrily at the way their army was portrayed, and the German ambassador in Rome was instructed to request the Italian government to ban the film. The French protested, too—at what they considered unfair emphasis on the American part in the war. For that reason, and because the Germans were depicted as "strong and splendid, though barbaric," it was urged that the film be suppressed. The League of Nations responded to the underlying message against war and provided representatives to address audiences. Marcus Loew sent a copy to the League's headquarters in Geneva.

Oddly enough, no one objected to the tragic ending—the death in battle of Valentino—even though Metro kept a happy ending in reserve. The New York *Times* singled out not the story but the cinematic interpretation: "The execution of the citizens of Villeblanche is done in pure cinematography, and is one of the most impressive incidents of the story. In bringing the symbolic Four Horsemen into the photoplay, Mr. Ingram again has done his work cinematographically, and with such a discerning sense of the unreal in reality that what might easily have been banal or incongruous has become a pervading and leavening part of the picture."[8]

Most Hollywood box-office successes set the mold for a flood of imitations. But this film stood alone—perhaps because the combination of exotic locales, marital intrigues, warfare, and mysticism was hard to duplicate. Perhaps because, coincidentally with the ending of the first cycle of war films, the motion picture industry experienced a serious slump.

REPARATION

In his column in *The Saturday Evening Post* in the early 20s, Carl Laemmle* appealed for money, food, and clothing for the stricken people of Germany:

"Possibly many of you haven't forgotten the war and maybe some hatred still lingers in your hearts, yet it is an American trait to forget and forgive, to soften and sympathize, when real distress steps over the threshold. There is no other nation in the world so quick to respond to a call for help.

"Can you imagine going back to your old home town and finding your old acquaintances starving—the prominent families going frequently without anything to eat and so utterly bereft of pride that they begged you for a dollar or a dime or anything you would give? That's what happened to me last summer, when times were not one-tenth so bad as they are today.

"The fact that these folks were enemies of America, in deed if not in heart—that they were misled by a fool Kaiser, thirsty for power, and compelled to become a part of his war machine, all slipped from my mind and the desire to help became uppermost. Yet, I am an American who profoundly respects all American beliefs and institutions.

"Will *you* help? Will you send me any kind of help you can afford—food, clothing, hats, shoes, money? All the employees of Universal are contributing, and

---

* Carl Laemmle was born in Laupheim, South Württemberg. Besides money, food, and clothing, he sent affidavits by the hundred to hopeful immigrants, who needed this proof that they would not become a burden to the U.S. government (Paul Kohner).

A street scene staged on location in Berlin by D. W. Griffith (center) for his story of postwar Germany, Isn't Life Wonderful? *(1924).*

weekly we are sending cases of supplies to Germany. We all feel it is incumbent upon us in the name of humanity."[1]

Mary Pickford, whose *Little American* had led the battalion of Hate-the-Hun films, now made a brave attempt to soften the raucous cries of hatred that still resounded against all things German. In *The Love Light* (1921), directed by Frances Marion from her own scenario, she again loves a German, and unwittingly collaborates in his scheme for sinking Allied ships. The German kills himself rather than be torn apart by the mob. *The Love Light* also proved too harsh for the Pickford fans, and it was given a very poor reception.

D. W. Griffith made an even more uncompromising attempt to make reparation for war hatred with *Isn't Life Wonderful?* (1924), his last independently produced feature. The idea of a film about the wretched conditions in Germany may have been sparked by humanitarian ideals, but Griffith, too, was in financial straits. German pictures were taking America by storm, and he was concerned about the threat they presented to his hitherto unassailable position. His *Orphans of the Storm* (1922) owed much to Lubitsch's *Madame Dubarry* (1919). It was hardly surprising, therefore, that he should attempt a German picture of his own.

With anti-German sentiment still smoldering in the Allied countries, Griffith made his leading characters Polish, and in an opening title, he provided further insurance against chauvinistic affront: "The story is laid in Germany only because conditions there were most suitable to show the struggle of love over hardship." Critics were puzzled why he should go all the way to Germany for authentic backgrounds, only to make a film about Poles. Furthermore, Griffith dropped all the bitter references to the French in Major Geoffrey Moss's story. (It was Germany's failure to pay reparations that led to the French occupation of the Ruhr.)

Reviewing the film in *The Spectator,*[2] Iris Barry considered it ridiculous and boring, and stated that there were no Polish refugees in Berlin after the war. She insisted that Griffith's depiction of the effect of inflation on the working class in Germany was absolutely false. (Years later, she called the film "a little masterpiece" and said, "among all Griffith's later pictures, this one wears best."[3])

The Germans rejected it. UFA producer Erich Pommer explained to Griffith in a letter, "the sufferings of the German nation were for the greater part different from those described in this film, although 'hunger' was indeed one of the most terrible." Pommer said the characters, such as the professor, would never act as they were supposed to in the film. "Too great an importance has been attached to the materialistic basis of the matrimony. Your film is pessimistic and we cannot see our way to propagate a production which glorifies a bushel of potatoes as the thing most coveted by German laborers and German citizens."[4]

Yet *Isn't Life Wonderful?* impresses one today as a film directed with compassion and subtlety. The location scenes, shot at Copenick, Potsdam, Old Berlin, Crampnitz, Sacrow, and Grunaw, give documentary value to a remarkable dramatic evocation. One unforgettable sequence is introduced with the title: "Then came the greatest financial disaster in all history. When a billion dollars, the wealth of a Rockefeller, fell to the buying power of one dollar." And Griffith builds suspense from the simple situation of Inga (Carol Dempster) rushing to take her place in the queue for a butcher's shop. "A cut of beef—only 9 million marks!" Policemen with carbines guard the queue. Inga must reach the counter before the butcher sells out, for wages paid today may be worthless tomorrow. As she waits, the price rises before her eyes. The butcher emerges to cross out one figure on the slate and replace it with another—11 million . . . 12 million. After a weary wait, Inga does not have enough money for meat, and she spends her wages on bread.

Griffith received no reward for making the picture apart from a few favorable reviews. In December 1924 he handed the negative and rights to the Central Union Trust Company as further collateral for outstanding loans. And from small towns across America, exhibitors' reports boiled with indignation: "They don't make 'em any worse than this one. Ten reels of Germans eating potatoes are too much for one picture."[5]

KING VIDOR AND *THE BIG PARADE*

When he first began making pictures, King Vidor told his wife that he intended to become a second D. W. Griffith. "He said this without conceit. It was just a simple statement," said Florence Vidor. In retrospect, Vidor achieved his aim. In the last years of the silent film, he directed an almost unbroken series of superlative pictures. But had *The Big Parade* been his sole contribution to the art of the cinema, his place among the screen's greatest artists would still be secure. What

The Big Parade *(1925) in production. King Vidor, standing top left; cameraman John Arnold, center, with cigar; and U.S. Army veterans, below.*

Veterans of the French and British armies recruited for Rowland V. Lee's Havoc *(1925).*

were the experiences that led to the development of this extraordinary director?

King Vidor was born in Galveston, Texas, in 1895. "Galveston was a very cosmopolitan place," he recalled. "On the block where I lived there was a French-speaking family next door and a German-speaking family across the street. It was a tremendous cotton port, so it attracted people of all nationalities. The houses were very close together and I grew up in this atmosphere of people from many countries and with many languages.

"At the age of six, I went through a flood, one of the greatest disasters of all time. Out of a population of twenty-nine thousand people, ten thousand were killed. All the wooden structures of the town were flattened and laid waste. The streets piled high with dead people. It was an indelible experience. You can't fear extinction so closely without lasting effect.*

"They had somewhat of a repeat of that hurricane some years later, when I was fifteen. By then I worked with a fellow who had built a camera out of part of a projection machine and cigar boxes. His name was Roy Clough; he was later mayor of Galveston. He lived fairly near the ocean, the Gulf of Mexico, so when the hurricane struck, I made my way to his house, and we went out and photographed it. By then, they'd built a sea wall, so the town wasn't inundated. There were two or three bath-houses, large frame buildings, beyond the sea wall. We were out there when one of these bath-houses was picked up and set down on top of the sea wall. Waves were coming over and it was disintegrating while it was sitting there. The wind was something like sixty miles an hour, and we were in some danger from flying timber. Roy Clough ran the camera, and I was holding the tripod down. My mother and father would have raised hell if they had known I was out there."[1]

Although Vidor describes the resulting film as "pretty awful," it was shown in local theaters. "I had been a witness and participant in recording an actual dramatic event on motion-picture film. It made an indelible mark on my psyche."[2]

Vidor quickly became addicted to moving pictures. They combined his interests in writing, acting, and photography. When he was eighteen, he telegraphed the Mutual Weekly, offering to be their representative for Texas. He received a swift reply:

> LONGEST MARCH OF MASSED TROOPS IN THE HISTORY OF THE UNITED STATES ARMY WILL BE UNDERTAKEN BEGINNING NEXT WEEK.† OVER ELEVEN THOUSAND OFFICERS AND MEN WILL MARCH THE HUNDRED MILES TO HOUSTON AND RETURN. WE WILL PAY SIXTY CENTS PER FOOT FOR ALL USABLE FILM. YOU ARE HEREBY APPOINTED OUR REPRESENTATIVE FOR TEXAS.

Vidor's enthusiasm had outstripped his concern for more practical issues. He had no camera. Roy Clough's machine had been abandoned. In desperation, he wired a New York raw stock supply company: "DO YOU KNOW ANYONE IN TEXAS

---

* Vidor wrote a remarkable account of the Galveston flood in *Esquire,* May 1935—"Southern Storm."

† The cause of the troop movements was the trouble in Veracruz.

WHO OWNS A MOTION PICTURE CAMERA?" They put him on to someone in Houston, and Vidor, with only a few days to spare, tracked him to the home of one of Houston's prominent families; he was John Boggs, the family's chauffeur. Vidor made a deal with him, but on the night before they were due to shoot, he found a note on his front door: "I have left the camera and tripod at the corner drugstore in your name. My folks are going on a picnic tomorrow and want me to take them. If the sun is shining, f11—if it is cloudy, f8—two turns per second—good luck."

Early next morning, Vidor was driven out with the equipment to a prearranged vantage point by an uncle, who helped him set up on top of a cotton warehouse. Vidor waited until the long, straight road was filled with troops; then he began cranking. Ambidextrously operating the handle of the tripod head, he slowly tilted up the column—when the camera jammed.

"I didn't want to lose the twenty feet that had already gone through, so we ran down into the warehouse and pushed cotton bales around, and made a kind of darkroom. I crawled between the cotton bales, took the film out, then ran up with an empty magazine, and went on shooting."[3]

The film was distributed throughout the world by Mutual, and it led to a local newsreel, organized by the editor of Houston's third newspaper, Ralph Spence (later famous in Hollywood as a title writer).

Vidor was chief cameraman, and he also undertook the production of some two-reel pictures. But Hollywood obsessed him, and despite a serious shortage of cash, he made the down payment on a Model T, and set off across the plains, covered-wagon style, with his wife, Florence. To help pay for the trip, he shot scenic footage en route for the Ford Motor Company with a newly acquired Ernemann.

By the time they had reached San Francisco, their total fortune was twenty cents. They lived by eating free samples from the San Francisco Exposition. When Vidor sold the car, the first use he made of the money was to see *The Birth of a Nation*.

After a brief period as an extra and writer, King Vidor became a director in Hollywood, and for a while ran his own studio. His early films were highly praised for their sincerity and talent, but his independent venture ultimately failed. At one time there was so little money that cameraman George Barnes, who was a talented musician, would leave the camera and pick up the violin, Vidor would crank at two turns per second, and Florence would emote.

By 1925, however, he was a successful director at Metro-Goldwyn-Mayer. Explaining to Irving Thalberg that he was tired of making pictures that played a couple of weeks, then vanished into oblivion, Vidor asked for a project of true value, a film that could achieve long runs throughout the country. He specified three themes: war, wheat, and steel. Fox had already made a war film called *Havoc*, directed by Rowland V. Lee, and MGM had the rights to a war book, *Plumes*. Thalberg thought he should collaborate with its author, Laurence Stallings, who had co-authored the Broadway success *What Price Glory?* Stallings came to California with five pages of a treatment and a title, *The Big Parade*. He had no intention of cutting himself off from the world in order to write a scenario. He decided he would return to New York, and Thalberg told Vidor to go with him, and to keep him talking. Vidor took a writer named Harry Behn, and joined the Super-Chief.

"Stallings had been a Marine, and had been at Belleau Wood, and had lost a leg," said Vidor. "That's why I had Gilbert lose a leg in the picture; he copied Stallings' leg movement for the last scene. Stallings was the biggest source of information about the war, not so much in writing as in talking. I had to sit with him and draw it out of him. The research that I did was more or less suggested by Stallings.

"One night I was reading about the horrors of battle on the train. He was in the upper berth and I was in the lower. I thought, I don't want to get too involved in this thing, otherwise I won't be able to sleep. I'll just say it's fiction. Stallings had hung his leg up, just as you hang your coat up, but he didn't take his shoe or stocking off the leg. The train started swaying and his boot swung over and kicked me in the face. At that point, I said to myself, well, it *must* have been real. It was just about gruesome enough for me to realize that I couldn't kid myself any more."

Although friendly with John Gilbert, Stallings was emphatic that Gilbert was entirely the wrong casting for Jim Apperson. Vidor tended to agree, but he so welcomed the chance to make an honest war picture, he was not as critical. "I don't think there had ever been a picture made from the soldier's viewpoint, never a film which asked 'Who's fighting this war? Men or orders?' It was always a story about officers in their shiny boots and tailored uniforms, always about handsome, very heroic men."

When Thalberg read the scenario, he envisioned the film as a love story with a background of war. Much of the detail was improvised by Vidor on the set. Its transformation into an epic crystallizing the spirit of the time was also Vidor's responsibility. But "epic" is a misleading term. The film is a collection of fragile incidents, directed with such affection and care that even the comic moments are strangely moving. Vidor's concern is with ordinary people—there are no villains, no melodrama, no heroics. And no lies.

Vidor was without combat experience, but he was not unfamiliar with the army. He went to the Peacock Military Academy, in San Antonio, Texas, which he regarded as a reformatory (he ran away after a few months), and he attended the Hollywood Officers' Training Camp during the war. He steeped himself in the atmosphere by watching thousands of feet of Signal Corps footage.

Yet Vidor never allowed himself to be enslaved by authenticity. "I always followed the attitude that technical correctness goes so far, then comes artistic control. No film can be absolutely authentic. After all, *The Big Parade* has eucalyptus trees in it. . . .

"We had two guys as advisers who had been in the Marines, and had been at Belleau Wood. (Stallings never showed up during the shooting.) Occasionally, they disagreed with me, and said, 'You can't do it that way.' That's how I learned the indelible lesson—do it the way you want, the way you think it should be, because no one person could be on all the fronts at the same time, and commanders had the right to make their own decisions about the handling of troops. For example, I had the troops spread out as they moved forward into open country. They said it was never done. There wasn't even a command for it. Well, I said, when I was in military school and officers' training camp, someone would say, 'Spread out, you guys!' That was enough of a command for me. Once you get into battle, there are no set rules. In any case, the graphic, artistic side has to predominate over someone saying, 'You don't do it that way.' After the picture was finished, I got verification from the War Department, who said, 'That's exactly the way it happened.' "

In some of the Signal Corps material, Vidor was intrigued to see a company of men pass the camera at a curious pace. In their deliberate slowness, they carried a strong intimation of death. A flag-draped coffin on a gun caisson explained the march, and Vidor decided to try to duplicate the slow, measured cadence in the Belleau Wood sequence. He used a metronome to record the pace and a drummer to amplify it when the scene was shot in Elysian Park, Los Angeles.

"There were a lot of men among the extras who had been in action in France. Their stock-in-trade remark was: 'I was there. I'll tell you how it was done.' Along comes a guy who was never there, and he's doing it his own way. They laughed, and wondered what the hell I was up to. One of them, an Englishman, asked if he was in some bloody ballet."

The Big Parade, shot only seven years after the war, employed many extras who had been in the war—if not in action, most of them had had military training, so it was comparatively easy to assign them to a sergeant who would separate them into companies and give them a rapid refresher course. This is one reason why the scenes of massed troop movements are so convincing. The art director, James Basevi, had been an artillery officer in the British Army, and one of the leading actors, Tom O'Brien, was also an experienced veteran.

Only one scene involved the cooperation of the U.S. Army. Vidor remembered the long column of troops he had photographed on their march to Houston and wanted a similar long, straight road jammed with trucks. He sent his assistant, Dave Howard,* to San Antonio, with a second unit, and provided him with drawings of what he required.

"There was no need for me to be there, since I was cutting the picture. Howard, who was a very good assistant, went to the army post at San Antonio, Fort Sam Houston, and got palsy-walsy with the General. He sent the film back—a lot of film—and when I finished running it, I called Thalberg. 'There's some good stuff,' I said. 'But he didn't get my shot.' Thalberg said, 'What are you going to do about it?' 'I'll have to go down there.'

"When I got down to San Antonio, I asked Dave Howard what had happened. 'Well,' he said, 'they told me it wasn't like that in France. There were no straight roads.' 'I don't give a damn,' I said. 'I want a straight road. There's got to be one *somewhere* in France.' The real excuse was that the only straight road near the army post was twenty-five miles away, and they didn't want to take all this stuff there. They had persuaded Howard to do it their way.

"I had to go out with him and meet the Commanding Officer, a tough general, noncommunicative, with big egotism, in command of the entire army post, and here am I, down from Hollywood, in my late twenties, my only army experience being military school. You had to have confidence in what you felt! 'I understand you don't like it,' he said. 'I like it all right,' I said, 'but you didn't do it the way I wanted.' 'We did it the way we thought it should be done.' 'That's the point,' I said.

---

* An assistant director with a high reputation, who had worked on such major productions as Edward Sloman's *The Westerners* (1919). He became a director of Western and action pictures in the 1930s.

In 1925 assistant director Dave Howard shot this scene for The Big Parade *in San Antonio, Texas, with army cooperation.*

The march through the wood from The Big Parade.

'You're going to have to do it the way I want it done.' This took all the guts I could muster up. We were asking a big favor, but I guess we had official recognition from Washington, or we couldn't have been so tough about it."

Vidor remained obdurate, and the general eventually agreed to restage the scene. Vidor then shattered army regulations by ordering the two hundred trucks to proceed down the road bumper to bumper. The scenes Dave Howard had shot on the zigzag road were not wasted, and form the sequence following the title: "It had begun—the Big Parade."

John Gilbert, as Jim Apperson, soared to stardom as a result of this picture. Although he was already a popular leading actor, no one imagined he could produce the kind of performance he displayed here. In a remarkable autobiographical article John Gilbert conveyed his feelings for the film: "*The Big Parade.* A thrill when I wrote the words. *The Big Parade!* As a preface to my remarks pertaining to this great film, permit me to become maudlin. No love has ever enthralled me as did the making of this picture. No achievement will ever excite me so much. . . . No reward will ever be so great as having been a part of *The Big Parade.* It was the high point of my career. All that has followed is balderdash. . . .

"[The picture] was to be my first starring vehicle for MGM. A little six-reel movie of the war, but something more behind it. Thalberg was the first to sense an underlying greatness in our story, which imbued Vidor and the rest of us with a knowledge of our responsibility. The camera was set up; Slim, Bull and Jim, caked with mud, were to plunge into a water-filled shell hole to escape an enemy's fire. It was the first scene to be photographed. As I was adjusting my gas-mask, King approached, his hand outstretched. Through a grin, he uttered prophetic words, the ultimate aspiration for movie makers, 'Grauman's Egyptian, baby.' "[4]

Gilbert described the making of the picture as an experience so filled with harmony and well-directed effort that he had little hope such good fortune would ever recur.

"Sequence after sequence was good. We knew it. There was no doubt in our minds, nor any display of ego. The chewing gum episode with little Renee Adoree. Only a suggestion was offered in the script, and no one really knew what would happen. Cameras started and away we went. Minute after minute; impromptu; inspired; both Renee and me, guided by some unseen power, expressing beauty. And when the film was exhausted, old Pop Vidor, age 30, murmuring 'I'll be damned if I ever saw a scene as good as that.'

"The shell hole scene with the German soldier boy. The only thing known about it being 'Jim offers him a cigarette.' And when it was over, Pop's question 'Do you think you slapped him too many times?'

"And my hysterical reply 'God, no, I felt it.'

"And King 'If you felt it, it's right.' "

The shell hole scene epitomizes the extraordinary quality of the film. It is dark. Jim Apperson, his two buddies killed, and a bullet in his leg, shoots a German and crawls after the wounded man until he corners him in a shell hole. Discarding his rifle in the pursuit, he uses the bayonet like a dagger, jabbing its point against the German's throat. The young German is in such agony that Jim lowers his bayonet with a gesture of disgust, and pulls open the man's tunic to reveal a serious wound. The German holds his fingers to his lips and in mime asks for a cigarette.

Refugees; The Big Parade.

Jim removes his helmet, pulls out one from the lining, and strikes a match, shielding its sudden flaring light with his hands. Remembering the death of his friends, a few moments before, he resorts to a gesture of contempt, and pushes the German's face away. But the man is in such pain that he twists to his former position. Jim laughs bitterly and pushes his face back. Concerned now with his own predicament, he leans forward to examine his leg. When he turns back, the German's cigarette has drooped onto his chin. Jim obligingly straightens it, but the man makes no response. He feels his pulse. The German has died. Muttering an imprecation, Jim grabs the cigarette and, as he eases the pain in his leg, smokes it himself.

Vidor designed *The Big Parade* musically, and he intended it to reach its climax right after this scene, as Jim yells helplessly from the shell hole, and American troops race forward on their advance. "Thalberg's attitude was that if you see a place to build it up, build it up. They said so many things about Thalberg the genius, he had to do something about this picture, so he thought it should have a night battle. It cost $40,000. I didn't shoot any of it—for one thing I didn't approve, but by then I was on to *La Bohème*."

The sequence, which involved complicated process work, was directed by George Hill, a former captain in the Signal Corps who had seen action in France.* Thalberg also requested Vidor to reshoot the family scenes with a more significant cast. Vidor gladly agreed, for Thalberg had influenced the original scene and now Vidor could do it as he wanted. Today, however, he feels these scenes with Apperson's parents are overly sentimental, and they form the one element of the picture he dislikes.

Vidor underestimates them. Claire McDowell, for instance, gives an excellent performance as Jim's mother, and most directors would have been content with that. But where most directors stop, Vidor is reaching his emotional high point; as

---

* Joe Farnham, title writer on the picture, had been a motion picture cameraman at the front for the Carnegie Peace Endowment.

Jim appears with a missing leg, and his mother embraces him, Vidor superimposes over her close-up flashes of memory of Jim as a boy, as an infant taking his first steps, as a small child grazing his knee. It converts a touching scene into one of unbearable poignancy.

These scenes were also shot to show Jim with merely a limp. It was a safety measure ordered by Mayer, in case audiences were too shocked to see the romantic lover so mutilated. Vidor ordered the shots not to be printed.

While the picture was in production, a vice-president of the Dupont company visited the set. "I told him that we didn't know if exhibitors would run the picture, since it questioned war. We thought somebody might stop it. Now this was the chief war manufacturer. He said, 'Let me know if you have any trouble. I'll set up a series of tents. If the studio tries to stop you, I'll give you all the Dupont film you need for nothing.' It was just the sort of backing I needed at the time. Although Thalberg was enthused about the picture, somebody bigger than Thalberg might easily have stopped it."

The picture's final cost: $382,000. Its earnings: $3,485,000.[5]

Vidor was surprised that his view of war aroused no criticism—except from England, where newspapers complained that it showed how America had won the war single-handed, and where the tougher scenes, such as the soldier in the hospital so mad with pain that he has been lashed to his bed, were censored.*

The hardest audience to convince were the veterans. Charles K. Taylor, a former sergeant, 102nd Engineers, painted a vivid picture in *The Outlook* of the ex-soldiers scrambling for tickets at a theater already crammed to the roof:

"It looked like a regimental reunion. Most of them were a trifle better upholstered than seven years ago. Men roared at times and slapped one another on the back . . . and then for a while sat in grim and breathless silence. In an hour or so they experienced anew the whole gamut of emotions that meant for them an infinity of experience. For the Great Adventure—hate it, if you will—is a very cherished memory to millions of us everyday, humdrum men.

"There were deft and cunning touches on the part of folk who knew what they were about. Little touches—even to the cow stable—the haymow and manure pile thereof! It made me ache to see those buddies getting it off their shoes. As for the company mess—well, you could actually smell those beans and that amazing coffee, so useful in getting gravy or grease off your mess kit, and—oh well, it was the real stuff, right down to the mademoiselles.

"And suddenly—just as it came to us—the war arrived. There was the abiding horror of trench warfare, barrages far too real, and that worst of all things, a heartbreaking 'walking charge,' timed walking, against those murderous machine-gun nests, with the wiping out of men—rows of men who dropped like a stone or who sank and scrambled about.

" 'This is no picture' declared the man behind me, 'this is the real thing. You can't fool me. That there's the road through Fismes! And you don't get a bunch of hard-boileds like that hanging around movie studios.'

---

* War films had rough treatment in England. *Dawn,* Herbert Wilcox's film about Nurse Cavell, was for a time suppressed by the British censor. There was a row over *The World War as Seen Through German Spectacles. Mare Nostrum* was withdrawn by MGM.

"Neither do you. The actual war scenes were so obviously true that if you forgot for an instant you were only looking at a picture you caught your breath and wondered how the Signal Corps ever did it, and how King Vidor ever got those films released for his picture!"[6]

WHAT PRICE GLORY?

What Price Glory? opened the week Broadway discovered the war. After a period in which the theater, like the motion picture, had ignored the war, three war plays opened within a few days of each other in 1924: *Nerves, Havoc,* and *What Price Glory?* Without any advance publicity, *What Price Glory?*, by Maxwell Anderson and Laurence Stallings, amazed its first-night audience with its blunt honesty, its raucous language, and its unprecedented lack of respect. There was talk of federal action to stop the play. A report was drawn up charging that subordinates were shown to have no respect for their superior officers, the public was permitted to believe that personnel of the U.S. Marine Corps were subject to debauchery at all times, and that there was a lack of discipline, which could only bring discredit upon the Army and Marine Corps.[1]

Producer Arthur Hopkins toned down some of the wilder profanities, but the play passed from mere success into Broadway legend.

Originally entitled *None but the Brave* (*A Comedy with a Few Deaths*), the play has acquired the reputation of being strongly pacifist, in contrast to the film version. Although the authors registered their protest against the ceaseless waste of young lives, their main fascination was in the two belligerents, Captain Flagg (Louis Wolheim) and Sergeant Quirt (William "Stage" Boyd), whose fight against the Germans was incidental to their desire to massacre each other. The two characters appealed so strongly to audiences that they inspired nostalgia for service life, and presented an irresistible picture to those who had never known it.

Laurence Stallings was signed by MGM. Fox bought his and Anderson's play once it became obvious, from the acclaim given *The Big Parade,* that war films would be commercial again. Louis Wolheim was set to play the same role, and Raoul Walsh was signed to direct.

Victor McLaglen was determined to have the part of Captain Flagg. A huge man, physically perfect for the role, McLaglen was half-Irish, half-Scots, and the son of a bishop. He ran away at fourteen to join the army, wandered the world, became a boxer, and took part in the gold rush at Kalgoorlie, Australia. During the war, he served in the Mesopotamian Campaign, and became provost marshal of Baghdad. J. Stuart Blackton gave him the lead in his British color production of *The Glorious Adventure,* then brought him to America to star in *The Beloved Brute.*

According to McLaglen, he was rejected for *What Price Glory?* because Walsh felt he could not possibly portray the prototype of the American marine. "I told him there were no soldiers in the world tougher than the men in my own old Middlesex Regiment." Borrowing a set for a Buck Jones picture, McLaglen per-

Recruiting in Trafalgar Square—a picture taken in 1914. The original caption, as printed in a number of newspapers, reads: "From among a large crowd listening to Lieut. McLaglen, the well-known boxer, come first an Indian British subject from Calcutta and then a Dutchman, both anxious to join the British Army."

From What Price Glory? *One man died during the shooting of this battle.*

suaded a British producer, George Ridgewell, to act as bartender, and he launched into a violent scene, snarling and blaspheming his way through the lines, thoroughly convincing Walsh.[2]

McLaglen's thirst for military life was unquenchable: in later years he formed a private army in Hollywood known as McLaglen's Light Horse.

Opposite him, as Sergeant Quirt, was the veteran film actor Edmund Lowe. The picture was shot at Westwood, at Fox Hills, where *Havoc*'s trenches had been dug.

Margaret Chute reported on the battle scenes for *Pictures and Picturegoer* in England: "When the explosion scenes were filmed, most of the residents near the Fox Hills Ranch got very little sleep for the best part of a week. I heard the steady bombardment in Hollywood, and was reminded of London air-raid days.

"Then I was taken to see some of the night trench scenes and at close quarters found the explosions terribly realistic. Nobody was allowed to stand in the open when the various mines went up. Cameras were under cover and we were told to stand behind a row of trucks and under big umbrellas which would catch the lumps of falling earth. Down in a hollow, in mud-filled trenches, hundreds of men crawled, and lay still, and crawled again.

"On the edge of the crater, Raoul Walsh, the director, shouted instructions to Edmund Lowe as he lay on his face in a shell hole. 'He's been down there for three hours, poor devil,' said Victor McLaglen and Leslie Fenton, grinning, as they consumed hot coffee and sandwiches at a friendly coffee stall that was travelling around the set. . . .

"Away to our left, five or six men edged their way along the hillside, stopping every few feet; they were laying the powder for the mines that were to be exploded in a few minutes. Everything was ready. A dresser rushed at Edmund Lowe, squirted some oil on his face, smeared some mud on the oil, and retired hurriedly. Raoul Walsh stopped joking; his 'army' stopped laughing at his witty remarks, made to ease the time of waiting.

"There was half a minute of silence, then one deafening explosion after another, earth flying in chunks, figures rushing for shelter. As we made a bee-line for a big umbrella, some other people dashed in the same direction. We ran a dead heat, and as we clung together, I heard a very English voice exclaim, 'My goodness! I *know* we'll all be killed!' I turned around and there stood Beatrice Lillie and Gertrude Lawrence—the stars of *Charlot's Revue*!"[3]

Raoul Walsh remembered the protests from the residents of nearby Beverly Hills during the shooting of the night scenes. "We had to get a different assistant director every night. The explosions broke windows in bungalows, and the sheriff would drive up and say, 'Who's in charge here?' And the assistant would say, 'I am.' They'd put him in the car and take him away, and I'd start again."[4]

The battles were every bit as dangerous as the visitors imagined, and one man was killed during the shooting.

Walsh was backed up by talented and experienced men. The art director was William Darling; the chief cameraman, Barney McGill; the second, Jack Marta. Daniel Keefe, first assistant director, was a U.S. Army veteran. Charles Griffen, technical adviser, saw active service on the French and Italian fronts. Salvatore A. Capodice, technical observer, served with the marines at Belleau Wood, alongside

Raoul Walsh, in sweater and plus fours, with veterans of Belleau Wood appearing in What Price Glory?

Stallings.[5] Production manager James Tinling served in the 63rd Artillery. All the extras, without exception, were veterans—eighteen had fought in Belleau Wood.

Revivals of the picture suffer from the legions of imitations that followed it.* Not that the picture, in the cinematic sense, has anything original about it. Apart from the language, intelligible only to lip readers, the element that sent the audience's temperature soaring was the utterly unabashed sexual content of the love scenes. Raoul Walsh was wickedly skillful in exposing more stretches of the female thigh than the Hays Office normally allowed, but present-day audiences are naturally blind to such subtleties. They do not react to Sergeant Quirt returning a hairpin to Charmaine the morning after—the kind of detail then regarded as revolutionary.

The raw comedy, another trademark of Walsh pictures, now seems dated and clumsy, whereas at the time it seemed a breath of fresh air after the awe that surrounded most scenes of military life. Not that it won universal approval.

"Remember the scene where the boys have the fight in Phyllis Haver's room?" said Raoul Walsh. "And a monkey jumped in the chamber pot? And he'd come up every now and then to look at the fight, and the fight would get rough and he'd duck? When Jack Ford saw the picture, he said, 'Well, when I have to resort to monkeys jumping into pisspots to get a laugh, I'm getting out of the business.' "[6]

The pacifist sentiments strike such an incongruous note that their message is totally lost. Two titles spoken by McLaglen sum up the schizophrenic nature of the film. Following the exciting night battle, McLaglen addresses his troops: "They

---

* The film itself had the sequels *This Cockeyed World* and *Women of All Nations,* and a John Ford remake. Ford shot one of the scenes in the original *What Price Glory?* of the troops moving up to the front just as he shot the taxis of the Marne sequence for *Seventh Heaven* (Lefty Hough).

sent me babies to baptize in blood. You've gone through it"—and McLaglen smiles his approval—"and as one soldier to another, I'm as proud of you as America should be."

The final shot shows Flagg and the wounded Quirt in close-up, marching to battle again with an eager comradeship. Quirt claps on a steel helmet and grabs a rifle with its bayonet ready fixed. That gesture, and the power of emotion behind the shot, sinks all the pacifism in the picture.

Raoul Walsh, allegedly a former cowboy, Mexico veteran, and director of *The Prussian Cur,* was not a pacifist. "They liked me in Washington," he said. "*What Price Glory?* promoted more enlistments in the Marine Corps than any picture that was ever made. See, in the picture they lived such a good life—happy-go-lucky guys with gals and this and that. People in the audience saw that and said, 'Hell, I'm going into the Marines. This is the life of Riley.' Time and again I would meet some officer who would say, 'You bastard. You got me into this thing.' "[7]

THE ELITE GUARD

To Hollywood were drawn former officers of former armies. Highest in rank was Archduke Leopold of Austria, grand-nephew of Emperor Franz Josef, and a cousin of the last Emperor of Austria, Karl I. Having fought on the Italian front, twice wounded and much decorated, he returned to Vienna to discover the Hapsburgs in almost as pitiful a state as the rest of the population, suffering from lack of food. After the war Leopold refused to renounce his title, and with his cousin, ex-Emperor Karl, tried to restore the monarchy in Hungary. In 1927 he came to America to auction some of the Hapsburg treasures; the sale was unsuccessful. While in New Orleans, he received a cable from Ben Westland, publicity manager for Erich von Stroheim, asking if he would inspect von Stroheim's new film, *The Wedding March,* in which many of his relatives were represented.

"I knew that Stroheim was anxious to get a favorable judgment from a member of the Imperial House. I decided, therefore, to visit the studio unannounced, in order to get an unbiased impression.

"My secretary found Stroheim in the midst of the work of cutting *The Wedding March.* It was a very hot day and the director was working without collar or coat, drinking ice water and, I might as well say, perspiring fiercely. The interruption did not seem to please him at all. He only growled 'What do you want?'

" 'I am Neuhardt, Secretary of His Imperial Highness, the Archduke Leopold. His Imperial Highness will be here immediately.'

"When my secretary introduced me to Stroheim, he was still speechless and it took me a half hour to pacify him so that he could show me *The Wedding March.*"[1]

The archduke was in dire financial straits, and he became an extra out of necessity. Too late, alas, for *The Wedding March,* his most substantial role was as a German officer in John Ford's *Four Sons.* (Ford paid his passage home.) While his aristocratic connections enabled him to eat—at Elinor Glyn's, Carl Laemmle's,

Von Stroheim's Elite Guard on the set of The Wedding March (1928). *Left to right. Ferdinand Schumann-Heink, Captain Peters, Carl von Hartman, Wilhelm von Brincken, Heinrich Reinhardt, Carey Harrison; von Stroheim.*

Pickfair—he was not exactly inundated with work. In six months he worked five weeks. "I have blue blood," he said. "Unfortunately, it doesn't photograph."

Among his fellow extras, the archduke encountered "The Former Officer"—as dispossessed as himself, but living on memories. "He still has his old military bearing," said the archduke. "He still salutes on every possible—or impossible—occasion. He speaks curtly, like a man issuing a command. In conversation, he stands at attention. Of course, he likes best to play in war pictures. Give him a small formation of Hollywood soldiers to command, and he is happy. He has one talent that is distinctly his own. When you talk to him, he has the remarkable ability of turning any conversation to the Great War in the shortest possible time.

"My presence in Hollywood gave new fire to the old feeling. Austrian and German officers questioned me with the speed of a machine gun about the possibilities of reconstructing the old monarchies. At a farewell dinner given to me, one of the Prussian officers made a short but pointed speech: 'Imperial Highness! If Your Highness goes back to Europe and starts a revolution, Your Highness can count on us. Just send us a postal card. We will join you soon!' "[2]

From the former comrades of these men, in Austria and Germany, vast quan-

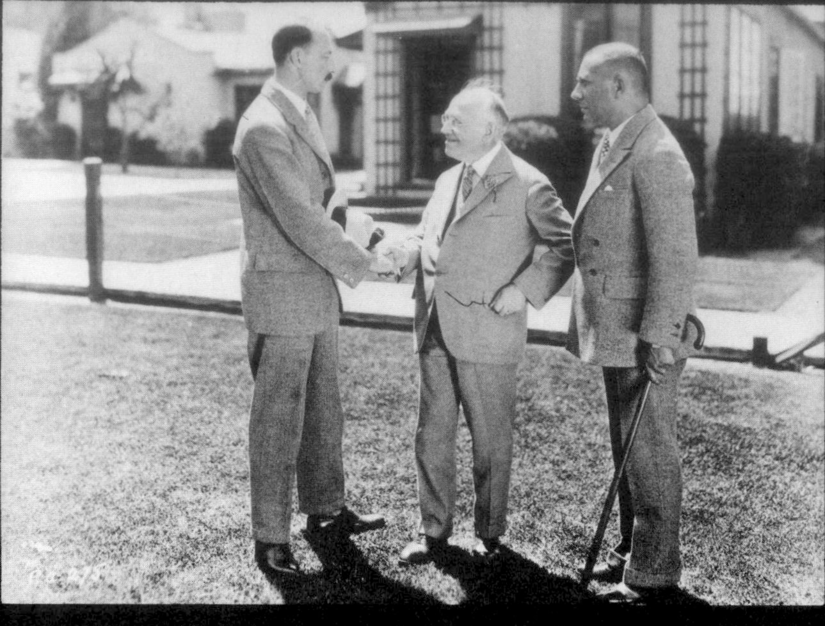

Archduke Leopold of Austria meets Carl Laemmle. Erich von Stroheim (then no longer working for Laemmle, but for his former rival Pat Powers) stands stiffly by. Such ceremonies belied the fact that Archduke Leopold was broke, and only too glad of the occasional bit part in pictures. His passage home was paid by John Ford.

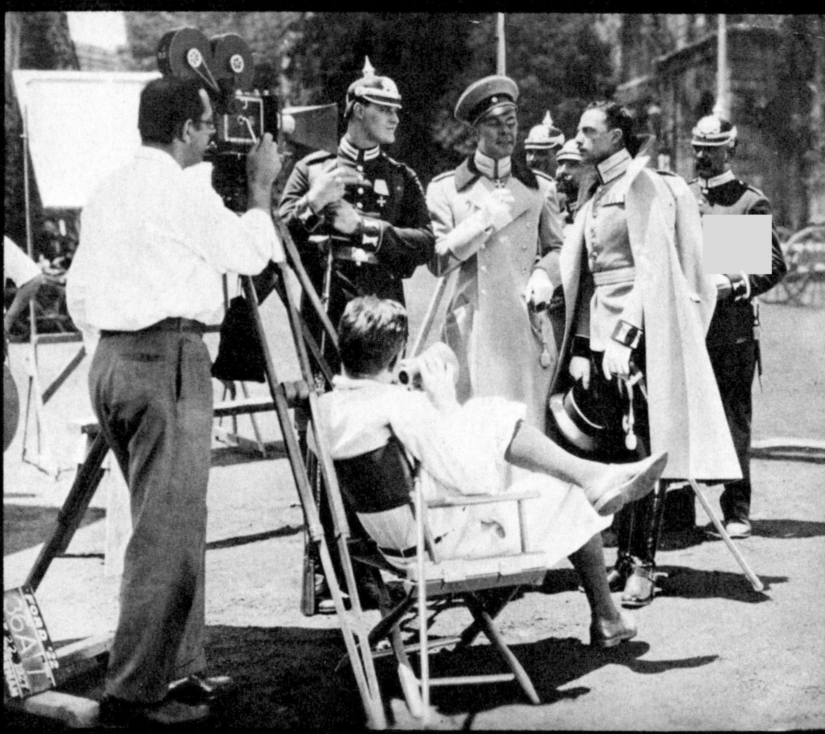

Archduke Leopold of Austria (without cap, right) as an extra in John Ford's Four Sons (1928), *with Francis X. Bushman, Jr., and Earle Foxe, founder of the Black-Foxe Military School. George Schneiderman at Mitchell camera. With the addition of a toupee, a uniform, and a row of medals, the archduke regains his former glamour.*

King Vidor's His Hour *(1924) was a Russian romance written by Elinor Glyn. To ensure the correct atmosphere, a Russian officer, second from left, acted as technical adviser and played in the picture. Allegedly an archduke, he disguised himself under the name of "Mike Mitchell." Vidor (left), Glyn, Aileen Pringle, and John Gilbert.*

The bordello scene from von Stroheim's The Merry Widow *(1925): members of the Elite Guard were expected to be past masters at this sort of thing. (John Gilbert's portrayal of Prince Danilo of Monteblanco was supposed to be sympathetic, but after the picture's release Prince Danilo of Montenegro not surprisingly won substantial damages from a French court.)*

tities of uniforms and insignia were purchased for use in Hollywood. The head of Western Costumes, Ned Lambert, requested assistance from his Austrian representative, Arthur Hansa, who obtained basket-loads of tunics, greatcoats, helmets, hats, and swords. The most elaborate cost about a dollar. These uniforms appeared in the von Stroheim films and many other Hollywood pictures. (After fifty years the company cleared out its stock and sold the gaudiest of the uniforms to Midwestern colleges for use by bands.)[3]

Before the wave of war films, the convulsions of European politics had deposited a strange band of refugees in Hollywood. "Between 1919 and 1923, perhaps twenty or more former Russian officers landed in Hollywood," said Robert Florey.[4] "They all said they were Generals. I never met a Captain or a Corporal." One of these, General Lodijenski, had led a motion picture squad on the Eastern Front, or so he told *Motion Picture Magazine*.[5] Florey, who knew him well, says that he was a "high ranking officer" in the Gendarmerie, not the army, and would therefore not have been at the front. "Almost as soon as he arrived in Hollywood, he opened the Double Eagle restaurant on Sunset, which was for a while successful until someone planted a bomb in the establishment."

Erich von Stroheim formed an Elite Guard of former officers: Ferdinand Schumann-Heink, the son of the opera singer,* who was born in Germany, but was a graduate of Fordham; Carl von Hartman, from Finland; Captain Peters of the U.S. Army; Marco Elter, a former Italian captain, who went on to direct some films in Italy and was shot by the Germans in World War II; Heinrich Reinhardt, who also became a director; and Wilhelm von Brincken, former captain of the Life Hussars of the King of Saxony and later military attaché at the German Embassy in Washington. He was technical adviser on *Flesh and the Devil,* and played Walter Byron's aide in von Stroheim's *Queen Kelly*.

"I was an assistant at the time," said Robert Florey, "and I kept the Elite busier than Stroheim did. I was with King Vidor on *Bardelys the Magnificent,* and we used the Elite for six or seven weeks, adding to their number, as a fencer and rider, young John Farrow, whom I had found at the gate wanting a job."

A close friend of von Stroheim's was Albert Conti, whose real name was Albert de Conti Cedassamare. He was born in Trieste in 1887 and spoke German and Italian. A professional soldier in the Austrian Army from 1906, he became a second lieutenant in 1914. By the end of the war he was a captain. Emigrating to America, he worked his way through the South as a laborer, and ended up at the California oil fields. He answered an advertisement, placed by von Stroheim, for an Austrian officer to act as technical research director, and was given the job. He played in *Merry-Go-Round, The Merry Widow,* and Clarence Brown's *The Eagle.* Until his retirement in 1962, he worked in the wardrobe department at MGM. He died in January 1967.

Some of these veterans proved to be liabilities. Curt Rehfeld, the German officer considered so resourceful on the Rex Ingram pictures, was less than helpful on Alfred Santell's *The Patent Leather Kid* (1927). Rehfeld's first directorial job, *The Greater Glory,* had flopped and he was back as assistant director. In status-

---

* Mme Schumann-Heink had sons in both the U.S. Army and the German Army (George J. Mitchell).

The uniform mystique affected the directors, who were always inclined to dress up. Al Santell, in his specially designed blue uniform, stands at extreme right; next to him is Richard Barthelmess, star of Patent Leather Kid. *His battle scenes were staged by the army under the stern eye of General Alexander (third from right), who had fought the original battle in France. Also in the group, Major John McDonnell, extreme left, and Will Rogers, third from left. Camp Lewis, Washington, 1927.*

conscious Hollywood, this was the equivalent of being stripped of one's rank, and Rehfeld was deeply humiliated. Alfred Santell wrote: "He was engaged by us as both technical adviser and first assistant. He had had one leg shot off, by our side, in the real war.* He was lucky to live to the day I sacked him. He had an insane hatred of American soldiers. The Army authorities refused to allow their men to wear German uniform, and the German soldiers were played by young ROTC (officer cadets) from nearby universities, but they were still American soldiers to Rehfeld. He took idiotic delight in moving up the early morning calls by two or even three hours. The poor lads playing soldiers were called upon to march all the way to our locations, some of them an hour's jaunt, only to sit on their butts and wait until the crew and I arrived. Naturally, the lads griped, sometimes taking their good time to do anything and ofttimes doing it badly . . . deliberately. Having been in the service myself, I smelled a skunk. I began consorting with the boys, and soon was told of the trouble. It had come to the point where they were talking about loading some rifles with real bullets and 'shooting off Rehfeld's good leg.' I knew the time to send him back to the studio had come."[6]

When Robert Florey directed a remake of *Hotel Imperial* in 1939, there were virtually none of these veterans left, except for two or three very old Russian generals. "One of the Russians died (of old age) during the shooting of a night battle, and his family wanted to sue me and Paramount!"

---

* Rehfeld actually lost the leg in a streetcar accident in Venice, California.

Dynamic action was the outstanding feature of Wings.

French air ace Charles Nungesser (left) with Jacqueline Logan (center) and Walter Miller in The Sky Raider *(1925), directed by T. Hayes Hunter. Nungesser played himself in the picture, although the story was fictitious.*

WINGS

The aviators constituted the most colorful group of veterans. The postwar slump forced many of them back to flying in the hope of making a living. Provided they could raise from $300 to $600, they could purchase a war-surplus plane, boxed-up and brand-new.

Congress had made a huge appropriation in 1917 for aircraft production. Yet a Universal industrial film of 1918, *The Yanks Are Coming,* shot at the Dayton-Wright Factory, which shouted the praises of the aircraft industry, was suppressed by George Creel. Charges of "aircraft lies," hurled at the CPI turned out to be all too true. The House Report of the 66th Congress stated that although more than $1 billion had been spent on combat planes, not a single aircraft reached the battle zone. With the lifting of the wartime ban on civilian flying, former military pilots applied to purchase the surplus aircraft. Enormous quantities were available—but they were mostly trainers. The combat aircraft were scrapped to keep them off the market.

The pilots, known as barnstormers, earned their living doing stunts at county fairs and taking passengers at a dollar a minute. To attract customers to the airfield they staged stunts. The movie studios hired the more skillful for serials and melodramas. Captain Nungesser, the French ace, who had shot down a reported one hundred and five German planes, was signed by the Arcadia Pictures Company of Philadelphia. T. Hayes Hunter directed him in *The Sky Raider* (1925). Nungesser was lost in an attempted trans-Atlantic flight in 1927. Thomas Ince encouraged civil aviation with a $50,000 prize for the first flight across the Pacific. But the most encouraging news of all was the announcement in 1926 of Paramount's massive epic of war in the air, *Wings*.

Irvin Willat's *Zeppelin's Last Raid* (1917) was one of the few pictures about wartime aviation, and most of the exteriors were achieved with miniatures. In 1918 *The Romance of the Air* featured Lieutenant Bert Hall, one of the only two surviving Americans of the original Lafayette Escadrille.* The other, Major William Thaw, declined to appear in the film, and his part was played by Herbert Standing. Adapted by Franklin B. Coates from Bert Hall's novel *En l'Air,* it was directed by Harry Revier and received government cooperation in the form of combat planes, observation balloons, and hydroplanes. This material was intercut with footage filmed by Lieutenant Hall's observer, including the destruction of a German biplane and the blowing up of an observation balloon. *Moving Picture World* considered the film little more than a publicity vehicle for Hall: "Lieutenant Hall rings true, but his story does not."[1]

Wings was the brainchild of John Monk Saunders, who had been a combat pilot at nineteen. Paramount was anxious for a war epic of its own, and, in February 1926, Jesse Lasky met Saunders in a New York hotel. Lasky was infected by Saunders's enthusiasm. "Go to Washington," he said. "Talk to the government. If they will help us with the picture, we will make it."[2]

---

* Film actor and director S. Rankin Drew, son of Mr. and Mrs. Sidney Drew, was killed in the Escadrille.

Official approval was eventually granted, subject to several conditions: Paramount must pay for all damage done in making the picture, must carry $10,000 insurance for each man who worked on it, must agree not to release it until it had been approved by the War Department, and must keep the fact of the government's cooperation out of the papers as long as possible, so that foreign countries would not think it was being made to intimidate them. Furthermore, the film was to be made in such a manner that it was training for those concerned.

Paramount agreed; the story was handed over to scenario writers Louis D. Lighton and Hope Loring. It became a West Coast production, which meant that B. P. Schulberg was in charge. When Schulberg had joined Paramount, he brought with him Clara Bow. She was given a leading role, along with former aviator Richard Arlen, Charles "Buddy" Rogers, and Jobyna Ralston. A small part was assigned to a young man from a Montana ranch, Gary Cooper. In giving the direction to William Wellman, Schulberg was taking a risk. But although relatively new to direction, Wellman had made a commercial and critical success, *You Never Know Women.* And he had one advantage over the other available directors—he had been an aviator in the war.* Wellman, before he took on this monumental task, watched *The Big Parade* again and again, just as Howard Hughes, before he made *Hell's Angels,* the subsequent aviation epic, ran *Wings* ceaselessly.†

Harry Perry, who had made several pictures for Schulberg in his independent days and had worked on *The Vanishing American* with the supervisor of *Wings,* Lucien Hubbard, took control of the cinematography. He was given several weeks to make tests. The usual method for shooting aerial scenes was to establish the planes in the air, then cut to close-ups shot on the ground, against the sky. But Wellman stipulated there was to be no faking; close-ups of pilots in the air had to be shot in the air. Assisting Perry on the tests were Captain (later General) Bill Taylor and Lieutenant Commander Harry Reynolds. They acquired a gun-ring, a scarf mount for a machine gun, and secured it to the cockpit of the camera plane. A camera mount was made, giving the operator complete freedom. The problem of filming the actors was more difficult.

"We had cameras shooting both forward and backward," said Lucien Hubbard. "There were many scenes where we shot over Arlen's head, as he dived to earth. You put that much weight in an unaccustomed place, and you're courting a crash. You're doing something that has never been accomplished before, and to do it so you don't crash and still get your picture, is really amazing."[3]

The cameras were attached to the aircraft on mounts made in the shape of a saddle, secured with two straps around the body of the plane, and situated in the rear cockpit. This mount was used mostly for motor-driven cameras, shooting forward over the head of the real pilot, showing the actor apparently in a single-seater.

One trick aroused widespread comment, and for a while Paramount refused to admit how it was done (the front office probably didn't know). Frank Clarke,

---

* In the Lafayette Flying Corps. See Kevin Brownlow, *The Parade's Gone By . . .* (New York: Knopf, 1968), p. 169, for Wellman's account.

† King Vidor says Wellman gave him one of the ideas for *Big Parade*—the episode where a German plane flies down over a column of troops and its wheels skim the helmets. Wellman himself had done this stunt during the war.

LEFT: *William Wellman playing a dying soldier in his production of* Wings. *Wellman, a former flier in the Lafayette Flying Corps, gave himself the ironic title: "Attaboy! Them buzzards are some good, after all."*
RIGHT: *William Wellman, right, and Richard Arlen, also a veteran flier (of the Canadian RFC).*

playing a German, was instructed to go up to six thousand feet, then come swirling down, his plane on fire and out of control. This was not so hard to do in a long shot. What astounded audiences—and technicians—was the fact that the camera stayed on him in close-up, the clouds wheeling round behind him. Clarke was equipped with a button-operating Mitchell camera, run by motor, using three 45-volt dry-cell batteries. He reached the required height, switched on the camera, jerked as though hit by a bullet, opened his mouth to release a gush of theatrical blood, released a gate in a box containing lampblack, let go of the stick, and kicked the plane into a tailspin with his foot.

Aviators acknowledged this to be one of the toughest stunts on record—to sit limp and useless while your plane does the one thing you have been trained to avoid.

For scenes involving actors who could not fly, a large headrest obscured the pilot in the rear cockpit. This automation meant that the exposure had to be adjusted on the ground, the result of guesswork and experience with previous attempts. Filters were dispensed with so lenses could work at the smallest aperture, thus carrying background focus. Harry Perry remembered that after two successive takes of a staff car being attacked, a scene involving hundreds of troops, a fly was found splashed across the center of the lens.

Perry was in command of an army of cameramen. One of the most important of these was Akeley specialist E. Burton Steene, former newsreel man who had served in Mexico, and in 1921 filmed the aerial scenes for a German picture about that country's wartime air supremacy. Steene had been flying since 1912 but regarded *Wings* as the greatest thrill of his life.

In addition to the Akeley, Steene had three Eyemos. Harry Perry, Faxon Dean, and Paul Perry filmed from another group of planes at 1200 feet. The pilot, Captain Stribling, used a thin rope to signal to Steene when to start cranking. A dud was dropped to get the range. Then came two tugs on the rope.

"It was a wonderful sight to see these death-dealing messengers speeding down—the terrible explosions took place right on schedule, due to the unerring eye and hand of Captain Stribling. For several seconds the ship shook and trembled with each explosion until I thought it might be out of control. The sensation of being rocked and thrown about in a giant bomber a scant 600 feet above the ground while dropping 1200 pounds of TNT is a thrill not often given to a man. In my cramped quarters it would have been very difficult if not impossible to get away with my parachute, but my confidence in the pilot kept me in repose."[4]

"There was a fatal accident," said Lucien Hubbard. "Some planes came over a hill and dove on the troops. Wellman and I were watching from a platform down below it. Suddenly he turned away and said, 'Oh, my God, no!' And I wondered what was the matter. He had seen a plane come down at such an angle it couldn't possibly go up again, and it crashed right behind us over the ridge. The boy was killed. We went back in our car and just at sunset we heard Taps—and we never forgot it. We thought they would stop the picture, but the operations officer at Kelly Field said, 'What's the matter? What are you so glum about? We don't think anything of it. Guys are always killed in training. It was his own fault. We told him to come in at a certain angle, he came in too short. These things happen. It'll never be heard of.' It never was."[5]

The cooperation of the U.S. government tied up thousands of soldiers, virtually all the pursuit planes the air force had, billions of dollars' worth of equipment—and some of the finest military pilots in the country. Several of those who flew for *Wings* became generals in World War II: Hoyt Vanderberg, Frank Andrews, Hal George, Earl E. Partridge, Clarence Irvine, Rod Rogers, Bill Taylor. The company had the use of the Air Service Ground School at Brooks Field and the advanced flying school at Kelly Field, both near San Antonio, and fliers came from as far away as San Francisco and Virginia.

The U.S. Army's 2nd Division, which had taken part in *The Big Parade,* was used for the big drive at St. Mihiel. This division was the same one that had participated in the original drive. The spot chosen for the location outside San Antonio was a section of ground about a mile long. The grass was so tall that Wellman climbed onto the shoulders of one of the crew to look out across the top of it. In a short time, the place was bombarded by field guns with live rounds—giving the gunners some useful practice—and a huge number of Mexican laborers dug trenches to strict military specifications. The effect was so alarmingly evocative that Wellman, flying over it for the first time, felt a wave of sickness and muttered, "God—I'm back in France."

The location was selected with aerial photography in mind, but when Perry made some tests, he found that at normal flying speed, the plane swooped over it too fast to capture detail. So a hundred-foot tower was erected, with platforms every twenty feet. It was from this huge tower that the main battery of cameras photographed the drive—although Wellman positioned hand-held Eyemos in other strategic positions.

In Washington, angry speeches were made about the frivolous squandering of military resources. The army, which had initially welcomed this chance of recreating warfare, grew sulky as scenes were shot over and over again. Troops grumbled that the aviators were stealing the picture.

The major battle was planned as carefully as a regular military operation; it was realized that with the intensity of explosions, men's lives were actually at stake. After the day's shooting, generals, officers, and engineers held a confer-

The hundred-foot camera tower built for the battle scenes of Wings (1927) *at San Antonio, Texas.*

John Monk Saunders, veteran flier and author of Wings, *overlooks the battlefield specially prepared by the army with an artillery barrage; this photograph was taken from the camera tower.*

ence with Wellman and Hubbard, and with blueprints and field maps, they planned the following day, making out a complete battle order for defense, attack, hour of advance, distance, troops, and equipment. This order went to under-officers, who relayed it to squad leaders. These appointed the "killed" and directed the survivors.

"When the director was not working on the picture," said *Motion Picture Magazine,* "he and the producer were settling the difficulties that arose because of army politics, smoothing over jealousies between different branches of the service, pacifying the impatient troops with barrels of beer and motion picture entertainments, giving the aviators dinners and dances and conciliating fuming officers with a diplomacy that would have avoided the World War. The Government cannot be hired, but at the close of the picture, Wellman handed over fifty thousand dollars as a gift to the mess funds."[6]

At the preview in San Antonio, *Wings* ran fourteen reels. The town went wild over it. Nevertheless, Paramount withdrew it, cut it to 12,267 feet, and premiered it in New York on 12 August 1927 with the additional attraction of Magnascope—a process in which the big scenes were projected onto a greatly enlarged screen. Some authorities declare a General Electric sound-effects track was heard at the premiere, but this seems to have been added the following year—effects machines duplicated the sound of machine guns and airplane motors until the actual sound-effects track was available.

Reviewers, whatever they thought of the rest of the story, were astounded by the aerial and action sequences. Technical faults were few, and the picture was regarded as generally satisfactory even to the aviator; the main criticism was that the Gotha bomber, in actuality a Martin MB4, flew in at a suicidal height—but otherwise it could not have been shown in conjunction with the village.

Moving Picture World interviewed veteran fliers, and invited them to submit a list of errors. Donald Hudson (DSC, Croix de Guerre, 27th Aero Squadron, 1st Pursuit Group, AEF) found a few faults, but declared that the action was so convincing that faults did not destroy the illusion of actual combat. "This was clearly demonstrated when the man sitting next to me, who saw several months of service at the front as a pilot, audibly called out 'maneuver' as the pilot on the screen failed to do so when attacked. The crashes are apparently real crashes, and it makes your blood run cold to see them."

Charles Porter (DSC, with Oak Leaf Cluster, Croix de Guerre, 147th Aero Squadron, 1st Pursuit Group, AEF) had been frankly skeptical about any moving pictures of aerial combat. "I had seen the official pictures of the Air Service taken in France by the U.S. Signal Corps. These pictures were not only uninteresting, but also unsatisfactory despite the best efforts of experienced photographers. After viewing *Wings,* however, I know that no one need miss seeing the actual manner in which our Air Force conducted its warfare in France."

Porter considered that the detail was so accurate that only someone familiar with the aerodromes in the zone of advance could find the slightest flaw. He pointed out that when a plane was shot down, it seldom burst into flames. He felt that Arlen, when attacked by Rogers, should have taken evasive action; "he could easily have spun or side-slipped to the ground and escaped with a forced landing." All the fliers objected to the ending of the picture, which they found "weak and improbable."[7]

Wings gets better the older it becomes. Values that once seemed overly sentimental now seem so much a part of their time that they no longer irritate. For most of its length, *Wings* avoids the grimness of war and captures exactly the fierce romanticism that so many veterans feel for it. But at the end Buddy Rogers shoots down his friend (Richard Arlen), escaping from the German lines in a German plane. Buddy Rogers lands in front of a war cemetery and steps out of his plane, in front of thousands of white crosses.

Otherwise, it is "the road to glory" and "the bravest of the brave" that figure in the titles, and the boys' initial hatred for each other is dispelled by a boxing match in which David is beaten to a pulp but refuses to admit defeat.

Wellman hurls his camera around the vast battlefield with exhilarating abandon. Even by today's standards, his setups seem remarkably bold. Although the troops die with rather operatic gestures, his epic handling of the big drive is overwhelming, and the superimposition of thousands of men marching into a horizon where their destruction is pictured in split screen, is a moment worthy of Abel Gance's classic *J'accuse.*

The film is dedicated to Charles Lindbergh, and the dedicatory title was adapted from one of his speeches: "To those young warriors of the sky, whose wings are forever folded about them, this picture is reverently dedicated."

BARBED WIRE

Metro-Goldwyn-Mayer, approaching the War Department for cooperation in the making of *War Birds* (to be directed by Clarence Brown), another tribute to American military fliers, received a flat rejection. They were told unofficially that a good, brisk war would be preferable to another movie.[1] *War Birds* was canceled. Another casualty was *The Big Gun,* an epic of the navy, which Irvin Willat was to have made.

Wellman used some of the combat scenes cut from *Wings* in his next picture, *Legion of the Condemned,* about the men of the Lafayette Escadrille. Count Jean de Limur, an Escadrille pilot who became a director himself, wrote the script. *Photoplay*[2] thought that, emotionally, it was above *Wings,* but we shall never know for sure. Paramount allowed the picture to decompose.

Another Paramount war film, *Barbed Wire,* was rescued from destruction by George Eastman House. This 1927 film was adapted from Sir Hall Caine's novel *The Woman of Knockaloe.* Caine was a pacifist who nonetheless supported the Allied cause; he wrote the book, not for publication, but to relieve his feelings, for it was highly controversial. It told the story of a girl on the Isle of Man who shares the conventional attitude toward Germans until Knockaloe Aliens' Camp is built on her farm. She falls in love with a German civilian prisoner. The two encounter such hatred that they are driven to commit suicide together. The book also depicted the tragedy of civilians who had lived perhaps fifty years in England, but who happened to have been born in Germany, and were brought over as infants; at the armistice, they were forcibly repatriated to a country they did not know, whose language they did not speak. An influential friend of Hall Caine

Clive Brook (who had been a British officer) in Rowland V. Lee's Barbed Wire *(1927). Surrounding him are the superbly chosen faces of German and Austrian veterans.*

read the manuscript and urged its immediate publication; it came out in 1923.

The adaptation by Jules Furthman set the action in France, around a conventional prisoner-of-war camp. The tragic ending was excised, and the new setting eliminated all the episodes detrimental to British policy. Nevertheless, the film was highly effective. Rowland V. Lee directed it, Pola Negri played the lead, and Clive Brook, who had seen the war as a British officer, was cast successfully against type as the German soldier. A story at the time related how Brook put on enemy uniform, went behind the set, and threw up. He described that to me as nonsense. He did not remember being highly criticized for playing a German, which he had already done in *Three Faces East* (1926), and, what was even worse, for making him sympathetic.

The general mood had changed, however. The commercial impact of *Variety* and other successful German imports led to each studio constructing its own German street on the back lot. John Gilbert's biggest hit after *The Big Parade* was a film in which he played a German soldier—pre–World War, it is true, but an officer and a Junker: *Flesh and the Devil.* Such films were regarded as peacetime diplomats, soothing the wounds caused by the Hun frightfulness pictures and insinuating themselves onto the commercial routes which favored UFA.

For this story of the degrading effect of blind hatred, an international flavor pervaded the studio, which Rowland Lee found exhilarating. "Directors, actors, writers, technicians, from both large and small countries, held important creative positions, exchanged ideas and worked side by side in an effort to improve the quality of the cinema. If our real League of Nations could harmoniously work together as these people did, there would be peace in the world."[3] The same international complexities worked themselves out in the cast: a Pole and a Swede played French parts, a German played a Frenchman, and a Briton played a German.

The German Hans Dreier was the art director; he built a farmhouse and prison camp at the Lasky ranch which were so accurate that it is impossible to believe the film was shot in California. A friend of Pola Negri, Baron von Katzian, was technical adviser, and since the star was inordinately temperamental, the German Erich Pommer was given the role of producer. His position was purely nominal, and he had virtually nothing to do with the picture, but since Pommer had been associated with Negri's earlier successes, Paramount considered his association a wise move. "Every time I ran into Pommer on the lot," said Lee, "he would say 'Excellent, excellent,' but I never saw him on the set." Pommer had already made his own Negri war picture, *Hotel Imperial,* directed by Stiller.

The Locarno Treaties of December 1925* had reassured the world that the Great War had in truth been the war to end wars. War nostalgia was an inevitable result, but the pacifist movement, determined to prevent any repetition of treaty-breaking, gathered momentum. *Barbed Wire* was, with Niblo's *The Enemy,* the first of the post-war pacifist films from America, and it was a minor masterpiece. The film is without villains, and, except for an over-symbolic and declamatory ending, without melodrama. Of course, it is a love story, and, for once, the film would be nothing without its love interest.

The whole tenor of the film is very much against war and against hatred between peoples, and the last speeches, by Pola's brother, returned from the front, are emotionally powerful. But the apocalyptic way the scene is presented is curiously theatrical, and out of key with the poignancy and subtlety of the rest of the picture: "I came home to my own people to find peace. Instead I find bitter hatred in your hearts—a hatred strong enough to start another war." As he talks, the dead—"Have you forgotten the dead?"—arise from the clouds, in the style of *J'accuse.*

Lee collaborated with Furthman on the script, and included incidents he remembered from conversations with German prisoners—many of whom he had captured himself. The final sequence sprang from an extraordinary moment Lee experienced just before a German attack at Consenvoye. "Company after company in more or less close formation was striding down the hill into the valley below us. The Boche had almost reached the bottom of the valley when we opened fire. I could see a number drop. But still they came—in their hundreds.

"I said to myself, 'This is it.' A strange calm came over me, blotting out any sense of fear in my mind and supplanting it with a feeling of exultation. Looking up at the sky I saw, or imagined I saw, thousands of soldiers. They seemed happy and stretched out their arms. Suddenly I heard the loud whirr of engines and over our heads came a squadron of American planes, which flew over the approaching Boches, dropping bomb after bomb. The surprise attack completely demoralized the Germans who broke ranks and ran for cover in the surrounding patches of woods."[4]

Not surprisingly, *Barbed Wire* opened to mixed reviews—the New York *Daily News* thought it had been directed with "restraint and artistry," while the New York *Daily Mirror* said, "it is so amateurishly moralistic that it perspires."[5]

Barbed Wire grew from communal experience and expressed an emotion shared by almost everyone concerned in its making. Basically, it was just a commercial star vehicle, but thanks to the sincerity and skill of its makers, it survives for posterity as a powerful statement on war by the very men who lived through it.

---

* Further antiwar treaties were signed at Paris by fifteen nations on 27 August 1928.

ALL QUIET

The apotheosis of the American war film was not a silent film (although a silent version was adapted for theaters not yet wired for sound) but one of the early talking pictures, *All Quiet on the Western Front.* Based on the book by Erich Maria Remarque, who had experienced most of the things he wrote about, it told the story entirely from the German side. Some of the dialogue is delivered with the awkward cadences of the early sound film, and for European ears, American accents don't go with German uniforms. But the film is a majestic achievement.

As a sound film, it is not strictly within the limits of this book. But no survey of war films could possibly be complete without referring to this extraordinary picture. Carl Laemmle, in the process of handing over his studio to Carl Laemmle, Jr., bought the novel at the instigation of Paul Fejos, who intended to direct it. Fejos was passionately interested in the documentary aspect of film-making and had made *Lonesome,* a study of ordinary people taking their leisure in New York, and *Broadway,* an early musical noteworthy mainly for its dazzling camera work, achieved with a huge crane especially built for the picture. Fejos, a Hungarian, quarreled with Laemmle when he discovered someone else had been offered *All Quiet.* Herbert Brenon, whose last big hit had been *Beau Geste* in 1926, was the front-office favorite for a while, but it was finally offered to Lewis Milestone, the former Signal Corps recruit, whose military comedy *Two Arabian Knights* was currently breaking records.* The original scenario was written by C. Gardner Sullivan, the author of *Civilization;* he became chief scenario supervisor, and the final credit was shared by Del Andrews (the first editor on *Civilization*), Maxwell Anderson, and George Abbott, the Broadway director. Dialogue director was George Cukor, the cameraman Arthur Edeson, who had had excellent training on *The Patent Leather Kid,* and the technical advisers were Hans von Morhart and Wilhelm von Brincken. Lewis Milestone, who was born in the Ukraine, went into pictures upon his discharge from the Signal Corps, and worked as an editor at the Thomas Ince studios.

Fascinated by the experiments of the Russian directors, Milestone brought to the battle scenes of *All Quiet* a flair for camera movement and swift cutting that put him at once on a plane with the finest practitioners of the art. He made creative use of Fejos's *Broadway* crane, which he sent hurtling across the battlefield with the speed and freedom of a bullet. Receiving no cooperation from the army, Universal hired soldiers from American Legion posts.

"I looked for a central theme for the battle," said Lewis Milestone.[1] "I wrestled a whole night trying to find something, and towards dawn I found it. In trench warfare, they used to send over wave upon wave. I thought that when the machine gun shoots, the men ought to drop with the same rapidity as the bullet leaves the gun. You have six, seven frames of the machine gun shooting, then immediately show the guys dropping, and they drop with the same impersonal, unemotional action as the machine gun spitting bullets. I thought that if I could keep that up, that would be something. And that became the central idea for the

---

* It won an Academy Award for its direction.

Lewis Milestone, left, who directed All Quiet on the Western Front (1930), *and former German officer Hans von Morhart, right, technical adviser, check John Wray's uniform.*

Several prominent people suggested that Carl Laemmle, left, as head of Universal, should receive a Nobel Peace Prize for All Quiet. *Here he poses with the man who wrote the book—Erich Maria Remarque, who had experienced much of the action at firsthand.*

Universal's camera crane, originally built for Paul Fejos's B[illegible]way (1929), on location at the Irvine ranch, near Santa Ana, California, for All Quiet. *Soundproof "barneys" cover the cameras. Arthur Edeson in cap.*

The magnificent re-creation of a German barracks square for All Quiet.

first battle. At the opening night, a couple of veterans who had been wounded at the front jumped out of their seats and said, 'Come on, let's get those guys'—and they charged at the screen. That's how close we came to the truth of the thing.

"I shot very little footage on the battles because the film was all figured out. Being an editor myself, I pre-edited the thing. My idea of drawing each setup was born on *All Quiet.* The front office was always sitting there waiting for me to say, 'Tomorrow I want 10,000 men.' I made the whole battle scene with 150 fellows, 75 Frenchmen and 75 Germans. Sometimes I only had half of them and they would exchange uniforms; 150—I never had more than that. That's what worried them to death—that I would blow the whole thing. One day when I said, 'Well, I'm finished, the war is over,' Junior Laemmle said, 'You haven't got anything. All I ever saw on the screen is guys running from right to left, and some are running from left to right. Where's the battle stuff?' I said, 'You've got to wait until the picture's cut.' He said, 'I'm not going to wait. I'd rather stop production now.' "

Milestone worked for twenty hours a day, sleeping in his car, which was chauffeur-driven between the Beverly Wilshire Hotel and the studio.

"I found a lot of things that I didn't even figure on, because film always has a habit of developing ideas of its own; no matter how closely you figure it out, you don't know all the stuff that's there.

"Anyway, a cut was finished. I remember it was three o'clock in the morning, and the only other guy alive around there in the cutting rooms was Paul Whiteman, the famous orchestra leader. He was cutting his picture *King of Jazz.* I said, 'I came in here, Paul, to ask if you would like to see, and be the first living thing to see, the battle of *All Quiet on the Western Front.*' He said, 'I'll be delighted.' It ran about 1,100 feet—no sound. And when the whole thing was finished, I said, 'Well, that's it.' He just went on sitting there, didn't say anything, didn't move. So I waited and finally said, 'Paul, are you still with us?' He said, 'Jesus Christ! I never saw anything like that. If the rest of the picture is anything like this, you've got the winner of all time.' "

But as the premiere date loomed closer, Milestone became desperate over the ending. "Remarque wrote the book in the first person singular. The central character was telling the story—like a camera which can see everything but itself. At the end of the book you suddenly came across a paragraph which said, 'He died on a day the official military report said: all quiet on the Western Front.' That is what we had to dramatize. We went wild and had all sorts of ideas. We thought of one idea—the armies of all nations marching towards a common grave. Well, it reads well, but you couldn't visualize it. I developed a blind spot and couldn't think of anything. I labored under the delusion that we had to stop the picture with a big crescendo finish. That was the blind spot. The guy who removed that blind spot from my eyes was Karl Freund—the cameraman who helped me by photographing the finish when my original cameraman had run out. I showed him the picture, and he came out very excited. He thought it was great.

" 'Now,' he said, 'what are we going to do about the ending?'

" 'Well,' I said, 'that's why I got you here. Let's meet tomorrow and start talking.'

"We went through a whole series of incidents. We had one finish, then another finish and a third finish. Nothing worked. Pretty soon the front office in-

Lewis Milestone's All Quiet on the Western Front: *so impeccably re-created that many scenes look like newsreels.*

sisted on getting the picture because they already had the theater booked and what not, and it had to go in for negative cutting. They threatened to take the print away. They said, 'You have one more chance, and that's it.'

"In the talks with Freund it became crystal clear, the mistake was that I tried to top the picture with a crescendo finish. We both realized that what the picture needed was a diminuendo. And that was the first step towards the true dramatization of the line: He died on a day . . . of all quiet on the Western Front.

"One day, I was coming back from Culver City with Karl. We had made one more attempt at an ending, and it was raining cats and dogs. We had to stop shooting. Karl said, 'You ride back with me. Tell your assistant not to dismiss the company, but tell them to go into the studio.'

"Coming from Culver City, we had the windshield wiper going, and Karl began mumbling to himself. I suddenly tuned in to what he was mumbling. He was mumbling to the tempo of the windshield wiper. He was saying, in German, '*der Schmetterling* . . . *der Schmetterling*,' which means butterfly; well, I knew that. So finally, I said to him, 'What the hell are you mumbling about a butterfly?'

" 'I don't know,' he said. 'All I can tell you is that the finish must be as simple as a butterfly.' That's what started the whole thing. I said, 'Wait a minute. As soon as we get into the studio, come into my office.'

"I had the whole book, torn into sections and pinned on the wall. So we go in and look up the section that deals with a butterfly. And in a minute, you could say, everything was hung up. We found out the following; the first time the butterfly came into being was when Paul was returning to the front. He makes his sister a present of his butterfly collection. So there he was, a butterfly collector. The first hundred times I went to the book I didn't pay much attention, it was such an insignificant detail. But coming now, knowing the whole picture was under our belt, that became very significant."

The final scene of *All Quiet* shows a day of calm. Paul's hand (actually Milestone's in the close-up) stretches out toward a butterfly that has settled on the earth. A French sniper takes careful aim. We cut back to the hand—it jerks, a split second before the crack of the rifle, and slowly relaxes.

> He fell in October 1918, on a day that was so quiet and still on the whole front, that the army report confined itself to the single sentence: All quiet on the Western Front.[2]

2

THE WEST

"What was the difference between the West of motion pictures and the West as you knew it?"
"There's only one thing I can answer that with, and that's another question. What's the difference between daylight and dark?"

—FORMER COWBOY TED FRENCH TO KEVIN BROWNLOW

The difference between the West of motion pictures and the real West is summed up in this picture. On the right is Jack Hoxie, who played Deadwood Dick. And on the left is the original Deadwood Dick, Richard Clark, a famous character when Deadwood, South Dakota, was a frontier town. Clark was an authentic Westerner, as his beautiful Indian coat and ancient rifle indicate. Hoxie was also a genuine Westerner, but of a very different era, as testified by his inauthentic outfit.

So affectionate have we grown toward the Western that to suggest it reflects more wishful thinking than history seems blasphemous. It is like challenging a Fundamentalist with the theories of Darwin. Why spoil the dream?

No one goes to a Western for a history lesson, so to charge most Westerns with inaccuracy is pointless. In any case, the history of the West is as plagued by myth as the history of the cinema, and to untwine the barbed wire of legend is all but hopeless. Long before the moving picture was invented, men had a financial interest in ignoring the facts and printing the legend. Western devotees, many of them, believe these legends should be sustained, for they have bred the romance they love. "Make it vivid," said Jack London. "Truth doesn't matter so much, so long as it lives."

Such an attitude may have been valid in the distant past, when cattle herding was more than just another branch of agricultural labor. The tales of the cattle drives, traversing plains larger than some European countries, plagued by wild animals, primitive savages, and the fury of the elements, captured the imagination, and set the men who accomplished such treks as far from the normal run of humanity as the astronauts of today.

But now the romance lies more and more in the actuality. The barest original account is of more absorbing interest than the raciest dime novel, just as an 1880 photograph is more precious than most 1880 paintings.

Some of the silent Westerns contain this emotionally stirring element of documentary. I make the claim hesitantly, for whatever their quality as films, the vast majority were intended as slam-bang entertainment. The only past being re-created in most of them were past box-office successes, and the men responsible would have been bewildered by talk of historical accuracy. But by carefully sifting through the facts behind these pictures (and many of the films are still available), it is possible to stumble across unique glimpses of Western history.

And one curious fact emerges. The Western offered employment to men who had known no life other than life on the range and for whom no security remained. It offered a rich prize to the rodeo rider. It gave outlaws a chance to vindicate themselves through re-enactments of their criminal past, to deter future crime. And it staged the last great drive of Texas longhorns. The motion picture not only reconstructed Western history—it became an extension of that history.

THE DIE IS CAST

Just as studios took a girl from the crowd, dyed her hair, straightened her teeth, redesigned her clothes, and aroused interest with invented escapades, so the archetypal hero of Western lore came into being. The origins of Buffalo Bill can be traced to the prolific dime novelist Edward Z. C. Judson, alias Ned Buntline.

Judson had traveled to Nebraska in search of a hero in 1869, setting his sights upon Major Frank North, a colorful commander in the Sioux campaign. But Major North would not cooperate.* "If you want a man to fill that bill," he said, "he's over there under that wagon."[1]

Buntline discovered a twenty-three-year-old named William Cody, who had won for himself a formidable reputation. Having started on his father's farm at nine, driven an ox team and served as express boy at eleven, he worked as a teamster with wagon trains, joined the Colorado gold rush at thirteen, rode for the Pony Express at fourteen, served in the Union Army on the frontier at fifteen, drove a stagecoach at nineteen, and earned the nickname of Buffalo Bill before he was twenty-one for his service as a hunter-supplier for the Union Pacific Railroad.[2]

Cody entertained Buntline with stories of life on the plains which became "The Greatest Romance of the Age!" in the New York *Weekly,* with vast commercial success. Financial inducements enabled Cody to overcome his initial shyness and to take part in stage productions of his exploits. Yet he did not abandon his former life and concentrate solely on play-acting. He confused historians by carrying his theatrical style, and his flamboyant costume, into actual events.

Buffalo Bill's Wild West was born in 1883, inspired by an "Old Glory blowout" he had attended the previous year in Nebraska. The Wild West—the word "show" was omitted—involved the same admixture of showmanship, stunts, and sentiment as the regular Hollywood Western of later years. And it involved the same, often accidental, historical links. Cody employed Sitting Bull in his show, and other celebrated Western figures, such as Chief Gall, field general in the defeat of Custer, and the scout John Nelson, joined the show when they ran into hard times. And Cody purchased an original Cheyenne and Black Hills Stage Line coach used on the Deadwood run—the famous Deadwood Stage.

Buffalo Bill's connection with motion pictures began the moment they were invented. In 1894 he and his company were photographed for the Edison Kinetoscope, a peepshow machine. Yet it was fifteen years before the trade press heralded the formation of the Buffalo Bill and Pawnee Bill Film Company, to produce spectacular historical Westerns. The announcement proved to be little more than ballyhoo for the merger of the two big shows, and no massive spectacular resulted. Since Cody's own company failed to deliver the goods, other outfits made their own Buffalo Bill films, and Cody, crippled by financial problems, took on the additional burden of court action. With all the trouble producers caused him, it is a miracle that Cody ever faced a camera again. But he did so as a last resort, when his days of glory were over and the props from his show had been auctioned off.

A new scheme to make a historical Western was a godsend, for Cody was

---

* He later cooperated to the extent of appearing in the Buffalo Bill Wild West.

In 1913 William (Buffalo Bill) Cody re-enacts the gruesome climax of his fight to the death with an Indian chief at Warbonnet Creek, July 10, 1876—"the first scalp for Custer." Cody is considerably older and stouter, but the fact that this legendary character plays himself gave the film enormous historical value.

Buffalo Bill leading Indian scouts at Warbonnet Creek.

The 7th Cavalry destroys Indian camp; a scene from the epic Western produced by William Cody at Pine Ridge, North Dakota.

William Cody, again playing himself, with two members of the U.S. Cavalry.

Generals Nelson Miles (left), Frank Baldwin (center), and Marion Maus, as they appeared in Cody's film. All were veterans of the Indian wars.

desperate to buy his freedom. The men who had forced him into bankruptcy—Fred Bonfils and Harry Tammen, owners of the Sells-Floto Circus and publishers of the Denver *Post*—were now his employers again. In association with the Essanay Company of Chicago, they had formed the Colonel W. F. Cody (Buffalo Bill) Historical Pictures Company in September 1913, and it is rumored that they paid Cody as much as $50,000 for his participation.* Cody owed Essanay's interest to G. M. Anderson, whose admiration for Buffalo Bill led him to adopt a career as a motion picture cowboy, Broncho Billy.

Cody was a national figure, and he exploited his advantage with direct approaches to both the Secretary of War and the Secretary of the Interior. He explained that he wanted to make a historically correct film that would be an education to the American public. It would show not just the Indian wars, but also the progress of the Indians, their schools, and their work. After consultation with the Indian agent at Pine Ridge, the government agreed to the film on that basis. Three troops of cavalry were sent to Fort Robinson, together with uniforms and matériel.

Fortunately, the government ensured that none of the soldiers were from the 7th Cavalry. For the climax of the film was to be the Battle of Wounded Knee.

WHAT HISTORIANS NOW ACCEPT as a massacre at Wounded Knee was at this period regarded as a conventional battle. The flame of Indian nationalism had been fanned by news of a Messiah, Wovoka, a Nevada Paiute, who promised to lead the tribes to their former glory. This belief was basic to the Ghost Dance cult, and was greeted by the Sioux with such desperate enthusiasm that the government dispatched several thousand soldiers to the Pine Ridge area. Their alarm was understandable, but Wovoka regarded himself as the reincarnation of Christ, and was therefore opposed to violence. The cult was an ironic result of the zeal of Christian missionaries, and was essentially mystical.

The general commanding the troops was Nelson Appleton Miles, a veteran of the Civil War, who had defeated the Kiowas, the Comanches, and the Cheyennes. He had also captured Geronimo. As the government had been alarmed by the Ghost Dancers, so the Sioux took fright at the troops. They evacuated the reservation and fled to the Bad Lands, where they were joined by a thousand more tribesmen. Sitting Bull had returned from exile in Canada, and General Miles decided to isolate him in case he tried to seize command of the Sioux. Miles asked Cody, on the staff of the governor of Nebraska and recently returned from a highly successful tour of Europe with the Wild West, to talk to his former trouper. Cody agreed, but he could not resist an all-night drinking session with cavalry officers. Next day President Benjamin Harrison, alerted by the local Indian agent, canceled Cody's mission. The agent sent a detachment of Indian police; Sitting Bull refused to submit and was killed. His white horse, given him by Cody, was trained to kneel at the sound of gunfire. As the Indian police shot Sitting Bull, the horse knelt—a source of wonder in Indian oral history.

A group of three hundred fifty Sioux, attempting to surrender at Pine Ridge, was intercepted by the 7th Cavalry. They were taken to a trading post at

---

* William Coleman was told by an actor in the film that he had actually seen the check.

The capture of Sitting Bull.

Wounded Knee (a rough translation from the Indian: "The creek where the man with the wounded knee was buried"). As the soldiers disarmed the Sioux, a rifle was discharged, probably by accident. The cavalrymen, many of them nervous recruits, thought this was the signal for the long-awaited uprising. They opened fire. Indians scrambling into a ravine in the hope of getting away were slaughtered by a battery of Hotchkiss guns—rapid-firers using two-and-a-half-inch shells. About two hundred men, women, and children were killed.

Was Cody's reconstruction of the "Battle" of Wounded Knee a high point of historical wishful thinking, or did it hint at the truth? William S. E. Coleman of Drake University has undertaken a great deal of research into the career of William Cody, and he suspects the picture was reasonably accurate. He interviewed Ben Black Elk, whose father, Black Elk, was in the picture. "It was made exactly as it happened," Ben Black Elk told Coleman. "Do you know what happened to that motion picture? The government put a ban on it. A friend went to Washington, D.C., to see the movie, but they had destroyed it." Other Indians hold contrary opinions about the film's accuracy, but it cannot be denied that Cody's film was given short shrift by the government, and that it apparently "decomposed" at the Bureau of Indian Affairs sometime in the twenties. Nitrate film decomposes eventually, perhaps after forty or fifty years; that it should do so in a mere decade is a trifle unlikely. No other print is known to exist.

The army originally saw the film as a useful recruiting device, since Mexico was at war and America's involvement was possible. Cody was therefore granted unprecedented cooperation, from both the regular army and from those retired officers who had taken part in the Indian wars. "My object of desire has been to preserve history by the aid of the camera," said Cody, "with as many living participants in the closing Indian wars of North America as could be procured."[3]

Acting as the main technical consultant, and playing himself, was none other than Lieutenant General Nelson Appleton Miles. General Miles had not been at Wounded Knee, but as the commanding officer he undoubtedly knew what had occurred. Yet his enthusiasm for the project shines through each of his statements. "They want me there to make sure that everything they do is historically correct," he told *Moving Picture World* on his way to Pine Ridge. "I shall take active part in it, too, perhaps. The idea is to give the whole thing from the start—the Indian dissatisfaction, their starving condition, the coming of the false 'Messiah' who stirred them to revolt, the massing of troops, the death of Sitting Bull and, finally, the surrender. All of these incidents will be gone over, just as they happened. Some of the Indians will be there who fought against us. They will fight again, but there will be no bullets. All that is over.

"We expect this will be one of the finest records in the government archives. I understand nothing of the kind has ever been attempted before. Having these officers of my own staff there will make it a splendid thing. It will be a regular reunion on the ground where we fought and bled together."[4]

Accompanying General Miles to the Pine Ridge location were Brigadier General Charles King, who had fought as captain of artillery and cavalry and who wrote the film's scenario; Brigadier General Frank Baldwin, brevetted major for gallantry in his attack on the camp of Sitting Bull on Red Water River in Montana; Brigadier General Marion P. Maus, who had graduated from West Point at the outbreak of the serious Indian troubles and had served in numerous campaigns, including several of the actions depicted in the film; and General Humphrey, decorated for Indian service in Idaho. Colonel Sickles of the 12th U.S. Cavalry also traveled up for this eerie reunion, among officers who had not seen each other for twenty-three years. Sickles had been a lieutenant of the 7th Cavalry, one of the few men present who had participated in the "Battle" of Wounded Knee.

Wounded Knee was not the only concern of the film, which also re-created the Battle of Summit Springs (1869) and the Battle of Warbonnet Creek (1876). Accounts of the making of the film are scattered throughout the trade papers of the time, in newspapers, and in some of the books about Cody. Piecing them together provides evidence of a situation so dramatic, and so full of irony, that it would make an impressive film by itself.

The picture was directed by Theodore Wharton (who was to make such wartime propaganda films as *The Eagle's Eye*) and photographed by Conrad Luperti and D. T. Hargan,* with Vernon Day as production manager. *Moving Picture World* pointed out that Wharton had a stupendous undertaking ahead of him, for besides handling the troops, Indians, and horses, in viciously cold weather, he had to cope with Colonel Cody himself, who, they warned, was something of a prima donna. Several other producers had attempted to film the life of Buffalo Bill, "but with indifferent results, mainly on this account."[5]

Nevertheless, Theodore Wharton managed an optimistic letter to the *World* in mid-production. "I am in the Bad Lands of South Dakota, hemmed in on one side by the U.S. Army and on the other by the Sioux Nation. As I look from my tent I see hundreds of tepees stretched over the hills. To give you an idea of the magnitude of the production, I will say that we are using more than 1,000 horses, and this is not a press agent's estimate either. Some job for little Willie, eh? It will either make or break yours truly."[6]

Since the picture was partly backed by the Denver *Post,* a reporter from that paper accompanied the production (I am once again indebted to William Coleman for making these articles available). The reporter was Ryley Cooper, described as "a crack war correspondent." (Cooper also ghosted the autobiography of Cody's wife,

---

* A year later Luperti and Hargan traveled to Central Africa for Essanay to make wild-animal pictures.

Louisa Federici, and in 1914–15 was a press agent for the Sells-Floto Wild West show and circus, which Cody joined when his old exhibition went bankrupt.)

Cooper's reports are suffused with nostalgia for the Indian wars and fascination with the complexities of Indian lore and customs. He is surprisingly blunt about the events of Wounded Knee. He stops short of the word "massacre" but does not omit the implications: "There the white man was the aggressor, they far outnumbering the Indians. The red men were crowded down into a ravine where lines of bullets sent them to death in scores."

Cooper also reported the campfire conversations of the Indian war veterans in a way that was not likely to appeal to the Bureau of Indian Affairs; despite the ferocity of the war, he wrote, "not only admiration but even sympathy for the redmen's patience is daily expressed by those who were forced by duty to meet the situation with a severity of reprisal to the limit."[7] Cooper constantly heard the phrase, "When did the white men or the government ever keep a treaty with the Indians?" "No matter how often or how loudly propounded by generations of questioners since the Mayflower days, no listener has heard the faintest response or echo from the walls of time. In this camp, filled with aged redmen wise in Indian lore, noted generals and scouts with records in frontier history, agents and friends, all memories (up to a few late years) fail to bring forth the date and location of 'a square deal.' "

Moving Picture World reported that the Indians regarded the arrival of troops with the gravest suspicion. "When they saw the Hotchkiss guns, the rifles, revolvers and cases of ammunition, there was a feeling of unrest, as though the time had come when they were to be gathered in by the Great Spirit through the agency of the white man."[8]

Fortunately, Cody was well regarded by the Indians—he had spoken for their fair treatment since 1872, when such an attitude was tantamount to treason—and he succeeded in enlisting the aid of several important veterans, including Short Bull, who had been blamed for starting the Ghost Dance war and who was still a religious leader, and Iron Tail.*

Cody's capacity on the film, apart from being its leading player, was equivalent to that of a producer. He considered film-making harder than "three circuses in one," since he not only had the sensitive feelings of the Indians to take into account but also the demands of General Miles. A stickler for accuracy, General Miles proved to be a monumental headache. This was a government-approved operation, therefore its historical accuracy had to be beyond dispute. Eleven thousand troops had taken part in the review after the hostiles had surrendered, therefore eleven thousand would have to be seen in the reconstruction. Cody and Wharton resigned themselves to squandering a few hours, while Miles led the three troops of cavalry round and round the camera. The cameraman carried on cranking, but exposed nothing after the first three circuits. (The result was unusually effective, since it was photographed in a snowstorm.) Miles's most tactless action, however, was to re-enact the Battle of Wounded Knee precisely where the massacre had occurred, over the graves of the victims. This led to an outcry from the Indians, and

---

* Both had been among twenty-five Indians held as hostages after Wounded Knee; Cody managed to have them transferred to his Wild West, which was about to leave for Europe. The army considered the absence of these men might prevent a war in the spring.

Chief Running Hawk, a veteran of 1890, re-enacts his tragic role in William Cody's epic of the Indian wars.

Preparing to film the scene of Indians being escorted to Wounded Knee.

the night before the battle was due to be staged, Chief Iron Tail warned Cody that some of the young braves intended using live rounds to avenge their fathers in symbolic but devastating style. Johnny Baker, Cody's adopted son, had already tried the standard technique for pacifying primitives; he had made one spokesman a colonel, the other a captain. Now Cody was forced to call a hasty conference in the middle of the night to determine whether there was any truth in the rumor. True or not, it frightened the life out of everyone who heard it. Cody pointed out the value of the film; it would be an epic record of the resistance of the Sioux. And it would show that the Ghost Dance cult was not, after all, a conspiracy to start a war. Furthermore, what was the point of threatening to use live ammunition when three troops of cavalry were present?

Before the shooting of the Wounded Knee sequence, reported *Moving Picture World,* the air seemed charged with danger. Both Indians and soldiers were extremely reluctant to begin firing at one another:

"During the entire taking of the picture, the squaws chanted their death song as they did years ago when they saw the brave warriors fall under the rain of bullets. Many of them broke into tears as the vividness of the battle recalled that other time when lives were really lost and everything was actual.

"Dewey Beard, still considered a hero among his tribe, appears in his ghost shirt, which still bears the mark of five bullet holes. Dewey Beard was the last to surrender at the time of the battle, and held off soldiers for fourteen hours from his place of vantage."[9]

Among the tragic and curious details—the squaws mourning, children playing on the graves, the raucous wheeze of a merry-go-round, provided by Cody, who thought film-making should be like a Wild West show, with its attendant attractions—were occasional comic moments. The Indians, falling from their horses in the battle scenes, kept forgetting, in their anxiety to watch the proceedings, to lie down and die.

The surrender of 1891 was re-enacted upon the parade ground of the Indian agency at Rushville, Nebraska. Present was one of the four scouts who had attended in 1891, P. Wells.

"It was a wonderful picture of many beautiful features that was taken yesterday morning," wrote Ryley Cooper. "Ranged on one side, at the delivering of hostages, sat in review Generals Miles, Maus, Lee and Baldwin, while on each side of the square where waited the army wagons were the troops, awaiting the order to move. A signal, and there walked forward Wells, with the hostages, and among those who came forward Short Bull, who once before enacted the scene and enacted it in earnest. In their great bonnets and masses of bead work were the Indians, clothed today as when they appeared for the finishing of the treaty.

"Watching carefully every feature, General Miles designated each action of the Indians and the soldiers so that it might conform with the original action in the years gone. The great general saw that the picture was historically correct in every detail and that not a feature was forgotten."[10]

Technical advisers like General Miles have never been popular with film people, for their obsession with detail so often seems trivial compared with the complexities of the whole production. General Miles was not a man to be deflected or patronized, however, and when he insisted that the events that occurred in the

Bad Lands should be shot in the Bad Lands, the Essanay people were dismayed. It would take days to transport the camp fifty miles to that miserable area and get everyone out again. Besides which, it was by no means certain they could secure the kind of shots that would make the journey worthwhile.

Cody and Miles argued the matter, and the argument developed into a full-scale quarrel, which ended their friendship. Cody realized that the additional costs would virtually break the budget. Miles stubbornly insisted. Johnny Baker brought the matter to a head. "I'll take the Indians and troops in there and I'll bring them out again," he volunteered. "And there will be pictures in the cameras when they come out."[11]

On 23 October 1913 the huge motion picture camp split, and the Bad Lands expedition set out across the plains. Ryley Cooper reported it as "one of the greatest achievements in the history of motion pictures." He noted that General Miles and his staff were willing to camp in soldiers' tents in order to be present. "The pictures were taken in places where, after the firing was over, ropes were used to drag some of the soldiers out of the great paths and up the steep precipices; taken where hours of climbing were necessary; taken where it seemed that descent and ascent would be impossible to anything except a mountain sheep. According to the view of General Miles, the Pass of Thermopylae lessens in strategic importance by the side of the Bad Lands, and it was here that history was reproduced."[12]

After three nights, camping in territory threatened by snow, the expedition returned. General Miles, smarting from his quarrel with Cody, departed for home. Wharton shot the Battle of Summit Springs with Cody as adviser. "All day long Buffalo Bill, his white hair flying in the wind, his gold-embossed rifle swinging at his saddle, directed the actions of Theodore Wharton."[13]

On 28 October 1913 work was complete. A great celebration was staged, whole cows were roasted, and the Indians danced. Cody announced that he would pay every Indian who had been with his show and suffered from its collapse. He handed out $1,313 and declared, "You have been my friends and I am going to be yours."[14] Wharton had displayed a similar talent for diplomacy throughout the production and was rewarded with the honorary title of Chief Wambli Wicosa (Eagle Man) of the Brule tribe of the Sioux and a gala dinner from the U.S. Cavalry.

A SIX-MONTH PERIOD FOR EDITING was unheard of at this time of one-reel-a-week, yet six months elapsed before the film received its first screening for the Secretary of the Interior, Franklin K. Lane, accompanied by other members of the Wilson administration. There was no hint of official disapproval; applause, cheers, and hisses indicated the unabashed enjoyment of the distinguished audience. Yet the government held the film back from release. Another six months elapsed before a version was shown in New York, and another in Denver, accompanied by an appearance of Buffalo Bill astride his horse on stage, with a group of Sioux warriors. When Cody died, in 1917, yet another version was released, together with veiled remarks about the government's attempts to suppress it.

General Charles King, author of the film's scenario and veteran of Warbonnet Creek, was undeterred in his loyalty to Cody's film. He called it "the most wonderful spectacle ever produced since motion pictures were invented." It was not

Filming the military review after the battle.

Hand-to-hand fighting follows the arrest and killing of Sitting Bull.

merely a photoplay or a series of staged spectacles. "It is war itself, grim, unpitying and terrible; and it holds your heart still as you watch it and leaves you, in the end, amazed and spellbound at the courage and folly of mankind. No boy or girl should be allowed to miss these pictures. If you are a lonely man or woman pick up some equally lonely kiddie and take him for an afternoon with the great leaders of our army, with the great chiefs of our Indian tribes and two hours in the open world that has been made sacred by heroic blood of the nation's fighting heroes."[15]

The picture received a violent attack from Chauncey Yellow Robe, Sioux chief from South Dakota, in a speech at the Society of American Indians. Cody and Miles, he said, had made a mockery of this tragedy to his race for their own profit and cheap glory. "You ask how to settle the Indian's troubles. I have a suggestion. Let Buffalo Bill and General Miles take some soldiers and go around the reservations and shoot them down. That will settle his troubles. Let them do in earnest what they have been doing at the battlefield of Wounded Knee. These two, who were not even there when it happened, went back and became heroes for a moving picture machine."

His audience laughed at his irony. "You laugh," continued Yellow Robe, "but my heart does not laugh. Women and children and old men of my people, my relatives, were massacred with machine guns by the soldiers of this Christian nation while the fighting men were away. It was not a glorious battle and I should think these two men would be glad they were not there. But no, they want to be heroes for moving pictures. You will be able to see their bravery and their hairbreadth escapes soon in your theaters."[16]

Whatever its defects, whatever its inaccuracies, the film would represent a historical prize of immense value if only it could be found. Perhaps it exists, unidentified, in a foreign archive, for it was known under a variety of titles—*The Indian Wars Refought, The Last Indian Battles or From the Warpath to the Peace Pipe, The Wars for Civilization in America, Buffalo Bill's Indian Wars, Indian War Pictures,* and *The Adventures of Buffalo Bill.* Perhaps the United States government has preserved it after all. The search for this extraordinary film should not be abandoned.*

MIGRATION WEST

In the very years when it was possible to document the last glimpses of the Old West, expediency led the majority of picture people only as far afield as the Catskills or Saranac Lake, New York. Some of the Eastern Westerns were such travesties on Western life and human intelligence, according to the trade press, that exhibitors in Western states dared not show them. Picture people were painfully aware of the drawbacks, but the journey west took longer than the entire shooting schedule of most pictures. In any case, a glance at the foreign trade papers showed that Westerns were made primarily for the European market, where audiences were not so critical. The French, in particular, loved them, and launched into production themselves with an enthusiasm that swept aside all considerations of accuracy. One Pathé film, *A Western Hero* (1909), caused a minor outcry in

* Part of the last reel has turned up in the collection of David Phillips of Chicago.

Canyon de Chelly: the Douglas Fairbanks company on location for Modern Musketeer *(1917). Fairbanks at center: Allan Dwan, seated to the right (with white headscarf).*

1913: Cecil B. DeMille (extreme left) and Oscar Apfel (above steering wheel) originally planned to make The Squaw Man *on location at Flagstaff, Arizona. According to one story, a cattleman-sheepman war deterred them, and they went on by train to Los Angeles. Dustin Farnum, center, in white*

the American trade papers. An exhibitor who had lived in the West for forty years exploded at the sight of Indians in gingham shirts and cowboys mounted on bob-tailed mares with English saddles, thundering along well-paved roads in pursuit not of a stagecoach, but of a horse-drawn omnibus.*

The French shamed the Americans when they expanded their empire; Gaston Méliès, the brother of Georges Méliès, the celluloid magician, established the Star Film Company in Chicago, and later in Texas, primarily to produce Westerns. And once in the West, the atmosphere affected even the most fanciful production. Méliès recalled how one of his 1911 pictures reinvigorated the lawless frontier days. A group of exhibitors, visiting the company, was persuaded to play the passengers in a stagecoach holdup. "With a good deal of banter to and fro, the visitors piled into the coach," reported *Moving Picture World,* "which went tearing down the road to where the bandits were hidden, and the stagecoach was held up in realistic fashion. In fact, it was so realistic that the bandits went through everybody's clothes and removed about $40 in small bills and change, charged into town with the proceeds of the haul and immediately proceeded to distribute it to various bartenders."[1]

As a handful of early film-makers reached the West, one element they shared with the outlaws and cattle rustlers of former days was the stealth with which their operations were conducted. Most of them used cameras that were violations of established patents. Edison had formed a trust from the major companies, all of whom paid royalties for their film and equipment. The idea was to force independent operators into liquidation. It developed into a vicious, and sometimes violent, campaign, with gangsters employed by both sides.

Allan Dwan made pictures in California at the time of the Patents Company scares, and not being a party to the trust was obliged to work in remote spots, guarded by armed cowboys. The atmosphere tended toward Owen Wister. "The Patents Company hired goons for gunmen. If they saw a bunch of people working, and it wasn't one of their companies, they'd shoot a hole through the camera. Without the camera you couldn't work, and cameras were impossible to get. The reason we came to places like California was to get away from these goons. Around Chicago and New York, your life was in your hands if you went out with a camera. You'd find a bullet whizzing by your ear—bang, a hole in your camera. And so we sneaked out to California and hid away in little places. We worked in areas where you could see everything around you, and we stationed sentinels. I got my cowboys, the three Morrison brothers, together with one or two they hired in the neighborhood, and told them, 'If these fellows bother you, pop at them. Hit them in the foot, or something, but don't kill. Just let them know you're there.'

"So I was more or less protected, until one day this character got off the train at San Juan Capistrano, and wanted to see the boss in charge. 'I'm the boss,' I said. 'What do you want?' He said, 'I'd like to have a talk with you.' So we walked up the road and he said, 'Get out of here and quit making pictures.' We walked across a little arroyo, a ditch, and people as usual had tossed some tin cans out there as they went by. He took out his sidearm and took a crack at a tin can

---

* *Indians and Cow-Boys,* a Pathé film of 1905, in the John E. Allen collection, contains similar delights, and includes an Indian village with painted tepees and totem.

The Eclair Company takes advantage of the Western atmosphere of Pawnee Bill's Buffalo Ranch, Pawnee, Oklahoma, 1910. Lucien Andriot at camera; William Haddock, extreme right, with megaphone. The cowboys are from the Buffalo Bill Wild West, which was in winter quarters at Pawnee. Joe Ryan, who eventually starred in serials at Vitagraph, is seated in the right foreground, wearing a white hat.

down in the gully, and missed it. God took me by the hand and I pulled out my gun and hit the can twice. And the fellow looked at me and put his gun away. He turned away to go back and he ran straight into the Morrison brothers with their Winchesters. They stuck these rifles in his fanny and walked him back to the train. He got on and left and we never saw a goon again. Our reputation was abroad—we had an army. People wouldn't even come to watch us work. They were scared. 'Don't go near them—they'll shoot you!' "[2]

AS THE INDUSTRY STABILIZED in Los Angeles, so the migration west increased, many of the optimistic individuals hoping to break into pictures being Westerners themselves. King Vidor, his wife, Florence—herself the daughter of a rancher—and a young man named Clifford Vick set out from Texas to Hollywood in 1915 in a dangerously overloaded Model T, on the back of which, in ranch-wagon style, was a chuck box. There were virtually no good roads outside the East, and their journey had all the drama of a covered-wagon trek. It was still necessary to wait patiently while cowboys drove great herds of cattle past.

On a railroad embankment in New Mexico, the Vidors encountered a line of covered wagons. But the occupants were not settlers.

"They were gipsies, the men with knives in their belts, the women with wild, flowing skirts. The embankment was so narrow that we couldn't get by if they didn't pull over a bit. We stopped, and suddenly the women were all over us, taking whatever they could, putting their hands into pockets of clothes in the car. We had stuff tied all over the car, food, buckets, guns. One of them reached over and turned off the ignition switch. I kicked it back with my foot just before the engine died—otherwise it meant getting out and using the crank. The car started off with all these women hanging on the running board. I started going faster and faster and two or three of them got frightened and jumped off, but some of them stayed on. We could still hear the men laughing and yelling, the women were still trying to grab stuff out of our pockets and claw our faces—so we pushed them off, prising open their fingers and pushing them in the face, and they went whirling through the air, skirts flying, hitting the dirt. That's how we got away. Soon afterwards, we met three fellows in a car with guns—a sheriff and two deputies. They asked us if we'd seen a band of gipsies. We told them our story and they said they had gone into a restaurant in Raton, New Mexico, and cleaned out all the shelves. Everything. I don't know why they didn't get shot. Plenty of guys out west were willing to shoot."[3]

The more conventional route for picture people was the train, but even this was an uncomfortable experience, stretching across several days from coast to coast. Once in the thick of cowboy country, passengers were sometimes treated to a hanging, the body strung up on a station pole and riddled with bullets. Apprehensive about frontier country in any case, the railroad tourist was unlikely to realize that the victim was no more than a straw dummy—for bored cowboys found a train-bound audience of gullible Easterners irresistible.

The moving picture companies exploited this inbred sense of display, and the scenario for the average Western was its celluloid equivalent. Regular cowboys took part, but if their role was prominent they gladly discarded working duds and climbed into a more extravagant and more appealing costume. Show business, in

The Cowboy Cameraman, A. D. Kean. The only known photograph. (Copied from Moving Picture World)

The original Californian stone ranch house used as location for Rose of the Rancho (1914), *directed by Cecil B. DeMille. In this house DeMille found a copy of the first census of the city of Los Angeles, the original of which had been lost. It listed the inhabitants by trade, said DeMille—"so many bakers, so many blacksmiths and so on—and one idiot."*

Jerome, Arizona, before it became a ghost town, was the location for The Hidden Spring *(1917). The company poses while miners watch from the background; Tony Gaudio (hand on camera), Harold Lockwood (white shirt), Billie West (on horse).*

*Filmed in the mining town of Randsburg, California—the times of the stage to Los Angeles via Mojave are visible in the background—*His Back Against the Wall *(1921) was directed by Rowland V. Lee.*

the Cody tradition, meant far more than the preservation of social history, a concept hardly among the cowhands' first considerations. But while the cowboys could avoid the truth, the camera could not. The Old West lingered on, and fragments of its reality were unwittingly captured by the early films. And in between the horse operas, companies often knocked off a split-reel "topical," since factual films were easy to make and required nothing in the way of actors or props. At the time, they were acknowledged to be inferior program padding. But today, if they could all be assembled, they would represent a visual encyclopaedia of Western life, invaluable to both historian and Western enthusiast. To take one year's output at random, the following factual films appeared in 1913: *Cowboy Sports and Pastimes* (101-Bison), which featured a cowboy called Ed Gibson (better known as Hoot) and Bertha Blanchard in "sensational riding on unbroken horses"; *Life Among the Navajos* (Majestic), photographed by Carl Louis Gregory (later chief instructor at the Signal Corps Photographic School), *Dredges and Farm Implements in the West* (Pathé), which showed the horse being eliminated from irrigation projects in the Far West and being replaced by dredges and engines; *Opportunity and a Million Acres* (Pathé), "homesteaders trailing in with their old-fashioned prairie schooners are shown"; *The Wild West Comes to Town* (Majestic), "merely a few pictures of the various wild west shows in action"; *Camping with the Blackfeet* (Edison), "a very able and interesting offering showing how the remnants of the once powerful tribe of Blackfoot Indians live on the reservation of North-West Montana"; *The New Red Man* (Edison), "shows the Carlisle Indian"; *Across Swiftcurrent Pass on Horseback* (Edison), "interesting pictures of western camp life are shown, cooking flapjacks for breakfast, loading pack animals etc."; and a cluster of rodeo films including *Duhem and Harter's 1913 California Rodeo, Pendleton Round-Up,* and *A Cowboy Magnate,* in which the Universal cowboys perform for California exhibitors.

A lone and unsung hero, who photographed several such documentaries, was a cameraman from British Columbia, A. D. Kean, known as the Cowboy Cameraman. A real cowboy and skilled operator with a high-speed Graflex, he was much in demand at sports and rodeos. In 1912 he made a widely distributed film of the Calgary Stampede, as a result of which Colonel Zack Miller hired him for the 101 Ranch film operation. Later he set up his own small company, and during the war made a pictorial record of every British Columbian battalion that went to the front. The trade press affectionately referred to Kean as Vancouver's most distinctive town character: "No public gathering is considered complete without the presence of the box on the tripod, the high leather boots and the big sombrero."[4]

By contrast, a kind of blindness to the history happening around them caused many Californian film-makers to grind out their Westerns in their own backyard. But the business was bursting with energetic and enterprising young men who saw a good deal further than the studio fence. Director E. Mason Hopper took a location trip headlong into Western history when he filmed Jerome, Arizona, as a thriving community.* (It is now a ghost town, a picturesque but almost empty tourist attraction.)

"Harold Lockwood's company found a typical mining town in Jerome," re-

---

* The film was *The Hidden Spring,* written by Richard V. Spencer, produced by Fred Balshofer.

ported *Pictures and Picturegoer.* "Houses built one above the other along the sides of a mountain worth three hundred million dollars in copper, streets filled with miners, owners of mines, stock speculators and prospectors, great mines and smelters where the output of precious metals runs up into the hundreds of thousands of dollars worth per week, all the atmosphere of a booming district of the mining country was found there.

"Right and left the Yorke Metro people were bombarded by salesmen of mining shares. Harold Lockwood and his director would no sooner seat themselves comfortably in the lobby of the hotel than half a dozen of the local mining men engaged them in conversation, telling of the rich profits to be gained by investing in their particular mines. The hotel man told Lockwood rather facetiously that so many men with samples of ore stood around in his lobby, that every evening when the porter swept the place, enough gold, silver and copper was 'panned' from the sweepings of dust on the floor to pay for all the help in the hotel."[5]

E. Mason Hopper had used Jerome as a location the year before—for *The Red Woman.* With a company consisting of a hundred and ten people, he set off for another location near Springdale, twenty-two miles up in the foothills. A storm broke suddenly, and with such fury that in the blinding snow even the guide became confused. Instead of traveling to the north, the company, wet to the bone and nearly frozen, stumbled upon a ranch known as Hacienda 104—six miles out of their way. The ranch house could not accommodate more than sixty-five, so the Mexicans and the cowboys attached to the company slept with the sheep to stay warm. Production manager George Sheer, remaining in Jerome, without any telephone, grew frantic about the company's fate until a cowboy rode over to reassure him.

Before unions were formed to protect picture people, actors and technicians were exposed to the full spectrum of climatic conditions; *On Burning Sands* was shot in the teeth of a genuine sandstorm, while the Kinemacolor company, making a Bret Harte Western, were snowed in on Mount Lowe, experiencing exactly the same rigors as the pioneers whose courage they were celebrating.

Erich von Stroheim claimed the accolade for the grimmest of all locations: Death Valley at the worst time of year for *Greed* (1924). A full decade earlier, the World Film Company, making a version of the same story, was obliged, under conditions agreed upon with the late Frank Norris, to shoot the relevant scenes in Death Valley and not to take them around the studio. *McTeague* (released as *Life's Whirlpool*) was not a Western, but its desert sequences involved the company in the kind of rugged adventure that quickly becomes Western legend.

Before leaving New York, director Barry O'Neill catalogued the terrors of the desert and the horrors of camping, and was surprised when members of the company pleaded to be included. The celebrated Death Valley Scotty (a former trick rider with Buffalo Bill's Wild West) acted as guide and met the company at the railroad station with a twenty-mule team from the Borax Mines. After traveling miles on the backs of the mules, the company reached Death Valley and ran into the worst sandstorm experienced on the desert for many years. The wind blew so hard that no one could manage to erect a tent and they unloaded the supply wagon and bunked in that instead. Then followed long, claustrophobic days filming in the mine workings. When the location was over, the company returned thankfully to the East. "I wouldn't take a million dollars for the experience," said one, "but I wouldn't go through it again for ten times the amount."[6]

WHILE COMPANIES LIKE BIOGRAPH and American re-created the struggles of the early pioneers in the pitiless desert, the California desert was being settled all around them. That the new settlers faced a situation no less dramatic than the one encountered by the pioneers was exemplified in an extraordinary film called *The Winning of Barbara Worth,* directed by Henry King for Samuel Goldwyn in 1926. Based on a popular novel of 1914 by Harold Bell Wright, and written for the screen by Frances Marion, the picture was intended as a love story to exploit the appeal of Vilma Banky and Ronald Colman. But the romantic sequences pale into insignificance alongside the magnificent scenes of civil engineering and desert reclamation. Superbly photographed by George Barnes (assisted by Gregg Toland), the picture tells the story of Imperial Valley, California, an irrigation project long considered impossible.

Henry King and location manager Ray Moore found the ideal location in Nevada's Black Rock Desert. Art director Carl Oscar Borg drew up plans for the three towns that had to be built in the desert, and the Western Pacific Railroad built a spur line to the new city of Barbara Worth, Nevada (Barba, in the film)—based on El Centro, California. A vast tent city housed the extras, and a mess hall, bakery, and recreation center were built; once the well had been drilled, hot water rose from 185 feet beneath the desert and fed the showerbath system. Yet Henry King felt that the company underwent greater hardship than the people who had settled Imperial Valley. The fierce temperature changes—from 120 degrees during the day to freezing at night—were accompanied by baby tornadoes. One of these destroyed most of the motion picture town Kingston, doing $10,000 worth of damage.

The editor of *Motion Picture Magazine* was invited to the location, and was appalled by the journey from Hollywood—it took two days, with a change of car in the middle of the night. He was equally appalled by the blinding sandstorms and vicious heat. But he was fascinated by the inhabitants of the desert towns Reno, Sulphur, and Gerlach, who worked as extras. "At night they gave us a real picture show and all the citizens were present. And such citizens! Most of them were natives of the surrounding country, all carefully selected by Henry King. It was a great sight to see them all huddled together on the floor watching themselves on the screen. There were mountaineers, cowboys, Indians, trappers and ranchers of every description and all in all the queerest looking specimens I had ever encountered. They not only looked and acted their part, but they *were* the part."[7]

The documentary reconstruction of *The Winning of Barbara Worth* is of such a high standard that it places the film on a level with the other Western epics, *The Covered Wagon* and *The Iron Horse.* But whereas those films were set in the nineteenth century, this is an epic of twentieth-century pioneering. The difficult transition between the Old West and the New is captured with fascinating fidelity, even though the exact date is smudged somewhat. How startling to see buckboards and prairie schooners sweeping through the desert, leaving in their wake an immobilized Model T Ford!

The film is frank about such modern miracles as the irrigation of Imperial Valley; financiers were promised such a staggering return on their investment that

The Winning of Barbara Worth (*1926*), *an epic of twentieth-century Western pioneers, shot in Nevada.*

Henry King (left) and Sam Goldwyn inspect an old stagecoach during the making of The Winning of Barbara Worth. *The original caption reads: "Made in St. Louis in 1850, it plied the Overland Trail before railroads penetrated Nevada, carrying gold bullion from Winnemucca and the Blue Hills district. Five million dollars worth of gold bullion was carried during its sixty year career with only four hold-ups."*

The Winning of Barbara Worth.

Gold from Weepah (1927) *was directed by William Bertram at that mining town while the gold rush was still in progress. Bill Cody, center, in white hat, wrote the story. Some of the extras are local prospectors*

gangsters were used to keep the work force under control. The picture is climaxed with a catastrophic flood—when the Colorado River burst its banks, flooded the valley, and created the Salton Sea. Ned Mann's special effects and miniatures are exceptional and the sequence has a terrifying reality. *The Winning of Barbara Worth,* which is still preserved by the Goldwyn Company, is essential viewing for devotees of Western history.

Recent Western history was also documented in less well-known films. Buffalo Bill's namesake, Bill Cody (son of a Winnipeg rancher), staged his *Gold from Weepah* (1927) at the Nevada boom town while the gold rush was still in progress. The director was Klondike veteran William Bertram. Western mining men had made their own reconstructed documentary in 1913, *The Tonopah Stampede for Gold;* the leading roles were played by Tasker L. Oddie, governor of Nevada, and Jim Butler, who discovered the Mizpah and Butler mines. Charles Pryor directed the picture, which showed "the early days of Tonopah, the rush for gold, the strikes, and also many scenes of the biggest mines in the world. See the thrilling race for claims. The Assay office. Sensational runway down the mountainside, every minute replete with action."[8] The picture was highly topical, since there had been a silver strike in 1912.

Vital to the California gold rush of 1849, the town of Sonora, with its dirt road untouched, was a favorite location for scores of early Westerns. Mark Twain once lived there. Directors were heartbroken when a garage wrecked the period charm. Sonora continued to appear in pictures, but a false front had to be custom-built for each modern addition that despoiled the town.

Farther out, towns like Tombstone, Arizona, looked much as they did in their heyday. Jack Conway's *Quicksands* (1923) was shot there, and assistant director Sam Marx discovered the disadvantages of authenticity when he forgot to water the street and galloping cavalry vanished in a cloud of dust. It was during this location that the *Quicksands* company witnessed the kind of hallucinatory experience that could only have occurred at this period.

"We went to Fort Huachuca, jumping-off point for General Pershing when he went chasing after Pancho Villa," said Sam Marx. "It was also the base for the New York 10th Cavalry—all black except for the officers. A few miles across the desert was a ghost town named White City that had been a mining town. The mine petered out, and it was deserted. On the first night of the month, this ghost town became the hottest hellhole in the world, because the commanding officer at the Fort was wise enough to know that you cannot coop up several thousand black men from New York on the Arizona desert with nothing to do. Sooner or later there is going to be hell to pay unless you give them a chance to break loose. So on paynight, once a month, he allowed White City to come to life. Gamblers came in and took over the old saloons. They brought girls, who took over the old hotels, and the bootleggers came in and this old town, deserted for twenty-nine days of the month, for one night came alive. It was a fabulous thing to see."[9]

By the 1920s, thanks to the growth of the automobile industry, more and more dirt roads disappeared under asphalt. A few isolated areas retained their appeal for Western locations; a favorite frontier town was Tehachapi, near Bakersfield, which required no major alteration whatever. Another was Independence in Inyo County, California, which kept its period flavor as a direct result of action, or rather inaction, by the city of Los Angeles. Inyo County was one of the sources of Los Angeles's water supply, and the city bought up vast tracts of land to control the water rights. The towns in those areas were thus frozen in time. Independence had been settled in the 1850s, during the gold rush, and was said to have fewer foreign-born residents than any other town in America.

The eventual modernization of these towns drove film-makers to the standing set of the Western street on the back lot of their studios. Occasionally, a Western town was built on location, and sometimes it was even left there to become an odd sort of ghost town. But on the whole, Western backgrounds now meant striking landscapes—Monument Valley in *The Vanishing American* (1925), Death Valley in *Greed* (1924). Thanks to Roosevelt's National Park scheme, these landscapes have been preserved. The Western towns, mostly changed beyond recognition, are preserved only in old photographs—and old motion pictures.

BRONCHO BILLY ANDERSON

At first sight, "Broncho Billy" Anderson seems the least interesting of all the cowboy stars. He had no hint of ranch or rodeo background; when he started in pictures he could hardly ride, and lost his role as a mounted outlaw in *The Great Train Robbery* (1903) because he kept falling off his horse. But Gilbert Anderson (his real name was Max Aronson) was an ambitious man, and he tackled the job of becoming a cowboy with determination. He was eventually taught to ride by Barney Pierson (Idaho Bill) of Hastings, Nebraska, a cowpuncher and promoter of Wild West shows, who considered him the least promising pupil he had ever had. "However, in spite of his numerous falls, and frequent bruises, he displayed his gameness time and again, until his progress began to prove a source of gratification to me."[1]

Anderson's inclinations were for the theater; he believed in a strong, simple story, played by colorful, easily recognizable characters, true to melodrama. Nevertheless, he was a pioneer who insisted that his Westerns had to be made in the West. He persuaded Colonel Selig in Chicago to let him travel to Colorado and join forces with a Selig crew already in Denver.

"I went out, and met 'Buck' Buckwalter, and we went over to Golden, Colorado, and I figured on making a Western picture there. I got an idea and wrote a very trivial story, and looked around for somebody to play the lead. I got together a few cowboys—I had to use a couple of girls as cowboys, couldn't get enough cowboys—and I made several pictures there in Golden.* I brought them back, but they didn't go so well. I thought there was something missing in them. I got to thinking, and I went to Selig to make a few more pictures, but he didn't want to make any more. So I went over to a fellow named George K. Spoor; he was in opposition to Selig, and they were deadly enemies. I talked Spoor into

* Francis Boggs was the director at this stage and H. H. Buckwalter the cameraman, who also organized the productions. See *Moving Picture World,* 27 June 1908, p. 541, which suggests there were plenty of cowboys available from local ranches.

setting up a company. He put up $2,500 and we formed a company called the Essanay Company—the 'S' was for Spoor and the 'A' was for Anderson."[2]

The historical importance of these early, pre–Broncho Billy films would lie (if only we could find them!) not so much in the story as in the backgrounds and the supporting cast—which invariably included real cowboys. In 1909 Anderson was back in Colorado, at Morrison, named for the family that produced three outstanding Hollywood cowboys, Pete (real name George), Carl, and Chick Morrison.* A report in the Denver *Post* supplied the atmosphere:

"Leaving at 8 o'clock, the company reached Mt. Morrison at 9, where the train was met by a bunch of trained cow ponies and riders under the command of the Morrison boys themselves. Up into the hotel flocked the company, the property man threw back trunk lids with a bang, and in a few minutes the principals were appareled and 'made up,' horses mounted, and away down the street, down by brawling Bear Creek, and on to a little farmhouse, tucked away in a clump of lofty cottonwoods. Permission had already been obtained, and seated at ease on the grass, horses hitched, the company listened to a reading from Mr. Anderson."[3]

Anderson traveled the West, filming in El Paso, Texas, Los Angeles and Santa Barbara, California, in search of a base for a studio with the right kind of scenery and the right kind of cooperation. His final choice was Niles Canyon, California, thirty miles from Oakland, and it was here that the Broncho Billy series was born in July 1910.

Niles Canyon acted as a magnet for cowboys. Among them were certain unsavory characters, who regarded moving pictures as a kind of foreign legion, a society into which they could melt and be immune to the law. Arthur Mackley, director for Essanay and sheriff in many Broncho Billy pictures, had to cope with them: "We have had in the Essanay Company some bad men—men who could not go back to Texas; and when you say that, you are talking a language that cowboys understand—fellows who will shoot at the drop of a hat. There was a time when it seemed if any cowboy got tired of his job he would look up the Essanay Company and apply for a place. We've had them by the dozens."[4]

Charlie Chaplin joined Anderson at Niles, and in his autobiography records his dismay when he first saw the bleak, glass-covered studio in the middle of a field, four miles outside the town. He lived in primitive conditions, along with Anderson's cowboys. Chaplin met his future cameraman, Rollie Totheroh, at Niles. Interviewed by Timothy Lyons in 1967, just before his death, Totheroh provided an entertaining account of his initiation into Westerns at Niles:

"When I saw the bunch, some of them recognized me, and they all came down jumping off their horses, shooting their gats off. A little fellow by the name of Spider Roach was to be my roommate; he was a fighter and a very good one. He said, 'Tonight the whole bunch of us are going to a little neighboring town over here for a party.' So I got into a buckboard with a whole bunch of these fellows—we'd been drinking quite a bit—and they tried to ride their horses right between those swinging doors of this saloon! We were only in there about a half hour when word came on that the Indians who took care of our stock in the corral were drinking and they had got mean and let all the stock out of the corral, and they were running

---

* James Morrison, boss cowboy at Flying A, was part of this family (Bob Birchard).

An accident occurred during the making of Broncho Billy's Christmas Dinner *(1911); the leading lady (Edna Fisher) was flung from the stage and broke her ankle. An alert photographer caught the crucial moment.*

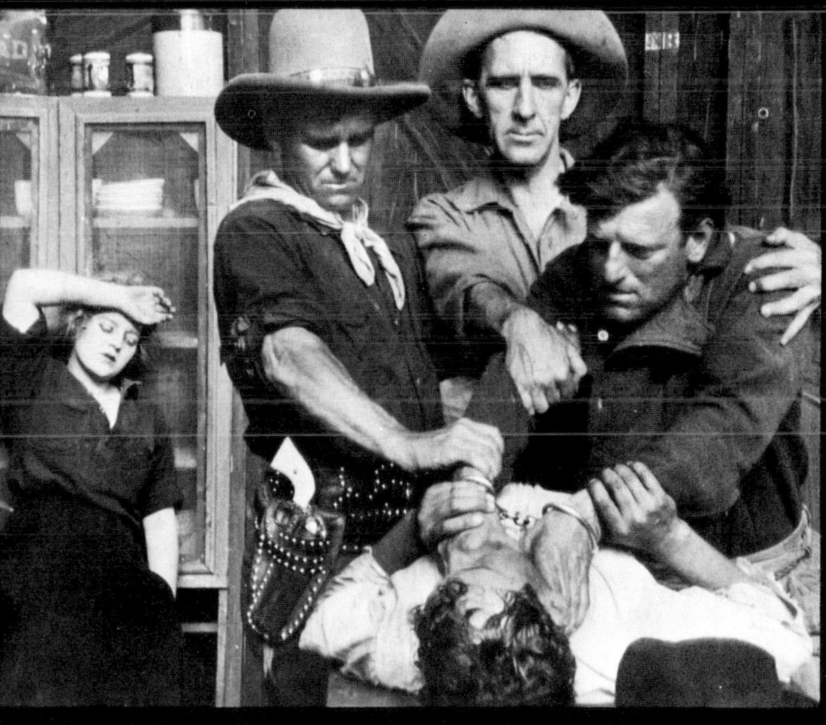

Broncho Billy Anderson (right) as he appeared in Broncho Billy's Cowardly Brother, *one of the vast number of Westerns he made at Niles, California, for Essanay. The man at left is one of the real cowboys who worked for the Anderson company.*

all over the mountains. Word was for everybody to come back and round them up because Broncho Billy wanted to shoot his picture tomorrow. So back we went to round up the horses. I had never ridden a horse, so I couldn't go after them—I was in a buckboard watching them go all around looking for them. Finally they came back and we were all ready to go in the morning—but I didn't know that I was going to be an actor.

"It seemed in this story that Mackley was going to produce, he said Spider and I were going to be twins. So, they gave me a hat, it was the only white hat amongst all the posse—it fit down over my ears. And they gave me a pair of chaps that were too long, put a bandanna round my neck and a big six-shooter on my hip and a pair of boots that were a mile too long for me and big spurs—I was all weighted down! They gave me a horse called 'One Eye'—he only had one eye—so I started to get on on the wrong side. I couldn't get on it so they boosted me up on this horse. I didn't even know that the stirrups were where you put your feet. Anyhow, when they rode through town on the way to location, they all yelled 'Whoooooooooooooppp!' and they'd be shooting their gats off. So they started out from the studio gates, and I was right in the center of them. They were all yelling 'WoooeeeeeeEEEEEEEWWWwwww!' One guy shot this gun off and my head snapped back; they tried to grab ahold of this horse. I held on to the saddle horn and away through town I went, bouncing all over the place."[5]

Totheroh was discouraged from the art of acting and became a cameraman instead, although Jess Robbins remained chief cameraman for Anderson. Referring to Anderson's chases, Totheroh said, "I'd make them very simple, of course. I'd shoot across from left to right on one side of the road without moving the camera around a lot, then I would have the posse come the other way. Stagecoaches used to knock me right off my tripod! I used to say, 'Come as close to me as you can,' and they would."

When the Patents Company lost its power, Essanay, as a member, lost its prominence. George K. Spoor bought Anderson out of Essanay and closed down the studio in 1916. Anderson returned to pictures in 1917, but without success.

"When I came back, they were idolizing Bill Hart, and it was a sort of second beginning. The Westerns I made were good, but they were not good enough to compete with Bill Hart's pictures. So I gave them up. Then I went to New York with Chaplin with the idea that I would make Western pictures, and he would make comedies. But Syd Chaplin, his brother, is pretty hard to get along with; we couldn't cooperate, so I gave up the idea."[6] Anderson produced a series of Stan Laurel comedies, which were not successful, and he returned to the theater. In 1926 *Photoplay* reported that he was broke, out of work, and ill, supported by contributions from friends.[7]

Robert Florey knew Anderson in the latter years of his life. "Whenever I went to the Motion Picture Country House to see some old friends I always paid a visit to Broncho Billy, and often brought along some French movie writers such as Charles Ford or Fronval—they were always more anxious to meet Anderson than the great stars of the day. We found him one day terribly excited as he was going to be picked up and transported to the Paramount Studio for a cameo in a Western quickie (*The Bounty Hunter,* produced by Alex Gordon) which, in fact, was his last screen appearance.

"Broncho Billy said that perhaps he had been wrong when he decided to quit Essanay—and the character he had created—selling his half interest in the company to become an independent producer. Spoor wanted to make features—Anderson was against the idea. He had not been happy with Chaplin (always quarrelling about time and money) and he didn't like Francis X. Bushman very much either. His favorite among the Essanay actors was William Cody, if one can call Buffalo Bill an actor."[8]

When he was asked by William K. Everson what he had been doing in his forty-year absence from the screen, Anderson's reply suggested that his halcyon cowboy days were not far from his mind: "Just drifting along with the breeze," he replied.

Gilbert M. Anderson died in January 1971. He was nearly ninety.

BISON 101 AND THOMAS INCE

This is the story of two enormous tracts of land, separated by more than a thousand miles, which were brought together, in an aesthetic sense, to create a fusion of Western lore and motion picture expertise. The results were the most impressive of all the early Westerns.

The first spread, of eighteen thousand acres near Santa Monica, was leased early in 1910 by the New York Motion Picture Company. Originally part of a Spanish rancho, Topanga Malibu Sequit, which took its name from three Indian villages in the area, the tract was scattered with orange and banana groves and grape vineyards. The film people had no thought of utilizing the whole area, but they were deeply embroiled in the patents war, and needed a secure refuge. The ranch had only one entrance, at Santa Ynez Canyon, and that entrance could be guarded.

The Bison Life Motion Picture Company, which was owned by the NYMP, had been forced to flee Patents Company detectives in the East and had settled in Edendale, outside Los Angeles, only to find the most tenacious detective, Al McCoy, hot on their trail. Bison's cowboys held him off until July 1911, when the patents company filed suit and Bison vanished into Bear Valley. Their Santa Monica ranch lacked drinking water, and the place was deserted in the summer. But as soon as the weather eased, Bison returned to it, put up fences and warning notices, and placed cowboys on regular patrol.

Not far away, at the resort of Venice, was the Miller Brothers 101 Ranch Real Wild West Show—or part of it—seeking the California sun to improve their motion pictures. Their manager, W. A. Brooks, was also their film director, and they worked in various locations, including the little town of Hollywood.

Their real home was near Bliss (now Marland), Oklahoma. The 101 Ranch was not simply a circus, but a vast spread, formerly virgin land in the Cherokee Strip, which had become the largest diversified farm in the world. Cattleman George Washington Miller participated in the second great Oklahoma land rush, in 1893, and staked enough land to start the ranch, which he named 101 for his

Thomas H. Ince with an original stagecoach, at Inceville.

cattle brand. Miller's three sons, Joseph C.,* George L., and Zack T., were as remarkable as their father; all three held the honorary rank of colonel, which was given to prominent citizens as a sign of respect, and all three were passionate Westerners. The Old West might pass from sight elsewhere in the land, but the Miller brothers ensured it would linger forever at the 101.

The ranch encompassed Indian lands, upon which the Indians were encouraged to stay; veteran cowboys were hired to train new hands, and buffalo herds imported to join the vanishing longhorn. Old Colonel Miller claimed to have originated the Wild West show in 1882, a year before Cody, but twenty-two years elapsed before his sons held the next 101 show, or roundup, as they preferred to call it. A rodeo arena seating twelve thousand was constructed, and at the height of its glory, a hundred thousand people a year visited the ranch. So many motion picture companies used it as a location that the ranch formed its own motion picture department and made its own films. From the 101 bunkhouses emerged the most prominent movie cowboys, Tom Mix and Buck Jones. So did Western director Cliff Smith. Among its performers was Mabel Normand, the brilliant comedienne. In later years, hopeful Western stars claimed association with the 101 as actors claimed association with Griffith.

The idea of the 101 Ranch joining forces with the Bison Company was such a good one that it is hardly surprising several people sought credit for it. "One day I hit upon the idea of putting on some Indian and Cowboy pictures in the mountain passes down Santa Monica way," said Thomas H. Ince. "So I leased the land and

---

* Joseph C. Miller appeared in the 101 production of *The Exposition's First Romance* (1915), made at the San Francisco Exposition.

The Miller Brothers 101 Ranch Real Wild West Show at Inceville.

Colonel Joe Miller (third from left), of the Miller Brothers 101 Ranch, with Thomas Ince (second from left, in cap) and Sioux at Inceville.

contracted with the Miller Brothers for the use of their entire stock, the '101 Ranch show' having just at that time arrived at one of the nearby beach resorts for the summer months."[1]

Ince was hired in New York as part of the reorganization of the Bison Company. He arrived on the West Coast early in November 1911. The deal with the 101 was announced in *Moving Picture World* of 2 December 1911, the *World* having a press date two weeks earlier. It is unlikely that negotiations on such a scale could have been finalized in a few days by a new arrival.

On the other hand, Bison already had a chief director, Fred Balshofer, a veteran of Western film-making whose stock company included such Indian players as James Young Deer and Princess Mona Darkfeather and such cowboys as Art Acord, Hoot Gibson, and Jess McGaugh. Balshofer was the man (with NYMP head Charles Baumann) responsible for securing the 101.[2] He even visited the 101 Ranch and considered moving his entire outfit to Oklahoma, until he found that while they had everything necessary for Westerns, they had nothing to compare with the Santa Monica Mountains for scenery.

W. A. Brooks, a cousin of the Miller brothers and an ex-cowpuncher himself, led to the Santa Ynez canyon a procession that must have delighted the Bison people who saw it, for it gave them the lead over every other producer of Westerns in the country: prairie schooners, stagecoaches, horses, oxen, bison, cowboys, cowgirls, and Indians. The Indians set up their tepees on the edge of the canyon, in isolation from the rest of the camp. The combined forces went into production with *War on the Plains,* under the direction of Thomas Ince. It was highly praised. "The true history of early life in the Wildest West is being written on film. The impression that it all leaves is that here we have a presentation of Western life that is real and that is true to life, and that we would like to see it again and again so as to absorb more of the details."[3]

Ince was an energetic and efficient director, but one of his best-developed talents was that of self-promotion. With *War on the Plains* he went so far as to take credit for the Western itself: "Forthwith the western sprang into instant favor," he said. "Producing companies everywhere set about the manufacture of cowboy and Indian films. Wild West shows were besieged with offers of employment to their members." And this flight of fancy was printed in *Moving Picture World,*[4] usually a paragon of accuracy, which had objected to the overproduction of Westerns the very year that Ince joined Bison.

Whatever his drawbacks, Ince proved a figure of heroic proportions in the development of the motion picture. When Fred Balshofer wrote his book with Arthur Miller, *One Reel a Week,* part of the Ince myth was punctured. Yet Ince was responsible for so many advances at this stage that he had no need to claim other people's.

Balshofer's interest in the NYMP was bought out by the owners, Kessel and Baumann, who were planning to form Mutual with Harry Aitken. But Ince was running the show long before Balshofer's involvement was relegated to history. He imposed Eastern business methods upon the easy-going Californians. He installed a water system so that work could continue throughout the summer. He streamlined production methods, and he rationalized the impulsive approach of those in charge of stories. When a steady run of bad weather threatened his schedules, he moved the entire company to Edendale in one night and resumed production the next morning. The picture people and the cowboys alike respected Ince because he was as rugged as they were and because he worked as hard as anyone. The ranch, called the Miller 101 Bison ranch, became more familiarly known as Inceville.

The importance of Inceville to the Western might almost be compared to the importance of Detroit to the automobile. Ince's improvement in production techniques allowed him to turn out longer and more elaborate films. As early as February 1912, three months after his arrival, his face glowered, Mussolini-like, from the cover of the NYMP magazine,[5] for he had achieved the Herculean task of producing no less than four epic two-reelers: *War on the Plains, The Indian Massacre, The Battle of the Red Men,* and *The Deserter.* "The world has gone wild over the 101 Bison pictures. Critics who have seen Mr. Ince's work proclaim him the Belasco of the moving picture business, and none can with fairness dispute his right to the appellation."[6]

But the Patents Company was still causing trouble for the independents. When NYMP joined the sheltering umbrella of Universal, a power struggle led to a resurgence of the kind of warfare the company had been formed to avoid. The NYMP laboratory in New York was twice attacked by gangsters, and Irvin Willat, who was there for the second raid, recalls several shots being fired. Universal's strong-arm men were all set to storm the Santa Ynez canyon in a similar manner. Had they done so, history might have recorded the first battle of a new Civil War, for the 101 people were spoiling for a fight. Wrote Balshofer: "Jim Brooks [*sic*], who was in charge of the Indians, had them dress in full regalia and cover their faces with war paint. He then asked them to parade on a ridge well in view of anyone approaching the canyon along the beach road, the only way to get in. One of the several prop cannons we used in our Indian and soldier pictures Brooks placed pointing in the direction the enemy was expected to come and he had his Indians carrying army muskets and jumping and hopping in an Indian war dance. The whole thing was staged by Brooks. Some of the cowboys joined in the fun and fired their guns in the air, using blank cartridges."[7]

Universal offered an armistice in return for a certain sum; they also demanded the name of Bison for their own product. The NYMP, caught out over a contract, submitted, and the unromantic Kay-Bee (for Kessel and Baumann) was substituted for the Ince product. Universal (which later won Francis Ford and other Ince personnel) shipped in their own Indians, cowboys, and longhorn cattle, producing elaborate Indian-and-military Westerns along the Ince lines, under the trademark of 101-Bison. Miller Brothers promptly sued to prevent this unauthorized use of 101, but Universal clung to the charismatic brand. Their 101-Bison pictures were often impressive, for former Ince directors like Ford and Frank Montgomery made them, but the magic—the Ince touch and the Inceville dust—were missing.

Historians have drawn the inevitable parallels between D. W. Griffith and Ince, showing how profoundly Ince was influenced. A striking example was *Custer's Last Fight* (1912), which bears astonishing resemblance in its treatment to Griffith's *The Massacre.* Yet the films were in production at the same time and finished on the same day.[8] It is taking nothing from Griffith to say that the Ince Westerns were generally superior and that *The Massacre* was an attempt to outdo

Thomas Ince with William Eagleshirt.

Inceville cowboys line up outside the schoolhouse.

The Inceville Sioux taking part in Custer's Last Fight *(1912).*

Part of the Sioux village at Inceville, 1913.

Ince on his own ground. Ince was an experienced director, but at Inceville he withdrew from active direction to a position where he could control all the pictures in production. *Custer's Last Fight* was the work of Francis Ford, who made many of Ince's very best pictures. As Ford observed, Ince had no scruples about claiming credit for direction, and often for the story as well.[9] Ince's methods were less heinous than they appear. Directors were not held in the same esteem as they are today, and Ince felt that by saying *he* had directed it, the film would stand a better chance with exhibitors. His technique can be most closely related to that of Walt Disney; the public had no interest in the dozens of animators who actually created Mickey Mouse—they responded to the name of the product. Ince was not concerned with who did what; he was building an industry.

His emphasis on business efficiency ensured that every item was exploited for its full value. At Inceville, actors were originally provided with tents for dressing rooms. When they complained that their clothes were visited by snakes and insects, the tents were supplanted by log cabins. These were eventually replaced by barrack-like structures that served as anything from costume store to commissary. "These studio buildings were built to be used as exterior sets," wrote Bessie Love. "Cutting rooms, dressing rooms, offices were in a Scottish fishing village or a far western town. If you were a cutter and your lunch break came and someone was dying right outside your front door, you would just have to wait until he was truly dead and the director yelled 'Cut!' "[10]

The sheer atmosphere of Inceville was responsible for much of the quality. According to John Gilbert, who began as an extra at Inceville, the camp had its own hierarchy. The cowboys under Pedro Leon were the aristocrats. They ordered the actors about from the heady heights of their steeds. The actors were hams, and the least distinguished were known as "bushwa." "The word must have been derived from the French *bourgeois,* which Webster defines as 'common people, lacking in distinction or refinement,' " wrote Gilbert.[11] "The itinerary of the bushwa from town to camp was as follows: a streetcar from Santa Monica to the Long Wharf (the longest in the world), a change there to a stagecoach, drawn by double teams of mules; a four-mile spin over a king's highway, past palisades and canyons and purple heathered slopes and a great, friendly Pacific which roared each early-morning greeting. When the last bend in the road hid the first glimpse of Inceville, twenty voices in unison called 'Yoo-hoo-oo-oo!' And as the camp came into view, an echo, rich but trembling: 'Yoo-hoo-oo-oo!' The old gateman had answered. My crusty old gateman who loved only the bushwa. Valleys filled with blossoming sage and poppies and yucca . . . a young world mad with ecstatic life, a fifteen-dollar-a-week world, but—swell!

" 'What'll we do today?'

" 'Bill Hart posse!'

" 'Yaa-hoo!'

"Into sombreros and chaps; long mustaches on seventeen-year-old kids; down mountain paths on bronchos, with cowboys just beyond the rise, and out of sight of camera, lashing the horses' rump with a blacksnake. 'Jump, you lousy bushwa!' Clouds of dust and a hundred-foot drop if you slip. What matter? Maybe you'll get a part tomorrow."

For the city dweller, Inceville was not such a paradise. "For my first chore," said Grant Whytock, "they gave me a horse, a camera and some camera cases, and said, 'Go find a company.' Well, I didn't know what to do. I started out and roamed the hills around Santa Monica and finally located a company—shooting one of Bill Hart's Westerns. I had to stagger down the ravine with the loads of equipment. So when I got back, I said, 'The life of an assistant cameraman is not for me. It's too hard!' I asked to be put in the cutting room."[12] But even that sedentary life had its perils at Inceville, for rattlesnakes would sometimes seek shelter in the cool of the film vault.

Enid Markey remembered it as the most delightful studio imaginable. "The long row of dressing rooms looked out on the sea. I came from a mountain village and it created such a love for the sea. We had a man named Gellow, who had been a cook for all of the cowboys at the 101 Ranch. We would come in from location, hungry and tired, and he would produce fried ham, fried eggs, steaming pots of coffee and thick cream."[13]

Actors at Inceville required more than ordinary skill with a horse, for in film after film they found themselves pursued by some of the finest riders in the world.

"In *War's Women* I was on this horse, with my arms around Frank Keenan, and thirty cowboys dressed as Arabs were coming down over the sagebrush, just as fast as they could possibly go. And suddenly I lost my hold and I slipped off the back of the horse and into the sagebrush. They couldn't stop the horses—these thirty kept on and I could hear the yells and I gathered myself into a tiny knot convinced that a hoof was going to come down on my head. Suddenly, someone was picking me up and saying, 'Are you all right?' I sort of shook myself and I looked over and everyone was terribly frightened—and the cameraman had fainted! They got a fresh cameraman, but they put me back on the horse again and we did the whole thing over."[14]

Other companies might boast Indian actors, but no one could match the Inceville pictures for their scenes of Indians *en masse*. "The Indians were of the Sioux tribe," wrote Ince, "from one of the government reservations,* who had been loaned to the wild west show. When I took them over, I had to sign an agreement with the Indian commissioner in Washington according to which the Indians were to have certain hours of schooling. I furthermore had to assume full responsibility for their well being and care."[15]

To intrigue the public, Ince's press agents conveyed the smoldering violence of the Indians, who had to be under careful watch; according to them, they severely injured an actor with tomahawks and tried to load their guns with live rounds for the battle scenes. All of which was rubbish; they were such peaceable people that Ince said, "Arousing their anger sufficiently to attack the enemy with any semblance of reality was one of the hardest things I ever had to tackle in my whole career in motion pictures."[16]

Threats from the elements—repeated brush fires, delays from sea fogs, and storms battering the coast road—led to an exodus from Inceville. Harry Culver, anxious to found a city bearing his name, offered Ince free title to as many acres as he wanted provided he would build a studio. Ince, who was now eager to follow the trend toward society drama, persuaded Kessel and Baumann to finance the operation in 1915. Inceville remained in existence as a kind of distant back lot, and was used

---

* Pine Ridge, North Dakota.

until 1922. It passed into oblivion in 1924, when a fire destroyed the few sets still standing. Only a church set escaped.

The Ince films made in Culver City reflected the new environment and tended to follow trends rather than set them. When an epic Western called *The Covered Wagon* took the country by storm in 1923, Ince was obliged to return to the kind of picture he had been making ten years earlier. He planned a vast Western called *The Last Frontier* (directed by Breezy Eason and John Ince, Tom's brother), a kaleidoscope of covered wagons, Indian raids, and cavalry charges, featuring historical figures such as General Custer and Buffalo Bill. A buffalo stampede was shot in Wainwright National Park in Alberta, Canada, with the help of hundreds of Cree Indians. For Ince it was a return to first essentials. But he never lived to complete it. He died in 1924. The project, taken over by Hunt Stromberg, was completed in 1926 by George Seitz. *Photoplay* described it as "a feeble version of *The Covered Wagon*."[17]

Two years later John Gilbert wrote: "Occasionally, I take a long afternoon drive up to the beach beyond Santa Monica. Where the buildings and stages and western streets of Inceville used to be, are now the red flags and orange placards of a new subdivision called Castellammare. My stomach sickens as I turn my eyes seaward and pass this hideous destruction of what was once my glorious playground. One piece of movie statuary remains; high up on a hill, the weatherbeaten legs and torso of a plaster horse which once ornamented the square before a great set representing the Kaiser's palace. A state of depression invariably follows my return from this drive, and lingers with me for hours."[18]

Filming a buffalo stampede with the last herd of any great size, in Wainwright National Park, Alberta, Canada, for The Last Frontier *(1926). (The same sequence was used as stock footage in a 1938 Tex Ritter Western,* Where the Buffalo Roam.)

WILLIAM S. HART

Historians have bemoaned the fact that Ince's great period of Westerns, which began in 1911, was over as early as 1914. "Apart from W. S. Hart's pictures," wrote William K. Everson, "none of Ince's post war pictures had the authenticity and conviction enjoyed by such earlier films as *War on the Plains*."[1]

The reason lay not in conscious decision or artistic failure, but in straightforward business expediency. Following a power struggle, in which the Millers nearly wrested control of Inceville, their contract, due for renewal anyway, was discontinued. Such fratricidal warfare was characteristic of the industry once the common enemy of the Patents Trust had been weakened. Yet this particular battle has never been mentioned in the history books. Apart from trade-paper references, it is spoken of only in a single sentence in the autobiography of William S. Hart,[2] when he describes his attempt to buy a horse from the 101. Joe Miller refuses, because he does not want any of their stock to fall into the hands of the picture people.

Leona Kelly, a cowgirl with the 101, was at the Anglo-American Exposition in Shepherd's Bush, London, when war broke out. The authorities immediately impounded all the horses for military use. "In the end they gave most of them back because the cowpony was not very useful for the army."[3] Nevertheless, the 101 concluded a business arrangement with the Allies, which contributed to their decision to leave Ince. In November 1914, five thousand head of horses were shipped from the West to the Miller Brothers ranch in Oklahoma, and from there to Europe. This included the majority of horses stabled at Santa Ynez canyon. Inceville was left with two dozen Indians, a hundred and fifty head of horses, and a small herd of cattle. The day of the epic Ince Western was over.

William S. Hart replaced it with a series of carefully mounted films that have become celebrated for their poetic evocation of the Old West. His films were animated by the same spirit of romantic realism that distinguished the paintings of Charles Russell, whom Hart knew. He firmly rejected the circus-comedy approach of Tom Mix and, like Russell, he was genuinely concerned about authenticity.

Hart was born in the East—at Newburgh, New York—but his early life was spent in the West. His father, an Englishman, was a miller, but Hart's irrepressible romanticism transformed him into a more impressive figure: "there are yellow gold and black gold (oil) pioneers," he wrote. "My father was a white gold (flour) pioneer." In interviews, he glossed over his father's humble trade. "I come from a family of English lawyers," he said, "but my father broke the line. He was one of the pioneers in reclaiming the waste land of the west."[4]

As his father traveled from mill to mill, so young Hart saw more and more of the West. He was fascinated by the Indians, and he developed a close relationship with a Sioux woman ("I cannot call her a squaw," he wrote. "The memory of her kindness to me, her honesty and her straightforward character will not permit me to do so"[5]), who took him on trips and spoke to him as an adult. He learned to speak a certain amount of Sioux and to converse in the Indian sign language.

Hart left the West at fifteen, intending to go to West Point. Instead, he became an actor. Twenty years later, he was celebrated for his Messala in *Ben-Hur* and as a leading exponent of cowboy roles. When Hart played in *The Squaw Man* in 1905, W. B. "Bat" Masterson, the celebrated lawman, wrote to thank him for sending him a photograph "in the picturesque cowboy garb that was once so familiar to me," and commented: "Your portrayal of Cash Hawkins the cowboy desperado is exceptionally good—giving as you do to the part the proper atmosphere in every detail."[6]

In later years interviewers often quoted him as talking in apostrophes—"git a bit o' writin' done"—in the vernacular of the West, forgetting that his training as a Shakespearean actor would scarcely permit such a lapse in elocution.

In 1917 Hart told *Photoplay* magazine that he made no pretense of having been a cowboy, so he set out to learn all about it.[7] By 1929, in his autobiography, he claimed to have been a trail-herd cowboy in Kansas, although very young.

Hart's love for the West, however, was genuine, and while playing in a show in Cleveland he reached a kind of emotional crossroads: "I saw a Western picture. It was awful! I talked with the manager of the theater and he told me it was one of the best Westerns he had ever had. None of the impossibilities or libels on the West meant anything to him—it was drawing the crowds. The fact that the sheriff was dressed and characterized as a sort of cross between a Wisconsin woodchopper and a Gloucester fisherman was unknown to him. I did not seek to enlighten him. I was seeking information. In fact, I was so sure that I had made a big discovery that I was frightened that someone would read my mind and find it out."[8]

During a period of poverty, Hart had shared lodgings in a New York hotel with a fellow actor named Thomas H. Ince. Touring in California, Hart went to see his old friend, who took him out to Inceville. Hart was enraptured. "The very primitiveness of the whole life out there, the cowboys and the Indians, staggered me. I loved it. They had everything to make Western pictures. The West was right there!"[9]

Ince was a shrewd businessman, and no one ever accused him of generosity. He set about dampening Hart's ardor.

"Bill," he said, "it's a damn shame, but you're too late. The country has been flooded with Western pictures. They are the cheapest pictures to make and every company out here has made them. You simply cannot sell a Western picture at any price. They are a drug on the market."

Just as Hart was leaving, Ince said, "Bill, if you want to come out next spring and take a chance, I'll give you $75 a week to cover your expenses, and direct you in a picture myself."

"Tom," replied Hart, "I'll be here as soon as we close."[10]

While he enjoyed the atmosphere of Inceville, Hart was dismayed at the standard of his first two pictures. Ince took Hart off two-reelers, and gave him his first feature, *The Bargain,* directed by Reginald Barker from a scenario by C. Gardner Sullivan. *The Bargain* is an extraordinary film on several counts. Despite its early date (1914), it is put together with casual skill, as though Barker had been turning out similarly accomplished Westerns for the past decade.

Moving Picture World considered *The Bargain* "a reckless attempt to revive a style of motion picture which we had hoped was a thing of the past. There can be no doubt whatever that a picture of this kind has a bad influence on youthful minds."[11] The Western had yet to become historical.

With these films completed, Ince suggested to Hart that he abandon acting and take up directing. Hart (perhaps noticing that the titles of *The Bargain* proclaimed Ince as director) decided not to forfeit a season's work, and to return East. *The Bargain* proved to be a smash hit. Ince realized he had created a star and offered Hart a contract as director-actor at $125 a week. The sum was ungenerous, compared to what other Ince stars were getting—Frank Keenan was earning $1,000 a week in 1915—but Hart was delighted.

From his first film as director, *The Passing of Two-gun Hicks,* Hart was dependent on former cowboy Cliff Smith; so much so that he asked Ince to promote him to codirector. Smith, a 101 Ranch veteran, occasionally played in his own pictures, and according to his own account in the 1921 *Wid's Year Book,* worked on forty-five William S. Hart pictures before moving on to direct other leading Western stars, such as Tom Mix and Hoot Gibson, who valued him for his immense experience. Hart and Smith's cameraman was generally Joseph August.

"My little western 'horse opera' company and myself were supreme at camp," wrote Hart.[12] "When I thought of my freedom and looked at those hills of throbbing hearts, full of the life of my boyhood, I was content, even if I failed to go higher. If this mimic world of toil, where I was earning my living and reproducing days that were dear to me, was to be the top of my mountain, I was content. I was surrounded by no greedy grafters, no gelatin-spined, flatulent, slimy creatures—just dogs, horses, sheep, goats, bulls, mules, burros and white men and red men that were accustomed to live among such things. If we wanted a snake, we could

William S. Hart helps to carry camera gear; with him is Ann Little, a heroine of many early Westerns, who was part Indian.

Hart (left) and his codirector, Cliff Smith, a former 101 Ranch cowboy, indulge in a gag shot

go out in the hills and catch one—one that would warn us that he was a snake, with his rattles. . . . I was happy."

As the main studio moved to Culver City, Inceville became Hartville. Although the Ince methods were used in the Hart pictures, Hart was his own master, and he set about his task of transforming the Western from a burlesque into a facsimile of the truth as he remembered it.

If Hart had spent roughly ten years in the West, he had spent twenty in the theater, and first and foremost his films were melodramas. Authenticity and melodrama do not complement each other. Nevertheless, Hart ensured that his Western streets and saloons were stark and simple. As far as costume was concerned, the cowboys dressed up for the part. Hart wore a particularly distinctive outfit, but he justified every last stitch of it:

"One of the many things you have to thank the movies for is that they have about banished the old 'stage' cowboy. The real cowboy clothes are all made for utility, not for effect. Even the silk handkerchief he wears round his neck has its uses. When he's herding cattle he doubles the handkerchief cornerwise, and puts it over his face just beneath the eyes to keep the dust out of his nose and mouth. There is another reason as well. A cowboy is usually a bit of a dandy and likes a silk handkerchief because silk is soft to the face and neck. This he fastens with a valuable ring when he can afford one; when he can't, he'll use a poker-chip.

"Have you ever seen a stage cowboy with a vest on? I don't reckon so, for these creatures have to look romantic, and a vest's a prosaic affair. The lariat the cowboy constantly uses would cut him up considerably were it not for the 'leathers' which cover his arms from elbows to wrists. These afford protection, and are usually from five to seven and a half inches long.

"I remember a friend of mine, an actor who made his name in western roles, being asked why cowboys always wear their cartridge belts loose. Well, he didn't know. He was famous for his interpretations of cowboys, so he didn't want to own up. He replied: 'In the West, cowboys wear their belts tight. We only wear them that way on the stage because it looks romantic.' Do you know what would happen if a real cowboy were to wear his cartridge belt tight? First, recollect the weight of a cartridge belt. Imagine this *tight* round a man's waist when he's riding sixty or seventy miles—mostly at a gallop. The man would stand a fine chance of being cut in halves by the end of the journey.

"His spurs are fastened to spur leathers. The 'bells,' as we call the small balls of steel which shake and jingle as the cowboy walks, go through a hole in the rowel and hold it fast so that it will not turn in the usual way when it touches the horse's flank."[13]

Hart's explanation, fascinating as it was, did not mark the writer as a man with a complete knowledge of Western lore. A correspondent wondered why he had selected the least important reason for each part of the puncher's outfit.

"Take the neckerchief—the first and foremost use for this is to protect such of his neck as escapes the shadow of his hat from blistering in the hot sun. Then again, the loose holster belt—the reason for this is because the hand falls more naturally to a weapon placed there; in fact, it is impossible to draw quickly a gun with a six inch barrel from a holster on the waist-line because your arm has to double up and your armpit gets in the way.

"Lastly the spurs—being large, they enable the rider to lock them in the girth, enabling him to pick up objects, etc., and to make a small target by lying along the horse's neck. The 'jangles' or 'bells' very often enable a man's favorite horse—it must be remembered that a puncher has upwards of six horses in his string in the remuda—to know the approach of his master at night when otherwise he might be scared and bolt. Possibly Mr. Hart takes it for granted that everyone should already know the above reasons, but from experience of Easterners I know very few who know the difference between a 'center-fire' and a 'double cinch' saddle."[14]

Such specialized details may seem picayune in the light of the achievements of the William S. Hart films. But it is precisely in such minute details, as Erich von Stroheim proved, that the difference lies between an exact representation and a rough equivalent.

In a sense, Hart had a more difficult job than von Stroheim. The cowboy was no more bound to wear a particular item of clothing than any other civilian. There was a great diversity of dress and behavior, and what was true for one area was unknown in another. Hart presented the West of the popular imagination, and in his Puritan Westerner people could see an idealized portrait of their fathers or uncles; his films brought to life the stories they told. The spirit of the West was there, for it was hard to shoot on those magnificent locations and avoid it. And occasionally, when the dust had covered the motion picture costumes, and Hart and his cowboys stopped acting, the camera recorded moments of absolute perfection.

It must be recorded that cowboys loved William S. Hart, and few criticized his sense of accuracy at the time. When he took a train to New York in 1917, cowboys gathered at the railroad stations to greet him. Their enthusiasm as well as their numbers might have been subject to press-agent exaggeration, but that same year the Cowboys' Reunion Association of Las Vegas, New Mexico, voted him, along with actor Dustin Farnum, the most popular cowboy in the world. (This Reunion was held in what was then the only primitive cattle country that remained unfenced.)

Life on location for the Hart company had its parallels to life on the range. An English journalist from *Pictures and Picturegoer* spent a day in the Mojave Desert with Hart and came away convinced she had seen the West as it really was.

"As many as two to three hundred people accompany Mr. Hart on his location trips and pitch their camp for a week or a fortnight, as occasion demands. Everybody bunks in tents, and a chuck-wagon is taken along to serve as a kind of perambulating cafeteria. There are no hors d'oeuvres, of course, but plenty of beef, beans, potatoes, peas and corn. There is a wonderful spirit of good fellowship on these location trips. . . .

"You would be amazed to see what children these great husky men really are. One of their favourite games is one that Bill himself learned as a boy with his Indian playmates, and which is known as 'Indian Blind Man's Buff.'

"Then there is wrestling, boxing, fancy roping and riding, and of an evening they play poker or shoot craps around the camp fire."

Hart explained that the boys kept order among themselves, without any interference from him. " 'They have their own "kangaroo" courts. The guilty party is promptly "chapped." In other words, the offender gets a spanking with a pair of

The William S. Hart company makes camp on the Mojave River. Locations for Western pictures often required the company to live rough, since hotels might be hundreds of miles away.

leather chaps. The punishment may be five to ten lashes, and if the offence is a grave one, they lay it on with wet chaps. And you may take my word for it, that a man wants to reform when he has once had a taste of damp leather.'

"'I'm glad,' said Mr. Hart, as we shook hands at parting, 'that you'll be able to tell the folks in the old country that the West I give them in the pictures is the *real* thing.' It sure is."[15]

Hart was extremely proud of his friendship with Wyatt Earp, William "Bat" Masterson, "Uncle" Billy Tilghman, and Al Jennings. He had a close acquaintance with Charles Siringo, the cowboy detective, and gave him small parts in *Tumbleweeds* (he appears in a barroom scene and in the celebration of the town, beating a drum). He also knew Charles Russell from his theatrical days, and one of his proudest possessions was a 1908 painting by Russell showing Hart in Western outfit (it appears as the frontispiece for his book *My Life East and West*).

Many of the stories he had heard from these old-timers, Hart admitted, would furnish finer material than any script ever written, but they would never be accepted by either the critics or the picture-going public. "Truth," he said, "is so frequently stranger than fiction, only you'll never get people to believe in it."[16]

It is a great loss to the history of both the motion picture and the West that Hart never really believed in it himself. For now that his melodrama has dated, his stories often have only curiosity value. This is not to underestimate the films, for the best of them have an epic quality that transcends the lurid melodrama. *Hell's Hinges* (1916), directed by Charles Swickard,* had Hart's bad-man character, Blaze Tracy, exact divine retribution upon a wicked township in a fire scene of breathtaking grandeur. *The Narrow Trail* (1917), directed by Lambert Hillyer, was a visual eulogy to Hart's pinto pony, Fritz, and brought the Western hero into city life at San Francisco, culminating in a devastating saloon brawl. Hart's fight scenes, which in his book he claims were not faked, were exceptionally brutal for the time. In *The Testing Block* (1920) he takes on his entire outlaw band to prevent them "visiting" a show girl, then, battered and bleeding, he seizes her himself. Occasionally, Hart's films were unrelentingly vicious. And despite Hart's professed admiration for the Indians, they generally appeared as primitive savages in his films.

Hart's attitude toward history was crystallized when he wrote *A Lighter of Flames;*[17] he had long wanted to write the true story of Patrick Henry, but when it came to it, he found it necessary to transpose some dates and incidents. "I have called it in my own mind fictional history—an effort to make that vibrant past and its heroic actors live again."

Fictional history was what the other Western companies produced, and Hart, for all his emphasis on accuracy, was actually in the same league. Although it pained him to see the liberties Westerns took with facts—"I have seen one western," he wrote in 1939, "*The Plainsman*. I'll never go again. I'm no good for weeks afterwards. It isn't what is wrong. There is never anything right"[18]—he took almost as many himself.

He was greatly concerned about his image with boys. He wrote a couple of books for boys emphasizing frontier virtues, and a slim volume "by Bill Hart's Pinto Pony" in which Fritz is made to say: "I suppose it must be fine for a boy to have something to look up to. A regular hero. It must be healthy for him, and give him a high mark to shoot at. . . ."[19]

If this naive attitude was a drawback where Hart's stories are concerned, it gave him the enthusiasm to produce them. Richard Griffith summed it up: "The west was opened by men whose tenacity in the face of hardship was matched by a boyish desire for adventure for its own sake. As the new country was developed, this latter quality became an anachronism, and soon *only* an outlaw could live what formerly was the normal life of all men on the frontier. Admiration for, as well as envy of, the glorified outlaw has persisted into our own period among that section of the population which retains an adolescent point of view; the worship of the gangster is its most recent manifestation. But the moral revolution which took place after 1920 made the Hart films seem suddenly rather naive. Hart himself remained personally popular, but exhibitors complained that his pictures were old fashioned."[20]

In 1924 Paramount informed Hart that future story decisions would be made

---

* *Hell's Hinges* is generally credited to Hart. However, he was taken off the direction (*Moving Picture World,* 2 October 1915, p. 87). Ince personally directed the fire scene.

by the studio, and he would be required to work under studio supervision. Rather than submit, Hart withdrew from Paramount altogether.

This was not his first setback. He had clashed with Thomas Ince—their final flareup, appropriately enough, was over Hart's pinto pony—and deeply disappointed in the behavior of his old friend, Hart refused to speak to him. He won a lawsuit against him, and he is harsh on Ince in his book. But it is a human trait to resent the person to whom one owes gratitude. James Card of George Eastman House says that the surviving scripts show Ince's controversial supervision to have been important.[21] And there can be no doubt that Ince's influence on Hart's style of production was indelible. Even when Hart moved from Hartville, his pictures bore the unmistakable stamp of Ince. Many of them were directed by Lambert Hillyer, a director trained at Inceville. Cliff Smith returned for such films as *Wild Bill Hickok* and *Singer Jim McKee*. J. G. Hawks, scenario writer from the Ince days, worked for Hart as an independent. The cameraman on most of the films was Joe August. And when Hart returned to the screen in 1925 to make *Tumbleweeds*, he hired C. Gardner Sullivan, who had written his first feature picture, to write this one, which proved to be his last.

MORE THAN ANY OF THE HARTS, *Tumbleweeds* looks like the sort of film a cowboy might have made. This is a two-edged compliment: Hart imbues the story with more dust-choked, wind-blown atmosphere than ever. But he adds the heavy-handed humor and simple sentiments of the cowpuncher to a story (by Hal Evarts for the *Saturday Evening Post*) which C. Gardner Sullivan, with characteristic severity, had already whittled down to its melodramatic bones. Joe August's photography is superb, and for much of its eight reels, *Tumbleweeds* is exquisitely shot hokum.

The film takes wings with the land-rush scene, among the finest sequences of pure action in film history. It was duplicated by John Ford in *Three Bad Men* and for Wesley Ruggles's *Cimarron*. So brilliantly conceived, edited, and photographed is this sequence that it is hard to believe it was the work of King Baggot. Baggot, who directed the rest of *Tumbleweeds* with Hart, was a competent enough director, but it took more than competence to achieve this scene. *Cimarron*'s land rush was shot by B. Reaves Eason, responsible for the chariot race in *Ben-Hur*, but no evidence exists to suggest that a second-unit director was employed on *Tumbleweeds*.

Photoplay reported that three hundred wagons, more than a thousand horses, and nearly a thousand men, together with dogs, goats, and other livestock, were involved in this one spectacular high spot, re-creating an event that had involved fifty thousand people competing for land which the government had purchased from the Cherokees at $1.25 an acre.[22] The land rush surged forward from the starting line at the Kansas border at the sound of an army cannon at high noon on 22 April 1889.

Said *Photoplay:* "With nineteen cameras trained on the scene, this thrilling fight for land was re-enacted at the La Agoura Rancho, some forty miles from Hollywood. And it had all the thrill of the old west. It was hard to believe that it was simply a picture. At the shriek of a siren and blasts from army bugles, the great horde of vehicles and stock swept into action across the softly sloping hollow of the hills. Hundreds of spectators lined the neighboring hills and cheered them

Hart's standing set at his Newhall ranch. Lambert Hillyer, director, on horseback; Joe August leaning on lefthand camera; Victor Milner, extreme right.

Preparing for the land rush at the Cherokee Strip—one of the outstanding action sequences in silent films—a scene from Hart's Tumbleweeds *(1925).*

on, almost forgetting in the excitement that it was but mimicry. King Baggot, assisted by J. H. McCloskey,* directed the spectacle and so well was it handled that not a man or horse was injured."[23]

The build-up to the cannon shot that starts the race is rhythmically cut in a style usually associated with the Russian film-makers, but since no Soviet films had yet been seen in America, such influence can be discounted. Close-ups of a watch held by the cavalry major (played by Captain Taylor E. Duncan, Philippine campaign veteran and formerly commander of the Lasky Home Guard) are intercut with the gun crew; the mass of wagons; the horses bucking impatiently; Hart trapped in his stockade; an elderly couple, tense and anxious; the Widow Riley with her family; the wagons, moving slightly as the horses strain. Then the cavalry commander again, the watch; ten seconds to go . . . the gun crew . . . close-up of a soldier's hand holding the firing string . . . long shot of the hundreds of wagons . . . big close-up of the watch—high noon! The cavalry commander lowers his hand. The cannon fires. Hart's horse, alone by a tree, starts in fright. The whole mass of wagons, buggies, carts, and individual riders bursts forward in an avalanche of movement.

Although almost every subsequent shot appears to be a traveling shot, virtually none of them are. Akeley cameras, with long-focus lenses, follow the wagons and riders, and the speed and precision of the following gives the impression of tracking. The long-focus lenses are used creatively, breaking up the jumbled blur and bringing one plane of the action into sharp focus. Extreme long shots, showing the massed wagons, are intercut with telling details: a horse, with one leg caught, being dragged along by the others in the team . . . Hart's knife, cutting its way out of the stockade . . . pit shots of hooves . . . an intrepid man mounted on a penny-farthing bicycle . . . a wagon careening over the side of a hill . . . excited children inside a wagon, clutching a pig. As the sequence reaches its height, plane after plane of action fills the frame. Finally, most incredible of all, a celestial shot of William S. Hart as a rider in the sky; the Akeley operator fills the picture with Hart (or rather his double), and the ground drops below the frame. The horse seems to be galloping through space. Then away goes Hart, the ground returns beneath his feet, and he is certain of victory.

Tumbleweeds was well received upon its initial showing in New York, but United Artists deliberately mismanaged its general distribution, as Hart proved in court. However, it was a bitter victory. He lost a great deal of money, and retired from pictures. In 1939 *Tumbleweeds* was reissued with music and effects, and with an introduction, photographed at Hart's ranch at Newhall, which, as William K. Everson points out, is virtually the film of a man delivering his own obituary.

Hart, wearing his Western costume, addresses the audience. His voice is melodious, deep, redolent with the tones of the theater. He overplays, as he did in most of his silent films, but there is no denying the majesty of the man, with his magnificent, hawk-like face. He concludes:

"My friends, I loved the art of making motion pictures. It is as the breath of

---

* Justin McCloskey was John Ford's production manager on *The Iron Horse* and later directed a couple of program pictures.

life to me. But through those hazardous feats of horsemanship that I loved so well to do for you, I received many major injuries. That, coupled with the added years of life, preclude my again doing those things that I so gloried in doing. The rush of the wind that cuts your face . . . the pounding hooves of the pursuing posse. Out there in front, a fallen tree trunk that spans a yawning chasm, with a noble animal under you that takes it in the same low, ground-eating gallop. The harmless shots of the baffled ones that remain behind, and then, the clouds of dust through which comes the faint voice of the director—'Okay, Bill, okay. Glad you made it. Great stuff, Bill, great stuff. And say, Bill, give old Fritz a pat on the nose for me, will you?' Oh, the thrill of it all! Adios, amigos . . . God bless you all, each and every one."

William S. Hart died on 23 June 1946.

Hart, stricken as he watches the breakup of the Old West, in Tumbleweeds.

LAWMEN AND OUTLAWS

The silent film was close enough to the frontier era to record not only the look of the Old West but, even more significantly, several of its outstanding personalities.

William Tilghman, last of the great Western marshals, was a former buffalo hunter, like Bat Masterson, for whom he worked in Dodge City. He spent six years as a lawman there, two of them as marshal, and then returned to his ranch. By 1908 he had retired, although President Roosevelt, with his predilection for colorful Westerners, brought him back to hunt for an absconding paymaster.

Tilghman had been associated with political campaign films and in 1908 had made *The Bank Robbery*, with outlaw Al Jennings, fresh out of jail. Jennings produced a picture about his exploits in 1914, and, as if in reply, Tilghman produced *The Passing of the Oklahoma Outlaws* (1915), which depicted the destruction of the Doolin and Jennings gangs. There was no plot, but Tilghman stressed the sordidness of an outlaw's life, rather than investing it with false glamour. Mrs. Tilghman records that each incident was staged with an eye to historical accuracy; Tilghman used official records when he needed them. "But his own mind was a storehouse of western history," she wrote. "He had a remarkable memory for events and dates and could relate instantly the story of any notable outlaw, or any bank or train robbery that occurred during his official days, whether he had any part in it or not. Newspaper men often called him for such information."[1]

Tilghman formed the Eagle Film Company, and Colonel Lute Stover, who had experience as a scenario writer, wrote the script for *The Passing of the Oklahoma Outlaws* from material supplied by Tilghman. J. B. Kent was cameraman and Marshal E. D. Nix, Chris Madsen, John Hale, and Caleb R. Brooks, United States attorney, appeared personally in the film. Arkansas Tom, the only survivor of the Doolin gang, who had emerged from jail after seventeen years, played himself, and provided inside information. The capture of Bill Doolin was filmed precisely where it happened, at Eureka Springs, Arkansas. The battle of the Spike S Ranch, and the later capture of the Jennings gang, was filmed with Marshal Bud Ledbetter playing himself and acting as technical adviser.

As the film neared completion in 1915, an event occurred which shows that at least on this occasion, the motion picture had a direct influence on Western history. One of the most notorious of all bank robbers, Henry Starr,* rode into Stroud, Oklahoma, with a gang of four, and held up two banks simultaneously, repeating the feat which had cost the lives of most of the Dalton gang. But Starr improved on their performance to a degree; his gang escaped with the money, until a seventeen-year-old named Paul Curry opened fire, bringing down Starr as well as the man carrying the money.

Tilghman was seventeen miles from Stroud, at Chandler. He stopped work on his film and raced over, reverting at once to the role of lawman and capturing a notorious criminal called "Alibi Joe" Davis.

---

* Nephew of Belle Starr (Myra Belle Shirley), who was the mistress of Jesse James.

A 1919 photo of Deputy U.S. Marshal Bill Tilghman (right) in front of a theater in Detroit, Michigan, showing his film The Passing of the Oklahoma Outlaws. *His collection of guns is on display, and one is playfully tucked into the belt of the man at left of center.*

LEFT: *Bill Tilghman (left) in his heyday—at the opening of the Cherokee Strip—with C. F. Colcord. Perry, Oklahoma, September 1893.*
RIGHT: *Henry Starr in 1915.*

Tilghman arrested a couple of other men, then resumed his role as film-maker; as the remaining bank robbers were brought in to Chandler, they were filmed by J. B. Kent, Tilghman's cameraman. The camera filmed Starr in the hospital, and caught Zack Mulhall, the well-known showman, coming to visit the wounded outlaw. Some years earlier, Starr had worked at his ranch.

Starr was sentenced to twenty-five years, which would have brought him freedom in the distant 1930s. But he spilled so much information that he was guaranteed parole and emerged from jail in 1919. Endeavoring to go straight, Starr purchased a one-fourth interest in the Pan-American Motion Picture Company of Tulsa, Oklahoma. The first picture he appeared in, *A Debtor to the Law* (1919, reissued 1924), was a careful reconstruction of his double bank-robbery, filmed at Stroud, with bank employees and townspeople cooperating, and even Paul Curry good-humoredly re-creating his own attempts to kill. With a degree of poetic justice, Starr's producer, W. C. Martin, cheated him out of his share of the profits. Starr received offers from a California company, but he could not risk going to California for fear that the Arkansas authorities would start new extradition proceedings. He did his utmost to recover the money due him—for the profits of *Debtor to the Law* and another 1919 picture, *Evening Star,* were said to have been $15,000[2] —and to recover a tenth of that sum in 1920 justified hiring a lawyer. But Starr could not afford lawyer's fees and pleaded for a mere hundred dollars from old friends to help him wage his war against Martin.

Bill Tilghman met Starr in Kansas City, discovered he was broke, and uncharitably went straight to Governor Robertson. "Henry's got that wild look in his eye," he said. "He's getting ready to rob another bank and you'd better revoke his parole."[3] Before the governor had such an opportunity, Starr, with three confederates, tried to rob a bank at Harrison, Arkansas, in February 1921 and was killed by the banker, who kept a shotgun handy in his vault.*

When his film was completed, Bill Tilghman was drawn into the role of showman. His associates in the Eagle Film Company were active lawmen, and they could not devote enough time to the exploitation of *The Passing of the Oklahoma Outlaws.* Mrs. Tilghman declared that the film frequently broke house records, and she quotes letters to prove it. "We are doing well at the Tabor Grand, are having the biggest run of any picture show in Denver. . . . My lecture is a drawing card . . . the proprietor said yesterday he wouldn't have the picture without me."[4]

But Colonel Tim McCoy remembered such successes as rare exceptions. "Bill Tilghman did what Buffalo Bill did—he made pictures of his exploits. But they were inferior pictures. He would go round the country and come into a town. He would hire a window in one of the main stores and put on show his collection of pistols. He had the damndest collection of six-shooters I ever saw. He gave his shows, and his lecture, took his percentage of the gate, and went on to the next town—starving to death. Hell, the public didn't know him. Unless they had a knowledge of the history of that country, they would never even have heard of Bill Tilghman."[5]

When William S. Hart's *Wild Bill Hickok* reached Oklahoma City in 1923,

* "My wife is from Harrison, Arkansas. Her parents knew the banker who shot Starr when he robbed the bank there in 1921, and they heard the story many times. The banker was a mild fellow who regretted the killing, although it was quite justified" (Jack Spears).

Bill Tilghman was brought out of retirement for personal appearances as "about the last survivor of the Hickok crowd."[6] The next year, at the age of seventy, he set out to clean up the oil town of Cromwell and was shot to death by an alcoholic gunman.

Tilghman was the most colorful lawman to involve himself in pictures, but several lesser-known personalities added color of their own to early pictures. Pat Fields, a nephew of Henry Starr, who became a lawman instead of an outlaw, was a friend of Tom Mix and spent several years playing supporting roles in Mix Westerns.

Ed Morrell, a member of the Sontag and Evans gang, was sprung from San Quentin by Jack London, who based his book *The Star Rover* on Morrell's experiences in prison. Morrell toured the lecture circuit with a film made by George Sontag.

Jesse Lasky, Jr., remembered family tales of Sontag and Evans as stagecoach robbers: "My father's mother, Sarah, used to take the stage from San Francisco to Los Angeles in the days before the railroad was built. She was very proud of the fact that on one occasion she had saved the other passengers' valuables. She was the only lady traveling in the coach. When she heard the shooting up ahead, she collected all the purses, wallets and watches and placed them under her bustles. When the door was flung open and everyone was ordered out, she pleaded sickness. There was a tradition of chivalry in the West—women were either whores or ladies—so they took what small change the passengers still had on them, and galloped off."[7]

The Folly of a Life of Crime was the censor-proof title given to the reconstruction of the activities of the Sontag and Evans gang. Sontag formed the U.S. Feature Film Company of Oroville, California, in 1914 to produce this film, and Chris Evans, also on parole, went to court to try to obtain an injunction to stop production. He failed. A bizarre trade-press announcement is all that survives of this fascinating film, directed by Harry Harvey: "This picture is vested, not from mechanical ideas, but of actual conditions of the original existence of the Sontag and Evans gang of California, FEATURING MR. GEORGE SONTAG, who has lectured along these lines throughout the United States in a fifteen-minute talk hypothecating this wonderful two and a half hour sitting, displaying throughout the early history and career of the said gang . . . showing the various systems conducted in stage robberies and train hold-ups; showing the hard struggles of the officers to follow this gang as is readily known; showing the capture of the gang; of the sentence of life imprisonment upon them; also showing the prison break made on several occasions at Folsom Prison; featuring the hardships and endurances these bandits have endured, and educating the young and old in this wonderful story and study. State Right Buyers Get Busy! This wonderful six-reel production, when shown, will thrill your thoughts of stratagems unquestionable."[8]

ALTHOUGH NEAL HART WAS born in New York, he went out West at the age of fourteen and worked on a vast horse ranch on the Sioux Reservation in South Dakota. At sixteen, he was driving a ten-horse freighting team from Fort Pierre to Rapid City in the Black Hills, moving on to Wyoming, where he worked with a trail herd into Rawhide Buttes. In 1898 he served aboard the U.S.S. *Panther* in the Spanish-American War. After a spell on the 101 Ranch, he became city marshal and deputy sheriff at Manville, Wyoming. He based his film *Butterfly Range* on incidents from his deputy sheriff days, when two important outlaw bands were brought to justice. Hart also directed the picture.

LEFT: *Outlaw Ed Morrell, whose experiences in jail inspired Jack London's* The Star Rover, *and who toured the lecture circuit with George Sontag's film* The Folly of a Life of Crime.
RIGHT: *George Sontag, stagecoach robber, formed a movie company to produce* The Folly of a Life of Crime *in 1914. This photo was taken at California's Folsom State Prison.*

Wyatt Earp in 1926. Earp had appeared in the background of The Half-Breed *(1915) but, according to director Allan Dwan, could not act convincingly enough to perform regularly in pictures.*

A fan from Torrington, Wyoming, wrote to *Motion Picture Magazine:* "A person was razzing Neal Hart because his name could be taken for Bill Hart. I knew Neal Hart before he ever thought of movies and he was Neal Hart. He was the first sheriff Manville, Wyoming, ever had, and the best one too."[9]*

The dividing line between lawmen and outlaws in the West was, to put it mildly, blurred. The celebrated Wyatt Earp, stern-eyed guardian of law and order in so many Westerns, had once been an outlaw himself, indicted by a grand jury on a horse-stealing charge. Years later Wyatt and his brothers were hired to keep the peace in Tombstone, Arizona, a task they conducted with a certain light-fingered permissiveness toward the roaring trades of gambling and prostitution. Their opponents referred to them as the Fighting Pimps. In his retirement Earp lived in Los Angeles and from time to time visited the studios to watch the making of Westerns. He tried to persuade William S. Hart to film his life story. But Earp was not the legend at this period that he became after his death.

Allan Dwan, however, used him in a picture. "He was a visitor to the set when I was directing Douglas Fairbanks in *The Half-Breed.* As was the custom in those days, he was invited to join the party and mingle with our background action. I think there was a trial of some kind. A group of people demanded that the half-breed be sent out of town. In that group was Earp; he only stood there and nodded his head.

"Earp was a one-eyed old man in 1915. But he had been a real marshal in Tombstone, Arizona, and he was as crooked as a three-dollar bill. He and his brothers were racketeers, all of them. They shook people down, they did everything they could to get dough. But they had the badge and they had the gun, and they won all their gunfights simply by shooting the man before he was told he was arrested. And so they were terrific heroes in the eyes of certain people.

"When I knew him, he was no longer a marshal, and there was no longer a West, and he couldn't be the symbol that he'd been. He looked for what anybody would look for. And the first person that got hold of him said he was a natural for show business. Well, he was and he wasn't. Our suspicion, because of the people that came around the set with him, was that he was looking for a place in law and order. He would have loved to have been Chief of Police of Los Angeles, or the marshal of the county. I think he was timid about being photographed, about acting and pretending. He knew inside himself that he wasn't an actor and had nothing to offer. I remember he saw Fairbanks bouncing around in the trees, and he said, 'Oh no, I'd not like to do that.' And I think for that reason he just finally took one last look and left.

"Years later, I made *Frontier Marshal* with Randolph Scott portraying Earp. One of his wives tried to sue us for suggesting Earp was ever in love with another woman. They didn't even let her in the courtroom, but she tried to sue for $50,000. We squared it by telling the wife that our leading lady was portraying her."[10]

Among the pallbearers at Wyatt Earp's funeral in 1929 were William S. Hart and Tom Mix.

---

* Neal Hart was a cousin of William S. Hart (Bob Birchard).

AL JENNINGS

The word "notorious" was often applied to outlaw Al Jennings, but it referred more to his failures than to his skill. He had the unhappy experience of blowing up the safe of a baggage car, only to find the car wrecked and the safe unharmed. In an attempt to save the day, Jennings robbed the passengers, grabbed a bunch of bananas and a jug of whisky from the wreckage, and rode away. What he lacked in expertise he made up for in humor.

Thanks to the intervention of Senator Mark Hannah, Jennings's lengthy prison sentence had been commuted by President McKinley, and in 1907 President Roosevelt granted him a full pardon. Jennings returned to his career as a lawyer, which he had practiced before he and his brother Frank turned to crime, and gradually became involved in politics. His memoirs, published in the *Saturday Evening Post,* coauthored by Will Irwin, attracted the Thanhouser Company, which hired him to play himself and act as technical adviser in a 1914 picture. Entitled *Beating Back,* a phrase Jennings used to describe his struggle to re-enter society, it was directed by Carroll Fleming and shot in New Jersey. It was an unusual Eastern Western, however, for its supporting players included several genuine cowboys, recruited from a Wild West show.[1]

Beating Back was permitted a showing at Sing Sing, where it received a rapturous reception, but it was banned by the Kansas City censor. He relented later when Al Jennings agreed to give a short lecture each time the film was shown. "I have been living an upright life for the last twelve years," he said, "and I could not, or would not allow anything to be shown on the screen that would have any immoral influence whatever, because it would immediately reflect upon me, and situated as I am at the present time, this would be very undesirable, if not dangerous."[2]

Jennings's earlier film, *The Bank Robbery* (1908), had a curious gestation.[3] Theodore Roosevelt was anxious to provide proof for a favorite story about a Rough Rider veteran, John Abernathy,* who could capture a wolf with his bare hands. He sent a motion picture cameraman, J. B. Kent, to Wichita National Preserve, where the wolf hunt was to be organized. In the nearby town of Cache, Oklahoma, Kent met the former outlaw Al Jennings, pardoned the year before and now trying to get into politics. Jennings and his gang had once robbed the Bank of Cache, and this incident so intrigued Kent that he postponed the wolf hunt and set about reconstructing the Jennings gang's exploits. Jennings's former adversary, William Tilghman, served as director, and can be seen escorting his prisoners past the camera in the final scene. Chief Quanah Parker† is also supposed to be in it, but he is rather harder to identify, for there are no close-ups.

What gives the film exceptional value is its documentary evidence: it is as

* Abernathy's children became national figures in 1909, when, at the age of five and nine, they rode on horseback from Guthrie, Oklahoma, to Santa Fe, New Mexico. In 1910 Jack Abernathy sent them on horseback to meet Roosevelt upon his return from his African safari. The Champion Film Company's first production was *Abernathy Kids to the Rescue* (Paul Spehr, *The Movies Begin* [Newark Museum, 1977], p. 66).

† Quanah Parker, the son of a white woman, was a Comanche war chief. He founded the Native American Church, or Peyote Cult as it was then known, which flourishes to this day.

Al Jennings (right) in Beating Back *(1914), with J. Morris Foster.*

primitive as any film could be while still remaining visible, yet here is a moving picture of the West, shot by Westerners before the Old West had entirely vanished. Cache, Oklahoma, resembles Hell's Hinges in the William S. Hart picture. The flimsy, false-fronted buildings might have been put up by Ince's art director, except that the film-makers, noticing nothing unusual, take little advantage of them. The film is composed with no aesthetic sense whatever, yet Kent and Tilghman capture in their first shot of the bank the essence of a hot day in a sleepy Western town; a dog hovers by the doorway, and a horse stands silhouetted in the background. An authentic stagecoach arrives. The bank robbery and the gunfight are staged as movies have always staged them—lots of smoke and wild movement, with everyone firing at once. According to Mrs. Tilghman, this scene was filmed at the close of business, by agreement with the banker. A citizen who failed to realize what was going on jumped out the window and ran to give the alarm, adding a bit of excitement that was entirely real.

The Bank Robbery can be singled out as perhaps the only Western in which horses relieve themselves without being censored. The cast, compared to later movie cowboys, are remarkably slow to mount their horses, but once aloft, at least they know what to do. On their feet, they stumble around with no direction of any kind. Such aimlessness is oddly attractive and helps to turn what would otherwise be a limp drama into the next best thing to a documentary.

J. B. Kent, or perhaps a second cameraman, was a somewhat eccentric technician. At the end of one shot, he pans his camera in a series of eye-thudding jerks, trying his best to follow a horseman, but going too far—picking up the little town and its church in a series of blurs and ending on a group of townspeople who have gathered to watch the filming. They are the original inhabitants of a town built in what was once Indian territory, and they wear the kind of clothes so few Western films ever get right. Only in such a primitive film could so fascinating an accident occur without being cut out before release.*

Wolf Hunt (1908), the third and last production of the Oklahoma Natural Mutoscene Company, is of equal fascination. John Abernathy is at last pitted against his wolf in a series of almost surrealistic scenes, and Al Jennings rides through the background of most of them. The sight of a man struggling with a wolf, his hands in its mouth or round its throat, is not particularly appealing, but the incidental documentation of Western costume and accouterments is rich.

Al Jennings was put forward as candidate for governor in the 1914 Democratic primary in Oklahoma, the very state that had once put $20,000 on his head. He polled a respectable number of votes and finished third. In 1915 he made another attempt to establish himself in pictures.

"I remember him as an ordinary little man who might have been cast as a grocery clerk," said Allan Dwan. "He came out to Hollywood, asked for work and got it. As soon as they knew he was Al Jennings, they opened the doors, because they knew who he was—and he had the usual book of lies all lined up. If you wanted something done in a Western the way it ought to be done, you asked him. How would you hold up a train? Not the way we see it done in movies. How did they *really* do it? It sounded awfully simple.

"In the first place, as he told it to me, two men would board the train at a station up the line. Fifteen or so would ride down the tracks to where they wanted to hold it up. The two men were ordinary passengers. As they approached the place, one would climb across the cars and down across the hollow section of the locomotive, into the cab, stick up the engineer and order him to stop the train at the spot selected. The fellow in the car, putting his handkerchief over his face, would stand up with his gun and tell the passengers to sit still.

"Meantime, the other members of the gang would unhitch the locomotive. That was a thing they always did. They would move it down the tracks a mile or two, away from the cars and the loot. Then they'd get in the baggage car, shoot the messenger if he made any interference, and toss the money out. The fellows on the outside would toss it up to the fellows in the saddle. The man in the car was joined by three others, and they went round and stripped the people of their valuables. Then they all piled off, got on their horses and rode off. By that time, the engineer knew he was safe, and he'd back the locomotive, hook on and take the train to where it was going. It was as simple as that."[4]

Allan Dwan hired Jennings in 1915 to supervise the bank and train robberies in *Jordan Is a Hard Road,* a story by Sir Gilbert Parker. Frank Campeau played a convict searching for the men who had framed him. He returns to his home town disguised as an evangelist, and Dwan staged a tent show, hiring Billy Sunday to work up the crowd. He got more than he bargained for. The people in the tent responded so wholeheartedly that they groveled at Billy Sunday's feet, begging for redemption. Jennings was in the audience, and he was so impressed that he and Sunday became close friends, and Jennings hit the evangelist trail himself.

Jennings used his criminal past as the foundation for his religious lectures,

---

* It happens again in another film by Kent and Tilghman, *Oklahoma Roundup,* also of 1908. J. B. Kent later took charge of the motion picture department of the 101 Ranch.

and after World War I, he extended these cautionary tales into moving pictures. Those responsible for promoting Jennings as an actor undoubtedly hoped that audiences would respond with the affection they reserved for William S. Hart, for they were both middle-aged men. But Jennings was the antithesis of the romantic Western bad man. Contrasted with the Hart image—tall, aquiline, mean-eyed—Jennings appeared insignificant and almost frail. His most distinctive feature, a crop of red hair, failed to register on film. His face had that rather deprived look one encounters in photographs of the Old West; it was an Irish face, and it could be mean, but a certain humor mollified the hard-etched features so essential for movie bandits.

Hart and Jennings had met when Hart was touring the West with a stock company. As Hart told the story—and it may be just a story—he came upon some rough-looking men preparing a meal over a campfire; they invited him to share their meal, and he told them he was playing at the Turner Opera House. He even gave them tickets for the show, adding that the new marshal who had just arrived in town for the purpose of capturing the Jennings gang had promised to attend. "Then their leader told me he was Al Jennings, and that the other gentlemen were members of his gang. That night, the first faces I recognized in the front row of the orchestra stalls were those of Al Jennings and his gang, whilst within a stone's throw from them, enthroned in a stage box decorated with flags and bunting, sat the very man who had sworn to get them."[5]

One of Jennings's first calls upon arriving in Los Angeles was on William S. Hart. He handed him a pass for the preview of one of his pictures, saying it was a return for the courtesy Hart had shown many years before, at the Turner Opera House in Muskogee, Oklahoma.

Jennings shared with Hart a respect for authenticity, but he went further. His films used real Westerners, they were shot in old Western towns, and Jennings wore the kind of clothes he had worn as an outlaw. Of the few that survive, several are outstanding. One is *Bond of Blood* (1919), directed by William Bertram,* a Westerner himself, who plays the sheriff. A modest two-reeler, *Bond of Blood* is one of the few Westerns to acknowledge the deep influence of the South upon the frontier country. Jennings commits a crime under the eyes of the sheriff, but as both are cousins from the same part of Virginia, the sheriff allows Al to give him the slip. As usual, it is not the story but the staging and the background that give the film its flavor. Far more accurate in costuming and setting than most of the Hart films, *Bond of Blood* is deliberately underplayed; the location is a rundown Western town,† and the acting is casual and naturalistic. There is probably more riding and shooting than Jennings experienced on such a minor raid, but there is no exaggeration of marksmanship. The outlaws' life is shown to be sordid and unpleasant.

"I'm not putting on 'wild west' pictures," Jennings told an interviewer. "These are *real* west pictures." He thought the Old West had been brutalized and manhandled for the sake of quick profits. "Every day we see '49 plots with 1918

* Veteran of the Alaskan gold rush, Bertram (real name Benjamin Switzer) started in pictures in 1912 as an actor with James Young Deer.

† Los Alamitos, Orange County, California.

Al Jennings, freed from a long sentence, demonstrating how the sensible bank robber concealed his armory. Taken on location for Lady of the Dugout *(1918) at Tehachapi, California.*

The atmosphere and authenticity of the Al Jennings pictures are summed up in this scene from Lady of the Dugout. *From left, Frank and Al Jennings, with Corinne Grant and Ben Alexander.*

settings. Producers have the idea that a gang of 'bad men' have to be fantastically masked, carry a whole arsenal in plain sight, plan for days on the details of the robbery, and carry it out with several hundred feet of thrills and romance.

"Let me tell you how it was actually done in those days. We didn't wear masks and we didn't carry our guns where they could be seen. There was very little bloodshed and no killing except in running fights. When my brother Frank and I decided to relieve a bank of some of its bullion, we went in quietly, he covered the cashier while I took the bags from the safe, then we'd lock up the cashiers in the vault for safe keeping.

"There wasn't any glamour in the life; there was much that was bad, much that was indifferent, and some that was good. But there wasn't any romance about it. It was hard, sordid and tragic."[6]

These elements are well evoked in *Bond of Blood*. Al Jennings in his crumpled clothes, anxious not to cast any glamour upon his criminal activities, captured a fragment of social history seldom seen on the screen. But he lost his audience. Romance was all they wanted in 1919, and romantic Jennings decidedly was not.

As a feature, *Lady of the Dugout* (1918) was very important to Jennings, and he had hoped that a first-class director would tackle it. Optimistically, he described it to George Siegmann, who had the ear of D. W. Griffith, but Siegmann, realizing Jennings's relative poverty, diverted him to a young director called W. S. Van Dyke.

Ironically, for a film about bank robbery, Jennings had promoted the backing from a banker friend. As he explained to *Photoplay,* the bank robberies were filmed exactly as they had occurred, twenty years before. "The first was unpremeditated, and was carried out by Frank and myself alone. We got five thousand dollars, but we rode off into the desert—hungry, and without being able to buy a sandwich for all our gold. That was when we met 'the lady at the dugout' who had been deserted by a drunken husband, and she and her little boy were starving. It was twelve miles to the nearest house, she told us, and Frank and I had ridden for almost three days without a stop, but we went that night and bought food for her and her little boy. She told us the sad story of her life, and how a banker in a Texas town had cheated her out of some land. That was enough. We got into our saddles and started for Texas. On the way, we picked up the gang, and we made for the town, several hundred miles away.

"That robbery was slightly more elaborate than the others I told you about, but say—any director living would turn up his nose at it, and say it lacked punch. Frank took care of the cashier, and I had a few words with the president. We got bundles of paper money which were lighter and easier to carry than gold, and we were almost out of the bank before the marshal fired at us through the door. Then we made for the horses, and the whole town was in an uproar, but no one knew who the bandits were. A man passed me at a run, waving his gun and yelling to me to get under cover, that there were robbers in town."[7]

Van Dyke and the Jennings brothers organized the production resourcefully, taking over the town of Tehachapi, California, for the Texas bank holdup. Although the story has been romanticized for the benefit of entertainment, *Lady of the Dugout* remains an outstanding Western. From the viewpoint of authenticity, it is one of the best surviving from the period. *Lady of the Dugout* has some unexpected

Hollywood documentation, too; it opens with a scene shot at the Beverly Hills Hotel, in which an English peer and an American editor meet Jennings, soberly dressed, and wearing pince-nez, who tells them his story. "Dugout!" says the peer. "You mean of the trenches?" "No," explains Al. "This dugout was a home dug in the soil of the western prairie." What other Western shows a family living in such conditions? The picture is full of backgrounds, rich in detail, and in subtle touches which prove that Jennings knows his subject inside out: a member of the gang annoys Al during a tense moment by roweling on the floor with his spurs. Another returns Al's hat as they gallop away from the robbery: "I knew you were redheaded and might sunburn easily."

Jennings ran out of money before the picture was complete. With one major scene to go, Van Dyke moved cast and props into the empty Essanay studio in Culver City, only to learn that the English actor playing the husband had vanished. He was discovered in a state of advanced inebriation, so they filmed him being shot, and his drunkenness registered satisfactorily as death.

Congress managed to discourage the spate of outlaw films in 1920. Congressman Herrold and Senator Gore introduced bills to prohibit the shipment of motion picture films "purporting to show the acts of ex-convicts, desperadoes, bandits, train robbers, bank robbers or outlaws."[8] All of which was a fair description of Al Jennings. As a result, Jennings never made the sort of impression in pictures that he deserved. He abandoned featured roles and played bits in pictures with Douglas Fairbanks, Art Acord, and Jack Hoxie. He worked as technical adviser from time to time, and in 1950 Dan Duryea played him in *Al Jennings of Oklahoma.* He died in Tarzana, California, in 1962, at the age of ninety-eight.

EMMETT DALTON

With fourteen years of a life term behind him, Emmett Dalton, like Al Jennings, became a churchman upon his release in 1907 and a crusader for penal reform. The only surviving member of the notorious Dalton gang, he used the moving picture to illustrate his wild past as a grim example to modern youth. *The Last Stand of the Dalton Boys* (1912) was a three-reeler, directed by Jack Kenyon, who had worked for Selig. Advertisements called it "the Triumph of Western Realism," and it undoubtedly contained a great deal of valuable documentary material; it was "taken on the exact localities" and "posed by people that actually took part in the raid."[1] The picture opens at the childhood home of the Daltons, where they were brought up by a devoted mother. The boys grow to manhood, and the oldest, Frank Dalton, enrolls as a deputy U.S. marshal, helping to stamp out bootleggers. He is shot in the performance of his duties, and his brothers, Bob and Emmett,* become deputies to avenge his death. Through political chicanery, the Daltons are ousted from the service without their back pay, and they turn to crime,

* Emmett, the youngest brother, did not become a deputy in actuality.

The last of the Dalton Gang, Emmett Dalton, appearing in the arena with the Pawnee Bill Show.

organizing the Dalton gang. They terrorize the Southwest until the final raid at Coffeyville, Kansas, where they stage the first double bank-robbery on 5 October 1892. The film ends with the shooting of Emmett and his arrest as he lies helpless in Death Valley. There was a coda showing his conviction and pardon.

In *Moving Picture World* of 18 April 1914, Emmett Dalton, who was at that time lecturing with his film, took out an advertisement: "This is to inform you that 'fake' Moving Picture Films, purporting to represent the lives of the Dalton boys are being shown throughout the country. My brothers' pictures and mine are copyrighted. I will prosecute anyone (Theater or Individual) who shows, impersonates or attempts to do same without my or my mother's consent."

It is typical of the perversities of film history that the original Dalton film should perish and one of the fakes should survive. A three-reel film entitled *The Dalton Boys,* it is put together with such dismal clumsiness that it looks as if it had been made in 1898 instead of 1914. To give it spurious authenticity, it concludes with a shot of Emmett Dalton bowing to the camera, presumably duped from a news weekly. Otherwise, there is not much departure from the story line of the original.

The climactic battle at Coffeyville, the Daltons' home town, is the only moment that generates the slightest degree of excitement. The town used in the location is not Coffeyville.* The film-makers have nevertheless taken pains to show each stage

* Another, earlier version of the Dalton raid was recently discovered in Coffeyville. Rescued from crumbling nitrate by Karl Malkames, for Thames Television's *Hollywood* series, it is

of the action in a parallel landmark. Bob and Emmett wore false beards as they entered the town; nonetheless, someone recognized them and raised the alarm. The local citizens were behind cover, heavily armed, when the Daltons emerged from the bank with their captives. The whole battle was over in ten minutes, with four townspeople dead and three wounded. Four of the Dalton Gang were killed, and the only survivor was Emmett. He might have escaped, but he tried to rescue his dying brother and was shot by a barber. The film muffs most of this. It concludes, like the original, with Emmett Dalton receiving his pardon in jail.

The fake draws attention to its doubtful origin by misspelling Emmett Dalton's name "Emmet" throughout.

In 1918 Dalton remade his film as an ambitious Western called *Beyond the Law*. Directed by Theodore Marston and photographed by Robert Olsson, it was made from a scenario by William Addison Lathrop, based on Dalton's own story. Dalton was very active in promoting the picture. "The motion picture industry has been flooded with pictures advertised as typical western features, and the public has come to regard the west in a light entirely foreign to its actual self. I have lived in the great west all of my life, and have roamed its prairies for years, so that it has become a part of my life. *Beyond the Law,* which I wrote, is an accurate account of western life, and depicts something real and typical of western life. Exhibitors can expect a western production which is perfect in every detail."[2]

Injustice and retribution are the keynotes of the story. The Daltons' first criminal act occurs in a gambling saloon when Bob, discovering a crooked game at the roulette wheel, takes his money back at gunpoint. A train robbery, wrongly attributed to the Daltons, goads them into living up to their reputation, and they rob an express of its shipment of gold. The picture re-created the Coffeyville double bank-robbery, and it ended, as before, with Emmett Dalton receiving his pardon.

According to the cast list for *Beyond the Law,* Emmett played not only himself but Frank and Bob as well. The picture was extremely successful; in March 1920 it was breaking records at the Symphony Theater in New York and the Rialto in Los Angeles. The same year Emmett Dalton announced a series of two-reel pictures, based on his experiences, and directed by Francis Powers. He remained in Hollywood for some time. His autobiography, written in collaboration with Jack Jungmeyer, *When the Daltons Rode,* was filmed in 1940.

When Dalton visited New York in 1914, he pointed out to reporters that his film never made heroes of those outside the law. He always delivered a talk before the show on the evils of a life of outlawry, especially advising young men against bad companions. Wrote a trade-paper journalist:

"Emmett Dalton was pardoned after serving fourteen and a half years. He is now forty-four years old. His appearance is that of a substantial business man, without a trace in manner or bearing of the characteristics usually ascribed to bad men. In fact, he seems to be all that such a man is not."[3]

---

now preserved in the Library of Congress. As primitive as *The Bank Robbery,* it is equally fascinating; what it lacks in filmcraft, it makes up for in authenticity, since it was shot where the raid took place a mere fifteen years earlier.

THE COWBOY IN HOLLYWOOD

As the cow towns paved their streets, installed electricity, and replaced feedbarns with gas stations, parts of Los Angeles grew more and more like a cow town. In front of certain studios was a hitching rail. Behind them was the statutory Western street, the sheriff's office, and the saloon, and, wafting over the fence, the smell of horses. For nostalgic Westerners the chance to earn money in such a congenial atmosphere was too good to miss.

Cowboys drifted into the picture business in substantial numbers in the silent days. It was estimated that in the mid-1920s, five hundred a year came to Hollywood, some of them when the big ranches in Arizona and Colorado went broke, others after watching film companies on location. Raoul Walsh recalled hiring cowboys from the Los Angeles stockyards at five dollars a day around 1914.

The movies were largely a seasonal employment in the years 1909 to 1920. Cowboys would follow the rodeo or the Wild West show circuit in the spring, then end up on a ranch for the fall roundup. They would work in pictures over the winter months. Tom Mix followed this pattern for a while, as did Art Acord, Buck Jones, and Hoot Gibson.

In Hollywood, when the first picture people arrived, there were only ten horses available for motion picture work. Jess McGaugh had the monopoly at first; then George "Tatobug" Champion brought in a string, followed by Slim Padgett, Fat Jones, and Curley Eagles. These horse dealers tended toward Edendale, where a cowboy rooming house was situated, near the Selig studios. Later, they dispersed to Burbank, Newhall, and Westwood.

Cowboys seeking work would head first for Universal, the company that churned out series upon series of Westerns. When Universal built on its mammoth ranch in the San Fernando Valley, bunkhouses were provided and cowboys engaged at thirty dollars a month. Hoot Gibson was the most prominent personality to emerge from the Universal cowboys; among the cowgirls was Jane Bernoudy, champion horsewoman of the world, a veteran of the 101 and Inceville, and once engaged to William S. Hart. Following the Ince tradition, the studio included a Chimallo Indian village. A Universal City rodeo was held each year. To hire extra cowboys, Universal ran up a white flag on the studio flagpole.

The corner of Cahuenga Avenue and Hollywood Boulevard was known as the Waterhole,* for here assistant directors could rely on rounding up cowboys whenever they were needed. It was the custom for drivers to stop off at the Waterhole and give cowboys a lift to Universal or the Lasky ranch. The men who waited there in vain, however, named Cahuenga "Go-Hungry Avenue." When Poverty Row was established, the corner of Sunset and Gower became the Waterhole.

The term "cowboy" was indiscriminately applied to anyone in Hollywood who dressed the part. As soon as a Western was announced, hopeful extras would don chaps and Stetsons and hover by the studio gates. The genuine cowboys were a

* The Waterhole Saloon forms the background for many of the tales in *Hollywood Posse* (Boston: Houghton Mifflin, 1975) by Diana Cary. She was known in silent pictures as Baby Peggy, and she was the daughter of cowboy Jack Montgomery. The book is full of Western lore.

Universal City attracted more cowboys than any other studio because it made more Westerns. Cowboys also doubled as soldiers—and knights in armor, and anything else that involved horses.

These authentic-looking cowpunchers, leading their mules in the Lone Pine district, are actually film technicians on location for The Roundup *(1919). Otto Brower, left, assistant director, and Harry Perry, cameraman (a few years later he was responsible for the majestic photography of* Wings*).*

The John Ford Wild Bunch at Universal. Teddy Brooks was an assistant, but all the others were the real thing. Back row, starting extreme left: Teddy Brooks, Pedro "Pete" Leon, Jim Corey, Bill Gillis, and, fourth from right, Whitey Sovern, Front row, from left: Bud Osborne, Neal Hart (former sheriff of Manville, Wyoming), Winnie Brown, Harry Carey, Olive Fuller Golden (later Olive Carey), Jane Bernoudy (champion horsewoman of the world), and Joe Rickson.

LEFT: *Al Hoxie as a Hollywood cowboy in Hollywood costume.*
RIGHT: *Hoxie as a working cowboy on a ranch in the Salmon River country in Idaho. He wears his best 7X beaver for the photograph.*

Raoul Walsh claimed to have been a cowboy, and here his skill is put to the test on a bucking horse for The Greaser *(1915).*

close-knit group, all for driving the "river-sand cowboy" or "scissorbill" out of the business. They refused to ride in pictures employing them, and they held out for higher pay for their own specialized work. Two hundred and twenty cowboys formed themselves into the Western Protective Association, to distinguish themselves from cowboys of doubtful ability. The association members were not fussy about where a man came from; all they demanded was proof that he could handle a horse. The country was full of competent riders from circuses and Wild West shows who had never worked on the range. Some of them were more expert with horses than real cowpunchers.

"We didn't feel malice because a fellow was a movie cowboy," explained Al Hoxie, a working cowboy himself, and brother of Western star Jack Hoxie. "Ken Maynard wasn't a range-riding cowboy, he was a circus cowboy. But he was a good rider and you respected good riders. The only ones we objected to were the Main Street cowboys sent over by Central Casting—those guys would doll up in great big hats and mufflers and, hell, they couldn't ride nothing. They were a danger."[1]

Faced with increasingly intensive stunt work, the cowboys' demands were perfectly reasonable. They had been trained all their lives for a certain job. Now boys, fresh out of riding school, were supplanting them as stunt riders. The veteran directors, however, knew their men. "I never seen a real cowboy refuse a director," said Al Hoxie. "If they could do it, they'd do it. If they couldn't do it, they'd fall off."

The studios who hired and fired their riders were careful to employ a boss cowboy to select the most skillful. The discipline of the range deteriorated quickly amid the relaxing surroundings of Hollywood. Cowboys who used to roll out at 3:30 a.m. without a whimper, circle beef herds all night, or stand guard twenty hours at a time over the cavvy,* loathed turning up at the studio for a 7:30 call.

They disliked actors, too, and this dislike was never more heartily expressed than when they had to wear make-up themselves. They often grew frustrated when they had worked their horses up for a scene and the director shouted "cut." As cowboy actor Bob Reeves said: "You've got to do some harder riding in motion pictures than you ever did on the range. The competition is very keen, but a man who can handle a rope well, ride, and has a good disposition can make a living in pictures. It's much pleasanter being a cowboy in motion pictures than on the ranch or the range. I would advise all the cow hands back in the hills to come to Hollywood and let the younger generation handle the cows back there a while."[2]

Cowboys were never more highly valued than when the big studios staged mob scenes involving horses. Universal laid great stress on the riding skills of the French soldiers in *The Hunchback of Notre Dame* (1923).

"They wouldn't let nobody but real cowboys ride into that courtyard," said Al Hoxie. "They wanted them to handle the horses so they wouldn't injure too many people. They had people laying around—and they weren't all dummies—and most of the extras had torches. They give us orders; if anyone hit our horses with a live torch, ride over them. They had a hospital tent right there on the courtyard, and they had stretchers, and they were carrying them in and out all the time."

---

* From the Spanish *caballada*, a band of saddle horses. Also known as "remuda."

As early as 1915 cowboys at Essanay went on strike, alleging that in riding for the company they were endangering their lives and that the pay was not enough to cover such risk. Essanay refused an increase and tried to hire replacements. There was another strike in 1920 when cowboys, already getting $7.50 a day, demanded a raise of $2.50.

Apart from the risks, working conditions were highly agreeable. On location the director and the leading players would generally stay in a hotel. But not the buckaroos. They would be accommodated in tents or in a bunkhouse. And they liked it this way. "We were separated off," said Al Hoxie, "and could play cards, shoot dice, or sit up all hours of the night if we wanted to. The bunkhouse was pretty much the same as a bunkhouse on a ranch, but you didn't have that smell—the old saddle blankets stowed in one corner, and old sweaty clothes hanging in another. But that was about all the difference there was."

Western companies preferred the chuckwagon to the box lunch, and to keep the cowboys happy, the cooks had to be the real thing. If you criticized the chuckwagon boys, you got a grasshopper in your coffee cup.

When they first arrived in Hollywood, cowboys tended to wear the clothes they were used to. They expressed scorn for the flashier outfits. But they soon realized that to gain any kind of prominence, the flashier the outfit, the better. "It was a day and a time and you just had to dress that way in order to get by," said Al Hoxie. "I don't think any of the boys really liked to be dressed up like that. In the first place, it was expensive. You had to pay for all your own clothes yourself."

The oldest established makers of boots and saddles in the country, Fursnows of Miles City, Montana, opened a branch in Hollywood; much of the stock was geared for the motion picture cowboy, with angora goat chaps dyed a vivid orange, and hand-carved revolver holsters. Prices reflected a Klondike atmosphere; cowboys were asked to pay $45 for a Stetson, $40 for Justin boots, $50 for a pair of gold or silver spurs, $40 for their chaps, and $50 for a gun. Such accouterments were essential for a public who expected the cowboy to wear chaps and guns at all times.

Said Harry Carr: "No one can escape the foolishness of the place. Just let a cowpuncher come in off the ranges to Hollywood where somebody wants him to ride a bucking bronc, and he isn't there twenty-four hours before he begins trying not to act like a cowboy. He puts on a huge two-gallon hat, which nobody would know what to do with on a real cow range—and wears fancy boots which torture his feet. He doesn't know what they are for; but he knows in a dim, dumb way that they go with acting like a cowboy."[3]

Emmett Dalton blamed the disappearance of the picturesque garb of the Old West on the arrival of the first Sears Roebuck catalogues from the East. But, as the 1920s began, it was still possible to identify where a cowboy came from by the style of his hat, the way the crown was pinched, and by subtly distinctive features of his rig. By the end of the decade, the movies had helped to standardize the cowboy's clothes. If life did not entirely imitate the movies, at least a fragment of fiction had splintered into fact.

With the enormous number of cowboys seeking work in pictures, it is surprising that so few of them dated back to the great cattle drives. But the movies were a young man's game, as the veterans quickly learned. Frank Murphy was among the oldest cowboys in pictures—he was seventy in 1928—and, with Si

Historic group taken at the Harry Carey ranch in 1923. Front row: Otto Meyer; Charles Russell, the celebrated cowboy artist; Harry Carey (in front of whom sits little Harry Carey, Jr.); Fred Stone, famous stage and film actor; and Henry Herbert Knibbs, the cowboy poet who wrote Overland Red. *Behind Carey are Will Rogers's children. Back row: Frank Spearman and Sam de Grasse (first and second at left) and Clarence Sovern (fourth from left), brother of Whitey (see photo, pp. 292–3).*

Franklin, he was one of the very few who had worked at trail herding in the great days. Murphy drove cattle from 1876 to 1888; he also claimed to be the first cowboy scout hired by the government, since trappers and hunters like Cody and Jim Bridger had, until then, been the men the government depended upon for information about the Indians. Milt Brown, ten years younger, was a 101 veteran. A stagecoach driver in the Rockies, he recalled being held up in true movie fashion. He was in pictures from 1909 and appeared in John Ford's *Straight Shootin'* and James Cruze's *The Covered Wagon.*

After examining the evidence, and talking to surviving witnesses, one is left with the inescapable impression that the Westerns we know so well were inspired not so much by Western history as by the atmosphere prevalent in Hollywood at this time. All the elements were there: the swashbuckling camaraderie, the donnybrooks, swinging fists, lethal liquor, wild-riding horses, and quivering trigger fingers. The Art Acord–Hoot Gibson fights were legendary. Tim McCoy explained, "They'd just stand up and beat the hell out of each other. And then they'd come to the bar and have a drink. They loved it. One time, Art launched a haymaker at Gibson, who ducked it, and Art struck a hitching post. 'Hey,' he said, 'I broke my hand.'

Two great figures of the Western: John Ford, left, and Harry Carey. They had no direct experience—although Ford used to say he had punched cattle in Arizona en route to California—but their deep affection for the West created many outstanding pictures. An advertisement, 1919.

Like much about Tom Mix, this is hard to believe. The caption says: "Sid Jordan takes aim to shoot the knot off Tom Mix's four-in-hand" (his necktie) "using live ammunition for the scene." (If Jordan, rear center, shoots at that angle, the bullet will remove not merely Mix's tie but some of his shoulder as well.) From The Coming of the Law *(1919). The director (in cap) is Lynn Reynolds, the cameraman Fred LeRoy Granville.*

Gibson said, 'Serves you right, you son-of-a-bitch,' and went and beat the hell out of him.

"They talk about drugstore cowboys. Those extras were far from drugstore cowboys. Those fellows came from Montana, Wyoming, Arizona, Texas, and New Mexico. Their work on the range had practically gone with the barbed wire and the closing of the big outfits. The only life they knew was the saddle. When they heard they paid seven and a half a day to take falls and ride horses, they said, 'How long has this been going on?' They'd been working for $40 a month, eighteen hours a day in the saddle. Some of them didn't just drift into Hollywood. They came hell-for-leather to get away from the sheriff. I would see fellows down there that I hadn't seen for years. Last time I'd seen S. Y. Slim he was riding out of Thermopolis on a stolen horse and the sheriff was six jumps behind him."[4]

They shot at each other, too. Explosive charges to simulate bullets striking home were tricky and time-consuming. The effect was much more frequently achieved by a sharpshooter, often the legendary Pardner Jones. Blank cartridges were used in gunfights, but for a scene in Cecil B. DeMille's *The Captive* (1915), a few guns were loaded with ball to make timbers splinter realistically. As the extras advanced, a young cowboy, Clarence Chandler, suddenly dropped to the ground, his head shattered by a bullet.[5] In 1927, during the making of *Red Raiders* (Al Rogell), an Indian chief was shot at close range during a battle scene. The incident occurred on the Custer battlefield, which was being used as a location, and the company feared reprisals by the Indians. But the murder proved to be a domestic affair—the chief was shot by his son-in-law—and production was resumed.

"I knew a cowboy called Tom Carrick," said Al Hoxie. "I worked with him in a barroom scene. He was dancing with one of the gals and his wife Sarah, she was part Indian, sat on the sidelines, tapping her toes. I says to Tom, 'Looks like she's getting pretty mad.' He just kind of grinned. I says, 'See you tomorrow, Tom,' and he says, 'Okay, Al.' I went to work next morning and the first thing I heard was, 'Tom's dead. Sarah shot him last night at a party.' "

Tim McCoy asserted, with pardonable exaggeration, that they knocked them off in the streets of Hollywood as often as they did in Dodge City. "There were still remnants of the Old West. There was a fellow called Yakima Jim, he was very belligerent, a big strong fellow. He'd pick a fight with anyone and he was tougher than a boot. He tangled with a fellow who was my double, Tom Bay.* Tom had killed a man over in Oklahoma before he'd ever come to Hollywood. Yakima Jim made a mistake this particular night. He whipped out a switchblade and said, 'I'll cut your belly open.' Well, he said it to the wrong man. Tom Bay reached into the waistband of his breeches and pulled out a six-shooter and killed him. And that was the end of Yakima Jim."[6]

By the end of the silent era, a new breed appeared. Tom Tyler, for instance, was a real cowboy, right off the ranch. Or so the FBO publicity department claimed. He was actually a New York boy who strongly disliked Westerns. He used to walk out on a film at the first flash of sagebrush. The only horse that failed to scare him was the vaulting horse at the YMCA gym. Here he trained for a career in pic-

---

* Tom Bay has a small part in *Red Raiders.*

The Harry Carey ranch, Newhall, California. Cowboys who didn't succeed in breaking into pictures often took work on California ranches, including Carey's—which was washed out in the late 1920s when a dam burst.

tures, taking a course at a screen school for good measure. As soon as he offered himself to a casting director, his dark good looks landed him a part as an Indian chief. And once he made contact with Westerns, he was lost. Groomed for stardom in program Westerns, he was condemned to spend his days galloping across the sagebrush he so abhorred, while the cowboys he replaced abandoned their dreams of cushioned comfort in Spanish castles and returned to the corner of Sunset and Gower.

TOM MIX

The most extravagant of all the cowboy stars, and the most successful, Tom Mix believed that his life was nowhere near colorful enough for his admiring fans. In his desire to make an impact, and thus make money, he retold his life story as it might have been written for the screen. In autobiographical articles—no doubt ghost-written—he told haphazard tales of adventure so wild that his career eclipsed for sheer action and breathless pace the first few chapters of the Bible.

He lived in an age that welcomed exaggeration—"if you believe it, it's so"—and adored unrestrained showmanship. With the shining example of Buffalo Bill before him, Mix and his zealous press agents set no limit on their audience's gullibility.

Yakima Canutt once overheard Mix tell a yarn of his law-enforcement days. "After the crowd left I said, 'Tom, you kinda handle the truth a little bit reckless, don't you?' He said, 'What the hell. They're here for entertainment. So I give them a reel out of one of my pictures.' That's the kind of fellow he was."[1]

When the Western stars refused to stick to the facts of their own lives, it is scarcely surprising that the facts of Western history were banged about a bit in their films. In providing a short outline of Mix's life, as perpetrated in his numerous autobiographical articles, I shall resist the compulsion to add exclamation points. For seeing the last glimmer of truth wither beneath the press agent's compost heap is salutary exercise for the film historian.

Mix was born in a pioneer's log cabin near El Paso, Texas, in 1880. His mother was part Cherokee, and her grandfather, a full-blooded Indian, lived on White Eagle Reserve and had translated the Bible into Osage. Mix himself learned to speak four Indian languages, but his hold on Osage was not too strong. He admitted to his poor education but composed lyrics and had a good command of Spanish. His father, Captain Mix, was an Irishman in the 7th Cavalry. At one point there was talk of young Tom being adopted by Buffalo Bill and being given the name of Cody. After becoming the youngest cowboy on the Texas ranges, in the great days of the cattle drives, Mix attended the Virginia Military Institute. By 1898 he was a lumberjack in the Pennsylvania forests, when he heard that America had declared war on Spain. He rushed to volunteer, and when the navy would not take him, he fought a group of high-ranking officers aboard a warship. He then enlisted in the army and went to Cuba. About to land, the officer in charge was bewildered by the horses. Tom Mix strolled up. "Throw them cayuses into the water," he said. "Put a bugler on shore and keep him tootin' stable-call. They'll swim ashore and I'll rope 'em." A lieutenant of Theodore Roosevelt's Rough Riders saw this and commandeered Mix's services. He fought with the Rough Riders and was wounded in their famous charge up San Juan Hill.* "I can't tell you a lot of details about these months of fire and fight," he wrote in *Photoplay,* "it all blends into one in my mind."[2]

As soon as he had recovered from his wounds, his unit was sent to quell the uprising in the Philippines led by General Aguinaldo, after which he was sent to China, to strengthen the U.S. garrison at Pekin. More excitement came when he was helping to build the railroad from Pekin to Tientsin, and a shell, fired from an ancient Chinese cannon, exploded in front of his Gardiner gun. A shattered wheel-spoke all but scalped him. Undiscouraged by military life, he shipped horses to South Africa for the British during the Boer War. (Later in his career, he became friendly with Will Rogers, who had actually done this job.) His sympathies lying with the Boers, he joined their ranks and fought the British, only to be captured,

---

* Mix was not aware that the Rough Riders' horses had been left behind at Tampa, and San Juan Hill was charged on foot.

sentenced to death, but finally shipped back to the United States. He drifted all over the West—"I haven't room here to tell you of the life I led"—joined the Miller Brothers 101 Ranch, where he became foreman, and traveled with their Wild West Show. He encountered Theodore Roosevelt, who remembered him from his Cuban days and who entertained him and his pals on inauguration day.

Then came a period when Mix served as sheriff of Montgomery County in western Kansas; Washington County, Oklahoma; and Two Buttes, Colorado. As a Texas Ranger, his accounts of desperate struggles with desperadoes included the capture of the notorious Shont brothers, which he achieved single-handed. He spent four days with his captives in a dugout, covering them with a revolver, not daring to go to sleep, until his posse arrived. Then he heard that the Shonts cared for their mother, and since she was now flat broke, he sent his reward money to her.

In 1910 Mix joined the forces of Madero fighting Díaz in Mexico. So convincing did he make this section of his story, that some of the standard histories of the revolution place him among the Americans who fought for Mexico's freedom.[3] Following the battle for Ciudad Juarez, he faced a firing squad. In later versions the firing squad shifted to Honduras, then disappeared altogether, being replaced by an offer from Madero of an important government position.

However far-fetched these stories sound, they were believed—and are believed. A correspondent to the magazine *Those Enduring Matinee Idols* went so far as to add another war to the overcrowded list: "Mix served a few months in World War One, was wounded and discharged. Most of the stories about his experiences in various wars are *true* and have been authenticated *many times* by *official documents*."[4]

Having amassed a vast quantity of this kind of material on Mix, I seriously considered journeying to Oklahoma and Texas in order to study old records and contemporary newspaper accounts. Then I discovered that a remarkable book, *The Life and Legend of Tom Mix,*[5] had been published by someone who had done just that—and taken a great deal of trouble over it. The author, Paul Mix, being related to Tom, remembered him as the topic of occasional family conversation. Paul's grandfather often denied the publicity stories, but the family felt that the best thing Tom had ever done for himself was to leave the Pennsylvania hills. Paul Mix was born only forty miles from Mix Run, Pennsylvania, which, as he explained, was named after Amos Mix, the first to settle in the Driftwood area in 1804. When Paul Mix's son was born—and named Tom—an aunt sent some news clippings; the contradictory stories fascinated Paul and led him to try to unravel the truth. It took him seven years.

Tom Mix was born at Mix Run on 6 January 1880. When he was ten, he was overwhelmed by the glamour of Buffalo Bill's Wild West, which visited Clearfield Fairgrounds. From that moment, he was obsessed with horses, guns, and the West. He received his first bullet wound when he and another boy had an accident with an old single-shot pistol. Meanwhile, he learned to ride extremely well and practiced stunt riding and roping. When the Spanish-American War broke out, some of Tom's friends joined the navy. Tom enlisted at Washington Barracks, and was assigned to Battery M, 4th Regiment, U.S. Artillery. He saw no action in the war; he was one of the men assigned to guard the Dupont powder works against the possibility of sabotage. By 1899 he was a sergeant, and following the Philippine

This picture was used to "prove" Mix's military background: he wears the full-dress uniform of a first sergeant of artillery, but he would have had to serve fifteen years to earn those stripes . . . and he's not much older than twenty in the picture.

Tom Mix (front row center) was a sergeant, and this rare photograph shows him in his regular uniform at the time of the Spanish-American War. But he never went to Cuba.

Tom Mix and his collection of sombreros.

insurrection, in which he took no part, he was honorably discharged. But the Boer War was still raging, and although the United States was not involved, Mix re-enlisted. In spite of rumors that the army allowed some of their regulars to go over to help the Boers, the records of Mix's battery show no such activity. After his first marriage, he was listed AWOL, and when that period elapsed, his army record ended with that most feared description: deserter.

Nothing was ever done about his desertion, and the matter was never raised again until Mix's death in 1940. His estate tried to secure an American flag from the Veterans' Administration to cover the casket during his funeral. The Veterans' Administration refused to provide the flag, and Mix's old director, John Ford, who was related to the quartermaster general of the United Spanish War Veterans, intervened. He was told that Tom Mix had left the army "without saying 'Good-bye to Uncle Sam.' " A flag was eventually obtained and he was buried with full military and Masonic honors.

Mix and his wife moved to the Southwest for the first time late in 1902. He ran a physical fitness class in Guthrie, Oklahoma, attending the St. Louis World's Fair in 1904 as the drum major of the Oklahoma Cavalry Band. Here he met Will Rogers, a rodeo clown for Colonel Zack Mulhall's Wild West Show. The two men became friends. After a period in Oklahoma City as a bartender and part-time ranch hand and with some occasional excitement helping law-enforcement officers round up desperadoes, Mix joined the Cowboy Brigade. Formed in 1905 by Seth Bullock to help celebrate the election of President Theodore Roosevelt, the Cowboy Brigade arrived in Washington on inauguration day. Late in 1905 Colonel Joe Miller hired Mix as a full-time cowboy on the 101 Ranch at $15 a month with board.

Mix said that his fondest recollections were of his days at the 101. "I attribute my present standing," he wrote later, "to the training I received and experienced when working under the 101 brand. I could name hundreds of incidents and scenes in my pictures that really had their origin along the banks of the old Salt Fork River."[6]

After marrying for the third time, Mix joined the Widerman Wild West Show in Amarillo, Texas, then started his own show with his new wife, Olive. Late in 1910 he returned to Miller Brothers.

Jack Spears learned that while researching dusty courthouse files, officials of Kay County, Oklahoma, discovered evidence that Tom Mix had once been arrested for horse stealing. "Technically, the charge was embezzlement, brought by the Miller Brothers 101 Ranch in 1910. Mix was arraigned on October 10 '10 but was somehow released without having to post an appearance bond of $1000. He failed to appear for trial the following January 16 and no further entries were made in the court records."[7]

Mix had apparently "borrowed" a horse from the 101 Ranch to enter a rodeo. He had broken his leg at the rodeo and the horse had vanished. Miller Brothers later brought a suit against Mix for breach of contract, which dragged on for more than twenty-five years, finally being settled out of court in 1937 for $50,000, long after the 101 Ranch had vanished (it was liquidated in 1932). Just to make life more difficult for Mix, who was in severe difficulties at the time, the 101 Ranch receivers had a new warrant issued on the horse-stealing charge. Mix was arrested once more, but the case was dismissed on technical grounds.

Although Paul Mix could find no evidence that Mix was ever a deputy United States marshal, he did find proof that Mix was a deputy sheriff and night marshal in Dewey, Oklahoma. Nothing much happened in Dewey during daylight hours, but the town's nocturnal activities demanded surveillance. Mix accepted a deputy sheriff's commission under Sheriff John Jordan, whose son, Sid, was also a deputy. Sid, part Indian, was a first-rate cowhand; he and Tom became firm friends and Sid joined him in the picture business, becoming such a popular supporting player that he was at one time considered for his own starring series. But Ken Maynard was selected instead.

TOM MIX'S INTRODUCTION to pictures came in 1909, while working with the Will A. Dickey Circle D Ranch Wild West Show and Indian Congress. The Selig Polyscope Company used the show, and Dickey was able to get him a job in Selig Westerns. His first big break was the documentary *Ranch Life in the Great Southwest,* directed by Francis Boggs. It was shot near Dewey, and Tom was hired to handle stock and act as safety man, but he asked Boggs for a chance to work in the picture. Boggs agreed, and Mix was featured as a broncho buster. *Ranch Life* was not, as its title implies, a factual film showing how cowboys lived and worked, but a series of rodeo events. It was advertised as "the greatest western picture ever put before the public."

The Selig Polyscope Company worked in Canon City, Colorado, through the summer months of 1910 and 1911, with William Duncan, Tom Mix, Joe Ryan, Myrtle Stedman, and Josephine West as the prominent members of the cast, and local cowhands, ranchers, and businessmen as supporting players. Residents welcomed the movies for their liberal distribution of dollars; livestock and buggies were rented locally, and a whole herd of cattle might be hired for one spectacular sequence.

Paul Mix interviewed Lonnie Higgins, now in his seventies and still riding the range, who was then a teenager. He frequently played the part of an Indian and

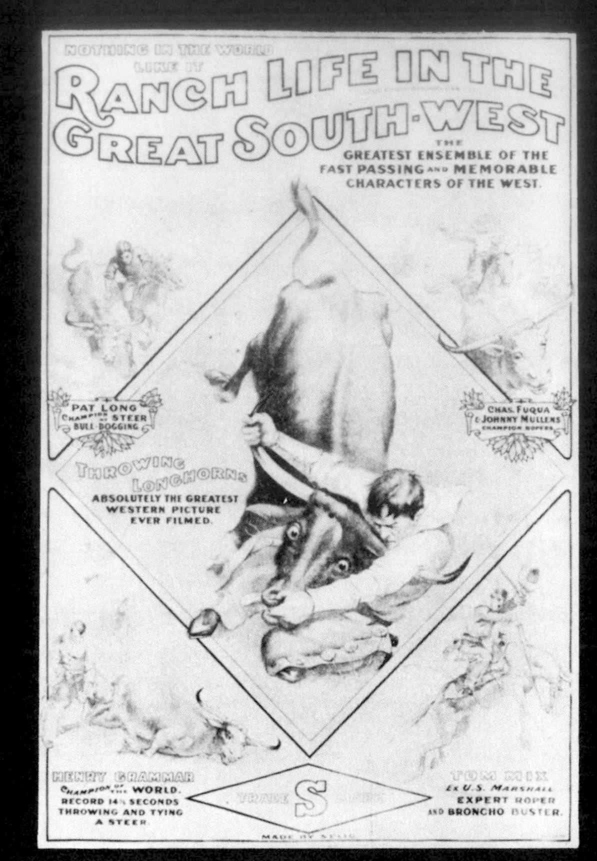

The legend begins—Mix's first film, 1910, describes him as "ex—U.S. Marshall, expert roper and broncho buster."

Tom Mix dressed accurately in an early Selig film, Starring in Western Stuff *(1916), shot at the Diamond-S Ranch, probably at Prescott, Arizona. Mix claimed in a 1916 advertisement that he was "the only honest-to-goodness cowboy in the movies." Well, there are five more behind him. (Copied from* Moving Picture World*).*

remembered that after a hot day on the range, the cowboys would gather at Hell's Half Acre Saloon, and Tom Mix would exhibit his skill as a marksman. Lemons were placed in a row of empty shot glasses and each man would attempt to hit them. Those who missed bought the drinks. They also visited the old coal camps, near Prospect Heights, where the activities consisted of "singing, drinking, dancing with the 'barflies' and raising hell in general."

These early Selig Westerns, even more than the pictures shot at Inceville, represent a fortunate historical accident, for they were photographed in the heart of the West, when cattle ranching was still more or less of a thriving concern and when the customs and characters of the old days were still very much in evidence. The foreground action may have been hokum, but the background was pure documentary. Regrettably Tom Mix directed himself in many of the early pictures, most of which were Western comedies, and his talent as director was little stronger than his talent as actor. One of the deficiencies of his films is the way so much action is played against the side of a shed. The backgrounds were as mundane to Mix and Sid Jordan as a service station to us, so the camera concentrates on the actors.

Some of Mix's films shot at the Diamond S Ranch* included references to motion pictures. In the hilarious rough-and-tumble of *Bill Haywood, Producer* (1915) the cowboys take up making pictures, but return to cowpunching—pictures are too hazardous. *Sagebrush Tom* (1915) has excellent scenes of the Selig company in action. Tom plays an ordinary cowhand, correctly attired, who brushes the dust off himself with a broom before meeting his film favorite.

The Heart of Texas Ryan (1917) is said to be a collection of Mix two-reelers rehashed into a feature. Admittedly, it is an unabashed mess, with jumps in the continuity and a total lack of smoothness or artistry, but it was originally Zane Grey's *Light of Western Stars*. Clearance problems forced the injection of a new story line. Shot on Mix's ranch at Newhall, California, the picture is notably devoid of artificial glamour. In a close-up a fly crawls across Mix's face. Racial prejudice is presented as a fact of life; a cowboy draws his gun at the mere sight of a Mexican. The camera is lined up with as much artistry as a theodolite, and the direction by E. A. Martin is neolithic. But *Heart of Texas Ryan* is probably more truthful to the West of its day than the most beautifully shot drama of William S. Hart.

Whatever Mix might have missed in battle-front action, he made up for in front of the camera, where everyone could see him. At a Wild West rodeo in Glendale, California, in 1915, he was seriously injured when he was trampled and crushed in a collision between two four-horse chuckwagons. Stunt man Harvey Parry said that Mix, even at the height of his career, loathed the idea of a double. But the studio insisted on it. "They'd take him down the road to show him something, and while they were doing that, I'd do the stunt. He'd come back, raise hell and fire me."[8]

Mix's success ensured that the silent-screen cowboy would never again wear the clothes of the humble cowpuncher. As Mix developed his individual style, so he elaborated his dress, which became more and more startling, with vast white

---

* Mix signed a new contract with Selig in 1913 and was provided with a ranch near Prescott, Arizona. It was probably this ranch Selig called the Diamond-S after their trademark, although a 1912 Selig release was *With Our Boys on the Diamond-S*.

Mix resented doubles and preferred to do his own stunts, an area in which he showed great physical courage. A scene from The Big Diamond Robbery *(1929), directed by Eugene J. Forde.*

For Big Stakes (1922)*: Mix and crew in a snowstorm on location at Victorville, California. Patsy Ruth Miller to left of Mix, director Art Rosson to right. The road is designated "National Old Trails Road."*

hats, nightclub jackets, and hand-carved boots. He made no pretense of showing the West as it was. Inspired by the Wild West show, it was to the tradition of Buffalo Bill he remained faithful.

"To explain Tom Mix you have to go back to Buffalo Bill," said Allan Dwan. "He set up the picture for the world. He said, 'That's the West'—tight white pants, a sharp coat, guns all over the place, and underneath, fancy white embroidered materials, with diamonds down the side of his pants. It was all a case of dressing up. It's like any style that people pick up—Beau Brummel swept through Europe with his clothes. Most rodeo cowboys were professional guys, and their clothes were practical. But when they went out on parade they had the damndest-looking outfits on.

"Tom Mix was a very likeable kind of a guy. Not a jolly fellow, and he didn't mix with everyone. He was reticent. But underneath, he was a philosopher. He recognized that he was in a phony business—show business—and he gave it the works. He went to New York on the train with a private boxcar for his horse Tony. And everybody along the road knew it. They came down to see Tom Mix and his horse, and he'd come out and say 'Howdy' and wave his hat and 'Whee, wow! There's Tom Mix!' When he got to New York, he rode down Broadway on this damned white horse and it stopped the traffic. People shouted and threw torn-up telephone books out of the windows.

"In the theater, he'd spin ropes with his patent leather boots that wouldn't have stood any minute of the real work around a ranch. He hated it as much as anybody did, but he did it because it was profitable. He got a fortune for it, built himself an estate and was a very unhappy man in general."[9]

By the end of the silent days Mix lost his lead, and some of his enthusiasm. Epic, all-star Westerns were forcing the routine cowboy pictures off the screen. The major stars and directors had allowed the picture business to fall into the hands of entrepreneurs; more and more producers were seizing more and more power. Furthermore, Mix's wife was suing for an increase of maintenance for their child. Like an aging cattleman, harried by homesteaders, he decided to go to South America, where he could work on the vast pampas without the barbed wire of interference.

"There wasn't much real West left when I knew you back on the 101 Ranch," Mix told journalist Herbert Cruikshank. "There ain't none at all now. And besides, you don't know how sick I am of things here. I've ridden every inch of this country on location for pictures. I've seen the same mugs and done the same things day in and day out for years. I can't work the way they work nowadays. With a lot of supervisors and yes-men and assistant yes-men and more red tape than an Indian agent. My last couple of pictures were very hard to make."[10]

Mix was signed to a new motion picture contract before he left for the pampas. He later toured with the Sells-Floto Circus, before returning to make talking pictures for Universal. His last picture was a 1935 serial.

In 1940 Mix paid a visit to his old studio, now known as Twentieth Century-Fox. R. Lee "Lefty" Hough was production manager. "He was a little seedy, with the boots, the hat, the white suit and everything. He said to me, 'I want to see Jack Ford or Sol Wurtzel [the studio manager] to find out what I can do in the picture business.' He had lost a million dollars in the circus, and there was no money

Tom Mix and his cowboys relax around the chuckwagon.
Dick Hunter, Mix, Sid Jordan (at left).

left. Ford was shooting *The Grapes of Wrath* but he took him to lunch. He told him, 'This picture business has passed you by a long time ago.' He got the same thing from Wurtzel. What the hell could they use him for? He came to my office and we sat there and talked a while and I could see he was quite depressed. 'Lefty,' he said, 'I don't know what I'm going to do.' I walked with him back to the gate. But the tragedy of the thing—he stood in the vestibule, and there were pictures of all the big stars, Tyrone Power and everyone else, on the wall. Here was the guy that had made the goddamn studio, looking for a spot."[11]

That same year Tom Mix died in a reckless but undeniably flamboyant accident. He drove past a detour sign at high speed and crashed at a washed-out bridge near Florence, Arizona. A year before he had turned his car over at that very corner. Mix was granted one final legend, one that would have amused him. When rescuers dragged him clear of the wreck, they found him impeccably dressed, unmarked by wounds. He had with him thousands of dollars in cash and checks. Apparently, a metal suitcase had struck him on the back of the neck, killing him instantly. Hollywood legend filled the suitcase with gold—twenty-dollar gold pieces—and fashioning a moral drama from this sad accident, saw Mix's life ended by the very element that, as far as he was concerned, gave it meaning.

WILL ROGERS

Will Rogers was born in 1879 in a ranch house in the old Indian Territory, later the state of Oklahoma. His parents both had Cherokee blood in their veins. They came from pioneer stock, and Rogers was fond of quipping: "My ancestors didn't come over on the *Mayflower*. They met the boat." Through his childhood, he rode with the cowhands on his father's ranch. In 1898 he worked as a cowboy on the Ewing ranch at Higgins, Texas, and the following year began managing the family ranch. He punched cattle in the pampas and sailed to the South African war with a cargo of mules. He broke horses at a remount station at Ladysmith, until the Boer War came to an end. At Johannesburg he joined Texas Jackie's Wild West Show and gradually worked his way home. He came to public prominence on the stage in the Ziegfeld Follies with his sleight of hand as a rope twirler. (His skill is evident in the 1922 two-reeler *The Ropin' Fool.*) His laconic wisecracks, delivered in a slow Oklahoma drawl, brought him immense popularity, and before long Will Rogers was celebrated throughout America as the Cowboy Philosopher. His observations about politics and international affairs were treasured for their warmth and common sense.

Rex Beach introduced him to Samuel Goldwyn, who enticed him into films in 1919. Commenting on Goldwyn's Bigger and Better Pictures campaign, Rogers said, "When Goldwyn decided to make fewer and worse pictures, he sent for me."

Largely dependent on vocal humor, Rogers's success was insubstantial in silent pictures; he was ideally suited to talkies. However, he wrote most of his own titles, and his shambling, shy cowboy was a charming, if minor, character in silent films.

Will Rogers, in Doubling for Romeo *(1921), plays a cowboy setting out for Hollywood. He is wearing what his pals think the movie capital expects.*

Doubling for Romeo was written by Elmer Rice, later to write the satire on movies *Voyage to Puerilia.* Directed by Clarence Badger, the photography was by Marcel le Picard and the art direction by Cedric Gibbons. The picture poked fun at Western film clichés in a way that would have delighted Westerners.

"We open our masterpiece with a scene of a western town." Fade in to an exquisitely photographed exterior of a street that, although contemporary with the film (1921), still has the false-fronted stores, the hitching rails, and the atmosphere of an earlier day. "Why?" asks the title, supplying its own answer: "Because they all do it." Sam (Will Rogers) is introduced as a sleepy cowhand. "To prove that he is a regular cowboy, we show him with the cows." "How do we know they're cows? Because here are the calves." Backlit shots of cattle herd with dust rising. "More cattle. We got 'em and it don't cost any more to show 'em to you."

Sam has a girl who is movie-mad and refuses to countenance Sam's courtship until he can make love as they do on the screen. "Don't you ever go to the movies?" she asks. "No more than I have to," replies Sam.

Realizing that the best way to learn to love is to go to the movie factory where they make it, Sam's friends, who decide that he can't work in movies as cowboys really dress, kit him out. They give him a dazzling shirt, a vest embossed with horses' heads and edged with lace, chaps like llamas, and cuffs decorated with silver studs. The other cowboys fall about with laughter. The contrast between the costumes is particularly strong in this film, for Sam's cowboy pals are wearing the kind of rig any ranch hand would have worn in 1920.

With a flourish, one of the cowboys produces a ten-gallon hat. "Here's a thing that was originally used for a tent," he says. "It's the nearest we could get to the one Tom Mix wears." Finally, a gigantic neckerchief is flapped in front of him. "What's this, a bedspread?" asks Sam.

"How's the poor feller goin' to get on his hoss with all them trimmin's on?" ask the cowboys. They give him a box to serve as a mounting block, and cheer him as he rides off up the street.

Sam arrives in Hollywood, at the Goldwyn studios. "We're not using any cowboys today," snaps the gateman. "What days of the week do you use 'em?" asks Sam. He encounters Willie Jones, a child star—"his salary supports his entire family in unaccustomed luxury"—played by Rogers's son, Jimmie. "Where d'you get that outfit?" asks Willie. "Sears Roebuck?" He gets him through the gate, and at last Sam is able to watch the way they make love in the movies. Suddenly the director (William Orlamond in pith helmet, looking like Otis Turner) catches sight of the full glory of Sam and his outfit. He calls the attention of the actors. "I want you all to take a look at a cowboy that's dressed right—the real thing."

Bashfully, Sam removes his ten-gallon hat, as the players gaze in admiration.

Will Rogers parodied the Western in other pictures—one of his two-reelers was a skit on *The Covered Wagon* entitled *Two Wagons—Both Covered,* and another was a send-up of his friend Tom Mix, which involved breathtakingly skillful riding and roping (*Uncensored Movies,* directed by Jay Howe). His career began again when sound arrived. In 1935 Will Rogers and his friend Wiley Post embarked on a flight around the world to visit the breeding grounds of war as Preparedness publicity. The plane crashed near Point Barrow, Alaska, and both men were killed.

ROUNDUP

The stars of the silent-era Western followed the traditions of the Wild West show almost to a man. Art (for Artemus) Acord was an early arrival; allegedly half Ute Indian, he had been a ranch hand and rodeo rider before starting in pictures in 1909. For some years, movies and rodeo alternated; he won the title of World Champion Bulldogger in 1912. When Acord arrived at the Flying A studios in Santa Barbara, he resembled a traveling circus. With him came his rodeo trophies—forty-two hand-carved saddles, thirty-six silver-and-jewel-mounted bridles, twenty-six pairs of chaps, silver hat bands, twelve pairs of hand-carved riding boots, and ten pairs of silver spurs. No doubt the scale was expanded by the Flying A press agent, but it helps to explain the title of the first of the Buck Parvin series, which was also a pun on the name of a celebrated Indian warrior: *Man-Afraid-of-His-Wardrobe.*

The Buck Parvin series of 1916 parodied the making of Western pictures. Writer Charles van Loan had based the character of Parvin on Acord himself. Playing in *Sandy, Reformer* in the densely wooded valleys of the Santa Ynez Mountains, Acord was required to ride down a steep slope among boulders and through

The Buck Parvin series, made by the American Film Company in 1916, were comedies about the making of Westerns. Art Acord (center, on horse) portrayed Parvin; Lawrence Peyton (far left) played the director and Hardy Gibson the cameraman. Ann Little was the girl in this first episode, Man-Afraid-of-His-Wardrobe.

Art Acord, as Buck Parvin in Buck's Lady Friend *(1916), a comedy about the making of Westerns, directed by William Bertram. (Frame enlargement)*

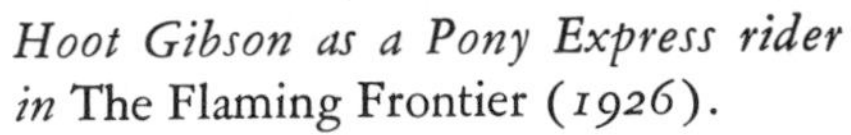

Hoot Gibson as a Pony Express rider in The Flaming Frontier *(1926).*

Art Acord, the wildest of the cowboys.

thick underbrush. "At one of the most perilous points," reported *Moving Picture World,* "the horse lost its footing, and fell sideways down the incline. Feeling the horse going, Acord attempted to spring off on the upside. One of his spurs caught in a worn cinch, and he was dragged after the rolling, pitching, struggling horse. Before the animal could regain its feet, it had rolled over on the rider, inflicting severe internal injuries."[1] Acord was not expected to live, but two months later he resumed work, and *Sandy, Reformer* was completed.

With both alcohol and fury in his veins, Acord was as spectacular a sight in the barroom as he was on a horse. Hollywood legend says that it was Acord who broke Victor Fleming's nose, when Fleming cast doubt upon his cowboy origins. Years later he was in court on a robbery charge, which came to nothing, and a scurrilous rumor of murder was whispered. In World War I, Acord served in France with the 4th Division and won the Croix de Guerre.

Acord's career never rose above the level of Universal Westerns, and it ended in tragedy. In 1931 *Photoplay* reported that he had committed suicide in Chihuahua, Mexico. "It seems, with fortune lost, Art had decided to make one more screen comeback. With another American, an unimpeachable informant tells us, he had planned to be kidnapped and held for ransom by Mexican bandits. But it all fell through. One suicide try at the Palacio Hotel failed—his American friend knocked a bottle of cyanide poison from his hands. But in his room Art had hidden another bottle of the poison. With this, he accomplished his tragic purpose."[2]

A FAVORITE SPARRING PARTNER for Art Acord was Hoot Gibson; they were in the same outfit together in World War I. Next to Tom Mix, Gibson was probably the most popular screen cowboy. He had impressive skill as a rider and an easy-going personality, with a delightful toothy grin. His pictures were mostly lightweight Universals. Ed Gibson was born at Tekamah, Nebraska, in 1892, and was for a while a ranch hand. He became a rodeo rider and at the Pendleton, Oregon, roundup of 1912 he won the Gold Belt for the best all-round cowboy in the world. During the winter months he worked around picture companies.

Helen Wenger was a 101 Rancher; she and Hoot first began working together at a rodeo in Salt Lake City in June 1913. "He and I won everything," she recalled, "the relay race, the standing woman's race, trick riding, and Hoot won the pony express race. But the promoter of the rodeo skipped town and we didn't get a cent of the prize money."[3]

They declared they were married for a firmly practical reason; at Pendleton, rooms were almost impossible to obtain, and married couples were given preference. Helen Wenger later took the name of Helen Gibson.

Hoot Gibson was not signed to a long-term contract as a result of his rodeo success. Far from it. As he told the story, he had returned from a tour of Australia with a Wild West show to a similar tour in America. "I was making a pretty good living, one way and another, but I didn't feel like there was much future in it. But still I didn't have nothing definite in my mind. . . .

"Well, one morning . . . I was in a little town by the name of Davenport up in Washington. I was going to ride there in a rodeo that day, but when I woke up it was snowing cats and dogs. . . . I didn't think much of that and I stood looking out there, and I put my hand in my pocket and found a letter from my mother. She was living down in Los Angeles, and her letter was all about sunshine, and flowers and things like that. . . . And I says to myself, 'If you can't make a living no other way, maybe you can ride in some of them moving pictures.' So that's what I done."

Like most cowboys, Gibson enjoyed riding and doubling, but he drew a line at acting. "Still, when you're trying to make a living at pictures, you got to take what comes. I rode when I could, and I was an assistant director, and a third cameraman, and I took care of horses, and there wasn't much I didn't do. But when things got too tough, I'd paint me up my face and go be an extra man. Then one day I made out I just couldn't stand that any more. So I seen where there was an automobile race in Fresno, and I went up there."[4]

While Hoot was working at Selig, in Edendale, with Tom Mix, Helen Gibson joined Kalem at Glendale, and by 1915 she had replaced Helen Holmes in the serial *The Hazards of Helen.* At Universal, Gibson worked with Harry Carey—a former Biograph actor with Griffith who became a popular Western star in the Hart tradition. After the war he went back with Tom Mix.

"It was a swell outfit, and I was eating regular. But I'd had a hankering after directing, and I'd made a few two-reelers off and on. So one day Universal sent for me, and wanted to know would I direct two-reel westerns? I told 'em I had a good job and didn't want to give it up unless it was sure about this directing thing, but they swore it was. I was getting $35 a week and they offered me $100 at the U. So I told Tom, and he said that was great if I could get a chance and to go take it. So I went out the next day and got my script and it looked like I had a real job. But before I got to work they said they were sorry, but it was all off, because the guy they'd been after all the time was going to take it after all. So there was I out of a job and felt pretty sick. But the chap that got my job directing was an old friend [Breezy Eason], so I went up to him and I says, 'Look here, I'm glad to see you got it, because you have been an assistant director for a long time, but I'm

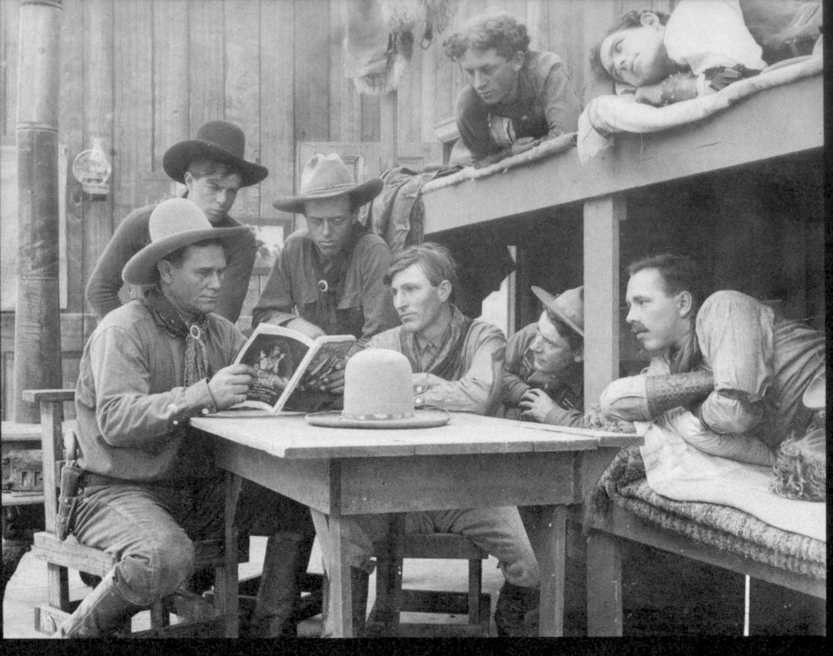

Hoot Gibson (in black hat) before his rise to fame, with other Universal cowboys in a bunkhouse scene.

Hoot Gibson.

Buck Jones, 1925.

BELOW: *Monte Blue (fourth from left), part Cherokee and a former cowboy, with Nez Percé Indians, on location at their reservation in Idaho for* Told in the Hills *(1919).*

out on your account. I don't see no reason why I couldn't play that young cow-puncher juvenile in there.' "[5]

In 1919 Gibson was playing leads, and in 1921 he went over to features. Before long, he was earning $14,500 a week.*

IN THE OLD TRIANGLE DAYS, Hoot Gibson and Monte Blue were cowboy extras together. Monte Blue's father was part Cherokee; a Civil War veteran, he was killed in a railroad accident when Montgomery Bluefeather was seven. Like his father, Monte Blue worked on the railroad, and also like his father was involved in a wreck. When he recovered, he joined a circus, worked as a coal miner, and decided next that life on a ranch would offer an agreeable contrast: "When I got out to Montana, I went to work at the Flying V ranch, in the Flathead Indian Reservation. I liked ranch life. It isn't so picturesque as it appears to be on the screen, but you're out in the open all the time, and if it's born in you to love the out-of-doors that means a lot. I learned horsemanship on the Flying V. My ability to do all sorts of stunts on horseback was to prove a drawback to me in my film career, but at the time nothing was farther from my thoughts than that I would some day become an actor."[6]

He had been fired by the idea of socialism in the coal mines; at a lumber camp in Washington he became a political orator, until run out of town by the police. He drifted to Wyoming and joined the Bar S Ranch at Big Piny. "It seems to me that Big Piny was just about the last of the real frontier towns. When I was there, the men were still carrying their six-shooters. It was a live cow town. But I couldn't seem to settle down to ranch life again."

After a series of more prosaic activities, he arrived in Los Angeles. He had heard of all the jobs available in the sunshine state, but found ten men chasing each one. After Blue had waited five weeks outside the Fine Arts studio, a man came out and said, "Say, fellows, I've got work for some of you." The extras rushed up. But it wasn't motion picture work—just digging telephone post holes at a dollar and a half a day. Once inside the gates, Blue continued his socialist speeches during the lunch hour, and one of these was overheard by D. W. Griffith. He thought Blue showed some potential as an actor, but when asked for a soapbox oration before the camera, Blue froze with nerves. Griffith overcame Blue's stage fright and created a special part for him in *The Absentees,* with Robert Edeson.

Monte Blue won a curious arrangement with Fine Arts; he was to continue as a day laborer, but whenever he worked in a picture, he would receive an extra five dollars a day. His ability on horseback, however, quickly typecast him as a stunt man. "Nothing more unfortunate could have happened to me at the time, for I was kept busy doing stunts and doubling for the more prominent players. It was a treadmill existence."[7]

Douglas Fairbanks rescued him and gave him parts in such pictures as *Wild and Woolly* (1917). Griffith used him as an assistant on *Intolerance,* and cast him in his most outstanding role, that of another labor agitator, Danton, in *Orphans of the Storm.*

---

* Gibson directed *Out of Luck,* a 1921 Universal two-reeler. In 1926 *Moving Picture World* announced he would direct Fred Gilman in *Range Terror,* finally assigned to William J. Craft (10 April 1926, p. 419).

To his surprise, he found himself more in demand for society roles in Lubitsch comedies, with patent-leather hair and dinner jackets, than for Western roles. Sometimes he ran across friends from the old days: "Pretty soft for you, Monte, these days." But, society roles apart, Monte Blue found pictures every whit as taxing as life on a ranch: "I was leading the Indians in a wild charge down the hillside," he said, when playing an Indian in *Told in the Hills,* "and I met a wide ditch right in my path. There was no time to pull up the horse—I was riding him with a rope bridle and no saddle—so I just hung on to his mane and let him try the jump. He missed, throwing me about forty feet, and I got up a pretty-looking object, with blood streaming from my mouth and ears. But I didn't intend letting those Indians see me fall down on the job, so I collared the horse again and rode him off. I was too shaken up to realise just what had happened to me, but when I went to take my shoes off after the ride, I doubled right up and couldn't straighten out again. They found, when they examined me, that I had broken three ribs."[8]

BUCK JONES WAS GROOMED for stardom at Fox as a threat to Tom Mix, in an attempt to keep that obstreperous cowboy firmly in line. But Jones was nobody's double, and in a remarkably short time he was a star in his own right, making action pictures that were so popular that his salary soared into the thousands a week bracket.

While Tom Mix's colorful career was mostly invention, Buck Jones's was real. Born Charles Gebhardt (often spelled Gebhart), he was raised on a farm in Vincennes, Indiana. Nicknamed "Buckaroo" when learning to ride as a boy, the shortened "Buck" remained. "When he was about sixteen," said Mrs. Buck Jones, "he became a little bit bored with home life and wanted to join the army. They wouldn't take him because he was too young. They said, 'If your mother will bring you back and vouch for you, we'll take you.' And she did. That's the reason for the discrepancy you see so many times in write-ups: 'Buck Jones was born in 1888 . . . in 1889. . . .' He was actually born in 1891 because his mother said he was two years older than he was."[9]

Enlisting in Troop G, 6th Regiment, U.S. Cavalry, in January 1907, he sailed for the Philippine Islands in September. "He was wounded at Mindanao. They were on the march and a Moro rebel shot him from the back. The bullet went in the back of his left leg and tore a hole five inches long in the front and he thought he was going to lose it. But he worked at it and he didn't."[10] Honorably discharged in December 1909, Gebhardt enlisted in the same regiment in 1910, becoming a sergeant two years later. He asked for a transfer to the Signal Corps aviation squadron and, in the hope of being able to fly, accepted reduction to the rank of private. He soon realized there was no chance of becoming a pilot and he let his enlistment expire; he was discharged on 23 October 1913.[11]

At the age of fifteen, Gebhardt had worked on a cow ranch with the Big V outfit, fifteen miles from Ponca City, Oklahoma. Now he joined three friends in a ranching venture near the Osage Indian country in Oklahoma. Fascinated by the 101 Ranch Wild West Show, which had its headquarters at Bliss (now Marland), Oklahoma, Gebhardt and his ranching friends decided to enter the qualifying rodeo, held to find the best riders for the road. The four boys agreed that if one failed, none would go. To their surprise, they all qualified. As Buck Jones put it, "The nag they gave me couldn't have thrown a wet saddle blanket."

Buck Jones in the first picture he ever made; he plays the sergeant holding the Indian. The man second from right is Duke R. Lee, who played in many Hollywood Westerns. The Indian girl is Princess Sunshine. Photographed at the 101 Ranch at Bliss, Oklahoma, in 1913.

After signing up with the show, Gebhardt found himself playing a soldier in a 101 motion picture. He soon gained a top position in the show and met his future wife, Odille (Dell) Dorothy Osborne, herself a champion rider. "I was born in New York, but raised in Philadelphia," said Mrs. Buck Jones. "I ran away from home when I was thirteen, and went to the 101 in New York, and told them I was older than I was, because they didn't want to take me. But they needed girls awfully bad for the show in New York and I tried so darn hard to make them want to keep me. I got into everything in the show, everything a girl could get into. Two or three of the top riders taught me to trick ride, so by the time the show closed in New York, I was a pretty valuable girl."[12]

Dell's mother caught up with her when the show reached Philadelphia, but the chief of the cowboys, D. V. Tantlinger, assured her that he and his wife would take care of the girl. "So they looked after me. But Buck and I managed to do some sneaking off to the side." They traveled all over the country. When the show departed for England, they left, joined the Julia Allen Wild West Show, and in 1915 they were married on horseback in the arena as a surprise feature of a show in Lima, Ohio.

After another spell with the 101 and one with the Ringling Brothers Circus, Dell became pregnant, and she and Buck decided to go to California. "We came in the winter of 1917 with the show. They needed all the riders they could get. There weren't too many of us trick riders out here, so we got all the work we could possibly handle. Buck and I both worked in pictures—he doubled Tom Mix, Bill Hart, and the others." Dell added that they were so hard up when they arrived that she doubled Bill Hart's leading lady when she was eight months pregnant.

"The boys used to line up at the Fox studios at Sunset and Western. The assistant director used to come out and look at them and say, 'I'll take you, and you,' and that would be it. The rest just stood out there. William Farnum* liked Buck awfully well. He asked for Buck, and so the assistant went out and got Buck and sent him in. Farnum asked him if he'd like to do a little part as a sheepherder. And that's one thing he didn't like, because he was a cowboy! Anyway, he got a part in this Farnum picture, and he was so good that Farnum went to Sol Wurtzel [Fox studio manager] and said, 'There's a man who's got looks, he can act, and he looks like he's part of a horse when he's riding. I think you ought to do something about him.' At that time they were having trouble with Tom Mix; every time he felt he needed a little more money, he'd refuse to work. Wurtzel contacted New York and they wired back: Sign him. They called Buck into the office and said, 'We're going to give you $100 a week. Don't come near the studio, don't tell anybody, don't call us, we'll call you. Every week you'll get the $100.' That was a million to us, after earning $35 a month on the circus. After a while, they called him and said, 'We're ready to start.' "

The studio anticipated grooming Jones for stardom in regular features, not just Westerns, and it was with some dismay that they noted that his customary rig consisted of Levis, boots, shirt, and Western hat. Winfield Sheehan, general manager of Fox, therefore issued instructions that read like those from the head of a finishing school: he was to comb his hair neatly (unless he was in a fight). His teeth required polishing and cleaning every two months. "It should be a practice of yours to open your mouth a little wider when you smile so that your teeth are seen more." He was to wear his new suits frequently so that he would not feel strange. "I have noticed that several actors seem uneasy in other than Western clothes." He was to keep his fingernails clipped and clean.[13]

Mrs. Jones explained why her husband changed his name: "He signed in October 1919, and that was so fresh after the war that putting a German name like Gebhardt on a marquee might have kept people away. They made a long list of names and Buck Jones just seemed to happen to gibe. After a few years, we changed it legally."

As soon as he was well established, Buck Jones bought a string of horses and contacted D. V. Tantlinger of the old 101. "The circus wasn't doing too well at the time, so Buck asked if he'd like to come out and run his horses and cowboys, and he was happy to come.

"When we first got here, we found quite a few fellows we knew from the 101 and other shows. They'd heard the pickings were good in California. We had no intention of staying. We decided to stay for the winter until our baby, Maxine, was born, then go back to the show. But we did so much work and made so much money, we stayed.

---

* Farnum's brother Marshall was chief director of the 101 Ranch motion picture department. Franklyn Farnum (no relation) featured Jones in several of his pictures and greatly aided his career.

"Tom Mix was just a son-of-a-gun when Buck first started at Fox. Oh, he was so nasty! But after a few years, when Buck made it, he admitted there was no way you could keep him out. So then they became good friends—the last eighteen years or so. He used to come over to our house and he and Buck would go into the barn, have a few drinks, and hash over old times. 'You know, Buck,' he used to say, ' I was an s.o.b. when you started. I hated your guts.' Mix came by our house just before he left for the trip to Arizona when he was killed."[14]

Buck Jones abandoned pictures for a while after a quarrel with Fox, and embarked on a Wild West show of his own. But union trouble combined with a crooked manager forced him to return to the screen. During the thirties he joined Tim McCoy, who had also had a Wild West show, and Raymond Hatton in the celebrated Rough Riders series.

He was on a bond-selling tour in World War II when he attended a party at the Cocoanut Grove nightclub in Boston. The entire place burst into flames. Buck Jones became the 487th victim, dying two days later on 30 November 1942.

"How sad that our industry doesn't realize that Buck Jones is one of the real heroes of the business," said John Wayne. "He went back into that Boston fire to rescue people, and he didn't come back out. But there's no memorial to him. They certainly forgot old Buck."[15]

BORN IN SAGINAW, MICHIGAN, in 1891, Timothy McCoy was the son of the chief of police, an Irishman who brought him up with a fascination for both military life and the West. He studied under the Jesuits in Chicago. "I always had two ambitions," said McCoy. "I wanted to be an army officer, but I also wanted to be a cowboy. I came home for a Christmas vacation and saw Dustin Farnum in the play *The Virginian.* From then on I knew I wanted to be a cowboy. A fellow in Saginaw shipped wild horses and sold them for use with delivery carts, truck-garden carts and that sort of thing. He brought some cowboys back to break them out. Well, like all kids I was hanging around these cowboys, and it didn't take me long before I had my hand on a rope. All of us, if our parents could afford it, rode western horses with western saddles, and down there with the cowboys we learned to rope."

McCoy quit college and bought a ticket to Omaha: "I didn't know whether I was going to Montana, Texas, Wyoming, Oklahoma, or New Mexico—I knew something would happen before I got to Omaha. On the train, I met a guy with a big black hat and mustache, and his business was rounding up wild horses in Wyoming and shipping them to New Jersey. He came from Lander, Wyoming. The result was I stayed with him. Lander was the end of the railroad and here I was in the middle of the damn cow country.

"The train got into Lander at 8 at night, and as I wandered up the street, the first thing that caught my eye were cowboys, talking outside the saloon. Ponies were tied along the hitchracks. You could hear the jingle of spurs along the wooden sidewalks. The sounds of the saloon. One of the fellows had a great big hat, a long black mustache and a pair of white angora chaps. I said, 'God, this is what I was looking for.' "[16]

McCoy learned later that this was Owen Wister country; much of the material for *The Virginian* was culled in the area. At first McCoy found himself pitching hay, but he soon became a cowboy, working in the Wind River country. Here he

Tim McCoy during his MGM period (1928).

came into contact with the Indians—the Arapaho and Shoshone. "It was my contacts with them, rounding up stray cattle, that enabled me to learn their sign language. I learned it so well that one of the Arapaho chiefs said I must have been an Indian a long time ago." The Arapaho later took him into their tribe as "High Eagle, one who leads the coyote."

McCoy's military career began when the European war broke out and Teddy Roosevelt announced the formation of his own expeditionary force. McCoy recruited one squadron of cavalry from Wyoming and Montana cowboys, along the lines of the Rough Riders. "Roosevelt embraced that immediately. I was to have been commissioned a captain. But then he wrote to me and said that unfortunately, for political reasons, the President had denied him permission to take troops abroad. So that was that."

After enlisting in the cavalry, McCoy was dismayed when his regiment was converted to field artillery. "When the war was over, I seemed to have attained a lot of rank. Too much rank for anyone as young as I was. When I got my majority, I know I was the youngest major in the army. At the end of the war they offered me the appointment as Adjutant General of Wyoming, which gave me the rank of Brigadier General. I was 28 years old."

McCoy accepted the appointment, which had resulted from his friendship with General Hugh L. Scott, the army's chief of staff from 1914 to 1917, and a cavalry officer in the Indian wars. McCoy was Scott's aide; when Scott retired he was appointed head of the Board of Indian Commissioners. The two men undertook an exhaustive enquiry into the Custer disaster, and quite by accident McCoy discovered two Arapaho who had been in the Sioux camp at the time. The information the Indians provided was handed over to Colonel A. W. Graham for his book *The Custer Myth.*

When Paramount was setting up production on *The Covered Wagon,* they asked McCoy for help. They needed a great many Indians and had no idea how to

McCoy's search for Wovoka, the Ghost Dance Messiah of 1890, is rewarded.

go about finding them. McCoy brought down two trainloads—"Indians, tepees, horses, dogs, papooses, everything there was"—and when it was over, he was asked to organize a prologue on stage at Grauman's Egyptian. So successful was the prologue—which included one of the Arapaho who had fought against Custer—that McCoy was asked to take it to London. He appeared at the London Pavilion for nine months.

On his return, he worked on Paramount's *Thundering Herd,* and it was while making that picture that he located Wovoka, the Ghost Dance Messiah. "No one had heard anything about him after the Ghost Dance thing was over," said McCoy. "I got interested in him because General Scott and I had looked into the whole Ghost Dance problem. I'd known an Arapaho scout called Sitting Bull—not the Sioux who was killed—who had spread the Ghost Dance religion from the Northern tribes all the way into Oklahoma. Scott called him John the Baptist. That whetted my appetite. So I picked up Wovoka's trail. Took me a long time. Went from one tribe to another. When I finally found him, he was rather reticent. He disclaimed a lot of things that were attributed to him about the Ghost Shirts. He was a man of peace."

McCoy was then put under contract by MGM as their sole Western star, and featured in a series of elaborate Western pictures. He announced they would be historically accurate. "I did as much as I could, until I realized that after all, it *was* entertainment. I learned as I went along that you can bring as much authenticity into it as you can, but don't spoil the entertainment. Furthermore, if you're going to be completely authentic, it'll take you weeks to do the things you're supposed to do in five minutes. Suppose you want to do the snake dance of the Hopis; well, the ritual calls for three days. But you can't stand and shoot for three days. That happens with so many of the details of Western pictures. Take the cowboy's life; you can't show men getting up while it's still dark, having breakfast by the light of the cook's fire, the boss detailing them to go out like the spokes of a wagon wheel and drive the cattle in. It would take you half a day to show that; you've got to get it over in three minutes and a half. I soon realized that this thing of being completely authentic is impossible."

In one area McCoy remained accurate. "When *War Paint* was shown in Oklahoma, I was told afterwards that old Indians would spend all day sitting in the theater. They couldn't read the captions. But they could read my signs."

McCoy has seen his films revived, and his career saluted with awards. But he derives most satisfaction from his memory.*

"When I met the old Indians and the old Western characters, I had both ears listening. I never forgot. I am so grateful that I was able to catch the end of the Old West. But I remember what General Scott said. He had a great career, but he joined the 7th Cavalry right after Little Big Horn. 'Too bad I wasn't born ten years sooner,' he said, 'or I might have amounted to something.' "

THE AMERICAN INDIAN

Ralph and Natasha Friar have written a controversial book called *The Only Good Indian . . . The Hollywood Gospel*,[1] which attacks Hollywood for its portrayal of the Indian as a gut-eating savage. They object to the term "Indian," explaining that since Columbus was under the impression he had reached the Indies when he discovered America, the term is a misnomer; they should be Native Americans. "No other race or culture depicted on film has been made to assume such a permanent fictional identity."[2] The book contains some strong arguments and is well worth reading, but I submit that the authors have gravely underestimated the silent era. A lot of melodramatic nonsense was produced in this period, as in every other, but a close examination of the years before World War I reveals that film-

* Just before his death in 1977, he published *Tim McCoy Remembers the West* (New York: Doubleday) in collaboration with his son Ronald.

Mona Darkfeather, a Seminole, at Universal (1912).

makers cared a great deal more about the Indian than the Friars give them credit for. To what extent the true culture of the various tribes was captured on film will never be known, for the majority of these early pictures, both fictional and factual, have been lost. But accurate or not, the number of films that presented a sympathetic view of the Indian is in marked contrast to later periods such as the thirties and forties. And the anger aroused by inaccuracy at the time matches the Friars' own.

Alanson Skinner, assistant curator of the Department of Anthropology at the American Museum of Natural History, protested to the New York *Times* in 1914: "From the standpoint of a student, most of the picture plays shown are ethnologically grotesque farces. Delawares are dressed as Sioux, and the Indians of Manhattan Island are shown dwelling in skin tipis of the type used only by the tribes beyond the Mississippi. If the Indian should stage a white man's play, and dress the characters in Rumanian, Swiss, Turkish, English, Norwegian and Russian costumes, and place the setting in Ireland, would their plea that they thought all Europeans alike, and that they had to portray the white man's life through standards of their own save them from arousing our ridicule?"[3]

Criticism of inaccurate productions had already reached a climax in 1911, when a group of Indian delegates visited Washington and charged motion picture producers with gross libel. Despite the protests, the flood of Indian pictures that poured from manufacturers included some highly praised productions. Alanson Skinner and other authorities were united in their commendation of F. E. Moore's 1913 epic *Hiawatha,* performed by one hundred fifty full-blooded Indians, with photography by Victor Milner.

Twenty, thirty years after the Indian wars, the tribes had been settled upon reservations, and they could at last be described by politicians as "docile." Those same politicians, even under Progressivism, were dispossessing the Indians as steadily as ever. Yet Roosevelt, with his pleas for conservation, aroused the nation to the plight of the Indian. And in response came a genuine concern. Born of guilt or romanticism it may have been, yet it crossed several generations and led to attempts at reparation by people who, with the disappearance of their country's native inhabitants, realized too late what they were losing.

As a result, there were many pleas for the downtrodden Indian: *The Friendless Indian* appeared in 1913: "Condemned to walk alone, a Red Man saves a life and is given only a nod for thanks—after all, he is Indian."[4] Edward Sloman, who was to specialize in films about another downtrodden race, the Jews, directed *Lone Star* in 1916. Described as "a strong tale of Indian life on the Nebraska reservation," it featured William Russell in the title role of an Indian who rose to fame as a surgeon; he becomes an outcast of the Indians for seeking the white man's civilization and is scorned by the whites because he is an Indian. This paradox reappears in the major pro-Indian films of the twenties such as *Braveheart* and *Redskin.* By contrast, *Her Own People* (1917) concentrated on the peaceful side of Indian life, spurring an English critic to remark that it savored of hypocrisy when an American producer sought to make heroes of a race his ancestors so sedulously subdued.

Moving Picture World offered an intriguing explanation: "Our feelings have undergone the same change that came over the English in their relation to the Scottish highland clans. Up to the time of William of Orange, the English, suffering very real hardship from the border depredations of the highland clans, regarded them as little better than highway robbers. A war of extermination was begun against them. Then, when all danger had passed, there came a formal union, the English went to the other extreme and could not seemingly go far enough in their admiration and fondness for highland history, highland customs and institutions, until the once despised attire of the Highlander was affected by the nobility, and even the royal family of England.

"Our Indians are no longer dangerous. We understand today better than ever that we have wronged them much and often, that we have misjudged and slandered them in the past. Now the reaction has set in, and it is surely a curious phase of the white man's civilization that his latest invention is helping to set the red man right in history. All of the more artistic Indian films exalt the Indian, depict the noble traits in his character and challenge for him and his views and his manner of life the belated admiration of his white brother."[5]

This awareness of the Indian problem was echoed in a review of Griffith's *Ramona* (1910): ". . . one wants to do something to help the unfortunates whose property is destroyed, whose land is taken and who are persecuted and driven ever farther into the wilderness. It is too late now for the reproduction of the novel to exert any influence in the rectification of a great wrong. But perhaps it will be worthwhile to show thus graphically the injustice which preceded the settlement of a considerable proportion of the United States."[6]

Yet it is Griffith for whom the Friars reserve their heaviest artillery. Certainly, one cannot defend the costuming of Plains Indians in Sioux war bonnets in the otherwise excellent *Last Drop of Water* (1911), nor the lurid portrayal of Indians in the 1924 *America.* But the Friars spare no praise for Griffith's sincere and compassionate attempts to show how the Indian had been wronged. For even in *The Battle at Elderbush Gulch* (1913), when the plot requires Indians to kill babies, Griffith establishes that hostilities were started by the white settlers.

The Friars object as virulently to the Noble Red Man as to the painted savage. Their objection is therefore to melodrama as a whole; at this period, in virtually all dramatic subjects, the characters, white or Indian, fell into one or the other of these categories. The early film was greatly enriched on the rare occasion when the bulwark of melodrama was breached with subtlety and realism, but such a film was seldom financially rewarding.

Among the Friars' most fascinating items of research, however, is a piece culled from the *Ladies Home Journal,* August 1923—an article called "My Own Story" by Mary Pickford, describing the making of *A Pueblo Legend* (1912), one of Griffith's least effective pictures:

"Undoubtedly this Indian picture was filled with mistakes. The dress of the Pueblos is very modest and they wear a sort of tunic or nightgown effect under the dresses. We obtained dresses like theirs, but did not use the under-dress and our arms were bare. So, too, were our legs, for we did not trouble to bind them with rawhide, which is worn as a protection against snake bites. . . .

"We proceeded to the Indian village of Isleta, sixteen miles from Albuquerque, where the inhabitants were shocked when they saw us in our incomplete dress. None of them knew what motion pictures were except a few who were Carlisle graduates. Among these was the chief's daughter.

"A Frenchman who was cast for the part of a medicine man had been given permission to select a costume for himself from the museum in connection with the Harvey Hotel at Albuquerque. He had the ill luck to choose a very weird one with a short skirt trimmed with bells. When he came dancing into the scene with bathing trunks underneath his short skirt the Indians were furious, because they thought we were trying to make fun of them. It seems that this was a sacred skirt, and they insisted that he take it off or that we all leave the village.

"The Indian chief demanded that our chief, Mr. Griffith, come to their kiva or councilroom, which was in the middle of the village. Mr. Griffith was detained there all afternoon. . . . There was only one Indian who spoke English, and Mr. Griffith had no idea whether he was translating his speeches fairly or not. . . . He offered them two thousand dollars if they would allow us to stay the rest of the afternoon; but the council decided that no matter how much money we had, we must leave the village. . . . Finding that there was nothing that would tempt them, Mr. Griffith sent me word that the camera was to be secreted and that I was to walk down their village street and steal the scene. If we did not get this particular bit, all that we had done before they stopped us would be wasted.

"I have never been so terrified as I was when I walked trembling down that street. . . . In those days the director was king Mr. Griffith's word was law and none of us would have thought of disobeying him. As I walked down that road I could feel eyes watching me from every corner and crevice. Finally there was a split in the tribe, and about one-fourth of them came with us when we went back to Albuquerque to finish the picture there. The chief's daughter acted as interpreter, and I heard afterwards that she had to leave the village, that her father was furious with her for going with us. Incidentally, the picture was not much of a success when released."

The Friars find preposterous the Hollywood habit of casting Indian roles with white actors. Yet in this early period, not only were there Indian actors—such as Chief Dark Cloud, who played in such Griffith films as *Song of the Wildwood Flute* (1910)—there was even an Indian director. James Young Deer (or Youngdeer, as he later styled himself) was a member of the Winnebago tribe, born in Dakota City, Nebraska. From childhood, he was involved in circuses and Wild West shows, among them Barnum and Bailey and Miller Brothers 101 Ranch. He entered the moving picture business almost as soon as it began, and his Wild West show background proved invaluable when it came to staging Western pictures. Soon he was writing scenarios and playing leading roles. He appeared in D. W. Griffith's *The Mended Lute* (1909), and worked for Kalem, Lubin, Vitagraph, and Bison. When Pathé Frères began producing in America, Young Deer joined them as director, becoming general manager of the Pathé West Coast studio. His Western pictures were often highly successful: *The Cheyenne Brave, The Yaqui Girl, Lieutenant Scott's Narrow Escape, Red Deer's Devotion.*

From the viewpoint of Western history, Young Deer's films would repay close study, for he made full use of what remained of the Old West, both in terms of locations and costumes. Many of his pictures were made at the S & M Ranch in Orange County, California. He once returned from a visit to his people on their reservation with trunkloads of Indian costumes. In 1912 he shot documentary footage of the Yuma Indians; Chief Dark Cloud thought so highly of Young Deer's

Chief Dark Cloud and Dove Eye Dark Cloud. D. W. Griffith used Dark Cloud in many early pictures; he even played a general in The Birth of a Nation, *his long hair concealed under a hat. His real name was Elijah Tahamont, and he was a celebrated lecturer. Griffith brought him to California in 1912, and he died in the flu epidemic of 1918. Dove Eye Dark Cloud wrote scenarios for pictures and played in them, and lived to the age of ninety one. Her granddaughter is the wife of Iron Eyes Cody.*

Thomas Ince (center) with the Inceville Sioux.

Young Deer working for the Bison Company at Big Bear in 1911, with Princess Red Wing; from Little Dove's Romance, *directed by Fred Balshofer.*

films that he used them on his lecture tours. Young Deer continued directing until about 1916, when he returned to acting. Pathé took him to France, where he directed some pictures at the end of the war, returning to America in the winter of 1919. The twenties were lean years for him; he operated an acting school and returned to direction on Poverty Row in the 1930s.

A director of great importance was Edwin Carewe, responsible for the discovery of Dolores del Rio and for such films as *Ramona* (1928) and *Resurrection* (1927); he was a quarter Chickasaw, his maternal grandmother being the daughter of Chief Tabuscabano. Carewe was proud of his colorful youth among the tepees; he had been expelled from four schools in less than a year, he ran away from home, punched cattle, and wandered the West as a hobo with Jack London. His real name was Fox—his brother was screenwriter Finis Fox—and his father, F. M. Fox, loaned the family's precious Indian relics from his ranch at Corpus Christi, Texas, for use in Carewe's Western *The Trail of the Shadow* (1917).

THE PRESENCE OF INDIANS in the cast did not guarantee accuracy, but no Indian film could claim authenticity without them. The most elaborate Indian dramas were those produced by Thomas Ince with the Inceville Sioux. These films were generally respectful toward the Indian, carefully balancing treachery and insobriety on the part of one group with honor and courage on the part of another. But the values were those of the whites: *Last of the Line* (reissued as *Pride of Race*) was directed by Jay Hunt from a C. Gardner Sullivan scenario late in 1914. Japanese star Sessue Hayakawa acted with the Inceville Sioux. Chief Gray Otter (William Eagleshirt), last of a line of powerful Sioux, proudly awaits his son's return from white man's college, and is appalled to discover his hope for the future lurching around the frontier station, drunk. Gray Otter has made a pact with the garrison commander that no white man shall be molested by the Indians. But his son, with a band of renegades, robs the paymaster's coach. Gray Otter is enraged at the attack and shoots his son, making it appear that he died defending the paymaster. The cavalry honors the boy with a full military funeral. As the soldiers march away after the ceremony, Gray Otter kneels at the grave and a title appears: "Alone."

Louis Reeves Harrison, critic of the *Moving Picture World,* was violently opposed to the sympathetic view of the Indian. He tolerated Ince's films because conditions alone were presented. The more radical pictures led him to expostulate: "The noble red man, who used to sell land that he never bought or paid for, drink the proceeds and then murder the purchaser in cold blood, is becoming immortalized."[7]

Harrison considered the Indian cruel, crafty, and predatory, with no universal language, no marks of gradual enlightenment, and incapable of contributing anything of value to human evolution.[8] Unfortunately, there was one character in early films who, in his celluloid form, precisely fitted this description. He was the half-breed, fair game as villain in anyone's picture. In Ben Wilson's *One Eighth Apache* (1922), written by Peter B. Kyne, it was enough for the heroine to discover in her husband the merest hint of Indian blood to cause her nervous collapse. While prominent Americans boasted of *their* Indian blood, the half-breed was portrayed as a menace to society, and usually half-starved as well: "A good hearty meal would work a revolution in their morals."[9] He did not appear in a sympathetic light until 1916, when Douglas Fairbanks played *The Half-Breed* under Allan Dwan's direction.

"I had a hell of a time getting it on its feet," said Dwan, "because Beth Fairbanks, Doug's wife and manager, didn't want him appearing as an unwashed half-breed. To fix that, I had him standing on a rock, nude except for a loincloth. He dives into the river, and scrubs himself thoroughly and rubs himself with sand to get himself oh, so very clean. So I asked Beth, 'How's that?' She said, 'That's fine.' He was a washed Indian, not a dirty Indian. I only put the scene in to satisfy her."[10]

WHEN THEY REACH 1916, the Friars fall with gratitude upon a factual film. Filmed by the Department of the Interior, the documentary material was shot on the Blackfoot Reservation in Glacier National Park, Montana, by Herford Tynes Cowling. These scenes, significant though they were, form only a small part of the collection of documentary material on the Indian, which was growing rapidly during the silent days.

In 1910 the American Film Manufacturing Company discovered that no film had been taken along the Old Santa Fe Trail, and they immediately began work in and around Old Santa Fe, heading on to the Indian villages of San Felipe, San Domingo, Isleta, and Laguna. Although much of this documentary footage would eventually appear surrounded by a fictional story, at least Flying A had the energy and enterprise to go and get it.

In 1912 Selig released *Life and Customs of the Winnebago Indians,* "an educational offering showing something of the industries, dances, games, sports and other customs of a tribe of intelligent-looking red men who live in the Black River Falls District of Wisconsin."[11] Ralph Radnor Earle, for Pathé's *See America First* series, made a film about the Blackfoot Indians in 1912. Bison produced *Indian Dances and Pastimes* about the Pueblo in 1912.

Potentially more rewarding for rediscovery even than these would be Rodman Wanamaker's* *History of the American Indian.* The film ran thirteen reels, an unusually ambitious length for 1915. Directed by Rollin S. Dixon, it was a careful documentary record of rites and ceremonies that were already forgotten by young Indians. Dixon was a member of the 1913 Wanamaker expedition and had persuaded the tribal chiefs at the Crow Reservation near Sheridan, Wyoming, that a more permanent record of rites and ceremonies should be obtained than the oral tradition. The chiefs agreed, for it was clear that the customs were not being maintained. The part of the film devoted to ceremonials included such mysteries as the medicine stick and the ceremonial steam bath. Dixon rounded up those warriors with combat experience and staged battle scenes, which the Indians ensured were scrupulously accurate. The modern section of the film depicted reservation life and featured the big ID roundup, showing the Indians riding the range and branding cattle.

As a result of the Wanamaker films, a motion picture company, Northwestern Film Corporation, was formed in Sheridan by John E. Maple, who produced a

---

* Wanamaker was a police commissioner. Some of his film survives at the American Museum of Natural History in New York.

A Nez Percé Indian, featured in Told in the Hills *(1919).*

Douglas Fairbanks as The Half-Breed *(1916). By having him dive from this rock and swim in the river, director Allan Dwan coped with Mrs. Fairbanks's objections to Fairbanks appearing as a "dirty savage."*

six-reel documentary on the Crow Reservation in 1918. Maple hired his technical staff in Los Angeles and was lucky enough to obtain two D. W. Griffith technicians, Paul Powell as director, and John Leezer as cameraman. Each reel was designed as an entity in itself, so that the documentary could support a program in serial form. John Maple, who had been adopted as a member of the Crow tribe, obtained a special permit from the Department of the Interior to operate on the Crow, Cheyenne, and Pine Ridge reservations. The film, entitled *Indian Life,* had a musical score by Vern Elliott.

The following year, Maple produced another all-Indian picture, *Before the White Man Came,* which was released early in 1920. A seven-reeler, directed by Maple himself, and photographed by John Fuqua, a former rancher, and E. B. Sonntag, the story was the work of William E. Wing. *Before the White Man Came* was not a documentary, although it incorporated rites and ceremonies; it was aimed at the regular Western market, in the hope that a Western shot on location with real Indians would carry more appeal than the straight factual material of *Indian Life.*

Very prosaically shot, *Before the White Man Came* is reminiscent of a primitive Eastern Western; yet, occasionally, a stunningly composed long shot appears that seems to belong to a different film. It almost certainly does; I suspect these wonderful scenes of mist-enshrouded tepees and Griffith-like perspectives of horsemen on the warpath come from *Indian Life,* and were shot by Paul Powell and John Leezer. Maple displays no talent whatever as a film-maker. The film makes an interesting comparison to *Nanook of the North,* for while Flaherty's technique is equally primitive, his fascination with people is transmitted to the celluloid. Maple seldom brings his characters close enough to the camera for the audience to recognize them. They are treated as impersonally as extras. Curiously, for a man who had lived among Indians for so long, Maple emphasizes their brutality.

The generous cooperation provided by the Crow Indians, which extended even to such violently anti-Indian pictures as *The Devil Horse* (see pp. 350–4), was not something film-makers could rely on from other tribes. "An attempt by the Cuauhtemoc Film Company to film the Indian snake dances at the annual San Xavier fiesta at Tucson, Ariz. this week came to naught," reported *Moving Picture World,* "when the Indians who performed the dance fled upon sighting the camera. The cameraman tried in vain to induce them to perform, but it was no use, and the film company officials departed. When the Eclair company was in Tucson, they endeavored to get a picture of the fiesta, and offered every inducement to the Indians, but it was in vain. In explaining why his people would not allow a picture to be taken, one of the chiefs said that if the camera caught them they could never die."[12]

Director Carlyle Ellis experienced difficulty in filming *Nurse Among the Tepees*, a 1920 public health documentary, on the Arapaho Reservation in Wyoming. The biting cold—forty degrees below zero—made life wretched for cameraman Goebel, who struggled bravely against freezing oil in his camera, brittle film, which could break at a touch, and static flashes on the negative. But the overriding problem rested with the Indians themselves. Many refused point-blank to pose for the camera. When Goebel cranked on a group of women, they preferred to hide their faces behind the children they carried in their arms, even though the purpose of the picture had been explained to them. The government-sponsored film drew attention to the importance of the public health nurse, who, from her log-cabin headquarters, provided essential medical aid to the Indians; the film highlighted a particularly serious eye disease, trachoma, very common at that time among children on the reservation.[13]

Herford Tynes Cowling, who photographed the Blackfoot documentary Ralph and Natasha Friar wrote about, became chief photographer of the U.S. Reclamation Service and contributed much valuable documentary material on Indian life, including 1916 films on the Pueblo and the Papago. Lawrence Grant, an English actor who played the Kaiser in propaganda films, was an acknowledged authority on Indians, and in 1918 made a film about their customs in Kinemacolor. Several 1920 films appeared in Prizmacolor: *The Land of the Great Spirit, Life in the Blackfoot Country,* and *Heritage of the Red Man.*

The most bizarre title among all the factual films was a Bray Pictograph of 1917, which dealt with the Sherman Institute in Riverside, California. It was called *De-Indianizing the Red Man.* Said the synopsis: "This is one of the largest and best of the Government schools for Indians, where by careful processes, the Government is striving to eliminate the Indian nature of its charges."[14]

This grim sentiment may have been government policy. But to judge from the examples of their work which survive, very few of the early film-makers would have supported it.

EDWARD S. CURTIS

The most gifted photographer of Indians was Edward S. Curtis, who set himself the enormous task of documenting a disappearing people. "What is it that lies behind this door that history wants to close so suddenly?" he asked. Criticized by classical anthropologists for his emotional involvement—for his humanistic rather than scientific attitude—this sympathetic quality of Curtis's now lifts his photographs from skillful documents into the realm of art. His faces, lit by a soft, almost inward glow, are characterized by an expression of trust rarely seen in such portraits. "While primarily a photographer, I do not see or think photographically. Instead, I have sought to bring art and science together in an effort to reach beneath the surface of what it appears to be."[1]

Curtis came to prominence through an exhibition of his prints at the Waldorf-Astoria, in New York, patronized by President Roosevelt. "Roosevelt understood as no other person I have ever known the great significance of my work; a few months later, through his help, I met with J. Pierpont Morgan. This event changed my life."[2]

Morgan set up a special trust fund to enable Curtis to continue his work and to produce "the most beautiful and lasting sets of books ever to be published." Unfortunately, the books were too beautiful, too expensive, and they vanished into

In the Land of the Headhunters: *filming Naida against a backcloth that obscures the timbers of an anachronistic barn.*

In the Land of the Headhunters (*1914*), *directed by Edward Curtis.*

A hitherto unpublished picture of the rarely photographed Curtis—taken by a fellow film-maker of Indians, Rodman Wanamaker.

the recesses of great libraries and private collections. Preserved in this lifeless manner, Curtis's work was forgotten.

One of those who brought about his rediscovery was Teri McLuhan, who republished a collection of his photographs in the same massive format as the original books. In 1974 Teri McLuhan completed a remarkable film about Curtis, called *The Shadow Catcher* (the Indian word for photographer). It dealt with Curtis as a film-maker as well as still photographer and ethnographer, and contained some unique footage:

"I started writing and contacting the people who knew Curtis. In the midst of editing the film, I had a call from Mr. Magnussen (Curtis's son-in-law), whom I had seen in California. I had asked him to let me know if he ever came across anything unusual relating to Curtis—in his attic, or in old papers. He said he thought he had found something, but he was about to throw it out. 'It looks like film footage,' he said, 'but it's completely rusted away.' I said, 'I'll be on a plane tomorrow.' There was 35 mm. film of the Hopi snake dance, and 16 mm. film taken by Curtis's daughter, Beth, of the 1927 Alaskan expedition. The 35 mm. footage was very badly corroded. A lab in Los Angeles did a poor job, so I had to take it to John E. Allen in New Jersey, a marvelous man, who worked on it day and night. And he rescued it."[3]

In 1947 an original nitrate print of Curtis's *In the Land of the Headhunters* (1914) was presented to Chicago's Field Museum, where Professor George Quimby was curator of the anthropology department. A 16 mm. safety print was made and the nitrate destroyed. When he moved to the University of Washington, Quimby took the film with him, and it is now available for sale or hire, complete with modern sound track.

Curtis's photographic work was of such a high technical standard that to copy it is to lose more than just the surface luster; tragically enough, such copying can obliterate the artistry. In the sharpness of detail lay Curtis's obsession with mystery. The film is of value now for what it shows, but not for the way it shows it.

Professor Quimby regards the film as a significant forerunner of *Nanook of the North,* Robert Flaherty's famous documentary about the Eskimo. Curtis provided his Kwakiutl actors with costumes and he reconstructed the living conditions of a past era, just as Flaherty did with the Eskimo. They were both romantics. It is this romantic element that still dismays some anthropologists. "It is very much a hokey film," says Kwakiutl anthropologist Gloria Cranmer Webster in *The Shadow Catcher.* "I saw the handbill from a theater in Seattle, and it made it seem as if these people were living like this in 1914. And this wasn't true at all. But if you forget about the story, it's a very important film."[4]

Curtis needed a commercial success to subsidize further his photographic field work. But he kept the story close to his knowledge of the American Indian. The picture entailed three years of preparatory work. "Women wove cedar bark capes and prepared the costumes," said Curtis, "while the men were busy painting the designs on housefronts, and carving masks, poles, implements, and canoes. On a protected beach on Deer Island [off Vancouver Island, Canada, and near Fort Rupert, principal village of the Kwakiutl] we assembled the Kwakiutl housefronts characteristic of the period before the white man. Many people joined in the work to make the film as much a document of the old times as we could."[5]

The film was a love story; woven into it were elements of war, revenge, and the struggle for supernatural power. To prove himself worthy of the love of Naida, the beautiful girl, the hero has to test his courage. One test involved the spearing of sea lions. Curtis enjoyed rough water and decided to sail thirty miles out to Devil Rock, which he knew would be packed with sea lions. (An amazing shot from his film shows a vast herd of bulls, splashing into the water in an endless row, one slightly behind the other, like a carefully rehearsed chorus line.) He had the foresight to check the chart and saw that the island would be clear forty feet above high tide. The boat left them, and Curtis and his assistant explored the rock. To their horror, there was no sign of driftwood, which meant only one thing: the government chart was wrong. There was no way of getting help. They packed their cameras in watertight bags, amassed their equipment on the extreme high point of rock, and hung on. Through the night, they were acutely aware that their lives hung in the balance. At dawn the high tide flooded over them. But their carefully rigged lifelines held: "To this day," wrote Curtis, "I cannot read about a human being sentenced to death without recalling that moment on Devil Rock."[6]

The picture won some ecstatic reviews—*Moving Picture World*[7] called it "a gem . . . it has never been surpassed. Overwhelmingly beautiful and impressive" —but it failed financially because of inadequate distribution. Curtis used a motion picture camera again, but he never produced another film of this sort, a sad loss for the documentary movement.

In the twenties Curtis established a studio in Los Angeles, and Cecil B. DeMille employed him to make still pictures on the set of such pictures as *Adam's Rib.* With this photographic genius in their midst, it is a dismal comment on the film business that no one financed another film. For men like Curtis, technically brilliant, with immense courage and tenacity and the additional dimension of empathy, have proved even rarer than the primitive people whose way of life they sought to celebrate.

Edward Curtis died in 1952, unknown and penniless. But by that time, he had recorded eighty tribes—he had exposed forty thousand photographs and made ten thousand sound recordings. He was not satisfied merely to document—he wanted to participate. He wanted to be accepted by this mysterious world that so enthralled him. He once took part in the Hopi snake dance, and the event proved to be a spiritual crossroads in his life: "these events are beyond words." When she set out on her own filming expedition, Teri McLuhan took some of Curtis's pictures with her. She found they acted as a passport to that very world Curtis strove so hard to join. "It is extremely difficult today to walk into an Indian community and film. But the emotional truth of Curtis's photographs struck home to every Indian who saw them. I explained my intention in making them more widely available. So Curtis's own work made it a little easier for us, and certainly permitted a greater depth to my film."[8]

THE VANISHING AMERICAN

For years, *The Vanishing American* was a legend among film enthusiasts. The film itself had seemingly vanished, and all that survived were some breathtaking stills, the memories of those who had seen it on its first release, and such enticing references as this one from John Grierson: "There is no greater story than the passing of the Indian—the picture had the desert, the canyons, and the plains to conjure with—there was something of the wilderness of space and of the infinity of time written on it that took one's breath away. The whisper of the winds of history was on it—[Richard] Dix was amazing."

When Paramount supervisor Lucien Hubbard was told that the company had acquired the rights to the works of Zane Grey—past, present, and future—and that he was to spend the next year of his life making them into movies, he was overcome with gloom. A promising career, he thought, sabotaged by Westerns. Instead of grinding them out as program pictures, however, Hubbard set out to secure the highest possible production values.

William K. Howard, who directed another Zane Grey story for Paramount, *The Thundering Herd,* was all set to direct *The Vanishing American.* But Hubbard and Howard had a disagreement, and Hubbard called in a serial director, George Brackett Seitz. The picture included a prologue, which was directed as a second-unit operation by Hubbard himself, with Harry Perry as cameraman.

The unusual contract with Zane Grey contained a clause which specified that the films had to be made on the exact locations of the author's stories. Hubbard's second unit traveled over rough trails to Monument Valley, a location now associated with the Westerns of John Ford, and the Betatakin Cliff Dwellings. Its job was to create a symbolic sequence, depicting the evolution of the Indian. Workmen from Paramount, under foreman Charlie Bocquet, opened up a road and constructed usable cliff dwellings for the spectacular attack sequence. While working with the Indians, the crew slept in the open. At Kayenta, Arizona, Hubbard and Perry stayed with trader John Wetherill, who had rediscovered the Mesa Verde cliff dwellings in Colorado, and in 1881 was reputed to be the first white man to see the Rainbow Bridge.

If the scenery was picturesque, life for the first unit was far from comfortable. They lived at an old Mormon settlement, eighty miles from Flagstaff. As the leading lady, Lois Wilson, described it: "We have had rainstorms, sandstorms, heat that sent the mercury up to one hundred thirty degrees, locations that could only be reached by long horseback rides, and sometimes only by mulepack. In some places, every drop of water had to be hauled over trackless rocks for miles, and conserved carefully, a bit at a time doled out to us; and several times we have skipped meals, not through any desire to diet but because there was nothing to eat."[2]

The Vanishing American was rediscovered by the American Film Institute, and an original tinted print presented at the Los Angeles County Museum of Art in February 1970, in the series *Here Comes the Parade*. It proved to be one of those "if only" films. If only it hadn't been so tied to a melodramatic story line, it might have been an enduring classic. For the problem of the Indian and his betrayal by the government was more clearly etched in this picture than in any other silent film. Ralph and Natasha Friar regard it as one of the most important films ever made about the Native American. "In the light of Hollywood's attitude, the fact that this film was ever made at all is incredible."[3]

The prologue demonstrates that while the Indian is a vanishing species, it was he who wiped out the races preceding him. Against the grandeur of a vast canyon at sunrise, a lone figure climbs to the crest of a rock, symbolic of his race. He passes on, to be replaced by another breed, stronger and more resilient. From the Basket Maker, the earliest recorded race, through the Slab House people, from the Cliff Dwellers to the Navajo, evolution has been maintained through violence and subjugation. The Cliff Dwellers are so secure, high up in their rocks, that war becomes obsolete; no attacker can reach them. They relax their guard and become indolent. The battle is shot in a style reminiscent of *Intolerance* and some titles have historical footnotes, in the Griffith manner: "Note: the eagle's feathers were intended to deceive an enemy into thinking the sentinel a captive bird." Among the invading Navajos is Nophaie, hereditary war chieftain, and Nophaie reappears in the sequence of the Conquistadores: "for every generation, a Nophaie would do what no one else would attempt." The prologue ends as the white race overwhelms the Indian, continuing the fierce, natural progression.

The body of the film begins just before the First World War. The Navajo are wards of the government,* living on reservations. Some members of the white race, such as Marion Warner (Lois Wilson), the schoolteacher, bring the benefits of white culture. But the majority of whites encountered by the Navajo are simply there to exploit them. Booker (Noah Beery), the unscrupulous Indian agent, is attacked by Nophaie (Richard Dix) when he forces his attentions on Marion. Nophaie is then obliged to take to the hills.

* The majority of Indians did not become citizens of the United States until 1924.

Richard Dix as Nophaie, banished from the reservation; from The Vanishing American (1926).

The Navajo depart for the Great War: The Vanishing American.

"The character of Nasja," says a subtitle in The Vanishing American, *"is played by Man Hammer's Oldest Boy, who has no name of his own. Nor will he have until he does something to distinguish himself among the people of his own tribe."*

When war is declared, the government sends an army officer, Earl Ramsdale (Malcolm McGregor), to requisition the Indians' horses. Nophaie persuades his people to hand over their horses and, with a group of Navajo, he proudly joins the colors. During heavy fighting in France, Nophaie saves Ramsdale's life. A depleted group of Navajo returns to the reservation to discover remnants of their tribe living in appalling conditions, under the vicious rule of Booker. The Indians are forced to resort to an armed uprising, and the film ends with a battle by the Navajo against the white man, during which Nophaie is mortally wounded. Marion reaches him with news that Booker has been discharged by Washington, and Nophaie, who tried to prevent the battle, dies in her arms.

Paramount bought a second-rate story, said John Grierson, and failed in a brave effort to turn it into a first-rate picture. The element of hokum was there to dog the film from the start. *Photoplay* thought it might have been one of the outstanding pictures of the screen. "Impressive, gloriously beautiful in its natural settings, yet robbed of greatness by mawkishly sentimental and overwritten titles and mediocre direction of its intimate scenes."[4]

Exhibitors' anxiety at the racial angle was reflected in *Moving Picture World,* which thought it might have a questionable effect on the box office: "here a ticklish situation is developed . . . many are liable not to care for this, even though the Indian is a wonderfully fine character."[5]

Wrote a correspondent from California: "I was thrilled when I first heard that such a picture as *The Vanishing American* was being contemplated, for I have lived in Navajo land and love it, and must say it contains material for an extraordinary picture that would equal *Birth of a Nation.*

"But it is a bitter disappointment that so worthy a production as this picture is ruined by the silly attempt of a white man to play an Indian. No white man can emulate an Indian. . . . The Red Man possesses certain inimitable traits, both in features and conduct, that no white man can achieve, and least of all, Richard Dix."[6]

An explanation for the lack of Indian stars was provided by Iron Eyes Cody, the veteran Indian actor and adviser. "Indians have no tradition of acting or plays. Our culture consists more of ceremonial. There were very few Indian actors because we weren't conditioned to it. In any case, the studios only put forward those names which the banks would put money up for."[7]

REDSKIN

Dissatisfied with his interpretation of Nophaie in *The Vanishing American,* Richard Dix had another chance to play an Indian when Paramount made *Redskin* in 1929. Directed by Victor Schertzinger, it had the advantage of Technicolor and, at its initial showing, Magnascope. The story and scenario were by Elizabeth Pickett, who made propaganda films for the Red Cross, and was one of the few people to win the confidence of the Pueblo Indians in New Mexico. They allowed her to make documentary films with cameraman G. O. Post in 1925.

The theme of the vanishing American was frittered away on vapid melodrama in the film of that title. Here the story takes second place to the magnificent backgrounds and a strong documentary sense. Schertzinger, a veteran of Inceville, was an excellent director (and a noted musician), sadly ignored by film history. Thanks to his sure hand, the action moves rapidly, and there is no sense of posing or of proscenium direction. The color in the original print is breathtaking; *Redskin* leaves an impression of a kaleidoscope of awe-inspiring backgrounds—with so much happening in the foreground that one hardly has time to take in the whole frame.

The color is used for emotional impact; black and white (toned amber) represents the world of the white man; color is reserved for scenes of Indian life.

The picture opens with a government agent, John Walton, dragging the small son of a chief away from the reservation to a government school. The film changes to black and white as the small boy, Wing Foot, is escorted into the school, sullen and suspicious. He is introduced to a Pueblo girl, Corn Blossom. "Navajo hate Pueblo," murmurs Wing Foot. He is lined up with the other children to salute the flag. Wing Foot refuses.

"Salute the flag," orders John Walton. "If you don't, I'll have to whip you." Wing Foot is adamant, and Walton hauls him away, ignoring the protest of the schoolmistress: "I've never whipped one of those children. Don't whip that boy!"

In a brilliantly directed scene, the cowed figure of Wing Foot staggers to the foot of the flagpole and, burning with pain, he slowly raises his hand to salute the Stars and Stripes. Even Walton has tears in his eyes. From then on, the children call him Do-Atin, Whipped One.

Wing Foot grows up and becomes the first Indian to enter Thorpe College, but his encounters with racial prejudice force him to return to his people. His

Richard Dix in Redskin *(1929), photographed partly in Technicolor.*

Redskin: *Jane Novak, as the schoolteacher, with Indian children.*

sophistication is not welcomed. When he tries to replace witchcraft with modern medical ideas, he is banished from the tribe. He becomes an outcast in the burning desert, neither white nor Indian. Just redskin.

The picture reaches its climax when Wing Foot stumbles upon oil, is attacked by white prospectors, and sets out to race the oil men to the nearest town to register his claim. He brings the news to the Navajo that half the wealth from the oil goes to them. And he gives his share to the Pueblo, to avert intertribal war. "I bring you not only a gift of the earth, but a greater gift—tolerance."

Henry Hathaway worked on the picture as assistant director. "For one scene, we had to have a sand painting. The design is done with different colored sand, and it takes a long time. It took the Indians from early morning until 11:30. So we didn't get started until this late, and then found out we couldn't finish that day. According to Indian religion and custom, that sand painting could not be on the ground at sundown. It had to be destroyed. When I found this out, I offered them money, offered them anything they wanted to leave it there. No way. So finally I had a still photographer take a picture of it, and then we painted that out on a board and covered it with a little sand—and kept the camera back so that it looked as though the sand painting was still there."[1]

The reason for the combination of color and monochrome had nothing to do with aesthetics, said Hathaway. It was purely financial. The production was more expensive than the front office had anticipated and Schertzinger was ordered to complete it in black and white. Schertzinger transformed a potential catastrophe into an asset. The documentary scenes are all in color and include footage of Acoma, the Pueblo stronghold on the vast rock that Robert Flaherty attempted to film for Fox. *Redskin,* which exists in the American Film Institute collection at the Library of Congress, is long overdue for rediscovery.

THE DEVIL HORSE

Without a trace of the liberalism of *The Vanishing American* or *Redskin,* the essential ingredient in *The Devil Horse* was hatred of all things Indian: "September 1874. The white man had invaded the buffalo hunting grounds—and red anger inflamed the heart of the Indian." A wagon train is attacked and the Montana settlers wiped out. As one of the evocative titles puts it: "Thunder of hoofs—whirl of arrows—snarl of rifles—and again the blood of two races stained the history of the west." The sole survivors are a small boy, Dave Carson (Fred Jackman, Jr.), and a colt. The colt is seized and tortured before the boy by the Indians.

Years pass and Dave Carson (Yakima Canutt) is now an army scout, with a never-ending hatred for the red man, who had robbed him of his parents. His hatred is shared by his colt, which has now grown up to terrorize the Indians—they call him Devil Horse. Like a winged steed from a Greek legend, it swoops down from its mountain eyrie and, able to outrun any other horse, picks its victims from the local tribes and tramples them to death.

The Devil Horse made no attempt at historical objectivity, and when it was shown at the Museum of Modern Art in 1970, the audience objected to such titles as "Keep your place, or I'll have you driven out of the post," and booed it off the screen. But on the level of entertainment, *The Devil Horse* is a fast-moving Western, with strong production values and frequently imaginative treatment. Yakima Canutt's stunt work is impressive, and the photography, by Floyd Jackman and George Stevens, does full justice to the magnificent backgrounds.

"We had our camp on the Little Big Horn River, Wyoming," recalled George Stevens. "The village was called Lodge Grass. This fifty-mile area was a Crow Indian reservation. The Crows had been what was called peaceable Indians, part of the Custer adventure. Every year, Indians came to this reservation for a pow-wow. Many brought their own tepees—which you see in the film—and this pow-wow was extraordinary. Throughout the night they'd beat out this rhythm on the big drums and dance, night after night, a variety of traditional dances."[1]

When George Stevens visited England in 1970, I screened *Devil Horse* for him. He pointed out that the opening shot of the wagon train was photographed on the Custer battlefield. The cavalry fort was built by the crew, which consisted of only seven or eight men. Rex, the Devil Horse, was a dangerous animal. "He took a bite out of Yak's face and it took a month to heal. If we let him get away from us, production would be stopped, and it would take all afternoon to catch him."

The idea of featuring a horse occurred to Hal Roach during a discussion about stars. "We were going off the Gold Standard," said Roach, "and for a time the banks closed. The big worry was how to pay the stars. I said, 'Why be concerned with the stars? They're in the same position we are. You don't pay them. They're not the most important part of this industry. If you have to, you can star a horse.' This idea was passed around, and my distributors said, 'Why not?' I sent Chick Morrison to find the kind of horse he could train. This guy was the greatest horse trainer I ever saw in my life, a very intelligent man. And he found Rex, the most interesting horse I ever saw. It had a brain ten times better developed than the average horse."[2]

Rex was a registered Morgan stallion. Because of his violent nature as a colt, his owner had left him to roam wild over the Colorado range—just as he does in the picture. Several attempts were made at capture, but Rex resisted until a full-scale roundup drove him into a corral. Rex—then called Casey Jones—killed a cowboy who tried to break him and injured others. He was ordered to be shot. But his beauty attracted the attention of the State Reformatory for Boys at Golden, Colorado, which specialized in breeding fine horses, and he was transferred. He was locked up and fed through the bars. Chick Morrison set out to conquer his fury with kindness. Rex responded by injuring him, but Morrison persisted. "The next day, the guy rode the horse down the main street of Morrison, Colorado," said Hal Roach. "This horse had hardly had a saddle on before. The only thing that went wrong was that the horse went right into the bank on the corner. Thought it was a stall, I guess."[3]

Although Morrison was on crutches by the time Rex was tamed, the trainer won. In 1924, however, an Arab stallion, selected to play the villain in one of Rex's pictures, killed him. C. P. Morrison was the brother of Western star Pete Morrison—the three Morrison brothers began in pictures when G. M. Anderson was making films in Colorado. Chick Morrison was at one time manager of the American

Rex, the killer: The Devil Horse (*1926*),
a Hal Roach production.

Film Studios and a partner in several ventures with Allan Dwan. The brothers came from Morrison, Colorado, a little town named after the family. Hollywood gave Chick a magnificent funeral.

Jack "Swede" Lindell, a former circus high diver, took over as Rex's trainer. "In the scene where Rex fights the pinto, Marquis, both horses had their muzzles taped," said George Stevens. "They'll naturally fight. They'll try to break each other's foreleg by biting it. They have very tender bones down there. But they never did hurt one another."

The Devil Horse opened at the Warner Theatre in New York in 1926 to enthusiastic reviews; supporting it was *Commander Byrd in America's Polar Triumph.* In September of the same year, Roach announced the end of his Western series: "the time and attention which must be devoted to such a series," he explained, "must be taken from the ambitious comedy series."[4] Rex, King of Wild Horses, was eventually sold by Roach to Universal.

YAKIMA CANUTT

Yakima Canutt is remembered for his epoch-making stunt work and for his direction of the chariot race in the 1959 *Ben-Hur.* He is the only man alive and active in the picture business who began life as a cowboy, entered pictures via rodeo, and survived half a century of Westerns.

His house in North Hollywood is dark with relics, souvenirs, and trophies. On the wall hang hats sixty years old. Over the fireplace, the gun carried by his grandfather across the plains. Ancient traps from the same period hang alongside spurs, and everywhere are horses—bucking, leaping, racing, in bronze, silver, and gold. Canutt's reputation was obviously hard won. He began in rodeo in 1914, and the advertisements that introduced him to the picture business read:

> The world's champion cowboy, unique among the riders of any country. Won the Roosevelt World's Champion trophy with the highest score at Cheyenne [Wyoming] Frontier Days and at Pendleton [Oregon] Round-Up against the best professional riders and ropers. Among his trophies are
> Police Gazette Championship belt '17–'19–'20–'23
> Gold and Diamond Medal, Calgary 1919
> He being the first and only one to ride Tipperary,
> the famous Canadian outlaw horse at Belle Fourche, 1920 and 1921[1]

When a rodeo was held at Curley Eagle's spread in Edendale, Canutt was filmed by the newsreel cameras. Ben Wilson, an independent producer, saw the newsreel and signed Canutt for a series of pictures.

"When I first came into the picture business, it was hard to take. They did everything the wrong way—backwards from the way you'd really do it. But after being in the business for some time, I began to learn that by putting showmanship into it, you're making entertainment. You can't be too authentic. You've got to add things to it to pep it up.

Yakima Canutt winning at bronc riding at Walla Walla, Washington, 1917. At Pendleton, Oregon, the following week, he won the Bronc Riding Championship of the World.

"When I started directing I fell right into the same trap. I did things they probably laughed about—some of the old-timers on the ranches. Nevertheless, it's showmanship. It's like the rodeo business. Today, they're dressing more like the cowboy used to dress. In my rodeo days, we feathered it up a little bit. I went into white riding trousers and two-tone shirts. I used to get some terrible write-ups: 'Who ever heard of a cowboy wearing white pants?' That kind of stuff. But it was rodeo and it was flash, and we were building the game up."[2]

Enos Edward Canutt was born in 1895 in Whitman County, near Colfax, in the state of Washington. At the age of eleven, he'd had his first taste of bronc riding ("But I rode him. By God, I stayed on him!"). At sixteen, he was champion of Washington state. In 1915 he tied for the world championship. In 1917, a veteran of the rodeo business, with a clutch of awards, he won the world championship.

Yakima is a nickname, the result of a misprint in a newspaper caption. Canutt was photographed with a couple of men from Yakima, Washington, and the caption came out as "Yakima Canutt." It is widely believed that Canutt is part Indian, to which has been ascribed his success with horses. "This is a mistake I can blame myself for. I'm not Indian. My blood lines are Scotch and Irish on my mother's side, Dutch and German on my father's. But there's a tribe of Indians called the Yakimas. So naturally everyone connects the name and figures I am part Indian."

Canutt remembers ranch life as an occupation not only unglamorous but often downright miserable: "You're breaking horses, for instance. You're working through

Yakima Canutt (center) receiving the Roosevelt Trophy in Los Angeles in 1923 from William Gibbs McAdoo, the politician who did so much for the Liberty Loan drives and for the formation of United Artists. Dorothy Morrell (left) and Tommy Grimes, champion roper (right). As a result of the newsreel coverage of this rodeo, Canutt was signed to pictures. Note how closely rodeo costumes resemble the motion picture cowboy's clothes.

a string of about twenty a day after you get them going. Each time you cut out a horse that's ready to go, broken long enough to sell, and pass inspection, you cut in another one. When you get through with the day, you know you've had a day's work. Before we went into World War One, the French were buying all the horses they could get here, and they had to pass what we call inspection—the measurements, the age, and then you saddled them, stepped on them, rode them down, turned them round, brought them back, spun round a couple of times, and often they went to bucking, or didn't handle. Then they rejected them. But I don't ever remember having a rejection that I put through.

"In my day, everybody had guns. But they didn't carry them around. In the South, I would gamble to this day that in Oklahoma and Texas you'll find plenty of fellows carrying guns—it's against the law there, too, but they carry them and seem to pay no attention to it. In Texas I saw a lot of gunplay one night at a nightclub. Fortunately, no one got hit. This is back in 1923, getting pretty late for gunfights. In my day, up in the Northwest once in a while you'd hear the shooting, but not too often."

Canutt's first starring role was *Ridin' Mad* (1924), directed by Jacques Jaccard. "I was a lousy actor, so if I had a couple of acting scenes I would transfer them to a bit of action—an argument, talked by hand instead of by mouth. When I first came into pictures, there were very few stunts done in Western pictures—a horse fall, a fall off the horse, ride up and drag a man off a horse, transfers to a wagon—and that was about the extent of it. So I started figuring out new stunts, putting a price on it—I figured the money angle pretty regular. Then I started writing action. I'd take a script and break it down, adding action sequences and bringing them back into the story in a smooth form. All through my picture career, I tried to figure out new stunts, thrills that would mean something to a picture."

For *The Devil Horse,* Canutt undertook several hazardous stunts, including a ninety-foot clifftop leap; a platform was hung over the edge, and Canutt dived from beneath the camera. During the attack on the Indian camp at dead of night, using flaring torches to panic the tribe, one of the flares blew up and Canutt's hands bear the powder burns to this day.

"We sort of made the stunts up as we went along, and I contributed quite a bit of the action. This old horse was kind of a dangerous horse to work with. Rex would just turn on you. I was making a scene where the trainer would send him in to me, and I'd send him back out through the fort gate. We did the scene several times, and the old horse finally turned and charged me. I got out of his way and managed to stop him. 'We'd better cut this out for the day,' I told the director. 'The horse is getting a little bit rank, and I'm a passenger out here.' I'd just gone through the explosion, and I had some pretty bad spots on me that I didn't want reopened. He said, 'Let's try it once more.' And the once more did it. The horse came at me. I stepped back and he snapped a chunk out of my cheek, knocked me down, and I rolled for thirty feet to the edge of a bank. The trainer was working on him with a buggy whip, but he just stayed right after me. I rolled, and kicked him on the nose. You need to get out of the way of their feet and teeth. They can really tear a chunk out. Well, it got to where he was charging me pretty regular. I made the director, who owned a half interest in the horse, let me take him to a barn and work him awhile. He said, 'Well, what are you going to do with him?'

" 'I don't know,' I said, 'I might kill him. But when I come out of there, he'll be ready to do the scene.' This was a scene where I was tied to a tree and the horse rears and strikes around me, but recognizes me as the boy he'd known. So I took him in, and the trainer came with me—he sat in the background and never said a word. I took a buggy whip and a billiard cue, and set this billiard cue where I could get it, and started putting the horse through his tricks. I worked him until he was hot and mad, and then he started charging me. And I just cut his nose off with that whip, until I backed up to the billiard cue, but he stopped and turned away. The buggy whip did the work. I really whipped it out of him, that's the only way you could do it. Then I made him go through his tricks, fed him, patted him, and the next day we did the scene. All I had to do was holler at him and he stopped. It was the only way you could do it, otherwise you'd find yourself on the way to the hospital."

Canutt was featured in Westerns until the coming of sound, when his career as a star came to an end. "My voice was very bad on the recording apparatus they had at the time. During World War One, I was in the navy for a year, and I contracted flu. Very fortunately, I didn't die of it—there were hundreds of people dying from the epidemic—but it left my vocal cords so scarred up that for a year I talked in a whisper. For years after that, I'd mouth a word and no sound would come out. It still happens once in a while. But my voice has never been strong. It was impossible for me to work alongside of an actor with a good, deep voice. So when talkies came out, I started making stunt work my full-time job. I did parts, bits, but my main livelihood was action."

SUNDOWN

Among the lost films of the silent era is one which, if the contemporary accounts are anything to go by, had rare value. *Photoplay* referred to the picture with unusual enthusiasm: "*Sundown,* which has for its theme the passing of the cattle barons and the cowboys, those picturesque figures who wrested the west from the wilderness and the Indians, and brought law and order, is undoubtedly a screen classic. . . . When the picture is over, you feel as if you had lived through something tremendous and still more than a little sad."[1]

The picture told the story of the last great cattle drive. Forced off their land by homesteaders, the ranchers vainly appeal to Washington for help, then take their families and possessions, along with their cattle, to Mexico, in the hope of re-establishing themselves there.

Wrote Theodore Roosevelt, in his autobiography: "It was right and necessary that this life should pass, for the safety of our country lies in its being made the country of the small home-maker. The great unfenced ranches, in the days of 'free grass,' necessarily represented a temporary stage in our history. . . .

"The homesteaders represented from the National standpoint the most desirable of all possible users of, and dwellers on, the soil. Their advent means the breaking up of the big ranches; and the change was a National gain, although to some of us an individual loss."[2]

Sundown was a eulogy to those who had suffered that loss. It included a scene in which Roosevelt (E. J. Radcliffe) makes these pronouncements to the cattlemen. It was directed by Laurence Trimble and Harry O. Hoyt, and it starred Bessie Love and Roy Stewart. L. William O'Connell was one of the cameramen.

"There were at least six cameramen," recalled O'Connell. "While working at the William Fox studios on Western Avenue, I was asked to accompany Larry Trimble on a trip to New Mexico for the purpose of rounding up horses for a forthcoming picture. Larry Trimble used to do the Strongheart pictures with Jane Murfin, and he had an uncanny way of getting the confidence of animals. We went to Columbus, New Mexico—to be exact, to a small village right on the border called Algadones. We holed up in a small adobe shack, with bullet marks on the walls, which had been shot up by Pancho Villa. Being a city boy [from Chicago], and this being my first real experience with the West, I have, tucked away in my brain, many

Sundown (*1924*), *a documentary-drama shot in Texas.*

unusual and happy experiences. I can still recall the overpowering aroma of the smoke from the slow-burning Pinyon branches in the open fireplace, together with the flickering light on the ceiling as I lay on the floor just before sleep.

"I recall walking into a herd of untamed horses and standing by while Larry slowly proceeded to make friends. You never saw a man with so much patience; one pace at a time, with outstretched hands, until the animal actually nuzzled him. After enough horses were bridled, they were turned over to a rancher and corralled. The Palomas Ranch extended along the Mexican border from Juarez about two hundred miles west."[3]

The *Sundown* producers wanted shots of Roy Stewart heading a herd of cattle, and since a second herd was to be driven from the upland grazing fields in the Kaibab Forest to Flagstaff, O'Connell was sent, with some other cameramen, to cover it.

"At this time, there were no highways, only trails through river bottoms, along the Vermilion Cliffs, and petrified forests, with an occasional Navajo village, hogans with goat herds. All went well until we arrived at the Colorado River, where we were to cross at Lee's Ferry. The approach was through a canyon with a road so narrow that we had to get out and hold up the car on the narrow side to keep it from plunging into the river. Lee's Ferry was a crossing where a flat barge was fastened to a cable. Night had set in, so we slept under an overturned boat.

"After a two-day wait, we heard the shouting of the cowboys and the bawling of the cattle. A few boys preceded the herd. General greetings all around, and the

Sundown.

Lunch break for the Sundown *company on their Texas location.*

cowhands looked over the possibility of crossing the river. It was planned to take the herd upriver about a mile, so that in swimming, the current would bring them down to the regular crossing. A problem arose when the first steer to cross got mired in the quicksand. It was a very heart-rending sight to see the animal slowly sinking to its death. But two of those experienced cowboys lassoed the horns—the last visible signs of the animal—and literally dragged the steer out of the sand to safety. While the animal lay prostrate on the ground, the boys poured buckets of clear water over it and washed it clean. After a short time, the animal revived, and jumped to its feet in the manner of a newborn calf.

"After several attempts, one steer was persuaded to swim out to clear water, and the others followed. The complete herd was assembled on the other bank and rested until the next morning.

"The cowhands knew nothing about motion pictures and cared less. The migration to Flagstaff was an annual, well-organized affair. They had their chuck-wagon, with a cook in charge. The wagon preceded the group until a proper place was located to rendezvous for the night. We had a truck to transport our gear and to keep ahead of the cattle. We were able to drive on ahead and locate advantageous spots where we could see the herd in its entirety, and shoot close-ups as it passed, leaving a cloud of dust against the setting sun.

"As the herd dragged along through the dry wasteland, I noticed that one could realize through a sense of smell that a water hole was in the distance. Here was where the cowboys had to break up the herd to keep the cattle from running into the water, the ones in the rear pushing those already there into the pool, and possibly drowning them. That all took time and patience.

"Now we are at the end of one of our days. The chuckwagon has stopped where the cattle can be watered and rested for the night. The cook is wearing a white jacket. The open fire is blazing away. The different pots are emitting steam and we all sit around on the ground and await our turn to serve ourselves. My highlight of the day was to whittle a brush stick to a point and spear a steak and dip it into a pot of hot grease and hold it there until I felt it was rare, or *just right.* The cook has baked a batch of fresh bread, large loaves. You whittle off large, thick slices, slap that steak between two slices of bread, and please don't bother me.

"You have seen the Jack Ford pictures where he opens up on an Indian sitting on his horse, on a high cliff overlooking a valley. If you were observant, that was a common sight during the day's travel. With a herd that size, there was always a straggler with sore feet, just plain unable to go on. The Indians stationed themselves along the way, and after the herd had passed by, they swooped down and took over the animal. Even though you did not always see the Indians, you were always aware of being spied upon. One day I was caught without a camera. The day was blustery: wind, dust, and snow, visibility almost zero. All of a sudden, out of this brown-gray atmosphere emerged a small group of goats, followed by a squaw on a pony, holding her baby in her arms. With the wind on her back, which seemed to propel her forwards, she passed in seconds. It was one of the most spectacularly beautiful scenes I have ever witnessed, and it's a scene I shall someday paint.

"The following days were broken up with the director taking over for close-ups, putting our leading man among the cowboys. We were allowed to hold up the cattle for a day in order to set up for shots of beauty through the timber country. Later, those scenes were much sought-after in other pictures."

O'Connell was sent down to Texas, in advance of the main *Sundown* company, to prepare the location. One of the jobs he and his colleagues undertook was the erection of tents for sleeping quarters. The huge task of feeding the cast, crew, and cowboys was entrusted to a man named Anderson; the experience served him in good stead, for he later won the contract to feed the construction workers on the Boulder Dam, through which he became a millionaire.

O'Connell explained: "In order to gather as many cattle as possible for the stampede, there was much dickering with the ranch owners around El Paso. They claimed that when cattle are stampeded they lose weight, and these cattle were raised for beef. We could never get as many as we needed from one ranch, so a location was fixed at the border of four large ranches. To keep the cattle from getting mixed up, a fence was built of wire, in the shape of an 'x.' Once you put the four herds together, they were separated, but you couldn't see the fence because of the cattle."

The stampede was shot with the aid of a mirror—an old Mack Sennett trick;

Despite the drought and the consequent depletion of cattle, the Sundown *company managed to stage this awe-inspiring drive. It was used, too, in* Tumbleweeds (*1925*).

Bessie Love, the daughter [illegible]

Bessie Love lay on the ground, and the oncoming herd was shown in the mirror, giving the impression that she was in danger of being trampled.

"There were days in that godawful, windy Texas when there was no letup in the wind. You were continually standing with your back to it. One of the best things for relief was to lie flat on the ground and cover your head with a saddle."

Bessie Love recalled that with the wind came the sand—"there was nothing to stop it but us"—and yet the company had brought a wind machine. One day she discovered the location surrounded by baby whirlwinds. Because of a seven-year drought, vegetation had perished and water holes had dried up. The cattle were in an alarming state; thousands of head had already died. Amid these conditions, *Sundown* could hardly fail to reproduce documentary scenes of outstanding value.

As the First National advertisement put it: "Here is a photoplay that has caught a climax of history in the making—the passing of the Old West. Never again can the story of *Sundown* be told in the motion pictures. It is drama that is real. The West of the open plains and the unnumbered herds is dying. Homesteaders—'nesters' the cattlemen call them—are narrowing the grazing grounds; winning the West from the pioneers who tamed it. You will see the last great roundup; the final drive of 150,000 head of cattle south into the grazing lands of Mexico."*

Some of the reviews were more excited than the advertisement. "Gigantic in every way," said *Moving Picture World*. "The long shots showing miles and miles of plains with thousands of cattle wandering slowly over them are most impressive. The photography is some of the most beautiful ever seen on the screen."[4] Exhibitors complained bitterly: "Too many cows!"

Wrote a correspondent from Muskogee, Oklahoma: "Reared on the plains of Wyoming as I was, I viewed *Sundown* with a grip upon my heart that was like pain. It was so true that it brought back 'the dear dead days beyond recall,' the days of happy, irresponsible childhood on the free range of Wyoming, as though they were today instead of my receding yesterdays."[5]

THE WIND

The wretched conditions of sand, wind, and drought that characterized the *Sundown* location were brilliantly evoked in bleak, Scandinavian style by Victor Seastrom in MGM's *The Wind* (1927, released 1928). Although more of a psychological than a realistic study, and more impressionistic than documentary in its treatment, *The Wind* is filled with remarkably expressive detail. For an utterly unromantic view of life on the desert, this film is unequaled. Lillian Gish plays a delicate Virginia girl who comes to live with her cousin and finds the life intolerable. The wind howls symbolically around the tiny shack, until nerve ends are

* Bessie Love said there were no more than seven thousand head. The long shots of the drive were used again in *Tumbleweeds* (1925).

stretched to the breaking point. Even the children, usually a sentimental high point of a silent film, are treated abrasively; Lillian Gish makes a friendly, playful gesture to her cousin's small child, and receives a slap across the face. The cowboys are equally unromantic, and expectorate on the floor Lillian struggles to keep clean. She braces herself to finding sand in the bread, sand in the water, sand in her bed. She eventually has to wash the dishes with sand. The carcass of a steer hangs in the center of the room, and her cousin's wife, already jealous of Lillian's presence, slices unmentionable sections of its interior while Lillian holds back her revulsion. Her affection for her cousin causes an outburst from the wife, and Lillian is faced with an ultimatum. Two men have asked her hand in marriage: choose one. With breathtaking economy, Seastrom bridges the next shattering events in her life with a series of dissolves: close-up of the ring being placed on her finger . . . a bowl piled with unwashed crockery . . . a heap of food waiting to be prepared . . . and a stunned Lillian, in her wedding outfit. The performance of Lillian Gish is beyond praise, and only the ending prevents *The Wind* from being a totally satisfying masterpiece. The picture originally ended with Lillian Gish wandering into the desert, insane, after killing a rancher. Eight exhibitors, reported Irving Thalberg, refused to run the picture with that ending, and a new sequence had to be shot showing her acceptance of her life. "It broke our hearts," said Lillian Gish.

Though the interiors were shot at the MGM studios, Seastrom took the company to the Mojave Desert for exteriors. Katherine Albert, reporting for *Motion Picture Magazine,* followed them out there, and quickly regretted it. She had to drive one hundred fifteen miles to the town of Mojave, where the company made their headquarters at the country hotel. "To reach the location, one had to drive over awful dirt roads into the sweltering heat—the thermometer was never lower than one hundred and fifteen degrees all the time the company was on location—into the blinding sun, the bleak, barren waste that is the Mojave Desert. That anyone could be active in that scorching heat is almost inconceivable. Yet there were cameras, generators and other studio equipment planted in the broad expanse of wasteland. . . . There were the usual number of workers, all wearing high boots in case they encountered rattlesnakes, and most of them had whitish looking stuff smeared over their faces to keep off sunburn. Goggles, making them look like men from Mars, were worn to protect their eyes from sand.

"But there was Lillian Gish in little, low-heeled slippers, hatless and without any protection for her eyes. As I drove up, I heard a frightful noise and in a second the scene was clouded by enormous drifts of sand. The noise came from the giant machines used to create wind. The nine propellers seemed to lift the desert and blow it before the cameras.

" 'It is, without doubt, the most unpleasant picture I have ever made,' said Lillian Gish. 'I mean by that, the most uncomfortable to do. I don't mind the heat so much, but working before the wind machines all the time is nerve-wracking. You see, it blows the sand, and we've put sawdust down too, because that is light and sails along in the air, and then there are smoke-pots to make it all look even more dusty. I've been fortunate. The flying cinders haven't gotten into my eyes, although a few have burned my hands.'

"I left Miss Gish burying the man she had 'murdered' in the sand. I have never been happier to leave anywhere."[1]

The Wind (1927–1928): *Lillian Gish struggles to bury the corpse of Montagu Love. Wind machines blasted sand, sawdust, and cinders at Miss Gish for the Mojave Desert scenes, and she regards this picture as the most physically arduous she had to make.*

Lillian Gish, right, newly arrived from the city, struggles to overcome her revulsion at the harshness of ranch life—The Wind, *with Dorothy Cumming.*

THE COVERED WAGON

Dedicated to the memory of Theodore Roosevelt, *The Covered Wagon* was based on a story by Emerson Hough, who had traveled the plains in a covered wagon himself. It enjoyed unparalleled success in 1923 as a ten-reel epic Western. It has come down to us in the form of a six-reel abridged version,* often in very bad physical shape. Some film historians, working on the basis of these poor-quality prints, describe it as "slow and pedestrian." Every so often I take a look at my toned Kodascope print, fearful that perhaps time has caught up with it. I take the precaution of showing it to an audience unfamiliar with silent pictures. And upon each occasion, the magic of *The Covered Wagon* sparks off the most enthusiastic reaction.

The picture gains new value with the passage of time, both in its simplicity of technique, once again becoming fashionable, and in its value as a historical document. One or two climactic scenes—a runaway horse, an Indian attack—have been filmed so often and with so many variations that Cruze's matter-of-fact coverage seems somewhat tame. The fact that the camera is not ubiquitous, however, helps the initial impression that *The Covered Wagon* is a documentary record of an original trek in 1848. For it is in its documentary scenes that the picture achieves its greatness. On a first viewing, particularly of a poor print when the long shots of the wagons look like bacteria under a microscope, one cannot appreciate the skill and hard work involved in creating that background.

When the film opened in 1923, the New York *Times* said: "You may think that such pictures make themselves. A long train of prairie schooners streaming across the open landscape, the wagons floating on a broad river through which the horses and oxen pulling them swim, prairie fires, fights with Indians, a buffalo hunt—these things comprise themselves into stirring scenes—or so you think.

"But the very size of it all, the necessity for coherence and individuality in the story and all the parts of it, make the job exceedingly difficult. . . . If Mr. Cruze had not mastered his subject, the result . . . would have been tiresome to the most faithful spectator."[1] Iris Barry[2] considers the picture stands with *Nanook* in heralding the series of documentary films that included *Grass* and *Tabu.*

The *Covered Wagon* began as just another program picture. According to Jesse Lasky, George Melford, a veteran Western director, had been entrusted with the project, which was to have starred Mary Miles Minter. Lasky disposed tactfully of both Melford and Minter by telling them that their talents were worthy of better things.

Lasky's grandfather had been a pioneer. "True or not," he wrote, "Grandpa's tales of covered-wagon days and skirmishes with the Indians along the Oregon Trail enthralled me. He must have spent far more time telling about his westward trek than the trip itself originally took."[3]

Reading Hough's story on the train, Lasky became absorbed in the struggles

---

* The Museum of Modern Art has an eight-reel version, which includes additional documentary material.

The Covered Wagon (*1923*).

Oxen rest between takes for The Covered Wagon.

James Cruze, from Utah, son of Danish immigrants, was the director of The Covered Wagon; *he knew the atmosphere of the film from his own childhood.*

of the pioneers, hearing again the tales of his boyhood: "Superimposing the past on the present by reading about that trek while actually retracing it myself, as I looked out the window of a speeding luxury train at the same scenery my grandfather had viewed from a lumbering conestoga, was an emotional, almost mystical experience."

Remembering that James Cruze had Indian blood, Lasky consigned the project to him. "To this day, I don't know whether he really had some Indian forbears—I never checked on it—but hearsay to that effect was what prompted me to call him in for a conference."

Cruze's powerful build and black eyes led to the belief that he was of Indian extraction. No one could have been more suitable to direct *The Covered Wagon,* for only a generation—if that—separated Cruze from the pioneers, and covered wagons had been a familiar part of his youth.

He was born in 1884; his parents, Danish peasants following the religion of Brigham Young, had come across the plains in a covered wagon and settled in Utah, where they lived on a ranch and raised a large family. On cold winter mornings, Cruze would come downstairs to find two or three Indian women sitting on the kitchen floor, waiting patiently for breakfast. As in many other ranch houses, the doors were never locked.

"The only thing I knew of the outside world," said Cruze (his real name was Jens Cruz Bosen), "was when covered wagons would draw up under our cottonwoods for the night, and I'd talk with the kids, and sometimes tent shows would come by. I suppose they were poor trash, but they seemed wonderful to me."[4]

Cruze was a man of little formal education. He played in medicine shows, graduating to the legitimate stage and reaching stardom in motion picture serials. By the time he was offered *The Covered Wagon,* he was achieving a reputation as a top-class director. Westerns had no prestige. According to Karl Brown, he hated the idea of being demoted to the level of Westerns and made the film much against his will. Yet Cruze had had the idea for such a film for years.

Jim Tully interviewed an old Mormon in Salt Lake City. "About seven years

The Covered Wagon *company in action. James Cruze with megaphone, Karl Brown at camera, Dorothy Arzner in chair.*

ago, a young fellow came down here from Hollywood and talked to a lot of us about filming the history of our coming across the country in wagons. He said he'd weave a love story through it and make it a big picture and we'd all make a lot of money, but we knew the youngster and didn't think he'd make good. So he went back to Hollywood and we decided to make use of his idea. We made a picture giving our entire history—but I guess it's no good. We're ashamed to show it to anyone now. Anyhow, the fellow who talked to us was Jimmy Cruze."[5]

The Mormon film came out in 1913—*One Hundred Years of Mormonism,* directed by Norval McGregor and produced by the Utah Moving Picture Company. It made no commercial impact at all. James Cruze's *Covered Wagon* was among the most financially successful films of the entire silent era.

THE MAIN LOCATION FOR *The Covered Wagon* was the Baker ranch in the Snake River Valley, on the borders of Utah and Nevada, eighty-five miles from the nearest railroad at Milford, Utah. Run by an old cattleman named Otto Meek,* the ranch provided as much land and water as the picture could require. Carpenters were sent ahead to lay down board-flooring for tents—an essential precaution against bad weather—and under the command of World War I veteran Tom White, an army-style camp appeared. Most company members were used to living in tents.

* Meek is a leading character in the account of *The Covered Wagon* in Karl Brown's fascinating *The Paramount Adventure* (to be published by Farrar, Straus & Giroux).

Some of the Mormon extras bedded down in the wagons and lived exactly like the pioneers. Accustomed to local conditions, they escaped the rigors of dysentery.

"Practically everyone suffered from it," said Dorothy Arzner. "I avoided it because my grandfather was a miner and I remember he said, 'If you ever go out on the desert, don't drink the water. Drink milk, but don't drink the water.' I didn't, and I was about the only one to escape. The others all looked green; they were sick for days."[6]

Dorothy Arzner, who later became the most successful woman director in Hollywood, was the editor of the film. "There was a wonderful spirit in those days—the pioneering spirit is what it was. Vernon Keays was James Cruze's assistant director, a marvelous assistant. He knocked himself out day and night. Everybody did. When we were delayed by the snow, even Paramount wanted us to come back and finish the picture on the Lasky lot. I remember Jim Cruze telling them, 'You'll have to come and get us!'

"He talked to the whole company. He said, 'We may not be paid.' To a man, everybody said, 'Let's stay.' And Jim was a wonderful man to accompany. He demanded work, and he wouldn't tolerate anyone who cried and complained. But on the other hand, he wouldn't demand any more than that. He carried his own responsibilities, and did not expect us to wait on him like a handmaiden, handing him his glasses one moment and his chair the next.

"And Karl Brown worked so hard. I can see him trailing off across the desert with that camera on his shoulder, keeping up with James Cruze. Everybody was geared at a high speed because he wanted to shoot fast and make it continuous, so that everybody could keep the mood."

In charge of the Indians was Tim McCoy. Some of the older Indians refused to come on the film because they believed it was a plan to break up the reservations. Among those who worked on the picture was a white woman known as Mrs. Broken Horn, captured as a child from a wagon train in 1865 and raised by the Arapaho. She could speak no English and had avoided her family because they were strangers to her. Another was Left Hand, who had fought Custer. McCoy would receive directions from Cruze and, as the only man present who could speak to all four tribes, he would tell the old men, through sign language, what to do, and they would pass the orders on.

Dorothy Arzner continued: "We were very friendly with the Indians, but we had a problem with some of the girls we brought out from Hollywood. They were fascinated by the beautiful silver bracelets and ornaments, and they would all casually walk into the Indians' tents. Then one night, one Indian decided to walk into the girls' tent and you should have heard the screams! Of course, they carried on about how they were going to tie up the Indian or chase him out of the camp. I defended him. I said, 'What can you expect? The girls have been walking in and out of *his* tent. What's wrong with the Indian walking in and out of theirs?'

"And James Cruze said, 'By God, you're right.'

"That Indian was my friend forever. I can't tell you how much attention I got. Yakima Jim was an outlaw, part cowboy, part Indian. When it snowed one night, I heard this noise outside my tent, and I said, 'Who's that?'

"He said, 'It's Yakima, tightening up your tent so it don't collapse with the snow.'

"He tightened Jim's tent and mine, and the next morning, all the tents were down but ours.

"One Saturday afternoon, everybody wanted to go into town. Not the railroad town, eighty-five miles away, but the little town seven miles from the camp. We went in and had dinner, and it began to get dark and it seemed as if it might snow. So I got on a horse, intending to ride back to camp before the snow hit us. After a while, I heard the clop-clop of a horse behind me. I looked back and there was Yakima Jim. He came up beside me and said, 'Miss Dot, I saw you riding out of town and I thought I'd better come along so you get safely back to camp.' He really was a tough outlaw. He was supposed to have killed a couple of people, and he looked like outlaws are supposed to look, dark and frightening.

"We rode along and it snowed heavier and heavier, and pretty soon there was no road to go by. It grew colder and colder and I said, 'Do you think we're going toward the camp?'

"He said, 'The horses know how to get to camp.'

"Pretty soon he pulled up my horse and said, 'I have to take your boots off, Miss Dot.'

"This scared me to death. I was awfully young and awfully innocent, and I was scared to death of anybody that might touch me. At the moment when this fright rode over me, he said, 'Now don't you be afraid of me. I just have to take your boots off so your feet don't freeze in them.' And with that, he pulled my boots off and rubbed my feet with snow until they were red, then put my boots back on, got back on his horse, and we rode on. We finally saw the lights of the camp, and Jim Cruze was fit to be tied because he was so worried about me."

Yakima Jim fell victim to a Hollywood gunfight some time later, as did another *Covered Wagon* cowboy, Tom Carrick (see p. 299). Property man Henry Hathaway remembered that a great many Hollywood cowboys worked on the picture; old Milt Brown, veteran of cattle drives, played in several scenes, together with Ed "Pardner" Jones.* One of the most colorful Westerners in pictures, Jones's real name was Garrett, and he was a relative of Pat Garrett, nemesis of Billy the Kid. Jones was a member of the Ford stock company, and lived with Ford and Harry Carey, Western-style, in Newhall. He came from Seligman, Arizona, and was a former sheriff. According to Ford, Pardner Jones was the lawman who killed the Apache Kid. A rifleman of uncanny expertise, Jones did all the critical shooting on *The Covered Wagon,* including the gruesome scene of the horse collapsing over the bluff in the Indian attack.

The cowboys on *The Covered Wagon* formed a remarkable group. Even Tim McCoy, whose gleaming white Stetson and fancy outfit attracted guffaws, proved his courage when a stampede broke out among the cattle, and he brought it under control. A few years later, James Cruze made an epic of the sea, *Old Ironsides,* and some of the sailors deserted. According to Dorothy Arzner, who worked on both pictures, Cruze replaced them with the cowboys from *The Covered Wagon*—Buck Bucko, Jack Padjeon, and the rest—and they manned the vessel thereafter.

---

* Karl Brown says the name is spelled "Podner."

FOR THE SPECTACULAR CROSSING of the Platte, the lake at Otto Meek's Baker ranch stood in for the river. The scene was attempted twice. The first time steel cables were lashed to the wagons. Since the cable was under water and would not be seen by the cameras, this was considered the safest method.

"Sure it was under water," said Karl Brown, "but it also weighed about two hundred and fifty pounds, and by the time I'd got the horses and wagons out in the middle of the lake, the weight of the cable dragged the horses under and they were drowned. The only thing to do was to go back to what the pioneers did. Caulk the wagons and swim across."[7]

At the second attempt, the wagons, horses, and stock were lined up on the bank. The animals stolidly refused to enter the water. "The cowboys yelled and fired their guns, but they just sat there. I sometimes have hunches and this one happened to pay off. I saw the leader—the one they followed almost as sheep will follow a goat—nose at the water. So I said, 'Start the cameras.' Gradually, first one foot, then the other, the animals moved into the water. The cameras started to move back and we went across that lake as smooth as glass. I had 3-inch, 5-inch, and 6-inch lenses on it from the various cameras. Every aperture was set at 5.6, every focus at infinity. Halfway across, my camera ran out. Four hundred feet was its full capacity. I think I broke all records in reloading a Bell & Howell. The other cameras were covering the same thing as me, so there was no disaster. Everything went beautifully."

Practically all of *The Covered Wagon* was shot out of doors, although the company carried a motor generator with them and full electrical equipment. Thus Brown could set up inside a wagon or a shack and depend upon regular studio lighting, even though he was in the middle of a desert.

"However, here's another case where my training with D. W. Griffith and Billy Bitzer came in on my behalf; we were shooting a battle scene, shooting down a canyon on the covered wagons, and there's an Indian attack from the top of the surrounding bluffs. It's a night battle. It was going to take everything the power wagons could give us to cover that canyon, because it was pretty deep and film wasn't very fast. But in the afternoon—just before this was to be shot—in fooling around with these power wagons they managed to blow both of them up. They backfired into the crankcase. We were shooting that night, the Indians were leaving next day. So it was up to me to take the reflectors off the sun arcs and place magnesium flares in the focus of the sun arc reflector and beam these like spotlights down on the canyon. That is what lit the shot."

James Cruze remembered a herd of buffalo on Antelope Island in Salt Lake, owned by the Buffalo Livestock Corporation. Karl Brown said, "There was a herd of about a hundred fifty, maybe two hundred buffalo—couldn't tell because they were scattered all over the island. The island was a pretty good size—five to six miles long, three or four miles wide—and we had the best cowhands in Hollywood to run them around. I came very close to getting killed on that location. We had to have a scene of a man [Buck Bucko] jumping from his horse onto a buffalo's back and riding him. That seemed impossible because these are wild buffalo. He was not only supposed to ride him, he was supposed to kill him with a knife. The only thing to do was to use a bucking rig, which would go round the buffalo, with two handles, one on each side. The mane was so thick that it covered everything.

Preparation for the river crossing. The lake on Otto Meek's ranch stands in for the somewhat more turbulent Platte.

Two horses were drowned in the first attempt at the river crossing; then The Covered Wagon *company staged the scene as the pioneers had done it, and all went well.*

All right, but first you've got to catch your buffalo. The boys were used to handling stock; one would be on one end of the island, and he'd run the buffalo as far as he could to the other end. And he could outrun him, on one of the best horses in Hollywood. There were fresh horses waiting, and they would turn him and run him back again. They ran that buffalo back and forth until they ran him almost literally to his knees. Then they pulled a rope on him and these other boys kept adding ropes and adding ropes until they had him spread out like Gulliver. I was watching the entire procedure from the back of the camera wagon, with a couple of horses who didn't like buffalo any too well, and a couple of Salt Lake boys holding these horses and trying to keep them from jiggling the camera. The horses would try to bolt for it, and the boys would pull them back, and I was trying to keep the camera steady while we're shooting this business.

"By now the rigging was on, so the boys let him up, they flicked the ropes and the ropes were open and came off. The buffalo got up, and there was something we didn't know about buffalo. As long as a buffalo doesn't get to smell you or touch you or be close to you, he's all right. But if you get close to that buffalo, or he gets your scent, he isn't afraid of you any more—he'll go after you. He particularly disliked horses, and the horses disliked buffalo, so the dislike was mutual. Here are these cowboys in a circle around the thing, and this bull just lowered his head. He didn't run, he didn't do anything to get away. He just lowered his head and charged at these horses on the camera wagon. He hit the first horse right under the belly with his sharp horns. The two horses lunged forward, I went out the back of the thing on my neck and here I was facing the buffalo and I couldn't move. I had a gun on me but I was afraid to shoot—there were all these cowboys around. The buffalo spotted me and started after me. Someone said, 'Shoot him!' and Ed 'Pardner' Jones threw his gun over on the wrong side of this rearing horse, pulled once—it was a .50 slug—and the buffalo just sprouted out about three feet from me. In fact he blew blood all over my pants. All over in five seconds—ten at most."

DESPITE ITS SIMPLISTIC PLOT, *The Covered Wagon* succeeds so impressively in documenting an era that one regrets its shortcomings all the more. The main shortcoming was its leading man. J. Warren Kerrigan was selected by Cruze more from friendship than conviction; Kerrigan had been a star of the early days, appearing in many Westerns at Flying A. When his mother fell ill, Kerrigan retired from the screen to look after her. Eventually, she recovered, and since Cruze and Kerrigan were old friends, Cruze invited him to take the part of Will Banion. Karl Brown said that his double, cowboy Jack Padjeon, would have been far more convincing.

It is the grease paint that makes Kerrigan stand out against the rough, tanned faces of the extras. Oddly enough, his face is not unsuited to the period of 1848, with its aquiline nose and finely drawn features. But the make-up removes any semblance of conviction. Besides which, his tight-fitting costume, although far from clean and in the correct style, is completely wrong for his figure. And it is hard to equate his spaniel-like looks at Lois Wilson with the character of a tough ex-army officer.

Lois Wilson was criticized because she always looked so immaculate. She commented: " 'Lois,' Jim Cruze would say, 'your costume looks too nice.' So I said, 'I'll sleep in it tonight.' But it photographed the same. And I do say this; a girl in

Ed "Pardner" Jones (left), formerly Ed Garrett, sheriff from Arizona, was the finest shot in the picture business. Here he prepares to demonstrate his uncanny skill in a rodeo staged during North of 36 *by shooting an apple from the head of director Irvin Willat (right). Such skill was needed, because real bullets were often used in silent Westerns.*

Jack Padjeon, standing between the musicians, was J. Warren Kerrigan's double and a skillful cowboy, much respected in the movies.

Sid Grauman, center, with Jesse L. Lasky, Colonel Tim McCoy (in Stetson), and Arapaho who appeared in the prologue to The Covered Wagon.

love does try to look her best, no matter what conditions she's living under. She washes her face and tries to look clean. And this was a well-bred young woman, so I think they were a little hard on me."[8]

The period of 1848 is an exceptionally difficult one to re-create effectively. Those familiar with the variations in length of hair, and the great differences in costume or breed of cattle, will find fault with *The Covered Wagon.* But the frequent flourishes offset the few failures; Banion and Jackson were in the army together under Doniphan in Mexico; so Jackson has been given the half-chaps of the *vaquero,* and Banion uses the wooden Mexican saddle.

State historical societies cooperated in the research: A. E. Sheldon, superintendent of the Nebraska State Historical Society, supplied valuable photographs and data about the Oregon Trail in that state, and Ennice G. Anderson, state historian of Wyoming, provided advice and references concerning Fort Bridger and other historic forts of Wyoming.

Publicity claimed that the countryside was scoured for original conestogas—named after the Pennsylvania valley where they were made from the eighteenth century. But the huge conestoga was seldom used on the long trip west; lighter wagons were more suitable. And many of these, some heirlooms, some still in use, were rounded up from farms and ranches.

Because the picture was so carefully researched, it is worth examining a few of the complaints leveled against it. Some people objected to the freshly laundered whiteness of the wagon tops. The same thought had occurred to the art department, who pelted the wagons with mud and daubed the canvas with dirt. They found nothing short of paint made any impression the camera eye would record. "Many of the wagons used in the production were very old. They were out in the western

Second cameraman lines up on the controversial box-canyon sequence. (All these production stills were taken by Edwin Willat, brother of Irvin, who was on the camera crew of The Covered Wagon.)

This looks like a scene from The Covered Wagon, *but it was actually taken in 1867 (at Russell's Tank, Arizona, by Alexander Gardner) and proves how successful was the restaging for the 1923 film.*

plains several months for the making of the picture alone. Naturally, they got dirty. But like sails at sea, they continued to look white."[9]

The most serious challenge to the authenticity of *The Covered Wagon* occurred when several former army officers protested officially against the proposal to file a print of the film in the archives of the War Department. They stated that the film was not truly historical since it made basic errors: "bull-trains never swam rivers with neck-yokes on . . . wagon trains never camped for the night in box-canyons . . . Jim Bridger was not that kind of man . . . four hundred wagons never travelled across the plains in a single caravan, for where would the oxen pasture? The largest number ever known to have travelled together was sixty-five, and they divided into three columns, four to five miles apart."[10]

While hardly likely to affect the massive box-office returns, the charges seemed likely to dent the picture's reputation in certain quarters, particularly when the allegations were echoed by William S. Hart. (Hart's *Wagon Tracks* of 1919, made for Artcraft, a division of Paramount, encouraged the company to proceed with *The Covered Wagon.* Hart should have played in the picture, since the Western owed so much to his leadership and imagination, but he was no longer a box-office draw.)

A letter from an ex-soldier from the years 1862 to 1865 appeared in *Motion Picture Magazine:*

"I say that at times no one could tell, unless one asked, whether it was one continuous train. For many days, there was just one wagon after another, and at times there were two wagons abreast nearly all day.

"Yes, how could all these cattle graze when there were from four to ten yoke of oxen to a wagon? Well, there were no fences on the plains then. At night, one could see the caravans camped about a mile apart and in daytime it was not only sixty-five wagons in a caravan, but often one continuous train from early morn until after sundown. . . .

"I know that the director of *The Covered Wagon* did better than any other man could do in organizing this train. . . . He shows the exact way the emigrants traveled, especially in the crossing of streams. I have often seen such a sight when the emigrants were crossing the Platte River."[11]

The circle of wagons in the box canyon is harder to justify. When McCoy raised the point originally, Cruze replied, "Well, I just want to show what a damn fool this wagon-boss is." The staging of the Indian fight also bothered McCoy. The answer was: "Who'll know the difference?"[12] Ralph and Natasha Friar point out that the Indians attack *en masse;* those on foot carry and hide behind branches and shrubs. "Now this is a perfectly legitimate tactic if you're in a wooded area. But not out on a flat, almost desert-like prairie."*

On the whole, however, Colonel Tim McCoy thought highly of the final film. "It was as authentic as you can make entertainment."[13]

A dispute over the authenticity of the portrayal of Jim Bridger gave Para-

---

* According to Houston Horn, they are all wrong: "Almost never in all the history of western migration did an Indian war party descend upon a circle of covered wagons" (*The Pioneers,* New York: Time-Life Books, 1975, p. 96). See Ralph and Natasha Friar, *The Only Good Indian . . . The Hollywood Gospel* (New York: Drama Book Specialists, 1972), p. 150.

mount a monumental headache. Bridger's daughter, Virginia Bridger Hahn, born at Fort Bridger in 1849, sued the company on the grounds that her father was shown as a drunkard who had two Indian wives. She claimed $100,000 damages to her feelings and social status. It is true that Bridger was a more outstanding figure than the film gave him credit for; he is said to have explored more territory than any other man of his century. He lived with the Indians, and although he did have two Indian wives, he had them one at a time. Tim McCoy tracked down survivors who knew Bridger, and took statements. And Mrs. Hahn lost her case. The court held that changing standards make it impossible to defame one's ancestors.

Paradoxically, the criticism attracted by *The Covered Wagon* bestowed upon it a unique status: it was the first Western to be taken seriously by historians. Said the New York *Herald:* "There is one adjective that one thinks of first. That adjective is 'honest.' The picture is honest in its simplicity, in its fidelity, in its sincerity and in its regard for the importance of the theme. It has been extensively advertised and exploited. Well, for once the advertisements don't lie. *The Covered Wagon* is worthy of the best in the way of superlatives that its press agents have to offer."[14]

NORTH OF 36

The theory that the history of the West was not simply preserved by the motion picture, but prolonged by it, is well substantiated in the case of *North of 36*.

Intended as a grand sequel to *The Covered Wagon, North of 36* (the title referred to the old slavery line) contained immense potential. Emerson Hough had written the story shortly before his death in 1923, and James Cruze was set to direct. Jacqueline Logan was to star, although Lois Wilson replaced her. Jack Holt, who had a rugged background in Alaska and the West,* was given the leading role, with Ernest Torrence and Noah Beery in support. Paramount expected to spend a million on it.

But before the picture was ready to go, the budget was cut. James Cruze was now far too expensive. Irvin Willat was assigned to direct. The budget sank from a million to $350,000, still a substantial amount, but not enough to do justice to the theme. Willat was faced with the biggest challenge of his career.

The first problem in this story of the great cattle drives was to find the right kind of cattle. Since 1900 the majority of cattle in the West showed a Hereford strain. Paramount sent letters and cables to stockyards and ranches in an attempt to locate a herd of longhorn. Without such a herd, the picture could not be made. In each case, the answer was negative. The picture was on the point of cancellation when James East, who had spent weeks location hunting in Mexico and the southern United States, reported that he had found a herd of four thousand longhorn on a ranch thirty miles out of Houston, Texas. By a remarkable coincidence, the ranch was on almost the exact locale described in Hough's story.

---

* Jack Holt, then called Charlie Holt, was a stage-driver in Alaska around 1908. On the opposition stage was Hal Roach.

The movies seldom showed cowboys working; this scene from North of 36 *(1924) captures graphically the tedious aspect of life on the range. Ernest Torrence, left, and the last of the longhorns in the background.*

Jack Holt, former cowboy and Alaskan stage-driver, in North of 36, *with co-star Alamo.*

"It was the first longhorn drive in almost thirty-five years," wrote chief cameraman Al Gilks, "and according to the owner of the cattle, Bassett Blakeley, there will never be another. Mr. Blakeley plans to ship the cattle to market and replace them with a more modern breed."[1]

The drive was virtually an exact replica of those staged in the period 1866–1875. The four thousand head of cattle, spread out across the plains, together with three covered ox-carts, and accompanying cowboys, covered a distance of more than four miles. High parallels had to be constructed before the cameras could encompass the scene. The cattle followed the old Texas-Kansas trails, and the routine on the trip was practically the same as if it had been a real cattle drive.

According to the group of cattlemen who acted as technical advisers and who had been over the trails in the old days, the herd sustained a pace of twenty to thirty miles a day for the first week of the journey. When the animals became tired, ten to fifteen miles a day was considered good time. The same speed was made on this motion picture drive.

"To handle the camera on *North of 36,*" wrote Al Gilks, "called for something in the nature of a cross between a cinematographer and a cowpuncher. The production was filmed under a broiling Texas sun from the start until the finish. During the ten weeks of location, we were living the life of the first part of the last quarter of the last century. We were not only living under primitive conditions but, cinematographically, we were photographing under like circumstances. We had to depend on nature, with its own light sources. We had to have our own laboratory unit on the field."

When the drive set out, many old cowboys came to watch from sheer nostalgia. Perhaps to put the fear of God into the movie people, perhaps because it was true, they said the longhorns were about the wildest animals they had ever seen. The production manager therefore took no chances. Cattle stampeded at sharp, unusual noises, and the company was instructed in the dangers of stampedes. To bring home this sense of responsibility, actors as well as cowboys were given a turn in the night watch. Jack Holt, Ernest Torrence, and Noah Beery stood in as night hawks.

The leader of the herd was Alamo, thought to be the oldest and the largest longhorn steer in the world. Alamo had a horn spread of six foot from tip to tip. Before Emerson Hough's death (just after he had attended the Chicago opening of *The Covered Wagon*), he had intended to purchase this animal himself. When the production was completed, it was planned that James East should tour the United States and England with Alamo, and when the publicity tour was over, the steer was to be donated to the Old Trail Drivers' Association of the Southwest to be sold at auction.

"I *loved* that film," said Lois Wilson. "It was not regarded as a great film, although I thought it was a good picture. But some of the things we went through! Miss Taisie Lockart was a real person, you know. I guess she was the only woman who ever led a cattle drive. It was the last drive of longhorns—they had mixed the Brahman cattle with longhorns—we almost got into war with India over that, because Brahman were sacred. We were not supposed to use them for beef.*

* When Paramount set out to make *The Thundering Herd,* no authentic longhorn herd remained in Texas, and they had to resort to whitefaced Herefords.

"I didn't have a double in *North of 36.* And we had to swim this river. You get out of your saddle, hold on to your horn, and swim with your horse. But the river we swam was infested with water moccasins and I don't like snakes of any kind. And a water moccasin is a pretty wicked snake. They were killing them right and left. They were swimming round us. Irvin said, 'Don't be afraid, Lois. As long as you're swimming, they won't do anything.' Well, after about the third take, Ernest [Torrence] and Jack [Holt] went up to Irvin and said, 'Lois is not going to go through that again.' Because I was terrified. I did it three times, and they said, 'You've got enough takes there. You've done it every way but nude.' And they wouldn't allow him to do it again. Irvin I liked very much, but he was a very hard-driving director."[2]

The fording scene set out to surpass the crossing of the Platte in *The Covered Wagon,* and with long-focus Akeley shots, it approaches the quality of the Karun River crossing in *Grass.* Flanked on each side by sixteen cowboys and led by Alamo, the four thousand cattle swam a river almost half a mile wide.

The old trailhead town of Abilene, Kansas, was reconstructed from engravings, sketches, and photographs, and from information supplied by early Kansas settlers. The company was satisfied enough with the result to claim that each house and store was an exact duplicate of its original building. The town was all but wrecked when the cattle stampeded through it.

The picture was very well received, but Irvin Willat considered it a profound personal disappointment: "There wasn't enough money to spend on it, and the finish was entirely inadequate. It was too conventional. It started off well, but it never got anywhere."[3]

North of 36 was rediscovered by the American Film Institute in 1971. It proved to be a fascinating failure. However, when one considers how few Western epics had been made by 1924, the lost opportunities seem more forgivable. It fails to make the most of its spectacle, but it piles on the action and is only sabotaged by Hough's simple-minded story. The documentary moments are more fragmentary than in *The Covered Wagon*—we hardly see anything of branding, or the way cattle were looked after, or how cowboys lived. It is purely an entertainment film, and as such, two-thirds of it is successful.

However, the sight of cattle coming from all over Texas to form one massive herd is highly impressive. And the scenes of cattle on the move begin to sound the tocsin of the epic. The river crossing has majestic qualities, too, with moments that concentrate as much on the cattle as on the people. It is strange how much genuine fear and alarm the cattle communicate in the close-ups. But then this is not play-acting for them. It seems almost as if the herd is struggling throughout the film to become a major character, but neither the story nor the director allows this to happen.

Perhaps because of the lack of money, perhaps because it was considered a fine idea, there is one extraordinary anticlimax. The Comanches are seen massing on the horizon in a superbly composed distant silhouette. The cattlemen are tensed for the overwhelming attack. The huge body of horsemen rides forward—and they turn out to be the U.S. Cavalry. The film dispenses with the Indian attack, and when the eagerly awaited battle occurs, it involves only a few outlaws.

Nevertheless, *North of 36* was greatly appreciated at the time. *Picture Play* thought that it followed the pattern of *The Covered Wagon* scene for scene, shot

North of 36 *river crossing. Ernest Torrence in the foreground; Lois Wilson on his left.*

With cameras partially camouflaged to avoid alarming the cattle, Ernest Torrence leads the herd of authentic Texas longhorns in North of 36.

for shot. "I have even heard bold heretics say that they liked it better than the Cruze picture."[4] And *Photoplay* said, "Put it near the top of your 'must' list. What the perfect 36 is to a beauty chorus, *North of 36* is to the western movie. It is a screen achievement."[5]

It was remade in 1931 by Edward Sloman as *The Conquering Horde,* and again in 1938 in a Lucien Hubbard production, *The Texans.*

THE IRON HORSE

Only one Western survives from the entire silent period that surpasses the scale of *The Covered Wagon:* John Ford's production of *The Iron Horse.* Ford was twenty-nine when he made the picture, which one critic called "An American Odyssey." The brother of director Francis Ford, who employed him as assistant, Ford received his training on the Universal ranch. He began his career there as prop man and assistant and later director with Harry Carey two-reelers. Both Ford and Carey were Easterners who identified themselves with the history of the West. Ford's identification was so strong that it materially affected that history; in 1939, when the Navajo of Monument Valley were severely hit by the Depression, Ford used the valley as a location for *Stagecoach* and provided desperately needed employment. He repeated this several times; the Navajo adopted him into their tribe, and called him Natani Nez, Tall Soldier.

Ford often talked of writing the story of the making of *The Iron Horse.* "My wife says it's more pornographic than even current literature," he told UCLA students in 1964.[1] But when I asked him about it, shortly before he died, he admitted it had remained an idea.

"I had four uncles in the Civil War," said Ford. "I'm a Civil War buff. I used to ask my Uncle Mike to tell me about the battle of Gettysburg. All Uncle Mike would say was: 'It was horrible. I went six whole days without a drink.' Uncle Mike was a laborer on the Union Pacific Railroad when it was built. He told me stories about it and taught me the songs they had sung. I was always interested in the railroad and wanted to make a picture about it."[2]

Ford had proved himself a reliable and inventive director of box-office pictures with Tom Mix, and Fox gave him the opportunity of his career with what was then known as *The Iron Trail.*

Ford, and his chief cameraman George Schneiderman, ran into the standard obstacle for spectacular Westerns at this period: cattle. They traveled to the Yaqui River in Mexico, where a sufficiently large herd of longhorns had been reported, and found that while the cattle were ideal, the living conditions were hardly Hollywood standard. There were no hotels, nowhere to house the company, so they spent a week, shooting from dawn to dusk, sleeping out in the open.

On the Mexican trip, property man Lefty Hough remembered a remarkable cowboy named Tom Smith. "He was a real, honest-to-God cowboy, who looked like Jesus Christ. We had about a thousand head of cattle we wanted to swim across this lake. It was an artificial lake. The Mexican cowboys wouldn't do it. So Tom

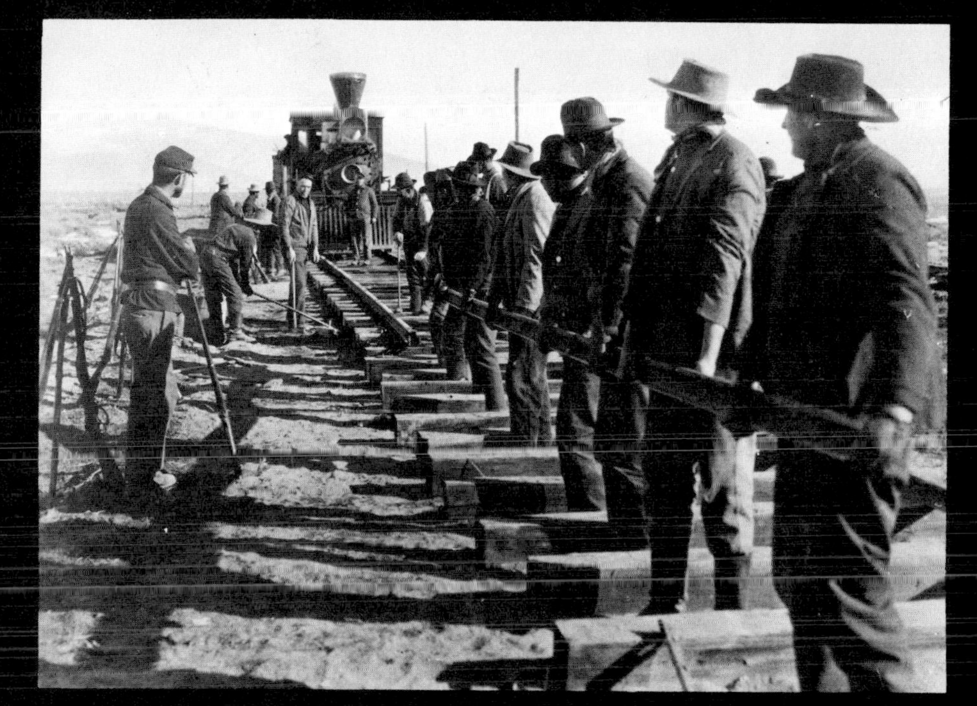

The Iron Horse (1924), *directed by John Ford.*

A forgotten epic of Alaskan railroad construction, The Iron Trail (1921), *based on fact, written by Rex Beach and directed by Roy William Neill.*

Smith went in the water with his horse and the Mexicans started to bless themselves. Tom Smith showed these Mexican cowboys how to do it. And this was an interesting sight to see. You know how they swim? They get off the saddle, and they grab the horse's tail, and as the horse turns they keep pushing water in the horse's face, and the horse will swim. He will go in a straight line. So that's the way we got those scenes. And these Mexican cowboys worshipped him after that."[3]

From Mexico the company moved to Lang's ranch in New Mexico. "It was here, for the first time in my life," wrote George Schneiderman, "that I had the experience of seeing my breakfast killed before me and then having it served a few minutes later. Well, the beefsteaks were nice and fresh to be sure, but my stay at the ranch was a period of self-imposed fast for me."[4]

Schneiderman and Ford hunted for locations throughout California, Arizona, and Utah. They required a spur of side track long enough to park a large number of railroad cars; since the location called for virgin territory, and hotel accommodation was unlikely, the entire company was to make itself at home in Pullman cars. The rail equipment of the Al G. Barnes Circus was rented for this purpose, together with an old locomotive, *Collis P. Huntington.* A spur of track in the division of the Southern Pacific Railroad was eventually selected at Dodge Flats, Nevada, the nearest town being Wadsworth. The art department (under Bill Darling), carpenters, and set dressers went ahead to prepare the two frontier towns required for the story, North Platte and Cheyenne.

Harold Schuster, later a director himself, worked on *The Iron Horse* in a general capacity, as actor, production assistant, and assistant film editor. He recalled how the adventure began. "On New Year's Eve, 1923, it was pouring pitchforks on the City of Los Angeles. At the Union Pacific station, a Barnes Brothers circus train was waiting, comprising two locomotives, and fifteen or so cars. With all on board, the long train pulled out into the night. As I recall, there was plenty of hearty conviviality. The ladies, the cowboys, and part of the crew and cast were singing, dancing, and drinking. Such numbers as 'My Darling Clementine,' 'The Yellow Rose of Texas,' filled the night air. Jack Ford was with the group and entered into the singing and story-telling—some of the stories were pretty raw.

"The next morning, I pulled up the shade of my lower berth, and looked out. The ground was a blanket of snow. It sounded as though there was plenty of activity going on: the whinny of the horses—the yells of the cowboys. A group of stolid Paiutes sat placidly on their horses watching the industrious white man scampering about his commercial activities. In the distance, I could see a Western town, mostly tents, and a few shacks. It represented North Platte, and later, with changes, it became Cheyenne and other towns that mushroomed and decayed as the rail-laying moved forward. I remember the Indian tepees encamped on the left of the town towards the mountains. They were the real thing, and the various nations brought their own. The Chinese were housed in tents back of the town. But most of the cast were housed in the circus train. It was freezing cold, for circus trains do most of their work in the summer, and lay over during the winter months. There was no heat, no hot water. We slept in long johns, Western shirts and long golf stockings."[5]

John Ford remembered the bitter cold: "I can see those boys and girls from Hollywood now. Some of them had on linen knickers. The Southern Pacific helped

The Iron Horse: *the survivors of the Indian attack return to the railhead. George O'Brien, left foreground.*

The railroad company forbade him, but John Ford did it anyway. Photographed in a camera pit, specially dug to film a locomotive passing overhead, are George Schneiderman, left, assistant cameraman Burnett Guffey, center, and Ford, cleaning his hands with his ever-present handkerchief. The shot has been successfully taken.

a lot and brought in several hundred pairs of long woolen underwear for us. We took the uniforms the studio had sent along as costumes for the soldiers and wore them because they were warm. I remember one girl wore a pair of soldier pants so big it came up around her chin. She cut holes in the sides for her arms and didn't care how she looked as long as she was warm."[6]

The next day the thermometer plummeted, and a blizzard sprang up. Ford recalled that Fox had permitted him a location schedule of four weeks. Helplessly, he asked Schneiderman, "What'll we do?" Schneiderman said, "There must have been snow when they built the railroad, so why don't we shoot anyway?"[7]

On another occasion, snow wrecked the continuity. Lefty Hough went to Ford, who was still in bed in his private car, and broke the awful news. Ford said, "Get some shovels and get everybody out there and get the snow off."

"And that's what we did," said Hough. "We brought the cattle in, the horses and everything else. We swept the whole town off. It may sound unbelievable, but I don't suppose we lost more than a couple of hours. Well, now, you take four hundred people, horses and cowboys and Indians and everything else—they can sweep a street in pretty quick time."

So well built were the sets that some people preferred them to the Pullmans, particularly when fleas were discovered aboard the aged circus train. The photographic staff, including Schneiderman, Sol Halprin, who handled the Akeley, Irving Rosenberg, second, Burnett Guffey, assistant, and William Walling, Jr., stills man and son of an actor in the picture, took over the set of the Pony Express office, filled in the missing wall with canvas to protect themselves against the twenty-below weather, and installed bunks. The laboratory building was disguised with a false front, but the roof blew off in a gale, causing both damage and injury. Film editor Louis Loeffler installed his cutting room in the relative comfort of a Pullman.

"I remember one night I went to one of the shacks and found an English actor named Cyril Chadwick living in there," said Ford. "I asked how he could stand it in a place like that. 'It's better than Vimy Ridge, old boy' was his reply. That was typical of the spirit of our troupe. Despite the bad weather and almost constant exposure to it, no one got sick. I suppose it was being out in the open air that kept them all healthy."[8] Lefty Hough, however, remembered that at one time or another, everyone in the company suffered from dysentery. And among the Indians, trachoma was rife.

"One day we were working out on the railroad," said Hough. "Now Cyril Chadwick spoke the King's English. And of course none of us could speak the King's English. Coming across the prairie was a big, beautiful automobile, with a chauffeur and a beautifully dressed woman. She got out of the car and she beckoned. So Ford said to Cyril, 'You're the only one who speaks English, you'd better go over there and talk to the lady.' So Cyril went over and he was gone about fifteen minutes. He came back and said, 'That's Madam Perkins. She wants to come out here and bring a tent and twenty girls.' She was from Reno, and she became a steady customer after. Everybody knew her."

The company had its own bootlegger. He operated at night, and in one furtive trip across the prairie, he hit a man, drunk on his own liquor, and killed him.

Naturally, the four-week schedule proved absurdly optimistic. *The Iron Horse* was made virtually without a script. The credited writer, Charles Kenyon, had written a synopsis, which only a handful of the company had seen. "This whole thing was actually made with ad libs," said Hough. "Ford injected and injected. He was the greatest improviser I have ever seen. Never seen anybody like him. But Ford's a very cagey guy—he'll never tell you anything you're supposed to know. That's your job. You're supposed to do it. It got so in a Ford picture that if you were an actor, you were afraid to leave the set. You know why? Because he's liable to change the scene and give you a plum—throw this character out and give it to you. Don't forget: many things happened on that picture. The steward in the dining car died of pneumonia. We had a marriage. We had a carload of coal brought in and the Indians stole the coal. The cooks in the cookhouse were selling big roasts to the Indians for fifteen cents. So we were running out of food. This is when the production man got fired. He was living in Reno in a whorehouse—which we could never find. We sent for the big boss of the studio, and he came up and fired him."

Otherwise, front-office interference—especially demands by wire for more rapid progress—caused Ford to grow choleric. "One day we were shooting out on the prairie when a rider came on like wildfire to deliver a wire to Ford," said Harold Schuster. "It was something like the pony express arriving. The wire was from the studio head, and had to do with the unit being behind schedule. Ford looked over towards Pardner Jones, who was about a hundred feet away, and yelled, 'Ed, I have a message here from Wurtzel. I'm going to fold it up and I want you to shoot a hole right through the name.' He walked out and stood there holding the wire with his right hand. Pardner put the rifle to his shoulder and fired. Ford never moved. He unfolded the paper and held it up for all to see. The bullet had gone right through the name. Everyone cheered and we all went back to work."[9]

In current films, the standard method to show bullets hitting the ground is to use electric charges. The same system was practiced then, but it was more realistic to use Pardner Jones. Toward the end of the picture, when George O'Brien runs through a hail of bullets to attack his enemy* in the blockhouse, the hail of bullets was real. Lefty Hough remembers that he and his assistant, Herbert Plews, were supposed to shoot back from the blockhouse, but Jones's bullets kept flying through the cracks. "We were lying on the ground, and Ford kept yelling, 'Fire back! Fire back!' I yelled back, 'To hell with it!' And Pardner kept shooting away, and we kept digging lower and lower."

Aside from Pardner Jones, the cowboys Schuster remembered included Tom Mix's pal Sid Jordan of the 101 Ranch (whose knowledge of horses proved of great value when Schuster directed *My Friend Flicka* in 1943). Jordan played the gunfighter in the saloon sequence. Herman Nolan was another 101 cowboy. Vinegar Roan, a cowboy so named because of his meanness, had drifted into pictures in the early days from the Texas panhandle. Jack Ganzhorn, who played Thomas Durant, was a small man and very fast with a gun. He had roamed all over the West before landing in California, where he worked in a great many Westerns. Jack Padjeon played Wild Bill Hickok and Governor Leland Stanford; he was a cowboy, part

---

* The villain in *The Iron Horse* is named Bauman (Fred Kohler)—probably a joke at the expense of Francis Ford's one-time employer Charles Baumann of NYMP. In the book of the film, the name has been changed to Deroux.

Irish and part Indian, who had doubled for Kerrigan in *The Covered Wagon.** Chief White Spear, a Spanish Indian, played the Sioux chief, and was in charge of the Indians. Chief Big Tree (a Seneca) played the Cheyenne chief.

Perhaps the reason the Ford company excelled at capturing the atmosphere of the Old West was because that atmosphere seldom evaporated when the camera stopped turning. "The Ford outfit was the roughest, goddamndest outfit you ever saw," said Hough, "from the director on downward. Ford and his brother, Eddie O'Fearna† [first assistant director], were fighting all the time. This goes back to the days in Maine when Eddie and the others ran a saloon and they used to kick Ford out of there and wouldn't let him drink. Ford never got over that. I had to break up the fights. When we were doing some of the stuff on the tracks, they got in an argument and O'Fearna went after the old man with a pickhandle."

The difficulty of finding ancient locomotives in any number forced the company to use their resourcefulness. "The railroad gave us two," said Hough, "and I know one of them was authentic. It had been used in the yard at Sacramento. Every time we turned these trains around, all we ever turned round was the smokestack. Then we had to repaint the cars—I had a sign painter up there—and work out whether they were going right to left or left to right. I got so confused I didn't know whether I was going or coming."

Ford went to Truckee, California, to film an old locomotive being shipped across the Donner Pass on skids. Publicity for the film described how the only way to do the scene convincingly was precisely the way it had been done originally—with two hundred fifty Chinese laborers and fifty head of horses. The Chinese were old railroad workers, most of them retired. Despite their advanced age, said the publicity, they heaved the locomotive across snow that was fifteen feet deep. The sequence was on the verge of disaster when half-inch cables began snapping, but even then there was no panic, and everyone stayed at his post. Actually, the locomotive stubbornly refused to move, no matter how hard the horses heaved. Ford tried dollying the camera past the engine. Only a few peremptory jerks of the skids can be seen in the film.

The Chinese had originally been imported by the railroad because of the lack of white labor in the West. There were about thirty of them in the film—not two hundred fifty as the publicity claimed—some were in their eighties (a cook was ninety) and the oldest of them had helped to build the original railroad. They doubled as Indians and soldiers.

Truckee was a favorite location for Hollywood pictures, and when *The Iron Horse* company arrived they found Edward Sutherland directing the Chilkoot Pass scene for Chaplin's *The Gold Rush.* Sutherland and Ford were old drinking companions, and even during Prohibition, Truckee was a wide-open town with a large number of saloons. "He had a drunken company," said Hough, "and so did we. I was one of them, so I know."

About fifty years earlier, the vigilantes in Truckee had decided there would

---

* *Hollywood Posse* contains much material on Padjeon, a name that is spelled differently whenever it is mentioned. According to William Julison, who has a photo signed "Jack Padjeon," he was actually John Duane of New Orleans.

† Ford's real name was Sean O'Fearna.

"Pulling 'Jupiter' over the Black Hills," says the caption in a scene from The Iron Horse, *shot at Truckee, California. But the locomotive proved impossible to move.*

John Ford, in cowboy hat, confers with Indians during the filming of The Iron Horse.

The wedding of the rails from The Iron Horse.

be no more Chinamen in the town. They hanged a number of them, and never again had a Chinaman been to Truckee. "Ford was using these old Chinese laborers," said Eddie Sutherland. "They wouldn't stop there. They stayed in their boxcars, which they had decorated with curtains and geraniums. As this train, with the old Chinese faces at the windows, pulled through the town, in back of us was the last of the vigilantes going in the opposite direction to be buried."[10]

Ford's pet name for the picture was *The Metallic Mustang.* The massive advertising campaign for this John Ford production was matched by Hollywood wags, who painted on their flivvers: "*The Tin Horse,* a Henry Ford production."

For the prologue, Sid Grauman persuaded Tim McCoy to repeat the success he had had with Indians in the prologue of *The Covered Wagon.*

Ford, characteristically, avoided the premiere and went fishing instead. The critics bombarded the picture with admiration and delight. "Neither Fox nor anyone else has brought to the screen so fine, so splendidly conceived a dramatization of the great West as that which is presented in *The Iron Horse.*"[11] The picture cost $280,000, and grossed more than $2 million.

The film was dedicated to George Stephenson, the man who built the *Rocket.* A title claimed: "Accurate and faithful in every particular of fact and atmosphere is this pictorial history of the building of the first American transcontinental railroad." No film can be accurate in every particular, but *The Iron Horse* makes a determined effort. Ford regarded himself in later life as a historian, and the documentary scenes are as striking as flashes of gunpowder amidst the murk of melodrama.

It was as though the scenario writer, Charles Kenyon, sat down and listed every incident in *The Covered Wagon,* for they are all in *The Iron Horse*—the love story, complete with misunderstanding, the girl engaged to the heavy . . . the river crossing . . . the buffalo hunt . . . the hand-to-hand fight between hero and villain . . . the parting of the ways before the final reconciliation. As in *The Covered Wagon,* the background cowboys wear their regular clothes, which are not entirely appropriate to the 1860s. However, George O'Brien is a much more convincing Western hero than Warren Kerrigan, and John Ford directs with a wider range of detail than Cruze.

The film doesn't show the epic endurance of the "rust eaters," or their triple-decker bunkhouses, or the staggering marvels of engineering. But to watch Ford's crowd scenes, to see one shantytown being demolished and another built as the railhead moves forward is to experience that surge of emotion that accompanies perfection. His direction of ordinary narrative is occasionally stiff and formal, but his reconstruction is staged with such authority that a viewing of *The Iron Horse* is the next best thing to being there.

Historical characters step in and out of focus: Abraham Lincoln . . . Buffalo Bill Cody . . . Wild Bill Hickok . . . Major North . . . Collis P. Huntington . . . Charles Crocker . . . Governor Leland Stanford . . . General Grenville Dodge . . . All of these appear on the cast list, but the action is so kaleidoscopic one cannot be certain that they all made it to the final cut. By the last reel, with the reconstruction of the wedding of the rails on 10 May 1869 at Promontory Point, Utah (for which, a subtitle insists, the original locomotives were used, a fact belied by the photographs), there is not the slightest doubt that the rails lie gleaming from sea to sea—and that the Ford company laid every inch of them.

The atmosphere off camera on a Ford film was much the same as it was on; the company was awakened by the romantic sound of a bugle. The bugler, Herbert "Limey" Plews, was a World War veteran from England who worked as a property man.

The U.S. Army Around the World aviators tour The Iron Horse *set; the aviators started on their flight right after this visit. This photograph is also notable as one of the few to show Milt Brown, oldest of the Hollywood Westerners and a former stagecoach driver in the Rockies. He stands at extreme left, next to Pardner Jones. John Ford kneels by camera.*

John Wayne in The Big Trail *(1930), with Tully Marshall, repeating his role from* The Covered Wagon.

Raoul Walsh puzzles out how to shoot the descent-of-the-wagons sequence, one of the most impressive in his The Big Trail.

THE BIG TRAIL

By 1930 the silent era was over. The Western film was undergoing a painful transition. Outdoor pictures were being avoided; they caused too many problems for the sound recordists. On top of the stock market crash, the enforced unemployment caused many cowboys to abandon Hollywood. But unexpectedly there came a reassuring surge of production.

President Hoover reminded the nation of a significant date; he asked for universal observance of the march of the pioneers from Independence, Missouri, on 10 April 1830.

The Fox company responded with the most spectacular Western so far mounted, Raoul Walsh's *The Big Trail,* and, appropriately, on 10 April 1930, a bugle call set in motion a long line of specially constructed prairie schooners. The picture was intended to surpass *The Covered Wagon* in every respect. For Walsh, it was an awe-inspiring responsibility. For one thing, the film was being shot in Fox Grandeur, 70 mm., as well as 35 mm. For another, he had taken a gamble on the leading man, and signed an unknown. A furious letter in the trade press charged him with insulting the acting profession: "Just how he can expect a youth to carry such a picture is beyond my conception. If he brings in a winner with Mr. Wayne he will be entitled to a Carnegie medal."[1]

"I selected Wayne," said Walsh, "primarily because he is a real pioneer type, but most of all because he can start over any trail and finish. *The Big Trail* means that everyone who goes over it while the cameras record will go through just as many hardships as the pioneers of 100 years ago encountered."[2]

The company traveled through seven states, from the blistering heat of the desert at Yuma, to the stinging blizzards of the Teton Pass. The picture has documentary scenes that have never been surpassed. Sadly, it was a box-office failure. Theaters could ill-afford to change their newly installed equipment to accommodate Fox Grandeur. *The Big Trail* has thus been as neglected as most of the silent Westerns.

Yet in its efforts to re-create American history, it made American history—on a minor but, for a picture about pioneers, a very significant scale.

"There was a place called Moran Camp, on Jackson Lake," recalled John Wayne. "It probably had five or six little shacks when we arrived. We came out with three hundred fifty people, and by the time we were through, we had about five hundred people working there, with a hundred and fifty wagons and horses. So we had to have a pretty big setup. We enlarged the place, built cabins and sets, and they ended up with an establishment that is now called Moran, Wyoming. It's a township. I don't imagine there's too many tall buildings out there, but still, we started it."[3]

3

THE WILDERNESS

"Those who have the courage and intelligence to make these records deserve to be rewarded with something more tangible than the satisfaction that comes from knowledge of a good deed well done."

—ROBERT E. SHERWOOD

The Kolb brothers hover over the Grand Canyon during their 1911 expedition.

THE FILM OF FACT

The factual film is the cinema's most noble endeavor. The desire to inform and to educate, as well as to entertain, is the highest aspiration of the film-maker. Yet how seldom do such films rise above the level of the dull and—a word that invariably follows—documentary?

The factual film holds an extraordinary power over the dedicated cineaste. It somehow represents a purity, an integrity, to which the commercial entertainment film can never aspire.

The factual film was born with the motion picture, although it took thirty years for it to be recognized as an individual art and dignified with the term "documentary." But while the documentary movement looks for its origins to the silent *Nanook of the North* (1922), it did not reach fruition until the 1930s. Its pinnacle of achievement occurred during the Second World War, subsiding in the late 1940s, to be given a new lease on life by television.

In the silent days, film-makers never realized they were making documentaries. They set out to make pictures about actual events, and they failed or succeeded, according to their individual talents. There was no formula. Some of them tried to emulate the feature film, some of them the lantern lecture. The only guide to their existence is an occasional review squeezed between comments on the dozens of feature releases. Despite the effort involved in making factual films, reviewers rarely considered them worth the same space as an entertainment film. They were considered an inferior species, rather like the people they depicted. Important documentaries like *Nanook, Grass,* and *Chang* were on the whole eulogistically received by the press, but lesser fry were given breathtakingly dismissive notices. Some pictures, which had literally cost blood to make, were sent winging into oblivion with a patronizing two-line review. *Up the Congo,* made by a woman explorer, Alice O'Brien, in 1929, was awarded this comment: "If you can work yourself into a lather over these expedition things into Darkest Africa, this particular one is interesting."[1] Of *Wild Heart of Africa,* a record of the Walker-Arbuthnot expedition, *Photoplay* said: "Someone who went somewhere saw something and brought it back for us to look at."[2] Exhibitors were no more enlightened. Said an Exhibitors' Report of *Wonders of the Sea* (Williamson, 1924): "a fine thing of its kind, but I could say the same about carbolic acid."[3]

"Mr. Roosevelt acknowledges the plaudits for his marksmanship." Colonel Selig's faked film of Roosevelt's expedition to Africa included the shooting of a lion; the authorized film did not.

Edison Company Canadian expedition, 1910, near Banff, Alberta. Director J. Searle Dawley, in white hat; Henry Cronjager at camera.

TRAVEL WAS THE MAINSTAY of the early moving picture. An intriguing use for the new invention at the turn of the century was to provide the very sensation of travel—in a railroad car, equipped with machinery to provide swaying, hissing, and banging. These *Hale's Tours* (named after their originator, George C. Hale, a former fire chief of Kansas City) transported their hypnotized passengers from Tacoma to Tokyo, from Vesuvius to Pike's Peak. A French device duplicated the movement of a ship, with a predictably rapid decrease in the number of spectators. Cameras were placed on streetcars, too, and the illusion was so effective that audiences yelled at jaywalking pedestrians.

If travel pictures could bring Boston, Tacoma, and even Tokyo to people who had never been there, they were capable of more impressive achievements. When Theodore Roosevelt announced his African safari, planned when his presidency came to an end in 1909, Colonel Selig,* the film pioneer, put forward a suggestion. He would train Roosevelt's son, Kermit, in the intricacies of a moving picture camera if he would record the trip for the benefit of posterity and the Selig Polyscope Company. The President had made a great impact as a popular hero, and such a coup by Colonel Selig would assist the industry in its struggle to attain respectability. The President thought it a good idea, but when the party sailed, no deal had been finalized.

Selig was piqued. He set about transforming his Chicago studio into an African jungle. A vaudeville actor who specialized in Roosevelt impersonations played the lead, and Otis Turner directed a film entitled *Hunting Big Game in Africa* (1909). The name Roosevelt was never mentioned, although the initials TR were plainly visible on the luggage. *Moving Picture World* thought it an audacious mixture of the real and unreal, although many would regard it with total conviction. "Unless we are mistaken, there is a mixture of Indian and African costumes in the dressing of the natives, but the whole thing is full of movement and shows great resource on the part of the producers."[4] It was photographed by Emmett Vincent O'Neill.

The authentic Roosevelt safari, photographed by Cherry Kearton, shows Zulu women at work, Roosevelt watching a native war dance and being carried across a stream on the shoulders of a porter. Kearton's great ambition was to film a lion, "but although he lay in wait for the king of beasts for weeks, he was unable to accomplish this object."[5]

And this was where Colonel Selig scored. In his faked version, a lion was shot dead, to be carried away on poles by natives. *Moving Picture World* expressed excitement not so much over the killing of the lion, but over the shots of the lion alive. "There is no doubt about this lion; he stalks majestically about the picture, thus enabling an audience to realize how a lion would look, not on the war path, but peaceably ambling about among natural surroundings. Your captive lion in a zoological park does not do much prowling about except in a small cage. This part of the film attracted very great attention; and we single the film out for special mention because we hope that it will be an encouragement to Mr. Selig and his merry men to cultivate the production of moving pictures of animal life, which are always attractive to moving picture audiences."[6]

---

* Colonel Selig's title was not military, but was adopted for his minstrel show.

Roosevelt caught up with the faked version upon his arrival in Berlin and was reportedly furious. Nevertheless, Selig profited so handsomely that he set up a zoo and produced a highly successful series of animal pictures.* When the authentic Roosevelt pictures opened, audiences were bitterly disappointed. "There is not a picture in the 2,000 feet that is fit to be called a picture," wrote an indignant exhibitor. "To tell you the honest truth, most any operator would be ashamed to run such a thing through a machine. Anybody could take a .22 rifle and go out in the sagebrush in Idaho and get more excitement hunting jack rabbits."[7] A journalist toured theaters where the picture was shown to discover why exhibitors were so angry. He quickly realized that audiences bred on melodrama expected excitement with their pictures, especially from Teddy Roosevelt. "They were expecting to see Teddy slaughtering lions and tigers and wallowing in the gore. It was of no use to explain the difficulties incidental to the taking of such a picture."[8]

The Roosevelt documentary created a prejudice against factual films which was consolidated by many of those that followed. But then, in 1912, appeared Paul Rainey's *African Hunt*. The film was a staggering success, running for fifteen months in New York and earning a fortune for its distributor, Carl Laemmle. Because the surviving print at the Library of Congress has been transferred from a paper positive, the quality is soft, gray, and lifeless. Nevertheless, viewing this material, one can see why the Rainey film had so much more of an impact than anything before it. The natives dance, and there are placid animals by the screenful, but, momentarily, there is drama; a fearsome scene as Rainey's Mississippi bear-dogs corner a lion, hold back, snarling and barking, and then close in for the kill. The moment of death, fortunately, is obscured, but the result is clear when men haul the carcass of the lion from the bushes.

A second series of Paul Rainey pictures, photographed as before by John Hemment, was released in 1914. They were airily dismissed as not being equal to the first. Rainey was a coal dealer and sportsman from Philadelphia, fired with the Roosevelt sense of adventure, and not too concerned about moving pictures. A far more serious film-maker was Carl Akeley, a vital, if neglected figure in motion picture history. Akeley's talents were spread across so many fields that he deserves the rank of Renaissance Man. His third trip to Africa was undertaken on behalf of the American Museum of Natural History, of which Akeley eventually became curator. On this safari, which lasted from 1909 to 1911, Akeley brought back eight specimen of elephant; he was almost killed at Mount Kenya when a bull elephant tried to gore him, and was laid up for three months. He took a motion picture outfit, but found the Urban camera unsuitable for tropical work; it was extremely cumbersome, unnecessarily complicated, and hopeless in emergencies. He designed his own, and in November 1915, patented the Akeley camera, which, equipped with gyro head, long-focus lens, coupled viewfinder, and a specially designed shutter, was revolutionary; ideal for game hunting, it could follow rapidly moving objects very smoothly, without blurring. It was soon adopted by news weeklies and by cinematographers in Hollywood, some of whom specialized

---

* In July 1911, Selig director William V. Mong made *The Way of an Eskimo* in Labrador, the majority of the cast being authentic Eskimos. (Mong later became a character actor and was featured in *What Price Glory?*)

Carl Akeley with his gyroscopic Akeley camera.

Carl Akeley and candidate for taxidermy.

as Akeley cameramen. During the war, the government commandeered the entire output of the Akeley Camera Company.

Carl Akeley was the author of several books, a sculptor (which perhaps accounts for the beautiful shape of his camera), and the inventor of a unique system of taxidermy. He also invented the cement gun, a machine for mixing and applying concrete by compressed air. A close friend of Theodore Roosevelt (he persuaded him to make his famous safari to Africa), Akeley shared his view of the importance of the motion picture, and he urged natural history museums to form film libraries and to make these records available to colleges, schools, and libraries. He was scathingly critical of producers who impaired the scientific merits of travel pictures by editing them solely with an eye for thrills (although he gave the blessing of his museum to the films of Mr. and Mrs. Martin Johnson, whose pictures fitted into just such a category). In 1921 Akeley penetrated unknown reaches of the African Congo to photograph the gorilla, and with this expedition he extended the frontiers of cinematography still further. For besides his Akeleys, he took another specially designed machine. This one was stereoscopic.

SUFFICIENT TRIBUTE CAN NEVER be paid to these pioneering cameramen; it is one thing to carry into the jungle a lightweight camera equipped with zoom lens —a courageous enough action in itself—but to lug a machine that, with its tripod, weighed anything from seventy-five to one hundred pounds, and to crank the handle evenly while positioned only yards from the fiercest creatures on earth—this took more than enthusiasm. "I find that turning the crank will not answer the purpose when the cameraman is looking into the eyes of a rapidly advancing lion," Akeley remarked, mildly. "It is not in human nerves to stand the strain without excitement."[9] However, not even he could provide as reliable an alternative, despite experiments with compressed air and spring-operated motors.

Whatever history we can see in photographic form, we owe to courageous and skillful cameramen. Our own lives are richer for the risks they took, and for their sheer hard labor. The most astonishing scenes ever put on the screen were captured by cameramen working for newsreels and documentaries. On occasion these men saved lives as they took pictures. The great newsreel cameraman Norman Alley flew over the Mississippi Delta in 1927, dropping food to the flood victims from his camera amphibian.

Why is it, then, that a factual film is usually so much less of an experience than a good fictional film? One reason lies in the factual film's denial of film craft. A dramatic sequence in a fiction film is a fragmented vision; to give the impression of a continuous event, an incident is repeated again and again, photographed from several different angles, and fused into one continuous action in the cutting room. Audiences have grown accustomed to this style over sixty years.

Most factual films use only one camera. To cover an incident as comprehensively as a feature film is impossible without restaging the incident. The audience thus finds the result flat by comparison with its fictional counterpart, like a newsreel of a horse race compared with the chariot race from *Ben-Hur*. The factual filmmaker is thus driven to artifice to recover some of this lost ground.

To create a little of the alarm generated by an elephant stampede, the filmmaker is obliged to inject reaction shots which, by their very nature, must be

The original caption reads: "The above illustration shows a cinematograph camera, constructed for Sir Philip Brocklehurst by Messrs. Newman and Guardia, for use on horseback. The photograph was taken in Africa, where Sir Philip was using the apparatus for taking nature pictures."

faked. The cameraman, concentrating on the charging elephants, is hardly likely to find time to focus on the faces of the terrified victims. In *Chang,* a shot of a helpless baby is inserted as elephants destroy a village. The baby was nowhere near the stampede, but his presence in the film, paradoxically, heightens the reality.

The bizarre truth is that the most effective films of fact have been subject to almost as much manipulation as fiction films. The more astounding they look, the less authentic they are.

The gulf between the so-called pure documentary, which records only actuality, and the reconstructed documentary, which is branded a fake, is not as broad as we have been led to suppose. There are precious few documentaries that have *not* resorted to some kind of restaging. Robert Flaherty, regarded as the purest film-maker of all, had no compunction about presenting his own romantic vision rather than unadulterated reality.

THESE EARLY FILM-MAKERS often felt constrained to escape civilization and to seek the primitive. It occurred to none of them to stay behind and record the primitive existence of the underprivileged in their own cities—primitive meant picturesque, and, in the Fenimore Cooper sense, noble. Films like *Nanook* and *Grass* had an underlying message to an increasingly materialistic nation: "Here is the spirit you have lost!"

A few of these documentaries were, admittedly, little more than bombastic home movies, rich men's conceits forced before the public. Others were worthy anthropological records, of interest only to specialists. A few of them masqueraded under provocative titles, hoping to delude the casual passerby into parting with his dime for some sensational sequences. *Primitive Love* justified its title with a single shot—all of ten feet—showing an Eskimo couple holding hands behind an iceberg. But there remain other lost exploration pictures, which may exist in private collections, geographical archives, or government vaults and which may prove of immense historical value.

A rare book by Leonard Donaldson, *The Cinematograph and Natural Science,*[10] refers to an expedition to the islands of the Torres Straits undertaken by one Dr. Haddon, which might have caused a stir in moving picture circles had anyone taken any notice of it. Haddon was not content simply to record the sights; he was determined to record the sounds as well. He carried with him a record-cutting machine, and when he returned with his pictures, he was able to accompany them with the original voices and music. Haddon was not unique, either; the 1901 Baldwin-Spencer expedition to central Australia recorded picture and sound, and in 1907 Dr. Rudolf Pöch filmed the tribes of New Guinea and recorded their language via the gramophone.*

Less adventurous technically, but an explorer of the first category, was Frederick Burlingham, an American who worked so much in Europe that his films are listed in the National Film Archive catalogue as English. Burlingham was an important contributor to the factual film, albeit a totally forgotten one; his first adventure with a motion picture camera was climbing the Matterhorn in the face of high winds, a feat that took nineteen hours. With two Italian crystal hunters, he took his camera into the crater of Vesuvius; all three were nearly killed when enveloped by a dense column of hydrochloric acid gas. After a trip to Borneo, Burlingham surprised Americans by relating that civilized man might learn from contact with savages. Yet some of his most popular films were revelations to the Americans of the beauty of their own country—such as *Suwanne River* (1919).

Dutch Borneo was the destination of cameraman William Alder, who left Universal City in 1919 with director Edward Laemmle (a nephew of Carl) to make expedition pictures. Exploring the mountains of China, they found themselves in the thick of the South China Revolution, which they obligingly filmed for Uncle Carl and the Universal Weekly. For propaganda services to a Chinese general, they were both decorated. Following a trip to Singapore, they penetrated to the interior of Dutch Borneo to search for the Dayak headhunters. According to the trade press, they nearly lost their lives when filming an attack on a village. "Alder and Laemmle were in a boat, which was propelled by several natives. The enemy tribe attacked with spears and poisoned darts. Laemmle fired both barrels of a shotgun into the savages and dispersed them."[11]

The film-makers borrowed a schooner from the Dutch colonial government

---

* An extract of the Baldwin-Spencer footage appears in Joan Long's *Pictures that Move* (1968), a history of the Australian cinema. To include the contributions to this field of Australian film-makers would dangerously increase the size of this volume. But Frank Hurley must be mentioned—he filmed the Mawson and Shackleton expeditions, was a front-line cameraman in the war, and made several important documentaries, including *Pearls and Savages* (1921) about New Guinea. For full details, see *The Australian Screen* by Eric Reade (Melbourne: Lansdowne Press, 1975).

and promptly wrecked it on a reef. Laemmle and Alder found themselves on a wild part of the New Guinea coast, inhabited only by cannibals. They were met with hostile demonstrations, but eventually they won the confidence of the people and remained in their midst for nearly two months. They were finally rescued by a Dutch patrol boat. Their picture, *Shipwrecked Among Cannibals,* was unusually well reviewed, but scarcely represented a box-office bonanza.

DESPITE THE MODEST RETURNS of the majority, factual films *could* smash records. *Hunting Big Game in Africa with Gun and Camera* ran for three months at New York's Lyric Theatre. As the American Museum of Natural History had lent its name to many expedition films, so well-to-do citizens of Oakland, California, decided to advertise their city with the same kind of museum; they employed H. A. Snow to produce the American specimens. Snow hunted with automobiles in the semi-arid American West, specializing in grizzly bear and puma. Now he sold the backers of the museum on the idea of an African expedition, and a motion picture. The party set sail in 1919.

Advised to use cattle to haul the equipment, Snow was dismayed when the lethal tsetse fly disposed of most of his oxen. He put all his faith in motor transport and sent an expedition ahead to establish advance depots of gasoline. Then the main party moved forward, and the picture became a hymn of praise to Detroit. The cars were put through grueling endurance tests, dragged across rivers with their engines underwater, and ploughed through swamps, in temperatures of 125 degrees. A wart hog, goaded by one Model T, attacked its chassis, ripped the tires with its tusks, and battered the radiator with its head. Yet the tin lizzie withstood the onslaught and provided a spirited sequence. From 1919 to 1922 H. A. Snow, and his son Sidney, the cameraman, exposed 125,000 feet of film in Africa. The Snows later produced a successful picture in the Arctic.

The northern regions offered an irresistible lure to factual film-makers; apart from *Nanook of the North* by Flaherty, Captain Kleinschmidt produced *Primitive Love* (1926), and former cameraman Earl Rossman directed *Kivalina of the Icelands* in 1925. Colin Campbell, who had made *The Spoilers* in 1914, directed *Balto's Race to Nome* (1925), another Alaskan story, about the desperate journey of Gunnar Kasson and his dog team, headed by Balto, to bring serum to a town afflicted with diphtheria.

Less accustomed to the perils of the Arctic than the rigors of the desert was cameraman Fred LeRoy Granville, whose experiences filming the rescue of the survivors of the Stefansson expedition in 1914 encouraged author Charles van Loan to include him as a character in his Buck Parvin Western series. Granville's assistant, George Zalibra, had been a cameraman in the Mexican Revolution. One of those rescued was Captain Bob Bartlett, leading character of several Arctic exploration films, who eventually lost his life making another.

When Stefansson went to the Arctic, he took with him a young Australian, Hubert Wilkins, who had filmed the Balkan wars for Gaumont. After two winters in the Arctic, Wilkins journeyed to the Western Front as official photo-historian for the Royal Australian Air Force. Wilkins graduated from expedition cameraman to become a distinguished British explorer, with a knighthood to his name, and Lowell Thomas has written a book about his experiences.[12]

H. A. Snow (right) and his son Sidney ruefully contemplate the damage a charging rhino has inflicted on their Universal camera: Hunting Big Game in Africa with Gun and Camera (*1922*).

Captain Kleinschmidt, a survivor of three fronts in the Great War, puts himself further to the test in order to make Primitive Love (1926).

Films of fact resorted to gratuitous titles to attract customers.

Hubert Wilkins as the cameraman on the Shackleton expedition—aboard the Karluk *(1913). He later served as an official war photographer and won a knighthood.*

Hollywood has been chronicled as such a self-serving community, completely cushioned from the world around it, that the number of Hollywood cameramen involved in expedition pictures comes as a surprise. A decade before he photographed Clara Bow, Victor Milner crossed the Atlantic on the *Lusitania*—the last trip before she sank—and filmed London during the Zeppelin raids. After months of battling with British and Belgian red tape, he embarked on a 1916 expedition to the Congo. "My only knowledge of the Congo country was such as I had been able to gather from reading the works of Henry M. Stanley. At Metadi I took the narrow gauge railroad to Kimsheda. Here the heat was killing. My assistant, Frank Farrell of Chicago, was taken down with a serious case of malarial fever. The state doctor told him he was to get out of the country quick if he was to get out at all. That left me on the job with sixty-seven cases of baggage, camera, chemicals and provisions to handle without the aid of another white man."[13]

Milner—still calling himself Miller, as in his Mexican days—was impressed by the steadfastness and fidelity of the natives, although one group misunderstood his intentions and attacked his party. He had to overcome their fear of the camera; missionaries explained it, and they named it "jijijingi," which, Milner said, meant the "reproduction of a shadow." Ultraviolet rays were so strong that Milner decided all developing should take place as soon as possible after exposure, to prevent the negative image being reversed to a positive. He did his best, but the malarial mosquitoes and tsetse flies drove him mad. "One time I had to run out of the tent and sacrifice four hundred feet of film. Remaining was impossible." Altogether, he exposed thirty thousand feet but sadly admitted that he lost the majority because he was unable to develop everything as he shot it. However, an authority in London congratulated him on bringing out a larger amount of successful footage than any of his predecessors.

Accompanying Lady Grace Mackenzie into Africa, Hal Sintzenich, cameraman on such D. W. Griffith films as *America* and *Isn't Life Wonderful?*, photographed a highly praised 1915 documentary, *Heart of Africa*. Lady Grace Mackenzie was hailed as the first woman ever to penetrate so far into the jungle and was said to have outdone Rainey and Roosevelt. Mackenzie Camp in Kenya was named after her. But she ran into financial trouble, and both her business management and her title came under suspicion. A lawsuit ended her courageous but brief excursion into pictures.

A well-known lecturer, Henry Howse, was responsible for Ernest Palmer's expedition to China in 1909. Palmer, who was later to photograph such classics as *Seventh Heaven* and *The River*, was twenty-two: "So seldom had white men made the trip up the Yangtse River to Chungking, and five hundred miles overland to Chengtu, that the authorities frowned on it," he wrote. "It was necessary for us temporarily to relinquish our nationality and become Chinese citizens."[14]

The American consul was worried not by their possible exploitation of the coolies but by the coolies' exploitation of them. "You have paid them one half," he warned. "Don't give them the other half until they deliver you safely to Chengtu, or they will run away and you'll be helpless. Do you have a gun?"

Palmer said he had. "Can you use it?" the consul asked. "You are forgetting that I come from Kansas," said Palmer. "We kids could knock over a jack rabbit on a full run with a .22." "Splendid," said the consul. "Tomorrow morning, as you

Negotiating the rapids on the Yangtse—a scene from Ernest Palmer's 1909 China expedition film.

The disgraced prisoner is highly amused by the camera, also from Palmer's 1909 China film.

With Byrd at the Pole (1930).

are about to leave, I will arrange that the head man lines up the coolies. Mr. Howse will throw a can up in the air, and you will take your revolver out of your pocket, be very sure you hit the can successfully, then place the gun in your pocket."

The scene was straight out of a Western, but Palmer said it worked like a charm. "I became very fond of the coolies. The peasants we met in that far country were always very polite, generous, and curious. To allow them to look through the finder of the motion picture camera was a wonderful experience. The film was made for a religious organization, the China Inland Mission."

Despite the example of these resourceful, skillful, and determined men, some expedition leaders were still blind to the importance of the moving picture.

Commander Byrd, departing for his Antarctic expedition in 1928, acknowledged that on his 1925 expedition he had paid far too little attention to his two Pathé News cameramen, Willard van der Veer and Bob Donohue.* "I didn't exactly neglect them. But I didn't give them much time and attention. I regret it. That expedition brought home to me the value of motion pictures as a scientific record as well as for the instructive amusement of the people."

Motion pictures, he declared, were undoubtedly the best way to bring back any record. Furthermore, he intended to make a proper film of the two years' sojourn in the Antarctic. "This picture will, I believe, do much to reduce the public's apprehension of exploration." Commander Byrd included in his equipment not only motion picture cameras, lights, and flares to ensure that shooting could continue during the dark winter months, but also projection equipment and a large stock of films.

---

* Joseph T. Rucker accompanied van der Veer on the 1928 expedition.

"We have taken mostly comedies, because the men can see them over and over and still get fun from them. And the other pictures I ordered were *Chang, Grass, Moana of the South Seas* and *Nanook of the North*."[15]

On its release in 1930, *With Byrd at the South Pole* contained this title: "The conqueror is still the Hero of Heroes. But war, once the Hero's only field, has given way to a grander campaign—the conquest of Nature."

BURTON HOLMES

Before the word "documentary" arrived to describe it, the factual film had endured a bewildering variety of categories: topical, graphic, educational, scenic, instructional, actuality. . . . Educational films were unpopular, although they had served their purpose in improving the reputation of the motion picture as a whole. In 1907, when censorship first came in, Sunday laws were enforced. Lecturers were suddenly in great demand. Audiences came to see thrills, and departed bored by natural history. The word "educational" was, from that moment on, the least pleasing adjective in the exhibitor's vocabulary.

While fiction films progressed, the educational film remained stunted from lack of money and lack of interest. Scenics were often thrown in by exchanges as part of a program, costing exhibitors virtually nothing.

To search for signs of support for factual film-makers from the motion picture industry is therefore a waste of time. The industry's record in this regard is scandalous. Were it not for an alternative cinema, the number of travel and expedition pictures produced in the silent days would have been even smaller than it was.

I can find no printed tribute to this alternative cinema in the annals of the documentary, yet again and again the encouraging certainty of lecture-hall bookings across the United States persuaded expeditions to include a motion picture camera in their equipment. Lectures had been a vital part of American life since the late nineteenth century, when culture was all the rage, and people filled their minds as they filled their houses. "The history of American education shows the far-reaching importance of the lecture," said *Moving Picture World.* "Free lectures have become a favorite medium of instruction in every large city in the US."[1]

The word "lecture," however, alarmed as many people as were deterred in later years by "documentary." Burton Holmes, who depended upon the lecture circuit, took evasive action with the word "travelogue." He is credited with inventing the term; an adaptation of the word "monologue," it was in use by 1908 to describe the short travel lectures delivered with slides between reels at motion picture shows.

Born in Chicago in 1870, Holmes's earliest desire was to be a magician, an ambition he shared with Willy Selig (later the film pioneer Colonel William Selig), who was apprenticed to the same master magician. The sight of Selig, publicly humiliated when an experiment misfired, helped to direct Holmes toward a less precarious vocation. He had long been fascinated by travel; he had toured America at the age of thirteen, and in 1886, when he was sixteen, he went abroad with his

Burton Holmes, photographed at the end of the Great War.

grandmother and a Kodak. His second trip, four years later, provided him with the material for his first public lecture, *Through Europe with a Camera,* which he presented before the Chicago Camera Club.

In 1892 he gave up his job and went to Japan. Upon his return, he lectured again in Chicago, in a hall hired especially for the occasion. It was a huge success, thanks largely to his family's acquaintanceship with Chicago society leaders. "They all came out of curiosity," Holmes said later. "They wanted to see what that 'lazy Holmes boy' was up to now."[2]

Searching for someone to project his slides, he hired Oscar Depue, who worked at the McIntosh Battery and Optical Company as a projectionist for the medical profession. Depue became Holmes's partner.

"In 1896," wrote Depue, "we realized that we had a growing rival—the motion picture. As a result, in 1897, at the end of the 1896 season, Mr. Holmes sailed for Sicily and Italy, and I sailed for London, the Mecca for motion pictures at that time. My intention was to search out and buy a motion picture camera. I found little from which to choose, and the prices were exorbitant. I was forced to go to Paris, where the situation was almost as bad—with one exception. Mr. Léon Gaumont had a Demeny camera for 60 mm. film—the only machine that I could find in all of Paris. It was not what you would call a facile piece of apparatus; it was cumbersome and its tripod was a piece of two-inch plank fitted with solid iron legs (not adjustable). I was somewhat fearful of what I could do with this equipment, but nevertheless I purchased it and took the train to Rome to join Mr. Holmes."[3]

For their first motion picture exposure, Holmes and Depue selected the piazza in front of St. Peter's Cathedral, where an old man with a flock of goats provided an unexpectedly picturesque shot.

The first showing took place in Chicago, at the Presbyterian church at Oak Park. The moving pictures were included after the lecture as a fifteen-minute added attraction. "With the spontaneous outburst of applause that followed the first roll, we had the great satisfaction of feeling that it was a real success," wrote Depue, "which it proved to be during the rest of the season. As far as I know, these programs in the fall of 1897 marked the first time that motion pictures were used by any public lecturer in this country."[4]

After a tour of Hawaii, Holmes and Depue filmed the Hopi Indians' snake dance at Oraibi, Grand Canyon, which they claimed as the first motion pictures of such a ceremony. Depue returned the following year, and projected his films for the Indians. "One of the pictures showed a storekeeper of the post who had since died. There was a shout from the Indians when they saw him and his dog on the screen. The 'magic' of the movies made fans of them very quickly, and the next time I wanted to film their games, I had no trouble in obtaining the assistance of the whole tribe. When the show was over, the audience was curious to know where the pictures came from; they touched the screen and looked behind it, but strangely enough paid no attention to the projector in the wagon."[5]

In 1901 Holmes and Depue embarked on a journey that took in Berlin, Warsaw, St. Petersburg, Moscow, and Siberia. They arrived at Pekin with the Boxer Rising freshly subdued. "It was an opportune time for our visit, because we were allowed, through the aid of our own troops, to see and film things which might not have been available to us otherwise."[6]

The 60 mm. camera was soon obsolete, and a 35 mm. Bioscope camera from Charles Urban's Warwick Trading Company in London replaced it. In 1903 they toured Alaska, a mere five years after the gold rush had started, filming the gold miners and their sluicing and hydraulic operations.

Burton Holmes managed to edge his pointed profile, with the sharp beard, into every one of his travelogues. But this was not mere vanity. It was his personal guarantee that what he was showing was real; he had been there himself, and this was his proof. Holmes was a sort of Baedeker of illuminated information.

Everest explorer Captain Noel remembered him with admiration: "He had a fabulous house in New York, with huge rooms, filled with Chinese temple ornaments. He had his own private film laboratories in Chicago,* and he had two women colorists who colored all his slides for him. He had two operators, and he used to do these whirlwind tours of America in all the big halls. He had his own circuit, his own management. He'd book the Orchestra Hall in Chicago; he had a motion picture projector of his own left in the hall, so he didn't have to transport it. He just carried the head and his films. He lectured to mass audiences, never less than two thousand; they paid two dollars a seat.

"He was a very fast speaker, and had a beautiful voice, which he synchronized perfectly to his films, and he'd show them on a huge screen. He never walked on the stage; he used to pull the curtain apart, and run on. The people clapped him and he talked rapidly, waving his arms about. Then the curtain would draw back and he'd slap the film on. A spotlight shone on him; it was very dramatic. He had five programs every winter which he'd made in the summertime. It was a marvelous bit of organization."[7]

Burton Holmes had been a platform personality for sixty-five years by the time he died, aged eighty-eight, in 1958.

---

* His lab, operated by Depue, was actually in his palatial apartment. Holmes cut and titled all his own films.

THE KOLB BROTHERS

My only encounter with one of these old-fashioned film and slide lectures occurred quite by chance, when my wife and I visited the Grand Canyon. Perched on the edge, like Chaplin's hut in *The Gold Rush,* was an old house containing the Kolb Brothers' Photographic Studio. Most of it was in use as a souvenir shop; over the entrance there was a sign: PHOTOGRAPHS MOTION PICTURES MAINLY U.S. GOVT TRIP THROUGH COLORADO RIVER BY BOAT 11:30 and 6:30.

Among the postcards and painted plates, I was surprised to find a 1914 publication entitled *Through the Grand Canyon from Wyoming to Mexico* by Ellsworth Kolb. Inside this book (reprinted for the seventeenth time in 1969) was an inscription by Ellsworth's ninety-year-old brother Emery.

A lady began canvassing for the motion picture show. "What sort of picture?" I asked, imagining a scratched, 16 mm. Kodachrome travelogue of 1949. "It's the film of the river trips by the Kolb brothers," she replied.

"When?" "1911, 1921, and 1923." That was all I needed to hear. My wife and I paid for tickets and went in to a large lecture hall, passing the projection box, fitted with lantern and Simplex 35 mm. projector. The hall was much like an early movie theater, with painted beams, a balcony, and an oblong screen. I have often been puzzled by pictures of old theaters showing screens of this shape, yet the reason was plain once the lecture began; it was for vertically framed slides.

Before long, Mr. Emery Kolb himself entered the theater, and in the declamatory tones that were once so much a part of the old travel talks, he announced: "Ladies and gentlemen. I generally narrate the motion pictures of our three river trips myself, but I have suffered an illness which has affected my voice. The story will therefore be told with loudspeaker. Thank you."

The lantern slide-projector was not equipped with the correct lamp for such a throw, and the glass slides, some of them hand-colored, were not as well defined as the motion picture, which had the raw sharpness of a print direct from an original negative. Filmically, one could find fault with the jump cuts and jerky pans, but the mere fact of carrying a heavy motion picture camera across mountains, down precipices, and through rapids transcended such aesthetic fastidiousness. The illustrated lecture was an extraordinarily vivid experience.

That evening, we met Mr. Kolb as he emerged from the evening show. He seemed quavery and uncertain at first, but once he understood what I wanted, he became rational and lucid. He answered questions helpfully and agreed to be photographed at his home the next day. "I worked on a shoestring," he said, pointing to his equipment. He opened a window at the side of the house, which gave him an ideal viewpoint for groups of tourists on mules descending the Bright Angel Trail. An old plate camera was aimed through the aperture, probably the same camera that accompanied the Kolbs when they arrived—among the first settlers in this Indian territory. It was held together with tape and operated with a bulb release. "It looks like a wreck," he said, sadly. He showed me his Akeley, which he had taken to Alaska in 1923 to shoot *The Valley of 10,000 Smokes.** I had to restrain

* Directed by Robert F. Griggs for the National Geographic Society.

Ellsworth Kolb running the rapids;
Emery filming him with Pathé camera.

him from swinging the heavy camera and tripod onto his shoulder to carry it outside for a photograph.

On the wall was a picture of Kolb as a first lieutenant in the Photographic Section of the Signal Corps in World War I. From his files he produced impressive pictures of the Colorado River trips. When they embarked upon the first, in 1911, this vicious, rapid-infested river had been negotiated only twice—and many deaths had resulted from ill-prepared attempts. As Emery Kolb said in his lecture, "The making and retaining of these pictures was almost equal to the work of the journey itself."

One of the most startling shots was made from a bucking boat as it hurtled through a rapid. Ellsworth Kolb wrote: "The two boats (*Edith* and *Defiant*) were fastened stern to stern, so that the rowing would be done from the first boat. My brother sat on the bow behind with the motion picture camera in front of him, holding it down with his chin, his legs clinging to the side of the boat, with his left hand clutching at the hatch cover, and with his right hand free to turn the crank. In this way we passed over two small rapids. After that one experience we never tried it in a large rapid. Emery had a great deal of difficulty to stay with the boat, to say nothing of taking a picture. Once or twice he was nearly unseated but pluckily hung on and kept turning away at the crank when it looked as if he and the camera would be dumped into the river."[1]

Emery explained that he was ill at the time: "My brother thought the best picture would be my expression."

The boats were damaged by storms, and sand—dangerous to intricate machinery—was beaten into their cameras, which were then filled with water and mud. The job of cleaning the equipment was endless.

In their hundred-and-one-day expedition, they passed frequent evidence of disaster to other river travelers. Although boats were seen, smashed and abandoned, more men starved in the attempt to navigate the Colorado than were lost by drowning, for the soaring canyon walls prevented landing and access to food. A picture that became famous when the Kolbs took their lecture across the United States was one of a half-clothed skeleton.

When shooting rapids, the motion picture camera acted as a kind of compensatory factor if an upset occurred, for the Kolbs were professional photographers, and a spectacular scene made up for much discomfort and danger. It was agreed that Emery would first of all film the wreck from the bank, then run to the lower end of the rapid with a rope and life-preserver. On one occasion, Ellsworth was thrown from the boat but clung to the gunwale. As he scrambled back into the cockpit, he noticed his brother, still at the camera, but white as a sheet, "turning at the crank as if our entire safety depended upon it."[2]

Mud and water could be cleaned, and the camera dried with an alcohol lamp. But when the brass tripod head was lost in Marble Canyon, the photographic results suffered. A hand-cranked camera cannot be operated effectively without a tripod, and it cannot be secured to the tripod without a head. Emery did what he could by supporting the camera on rocks, but the accident accounts for the jerky pans. At one point the camera was under water for an hour, and plates and film were always being subjected to frequent soakings. They tucked the precious film in the toes of their sleeping bags; somehow, most of it survived.

They interrupted their journey upon reaching home, the Bright Angel Trail at the Grand Canyon. Tourists cheered their welcome.

"On nearing the top our youngest brother, Ernest, came running down the trail to greet us. One member of a troupe of moving picture actors, in cowboy garb, remarked that we 'didn't look like moving-picture explorers.' "[3]

Perhaps influenced by the moving picture people, the Kolbs staged their own drama on the next phase of their journey, using some of the men helping them for the cast. It was a Western. "Dodd, a big Texan cowboy, was cast for the role of horse thief and bad man in general. Morris Lauzon was the deputy sheriff, and had a star cut from the top of a tomato can to prove it. Emery played a mining engineer, arriving on the scene in his boat."

The hidden desperado, on the run, made his escape in the engineer's boat. Little does he know that a second boat is in the area. A chase ensues, over the rapids. Emery Kolb was director, scenario writer, and star.

"The thrilling drama will not be released in the near future," wrote Ellsworth. "One day later we found that a drop of water had worked into the lens cell at the last upset. This fogged the lens. Nothing but a very faint outline showed on the film. We had all the film we needed for a week after this, for kindling our fires."[4]

HERBERT PONTING

Herbert Ponting was to the expedition film what Charles Rosher was to the feature picture—a photographer and cinematographer of unparalleled artistry. Captain Scott's Antarctic expedition of 1910–1913 was fortunate to have Ponting as official photographer, for his technical mastery and his highly developed sense of composition ensured that his work would live, to bring a kind of immortality to that tragic adventure.

As Captain Scott himself wrote: "The composition of his pictures is extraordinarily good; he seems to know by instinct the exact value of foreground and middle distance and of the introduction of 'life,' whilst with more technical skill he emphasises the subtle shadows of the snow and reproduces its wonderfully transparent texture. He is an artist in love with his work."[1]

An Englishman, Ponting resembled a successful banker rather than a great artist, which is ironic, for Ponting's father had actually been a successful banker and he fully intended that Herbert should follow suit. Herbert did his best, but after four years he acknowledged defeat. He set out for the West Coast of the United States, where he bought a ranch and became a partner in a gold mine. Although completely at home in America, he was cast in the mold of the British Empire: immensely patriotic, rather genteel, extremely courageous, utterly single-minded, and slightly pompous. He was never guilty of underestimating his own achievements, although he could be bitterly self-critical. The mock modesty with which his book, *The Great White South,* opens is characteristic: "Before going to the Far South with Captain Scott's South Pole Expedition, my life—save for six years' ranching and mining in Western America; a couple of voyages round the world; three years of travel in

Japan; some months as war correspondent with the First Japanese Army during the war with Russia; and in the Philippines during the American war with Spain; and save, too, for several years of travel in a score of other lands—had been comparatively uneventful."[2]

He took up photography seriously in 1900 and was immediately enamored of stereo-photography. He won major awards with his early pictures and was sent round the world by magazines and by such agencies as Underwood & Underwood. In an excellently researched biography, *Photographer of the World,* H. J. P. Arnold revealed that Ponting was so obsessive about his work that he abandoned his wife and two children, a fact that proved a source of melancholy in later years: "I could be walking down Oxford Street, with my son passing me, and with me not knowing that it was him."[3]

The Antarctic expedition was his finest hour, and the film that resulted—a version of which is still in circulation—was inspiring in every sense.* His association with the expedition occurred by accident. Ponting had met a young man named Cecil Meares in 1905. Meares's favorite topic was polar travel and, because of his infectious enthusiasm, Ponting took Scott's book *Voyage of the Discovery* on a journey he made across Russia in 1907. When Scott began to form his party, Meares volunteered and introduced Ponting to Captain Scott in 1909.

Like all those who came into contact with Scott, Ponting was deeply struck by the force of the man and by his warmth and humor. His book is careful to praise every member of the expedition, but he reserves his most spontaneous affection for Captain Scott and his right-hand man, Dr. Wilson. Although his book is written in the mannered style of the travel talk, the final section on the deaths in the polar party achieves an epic quality and is profoundly moving.

Ponting took two moving picture cameras with him: a Prestwich, which is now in the Science Museum in London, and a Newman Sinclair, specially adapted by Arthur Newman from a No. 3 model.

The expedition ship, the *Terra Nova,* set out from the London docks for the first leg of the journey, to Australia and New Zealand, in June 1910. Ponting had many preparations to complete, and he joined the ship at Lyttleton, where he was horrified to discover that some of his equipment had been damaged by water. It sustained a further battering during storms in which Ponting was injured, his darkroom flooded, and some of the Siberian ponies killed. The sailors had suffered even more than Ponting. "In the vocabulary of the forecastle," he observed, sociologically, "I detected a strong affinity to the vernacular of the American gold-miners and cowboys, with which, in my 'Out West' days, my ears had not been unfamiliar. It was like the voice of an old friend."[4]

Eager to film the bow of the *Terra Nova* slicing through the pack ice, Ponting had a camera platform rigged up. This consisted of planks, jutting out ten feet from the starboard side of the ship. "Spreadeagling myself on the end of these planks, I had a field of view clear under the overhanging prow. As the ship bumped into the floes, I hung on as best I could, and with one arm clung tightly to my precious camera lest it should break loose and fall into the sea, whilst with the other hand I turned the handle. Fortunately, no mishap occurred; and the result—showing the

---

* *90° South* is available on hire from the Distribution Library of the British Film Institute.

Herbert Ponting and Prestwich camera, 1910.

Herbert Ponting, on a specially constructed camera platform, filming the Terra Nova *breaking the ice, 1910.*

One of Ponting's marvelous pictures: Captain Oates (later to die on the expedition) and his ponies, on the Terra Nova.

ironshod stem of the ship splitting and rending the broken ice into the foaming sea —proved to be one of the most thrilling of all the moving-picture records of the Expedition."[5]

Ponting was confined to his bunk by seasickness for two days, after which he proceeded with his work as though he had recovered. Captain Scott's dairy made it plain he had not: "Ponting cannot face meals, but sticks to his work. . . . I am told that he posed several groups before the cinematograph, though obliged repeatedly to retire to the ship's side. Yesterday, he was developing plates with the developing dish in one hand and an ordinary basin in the other!"[6]

Scott appreciated the value of the moving picture records, regarding them as one of the most important aspects of the expedition, but instead of passing the Great Ice Barrier slowly and closely, as had been arranged for the benefit of the camera, he steamed rapidly away from this "eighth wonder of the world." The ship had been so delayed by pack ice that Scott had no alternative. Ponting, who had sacrificed everything for his art, felt the schedule should be sacrificed too. "In the hope of illustrating it, so that others may see it too, I had come over more than a third of the circumference of the globe."[7]

Once the party had landed, Ponting was startled by the sight of eight killer whales. He ran forward as they dived under the ice, adjusting his 5 x 7 reflex, when the ice heaved violently beneath him, and the killer whales reappeared. The episode would be highly suspect were it not for the fact that Captain Scott witnessed it, and wrote an identical account in his diary. "The head of one was within two yards of me," wrote Ponting. "I saw its nostrils open and at such close quarters the release of its pent-up breath was like a blast from an air compressor. The noise of eight simultaneous blows sounded terrific, and I was enveloped in the warm vapour of the nearest 'spout' which had a strong fishy smell. Fortunately, the shock sent me backwards instead of precipitating me into the sea."[8]

The whales caused such a commotion that the floe on which Ponting was standing began to rock furiously, and the whales moved to the attack. Like a nightmare from *Way Down East,* Ponting jumped from floe to floe, struggling toward the ship, sixty yards away. "As I reached the last fragment, I saw that I could not jump to the firm ice, for the lead [gap] was too wide. The whales behind me were making a horrible noise amongst the broken ice, and I stood for a moment, hesitating what to do. More frantic shouts of 'Jump, man, jump!' reached me from my friends. Just then, by great good luck, the floe on which I stood turned slightly in the current and lessened the distance. I was able to leap across. As I reached security and looked back, a huge black and tawny head was pushed out of the water and rested on the ice, looking round with its little pig-like eyes to see what had become of me. I saw the terrible teeth which I had so narrowly escaped."[9]

Captain Scott considered this "the nearest squeak I ever saw." Watching Ponting at work and learning the craft of photography himself, Scott made the remark: "This photographing is the coldest job I have ever struck, as well as the most risky."[10]

The Antarctic was peculiarly hostile to photography. Ponting was not only attacked by whales and seals, he was dive-bombed by skua gulls, and so badly injured by one blow that he was convinced he had lost an eye. Threading the motion picture camera in the open was like juggling with nitro-glycerine, for whenever his fingers touched metal they were instantly frostbitten. "On another occasion, my tongue came into contact with a metal part of one of my cameras, whilst moistening my lips as I was focussing. It froze fast instantaneously; and to release myself I had to jerk it away, leaving the skin on the end of my tongue sticking to the camera, and my mouth bled so profusely that I had to gag it with a handkerchief."[11]

Ponting's patience was inexhaustible. But after waiting motionless for hours in temperatures of minus thirty degrees, hoping for a skua gull to steal a penguin's egg, he gave up. "I finally decided that the incident would have to be 'produced'—just as any drama film is produced—and the various characters concerned would have to be *made* to play their parts."[12] He removed the penguin and tied it up, and in a few minutes the skua gull swooped at the eggs. But as soon as the handle turned, and the machine began to crank, the gull flew away. Ponting kept his hand moving, as though cranking, and eventually, the skua gull's greed overcame its fear. He vowed to have a noiseless camera constructed when he returned home.

It was not enough for Ponting to be a brilliant photographer; with so much of scientific value depending on the results, the knowledge of what to photograph was almost more important than how to photograph it. During the dark winter months in the hut, Captain Scott organized lectures, with each specialist explaining his role in the operation and enlightening the others on his particular branch of science. For Ponting, who surprised and delighted everyone by producing a lantern and five hundred slides, these lectures were the equivalent of a high-pressure university course. When daylight returned and he was able to film again, he went to great lengths to provide cinematographic proof of certain animal habits which had been discussed, but for which no one had recorded evidence.

Wrote Captain Scott: "Ponting would have been a great asset to our party if only on account of his lectures, but his value as pictorial recorder of events becomes daily more apparent. No expedition has ever been illustrated so extensively, and the only difficulty will be to select from the countless subjects that have been recorded by his camera—and yet not a single subject is treated with haste; the first picture is rarely good enough, and in some cases five or six plates are exposed before our very critical artist is satisfied."[13]

In the final race to the Pole, Captain Scott, with four companions, experienced worsening conditions; their tractors failed miserably, heavy snow made progress almost impossible, snow-blindness and crevasses were a constant danger. But to Scott, their arrival at the Pole was certain—"the only appalling possibility the sight of the Norwegian flag forestalling ours." Roald Amundsen, the Norwegian explorer and first man to navigate the Northwest Passage, had set sail for the North Pole, but upon hearing of the British expedition, he had turned his ship southward.*

After all they had endured, the word "disappointment" hardly describes the reaction of Scott's party as they approached the Pole to discover the remains of the Norwegian camp and a note from Amundsen. Scott planted the Union Jack, and Lieutenant Bowers took a photograph by remote control, so that all five men were in the picture. Then they started upon the return, described as "The Worst Journey

---

* Amundsen also regarded motion pictures as a vital element of exploration, and he delegated his brother Leon to film the expedition (*Moving Picture World,* 29 November 1913, p. 997).

Ponting's breathtaking picture of the Terra Nova from an ice cave

Herbert Ponting filming skua gulls, some of which attacked and injured him.

Another of Ponting's beautiful photographs of the Antarctic.

in the World." Incredibly, under such conditions, Captain Scott kept a diary—in itself an extraordinary achievement. It told of the gradual disintegration of each member of the party through frostbite and snow-blindness. It told of the death of the man they most depended on, Petty Officer Evans. In sixty to eighty degrees of frost, with gale upon gale causing them to lose their way, the daily marches averaged a pitiful five miles, whereas thirteen was essential. Captain Oates, suffering agonies with frostbitten feet, walked from the tent into a blizzard, with the remark, "I am just going outside, and may be some time." But even this self-sacrifice did not save the others. Frostbite seized each in turn: "Amputation is the least I can hope for now," wrote Scott, "but will the trouble spread?" They struggled on, knowing there was no hope: "We shall march for the depot, and die in our tracks." Only eleven miles from a depot of food and fuel, the party perished. Scott's final entry in his notebook showed deep anxiety for the families they were leaving behind: "Had we lived, I should have had a tale to tell of the hardihood, endurance and courage of my companions which would have stirred the heart of every Englishman. These rough notes and our dead bodies must tell the tale, but surely, surely, a great rich country like ours will see that those who are dependent upon us are properly provided for. R. Scott."[14]

THE GAUMONT COMPANY, UNDER its agreement with the expedition, showed Ponting's film in 1913 as *The Undying Story of Captain Scott.* In 1914 Ponting purchased all rights to it for more than £5,000, presenting it, with slides and his lecture, at the Philharmonic Hall in London. In May 1914 Ponting gave a Royal Command Performance of his lecture at Buckingham Palace. At the outbreak of war, he offered his services to both the War Office and the Foreign Office but was told that his lectures were of great value to the nation and he should continue his work. A set of the films was sent to France in 1915; they were shown to 100,000 officers and men. Wrote the senior chaplain to the forces: "The splendid story of Captain Scott is just the thing to cheer and encourage out here. . . . The thrilling story of Oates' self-sacrifice, to try and give his friends a chance of 'getting through,' is one that appeals so at the present time. The intensity of its appeal is realised by the subdued hush and quiet that pervades the massed audiences of troops while it is being told. We all feel we have inherited from Oates and his comrades a legacy and heritage of inestimable value in seeing through our present work. We all thank you with grateful hearts."[15]

A second series of lectures in 1917, also held at the Philharmonic Hall, was a heartbreaking failure. "Since Xmas," wrote Ponting, "I have had to close six nights as no one came."[16] The silent film was re-edited and shown as *The Great White Silence,* and re-edited once more and released with sound in 1933 as *90° South.* The ill-fated journey was not, of course, covered by Ponting's camera; he resorted to diagrams and animated maps. But the arrival at Ross Island and the kind of life led by the expedition is celebrated by Ponting with a graphic excellence rare in early films of fact. His achievement is all the more remarkable since he had virtually no previous experience with moving pictures. Ponting's still camera captures the clouds and the effect of light glistening upon ice; he reserves his moving pictures for scenes of movement—Siberian ponies, released from the ship, rolling in delight upon the ice . . . penguins, and their ceaseless battle with skua gulls . . .

seals and their fight with killer whales . . . hundred-foot waves thundering in natural slow motion against towering ice cliffs. We glimpse comparatively little serious scientific work (this was covered by still pictures and flashlight, as Ponting lacked motion picture lighting); the atmosphere is that of a grand outing with highly congenial company. The tragic end to the expedition is all the more poignant after we have seen a little sequence, shot at base, of Scott and Oates pretending to make camp, squeezing into their sleeping bags, unable to suppress their amusement at acting for Ponting's camera. Ponting remembered Scott's remark upon this occasion, "What fun it'll be when we're home again and see this at the cinema."

Ponting was older than most members of the expedition. The remainder of his life was haunted by business failure and an unequal struggle with the film industry. He died in 1935.

"The Kinematograph, properly applied, is the greatest educational contrivance ever conceived by the genius of man," he wrote. "In it, the art of photography finds its highest mission."[17]

CHERRY KEARTON

Through his books, photographs, and prolific wildlife films, Cherry Kearton became a sort of official guide and adventurer to a whole generation.

Born in 1871, in Yorkshire, he joined his brother Richard in Fleet Street at the age of fourteen, forced to work by the death of his father. As soon as his wages as office boy had amounted to enough, he bought a secondhand camera and, as his brother put it, "speedily began to produce the usual atrocities of the juvenile amateur photographer."[1] In 1892 the Keartons were invited to spend the day with some Yorkshire friends who were living near Enfield. Cherry took his camera with him, and when Richard pointed out the nest of a song thrush, he took great care in photographing it. The result was so striking that Richard, an ornithologist, was converted to the importance of photography and decided the two of them would embark on a book, *British Birds' Nests,* to be illustrated with their own photographs.

The Kearton brothers went about their work in England as though exploring in Africa. Birds' nests were situated in inaccessible places, therefore trees had to be climbed and cliffs scaled. To give himself the advantage, Cherry Kearton became a proficient gymnast and won the National Physical Society's Bronze Medal. On the bird sanctuary island of St. Kilda, his death-defying climbs on the giant cliffs alarmed even the inhabitants, who were considered among the finest cragsmen of the world. Although a heavily built man, he had a phenomenal head for heights and was as nimble-footed as a goat.

"One of the very narrowest escapes from death my brother has perhaps ever had also illustrates his coolness in face of imminent danger," wrote Richard Kearton. "We required a series of moving pictures to illustrate our methods when engaged in photographing the eyries of birds which breed in inaccessible situations, and I

Cherry Kearton during the making of Dassan *(1930).*

Teddy Roosevelt conferring with Cherry Kearton (1909).

was therefore lowered with a kinematograph camera to a ledge, which commanded a good view of him on his perilous journey. When he had walked backwards over the edge of the escarpment, and descended some twenty or thirty feet, I was horror-stricken to observe a lump of rock almost as large as a man's head slip out of its position high above, and shoot straight down towards him. It missed his face by a hair's breadth, and, pursuing its mad career downwards, broke into a thousand fragments on the great boulders far below. I was so overcome by the sight that for a moment I ceased to breathe and to turn the handle of the kinematograph camera, but, so far as I could see, my brother neither turned a hair, nor changed colour, and, in comparing notes after the incident, he teased me unmercifully, and wound up by saying: 'Call yourself a photographer! Why, you missed the very feature that would have made the picture valuable as a record of the dangers of cliff work.' "[2]

A certain *Boy's Own Paper* exuberance lay behind some of these feats of daring, and it was only natural that before long, Kearton should find himself retracing the footsteps of his boyhood heroes in Africa, Ceylon, Borneo, and India. He also traveled to America, where his characteristic good luck protected him on more than one occasion. He booked a passage on the last voyage of the *Titanic,* but was forced by last-minute business to cancel the trip. Returning from filming in the Rocky Mountains, a minor informality on his ticket prevented him from taking a train that was wrecked with great loss of life.

Any account of Kearton's activities will necessarily stress the enormous risks he took—because these are what he emphasized in his books. In a sense, the experience was more important to him than the result, for while his chronicles are full of disappointment over lost slides and ruined film, the memory was nonetheless an immense compensation. "By merely closing my eyes and calling up the old memories, I can see again every detail of the scenery. It is quite unnecessary for me to look at my photographs."

Kearton was convinced that in the tropics to delay the developing of exposed film was an invitation to disaster. He was therefore obliged to carry with him the necessary chemicals and apparatus. "Once the light has been on it, all sorts of chemical actions and reactions take place. It is better to use the roughest and most inconvenient of dark rooms than to wait."[3]

Working in Borneo, in a makeshift darkroom underneath a house, he was forced to leave some space uncurtained because of the stifling heat. Constant flashes of lightning intermittently fogged much of his film; at such times, Kearton's self-imposed rule must have seemed idiosyncratic, even eccentric. Experience has shown that tropical conditions demand special packing, for film can be affected by condensation. But developing in a half-built darkroom in the midst of a thunderstorm is hardly an answer to the problem.

Kearton's films were valuable from many points of view. One of his most devoted fans was Theodore Roosevelt, for Kearton had filmed his 1909 expedition. Roosevelt invited the brothers to the White House, and supported Cherry Kearton on his American tour. Kearton was a pioneer in the field of natural-history cinematography, and he made many fascinating documentaries. But one senses that he was not at heart an artist. He was excited by photography more than anything else because it provided evidence of his adventures and perpetuated his reputation as a daring explorer. "Nothing can be more splendid than to see the pictures come out sharp, unspotted, an actual record of an exciting moment, infinitely more convincing than a word-picture can ever be; and nothing is more dreary than to find in some developing tank foot after foot of absolutely worthless stuff, and to know that you cannot spare the time to go back and try again, and that, even if there were the time, the opportunity would probably not recur."[4]

In 1909, in the company of James L. Clark of the American Museum of Natural History, he went on a photographic safari in Kenya. It was a punishing ordeal. Kearton had spent one day in excruciating discomfort, attempting to film hippos while ants crawled over every part of his anatomy; eventually he had given up in disgust. Returning to camp along the river bank, he spotted a leopard, half-hidden by overhanging leaves, crouching by the water's edge. The animal did not seem aware of Kearton's presence. As he feverishly set up his camera, the leopard sprang out on the bough and climbed down to the level of the stream. "When he was well out on the bough, he began to make a most peculiar noise, at the same time striking downwards with his paw. Then I discovered the reason for his action. In the water was a dead hippo, or rather, the putrid remains of one. All round it were crocodiles, and the leopard was trying to drive them off while he got his share.

"It was a wonderful chance for me. I secured some fifty feet of film of it without the least difficulty. Then Clark came up and I pointed the leopard out to him. I shall never forget the look of astonishment on his face. At first he could only stare. As he said later, he had spent nine months up there in quest of wild animals, and during that time had never seen a leopard come out into the open. The animal went on with his fishing—I suppose he was starving. I continued to turn the handle until I had used up all the film in the machine. Even then we remained watching him for some time longer.

"Needless to say, I was excited about my pictures, and as soon as I got into camp, I started to develop them. To my horror, however, the test pieces simply fogged off in patches, with little bits of the leopard visible here and there. I had had the chance of a lifetime, of ten lifetimes, perhaps, yet the whole film was valueless. It was terribly hard luck."[5]

Kearton wastes little space in his narratives complaining about the cumbersome apparatus he was condemned to use in 1909. But he does remark, with admirable sang-froid, that it was not a simple matter to move noiselessly, stalking lions, with a seventy-pound camera slung over your shoulder.

"Without boasting unduly, I may say that the naturalist-photographer usually takes infinitely greater risks, and certainly displays infinitely greater skill and patience, than does the pseudo-sportsman. It is much easier, much less dangerous, to shoot a lion, after your boys have led you up to him, and your white hunter—who is by your side, ready for emergencies—has given you explicit instructions, than it is to creep close to that lion and take a moving picture of him."[6]

Kearton shared with the greatest naturalists that all-important quality of patience—a quality which has to be supported by a certain amount of fanaticism. Discovering a water hole that attracted vast numbers of animals, he built himself a blind. It had to be large enough to conceal him and his camera, but it could not impose itself suddenly on the familiar landscape. It had to be constructed at the rate of a foot a day, so that the animals grew accustomed to it. Elephants, who create the water holes in the first place, were instantly aware of Kearton's handiwork and ripped it to shreds every night, scattering the blind in all directions. Kearton began again, and discovered that if he threw wet sand over each stage of the construction, the elephants left it alone; they were unable to scent the human involvement.

"At one water-hole, I waited in hiding for my 'sitters' exactly thirty days, and the picture I show on the screen does not occupy more than thirty seconds. The heat was unbearable, and when a couple of days had gone by, I felt like an old man of seventy and had to take a rest. The rays of the sun have a terrible racking effect on the system, but luckily you do not think of the torture when you are expecting to get a good picture."[7]

The natives involved in these photographic safaris were nonplussed by what seemed to them their utter futility. Hunting tigers in India, Kearton's determination to secure a powerful shot put himself and his companions at enormous risk. "I gave the beaters the signal to start, and awaited events. Soon I knew the tiger was coming. Moreover, it was evident that he was in a furious rage at having been disturbed. Just as he got near me, he gave one of those terrible coughs which the Indian hunter knows so well, the real danger-sign. I was turning the handle then, and in my moving pictures the brute can be seen looking at the lens and quivering with fury."

The tiger passed Kearton's blind with a growl and disappeared into the jungle. The game ranger emerged, bathed in perspiration, declaring he would not go through the same thing again for a thousand pounds. Kearton and he were discussing their next moves with the native spearmen when a violent and appalling cough, emitted by the tiger, sent them rapidly up the nearest tree.

"For my part, I was well satisfied. But the boys were far from pleased. They were not in the least degree interested in photographs, whilst they had a hereditary hatred of the tiger. I shall never forget the disgust with which they regarded the camera. They had expected it to rain leaden bullets into the enemy, and lo! it appeared to have done nothing. Yet I had closed it up again, and was obviously satisfied with the result of my foolishness. Their opinion of me had now gone to zero. I had risked my life out of mere childish curiosity, they decided."[8]

Kearton's attitude toward the natives was standard among British colonials of the time. He treated them, as he thought, fairly, and when they stepped out of line they were severely punished. He saw nothing paradoxical in his praise for British colonial achievement—"Nowhere in the world has the British Government done more splendid work than in Southern India"[9]—and his contempt for the poverty that surrounded him there. He was a successful pupil of Victorian propaganda: "With the exception of the Latins, all the Great Men came from the British Isles. The really big things are ours."[10] His chauvinism was not even dented by his trip to America, although he was charmed by the Americans he encountered. But he had no sympathy for the original inhabitants of the continent.

"The Red Indian had to go, of course. His is one of the races which simply cannot live side by side with the white man. No amount of legislation or care would have preserved him for long. Really, he was out-of-date, doomed, when the first settler began to build his log hut."[11] But game, he felt, was different. He con-

Colonel Charles "Buffalo" Jones, who brought Western methods to Africa for a film. (*From* Moving Picture World)

sidered it a scandalous waste of national wealth that a host of species should have been wiped out.

"Last year I travelled from Cape Colony right up into the Congo, and although I was on the look-out all the way, did not see half a dozen animals throughout a journey of hundreds of miles. Fifteen years ago, I journeyed from Mombasa to Nairobi and was so excited that I could not sit still, for on both sides of the railway right up to within fifty yards of the train game of every description abounded."[12] The destruction of game Kearton blamed not only on the activities of the settler and the hunter but on a type of photographic expedition that, while ostensibly forwarding the interests of natural history, was as deadly as the regular big game hunt.

On his journey through Canada in 1911, he wondered how many animals he might have seen had he followed the same route fifty years earlier. "A tally of them would certainly have run into thousands. As it was, I saw ten or twelve moose and many, many dams where, on former days, the poor little beaver had worked so hard and so patiently to build his home, and had been rewarded by having the poacher mark him down and wipe out him and his whole family."[13]

The object of the Canadian trip was to secure moving pictures of moose. Kearton was so excited when he finally glimpsed a moose through the viewfinder of his new Aeroscope that he stood up to get a better view. Such an action was normally problem-free, for the Aeroscope operated without a cumbersome tripod. But on this occasion, Kearton was standing in a canoe. "When I came to develop the film, I found a few feet with the moose on it, quite nicely; then the moose seemed to turn skywards, and after that everything appeared to be going round in a circle. The end was darkness. I had lost my balance, and landed in the lake with a mighty splash. Still, I had not lost my head, but had retained my grip on the camera, and had scrambled back into the canoe with it."[14]

Kearton received cooperation from the State Department when he arrived in the United States, although the telegram to the regular troops stationed in the country's first National Park, Yellowstone, was somewhat ambiguous; Kearton was apparently coming to *fake* natural history photographs. At Yellowstone, Kearton worked with Colonel Charles Jones, known as Buffalo Jones, and famous for his experiment with the cattalo, a cross between a cow and a buffalo, with which he intended to populate the plains. Kearton's most remarkable exploit was the Kearton-Jones expedition. One of the abortive 1930s film projects of the team that was to make *King Kong*—Cooper, Schoedsack, and Willis O'Brien—was a picture about cowboys rounding up big game in Africa.* Kearton put this idea into practice in 1911, although he had but two New Mexican cowboys, Loveless and Means, under the command of Colonel Jones. Said Roosevelt: "They make my own efforts look like thirty cents."[15]

If the native carriers in India had doubted Kearton's sanity for attacking a tiger with a harmless box, the men on this expedition were convinced of his madness. They just gazed at the proceedings with resignation. They watched the cowboys, wearing solar topees instead of Stetsons, thundering after such animals as wart hogs, roping them with expertise, and dragging them before the camera. Once photographed the animals were released. The natives, disgusted by the waste of meat, were not at all pleased to be aiding such a foolish enterprise.

A lioness sparked the most dramatic confrontation. Remembering the use that the great hunter F. C. Selous made of dogs in lion hunting, Kearton did the same. Forced by the pack of dogs to move from concealment, the lioness raced over to an opening in some rocks, where she stood at bay. Kearton managed to get some scraps of film at close quarters, but the cowboys could not maneuver their horses near enough to use their ropes. Buffalo Jones, as a last resort, decided to slip a noose over her by means of a pole, but the lioness surprised her pursuers once more, raced across the veldt, and stood among some scrub on the bank of a small spruit. She was tired, and angry. In this interval, Kearton managed to move his camera and adjust the lens. One of the cowboys, Means, moved forward with immense care, his rope at the ready.

"Before he could throw it, she seemed to realise her danger. With mouth open, she was at him. For a moment, it was touch and go whether he could avoid her, but he managed to gain a few yards. Instantly she saw that the first man had escaped, she swung round and directed her attention to Jones. But he, too, evaded her, and in savage disgust, she abandoned these tactics, and took up her position at the foot of a thorn tree. All this time I had been turning the handle of my machine, recording the whole incident on the film. It was an amazing opportunity, and I was well repaid for all the previous disappointments."[16]

She was now in a more vulnerable position for the cowboys; one kept her attention by shouting and swinging his rope while the other crept closer. The noose fell over her neck, but the lioness skillfully slipped out of this and the next throw before racing off to a more secure hiding place.

"It was here that we finally got her. Whilst I brought my camera up to within twenty yards Loveless threw his rope so that the noose rested on the grass above her head, while he passed the other end over the branch of a thorn tree. Then,

---

* Elements were incorporated into *Mighty Joe Young.*

as coolly as though he were trying to catch a sheep, Jones went forward, a long stick in his hand, and from the bank above, pushed the noose down on the lioness.

"Naturally, she sprang at him, but was caught by the noose, and after one of the most exciting struggles that white men were ever engaged in with a savage beast, she was captured, caged, and sent to the Bronx Park Zoological Gardens, New York. It was a unique and wonderful piece of work, requiring unstinted skill and pluck on the part of the cowboys."[17]

In 1913 Kearton's films were presented before an invited audience at the Playhouse in New York, under the aegis of Adolph Zukor, who later presented them publicly. The showing was introduced by Teddy Roosevelt, who described his intense interest in moving pictures of big game.

"In moving pictures of wild life," said Roosevelt, "there is a great temptation to fake, and the sharpest discrimination must be employed in order to tell the genuine from the spurious. My attention was particularly directed toward Mr. Kearton's work because of its absolute honesty. If he takes a picture it may be guaranteed as straight. With regard to the pictures of the Masai warriors I can personally vouch for their fidelity to the actuality. His views of the charging lion, in which several natives are trampled and torn by the infuriated beast, are wonderful—really wonderful! It is a really phenomenal record of a really phenomenal feat, and I congratulate Mr. Kearton with all my heart on what he has done."[18]

Kearton was a stubborn eccentric, and to that characteristic we owe some of his more startling material. For a scientist he had some odd shortcomings; he believed in mermaids—he claimed to have seen one in a New York Museum—and accepted the existence of fairies. But his ornithological books, *British Birds' Nests* (with Richard Kearton; London: Cassell, 1898) and *Our Rarer British Breeding Birds* (London: Cassell, 1900), became standard works. His other books were popularly styled, breezily written, and responsible for sparking an interest in natural history among thousands of people who were young in the first two decades of the century. The influence of his films was equally far-reaching, and his strictures against the unnecessary killing of animals were a vital part of these films, even if the most thrilling scenes were the most barbarous.

"It is as a naturalist that I view the wanton slaughter of game with such abhorrence. I have travelled across the world to secure photographic records of wild animals at home, and my work has been a labour of love. That men and women of this and future generations may share the pleasures I have enjoyed I raise my voice with all its force against the wicked and wanton destruction of big game, and if through my books, still pictures and films the public can gain a wider knowledge of the animal creation, and consequently a deeper sympathy, I shall be satisfied."[19]

LOWELL THOMAS

The career of Lowell Thomas is so multifaceted that to describe his work in terms of motion pictures alone does him less than justice; it is like filling an atlas with just one map. His is a voice inescapably associated with American broadcasting,

Lowell Thomas, with Sudanese bearer, during the Palestine campaign, 1918.

from the very beginning to the present. He holds a wide variety of records for his work in newsreels, journalism, television, on the platform, and in publishing.

Lowell Thomas, a true Westerner, was born in 1892; his father, a doctor, set up his practice in the gold-mining town of Cripple Creek, on the slopes of Pike's Peak, Colorado.* His Sunday School teacher was, incredibly, Texas Guinan, later a vaudeville entertainer, then a Western movie star, and most celebrated as Queen of the Speakeasies in the Prohibition era. His first job on leaving college was in the mines; he also did some cowpunching on his father's ranch. He then moved into the newspaper world.

Lowell Thomas's parents did not regard moving pictures as a vital part of their son's education, and he saw comparatively few before starting to make them himself. Thomas remembers little of his first pictures; he took two trips to Alaska, in 1914 and 1915, operating his own Ernemann camera. Russel Crouse, in the *Reader's Digest,* described Thomas persuading a gold rush survivor to shoot Miles Canyon and Whitehorse rapids as he had done in '98, with Lowell Thomas for a passenger, and being scared to death when he did it.[1]

"On those early trips to Alaska," said Lowell Thomas, "when I carried that rather heavy movie camera and tried to do the filming myself, I never did become too adept. The threading was complicated, and the thing frequently jammed. I came to the conclusion that the intelligent thing would be to hire the most competent cameraman available, and then direct him."[2]

For a time, Thomas hoped to follow in the footsteps of Burton Holmes. But while Holmes took his audiences to places where travelers normally go, Thomas was more interested in remote parts of the world, where travelers seldom go. "Each of my journeys was an expedition, not a tourist trip."

Shortly before the United States entered World War I, Thomas became acquainted with a member of the Wilson cabinet. "At the time I was on the faculty of Princeton University, and spending my weekends presenting illustrated talks about Alaska in nearby cities. Mr. Wilson's Secretary of the Interior was a Westerner, a man of imagination by the name of Franklin K. Lane. Mr. Lane had heard me on Alaska, and had asked me to head what he called a 'See America First' campaign, the idea being now that Europe was off-limits, to arouse the American people, get them interested in the wonders of the West—Yosemite, Yellowstone, the Grand Canyon, the Pacific Northwest, and so on.

"But when we became involved in World War One, he called me to Washington and told me he thought it was a poor time to talk about 'the quiet charms of nature' and asked if I would be willing to take a cameraman or two abroad, cover as much of the war in Europe as possible, then return to America and help arouse our people. The Americans at that time were not too enthusiastic about the war, largely because President Wilson had promised they would not be involved.

"Secretary Lane introduced me to two other Cabinet members, Newton D. Baker, Secretary for War, and Josephus Daniels, Secretary of the Navy. Through them, and with the help of President Wilson and his Director of Information, George Creel, I was given papers to pave our way when we arrived in Europe. But

* The Pike's Peak gold rush was in 1858. The area was relatively seldom seen on the screen, but Universal made *The Ranger of Pike's Peak* on location in 1919.

first it was necessary for me to raise the money for the undertaking, privately—which I did. I also married a Denver girl [Fran Ryan], and off we went to the war, on our honeymoon.

"With us was an unusually able cameraman, Harry A. Chase, of East Orange, New Jersey. Harry, a man of wide experience, had originally been a still photographer. From then on, for some years, we worked as a team. While my bride joined the Red Cross in Italy, looking after refugees driven out of Venice, Chase and I went from one battle front to another.

"First we were with the Allied forces in Belgium, then for a time in France, and on the Italian front. One day when we came in from the lagoons outside Venice where the Allies were attempting to hold back the onrushing Austrian and German armies, on a sandbag in front of the great cathedral of St. Mark, I read a bulletin announcing that the British had appointed a new Commander-in-Chief to succeed a general who had not been too successful in the Near East. The name of the new man was Sir Edmund Allenby. I knew something of Allenby's record on the Western Front, also as a cavalry leader in the Boer War. With him now in command in the Near East, I correctly guessed that major developments might soon occur out there."

Thomas sent a lengthy telegram to the Foreign Office in London, explaining what he was doing and asking for permission to join Allenby. The request was handed over to Colonel John Buchan, head of the Department of Information, who approved the scheme. "I suppose the greatest stroke of good luck that ever came my way was when I was allowed to join Allenby, and soon after had the rare good fortune of being the only observer attached to Lawrence and the Arabian Army. Undoubtedly, that was a major turning point in my career."[3]

T. E. LAWRENCE WAS THE most enigmatic figure of his time, and his exploits are clouded by romance. This handsome, twenty-nine-year-old colonel dressed in Arab robes and swept through the desert on a camel, at the head of an Arab army, dynamiting Turkish troop trains. Recommended for almost every award the Allies had to offer, including the Victoria Cross, Lawrence shrank into the background. He was petrified by publicity. "We saw considerable of Colonel Lawrence in Arabia," explained Thomas, "and although he arranged for us to get both 'still' and motion pictures of Emir Feisal, Auda Abu Tayi and other Arab leaders, he would turn away when he saw the lens pointing in his direction. We got more pictures of the back of his kuffieh than of his face. But after much strategy, and using all the artifices that I had learned as a reporter on a Chicago newspaper, where it was worth one's job to fail to bring back a photograph of the fair lady involved in the latest scandal, I finally maneuvered Lawrence into allowing Chase to take a 'sitting shot' on two different occasions. Then while I kept Colonel Lawrence's attention away from Mr. Chase by keeping up a rapid fire of questioning regarding our projected trip to the 'lost city' of Petra, which he believed to be the primary object of our visit to Arabia, Mr. Chase hurriedly took a dozen pictures from as many different angles."[4]

The very unconventionality of Lawrence's behavior cast him irrevocably in the role of Eccentric British Hero, and his military exploits were so successful that Lowell Thomas characterized him as "Britain's modern Coeur de Lion," in the

Colonel T. E. Lawrence—"Lawrence of Arabia"—photographed by Lowell Thomas's cameraman, Harry Chase (1918).

mold of Raleigh, Drake, Clive, and Gordon. But historians are sharply divided over his desert campaign; the accepted explanation for his postwar retreat was that he felt the Arabs had been betrayed by the peace treaties. Revisionists claim he knowingly betrayed the Arabs, and it was for atonement that he sought monk-like seclusion.

"Near the end of the desert campaign, and when we left the Near East, the war on the Western Front was still in progress. So we had time to see more of what was going on there, this time mainly with the American forces. Then, when the war in Europe came to a conclusion, obviously there was no longer any need for me to hurry home to help arouse my countrymen. So I stayed in Europe a little longer. All the world wanted to know what was going on in Central Europe. Rumors were coming through to the effect that the German people were starving,* also that communists were taking over. An able editor and journalist by the name of Webb Waldron (of *Colliers*) joined me, and after some rather wild adventures, including a night in a Swiss jail, we succeeded in getting through the Allied lines into Germany, where for some weeks we followed the German revolution. One of the leading German film companies of that era was known as UFA, and in Berlin I was able to get the cooperation of their cameramen. As a result of this, I brought back the first film record the world saw of events in Germany following the downfall of the Kaiser.

"Shortly after Christmas, 1919, I returned to America. But when a war ends people are searching for escape, and they want entertainment. They are not at all interested in hearing about the tragic days through which they have so recently lived. But I had a vast mass of material; what was I to do with it? Being young and somewhat naive, I went ahead and launched myself in New York at what was then the largest theater in Manhattan. Theater managers and owners were not a bit interested; nor were the heads of the motion picture companies. To them I was neither fish nor fowl. Therefore, I had to raise enough capital to rent a theater, and go it alone. All of which turned out to be quite an adventure.

"I had a series of five film productions; one of the American army in Europe, one on the Italian campaign, another entitled *With Allenby in Palestine,*† one that I called *With Lawrence in Arabia,* and *The German Revolution.* I soon discovered the public wasn't interested in the first two, but when I put on either my Allenby or my Lawrence show, I had packed houses. There were several reasons for this; Americans have always been interested in the Holy Land, and they had heard almost nothing about Allenby's campaign. Also, those productions included Biblical places, camels, veiled women, palm trees, Jerusalem, Bethlehem, deserts, Arabs, cavalry charges—and the story of a mysterious young hero named T. E. Lawrence, of whom no one had heard a word until I came back from the Near East.

"I had such a surprising success with these two shows that we finally moved from the huge Century Theater to the even more vast Madison Square Garden, one of the largest places of entertainment in America. On my final night, a famous

---

* The British blockade continued despite the armistice.

† The lecture was originally entitled *With Allenby in Palestine and the Conquest of Holy Arabia* (Phillip Knightley and Colin Simpson, *The Secret Lives of Lawrence of Arabia* [London: Penguin, 1975], p. 160).

British impresario, Percy Burton, dropped in. He had managed such famous stars as Sarah Bernhardt, Sir Johnston Forbes-Robertson, and Sir Herbert Beerbohm Tree. Impresario Burton just happened to hear me on my final night at Madison Square Garden. If he hadn't done so, who knows what my future might have been? He was stunned at what he saw and heard. Here I, an American, was telling a story about a great British hero, Lawrence of Arabia, of whose name he hadn't even heard. Right away he saw possibilities, and determined to lure me to London. However, I said that was impossible. Because of my New York success, by then I had booked myself on a tour of the U.S.A. from coast to coast, with deposits made on a series of dates.

"But as we talked it over, I jokingly said that maybe I could make a quick trip to London just for part of July and August. In those days, there was no air conditioning in auditoriums, and theaters in American cities closed down during the hot weather. For those few weeks, if he wanted me to do so, why I could go to London—but only if he would put me on in the most famous theater in the English-speaking world. Also if he would get an invitation from the King. I was just pulling his leg.

"Burton hurried over to London, and soon wired me he had succeeded in getting the invitation from the King. As for Drury Lane, it was booked, but he could get Covent Garden.

"When I left New York, I figured it would be impossible for either of us to make any money. I wouldn't be in London long enough. So I decided to do some experimenting. First, I combined my two productions, the one on Allenby and the one of Lawrence, and made them one show with an interval between. I also cabled Burton to line up the finest musical organization in the British Isles, which he did in style. He hired the Band of the Royal Welch Guards. In their bright scarlet uniforms, we put them on the stage for twenty minutes, while the audience was coming in. Then they were shifted to the pit, where for another ten minutes they played atmospheric Eastern music that my wife had arranged. When the lights went out something else happened that had never been done before. You remember a spectacular film called *The Covered Wagon*? They copied the thing we did with our Allenby-Lawrence show, when we launched it at the Royal Opera House, Covent Garden, and for some time after that, many feature pictures copied our 'live prologue' idea.*

"When I made my entrance, it was not in the usual way. There was no chairman saying, as was usual in lectures, 'Ladies and Gentlemen, we have with us tonight . . .' I merely stepped out into the spotlight and said, 'Come with me to lands of history, mystery, and romance.' These words were spoken as the first scene appeared on the screen. I told the story of the Palestine and Arabian campaigns with each sentence beginning just a split second before each scene came on—so the sound of my voice would reach the audience simultaneously with the picture. The Guardsmen played softly in the background, but whenever there was a scene that needed something special they would produce it—charging cavalry, grunting of camels, and so on.

---

* George Pratt points out that stage prologues are mentioned in the trade press as early as 1911.

The legend, and the man who broadcast the legend: Colonel T. E. Lawrence (left) and Lowell Thomas, 1918.

"For our opening night Burton had filled the boxes and the main floor with the most distinguished audience that had been assembled in London since before World War One.

"The following day, the London newspapers reviewed it in an unprecedented way by publishing their reviews on the first page. It finally dawned on me that we were enjoying an unexpected and fabulous success. In the days that followed, I would occasionally walk down to Covent Garden around nine a.m. to have a chat with Burton, pick up the mail, and so on. There I would find hundreds of people sitting on camp stools, where they sat until evening, just to get the less expensive seats. Members of the Royal Family paid us a visit—separately. One night David Lloyd George sent word that he was coming, accompanied by several members of his cabinet, one of whom turned out to be a rather cherubic-looking dignitary by the name of Winston Churchill. Parliament was sitting at night; as a consequence, the Commons actually gave the Prime Minister a vote of 'no confidence,' on the grounds that he should have been in Parliament and not at Covent Garden listening to me. So, as a result of the Prime Minister's visit, you can imagine all the publicity."[5]

One unpublicized visit was that of Lawrence himself. He had disappeared from public view, but a note was received in characteristically cryptic style:

> My dear Lowell Thomas:
> I saw your show last night. And thank God the lights were out!
> T. E. Lawrence[6]

Lawrence wrote to his mother: "We went to a Covent Garden entertainment yesterday. Lowell Thomas had asked us to accept a box. I had a very enthusiastic reception, and was often vociferously cheered by the entire house."[7]

A few days later, Lawrence came to tea and implored Lowell Thomas to stop glorifying his exploits. The Covent Garden show had wrecked his life, and he was hounded by women, reporters, and autograph hunters. When Lawrence learned that the lectures were being extended, he fled from London.

Emir Feisal came to the show, as did Field Marshal Viscount Allenby; Thomas was then invited to present the show to the King and Queen at Balmoral Castle.

"Sir Thomas Beecham, who owned the opera company, had a lease on Covent Garden. This meant he was sharing in our take. He admitted he was doing so well he could even afford to keep his opera company in the Provinces longer than he had intended. But finally he said he had to bring them in, which meant we must either end our London season, or find a new home.

"Burton found only one place available, the huge Royal Albert Hall, which holds six thousand people. Although I thought I should have been on my way back to America to continue my tour there, it somehow dawned on me that something incredible was happening to us in London, something unlikely ever to happen again. So I decided to cancel my American tour, and we moved to the Albert Hall. Later on, we moved to Queens Hall, and finally to the Philharmonic Hall.

"In those days, we had to carry our own projectors, equipment so bulky it filled half a railroad car. My cameraman, Harry Chase, built a tunnel out of black cloth, and then set up his equipment in the upper foyer, shooting through the tunnel. He was using a high-powered arc projector that gave as much illumination as you can get with the best modern equipment today. We also used a huge screen.

"Sir Ernest Shackleton returned from one of his expeditions when we were at Covent Garden and Albert Hall. When he saw what was happening, he was amazed, and hoped he could do something similar with his Antarctic films. The first thing he tried to do was hire Chase. But he had no luck on that. Sir Ernest concluded that our superior projection was an important factor in our success, which I am sure it was."[8]

After London, Lowell Thomas was invited by the Prime Minister of Australia to give his show there, and this trip initiated a tour of the English-speaking world. Thomas was so weary from giving the same speech over and over again, he was convinced his mind would petrify. He decided to return to the field to gather new material. He chose Malaya, moving on to Burma and India, where he spent over a year, and secured what he considered the first motion picture record of life in Afghanistan.

"When I got back to America, I found that Merian C. Cooper and Ernest Schoedsack had come out with a picture called *Grass*. And I mention this because the Cooper-Schoedsack picture was a great success, but it was more of an artistic than a financial success. They didn't make any money, they didn't have any big audiences. They just had a very fine moving picture; the struggle of man against nature. Bob Flaherty's *Nanook* had been more of a financial success than *Grass*. *Grass* was important because it was such a fine job that it made a great impression on Hollywood. So much so that Jesse Lasky backed Cooper and Schoedsack in the making of another picture, *Chang*."

Somewhat ruefully, Thomas recorded how Schoedsack and Cooper were lost to the factual film. "Everything I have done in my life has been a hundred percent reality, without any Hollywood in it. But Cooper and Schoedsack gradually went Hollywood. *Grass* was a hundred percent reality. In *Chang* they went fifty percent Hollywood. Then they went seventy-five percent in another one called *The Four Feathers,* in the Sudan, which was seventy-five percent hokum and twenty-five percent authentic. Finally, they went a hundred percent Hollywood with *King Kong,* which was a fantastic success. Then Cooper became President of RKO, and a top Hollywood personality."[9]

DURING THE NEXT TWENTY YEARS, apart from his radio commitments, his publishing, and his traveling, Lowell Thomas played a part in the production of hundreds of one- and two-reel shorts for Twentieth Century-Fox, Paramount, and Universal. He also edited and narrated many feature-length films, all nonfiction, such as the aerial conquest of Mount Everest by Air Commodore Fellowes, the Marquis of Clydesdale, and their companions, in 1933. His motion picture activities culminated in the Cinerama venture, into which he brought first Robert Flaherty—who died shortly after he joined the company—and then Merian C. Cooper.

The early career of Lowell Thomas, acting as a bridge between the travelogues of Burton Holmes and the expedition feature films of Cooper and Schoedsack, is yet another example of the vagaries of film preservation. As far as I can determine, all that remains of the Allenby-Lawrence film is in the National Film Archive. It consists of ninety feet . . . little more than a minute.

But coincidences abound in film research, and historians often find themselves dependent upon the happy accident. I had no sooner written the previous paragraph than I heard from the Imperial War Museum that a man had paid them a visit and allowed them to copy two reels of 16 mm. toned film. One of the reels was entitled *With Lawrence in Arabia,* the other *With Allenby in Palestine, A Lowell Thomas Adventure.* The discovery turned out to be enticing but minor; the Thomas footage added up to no more than five minutes before it turned into a travelogue on the Holy Land. But the material was excellent, and Anne Fleming of the IWM's film department realized that it was duplicated in some Allenby footage they already had in the vaults on 35 mm. This material proved to be the real discovery, for it was the uncut Lowell Thomas film, as it had come out of Harry Chase's camera.

One can see how the Lawrence legend caught fire as soon as these pictures hit the screen, accompanied by the romantic background provided in the Thomas production. Lawrence hardly appears at all. But the Arab irregulars, charging across the desert, their rifles held up assertively against the sky, create images of breathtaking excitement. Of course, in common with most war films of the period, there is little real action. Lawrence might have referred to his railway raids as cinema shows,

Lawrence's Arab irregulars. A frame enlargement from Lowell Thomas's With Lawrence in Arabia (*1918*).

but he would scarcely have permitted them to turn into one. Yet there is much vitality. Whether the camera films children in a market or Tommies in an armored car, the shots are *alive.*

Swooping over the brow of a hill and charging toward the camera, the camel corps puts on a grand show for Thomas and Chase. The Arabs, filmed as individuals, regard the camera gravely. The British soldiers, in contrast, giggle self-consciously and pose as if for a still picture. In lingering long shots, Lowell Thomas sometimes strolls into the picture in his distinctive American officer's uniform, and sits down, surveying history-in-the-making in Burton Holmes style.

Even in the disjointed form of camera rushes, the infectious fascination of the desert war takes hold, and for days afterward one remembers the images: the charging camels, the bombardment of Jedda, the winding road leading down to the desert, filled with a procession of camels, military trucks, motorcycles, and waving palm fronds. . . .

Years later, T. E. Lawrence corresponded with Hollywood director Rex Ingram, who shared his fascination for Islam. Ingram asked if he had ever been approached about a film of his wartime exploits. Replied Lawrence: "They babble sometimes to me of making a film of *Revolt in the Desert.* I have no wish to see myelf parodied on the pitiful basis of my record of what the fellows with me did."[10]

Whatever the cause of this modesty, Lawrence was perhaps the most camera-shy personality of the age. He may have regretted the determination of Lowell Thomas. But posterity will be grateful.

CAPTAIN NOEL

The British expeditions to Mount Everest in the 1920s were regarded as epic adventures laced with tragedy. On the 1921 exploring expedition, a veteran climber died of dysentery. On the 1922 attempt, seven Sherpa porters were swept to their death by an avalanche. In 1924, two climbers, Mallory and Irvine, failed to return from a final assault on the summit. Although Everest was not to be conquered for another thirty years, these early expeditions cannot be dismissed as failures. They yielded side effects of value both to science and to the art of climbing.

The official photographer on both the 1922 and the 1924 expeditions was Captain J. B. L. Noel, whose book *Through Tibet to Everest*[1] was a best seller in America in the late twenties.

Captain Noel was interviewed by the BBC for the program *The Mystery of Mallory and Irvine on Everest,*[2] and thanks to the program's producer, Stephen Peet, I was able to talk with Captain Noel at his cottage in Kent.

"As a boy in Switzerland, I spent more time climbing mountains than going to school. The school didn't bother with foreign students, and I and another English boy climbed many of the big mountains in the Alps together, without guides. And I was very fond of mountain photography.

"I worshipped a man called Vittorio Sella, who was reputed to be the finest photographer of mountains. He had accompanied the Duke of Abruzzi on his famous 1909 expedition to the Karakoram Mountains in Kashmir. He was one of the old school; he carried a whole-plate camera, with glass plates, and he thought nothing of taking eight hours over one single picture. He'd sit on the mountain

Captain Noel, with Newman Sinclair camera and long-focus lens, awaiting the return of Mallory and Irvine from the peak of Everest, 1924.

slope until the mist was just right, or the sun sparkled on the ice ridges. I thought that was very wonderful.

"I was sent to art school in Florence, and was trained there as an artist. But my father was a soldier; he didn't want me to be an artist. He wanted me to be a soldier.

"I wanted to go into the Indian Army, but that was reserved for the elite. It was a prize job, the Indian Army, because it was a very fine life, and double the pay of England. In my day, you joined the army for the social standing. For sport and for adventure. You couldn't exist without a private income. Pay as a subaltern was five shillings and twopence a day. Out of that you paid for your own uniform, your own mess bill, your batman, and you contributed to the upkeep of the regimental mess. When I failed to get into the Indian Army, I asked for the British Army and chose a regiment in North India, so I could be near the Himalayas. I chose a regiment that had a very hot station. I worked it out in my small mind that at a hot station, there wouldn't be too much military training to do. And it worked out that way. It was so hot where I was stationed that no military training could be done six months of the year, at the height of the day. You did some office work, and the rest of the time you retired to your bungalow in a temperature of 90 degrees. I studied maps of the Himalayas.

"I used to get four months' leave every year to go to Sikkim. Here, I photographed the Himalayas very extensively, and I set myself the task of trying to find a way to Mount Everest. Even in those days, Mount Everest was known to be the world's highest mountain.* It had been measured from India by long-distance triangulation. But nobody could go to it because it lay in forbidden Tibet. No map existed; it was in totally unknown country.

"After making three attempts in three years, I found a high mountain pass (19,000 feet) that the Tibetans didn't watch. There was a wall across the valley, built by the Tibetans, but they had no soldiers guarding it. It was more or less a ruin, a sort of Hadrian's Wall. In 1913 I went with five natives over this pass. It was completely desolate country, and we had to carry our own food. I was in disguise; my hair was dyed black, and my skin was dyed brown. I pretended to be a half-caste Indian."[3]

Noel and his party avoided villages because they knew their presence would be reported. But when their food ran out, they climbed down the valley into a village, secured food, and continued on their journey. Within a short time, their camp was surrounded by soldiers under the command of a governor, the Dzongpen of Ting-ki. Noel had invented a story for use in such circumstances; he explained he was a tea planter from Darjeeling who had employed a Tibetan from this part of the country. The man had absconded with property from the tea garden, and he was determined to find him. The governor accepted the story, but insisted that as foreigners, Noel and his party were not permitted in Tibet and must leave at once. Noel agreed on condition he was supplied with food. The governor obliged, and the party turned back—a mere forty miles from Everest. It was then the closest any explorer had approached to the mountain. Noel made a prismatic-compass sketch map of the route and the country he had explored.

---

* Then its height was calculated at 29,002 feet, later determined to be 29,028.

When war broke out in 1914, Noel was on leave in England. Instead of being returned to India, he was sent to join a regiment leaving for the front. He took part in the Battle of Mons. "It was like manoeuvres, except we were firing at live targets. It was a big show, with hordes of Germans attacking us in mass formation, and outnumbering our little army four to one. We enjoyed it—except now and then, there'd be a tragedy as the chap next to you fell with a bullet through his head."

With the end of the war, Britain was peripherally involved in the fight against the Bolsheviks. Noel was assigned to the Norpa Force, a small army of about six thousand men in North Persia, whose job it was to guard against the possibility of the Bolsheviks seizing the oil fields of Mesopotamia. The general ordered him to explore the south shore of the Caspian Sea, to calculate the chances of the Bolsheviks invading Persia through the Elburz Mountains. Noel set out by horse, and since restrictions on photography had been relaxed, he took with him his Debrie motion picture camera and made a film about the caviar industry.

At a meeting of the Royal Geographical Society, 10 March 1919, he delivered a lecture about his prewar invasion of Tibet, which aroused intense enthusiasm among his audience. The president-elect of the RGS, Sir Francis Younghusband, who had led a full-scale invasion of Tibet in 1904, recalled that Noel's lecture made no reference to anything more than approaching the mountain. But in the discussion that followed, the president of the Alpine Club, Captain Percy Farrar, spoke of the summit itself. This, said Younghusband, was the decisive leap forward. Younghusband determined that Everest would be the main goal of his three years in office.

Younghusband induced Sir Charles Bell, Political Officer for Tibetan Affairs, and Political Resident in Sikkim, to visit the Dalai Lama, the mysterious ruler of Tibet at Lhasa, and ask his permission. Bell was the only European who had ever won the confidence of the ruler of Tibet. He spoke the language fluently and was the author of a Tibetan-English dictionary. Bell returned with a parchment (preserved in the archives of the RGS)—a passport for the British expedition:

"Be it known to the officers and headmen of Pharijong, Kamba, Ting-ki and Shekar, that a party of Sahibs will come to ascend the sacred mountain, Chomolungma—you shall render all help to the party and safeguard them—we have requested the Sahibs to keep the laws of the country and not to kill birds or animals as the people of Tibet will feel very sorry for this—His Highness the Dalai Lama is now on great friendly terms with the Government of India."

Having proved a catalyst, Noel was an obvious choice for the project. He was selected as one of the members of the 1922 expedition but was obliged to resign his commission in the army, because the War Office refused him sufficient leave. Noel explained: "The Royal Geographical Society was a very conservative body; they didn't want an ordinary professional person from a film company to make the pictures. Half of them didn't want any pictures at all. It was just a scientific climbing expedition. They didn't want any vulgarity in the newspapers. So they invited me. The idea was that the film, when it was eventually shown, would produce money for the expedition."

Noel had been greatly impressed by the record of Scott's expedition, filmed by Herbert Ponting, and he haunted the Philharmonic Hall, watching the show again and again. In later years, he became a close friend of Ponting. The lightweight camera, especially designed by Arthur Newman, proved so successful in the Antarctic that Ponting advised Noel to acquire a similar machine. The result was superb, constructed of Duralumin metal, strong as steel and as light as aluminum. Fully loaded, with four hundred feet of 35 mm. film, it weighed less than twenty pounds.

According to Noel: "It was specially made to withstand the cold. The bearings were point bearings, and didn't need any oil at all. That obviated any friction. Remembering Ponting's description of his tongue freezing to the camera, I asked Mr. Newman to make a rubber cover, so if I had to press my face against the camera, to steady it in the wind, I wouldn't be in contact with the cold metal."

The starting point for the Everest expeditions was Darjeeling; the route followed was the trade route of the Jelep Pass (14,600 feet), the Chumbi Valley, and Phari, to Tibet. The 1921 expedition, which included G. Leigh-Mallory, reached 23,000 feet and established that the mountain could be climbed. The world record was held by the Duke of Abruzzi's team, who reached 24,600 feet on the Bride Peak of the Karakoram, and who claimed that the human body could ascend no farther without oxygen. Perhaps the most significant contribution of the Everest explorers was their realization that the Abruzzi theory was wrong.

"When we came to Tibet, which is at 15,000 feet, we were panting. So would you be if you took a train to Switzerland, and went up Mont Blanc. You'd be gasping for breath at 8,000 feet. But stay in a mountain hut on the slopes of Mont Blanc for a couple of days, and you'd find you'd manage the height more easily. Our ability to adapt was unknown before, and it was discovered on the Everest expedition. If an expedition allowed itself enough time, then there is no limit to which the human body could go. You could walk up Mount Everest with a walking stick, if you took two years to do it, and you had little hotels all the way up."

But one thing none of the expeditions had was enough time. Due to the monsoon, the whole summer was obliterated by storms, and the only clear climbing weather lasted from the beginning of April to the end of May—with another two months in the autumn. The monsoon arrived, as regular as clockwork, during the first week of June.

Noel considered Tibet, in spite of its scenic magnificence, to be the most frightful and desolate country in the world. "The people live in the most extreme hardship," he wrote in his book. "It is so cold, and the land is so poor, that the only crop they can grow is barley. There is even a scarcity of air to breathe. Yet the icy winds blow endlessly with biting velocity."[4]

The Dalai Lama's passport opened the gates of the Rongbuk Monastery, twenty miles from the foot of Everest, where the expedition was received with great courtesy and hospitality. Despite the harshness of their life, Noel found that Tibetans generally were remarkably cheerful, and these monks in particular expressed their religion with joy. To them, Everest was a sacred mountain: Chomolungma, Goddess Mother of the World. They predicted mournfully that the Goddess would undoubtedly destroy the explorers. "They found it difficult to see why we'd come all this way for mountaineering—they had no conception of sport. They thought we were insane. We explained it simply as our enjoyment of high places."

The porters for the expedition were hired in Darjeeling; they were mostly Sherpas, an incredibly resilient mountain people, part Nepalese, part Tibetan, each of whom achieved miracles, selecting the heaviest weight he could bear. Wrote Noel in 1927: "Should they ever become animated by a sporting desire to reach the top of the mountain, they could undoubtedly do it more easily than any white man."

Noel supplied himself with four cameras on the 1922 expedition, together with tripods, raw stock, developing tanks, a developing tent, and ancillary equipment. The other members of the expedition did not take kindly to the presence of a camera. This was understandable; no one wants his mistakes recorded for posterity, and the camera was a constant reminder of the expectations of the world. "The climbers thought of a film as a vulgar thing—only for people in the street. They didn't want any money made from them, or for people to remark about their antics on the films."

Noel was unable to film casual, intimate shots. He was anxious not to annoy the climbers, and avoided shooting them unless they were prepared. Mountaineers are traditionally rather quarrelsome; Mallory once said that each expedition started out as one party of twelve, and returned twelve parties of one.

Above a certain height, there was no possibility of the motion picture equipment accompanying the climbers. Anticipating this, Noel had had a twenty-inch Cooke telephoto lens made by Taylor, Taylor & Hobson. "It had a six-power finder telescope, which clipped on the camera. It was synchronized with the optical axis of the lens. So whatever you saw in the finder telescope was in the aperture of the lens."

Noel used panchromatic film, which had been a feature of certain natural history films, in order to capture dark skies and cloud formations, with the help of red and yellow filters.

"On the 1922 expedition, I had a photographic tent. This tent was completely lightproof in tropical sunshine, and we put it up on the banks of the little stream that runs out of the snout of the glacier in the month of May. That was the only water there was. It was quite a roomy tent, ten-foot-square base, and in it I developed 8,000 feet of 35 mm. film, using pin frames holding two hundred feet at a time, in special plywood tanks lined with silver. I developed and fixed it in these tanks, then washed it from river water that was pumped by Sherpas and filtered to remove the grit. Then it was warmed to 65 degrees by means of a special stove, which burned the only fuel in Tibet—the dried dung of the yak. When you light it, this dung emits a nasty, dense smoke. But it soon goes into a red-hot ash. It remains as red-hot ash, retaining a high temperature, for a long time. It's an ideal fuel for slow combustion in a stove. Developing on the spot was necessary to find out what results I was getting. I didn't know what troubles we were going to get. We foresaw that the great difficulty would be static—electrostatic markings on the film, because the air was so dry that the static charge could collect on celluloid film very readily.

"In England, I had had long discussions with Mr. Newman, and he had invented a little retainer, with a sponge of water, inside the camera, which released a certain amount of humidity. But you had to be very careful that the water didn't get on the film when you moved the camera about. We introduced a magnet into the gate mechanism in the hope that it would attract the static charges away from the film's surface. If you pulled film through the velvet light traps on the magazines,

North Col camp, 23,000 feet, photographed by Captain Noel.

A group of the 1924 Everest expedition members at their base camp. Back row (left to right): Andrew Irvine, G. Leigh-Mallory, Colonel Norton (leader), Noel Odell, MacDonald (interpreter). Seated (left to right): E. O. Shebbeare (transport officer), Captain Geoffrey Bruce (adjutant, general manager, nephew of General Bruce of the 1922 expedition), T. Howard Somervell, Bentley-Beetham. (Photo by Captain Noel)

you got it covered with static. So the camera had magazines whose mouths opened when you shut the camera door, so the film came through an open gate and didn't rub against anything."

The worst problem was physical exhaustion from lack of oxygen. "Your movements are very slow, and the trouble with high altitudes is that the lack of oxygen to the blood not only slows you down physically, but it slows your brain. You don't think quickly. You are muddled, and you often look as though you're drunk. The idea of using the camera fills you with horror. You have to fight against yourself. You're lethargic, you just want to do nothing. Your fingers fumble with a screw, and you drop the screw. You just don't care."

One of Noel's Sherpas collapsed and almost died, while two others fell ill with mountain sickness. Noel managed to take some long-focus shots of Finch and Bruce climbing to 27,000 feet. When the two climbers failed to return, Noel set fire to his spare, unexposed film as a signal. Eventually, they returned, but they were at their last limits of endurance. Finch broke down and was sent back, together with other members of the party who were in serious condition. There was still a short period left before the monsoon, and three other climbers, Mallory, Somervell, and Crawford, made a final attempt. The exhausted porters were unable to carry the photographic apparatus to the North Col (23,000 feet), so Noel set up camera stations on the glacier below, at 21,000 feet and 22,000 feet.

"It happened in the late afternoon. We were watching the men going up the sheer face of the great Ice Cliff of the North Col. Suddenly they disappeared and there was nothing. We coupled that with a noise like artillery, and we knew an avalanche had swept them down. Everybody collected blankets and food, and I heated up soup in two Thermos flasks and went out with my Sherpas. I didn't bring a camera—I just went out and helped."

Although the climbers were safe, seven Sherpas had been killed, their bodies smashed on the hard ice of the glacier below. The disaster ended all further hopes for the 1922 expedition. Surprisingly, the Geographical Society and the Alpine Club were determined to renew the attack. Only two thousand feet remained unscaled; with the confidence provided by the discovery of acclimatization, a final assault was called for by everyone concerned.

When Noel assembled his film, *Climbing Mount Everest,* the Wardour Street film trade, as he had suspected, showed no interest. "I told the Geographical Society that we should do the same as Ponting; we would hire the same hall. They said, 'It'll cost a lot of money.' I said, 'Well, we've got to find it.' We rented the hall for ten weeks. We had a very fine operator, and we installed two Ross projectors. We had a big lunch at Frascati's Restaurant for the newspapers, and we gave them a private showing. We opened up—and lost £400 the first week. The Geographical Society got very frightened about this. I said, 'Don't bother. The press reports are marvelous, you just wait till people read them. Then they'll come.' We made a small profit the next week. Every week showed an increased profit and on the last of the ten weeks there was a board up outside the hall: 'No Seats.' We couldn't have continued because the hall was booked by somebody else. But it had a smashing run, with over £10,000 taken at the door."

Once it had proved a popular success, the trade was only too delighted to reap the rewards of Noel's efforts and release the film to selected theaters.

CAPTAIN NOEL WAS AGAIN selected to photograph the 1924 expedition, but this time he arranged it on a fresh basis. He formed a company, Explorer's Films, which paid the expedition for the right to film it. The backers included Archibald Nettlefold, engineer Charles Merz, Lord Salveson of the Scottish Geographical Society, the Aga Khan, and Professor Chalmers Mitchell. Sir Francis Younghusband was president of the company.

The problem of how to remain faithful to the subject, but at the same time win the widest possible commercial interest, was highlighted as the preparations got underway. "Film experts, in a business-like manner, said cheerfully, 'Without a love interest the picture will be a certain failure,' " wrote Noel. "They asked: Could we not bring out actors and actresses and make a romance in the snow?"[5]

The 1922 film inevitably lacked the drama and agony of the expedition, while providing an abundance of shots of scenic grandeur. Bernard Shaw saw it at the Philharmonic Hall and said afterward, "The Everest Expedition was a picnic in Connemara surprised by a snow storm."

Noel's primary task was to act as photographic historian. But he strove to capture, as he put it, the feeling of power and majesty of the mountains, the intangible mysticism of Tibet, and above all, something that would make the spectator feel the immensity of this struggle of men against nature. The aesthetic standard demanded by the theme called for effects both subtle and stupendous.

He had Arthur Newman fit an electric motor to his camera, operated by a six-volt nickel-alkaline battery, and geared so that time-lapse photography was possible. For the film's opening scene, he set up his camera at base camp before dawn, and by exposing one picture every four seconds, he captured the sunrise in a violent, sweeping display of light. He was fascinated by the patterns of light upon snow and the Streamer of Everest, caused by evaporating mists from the Kangshung Glacier, and converted them into dissolving patterns on celluloid by the same process. Time-lapse photography is familiar today, but it was a technique rarely tackled in the silent days. Noel was an admirer of the work in California of Arthur Pillsbury, whose time-lapse films of flowers were a feature of the lecture circuit in America.

Experience on the previous expedition was put to good use on this one, and Noel managed to create a streamlined organization. "In the field, my aim was to make myself independent and mobile, so that I could be well ahead, or if I remained behind to get a shot, could catch up again. The cameras were carried on two chosen mules, fitted with special carrying saddlery. The cameras were contained in metal boxes, with clip handles, so that the lid opened at once. If it was raining, the lid acted as an umbrella. The boxes were watertight; you could leave them in a pond for a month and there wouldn't be a drop of water inside. They were double-cavity metal, quite light, and painted white to reflect the sun."

Noel had two mule men who became so expert they could have the camera out of its box and onto its tripod in thirty seconds. "Thus, as we marched across Tibet, we obtained spectacular pictures of men and animals crossing stupendous passes and bleak plateaux."[6]

The expedition members were mostly new, although Mallory, Somervell, and Odell were veterans. They were still prejudiced against photography, too, although

Fairyland of ice—East Rongbuk Glacier. A Sherpa porter in the right foreground. (Photo by Captain Noel)

their objections were less vehement. "I had to be very tactful not to pester them with picture-making all the time, pushing a camera in front of their faces."

Noel had the advantage of an expert technician for his base laboratory—Arthur Pereira. "We bought a piece of land in Darjeeling, and we got a party of natives to dig it out flat, because everything in Darjeeling is on a steep incline. A laboratory was built there. We brought in all sorts of equipment—developing tanks, drying apparatus, electric generator, and chemicals. The film was carried down by dispatch riders on relays of ponies, to Darjeeling. Sections were sent to Europe for inclusion in Pathé News."

The long-focus lens was the same one that had proved its value on the previous expedition, but now it had been provided with additional steadying supports. The shot Noel aimed at above all others was that of the climbers reaching the summit of the world.

Wrote Noel in his book: "In photographing the high climbing I had to fit my plans and wait on the climbers. I could not ask them to modify their plans or 'act' for me. I had to be on the spot whenever I could and photograph what might come by chance. This meant hours of patience, hours on the watch. But such scenes are more convincing than any acted episodes because they are stark reality.

"Such scenes must be caught immediately because they will not be repeated. It is not work that the ordinary 'Pro' could do. The operator has to have the heart for it. There is no money in it. He must do it for the love of it. I considered it a privilege to undertake this work for the expedition, although some members of the Organising Committee, and even some members of the Expedition itself, seemed rather to resent the presence of the cinematograph. I remember Mallory told me once in a laughing way that I had converted him. He told me that on the first visit of 1921, he said, 'Thank God, there is no cinematograph with us.' But now he quite liked me and my picture-making toys."[7]

Abnormal weather caused a severe setback that all but wrecked the expedition. Furious gales tore the tents and generally shattered morale. One of the porters fell into a crevasse and broke his leg. Two more died, one of a hemorrhage, one of frostbite. The expedition was forced to retreat to base camp. After a serious loss of time, the climbers set out again.

"I had an arrangement with the expedition to provide me with ten cylinders of oxygen and two sets of breathing apparatus—one for me, and one for my native assistant and interpreter—and ten Sherpas allotted to the photographic party alone. Well, we had such a strain on the Sherpas that they became exhausted and ran short of porter power. So I contributed my Sherpas and my oxygen to the climbing party. They needed them; I was only really a supernumerary. But I got on without the oxygen and carried my camera up to 23,000 feet.

"That is the highest that a 35 mm. camera has ever been used, and it is also a world record for altitude living. No one has ever lived for so long at such a height as I have. It is a world record no one has broken—not that anyone would want to break it. It happens to be an accidental record—nine and a half days at 23,000 feet without oxygen and without deterioration. That's an interesting point, because even today doctors and scientists consider that 21,000 feet can be taken as the limit of acclimatization; every day a man lives beyond 21,000 feet, his physique will deteriorate. But my experience disproves that.

"When I first reached 23,000 feet I was done in. I could do nothing but stay in my sleeping bag. My Sherpa cook and servant became ill, and I had to detach three of my Sherpas to carry him down the Ice Cliff, and he never came up again. I did my own cooking after that, and cooked for the Sherpas, too. Next day I felt better. I couldn't do any pictures, and still nodded about in my sleeping bag. The third day, I felt much better. I ate well and slept without oxygen and operated the camera. Each day I improved."

One of the most remarkable telephoto scenes captured by Noel was the rescue of four porters, who had been marooned by a heavy snowfall for four days. Norton, Mallory, and Somervell achieved the rescue, which was made under circumstances of extreme danger—not the least being a possible repetition of the avalanche which caused the tragedy of 1922.

The rescue crew reached the porters late in the evening. "The men were by this time so reduced and so frightened, despairing of their lives, that they were crying like little children and this made Somervell's difficulties worse. His rope, held at the other end by Norton and Mallory, was not long enough to reach across to the men, and he did not dare go without it. The snow threatened to slip at any moment from the steep ice beneath, and a slip would have meant a crashing fall of a thousand feet to the glacier below. At last the men cut steps one by one and reached the end of Somervell's rope, made fast to his ice axe, driven into the ice beneath the soft snow covering."

The porters were completely exhausted and dangerously frostbitten. They had given up any hope of rescue. They remembered the 1922 disaster all too clearly, for they were all related to the men who had been killed. They were relieved from further duty and sent back to base camp to recover.

Demoralization swept over the camp like a mountain mist, and Mallory's last climb, Noel considers, was made entirely on his nerves, for his strength was sapped. With him was a somewhat inexperienced climber, twenty-two-year-old Andrew Irvine.

Noel set up his camera at daybreak, the long lens aimed at the summit; scanning the area through the telescope were two Sherpas, in alternating shifts. They watched for hours.

"Think of what the effort had cost those already tired men struggling towards the pinnacle," wrote Noel. "Think also of us; our initial joy and expectation sinking into as deep a dejection and anxiety when every fresh hour brought the certainty of disaster and death more overwhelmingly upon us. How we had desired victory! Did we not deserve it? This was the third time we had returned to the task."[8]

At last, after two days of anxious waiting and constant watching, figures became discernible through the telescope—a line of men returning to the camp. It was Odell with his support party. They approached the edge of the Ice Cliff. Noel switched on his camera as they began to make a signal.

"As we watched we again hoped, against hope, that they would tell us they had found the men—frostbitten—exhausted—incapable of moving—anything, but still alive. While life existed, we could go to the rescue and do our best, our utmost. What would the signal be? Life, or—? I saw them place six blankets in the form of a cross. Then they went away. That was the signal.

"I remember the moment vividly. I saw this signal through my telescope as I was making the photograph of the scene through my high-powered lens. An electric battery was operating the camera. I was so agitated to read the message that I could hardly have turned the handle of the camera myself."

Odell had seen Mallory and Irvine within six hundred feet of the summit, and going slowly, step by step, toward it. Then driving mists obscured them from Odell's vision. He never saw them again. "When the time came for [Mallory] to make that great climb from which he never returned he discussed his route minutely with me, and told me where to look for him with my telephoto lens on the final pyramid. I told him I would get him, if the light were right, even three miles away. The night before he was killed, he wrote me—what was perhaps the last note he ever wrote in his life—a little letter, reminding me where to look for him the next morning at eight o'clock, and he sent the note down from his camp of 27,000 feet by one of the returning porters. I have kept that little crumpled note ever since. I wish everybody would realise the real service a motion picture can do for a work of this kind. It can do in a sense more than writing can."[9]

A cairn of stones built near Rongbuk Monastery, base camp. Inscribed on the stones are the names of the thirteen men (including Mallory and Irvine) killed on Everest before the end of 1924. (Photo by Captain Noel)

CAPTAIN NOEL'S FILM, which was edited by Nelly Williams, was presented at the Scala Theatre in London. He persuaded seven Tibetan monks, from a monastery in the interior of Tibet (the Palkor choid, Gyantse), to come to England and to appear in a prologue. The orchestra included members of the Goossens family—father conducting, Sidonie playing the harp, Leon the oboe.

The opening night was presided over by Prince Henry (the Duke of Gloucester) and Sir Francis Younghusband. The press notices were exceptionally good, although the *Kinematograph Weekly* complained about the London weather; how could the critic be expected to judge the quality of the photography when the theater was full of fog?[10]

"Immeasurably fuller and finer in every respect than the previous Everest film," said *The Bioscope.* "There have never been screen studies more impressive than the spectacular glimpses of the icy caves and frozen precipices which make Everest's heights like a bizarre giant's palace.

"Thanks partly to the restrained, yet forcefully expressive sub-titling, partly to the realistic illusion created by these wonderful pictures, one gains a very strong sense of the drama of the climb. With the baffled explorers one begins to fancy that this dreadful pile of rock, lowering demonically behind a veil of mist, is actually a living thing."[11]

Captain Noel toured the United States and Canada, showing his film—*The Epic of Everest*—and slides to more than a million people. The film has been preserved by him, together with its predecessor, *Climbing Mount Everest.*

A comparison of the two reveals that each has distinct attributes. The first film spends more footage on the approach to the mountain. Intriguing shots taken from the tiny Darjeeling railway, together with scenes of the porters straining through leech-infested forests and hauling reluctant mules across freezing mountain rivers, create a sense of anticipation, which is increased by the carefully photographed religious dancing. But the Everest material is necessarily anticlimactic; it ends with Finch and Bruce setting out for their oxygen climb, which created a new world record of 27,250 feet. "Though defeated this time, still our climbers will not accept defeat. They will make another expedition soon to complete the conquest of the mountain," reads the final title.

So many technical advances have been made in the field of time-lapse and reportage photography that it is hard to see the second film with the fresh eyes necessary to appreciate what it meant at the time. Today, one is all too aware that the mountain gets favored treatment at the expense of the people—and in most documentaries the people are what matter. Abandoning the task of characterizing the expedition, Noel contrasts the mystical purity of the virgin slopes with the wretchedness of the villages beneath. His fascination and affection for the Tibetans, which so strongly permeate his book and the first film, are absent from this version.

Some of the scenes of the expedition on the move, with yaks and ponies, are reminiscent of *Grass* (1925). Crossing icy mountain streams is as much of an ordeal as in the Cooper-Schoedsack film, with animals ferried across by hardy Sherpas, immersed up to their thighs. The English climbers seem dressed for the grouse moor. Their tweed jackets and floppy hats are apparently sufficient protection when augmented with goggles, cardigans, and four pairs of socks, for while the temperature drops to fifty degrees below at night, during the day one can get sunstroke.

The film perpetuates a tragedy that no one saw. And it ends by trying to pluck a shred of inspiration from the wreckage of the expedition's hopes: "As you look back over the solitude of the glacier, where those men remain behind, there might come this thought to you—if you had lived as they had lived and died in the heart of nature, would you, yourself, wish for any better grave than a grave of pure white snow? Or to your memory, just the building of a simple cairn of stones?

"Now could it be possible that something more than the physical had opposed us in this battle where human strength and western science had broken and failed?

"Chomolungma—Goddess Mother of the World."

MR. AND MRS. MARTIN JOHNSON

For a while in the 1920s, it seemed as if Mr. and Mrs. Martin Johnson had a copyright on the African continent. Backed for a time by George Eastman, inventor of the Kodak, they brought a technical expertise to their work that gave their productions a lasting quality. Their safaris were undertaken purely for photographic purposes, and their films, as popular for their entertainment value as for their educational content, received full distribution and were not dependent on the lecture circuit.*

To the pure documentarian, Mr. and Mrs. Johnson are beyond the pale, for

* Martin Johnson prepared both commercial and lecture versions of his films.

The transport needed for a Martin Johnson motion picture expedition: Willys-Knights with safari bodies.

Martin and Osa Johnson, unlike other expedition film-makers, occasionally employed Africans as auxiliary cameramen. Osa embraces the Akeley, the Africans have Universals, and Martin a Bell and Howell.

they regarded the African continent as a kind of special effects department. They were obsessed by adventure, in the Theodore Roosevelt sense, and aimed exclusively for thrills. They laced their sensational material—and much of it was sensational—with scenic and comedy material, but they had no scruples about authenticity. Their 1928 production *Simba,* although made under the auspices of the American Museum of Natural History, resorts to the full range of editor's tricks to extract the greatest punch from the material. Some of the devices are legitimate: rhinoceri are shown at a water hole. "The Rhino," says a title, "is always looking for trouble and hoping for it." A rhino is seen with Osa (Mrs. Johnson) in the same frame. The rhino seems indifferent and wanders away. But after a cutaway to Osa, the rhino advances. Cut to Osa cocking her gun. The rhino runs away, but sweeps round and charges. Osa fires. The rhino tries again. Osa brings him down.

Due to the skillful editing, the scene is totally convincing. Where it becomes suspect is in *Congorilla,* the couple's first talking picture, in which the rhino sequence pops up again—the footage revealing that the rhino was killed not by Osa but by the editor, for in this version the animal is scared away by the shot.

But however good the footage, a motion picture cannot hint at the danger lurking unseen for the expedition cameraman. Osa and Martin Johnson regarded the narrow escape as a source of pride and their books sometimes reveal them to be a trifle callous in their methods. Despite their patience, they are not beyond rousing animals and goading them into action spectacular enough for the movies. When an angry elephant is thundering toward thousands of dollars' worth of motion picture equipment, the only way to end the scene is with a bullet. Yet in his book *Lion,* Martin Johnson wrote: "To kill in the sense of destroy, to slay in the cause of conceit, is surely an offense against the Almighty and a symbol of human stupidity."[1] Despite his disapproval, Martin Johnson packed two revolvers, four shotguns, and twelve rifles along with his twenty cameras.

The influence of the Martin Johnson pictures was considerable. Their wide acceptance by a public normally averse to educational films led to Hollywood incorporating more and more documentary backgrounds, culminating in Van Dyke's African epic *Trader Horn.* It was the early Johnson films that sent Frederick O'Brien away to write *White Shadows in the South Seas.* Akira Kurosawa remembered the African pictures, and a sequence of a lion influenced the performance of Toshiro Mifune in *Rashomon.*

Born in Rockford, Illinois, in 1884, Johnson was expelled from school for making a composite photograph that showed the staff in a comic light. As a young man, he crossed the Atlantic in a cattle boat for a bet, and the experience gave him the confidence to apply to join Jack London's expedition—as cook. He had never cooked in his life. London hired him, and the crew of the *Snark* endured his food as long as they could, recognizing his talents lay in other directions. Jack London was struck down by illness, and the ship put in at Penduffryn, in the Solomon Islands. Three cameramen from Pathé in Paris were at work there. They had been filming the arrival of the American fleet in Sydney—the cruise was Roosevelt's gesture to show the world that America was as entitled to the Pacific as to the Atlantic. Now they wanted pictures of the cannibals in the interior of Penduffryn, and two traders organized an expedition. Martin, meanwhile, was fascinated by the cameras.

Cannibals of the South Seas (1922). *Original caption: "Nagapate, great cannibal chief of the Big Numbers tribe of Malekula, second largest tribe of the New Hebrides, was very interested in the screen—on which motion pictures were shown of himself and his tribe. On several occasions, he jumped behind the screen as if expecting to find someone or something there that would explain the mystery of motion pictures."*

His father, a jeweler, had acquired the Eastman franchise, and he was accustomed to handling photographic equipment. The Frenchmen showed him how to thread and how to crank, and when all three were stricken with fever, Martin took over.

He bought a print of his film in Paris, returned to America, and became an impresario, presenting *Jack London's Adventures in the South Seas* in 1912. He employed a young girl named Osa Leighty as a singer for his theater, Snark No. 2, which was one of a chain of Snarks. "I couldn't afford to hire her," Johnson used to say, "so I married her." Johnson's wanderlust, combined with diminishing returns, encouraged him to sell the business and to embark with Osa on a return voyage to the South Seas. Osa had never traveled, but she courageously agreed to the trip. In Kansas City, Emmett Dalton was making money with pictures reconstructing the Dalton Raid. Inspired by Dalton, the Johnsons went on tour, lecturing on Jack London and on their own projected voyage. Osa danced, sang "what passed for Hawaiian songs," and Martin ran his film. They won an Orpheum contract, appearing on the same bill as Will Rogers, and eventually amassed enough money to set out on their voyage.

Osa had to struggle hard to persuade Martin to take her on the most dangerous parts of the trip, and they were beset by experiences as far-fetched as any serial. The islanders of Malekula abandoned their polite curiosity and attacked the Johnsons; only the appearance of a British patrol boat saved their lives. If this sounds as pepped up as a movie scenario, Osa provided documentary evidence in her book *I Married Adventure*[2] in the form of a letter from the British Commissioner requesting them to call off their expedition. The letter was delivered by the same patrol boat—the *Euphrosyne*—that had unhelpfully steamed away before rescuing them.

Martin Johnson's film was called *Cannibals of the South Seas* ("photographed at the risk of life"); its reception encouraged him to return to Malekula with a projector—and an armed guard—to win the islanders' support by showing them themselves on the screen.* Osa recalled that because Nagapate, the chief, was now a screen personality, she had lost all her terror and strode forward to greet him. "The cannibal chief seemed puzzled at first, but he could see we held no grudge for his apparent culinary intentions on our first visit, and became almost genial."[3] When the darkness came, and the picture faded in on the screen, the Malekulans were struck dumb. "Here I was on the beach, sitting beside Nagapate—and there I was on the screen as big as a giant. Then the picture of me winked at them. This threw them into a furor. They shrieked with laughter. They howled and screamed." Practically everyone in the audience made his debut on the screen. "As each man appeared, the audience shrieked his name and roared with laughter. Suddenly, the roar became a hushed murmur as the figure of a man who had been dead for a year was shown. Martin's 'magic' had brought a dead man from his grave."[4] The Johnsons experienced a complete change of attitude from the islanders, which enabled them to make a more elaborate film, *The Wild Men of Malekula.*

The simple expedient of taking a projector and portable generator opened other islands to them. "It would have done you good," wrote Martin Johnson to the president of the Pathéscope Company, which manufactured the Peerless projector, "to see the Peerless and the generator going over mountains and into valleys, on the backs of savages, and at night to have seen hundreds of cannibals squatting around the devil-devil grounds, watching the wonderful things they never dreamed of before. Many a time the trees and houses would be full of human heads—dried—all about us. The savages liked a five-hundred-foot piece of Armistice Day in New York City better than any of the other films. It shows hundreds of thousands of people on the streets. These cannibals never dreamed that there were so many people on earth."[5]

A CABLE FROM ROBERTSON-COLE, who were marketing Johnson's films, changed his life. "The public is tired of savages. Get some animal pictures." The Johnsons were deeply discouraged, for they were fascinated by wild men but had no interest in wild animals. A few months in Borneo converted them, and Johnson found his métier as a wildlife film-maker. In order to graduate, he had to face an utterly miserable safari in Africa—during which he tramped wretchedly across Kenya, losing face with his companions and losing money, too—desperately trying to shoot something, whether with camera or with rifle, but missing with doleful

---

* Chaplin provided a one-reel comedy and some mustaches for the islanders.

regularity. He charged the ten months up to experience; thereafter his luck changed. The Johnsons discovered a lost lake, missing from maps and mentioned only in one nineteenth-century account. Naming it Lake Paradise, they established their headquarters and began their task.*

Martin Johnson's objective was to film, more completely than ever before, a record of Africa's fast-vanishing wildlife, so that posterity might be able to recall it as it had existed in its last and greatest stronghold. How was he to know that posterity would be spending weekends in the local safari park, examining lions in bold close-up? Or that television would bring into the home natural-history films of color, detail, and clarity that would have astounded him? The Martin Johnson films pall only when they present scenes that have become all too familiar. The last couple of reels of *Simba,* intended as a staggering climax, now seem a routine series of shots of lion, giraffe, and rhinoceros. When they originally appeared, they must have seemed a treasured and privileged glimpse into a forbidden world.† After the release of *Trader Horn,* W. S. Van Dyke acknowledged his admiration for Johnson's infinite patience: "Shooting big game with a camera is heartbreaking work. I know for a fact that Martin Johnson and his wife spent five months on one lion location getting lion stuff only."[6]

Johnson was probably the best cameraman of all the African explorers. Apart from his association with George Eastman (who appears in *Simba*), he was a friend of Carl Akeley. Johnson's Akeley cameras, fitted with long-focus lenses, were responsible for the fluidity of his later pictures. He even mounted two together, one to film at normal speed, one geared for slow motion. (He also relied on the Bell and Howell 2709, with its turret head offering a wide range of lenses in seconds.) As an unconscious tribute to Akeley, who died in Africa in 1927, his camera was featured as the chief character of *Simba.* Putting the audience behind it made an unusual and highly effective framework.

In his books Johnson was ambiguous about the native reaction to photography. On the one hand, he claimed they had no concept of a photograph. "They turn it upside down and on its side trying to find out what it is all about. I have shown them the best of my flashlights and daytime stills and often they cannot tell an elephant from a rhino." On the other hand, an African who worked as laboratory assistant became a photographic expert, and *Simba* shows tribesmen grinding away at Akeleys with the expertise of professionals.

Johnson suggested that the absence of depth and stereoscopic effect made the pictures meaningless. He might, too, have mentioned the absence of color. Yet no one had any problem understanding moving pictures. Johnson was a born showman, and he loved to show his work. Boculy, a tribesman whom Johnson describes reverently as the greatest elephant hunter in the world, had never seen a movie before. "When he saw all our adventures over again and himself in many of the pictures, he was simply stunned by the wonder of it. He kept repeating 'A-h-h! Ah-h-h!' He was too full of astonishment even to put his emotion into words. He never once took his eyes off the screen and when he saw the elephants close up he

---

* This seems to be Martin Johnson publicity; according to the local district commissioner, the Johnsons removed the remains of his house to build their own.

† *Simba* made $2 million in the United States and abroad.

was the most excited person I have ever seen in my life. The porters talked and yelled and 'Ah-h-h-d' for hours after the show."[7]

To capture such pictures required dedication of an almost religious intensity. Some of the animals were as hard to photograph as a vision. Dependent on water holes for glimpses of the rarer African game, the Johnsons had blinds constructed of thorn bushes. Thorn branches were also scattered strategically to bring the animals within camera range. To prevent the animals detecting the slightest sign of life from the blind, a blanket was hung over the thorn-bush door at the back. Then it was just a matter of waiting—the Johnsons' patience was eroded in particular by zebras, who were so cautious that two hours might elapse from the time they came into view to the moment they reached the water. Zebra, giraffe, and oryx were always aware of the camera, even if they could not see it.

"The minute I start turning the handle the animal looks round. But as the sound continues and nothing happens, he goes ahead drinking. When I stop, he gets another start and looks around again. Strange to say, the click of the still camera frightens him more than the whirr of the movie camera."[8]

By contrast, the alarums and excursions of camp life were invigorating. Boculy alerted the Johnsons to an elephant herd. "This time Osa took the crank while I went forward as a 'movie director' to start action among the animals. I was afraid for her to go forward. There was no cover in case the beasts charged. She cranked away for all she was worth while I walked gingerly toward the herd. The first thing I knew the big bull saw me. He raised his trunk and spread out his ears, shifting his feet about angrily. Then with a furious grunt he charged. I ran."

Sometimes Johnson was able to stop an elephant simply by yelling and waving his hands. But this elephant was too fast and too close. Johnson tried to dodge, but the bull narrowed the distance between them; behind the bull were seven other elephants and behind those a dozen more no one had noticed. "Osa was scared stiff but she kept turning the crank. She knew she was getting a superb picture and there was nothing she could do about me yet. By the time I reached the camera, the elephants were only a few feet behind. Osa's gun bearer had been at her elbow every instant. Now she took her rifle from him and fired. Her shot didn't kill the elephant at once but it diverted him from his murderous course. He nearly knocked the camera down when he passed it. He fell a little further on. The herd hesitated for a moment. Then all turned and ran."[9]

As Johnson admitted, the scenes of animals in repose were even more difficult to obtain than the more dramatic episodes. He commented wryly, "African animals have only two lines of action with reference to the camera. They either run from it or at it."[10] Game melted like summer snow whenever cameras approached. The long-focus lenses were incapable of penetrating the vibrating heat waves. The Johnsons were forced into making a totally new and costly safari to an area where there were far fewer water holes. But here they discovered natives watering their stock by day, the game drinking only at night.

Animals were only part of Johnson's overall plan; his films always contained material of an anthropological nature. In dealing with pygmies, Johnson came up against a business sense as shrewd as his own. He wanted to photograph them shooting an animal or bird, but they steadfastly refused. They were only too happy to shoot arrows at trees, but that was all. He learned that if a monkey was shot, the white man would expect the pygmies to eat it—and then the meal of good rice and sugar, which the Johnsons had provided before and which they were greatly looking forward to, might not be served.

At first sight of the Johnsons, the pygmies thought their last hour had come; they huddled together and cringed silently. Yet such was the Johnsons' ability to communicate that they persuaded the pygmies to lead them to their village in the jungle. At the village the pygmies put on a dance, and the atmosphere became relaxed and highly enjoyable. Johnson lined them up for close-ups, and through an interpreter directed a different expression for each one. "To our surprise they were not only obedient, but they were exceedingly good. Some had real histrionic ability. And while the one 'acting' did his or her trick, the others would crane their necks down the line and roar with laughter. I am sure they hadn't had so much fun and excitement for years."[11]

One woman put on a special show, running the gamut of emotions as though trying to qualify for a role in a Hollywood picture. "It was perfectly superb; one of those jungle miracles that makes travel in the wild parts of the world an unending adventure even without the fiction writer's melodrama."[12]

Enduring fever is a cliché of travel stories, but Johnson's account of a horrific endurance test, when he contracted bronchitis on top of influenza, and Osa suffered double pneumonia, has a grim ring of truth. Osa nearly died. And yet despite the insects, the disease, the vicious animals, and the fact that they seemed to set off on safari with only a bottle of aspirin between rescue and the vultures, Osa and Martin Johnson returned again and again to this extraordinary country. For the word they regarded as the most exciting in the language was "Africa."

ROBERT FLAHERTY

Robert Flaherty, the sole figure among the factual film-makers of the silent era to be accorded the status of artist, produced only two full-length silent films. The impact of his first commercially released production, *Nanook of the North* (1922), inspired attempts at similar films all over the world. The very word "documentary," adapted from the French "*documentaire,*" was coined from a phrase used by John Grierson (in the New York *Sun,* 8 February 1926) to describe Flaherty's *Moana* (1926).

Flaherty's struggle to make his films, his utter disregard for commercialism, and his endearing personality brought him gratitude and undying affection from a group of young film-makers in Britain whose talents coalesced into the British Documentary Movement.

In a sense, Flaherty's films are more important for their effect on others than for their integral artistic value. Like Griffith, whose counterpart he has become, his films contained an extraordinary inspirational quality. Their apparently artless techniques were analyzed, and imitated, and perpetuated, until their original spontaneity was buried under the sheer weight of repetition.

While a well-made feature film of the late 1920s can still hold its own against

A rare portrait of Robert Flaherty taken on the second expedition, which produced Nanook of the North (1922).

Robert Flaherty on his 1916 expedition, with a Bell and Howell camera, which proved unsuitable for Arctic temperatures.

a current feature, despite the handicaps of silence and monochrome, *Nanook* seems as primitive as a cave painting alongside a professionally shot documentary of the 1970s, with its direct sound, color, and the inestimable advantage of the zoom lens. *Nanook* was hailed as the first poetic film of fact, but poetry is hard to perceive when the print is well-nigh invisible, and the Eskimos register as shuddering silhouettes. Much has been written about *Nanook,* some of it at odds with the truth; it is, for instance, claimed as the first feature-length documentary, even though Captain Kleinschmidt's film of the Carnegie Museum Alaska-Siberia expedition (1911), to take an example at random, exceeded it a decade earlier by four reels. What is undeniable is that *Nanook,* in its original form, evoked the spirit of a forgotten people, and thus had a quality which captured the imagination. It was a film of utter simplicity and stark realism. *Moana,* too, was a film of simplicity, its indolent, lyrical beauty in sharp contrast to the earlier film. Simplicity in a film of great reputation invariably transmits itself in the form of anticlimax. Students of the cinema, eagerly expecting the storm in *Nanook* to outdo the one in *Storm over Asia,* watch the wind sweeping snow across the wastes with deepening disappointment. They cannot hear it. In most modern prints they cannot properly see it.* And they expect bravura treatment where the mere presence of a camera is epic enough.

Robert Flaherty, born in Iron Mountain, Michigan, in 1884, was of Irish origin. His father was the owner-manager of an iron-ore mine, and it was mining and prospecting that brought Robert into contact with motion pictures. His formal education was negligible; instead, he learned about life in the wilderness at first-hand, building up a set of experiences, such as hunting with Indians, that enabled him to develop into an explorer. In 1910 he was commissioned by Sir William Mackenzie, builder of the Canadian Northern Railway, to explore the Nastapoka Islands, Hudson Bay, and prospect for iron ore. His natural affinity with primitive people made it possible for him to communicate with the Eskimo, mostly through mime, for he could not at first speak a word of their language. His experiences on this and subsequent trips, some of them as rigorous as those described by Ponting, gave him a deep admiration for the Eskimo. In commissioning him for another expedition, Sir William Mackenzie made a suggestion, probably as a result of Flaherty's graphic tales, which ultimately lost him a consultant engineer.

"Sir William said to me casually, 'Why don't you get one of these new-fangled things called a motion-picture camera?' So I bought one, but with no thought really than of taking notes on our exploration. We were going into interesting country, we'd see interesting people. I had not thought of making a film for the theatres. I knew nothing whatsoever about films."[1]

Flaherty purchased a Bell and Howell, an extremely sophisticated camera for 1913. The metal model had appeared on the market only the year before. (Ideal for studio work, it proved unsuitable for extreme cold, since the oil thickened and it had to be warmed between takes.) Flaherty took the precaution of spending three weeks in Rochester, at Eastman Kodak, learning the craft of the cameraman. He pur-

* David Shepard's restoration, undertaken for Frances Flaherty's International Film Seminars, is available from Blackhawk on 8 mm. See his account of the restoration in *Blackhawk Bulletin,* February 1975, p. 50.

chased a portable developing and printing outfit, intending to process his films as he shot them. Arthur Calder-Marshall thinks that Flaherty regarded film-making as an occupation to combat boredom. Yet in 1915 Flaherty told *Moving Picture World* that the principal purpose of the expedition was to obtain pictures, and "many hazardous ventures were made, especially while taking pictures of natural phenomena."[2] Either way, the Eskimos took picture-making deadly seriously.

"We did not want for co-operation. The women vied with one another to be starred. Igloo-building, conjuring, dances, sledging and seal-hunting were run off as the sunlit days of February and March wore on. Of course there was occasional bickering, but only among the women—jealousy, usually, of what they thought was the over-prominence of some rival in the film. One young mother, whom, with her baby, I was in the midst of filming one clear day, suddenly got up, and despite my threats and pleas, walked away. Neither she nor her husband had been up to snuff of late, so I decided to send them away. 'Don't care,' said she when in the most impressive way we announced her fate, 'seals are the best food anyway.' But old Yew, ever father of his flock, interposed, and what was finally picked out from the crazy-quilt of his pidgin English was that she was not altogether wrong. Two times in as many days I had given Luliakame's (her rival) baby candy, but I 'no see him hers.' "[3]

One of the documentary film-maker's first preoccupations is with the people he has chosen as actors, for they regard themselves as special, indispensable to the project, requiring their reward in extra rations of diplomacy and tact. Flaherty was a man of immense personal charm, prejudiced in favor of primitive people before he even met them, and on the whole, his Eskimo associates loved him. If other explorers used beads to gain the good graces of the natives, Flaherty used his camera to enter their world. It engaged the attention of the Eskimos, allowing him to probe their character and way of life, absorbing rather than distressing them. And inevitably his camera led him into some hair-raising experiences. For a deer hunt, he mounted it on a sledge.

"Dragging his six-fathom whip ready to cow the dogs before they gave tongue, Annunglung went on before the team. We swung in behind the shoulder of an intervening hill. When we rounded it we were almost among them. The team lunged. The deer, all but three, galloped to right and left up the slope. Three kept to the valley. On we sped, the camera rocking like the mast of a ship at sea. From the galloping dogs to the deer not two hundred feet beyond, I filmed and filmed and filmed. Yard by yard we began closing in. The dogs, sure of victory, gave tongue. Then something happened. I am not altogether clear as to how it happened. The sledge was belly-up, and across the traces of the bitterly disappointed team Annunglung was doubled up with laughter.

"Within two days we swung back for camp, jubilant over what I was sure was the film of films. But within twelve miles of the journey's end, crossing the rotten ice of a stream, the sledge broke through. Exit film."[4]

When Flaherty returned to safety from that expedition, during which his ship sprang a leak, he fired his rifle to attract attention from the trading post. No one emerged. The place seemed deserted. It turned out that news of the war in Europe had reached the post and Flaherty had been mistaken for a German.[5]

Flaherty married Frances Hubbard, daughter of Dr. Lucius L. Hubbard, who had been state geologist of Michigan. She shared her husband's fascination for the wilds, and became an important contributor to those later films on which she worked. Flaherty, who had spent the winter months editing his film, returned north in the summer of 1915 (Frances Flaherty went part of the way), and by February 1916, his prospecting complete, he turned his whole attention to motion pictures.

"Much has been written about the birth of Flaherty the film-maker," wrote Arthur Calder-Marshall, "much of it pious poppycock. The deepest experience in Flaherty's life had nothing to do with films, art or for that matter exploration. It was the discovery of people who in the midst of life were always so close to death that they lived in the moment nobly."[6]

Flaherty had shot 25,000 feet of film[7] and in Toronto cut together a 6,000-foot print, which was sent to Harvard for a special screening. But while working on the negative, he ignored one of the most rigorously imposed rules of professional cutting rooms and smoked a cigarette. As Terry Ramsaye told it: "There was a burst of flame. Flaherty was thrown across the room, burned deep by the blast, scorched as though he had stepped into the roaring vortex of a giant blow-torch. He struggled out of the room and ran to the street in a frenzy of pain, clothes afire. Weeks later, he recovered in the hospital."[8]

The pattern of Flaherty's career shows that he needed the period of discovery, enjoyed by other artists but generally denied film-makers, in which to find the style and content of his films. The loss of the negative was therefore of crucial importance, for, as Calder-Marshall points out, had it survived, Flaherty would have tried to sell his picture, and he would have failed, thus proving to himself that he was a flop. He would have abandoned film-making and returned to his former work as mining engineer.

He had the print to remind him of his mistakes, but he failed to make a duplicate negative, declaring that the quality of such negatives was far from satisfactory. This cannot have been the whole truth, for successful dupe negatives had been made as early as 1904. Besides which, his film had been highly praised. Nevertheless, Flaherty was happy to have an excuse to try again. "Though it seemed a tragedy at the time," he wrote, "I am not sure but what it was a bit of fortune that it did burn, for it was amateurish enough."[9]

Flaherty took the print on the lecture circuit. As he described it, the film was untitled, and since he knew little of editing techniques, it ended up as a series of disconnected scenes—sub-Arctic home movies.

"People were so polite, but I could see that what interest they took in the film was the friendly one of wanting to see where *I* had been and what *I* had done. That wasn't what I wanted at all. I wanted to show the *Innuit* (the name the Eskimo call themselves).* And I wanted to show them, not from the civilized point of view, but as they saw themselves, as 'we, the people.' I realized then that I must go to work in an entirely different way."[10]

Flaherty and his wife had worked out the reason for the failure of the existing film and discussed the idea of a film showing a single Eskimo and his family, and his constant fight against starvation in the cruelest climate in the world. At a

---

* The Eskimo were called Eskimo by the Cree Indians. Their own name, like so many tribal names, means simply "people."

cocktail party, Flaherty encountered Captain Thierry Mallet of Revillon Frères, a world-famous fur concern of the Far North; he showed his film to both Mallet and John Revillon. *Nanook* was sponsored by Revillon Frères, but the degree of direct advertising was not decided upon. David Shepard has seen *Nanook* footage in which "Revillon Frères" was painted on a side board of an Eskimo sledge, suggesting that Nanook was to have been depicted as a trapper who spent the year gathering furs for the company. Shepard said, "I asked Frances about this and was told yes, that Flaherty had shot coverage both ways and the Revillon-identified shots had been replaced after soft-pedalling of the sponsorship proved the only way to sell the picture."[11]

In June 1920, by schooner and canoe, Flaherty transported 75,000 feet of film, two Akeley cameras, a printing machine, a Haulberg electric light plant and projector, together with all the equipment needed for such an expedition, to Cape Dufferin, on the northeast coast of Hudson Bay, eight hundred miles north of the rail frontier in northern Ontario. He cast his film from the Eskimos who were familiar to the post. Nanook—a common name among Eskimos, meaning "bear"—was a well-known character, and Flaherty gave him the lead.

Although *Nanook of the North* was presented as a film of actuality, it no more reflected Nanook's ordinary life than *Man of Aran* reflected life on that island in the 1930s. "In historical terms," wrote Calder-Marshall, "*Nanook* was a costume picture, as in far cruder terms the Wild West shows of Buffalo Bill Cody were."[12] Flaherty took great pains to procure genuine Innuit clothes, for his cast were not correctly dressed to take part in his vision. Flaherty, in all his work, behaved as an artist rather than a documentarian. Like an art director on a period picture who avoids telegraph posts, so Flaherty presented his subjects untainted by the white man's presence.

"I am not going to make films about what the white man has made of primitive peoples," wrote Flaherty. "What I want to show is the former majesty and character of these people, while it is still possible—before the white man has destroyed not only their character, but the people as well.

"The urge that I had to make *Nanook* came from the way I felt about these people, my admiration for them; I wanted to tell others about them."[13]

Captain Kleinschmidt, in his Arctic exploration films—made long before *Nanook* was released—selects far more prosaic and therefore more truly documentary scenes of Eskimo life than Flaherty would have considered. In the Carnegie Museum expedition film of 1911 (Alaska-Siberia) the camera tracks past Eskimo houses, built upon stilts along the shore. Eskimo children, excited by the camera and slightly alarmed by it, are dressed in department-store overalls. One of them sports a peaked cap. Telegraph wires stretch across the landscape. The fact that this post is closer to civilization than Cape Dufferin is borne out by the sight of huskies sitting on a trolley as it proceeds down a railroad track under its own steam. Nevertheless, Flaherty's exclusion of all elements of modern life places *Nanook* in the category of reconstructed documentary, like *Chang* and *The Silent Enemy*. And when Kleinschmidt himself released *Primitive Love* (1926), a picture about the Siberian Eskimo that included footage from the 1911 Alaska-Siberia expedition together with fresh material, he followed Flaherty's example and produced a drama of primitive man struggling against the elements.

Eskimos with an Akeley camera on Nanook of the North.

Sleight of hand was required even for so realistic a documentary as Nanook.

The sequence of the walrus hunt was staged at Nanook's behest; he repeated again and again that it was many moons since he had hunted walrus. He persuaded Flaherty to cross to an island where no one landed in summer because of the heavy seas but where walrus were in abundance. They managed the landing after a three-day wait.

"By the night all my stock of film was exposed. The whaleboat was full of walrus meat and ivory. Nanook never had such walrus-hunting and never had I such filming.

"Three days later the post bell clangs out the welcome news that the kablunak is about to show his iviuk aggie. Men, old men, women, old women, boys, girls and small children file in to the factor's house. Soon, there is not an inch of space to spare. The trader turns down the lamps. The projector light shoots over the shocks of heads upon the blanket which is the screen.

"Then the picture. A figure appears. There is silence. They do not understand. 'See, it is Nanook!' the trader cries. The Nanook in the flesh laughs his embarrassment. 'Ah! Ah! Ah!' they all exclaim. Then silence. The figure moves. The silence deepens. They cannot understand. They turn their heads. They stare at the projector. They stare at its beam of magic light. They stare at Nanook, the most surprised of all, and again their heads turn towards the screen. They follow the figure which now snakes towards the background. There is something in the background. The something moves. It lifts its head. 'Iviuk! Iviuk!' shakes the room. The figure stands up, harpoon poised in hand.

" 'Be sure of your harpoon! Be sure of your harpoon!' the audience cries.

"The figure strikes down; the walrus rolls off into the sea. More figures rush in; they grab the harpoon line. For dear life they hold on.

" 'Hold him! Hold him!' shout the men. 'Hold him! Hold him!' squeal the women. 'Hold him!' pipe the children.

"The walrus' mate dives in, and by locking tusks attempts rescue.

" 'Hold him!' gasps the crowd.

"Nanook and his crew, although their arms seem to be breaking, hold on. But slowly and surely, the thrashing walrus drags the figures nearer the sea.

" 'Hold him! Hold him!' they despair. They are breathing hard. 'Dig in! Dig in!' they rasp, as Nanook's feet slip another inch through the sand.

"Deep silence. Suddenly the line sags, the crew, like a flash, draw in the slack, and inch by inch the walrus is pulled in to shore. Bedlam rocks the house.

"The fame of the film spread far up and far down the coast. Every strange Eskimo that came into the post Nanook brought before me and begged that he be shown the iviuk aggie."[14]

The Eskimos were now converted to the true value of moving pictures and helped Flaherty in every way possible. A curious parallel to Martin Johnson's experience with Africans was recorded by Flaherty; the Eskimos examined still pictures of themselves with the same bewilderment. Often, they would look at one upside down. Flaherty would lead them to a mirror and place the photograph beside it. Then, with a broad smile, they would make the connection. Yet the mechanical skill of the Eskimo enabled one to reassemble the intricate insides of a Graflex camera, when Flaherty himself had given up, and several Eskimos loaded the Akeley magazines and operated the cameras when necessary.

The perils of expedition film-making are well illustrated in this picture of Flaherty filming Nanook.

The disaster to the earlier film kept Flaherty's reflexes alive on this one. His hut was warmed by a stove, but Flaherty preserved his negative with loving care. He greatly missed one convenience of civilization—running water. Three barrels of water were required for the developing of every hundred feet of film. A water hole had to be maintained all winter, and water, with chunks of ice in it, had to be carried by sledge to Flaherty's laboratory, a quarter of a mile away. Fifty thousand feet were developed during the winter, with Eskimo assistants clearing the ice from the water before it touched the film. Another peril was deer hair from clothing, for hairs adhering to negatives produced unsightly prints.

A kind of studio igloo was required, since the ordinary igloo was far too small. Instead of the standard diameter of twelve feet, Flaherty asked for one of twenty-five feet, but Nanook and his companions had never constructed such a huge edifice. Their first attempt kept falling to pieces. The more it fell down, the funnier they found it, until they could hardly work for laughing. When a structure finally remained intact, Flaherty could not get sufficient exposure from the ice-windows, and the crown of the igloo was sliced away to produce the equivalent of an open stage.

The arduous nature of film-making in such conditions was emphasized by the stories Flaherty told Terry Ramsaye. Flaherty was a born raconteur and, in Calder-

Marshall's phrase, he hid the truth in fancies as a buddleia hides its blooms in butterflies. Substantiation for such tales is nonexistent. One can only ask oneself, are they *likely?*

Ramsaye tells how Flaherty had to burn precious rolls of film to melt snow for tea water when no other fuel was available. When in raging pain from an abscessed tooth, he made a crude drill from a file and a nail, and he instructed an Eskimo in the operation of extracting the tooth without anaesthetic. The extreme cold—sometimes 37 degrees below zero—caused the film to become as brittle as glass and to break into flakes when he attempted to thread it. The only remedy was to warm the film in the igloo at camp and wrap it in clothes until it was needed.[15] Flaherty told cinematographer George Folsey, however, that he had shot part of *Nanook* in the area around a hotel—"because snow was snow, and you couldn't tell whether it was the North Pole or somewhere else."[16]

When Nanook persuaded Flaherty to cap the walrus hunt with a sequence of bear hunting, he unwittingly led him on a journey that almost killed the entire party. They traveled in wretched weather and were soon hopelessly lost. Poor Nanook was deeply humiliated. Two dogs died of starvation, and the other dogs were too weak to work. The food supply was practically gone when Flaherty discovered that the Eskimos had not touched Flaherty's own rations, which he willingly shared with them; Nanook had been afraid Flaherty's might be insufficient. When a large seal saved their lives, Nanook declared, with satisfaction: "Now we are strong again and warm. The white man's food has made us much too weak and cold."

Ironic footnote: Nanook starved to death two years later.

INSTEAD OF THE LECTURE CIRCUIT, Flaherty took *Nanook* around the distributors. It was a humiliating experience. Paramount would seem to have been an ideal company to handle the film; Jesse Lasky was fascinated by travel and wildlife, and Adolph Zukor had handled Cherry Kearton's picture in 1913. But evidently, the wrong people saw the film. "They all pulled themselves together and got up in rather a dull way, I thought, and silently left the room. The manager came up to me and very kindly put his arm round my shoulders and told me that he was terribly sorry, but it was a film that couldn't be shown to the public."[17]

First National representatives saw the picture, and refused even to comment on it. Eventually, Pathé, perhaps responding to the French name of Revillon, acquired the picture. Carl Stearns Clancy, editor-in-chief of Pathé News, was credited in the *Nanook* press book for his editing and titling, which suggests that Pathé reworked the picture before its premiere at the Capitol Theater in New York, with one of Robert Bruce's *Wilderness Tales* (not with *Grandma's Boy,* as Flaherty stated).

Film historians have implied that *Nanook* was ignored by the professionals in the picture business. On the contrary, it aroused envy; a story was put out that the picture was simply a clever editing job. Eskimos all look alike; "Nanook" was created at the editing stage by the title-writer. Generous praise, however, came from Rex Ingram, director of *The Four Horsemen of the Apocalypse,* who was a documentary director *manqué:* "*Nanook* is one of the most vital, dramatic and human films that has ever flashed across the screen. Because its drama is made tremendous by its naturalness and sincerity. Because its story is the first and most dramatic of all stories—man's fight for his daily bread. And vitally important, its director was unhampered by studio methods, traditions and equipment."[18]

One unexpected critic of the film was Iris Barry, a pioneer of film appreciation. As a former secretary to the Arctic explorer Vilhjamur Stefansson, she could not accept *Nanook* as a film of fact. In her book *Let's Go to the Movies,* she described it as an "enchanting romance." "*Nanook* was actually taken in the latitude of Edinburgh and acted by extremely sophisticated Eskimos." Stefansson, she said, had called it "a most inexact picture of the Eskimo's life." Calder-Marshall, however, records that Stefansson had shown great understanding of the sort of difficulties Flaherty had been forced to work under, and, although he tried to dispel the idea that the Arctic was essentially a hostile region, he was most generous in his book toward Flaherty, the poet of the "Bitter Arctic."[19]

A comment of Flaherty's should be stamped upon the front of every documentary film script: "One often has to distort a thing to catch its true value."

Now enters upon the scene, a little late in the day, that figure of major importance from Paramount—Jesse Lasky. Pathé's modest success with *Nanook* caught Lasky's enthusiasm. Lasky had the right idea; he had already commissioned an expedition to Africa, headed by Leonard Vandenbergh. An admirer of Theodore Roosevelt, Lasky had embarked on expeditions of his own, which included a camping spell with Zane Grey and journeys to the High Sierras, the Canadian Northwest, and the Colorado River. At the time of the gold rush, Lasky had struggled through Alaska as an unsuccessful prospector.

Lasky cabled Flaherty, inviting him to make a picture for Paramount—"Bring back another *Nanook of the North*!" Robert and Frances Flaherty went to New York to see Frederick O'Brien, author of *White Shadows in the South Seas,* who urged them to capture something of South Sea culture before it was entirely eradicated. Filled with enthusiasm, they sailed for what O'Brien described as the last island uncorrupted by Western civilization—Savai'i.

Flaherty was as innocent of South Sea culture as the average tourist. No artist of his integrity could hope to produce a worthwhile picture until steeped in the subject. He made conscientious attempts to film *something* to fulfill his contract with Famous Players–Lasky, but the approach was wrong, and he gradually realized that he was getting nowhere. Wrote Frances Flaherty: "We thought we knew all about how to make our film. Just as in the North the Eskimos hunt animals, so here we would have the Samoans hunting creatures of the sea. We went all over everywhere hunting up tiger sharks and giant octopi that these gentle people might do battle with them. We got nothing for our pains. There were pictures we got, but there was nothing in them. Our camera had lost its cunning. It no longer gave us the feeling of looking into life. It balked, baffled us. We packed our cameras away and sat down to think."[20]

Every element of Samoan life seemed to be a negative image of *Nanook.* There was no struggle for existence. Where was the conflict in surroundings so benevolent that a meal could be plucked effortlessly from the warm waters of the sea? Distressed by his creative block, Flaherty found his health undermined by the unaccustomed heat; production was delayed a month by illness, and a year by indecision.

The film came to life as soon as Flaherty concentrated upon the very antithesis of what he had intended to film: the slow pace of life, the indolence, the gentleness, the beauty of the surroundings, of the people, and of their every movement.

"For so many generations," wrote Frances Flaherty, "have they been practicing these beautiful movements that beauty has entered into even the commonest things they do, whether they sit or stand or walk or swim, there is that beauty of movement, rhythm, the philosophy, the story of their life. So that simply in the beautiful movement of a hand the whole story of that race can be revealed. Now we had the secret. Here was the matter for our philosophical camera's eye. We unpacked our cameras again."[21]

The extraordinary richness of the photography of *Moana*—the word means "the sea," and is the name of the chief character—is due in part to Flaherty's use of panchromatic film. This has been portrayed as an accident, also as an innovation. In fact, it was neither. Panchromatic had been used by Hollywood cameramen for years. It was the staple diet of the old Kinemacolor process of Charles Urban. Flaherty planned *Moana* as a panchromatic picture from the beginning, probably under the influence of Carl Stearns Clancy, whose one independent production, *The Headless Horseman,* had been shot on panchromatic and was ready for release when Flaherty left. At the request of the owner of the Prizmacolor Company, Flaherty took a Prizmacolor camera; like all additive processes, Prizma depended upon panchromatic film.* But the story that the color camera broke down and Flaherty loaded his Akeley with the panchromatic stock as an experiment is a denial of his wide knowledge of photography.

The climax of *Moana,* if such a film can be said to have a climax, is a clinically filmed ritual of tattooing. (Flaherty, like Hemingway, could not admire gentleness unless offset by suffering.) "Tattooing," wrote Frances Flaherty, "is the beautification of the body by a race who, without metals, without clay, express their feeling for beauty in the perfection of their own glorious bodies. Deeper than that, however, is its spring in a common human need, the need for some test of endurance, some supreme mark of individual worth and proof of the quality of the man."[22] The young man who underwent the ritual would never have done so had it not been for the film; he endured the six agonizing weeks because, said Flaherty, his pride, and that of all Samoans, was at stake.

Flaherty had been supplied with a number of feature films by Paramount, including *It Pays to Advertise,* with Bryant Washburn, *Sentimental Tommy,* with Gareth Hughes and May McAvoy, and *Dr. Jekyll and Mr. Hyde,* with John Barrymore. *Dr. Jekyll* was received with reverence, because its author, Robert Louis Stevenson, had lived in the South Seas. One film that was not particularly well received was *Nanook.* The most popular was the 1920 German film *The Golem;* Frances Flaherty remembered Samoan children being named Golemii in honor of the robot.

Moana of the South Seas, "this lyric of calm and peace," as Calder-Marshall calls it, would have been as popular at an exhibitors' convention as Chinese eggs. Flaherty sneak-previewed it to Laurence Stallings, who ran a column in the New York *World.* "I do not think," he wrote, "that a picture can be greater than this Samoan epic."[23] Paramount chiefs Lasky, Zukor, and Walter Wanger thought highly

---

* Harold Horton had shot *Bali the Unknown* in Prizmacolor in 1921.

The Samoan kiss—Tu'ungaita and her granddaughter—from Moana *(1926), directed by Robert Flaherty.*

of the picture but declared it too long at eleven reels. Cut to six, they might consider roadshowing it. But the salesmen were mutinous: "Where's the blizzard?" one asked. The roadshow idea was quietly dropped; the picture survives in seven reels.

Eventually, a trial run was held at six tough towns. Flaherty enlisted help from the National Board of Review, who alerted lecture societies and groups of people who might respond warmly to the picture. Business, though not outstanding, was better than average. The original title was *Moana of the South* ("Bring back another *Nanook of the North!*" Lasky had said). Known as *Moana of the South Seas,* it was altered to *Moana: A Romance of the Golden Age* to avoid confusion with Maurice Tourneur's *Aloma of the South Seas.*

A notable account of the film appeared in the New York *Sun,* written by C. E. Hall, a resident of Samoa: "A large number of chiefs were present, and I observed them closely during and after the showing of the picture. To them, the film possessed no new beauty. They watched silently the feats of climbing, swimming, pig-hunting and canoe adventures as commonplace events in the old Samoan life. But they missed nothing of the scarcely perceptible gestures and detail of ceremony so full of significance to them.

"The picture faded from the sheet, and they turned sadly away, knowing full well that never again would these things be.

"To my inquiries, the picture was *lelei lava* (good exceedingly). Their only other answer to my many questions was that it was *fa 'a-Samoa;* setting it aside at once as something *sa* (sacred) and beyond the comprehension of the alien *palagi* (white man)."[24]

Moana's distribution was not well handled. In 1926 Flaherty made a short film, financed by Maude Adams, entitled *The Pottery Maker.* The same year he made *Twenty-four Dollar Island,* a film about New York on the lines of *Manhatta.* Instead of recording the primitive struggle for existence in that harsh city, he produced an abstract picture. "I shot about thirty thousand feet," said Flaherty, "which will be boiled down to about two thousand, but really I don't know what I have got. But this I do know; it is a great idea for a picture and somebody is going to make a great picture of it some day. I'd like to have three years to devote to it. Yes, it would take that long to do it right."[25] The film was shown with a Stiller picture at the Fifth Avenue Playhouse, and eventually used as a backdrop for a stage ballet at the Roxy Theater. This was not the insult it has been made out to be. S. L. Rothapfel (Roxy) genuinely admired the film and surrounded it with an exclusive presentation.

Flaherty was an intuitive artist who worked entirely by instinct—hardly a quality attractive to potential financiers. Studio executives, anxious to release fifty pictures a year, were all too aware that *Nanook* was an exception. No factual film had ever grossed more than a popular feature (*Nanook* made $251,000 worldwide), and setting one up, supplying it, and controlling it was just too much trouble. Flaherty was therefore not overwhelmed by offers. As David Shepard put it, "I think perhaps Flaherty's and the industry's concepts of life and its meaning were so different that beneath the veneer of a common language, there was simply no communication."[26]

But what the industry did not yet know was the extent to which Flaherty, and the tiny group of expedition film-makers, had obliged feature producers to change their style. The Selig Zoo was no longer an acceptable location. Audiences across the world had grown too familiar with the topography of Africa, the Arctic, and the islands of the South Seas. Hollywood fiction films began to incorporate the values of the factual films. And to ensure success they had to have Flaherty.

FROZEN JUSTICE

An admirer of Robert Flaherty, the German director F. W. Murnau decided to follow his first American films, *Sunrise* and *The Four Devils,* with *Frozen Justice,* a story of Eskimo life before the advent of the white man. The Fox Company contacted the Loman brothers in Alaska, who suggested that suitable conditions might be found at Point Barrow, the northernmost point of the continent. But they were doubtful whether the old skin boats, harpoons, or fur costumes would still be in evidence; after all, they said, the Eskimo had been in contact with the white man for a hundred years. But the Flaherty film was still fresh in the memory. And Murnau was anxious that the Einar Nickelson story, with its whale-hunting episodes, should be told with full use of authentic background footage.

A special unit was formed to film the documentary material. Charles Clarke, a young cameraman and AEF veteran who had just finished *The Red Dance* for Raoul Walsh, was assigned as director-cameraman. With him went an Eskimo assistant cameraman, Ray Wise,* to act as interpreter; Virgil Hart, unit manager; Ewing Scott, in charge of props and costumes; and Captain Jack Robertson, an experienced Alaskan explorer and film-maker, responsible for two feature-length documentaries—*True North* (1925) and *Alaskan Adventures* (1926).

In April 1928, the unit traveled by train to Seattle, where Virgil Hart contacted one of the "Byrd of the Antarctic" men to build a shortwave transmitter for them and ship it to Anchorage. The unit outfitted themselves for the Far North, took a steamer to Seward, Alaska, and a train to Fairbanks, where they chartered aircraft. The first flight of two planes ran into fog and made a forced landing on the snow wastes. One of the planes took off again, intending to return with assistance, but it never reappeared. Charles Clarke, Captain Robertson, and pilot Russell Merrill waited hopefully, surviving on the pilot's emergency rations.

They encountered very few animals in this barren area, although Clarke shot a squirrel: "I was dubious about eating it, for it had the smell of a rat, but this was no time to be fussy."[1] Their snow house, two and a half feet wide and eight and a half feet long, was cramped and uncomfortable, and Clarke ached for somewhere to stretch out and relax. He made a little film of their predicament and read *Trader Horn* to keep himself occupied. Constant use of the sleeping bag, in shifts, melted the ice on the floor of the hut and soaked the occupants. They moved to the cabin of

* Ray Wise was the star of Van Dyke's 1933 *Eskimo,* a dramatic documentary with dialogue in Eskimo. Van Dyke and explorer Peter Freuchen had prominent roles.

One of the two planes carrying the Fox crew to Point Barrow, Alaska. Both were forced down by fog. One took off again, and never returned

the plane, but it was lined with frost, and snow filtered through every crack and seam. But they were now too fatigued and hungry to care.

"May 20th," Clarke wrote in his diary. "The storm is still on. We have been here seven days now. We sang songs and joked about which one of us we would eat first when the rations were gone. I went out into the storm to get the things from the snow house. The snow had drifted in front and completely blocked the entrance. A little rice for supper. I finished *Trader Horn* and tried to get some sleep by pretending I was in the hot climate of the Belgian Congo."

The lack of food began to affect them the following day. "My stomach keeps twisting and contracting as though it is trying to turn each fold and crevice inside out, in the hope of finding a bit of food that was missed before."

The camera equipment was unloaded from the plane to save weight, and piled in the snow, marked by the black flag of a changing bag, held aloft by a tripod leg. But the plane stubbornly refused to take off. They had waited nine days. Clarke and Robertson decided that to remain longer was to risk starving to death. Merrill thought that with the right wind, and an empty plane, he might take off, in which case he would send help. For the moment, anyway, he would stay with his plane.

"Fortunately," said Clarke, "I had bought a dollar compass in Seattle. Our plan was to walk north until we picked up the shore, then follow the shore to Point Barrow. We had little food and we dared not sleep."

Captain Robertson wore the Eskimo costume that had been brought along for the film. Thanks to the mukluks, the Eskimo shoes, he found walking far easier than Clarke, whose boots constantly broke through the ice crust, causing great strain to his muscles. "We would walk until we were exhausted, then catch our breath and go on again. After the first twenty-four hours, the muscles in my leg were so rigid from this unaccustomed activity that I didn't think I could make it any more. It was a constant ordeal to try to keep a compass course because there was nothing to set a compass on. Besides, the light was deceptive. You would see a post set in the ground about a mile away, and after a few more steps it would turn out to be a blade of grass in the snow. Captain Robertson carried a .22 pistol, and one day we saw a goose circling over us. We had visions of shooting it and drinking the hot blood. We had no way of cooking it, but that didn't matter at our stage of hunger. But nothing came of that. We kept on without sleeping, eating snow when we were thirsty, until eventually we found something good to walk on; a frozen lake."

Captain Robertson began to drop behind, his stomach causing him pain. The two men reserved their energy for walking and talked little. But they did discuss what they would eat when they arrived at Point Barrow; Captain Robertson had visions of canned pineapple, while Clarke longed for canned grapefruit and dried apricots.

"Our lips were by this time badly swollen and cracked from eating snow. We had been using the minerally deficient snow-water for two weeks now, which is probably the reason we craved acid fruits. We had no idea of where we were, or how far Barrow was. We imagined it about sixty miles from the plane."

The endless trek continued. At last they reached the coast. Some empty tin cans and blackened stones raised spirits, which sank when there was no further sign of habitation, and the coastline proved to be pitted with crevasses. The two men shared an owl's egg. They came upon a deserted igloo, and salvaged every trace of food from discarded cans. But remembering the plight of the pilot, they dared not stay, and set off again on their painful journey. After seeing no other traces of the coast for thirteen hours, Captain Robertson decided their course was suicidal, and veered due north. His stomach was still causing him acute discomfort. The sight of some posts aroused their anticipation, but they proved to be nothing more than the corner posts of four oil claims.

"About midnight, I crashed through a deep pocket of snow and could not help letting out a cry of pain. The tendon of my left leg had turned into a jelly-like cavity just above the heel. I had torn the Achilles' tendon, and my foot folded up like a hinge. The pain was awful. By walking arm-in-arm with Robertson I could make it along, shifting the weight on to my right foot. By keeping in step we plugged along until morning."

Robertson's strength was giving out. Clarke found a piece of driftwood which he tied to his left foot, enabling him to walk unaided. Nevertheless, the situation was becoming graver by the hour. A couple of planes passed, but too far to spot them. Clarke discovered an immensely encouraging sight—the fresh trail of a sledge, which suggested a settlement was not far away. Robertson agreed to fight it out, and the two men hobbled forward, hanging on to each other.

In melodrama, the nick-of-time rescue is a smooth and standard operation. In reality, such rescues are often fraught with misunderstanding. A pilot, searching for the three men, caught a glimpse of Clarke and Robertson and flew closer. The terrain was unsuitable for landing, and he had to be absolutely sure of their identity before he risked his machine. He circled the men, who waved their arms to attract his attention. He saw Captain Robertson, dressed in his motion picture costume, and decided he was simply an Eskimo excited by the airplane. He flew away.

The two men were not cast down by this apparent setback. Having no idea what was in the pilot's mind, they were overjoyed; at last somebody had seen them and knew where they were. In any case, they realized that no plane could land on that stretch of tumbled ice blocks. They continued hobbling forward until they reached a sandbar. Then they heard the sound of the returning plane. The sandbar was an excellent landing strip, except that it was covered with driftwood. The two men expended the last of their energy in an attempt to clear the driftwood. But the pilot paid no attention to such details. He had changed his mind about the two men. He came bouncing down over the driftwood, switched off his engine, and strode forward with his passenger. "I must say we were a horrible-looking mess. We had eighteen days of beard, our lips were terribly swollen, and we were crippled and generally emaciated. We were very emotional and our voices wavered."

The passenger was Sergeant Richard Heyser of the Signal Corps, a radio operator engaged by Virgil Hart to operate the "Byrd of the Antarctic" shortwave transmitter. The pilot began to cook right away, but decided that in their starved condition, the wrong food, or too much of it, might be dangerous. He unloaded the equipment, leaving Sergeant Heyser to look after it, and flew the men to Point Barrow. They learned from the awe-struck inhabitants that they had walked more than one hundred fifty miles.

Russell Merrill had damaged the propeller as he tried to nose his plane forward. He followed Clarke and Robertson's trail, and was discovered, snow-blind and fast asleep, near the spot where his comrades had been found. It was another

Trying to dig a runway on the snow-covered lake, about one hundred miles south of the Arctic shore.

Charles Clarke (left) and Captain Jack Robertson upon being picked up on the Arctic shore near Point Tangent. Both have eighteen days' growth of beard and cracked lips from eating snow. Robertson is wearing an Eskimo costume brought from Hollywood.

nick-of-time rescue, for Merrill would have frozen to death had he remained in the open much longer. Another important rescue operation restored to Clarke his precious camera equipment, which had sat in the snow for three weeks.

The irony of their situation became apparent as soon as Clarke and Robertson were fit enough to leave the hospital. They discovered that none of the vital sequences for *Frozen Justice* could possibly be filmed. The whaling season was over, and the Eskimos lived very differently from their ancestors. The only skin whaling boat was in a museum at Juneau. Instead of harpoons, they used guns and explosives. While their clothes might have been lined with fur, they were covered with the gayest-colored calico they could purchase. Instead of igloos, they built their homes with lumber. Furthermore, they had abandoned many of the Eskimo customs and taboos.

The unit advised the studio. Meanwhile, Clarke filmed an Eskimo ritual called Nalaqataq, held in honor of the end of the whaling season. His camera was only slightly corroded, and he was able to secure excellent footage of the celebration, in which, with a trampoline made of walrus skins, the Eskimos toss their friends high in the air.

Some walrus-hunting scenes were also filmed—this time by Captain Robertson, who was expert with the Akeley camera. Apart from that, the only valuable result of the expedition was the creation of a permanent radio station at Point Barrow, operated by Sergeant Heyser with the Byrd equipment.

Charles Clarke returned to the Fox studio on 3 July 1928, and was assigned to a new picture—John Ford's *Riley the Cop*—two days later. He suffered pain from his leg and experienced an insomnia that troubles him still. Captain Robertson returned with his footage of the walrus hunt, and two years later released a third feature-length documentary on Alaska called *The Break-Up*.

Said Clarke: "The Fox Film Corporation was still committed to deliver a picture called *Frozen Justice,* so a dance-hall-of-the-Klondike story was dreamed up and made that summer by Allan Dwan. It was hot work for the actors, wearing those fur parkas during the summer heat. The story they made had nothing to do with the book, about the primitive Eskimo before the white man."

Charles Clarke was assigned next to a picture called *Sin Sister,* which, by coincidence, was also set in the Arctic. The director, Charles Klein, objected to Harry Behn's script: "The idea of people being lost in the Arctic for a week is unrealistic," he complained to the studio manager. "They'd be dead." The studio manager informed him that his cameraman had just gone through an identical experience—for three times as long. "And that," said Clarke, "ended the discussion!"

WHITE SHADOWS IN THE SOUTH SEAS

Despite the cooperative nature of film-making, collaboration has seldom been popular among Hollywood directors. Apart from such partnerships as Schoedsack and Cooper, the coupling of names on the credits usually implied that one director had been fired and replaced by the other.

White Shadows in the South Seas (*1928*).

When Robert Flaherty was invited to join MGM to make *White Shadows in the South Seas,* he had never worked on a commercial production, to a feature schedule. He was at heart an amateur. Frederick O'Brien's book, published in 1919, was a series of sketches, a romantic travel book. It had no story. MGM apparently acquired the property for its title, even though, at one point, the picture was retitled *Southern Skies.* Irving Thalberg planned a prestigious production. He asked Flaherty to accept W. S. Van Dyke on the picture as associate director. Van Dyke had made the Al Jennings picture *Lady of the Dugout* and had specialized in Westerns starring Tim McCoy. The selection of Van Dyke was entirely due to his superb generalship on location. He was a professional to his fingertips, one who would keep the machinery running smoothly, directing the odd straightforward scene, while Flaherty was in overall artistic control.

Flaherty accepted the situation, for organization was not his strong point. Once at Culver City, he was put to work with Laurence Stallings, who had so admired *Moana* and who had initiated *The Big Parade.* They found it hard to extract a strong motion picture situation from the O'Brien studies and suggested that a more effective picture could be made from Melville's *Typee.* But Thalberg paid no heed to the idea, and Stallings did his characteristic vanishing act. The project was handed to a former Chicago newspaperman, Ray Doyle.

Van Dyke had worked on the Tim McCoy Westerns with a producer named David Selznick. As a comparative newcomer, Selznick was given the job of assistant to producer Hunt Stromberg. Selznick remembered that the term "associate director" was a euphemism. "The decision was whether to have Van Dyke do it, or Flaherty," said Selznick. "To my astonishment they decided to have them co-direct it. Knowing both men extremely well and being an admirer of the two men and recognizing that they were miles apart in personality, I said that this was an outrage and would not work. That either man could do it perfectly as well, but not the two of them. But they insisted on this. And in any case, I got into a terrible argument with Stromberg,* and that was the end of my connection—my abortive connection—with *White Shadows.* What also appalled me was that they were very excited at the opportunity of getting away with very revelatory scenes of naked girls. But Flaherty was a real poet, a marvelous man who clearly could never work within the commercial setup. He had to work on his own."[1]

Rex Ingram's editor, Grant Whytock, took over as Hunt Stromberg's assistant. Whytock remembers that Van Dyke's enthusiasm for the picture was minimal. He did not particularly want to go to Tahiti (although Robert Cannom, in his book on Van Dyke, declared that he did). Stromberg approached another director, John McCarthy, to serve in his place, but MGM could not make a satisfactory deal with him. It was now almost time to leave for Tahiti. The company was having enormous trouble finding the right girl—Thalberg wanted an unknown for the lead opposite Monte Blue, whom he had borrowed from Warner Brothers. Whytock, almost at the last moment, found a girl sitting in the casting director's office who seemed ideal. "I took her right to Hunt's office. I'd already tested her two weeks before, but I didn't tell him this. He said, 'Test her right away.' We were now getting to

---

* According to Bosley Crowther, the row was over status. Selznick thought he would supervise, but his job was no more than unit manager.

Waiting to do a swimming scene for White Shadows: *Clyde de Vinna, at camera, peers at the sun; Robert Flaherty sits beneath camera with megaphone.*

W. S. Van Dyke in the director's chair; Flaherty, behind him, right of camera, is already relegated to the background in this production still from White Shadows. *Grant Whytock squats at right, next to Monte Blue.*

A generator attracts a crowd during the filming of White Shadows.

urgency point. So we just dug out the old test and ran it, and Raquel Torres got the part."[2]

Just before sailing, Van Dyke was warned again that under no circumstances was he to interfere with the documentary scenes; he was to concentrate on the straightforward narrative material. "Each director had his own sections of the script," said Whytock. "The scenes were kept entirely separate. That had all been worked out. Flaherty was to do all the utopian scenes among the natives. But he wanted to work like he'd worked on *Moana of the South Seas.* He'd make it, then he'd want to remake it. He had a quality all right, but he didn't get along with Monte Blue. Monte didn't know how to work this way."[3]

Richard Griffith stated that Flaherty was upset by the sight of the camera crew, sprawled in the sand, listening to the band at the Coconut Grove in Hollywood on the radio. "Why not go back to California and make the picture in the Coconut Grove there?" he is reported to have said.[4] Yet was it not Flaherty who had given such joy to the Eskimos with his gramophone and his records of Harry Lauder and Al Jolson? In any case, the radio ham was Clyde de Vinna, former official photographer of the Pacific Fleet, who proved himself one of the great exterior cameramen of Hollywood and who won the Academy Award for his work on the picture.

Flaherty was out of sympathy with the project. He knew from his own experience on *Moana* that it was fatal to impose a story on the South Sea islanders. Denied his customary period of discovery and forced to follow a set scenario, he suffered a creative block. Van Dyke's material arrived at Culver City on schedule, but Flaherty's was long delayed. Had he been the sole director, MGM might have given him more leeway, as they had with Rex Ingram. But Ingram had an impressive commercial record; Flaherty was a newcomer to the studio.

Flaherty's material was slow in coming through for another reason. His interpreter was jailed for some previous transgression on Tahiti, and local suspicion spread to the film crew. Conditions became more and more unsuitable for Flaherty's style of film-making until the inevitable crisis was reached. Officially, Flaherty resigned, but Whytock remembered that he fell ill and was sent back. In a letter, Hunt Stromberg wrote: "Mr. Robert *Moana* Flaherty is, well, the bunk. I didn't expect him to have a sense of the 'drammer' but I did think he knew the South Sea natives—and could choose a location!"

With remarkably poor judgment, Flaherty was seduced into a further collaboration on a project in the South Seas. F. W. Murnau, who had failed to make his picture of primitive Eskimo life, turned to the tropics. Flaherty, who had failed to make a picture for Fox about the Indians of Acoma,* fell prey to Murnau's disillusion with Hollywood. He told Murnau the story of a pearl fisher he had heard about on *White Shadows.* "This," said Murnau enthusiastically, "will be the first Murnau-Flaherty production." Flaherty sailed into another sea of crisis. Financial disaster and personal conflict caused him to withdraw once again. The resulting film, *Tabu,* despite, or perhaps because of, all the anguish, developed into one of the silent era's last great classics, even though it was released as late as 1931. Said Richard Griffith: "Flaherty's name loomed large on the credits. What was lacking was his signature on the film itself."[5]

PRODUCTION DIFFICULTIES ON *White Shadows* did not evaporate with Flaherty's departure. "Our great problem was the usual thing you hit on location," said Grant Whytock. "You can't work fast. There's no possible way you can make a picture in twenty-eight to thirty days down there, because you've got to wait for things to be built, and you don't have the mechanics, and then the weather gets you."[6]

It says much for his stamina that Van Dyke returned to Tahiti for his next production, *The Pagan* (which he scheduled at thirty days!), and then went to Africa for *Trader Horn.* For he suffered greatly from the heat. "I've never felt such heat," he said. "Wet heat, steamy. I'd put on a fresh suit of white ducks and ten minutes later they'd be wringing wet. At night the bed sheets would be sodden a few moments after I got between them. I didn't even try to sleep. I'd get a few drinks just to cast a rosier light over the prospect of more months in Tahiti, and then I'd read or write all night. The next morning it would be raining. It rains every minute of the day, somewhere on the island."[7]

MGM press releases contained highly colored accounts of the company's experiences: "They encountered terrific hardships, climbed mountains seven thousand feet high, braved tropical storms, lost themselves in the depths of jungles never before explored. . . ." Van Dyke, Monte Blue, and company complained far more vehemently of the cockroaches in the stew, the centipedes in the bed, "squeaky tin phonographs grinding out ten year old tunes, poor champagne at terrific prices, daytime in the South Seas, night-time in the South Seas and a mail steamer only once a month."[8]

---

* Leon Shamroy was at the camera for the few scenes which were shot in 1930. The front office at Fox demanded a love story, and a warehouse fire destroyed the print of *Acoma—the Sky City.* Shamroy made a two-reeler based on an Indian legend, then joined the Huntington Ethnological Expedition to the Far East. His assistant, Floyd Crosby, photographed *Tabu.*

The unglamorous side of expedition film-making (White Shadows).

W. S. Van Dyke, director of White Shadows, *and local inhabitant who has discovered how to charm the men in the food store.*

To relieve the monotony, MGM films were screened for the cast, crew, and islanders. Whytock recalled that they seldom received the reverence due to them. "The interpreter had a little box up high alongside the audience, and instead of reading the titles he would interpret them the way he thought they should be. He had them roaring with laughter at the dramatic scenes half the time. I never could get anyone to tell me what he was saying. As a result, we had a problem. If we were shooting a scene where someone was dying, they'd burst out laughing. We finally got a phonograph and played sad music. That sobered them right down."[9]

The native characters were all paid the same salary—a dollar a day and lunch. "The extras that we ran up and down the hills came in a body and complained. They felt they should get more money because they were doing all the work—these other fellows, playing native chiefs, were just sitting there. Then the cast started to disappear. We had to sign them to contracts, which they honored. And the way we evened it out, the contract was a letter that we guaranteed to pay them and at the end of the picture we gave them a little bonus.

"Van Dyke had brought out his Western crew. They were all tops in their way. The grip was as strong as a bull. He used to get under one of those big parallels and move it all alone.

"We had three cameramen—Clyde de Vinna, George Nogle, and Bob Roberts,* and no assistants. That's how MGM economized. They took the boys from the islands and made assistants out of them. We opened our own lab there, too."[10]

Robert Cannom, in *Van Dyke and the Mythical City, Hollywood,* says that Van Dyke's experience in handling the Indians on the Tim McCoy Westerns helped him considerably in his relations with the islanders. "In re-enacting the scenes of past native life—before the white man came—the oldest natives of several islands were called into consultation for assurance that nothing of white civilization would creep into the spirit of the pre-white days on the islands. Relics were borrowed from museums and island families and used as hand-props in production."[11]

Van Dyke's determination to get the picture made was balanced by a certain cynicism as to its commercial chances. "Van used to laugh about the picture," said Whytock. "But I said, 'Van, you've got a picture that's going to the Chinese [Grauman's Chinese Theater].' And I had the privilege of sitting next to Van Dyke and D. W. Griffith at the opening night at the Chinese. And Griffith asked Van Dyke how he did the undersea stuff. I didn't hear the reply. But I shot the undersea stuff when Van and the main company had left. I kept the second cameraman, George Nogle. We shot ten days, and got some acceptable stuff, but suddenly the water cleared, the rain stopped for a while, and we didn't get any sediment from the rivers. And the shots came through crystal clear. We had a month, so we started all over again—we just did everything over and threw the other stuff away."[12]

Whytock also shot other second-unit scenes, including the traveling shot that opens the picture. He made a first cut on part of *White Shadows,* although the main editor was Ben Lewis. Whytock considered him a marvelous editor; he particularly admired the way Lewis worked in apparently irrelevant cutaways of sea creatures, upon which so much footage had been expended.

---

* Bob Roberts had also worked on *Moana,* and all three worked on *Trader Horn.*

White Shadows in the South Seas. *Clyde de Vinna won an Academy Award for his photography.*

Despite his experience at the hands of Stromberg, David Selznick echoed the press reports and the audience preview cards; he thought it "a beautiful picture"—a description that holds good today. Yet the film has been dismissed by historians simply because Flaherty had abandoned it. Bosley Crowther referred to the weak story and the atrocious acting in his book *The Lion's Share.*[13] Calder-Marshall implied that the central theme of the book—the degrading impact of the white civilization—had been intentionally omitted by MGM. This is not so. *White Shadows* is as sharp an attack on the exploitation by the white man as had been made up to that time. One of the opening titles sets the mood: "But the white man, in his greedy trek across the planet, cast his withering shadow across the islands, and the job of 'civilizing' them to his interests began."*

The film is as romantic as anything Flaherty might have made, and its documentary detail is as rich. Its one drawback might have been eliminated had he stayed on the picture, however. One feels too strongly the opposition; one gets to

* The white man cannot take the whole blame for the despoiling of the earth. Thor Heyerdahl says that Easter Island was once covered by forest—obliterated long before the white man came.

know all about the destruction of this primitive paradise, but one does not know the islanders. They provide a picturesque background. One sees their customs in affectionate detail, one sees the way they live. But unless one can feel for the islanders themselves, the final tragedy of their "civilizing" is muted. Nevertheless, *White Shadows* is a sensitive, often moving film, remarkably uncompromising, and a tribute to the talent of its director. As D. W. Griffith said on the opening night at the Chinese: "*White Shadows* is a work of art. And Woody Van Dyke is the artist who brought it into being."[14]

STARK LOVE

The unpromising title of *Stark Love* conceals one of the most unusual films ever made in America. A dramatic documentary, the film was shot in the mountains of North Carolina, among the isolated and primitive mountain people, descended from Scots-Irish settlers, who inhabit the Smokies and who are notorious for their violence toward intruders. Bruce Barton called them "our contemporary ancestors."

"In their inaccessible mountains these people remain undeveloped by culture," reads an opening title, "and their law of the wilderness is expressed in the cruel principle: Man is the absolute ruler—woman is the working slave."

Unlike most of the films about primitive people, in which civilization's encroachments are seen to be ruinous, *Stark Love* stresses the liberating value of education. The only member of Wolf Trap Creek capable of reading is young Rob Warwick (Forrest James). Books have brought, first, discontent, then raging ambition. His girl, Barbara (Helen Mundy), fired by his enthusiasm, dreams romantically of the outside world, her ideas formed by the tales of ancient chivalry Rob has read her.

Once a year the mountaineers assemble for the "funeral feast," which is celebrated for generations of past dead. If on this day the circuit preacher should come, all "wild marriages" are legalized. This year, the preacher arrives, and Rob makes a momentous decision. He asks the preacher to take him back to the city; there, he will sell his horse and pay the school not for his education but for Barbara's.

Rob's mother dies, and his father, Jason Warwick (Silas Miracle), cannot cope without a woman to work for him. Barbara goes to help out and finds the house in complete disorder. She takes over, cleans the place thoroughly, puts the children to bed, and so impresses Jason that he decides to marry her. Barbara's father suggests that Jason wait while he gives the matter proper consideration.

"I can't wait. The river's flooding, and if I don't take Barbara now I'll be cut off from you. When the preacher comes again we'll be properly married. What do you say?"

Decisions about marriage are a concern purely for men in this society. They shake hands, and the deed is done. But Barbara's dreams of reaching the outside world are not to be shattered so easily. When Rob returns from the town, anxious to take Barbara back with him, Jason introduces his "new maw."

Stark Love (1927) *utilized Karl Brown's acetylene lighting system, adapted for shooting in the wilds. Brown (in chair) directs Forrest James and Helen*

Mundy, watched by Captain Paul Wing and Robert Pittack, assistant cameraman (standing).

An argument develops into an impassioned fight, human anger echoed by the fury of the elements as the swollen river thunders past the shack, plucking Rob and Barbara from their natural habitat and sweeping them down the mountainside toward a new life. Struggling desperately against the violence of the current, they manage to reach the shore, and, when morning comes, they set off together to leave the mountains for good.

Director Karl Brown's decision to make the whole picture on location meant the difference between just another hillbilly melodrama and a work of art. Apart from the two leads, every member of the cast is an authentic mountaineer. There is no make-up; the quality of the faces, the texture of the rough skin, is carefully and affectionately captured by the camera, and the effect is reminiscent (in original prints) of seventeenth-century Dutch painting. The compositions crystallize the atmosphere but are never obtrusive.

Every new scene carries the pleasure of discovery. Brown tells us exactly what we want to know; he explains the origins of the settlers, he illustrates the way they live, their manner of dress, and their customs and traditions. He shows how, when they die, their bodies are placed in miniature cabins as protection from the wolves. He shows us women skinning an animal in the one room of the cabin, while the men sit at ease, drinking moonshine. But none of this is presented in the dry, educational manner of so many factual films. Every facet of mountain life is woven into the fabric of the story. *Stark Love* stands as a priceless record of a forgotten people.

The idea for *Stark Love* developed from the big outdoor pictures such as *The Covered Wagon* and *Pony Express.* "I saw pioneer families doing what they had been doing all their lives. It was so effortless and so natural, I realized no actor could ever duplicate what had been bred in the bone of these people for centuries past."[1]

Brown has kept a copy of a book called *Our Southern Highlanders,* which served as a guide. Its author was Horace Kephart, whom he knew well. Brown had also traveled through the country as a cameraman, and the idea gradually came into focus. The first problem was to convince the Paramount hierarchy—Jesse Lasky and Walter Wanger—to let him do it.

"Well, they sent me ahead on a sort of exploration trip. They gave me six weeks and a camera and a business manager to make arrangements in case I liked what I saw. So I went into the country just at the turn of the year. I had spent so much time out of doors—Wyoming, British Columbia—that I didn't mind at all. I was used to roughing it; you come to a stream, you learn to cross it, you build a fire on the other side to dry your feet because that's wisdom. A trick that Kephart taught me gave me many a comfortable night when others could have frozen. When it's very cold at night and the wind is blowing and the ground is so hard that it's just like rock, you may have nothing but your blanket. You could very well freeze to death. The idea is to build yourself a big bonfire—you can always find plenty of dead wood in the forest. A big bonfire as high as this ceiling and let it burn down to coals. Rake some of them out, cook your dinner over the rest, then brush the fire aside. The ground is not only thawed, it's heated maybe two or three feet deep. You spread your blanket over that natural hot bed, curl up and go to sleep. The snow can be hitting your face, but your body is warm. Nobody need ever freeze to death as long as there's wood. It's just so simple that nobody thinks of it. And of course if you're in luck, and can find a niche between a couple of good-sized boulders, and you can build your fire there, then you're all set—you'll have radiant heat all night.

"The business manager who accompanied me was Captain Paul Wing—he had been with me on two or three pictures.

"To make contact with the mountain people, I first of all went to Kephart. He told me what not to do, and he wouldn't tell me what to do. He simply illustrated a thing I'd known a long time and has yet to fail me; that if you go into any country—that is, if you're not at war—and behave yourself as a gentleman should, nobody will ever bother you. Mind your own business, keep out of other people's trouble, don't interfere with anything, just do what you're supposed to do. That's the way with the mountain people. They're naturally suspicious and so you just go about your business until they observe, or by some sort of psychic osmosis learn, that you are not up to any harm, you're not going to turn them in, you really are going to do what you're supposed to do. From that point on, everything is plain sailing."

"Plain sailing" was hardly the term to describe the Paramount reaction when they saw the documentary material. Brown countered their distaste with a publicity campaign, citing *Grass* and *Nanook*—an approach that appealed to Lasky. The low budget appealed to Zukor. The film got the go-ahead.

"I had discovered, quite some time before this, that the easiest actors to handle are children. They are naturally imitative, that's how they learn. Now if you try to tell anybody, even a pretty good actor, how to do something, he'll unconsciously resent it. He feels that he knows his business. And so I had learned, mostly from watching Griffith do the same thing, and later on Cruze—never tell an actor what to do. Tell him what is to be done.

"And so in this case, take them from the viewpoint of casting. If you've got a big strong guy like Jason Warwick, you need a big barrel-chested fellow who looks like General Grant. Just look over and find a contrasting type—and here comes the fellow they called Reb—he was the little skinny one who played opposite. He had a little white beard.

"Helen Mundy was the most difficult person I ever had anything to do with. I didn't find her. Wing was the one that found her; she came from Knoxville. I found a girl who was much better than Mundy. She lived on the mountain and was everything she was supposed to be. And when it came to getting parental consent, her hillbilly father said, 'I'd see her dead an' in her coffin before I see her play actin' for nobody.' "

Wing went to Knoxville. He asked a girl behind the counter of a drugstore if she knew anyone willing to star in a picture. Yes, said the girl. A friend of hers, whom she expected any minute, might do it. And in came sixteen-year-old Helen Mundy, from Knoxville High School. She thought Captain Wing was kidding, so she kidded back. Oh no, she flounced. She hadn't *any* idea of getting into movies. It took a great deal of persuasion before she would take him seriously. And then he had to deal with a tougher obstacle still—Helen's mother. Eventually, he succeeded in packing Helen off to Asheville, North Carolina, for a camera test.

"I was so desperate at the time that I didn't ask too many questions," said Brown. "I took her out and made some still pictures of her, and a few tests, shot them back to New York and they practically burned up, saying, 'How did you ever find her down there?' But the famous ones, like Pola Negri, were nothing compared to this one. She learned very early in the game that she was the only girl in the picture, that without her the picture could not be made, and so it was virtually a case of blackmail. 'Give me this' or 'Get me that—or I'm gone.'

"I said, 'All right, Helen, go ahead.'

"She said, 'You think I won't?'

"I said, 'Well, what are you sticking around for?'

"So she went. The others said, 'Well, there goes your picture.'

" 'Maybe it does,' I said, 'but I'm not going to make a picture at the cost of all this.' About two hours later, she came creeping back, scratched by briars and very hungry.

"We had magazines coming in, and Helen read everything she could about the movie people. She came on the set one day with the damndest face you ever saw. Cheeks that looked like a Russian ballet, very badly applied lipstick, which made her look as if she'd been eating raw, live meat, and her eyes were just two black holes. I had to take her down to the creek and wash her face before I could do anything with her.

"Wing and I were having dinner in Knoxville one night and about three tables away were four boys, laughing and having a fine time. The one farthest from me was exactly the type that I had in mind for the boy. I said, 'We should try to meet that fellow.'

"Wing just got a waiter over, wrote a note and said, 'Give it to that gentleman over there.' He read it, came over, and I let Wing do the talking. Yes, he was willing to do it. He was part of a football team and they had just won something somewhere and they were celebrating. So we took him in and he made the picture. He was very silent. He would sulk in his tent like Achilles. He had very little to say to anybody. But he got through with his part and as soon as he got through it he was gone. Nobody ever heard of him again.

"All the rest of the cast were real mountain people."

"IN THE EIGHTEENTH CENTURY, before the Revolution, the British officers were very fond of a sport called pig-sticking. There were no wild boars in America, so they imported some from Central Europe, especially savage ones. Some of them got away and overran the entire mountain area, and they are very, very dangerous. They are hunted on horseback because you can't get away from them on foot. So we were well equipped with .45s strapped to our belt, because they will attack you without warning, just rip out your shins, kill you in a minute. Fortunately, we never met one. We were all prepared and they kept away.

"We discovered a rocky outcrop that would block any sort of wagon road. We had to get our supplies in and out, so we decided to blast it out. They were building a dam on the river forty or fifty miles away, so we had a ready supply of dynamite and experienced men to use it. We simply blasted that ridge away.

"Instead of shooting the interiors in a studio, we used an actual cabin and took two walls out—so we could get cross shots. Part of the roof remained in place. We used reflectors for daylight shots, and for night shots, with the firelight glowing, I used special acetylene lights.

Stark Love. *Helen Mundy brandishes an axe in the censored rape scene.*

"We were in the mining district—it was stuffed full of coal and miners—and they all had acetylene lamps fastened on top of their helmets. Two jets of acetylene are projected so they meet and flare out and give a pretty bright light. So we got a lot of these lamps and made a whole battery of them inside a regular Klieg light.

"For the river scenes, we had to create our own flood. We built a dam upstream with a breakaway arrangement. When the water got up to six or eight feet we could blow up one end of it and the whole river would rush on down.

"One connecting shot was made in the studio at Astoria. I not only did not want, I did not *like* any part of the water sequence that ends the picture at the present time. To me, that was just a cheap melodramatic trick, completely out of key with the picture."

Unfortunately, Brown had shot a rape scene that was violent but, he hoped, not censorable. Paramount thought otherwise; the scene was cut and the river sequence substituted to provide the standard "thrill" ending.

"Once the girl moved out and joined the boy and started to walk down the mountain, that's the end of the story. You don't have to do anything else, but New York insisted. And so I had to go back and shoot that water stuff later, and we needed a connecting shot to get the thing to flow through. So we took it in one long

Authentic mountain people played in Stark Love, *as this photograph attests. Silas Miracle (left) and Mrs. Queen. The boy at right is obviously suffering from malnutrition.*

shot at Astoria—they duplicated the interior from stills, duplicated the costumes, and stuck on beards and that was it. But it was a whole day's work for one scene.

"We had no rushes on location. Everything was blind. We took the standard amount of stills, but we never showed them to the mountain people. They had a complete lack of interest. They had no curiosity, they had no understanding. They just didn't care, that was all there was to it. It was no use explaining anything, they thought you were crazy anyway. We were paying such enormous salaries—everyone got $25 a week, leading man, leading woman, everyone. That way there could be no quarrels, no jealousy.

"Walter Woods thought up the title *Stark Love.* I didn't particularly like it, but nobody came up with a better one, so we let it go.* When it was released it did pretty well in America—I understand it did very well indeed in Europe. I say pretty well—it ran about two or three weeks. Ordinarily, a picture would run a week. But it wasn't one of those things like *The Covered Wagon* or *The Birth of a Nation* that ran for a year. It also had the handicap of being the first of its kind. It was a stranger in town—nobody knew quite what to make of it. I don't want to take too much credit upon myself, because Bob Flaherty had already made *Nanook of the North,* but that was a straight document—no attempt was made to tell a story.

"As a matter of fact, *Stark Love* was such a maverick in design, conception,

* Karl Brown wanted a generic title like *The Covered Wagon*—something along the lines of *The Log Cabin.* But Paramount insisted on the word "love" in the title. Brown describes the making of the film and his struggles with the front office in his remarkable book *The Paramount Adventure,* to be published by Farrar, Straus & Giroux, New York.

and everything else that nobody in the sales department knew what to do with it. And there was considerable talk about simply shelving it. It didn't cost much and it wouldn't be much of a loss. But they did put it out and everybody was astonished —including myself."

"A mighty fine picture," said *Photoplay,* "in some ways as noteworthy as Robert Flaherty's *Nanook* and *Moana. Stark Love,* despite its garish box office title, is a picture of genuine merit. It is astonishing how well the mountaineers act. Helen Mundy, a school girl hired in Knoxville, Tenn., is excellent as the heroine, while a hill boy, Forrest James, gives an amazingly good performance. An old timer, Silas Miracle, plays the boy's father in a way to outshine Wally Beery's best work. Don't miss this film."[2]

But the great financial success the film deserved was not to be.

"It gumshoed into an intimate theater on rubber heels," wrote George Kent Schuler, editor of *Motion Picture Classic.* "Were its sponsors afraid of the fate of other naturals—like *Moana?*"[3]

Said Brown: "Many of my friends of that day, such as Larry Stallings, Ben Hecht, and Bob Sherwood, expressed regret that I could not have waited a few years to get the sound of the mountaineers' voices, who spoke Elizabethan English, and the magnificent colors of the mountains in spring, when the mountains are solid masses of azaleas and rhododendrons in full bloom—a sight of breathtaking beauty not to be found elsewhere.

"The real cause for genuine regret is that I made the picture at a time when the screen was heavily censored and that some of the more powerful scenes were banned by the censors. I regard the picture as a pallid ghost."

STAMPEDE

Checking through the documentary catalogue of the National Film Archive, in London, I selected *Stampede* for viewing simply because it seemed relevant. I had no expectations beyond a conventional African travelogue. *Stampede,* despite its incompleteness and its rough edges, proved to be an elaborately reconstructed documentary in the tradition of *Chang.* It set out to exploit the Sudanese background; by focusing upon the migration of a tribe, in the manner of *Grass,* highly dramatic incidents were woven into a quasi-factual story.

The film was made by Major Court Treatt, of whom no one seemed to have heard. Imagining he was an Englishman, I tried to track him down. The London telephone directory listed no Court Treatts, but there was an R. C. Treatt; the spelling was similar enough to justify a try. R. C. Treatt turned out to be a firm specializing in perfumery compounds. The managing director remembered Major Court Treatt, but said he had died many years before. He put me on to a relative, who diverted me to South Africa. Stella Court Treatt, the major's wife, who had scripted the film and helped in the direction, replied from Johannesburg; she in turn put me in touch with her brother, Errol Hinds, who had photographed the picture.

Stampede (*1928*): *Fatma as Loweno.*

This family undertaking had developed from an earlier picture, a straightforward travel film called *Cape to Cairo,* which had been photographed by T. A. Glover. The word "straightforward" can be used to describe the film (although only a minute fragment survives in the National Film Archive), but it hardly applies to the expedition itself, which was the fulfillment of an ambition for Court Treatt. A member of the original British Expeditionary Force of 1914, he fought as an infantryman before transferring to the Royal Flying Corps in 1915. He flew as an observer until 1916, when he was shot down and badly wounded. He ended the war as a staff officer in Egypt; after the armistice he was put in charge of the third section of aerodrome construction for the Trans African Route in preparation for the first flight by Sir Pierre van Ryneveldt. Both on this project and in the RFC, he had used a Crossley car and considered it the best possible vehicle for rough work. He dreamed of using one to cross Africa from Cape Town to Cairo, and of making a film en route. Captain Kelsey, who had attempted the journey in 1913–1914, experienced setback after setback, until he was eventually killed by a leopard in Rhodesia.

The cinematographer, T. A. Glover, had recently returned from an expedition with Captain Angus Buchanan through the Sahara from Lagos to Algiers. The Court Treatts had seen his film *Across the Great Sahara* in London, and so admired it that they invited him to join them.

The Court Treatts, like so many explorers, had a deep disdain for most aspects of civilization. Having literally hacked their way through impenetrable jungle, they felt it very galling to reach their goal only to find it swarming with tourists. Travel in Africa was becoming easier, and the tourists, with their immacu-

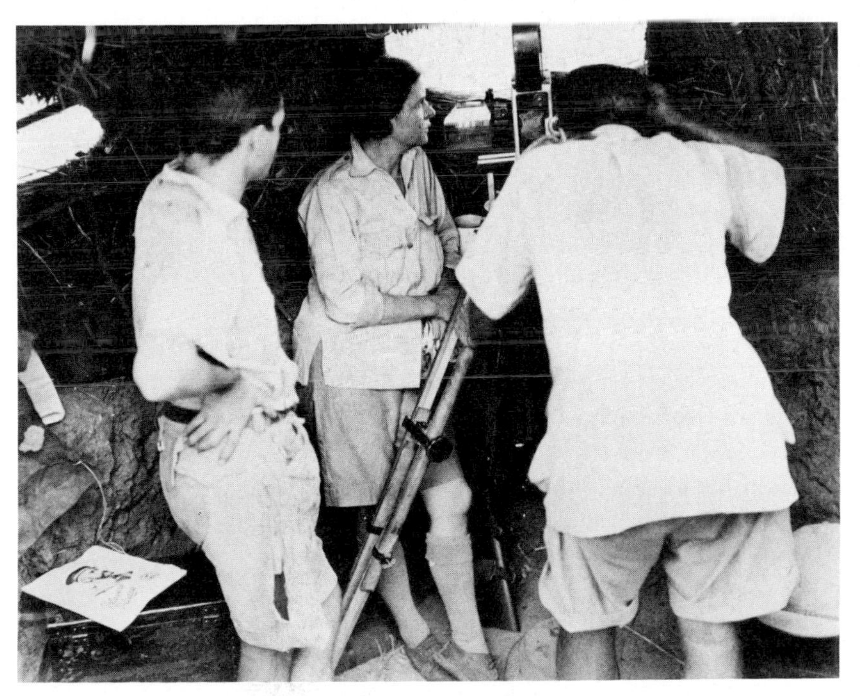

Photographing game from a hide at a water hole—a job of profound tedium, common to most expedition films, and one demanding the strongest sense of dedication. Errol Hinds with Stella and Major Court Treatt.

late white helmets and bone-rimmed goggles, infuriated the scruffy, insect-bitten explorers, whose endurance seemed challenged by their very presence.

The trek was described by Stella Court Treatt in *Cape to Cairo*.[1] The picture opened in London, and, according to Errol Hinds, the Polytechnic Cinema was crammed every evening. "Then the 1926 General Strike occurred and almost immediately attendances faded right out," he wrote.[2]

The successful conclusion of the expedition inevitably led to thoughts of another. The Court Treatts and Hinds spent long hours discussing the possibility; they agreed that the next attempt should be made in the virtually unexplored regions of the southern Sudan.

The inevitable drawback was lack of money. Major Court Treatt had made the first trip possible by financing it himself. He could not manage such a huge outlay again. The family approached British Instructional Films, which agreed to sponsor the expedition and to handle the distribution of the resulting film. The Court Treatts spent two years in England, studying the latest developments in cinematography and watching the current documentaries. Realizing that a story line was now essential even for expedition pictures, Stella Court Treatt wrote a scenario. From Southampton, they sailed to Port Sudan, driving their Morris Commercial, named "Star of the Desert," to a small Habbania Arab village named Buram, five hundred miles from El Obeid.

The expedition was a source of fascination in this remote spot, for the only white people who ever stayed there were district commissioners. A collapsible darkroom, built to the design of Court Treatt and Errol Hinds, was erected. "The portable darkroom consisted of sheets of prefabricated three-ply covered with duralumin," wrote Errol Hinds. "The crates in which sheets were packed formed the floor on which the darkroom was erected and bolted together. We erected it under a giant wild fig tree which grew near the one we used for the python and the baby scene. For extra coolness, we erected a thatched roof. It worked like a charm. Suspended from a branch outside the darkroom we had two large canvas buckets with wooden taps. The buckets were filled from the local well, and a teaspoon of alum fairly soon precipitated all colloidal matter to the bottom. Trouble started as the well, which was the water supply for the whole village, began providing less and less water. It soon became apparent that we would have to give up, and our carefully designed darkroom project took on the semblance of a large white elephant. The only thing I could do was to make a short test strip of each magazine and send the film to England for processing."

Casting was difficult; a large number of local people were interviewed, but it took a great deal of searching before the right faces appeared. Three hundred piasters had to be paid before the leading men would agree to shave their beards—shaving is not an expense that appears on many documentary budgets, but the Court Treatts regarded it as essential for their story.

The Arabs hired for the picture found the chores very boring. Construction work, such as digging a mock river, may have excited the Court Treatts, who knew what it was for, but to the locals, it was just another hot and tedious job. They disappeared whenever they could. The Court Treatts acquired a sergeant of *askari* who bullied the Arabs into working hard.

"With a view to collecting as many animals as possible for use in the fire sequence," wrote Errol Hinds, "we offered cash. You would have been amazed at what turned up—ant bears, baby cheetahs, young guinea fowl, hyenas, gazelle. . . . One of the acquisitions was a full-blooded young python which we decided to use in the baby scenes. The whole scene was rigged but not faked. Where it took place was under a colossal wild fig tree. My camera was set up for a medium shot showing the obliging python draped on a limb of the tree above the baby's head. All I had to do was to wait until the python finally decided he was bored with the fig tree, and as it uncoiled, it came down slowly, head first. I changed lenses on my Bell and Howell to get a close-up of the head and body descending through the frame, and close-ups of the baby to intercut with the action of the python."*

This scene caused much comment when the picture was released, for the python appeared to be creeping closer and closer to a crying baby—which was achieved purely by editing. But in the final shot, the mother rescued the baby at the precise moment that the python fell to the ground, a startling piece of showmanship that was climaxed when an Arab hunter wrestled with the snake and killed it.†

Disaster struck the expedition when Major Court Treatt connected flashlight batteries; a short circuit caused the powder to explode in his face. The major and two Arabs were blinded, their faces masks of burned flesh. "Stella," said Court Treatt, deliriously, "those damned Huns have started again." Stella and Errol Hinds treated the victims, and when a Syrian doctor arrived, he told them they could not have done better for the patients. None of them would lose his sight.

The motion picture village was now complete, and a deluge had filled up the mock river. But some well-meaning Fellata cut all the grass and ruined the set. The grass had to be replanted.

"Monday September 10 1928," wrote Stella Court Treatt in her diary. "Today everything has been supremely successful in everything. We find that the people can act naturally, and that Fatma, the lovely girl we have to play the part of Loweno, the heroine, is a positive gem. She is a poem of grace and very beautiful. All her actions are pretty."[3]

Once the cast was set, they were screen-tested before the camera, which ran without film, and they performed superbly. "It was amazing how easy it was for them to accept direction," wrote Hinds. "We had a first-class interpreter and he carefully explained to them what it was all about, giving chapter and verse of the scenario, and they very soon got the idea. The main difficulty was in getting them not to look at the camera, but a few well-chosen adjectives in rich Arabic overcame that problem! They very soon entered into the whole spirit of the exercise and, in fact, thoroughly enjoyed themselves—especially the building and subsequent burning down of the village and the flight across the river from the approaching fire."

Continuity was one concept the Arabs failed to comprehend. They changed not only their clothes but their ornaments as well. Major Court Treatt and Hinds had enough to do with their two Bell and Howells and two Newman Sinclairs, so

---

* Court Treatt later developed a device for the Newman Sinclair camera that enabled it to be operated by remote control. It became officially known as the Court Treatt release.

† The scene had to be shot twice, since the first mother left the picture.

Stella had charge of continuity. An actor might enter one shot with a walking stick—another shot with a cast-off solar topee.

"Monday October 1. We got the shot of shots today—people, bulls, horses, donkeys and cows, all crossing the little river. I've never seen such movement and color, and incident, too. People fell off—loads crashed—there was so much shouting, and cries and laughter that I could hardly hear myself think. I noticed that the horses and people on the bank were marvellously silhouetted in the water, and got C.T. to photograph the reflection as well. If it comes out on the screen, it's going to be beautiful.

"Then we photographed them all on the other side—got pictures of camping scenes at dusk; fires, cooking pots, horses and animals tethered to near-by trees. Then night shots of the sheikh with his wife and two babies—the future heroes of the picture. We got our magnesium flares placed in holes two feet deep in the ground over which wood was stacked. When the flares were lit the effect was just like that of real wood fires."

Some of the Arabs were suspicious of the film-makers' motives; they suspected their intention was to force them back to England to be enslaved—"just like the Turks did."[4]

Errol Hinds took advantage of an unusual location: "It must have been a perennial stream from which extended a beautiful green lawn, such as you might find in England. We found a tree, which had probably been uprooted by elephants, lying on its side. By doing a little pruning we were able to make a hide just large enough for the camera. One morning, I took my stance in the hide before dawn. A most extraordinary day. A leopard came down to drink. This was unusual and unexpected as one rarely sees them during the daylight hours. I still feel rather bad about this, but knowing from experience how incredibly dangerous leopards are under these conditions, I shot him. Later a huge lion came down, more or less in the same spot, and he must have had a most fantastic hangover because he drank and drank and drank. All the while, using different lenses, I cranked my camera. Having satisfied his thirst the lion walked away. Quite suddenly I remembered the sequence in the script which called for a lion stalking. Still cranking the camera, I did what could have been an extremely stupid thing. I suddenly made a noise mimicking the bleat of a goat. The result was electric. The lion whipped round in his tracks, then stalking slowly forward he got so close to the hide that I became nervous. I stopped filming and picked up my .350 Rigby magnum. By this time he had moved round behind the hide and as I cautiously emerged, rifle at the ready, I was surprised to see him running towards some distant bushes. I deliberately smashed a bullet into the ground behind him to help him on his way, and said thank you for your co-operation. It was a gusty day and probably what happened was that with a shift of wind he must have got my scent—happily for me, a scent quite unlike that of the expected goat."

When the picture was completed, and the expedition returned to England, Errol Hinds was horrified to discover that the laboratories had not processed a single roll. As if to disprove Cherry Kearton's theory that film must be developed at once, the negative proved to be flawless.

Stampede was successful enough for two books to be written about it—Stella Court Treatt's *Sudan Sand,* about the expedition, and *Stampede,* the story of the film

This scene became the most famous of all from Robert Flaherty's Nanook of the North.

Major and Mrs. Court Treatt, remembering that scene, try the phonograph on one of their cast.

Photographed by Errol Hinds during Stampede.

Stampede: *camera boom improvised from a deck chair by Errol Hinds.*

illustrated with stills. Major Court Treatt, an admirer of the work of Walt Disney, attempted later on to mount another expedition with Disney's backing. He returned to England at the outbreak of war and served in the RAF as an aerial photographer. He died in Los Angeles in 1952, aged fifty-six. Stella Court Treatt married again—she is now Mrs. Mosley-Yeo—and Errol Hinds, after an eventful desert war as a combat cameraman, became head of the National Film Board of South Africa, a position he still holds.

GRASS

Had it not been for the guaranteed outlet of the lecture circuit, the partnership of Merian C. Cooper and Ernest B. Schoedsack might not have been formed, *Grass, Chang,* and *Rango* might not have been made, and the film industry would have been denied its legendary box-office sensation *King Kong.*

The man who brought the two together professionally was Captain Edward Salisbury, an explorer and a veteran of expedition films. Salisbury was a Roosevelt-like conservationist: "For three years he has labored to assemble a film library in which may be found all that pertains to the natural history of North America."[1] In 1915 he sailed in *Wisdom II* for Central and South America, on an expedition with Rex Beach. Salisbury's cameraman, Charles Dahl, succeeded in filming the diminutive San Blas Indians, who had never before been photographed. In September 1917, Salisbury reported from Pekin that he had filmed an uprising there in Prizmacolor. An expedition to the South Seas resulted in a 1923 documentary, *Black Shadows of the South Seas.*

Captain Salisbury was about to embark upon another expedition and hired a young journalist, Merian C. Cooper. Cooper, born in Florida in 1894, had served in Pershing's army on the Mexican border, and as an aviator in the war he participated in the Battle of St. Mihiel. Shot down in flames over the Argonne, he became a prisoner of the Germans. After the war, he went to Poland with the U.S. Food Administration, which was headed by Herbert Hoover. The Allied intervention was at its height when, with Major Cedric Faunt le Roy, he formed the Kosciusko Squadron to fight the Bolsheviks. Again he was shot down, this time by Budënny's cavalry, and he became a prisoner of the Red Army. Sentenced to death, he made an epic escape and returned to the United States.

Cooper had been impressed by Theodore Roosevelt's *Through the Brazilian Wilderness,* and by its message: "If you want to be an explorer, make sure you do it while you're young." Determined to follow this advice, Cooper spent his evenings studying at the American Geographical Society. "I learned to be a good mapmaker. I learned survival techniques and I learned that you had to have money to be an explorer. I didn't have any money. A man wanted a navigator who could write, so I joined a sailing ship at Singapore—the *Wisdom II.*"[2]

The purpose of the voyage was to visit little-known places, to collect material for a book (*The Sea Gipsy* by Edward A. Salisbury and Merian C. Cooper)[3] and magazine articles, and to make motion picture films. Unfortunately, the ship ran into a typhoon which so demoralized the American cameraman that he jumped ship at Colombo, Ceylon. Cooper seized the opportunity and contacted an old friend, Ernest B. Schoedsack.

Schoedsack had first met Cooper on the station platform at Vienna, and they had traveled to Warsaw together. Schoedsack filmed the Polish intervention and the Greco-Turkish War of 1921–1922, an experience that sparked his fascination for the Near East. Returning to Paris, he received Cooper's message and joined the expedition at Djibhouti.

When Captain Salisbury fell ill, Cooper and Schoedsack made their first film together in Addis Ababa, with the cooperation of Ras Tafari (later known as Haile Selassie). The footage was destroyed, supposedly, when *Wisdom II* put into dry dock for repairs and a careless workman set her ablaze. Yet the *Golden Prince* was eventually released as a short subject.

The *Wisdom II* lost her keel in a heavy storm and her crew nearly lost their lives. The expedition came to a full stop. Cooper and Schoedsack, certain they could do better than travelogues, discussed a full-length production. The theme would be man's struggle against nature, as in *Nanook of the North,* a film they had heard about but had not yet seen. While the battered ship limped toward port, the basis of *Grass* began to take shape in their minds. The dramatic conflict of the film was to be exemplified by a nomadic Asian tribe, which is forced to migrate each year in order to survive. The people selected were the Kurds, who, the film-makers were told, had the most picturesque costumes and customs and lived in highly photogenic country.

Cooper went to New York and raised a loan of $5,000 from his father and brother. Schoedsack returned to Paris. His contribution was a Debrie camera.

When Cooper rejoined Schoedsack in Paris, with him was Marguerite Harrison, who had invested a further $5,000. Cooper had met her in Warsaw. "She was supposedly a war correspondent for the Baltimore *Sun,* but she was actually a professional spy, the only one I ever knew. She was a prisoner in Russia twice, and she saved my life when I was a prisoner by sending me food, blankets and books." The presence of a woman on the expedition did not please the two men—the situation is parodied in *King Kong*—but Cooper's indebtedness overcame his misogyny. To help her chances with the lecture circuit, she was to be the only one of the three to appear before the camera. (Marguerite Harrison later wrote a book, *There's Always Tomorrow,* which contains an account of the expedition and an entertaining description of Schoedsack and Cooper.) The trio set out for Turkey, intending to cross Anatolia to Turkestan.

The Turks, however, led by Kemal Ataturk, had recently driven both French and German invaders out of Anatolia and had ended the Allied occupation of Constantinople. They were highly suspicious of all foreigners. "I believe now," wrote Schoedsack, in his account of the trip, "that the Turks thought we were British spies, trying to get across to see some starving Armenians, or to stir up more trouble in Kurdistan. At any rate, they kept us waiting in the ancient town of Angora [Ankara], the new capital, while they stalled on permission to travel any further East."

The prevarication lasted some weeks; the officials evidently hoped that discouragement would drive the travelers back where they came from. Eventually,

The triumphant descent from Zardeh Kuh— the end of Grass *(1925), as the tribes sweep down to the fertile Iranian plain.*

Ernest Schoedsack near Kiev during the Polish intervention in Russia, 1919.

Merian C. Cooper (back row, second from right) with pilots of the Kosciusko Squadron, on leaving Paris for Poland in September 1919. Front row (left to right): Shrewsbury, Noble, Crawford, and Kelly. Back row (left to right): Clark, Faunt-le-Roy, Cooper, and Corsi.

In the Taurus Mountains, January 1924. Guide, Schoedsack, Marguerite Harrison, guide, Cooper.

however, they managed to penetrate Anatolia, traveling by horse and wagon.

"For lack of anything else to do, and because we didn't know whether we'd get anything better, we made some travelogue footage—some of which is still in the picture. Also an occasional newsreel shot—so long as we could get it back. This was just to support our anti-poverty program. Of course, none of it was what we came for. We were only wasting our precious capital and film, and we knew it. And I had every reason to believe that we were always kept track of by the secret police. They wanted to make sure we did not turn East toward Armenia and Kurdistan."

They were told of a tribe of nomadic shepherds—the Uruks—who inhabited the Taurus Mountains, to the west, and they set out to find them.

ONE MORNING, WHILE CROSSING an ancient pass, they met two mountain-goat hunters, who invited them to their village, high in the Taurus. The last foreigners that these peasants had seen were French troops, whom they had fought and defeated in their own valleys just a couple of years earlier. But they could hardly have been more hospitable. Schoedsack filmed a sequence of a hunter, shooting a goat from the camouflage of a shield, which went into the picture. The Uruk tribe, however, proved to be something of a myth.

One of their forays into the mountains almost put an end to the expedition. Accompanied by a local guide, who led the pack horse, laden with camera equipment, Cooper and Schoedsack were caught in a blinding blizzard.

"I have never, before or since, seen such a heavy, wet snowfall," said Schoedsack. "It was soon up to my waist, and higher on Cooper. As for our guide, he quit entirely, and implored Allah to save us. Which may be why we got through, for all I know. Being taller than Cooper, I went first, kicking sideways at the snow to make a sort of ditch through which he followed, dragging the guide and the pack horse. Progress was very difficult. The only way we could keep going was

A desert caravanserai. Schoedsack with rifle, during the making of Grass.

Grass: *the Baba Ahmedi celebration before departure.*

Haidar Khan, fourth from left, and his son Lufta, kneeling, with rifle—the leading characters of Grass.

to pick out the nearest tree we could see, and determine to reach it. Having done that, we picked out the next one and made for that. We knew if we stopped to rest we'd be frozen."

As dusk gathered, the snow gave way. Avalanched into an icy stream, they found that progress through the shallow water was much easier, although large blocks of ice frequently swept down the stream and knocked them over. The stream led them to a caravanserai and safety. In later years Cooper declared that Schoedsack had saved his life. "I was doing myself a favor, too," said Schoedsack.

The snows melted a few days later and the little group moved on. They crossed the border into French-occupied Syria, but the only nomadic tribe they could find were Bedouins. They still had their dream of Kurdistan; at Aleppo they hired a Model T and drove across desert trails to Bagdad. While Cooper undertook the diplomatic negotiations, Schoedsack went north to investigate the Kurdish situation. He was discouraged to learn that border skirmishes were frequent.

Cooper, meanwhile, had made friends with a prominent British official, Sir Arnold Wilson, who told him about the Bakhtiari tribe in southern Persia. Wilson had been High Commissioner for Mesopotamia, and he was also the chairman of the board of the Anglo-Persian Oil Company. The oil-bearing lands were owned by khans, who received dividends from the oil company's profits. The khans were thus extremely wealthy.

Cooper, Schoedsack, and Harrison were invited to meet the khans at Shustar, capital of Arabistan—as far as a Ford could go over the old chariot trail—and state their case. The khans were represented by Rahim Khan, who had been educated at the American University at Beirut; he led them to his uncle, who was highly amused by the idea of the foreigners accompanying one of his tribes on a migration.

Now that permission was forthcoming, Cooper had mixed feelings. Before reaching Shustar, he had read a description of the Bakhtiari in a nineteenth-century book by Sir Austen Henry Layard called *Early Adventures:* "The Bakhtiari bear the very worst reputation in Persia. They are denounced as a race of robbers, treacherous, cruel and bloodthirsty. . . . I had been repeatedly warned that I ran the greatest peril in placing myself in their hands, and that although I might possibly succeed in entering their mountains, the chances of getting out of them again were but few."[4]

Accompanying the film-makers were an interpreter named Mahomet, a muleteer with two assistants, and a servant for Marguerite Harrison. The little expedition had already spent most of its money and had cut deeply into its film supply—and there was not much to show for it. The Bakhtiari were about to leave on their annual migration—taking their flocks and herds, upon which their living depended, to the cool green pastures of the highlands for the summer. Prudently, the two men had abandoned their weapons.

"We slept on the ground," said Schoedsack. "We ate the food they gave us—we had no supplies of our own—and it was very good. They'd bring us their food every night. We'd stretch out on our bedroll, and they'd give us barley, which they stored in goatskin sacks, and every few days they'd have a shish kebab—and always plenty of yogurt. Eat a lot of that stuff and you always go to sleep. They'd feed us first then the men would eat, and then they'd feed the dogs. And the women got what was left."

The Great Trek began on 17 April 1924. Cooper's diary records at least fifty thousand people and half a million animals on the move. "The Bakhtiari move up over the mountains in five main groups. There are five ways to pass up and over the mountains. On our route—the hardest—go five thousand people. They do not all start together, but come converging in from different points as the migration progresses, until somewhere far up in the wilderness, they gather together in a big mountain valley."[5]

Camp was generally broken between midnight and two a.m. Among the many spectacular events, which Schoedsack could not shoot since they took place in darkness, was the hauling of animals up steep cliffs by sheer manpower.

But no film-maker could hope for a more astounding scene than the crossing of the vast Karun River. Schoedsack went ahead with his equipment to secure a long shot of the river before the crossing took place. He left a note: "Coop! I hate to say it before we start shooting, but this is what we have been traveling months to see. Better be here before sunrise tomorrow. This is it!"

Cooper wrote in his diary: "Consider it! Here's a river a half-mile wide. Its waters are swelled to a rushing torrent by the melting snows of a hundred mountain peaks. The river is icy cold. It is filled with whirlpools, cross-currents, rapids. It is tearing through mountain gorges with cliff-like jagged shores, and it is bridgeless and boatless. Now here's the problem. On one side of this river are five thousand people with all their worldly goods and perhaps fifty thousand animals. It is spring, and the herds and flocks have any number of baby animals. When I first rode along the rocky trail, on my way to the river to join Schoedsack, and saw the terrific speed of the current and the jagged shore line on either side, I was almost ready to say, 'It can't be done.' It would have given any army commander heart failure. But I knew it could and would be done. For centuries, twice a year, the tribes have been crossing it. But how?"[6]

The crossing was accomplished with the aid of goatskins, which were inflated and fastened to a row of sticks. A heavy rug was laid on top, providing a serviceable raft. The chances of this frail craft surviving were good, for the crossing point had been carefully chosen. The Karun made a sharp turn here, so that animals driven into the water were swept along by the current, to scramble ashore farther down. Rafts took the women, the children, and the baby animals. The flocks and herds had to swim—escorted by men using goatskins like water wings.

"But recall that the river torrent is cold, snow cold, ice cold," wrote Cooper. "I defy your strongest cross-channel swimmer to plunge into that stream, fight a steer by the horns and swim it across, then return and do it again and again many times in a day.

"It was a show all right. For five days, Schoedsack and I, rushing about with the cameras, watched the greatest piece of continuous action I have ever seen."[7]

Perhaps the most alarming moment in the picture is a scene in which sheep are drowned—sucked beneath the boiling current—before the camera's unflinching eye. "We found a big whirlpool," said Schoedsack. "Everything was going under. Most of them came up again. They probably lost a few hundred animals. I know two men were drowned."

Some shots give the impression that the camera, too, was mounted on a raft, but Schoedsack says everything was taken from the shore. Sometimes, a six-inch

Grass: *goatskin raft for an emir.*

Original caption from Asia *magazine reads: "With his young son, Haidar Khan, chief of the Baba Ahmedi, with which the three Americans made their migration over the Zardeh Kuh Pass, inspects Ernest B. Schoedsack's motion-picture camera. The mechanical contrivances of the West neither surprise nor overawe the independent, high-spirited people of the Orient, who view machinery as somewhat akin to children's playthings."*

lens followed the tribesmen, furiously paddling, yelling the tribal cry "Yo Ali!"

Cooper wrote: "There was one thing about the river crossing that I shall always remember. Horses, sheep, cows and donkeys—all can swim. But goats won't swim. Goats are the only adult animals that didn't swim that river. They crossed, like the women and children, on rafts.

"We crossed like the goats."[8]

As the tribes reached higher country, and the heat moderated, so the marches became longer. When it rained, the tribes stopped to protect their supplies of grain. "You were so tired," said Schoedsack, "that you just lay there and let it rain right through you. Wonderful!"

The equipment, carried on donkeys, consisted of two fiber boxes: one held the film supply and the still camera, the other held two Debries. Personal equipment included a mess kit, a piece of towel, a blanket, a change of socks and underwear, and a safety razor. A small laundry bag served as a pillow, being stuffed with a tuxedo, for possible use in Teheran.

Whatever time they had to rise, and it was often two a.m., both men agreed that they woke fresh and fit, with none of the sluggish, bad taste feelings of early rising in the city. "The water was so cold," said Schoedsack, "it splashed on the rocks and froze. They used to watch me take a bath—and they named a rock after me."

Mrs. Harrison, who had her own tent, acted as doctor for the tribe. She dressed wounds and distributed medicines for internal illness. Once, she saved the life of a small boy by forcing him to drink a strong salt solution after a leech, acquired by drinking from a stream, stuck in his throat.

The motion picture camera required some explanation before the tribesmen could learn to ignore it. One of the few Persian phrases learned by both men was "Don't look at the camera." No one understood the word for camera, so the phrase became "Don't look at me." Schoedsack was able to develop only the 5 x 7 still pictures he took en route. Using portable developing tanks filled with muddy ice water, he would crawl under a blanket and emerge with portraits of the tribesmen. At first, they failed to recognize themselves on a flat plane. "Then they were all very cross because the pictures only showed their heads and shoulders."

COOPER WROTE IN HIS DIARY, 12 May 1924: "Now, how they are going to do it is beyond me. Schoedsack and I have been looking at it for half an hour trying to figure it out. There it stands, directly in our path—fifteen hundred feet of sheer rock cliff. And when I say sheer I mean it is vertical. And here the tribes are camped all along its base with the intention of going up and over tomorrow. Women and children and overladen cows and donkeys up a vertical rock cliff!"[9]

The tribes moved upward. If any person or animal paused, they caused a complete halt, for there was no room to pass. Cooper and Schoedsack, however, *had* to pass in order to film the ascent. Cooper jerked the camera donkey off the diagonal trail and tried to persuade it to climb almost straight up. It fell, and the motion picture equipment rolled with it among the stones. The two men held on desperately, prevented it from falling farther, then unloaded the equipment and forced the donkey back on the trail.

"Now Schoedsack swung the camera across his back and I had the tripod on my shoulder, and clinging to handholds up we went—up the cliff, climbing among the goats, working our way steadily upward, holding to our maximum speed. Below us, the little lines of pygmies, toiling up the tortuous trail in deep zigzags, seemed to move not at all."

Schoedsack and Cooper worked for four or five hours filming the ascent, having to cope with mist and cloud as well as perilous camera positions.

"As we came over the mountain top," wrote Cooper, "we stopped dead still—we stared. There before us, forty miles or so away, towering giant-like over the rough country between, was a great row of solid snow–mountain peaks! This was the mighty monarch of this part of the South-Persian Mountains—the dreaded barrier of the way to Grass—there was Zardeh Kuh!"[10]

Mrs. Harrison fell ill with malaria. Haidar Khan (chief of the tribe) held up the tribes until she recovered. As soon as the news of her illness spread, each of the Baba Ahmedi khans brought her the quinine pills saved from doses she had given them.

The crossing of Zardeh Kuh was made possible by Haidar Khan and his volunteers, who dug a zigzag trail through the snow. Cooper and Schoedsack went with them to photograph the operation and to lend a hand, and were astounded to see Haidar and his helpers removing their shoes. The soles of these cotton shoes were made of pressed rags and disintegrated when wet. The men worked for hours in an unrelenting wind. Barelegged, they wore only thin cotton garments, without heavy coats. Behind them marched the rest of the tribes. Some of the women were barefoot, too, and their bruised feet left blood in the snow.

To avoid delaying the march, Cooper climbed off the trail onto the mountain slope. "Mahomet and I perched quite safely on the edge of the trail, hanging our feet down in it, but Schoedsack had to set up his camera well outside the trail. With cool courage he started out, thrusting the ends of his tripod deep into the snow for support. Once he began to slide, and I thought it was all over except the shouting. But the very weight of the heavy apparatus saved him. The steel points of the legs of the tripod dug deep into the snow and gave him the necessary second to get his balance and hold on."

Both men still wore the light clothes they had found suitable for the hot country. Nevertheless, after the first day's climb they elected to stay the night on top of the mountain. They had no food with them, so they robbed their donkeys of their nosebags and ate the cold, hard barley. They then dug into the snow and waited for the dawn. "I know we nearly froze to death," said Cooper. "We said, 'We'll probably die up here, but let's make the goddam picture.' "

For three days, they recorded the ascent, climbing to a new vantage point each morning before returning to camp at the foot of the mountain. They captured one of the most unforgettably epic shots of documentary history. It was based on a painting of Napoleon crossing the Alps, which Cooper had seen in Paris. Taken from an adjacent mountain, it depicted the tribes as a procession of flies, flattened against the snow wall in a gigantic zigzag.

When they finally crossed the summit, and began the descent, they passed animals lying dead in the snow.

"The old, the young, the weak were strapped backwards on donkeys and cows. And whooping, laughing, shouting and weeping, stumbling and falling, with frost-

Merian C. Cooper, Ernest Schoedsack, and Bakhtiari guide—Grass.

bitten legs and feet, the cotton-clad horde swept on down . . . down . . . down the mountainside.

"At last the snow and mountain ended; we broke out of a gorge into the open. Here, out to the horizon stretched green valleys through which, in the golden sunshine, rippled silver streams feeding the luxuriant young grass. Here was the prize of the gallant fight. Here was the land of plenty. Grass, Grass and Life!"[11]

Schoedsack's efforts at conserving stock were well judged; he had exactly eighty feet left to contrive an ending for the picture.

Despite their sense of achievement, the two men realized the film was far from finished. With Marguerite Harrison, they formulated a plan; Cooper would go home and try to raise more money, returning in time to join Schoedsack for the autumn migration. With light conditions reversed, and a great deal more favorable, they would know just what lay ahead and could secure whatever they missed the first time. Schoedsack should remain in Persia, get hold of some film, and go back to the Baba Ahmedi for the summer. He would photograph the family of Haidar, his two wives and his son Lufta, who had been briefly established, and their life between migrations. Schoedsack and Cooper would show that family in the foreground of the return journey. Thus they hoped for a full-length feature picture, with a great deal of human interest, plenty of action and spectacle, and the essential ingredients of a Cooper-Schoedsack production—a beginning, a middle, and an end.

"To my dying day," said Cooper, "I regret that we did not go back and complete *Grass*. But until we released it we couldn't get any money."

LITERATURE AND TOURISM HAVE PAID tribute to the romance of Paris in the twenties with its echoes of Hemingway and Miller and Joyce. Outside the city walls, in the Moroccan quarter, Cooper and Schoedsack rented the cheapest room they

Ernest Schoedsack (1924).

could find. At a little laboratory, they hired two girls and began developing their film. "But we couldn't get home with all the stuff," said Schoedsack, "so we had to throw a lot of it away. We couldn't afford the duty."

Cooper wrote some stories for magazines, and Schoedsack sold a great many still pictures, and they earned enough to rent a room in New York in which to edit the picture. "What made the editing tough," said Cooper, "was that we knew we had just half a picture. But cut it we did, with our own hands. We put it together, with mediocre titles, then hired a Hearst man, H. P. Carver,* and his son Richard to try to market *Grass* as an educational film."

Schoedsack, in order to support the firm of Cooper and Schoedsack during this difficult period, joined a New York Zoological Society expedition to the Sargasso Sea and the Galapagos Islands, headed by William Beebe. Another member was Ruth Rose, whom he subsequently married.

Cooper, meanwhile, had found a publisher for his diary, to be illustrated with Schoedsack's stills, and the publisher, George Putnam, secured him a lecture agent. Cooper lectured with the film at universities and colleges, principally in the Midwest. Putnam also arranged for a full hour's talk on the radio, sponsored by the Goodyear Tire and Rubber Company, which paid the incredible sum of $1,000. This income he divided among Schoedsack, Harrison, and himself, as equal partners in the expedition.

Jesse Lasky saw the picture at a private dinner party and offered to release it. Paramount acquired the film on 29 January 1925. They discovered that in all the mass of footage, there was no shot of the men who had made it. So they sent down to the wardrobe department for a couple of soft shirts, and the shots that open the

---

* General manager of Cosmopolitan Productions. See *The Silent Enemy*, p. 550.

film were taken by a rock behind Paramount's Astoria Studios. Terry Ramsaye was involved in the editing, cutting the film to Paramount's specifications. The sales department boosted it to ten reels, but eventually it was cut to seven—the English release running only four.

Schoedsack and Cooper disliked the "damned half picture," yet it made money for them. After paying off the Carvers, the lawyers, and the lecture agents, they were left with several thousand dollars each. "Nevertheless," said Cooper, "we had one of the worst distribution deals in history, because neither of us knew the difference between paying 25 percent of the distribution, or 50 or 75 percent. After I had run a studio for a while, I wondered how two young men could have been so financially ignorant—but we were, period."

A preacher in Southern California announced that *Grass* was a fake—he happened to know that it had all been shot in the San Bernardino Mountains, a hundred and fifty miles from Los Angeles. And students at Princeton, who expected sex with their movies, voted *Grass* the worst picture of the year. The Soviet government approached Paramount Pictures, hoping that Cooper and Schoedsack would make a similar film for them, to discourage peasants in remote areas from their traditional migration. But Cooper's record in the war against Bolshevism ruled out this propaganda project.

Said Schoedsack: "I have always considered *Grass* to be a lost opportunity, and a great missed chance."* Nevertheless, *Grass* became celebrated as a classic of documentary, rated by historians as second only to *Nanook*.

CHANG

The exception to every rule, *Chang* (1927) was no more a documentary than *King Kong*. It was conceived as a spellbinding "natural drama," utilizing the central family missing from *Grass* and depicting that family's struggle against the jungle. Sequence by sequence, the picture was planned to seize an audience by the hair, to excite them as no ordinary film had ever excited them. And the magic works today. *Chang* is the audience picture supreme. Its slow start lulls them into condescension; its savagery takes them unawares. The rhythm builds, with sights unfamiliar despite the hundreds of wildlife pictures since, to a climax that belittles such publicity terms as "stupendous." As a piece of film craft, it is masterly and stands far beyond the other documentaries in that regard. But since it was not an unrehearsed record of real life, it was hard to categorize, harder still for historians to praise. *Chang*, overshadowed in Cooper and Schoedsack's career by *King Kong*, was cast aside, to join the ever-growing legion of lost films.

No script existed for *Chang*—and no title—when the two men set off for the jungles of Siam. They had the support of Jesse Lasky and some firm ideas about

---

* *Grass* was attempted again in 1956; Lowell Farrell directed, Winton Hoch at camera, with Cooper producing from the United States. In 1971 Anthony Howarth made *Bakhtiari: A Persian Odyssey* (also known as *People of the Wind*), with Shusha Guppy.

Chang (1927), *made by Merian C. Cooper and Ernest B. Schoedsack.*

what they were going to shoot. When they arrived in Siam, they set out on location trips, each covering a separate area. Schoedsack went to Saigon, but reported little of interest apart from French professional hunters' camps. Back in Bangkok, they enquired about the most likely areas for tigers and elephants; they were told that tigers no longer existed in Siam. But some Presbyterian missionaries disagreed with the official view. "Tigers?" they said. "Plenty of tigers up at Nan. Last winter they killed nineteen people."

Schoedsack set off for this location, while Cooper investigated South Siam. "Without the missionaries we couldn't have done anything," said Schoedsack. "They supplied us with carriers and interpreters, and did everything for us. Of course, they were surrounded by rice Christians, but they were a good crowd."[1]

Schoedsack's first encounter with the jungle was a route-march of a hundred miles along the trail to Nan. One night after he had shared dinner with an elderly missionary, there was a disturbance on the path in front of them. A leopard burst from the undergrowth and bounded away. "Well," said Schoedsack, "this looks like a good place. What about tigers?" The missionary replied that several tigers had been reported in that area—all of them man-eaters. From a little one-wire government telegraph station, Schoedsack wired Cooper to come on up.

The missionaries provided the men with a deserted house, and helped them find local people to play in the film. The family was put together artificially: The mother, Chantui, was the wife of one of the carriers. The children, Nah and Ladah, came from other families. The husband, Kru, was the local carpenter. And there was a pet gibbon—Bimbo.

Cooper was kept occupied during these early days building traps for tigers. These were glorified rat traps, baited with live animals. One day a tiger was reported in a trap at the Kamuk village, and the villagers were afraid he might break out. While Schoedsack jumped to the task of getting the boats ready to send upriver with a cage, Cooper, Muang the interpreter, and Douglas Collier, a young missionary doctor, set off into the gathering darkness of the jungle on ponies.

"Neither Collier nor I had ever caught a tiger before," wrote Cooper in *Asia* magazine. "The few natives who had trapped tigers and leopards had always stabbed or shot them to death in the trap without attempting to remove them until they were dead. So we had to figure out our own method."[2]

When the boats arrived with the cage, the villagers looked at it and laughed. "The tiger will jump out of it," they said. Cooper realized it was too weak and had it strengthened in a hurry. The next problem was how to persuade the tiger to leave the trap and enter the cage. The villagers tied trap and cage together. Anticipating that the cage would make the canoes top-heavy, Cooper had arranged for thick bamboo poles to be fastened to the sides to act as outriggers. The cage was lowered and the canoes cast off. Cooper and Collier, relaxing in folding chairs, congratulated each other. Ten minutes later, a tropical storm burst upon them—thunder, lightning, and torrents of wind-lashed rain.

Cooper wrote: "Above the sound of the storm, a new noise struck my ear. Something gnawing wood, mixed with deep growls and grunts. A sound of something ripping. 'Now what in hell is that?' I grabbed Collier's flash light, jumped on the outrigger, almost knee-deep in water as it swung low with my weight, and hanging on the side of the cage, peered down. Then I jerked my head back like a shot.

One log had been clear gnawed away or jerked out, another, half-way out. There, staring into my eyes through the ruin, were two big green eyes, and below them was a flash of red jaws filled with white teeth."[3]

Collier and Cooper worked hard fastening logs into the gap. In five minutes the tiger had pulled them into the cage. They fastened more. Again the tiger destroyed their work. They could hardly hear each other above the roaring of thunder, rain, and water.

"Just as we began working the third time, the boat stopped with a shock and almost overturned. We were aground. The boatman had found it impossible to see the way, and the boat had run on a shallow near the middle of the river."[4] Collier saved the day. He had brought a bottle of chloroform with him, "just in case we might want to put the cat to sleep." Cooper had ridiculed the idea, for in laboratory tests, feline animals had been set crazy by chloroform. But now he was ready to try anything. Climbing onto the outrigger, Cooper thrust a bamboo pole into the jaws of the tiger, while Collier poured down a shot of chloroform.

"The tiger gasped and coughed, but jerked the bamboo out of my hand and into the cage, where we could hear him chewing it to pieces in an excess of rage. Then he came back again, trying to tear his way out. We repeated the dose and the tiger repeated his performance. But the third time he didn't come back for more. He lay quiet, grunting and breathing hard, long enough for us to patch up the side of the cage again."[5]

Cooper and Schoedsack gained their knowledge about tigers through such practical experience. They discovered that many of the facts in supposedly authoritative books were not correct at all. "The books tell you no tiger jumps over eleven feet high," said Schoedsack, "so for the shot where the tiger leaps up the tree, I built my platform at thirteen feet. I think he jumped about twelve and a half." The tiger literally nudges the lens, and since the Debrie was provided with a lever for such a purpose, Schoedsack calmly pulled focus to ensure a crisp rendition of this magnificent close-up. "There was nothing else I could do, so I figured I might as well keep on cranking."

Cooper covered Schoedsack with a rifle whenever risk was involved. They began the expedition with a Springfield, which was not powerful enough to kill a tiger. Schoedsack acquired a heavier, Belgian-made gun during his trip to Saigon. It proved to be of limited value, for once fired it could not be used again until it had cooled.

"I knew nothing about tigers," said Schoedsack. "For the first tiger we beat out, I had the camera platform surrounded by barbed wire. I didn't know at the time, but any cat animal can go through anything that his skull can go through. This tiger saw me, rushed at me and got his head through the wire and his paws on the platform. I yelled at Coop—'Don't shoot . . . it's our only tiger!' Finally, the tiger ran away."

They learned, too, that a tiger would not always follow through on a charge, unless the victim turned and ran. "He stops about ten feet away, with a roar like a Ferrari racing car. That's his trick. We tried it with the dummy, and when the dummy didn't flinch, he'd generally turn away. Sometimes, when we yanked on the rope and the dummy moved, he would jump—and we could see how he attacks. A tiger holds and bites the head off. A lion strikes with his paws. A leopard is the

Chang: *Ladah and small relative of Bimbo.*

Ernest Schoedsack films a marauding leopard in a stockade, using a Debrie camera. From Chang.

worst of the lot. He doesn't stop for anything. In the shot of the dummy over the covered pit, you can see how they attack. They jump on the victim, and bite at the face while the hind feet are tearing the intestines out. I timed them with frames of film, and their take-off speed was forty-seven miles an hour. And they always seemed to go for a man with a gun."

The approach for *Chang* was to achieve dramatic realism by observing how certain things happened and then causing them to occur again for the camera. Cooper separated a mother elephant from her baby and tied the baby to a house. With the camera ready, the mother was set free. "She came like a bat out of hell. She just wanted to free her baby, and there's nothing staged about that. I knew she would get the baby loose—but I didn't know she was going to tear down the house."

The actual method used to obtain the startling animal scenes remained a secret Cooper steadfastly refused to divulge. He came upon it, he said, in a book published in the early nineteenth century. This device, which he termed his invention, was tested first with the film's two children. "I was practicing running the children across, and releasing the leopard when they were in complete safety. Unfortunately, the native in control of the box must have released the leopard, being in a safe spot himself, not realizing that I had given no signal. The leopard went right for the kids. For once I didn't kill with one shot—I wounded the leopard, and he crawled into the brush. The kids ran like hell. I followed him into the brush. I was on my belly, because you couldn't see much in there. I just saw his eyes as he jumped at me, and I shot him in mid-air, or mid-brush, and he landed with his paws either side of my head. I was very thankful the two kids weren't hurt. I don't think I ever told anyone about this. I was too ashamed."

Schoedsack brought his Debrie camera, the veteran of *Grass*, and augmented it with a metal-cased Debrie purchased in Paris; in these tropical conditions, the metal-cased camera proved marginally superior. He had ordered panchromatic film especially wound for a Debrie, emulsion out, and packed for the tropics. The film was in 400-foot cans, sealed with adhesive tape, and placed in a 1,000-foot can, the edges of which were soldered. On location, the outer can was opened with a can opener, the smaller one placed in a changing bag. But Schoedsack received a shock when he ordered fresh stock from the United States. "When I opened the first pack, do you know what those stinkers had done? They had electrically welded the 400-foot cans. The only way to get them open was with a can opener. That meant ruining the outer layer of film. And the only place to open them was the changing bag. The bag never got dry between the perspiration and blood from my hands off the jagged edges of the can. You were lucky if you got 300 feet out of a 400-foot roll. Pull it out, and it stuck in the jagged tin. That's the way the picture was made."

The all-pervading mildew threatened film and machinery; Schoedsack invented a tropical drying pack that worked well, using blotting paper soaked with calcium chlorate, baked crisp and placed between wax paper so that it would not come into contact with the film. This dried out each roll. The cameras and lenses were kept in boxes and the same technique used.

The major sequences with the elephants were shot at Chumphon, in the south. Cooper went ahead via Bangkok to handle the arrangements, and Schoedsack es-

Ernest Schoedsack invented this contraption as a method of creating a traveling shot of the two men and keeping them in focus—Chang.

Chang—*the cast and crew.*

The elephant stampede from Chang. *(Frame enlargement)*

Ernest Schoedsack attempts a tracking shot with a Debrie camera.

corted their little family—Kru, Chantui, and the two children. "It was the rainy season at Nan, and of course all the relatives wanted to come with us. They'd never been away from home. I had to march them a hundred miles in five days to the railway. They'd never seen a railway. The train ran alongside the ocean, and they'd never seen the ocean, so that was another big thrill. At Bangkok, the missionaries took care of them."

No one was allowed to kill an elephant in Siam, although trapping was permitted. Thousands were in captivity, thousands more roamed the jungle in wild herds. Each area had its own method of trapping.

It was only through Prince Yugala of Lapburi, brother of the King of Siam, that Cooper and Schoedsack were able to secure the elephant sequences at all. The authority of the royal family was absolute; the King was supreme law and could make and unmake laws at will. The King had his own private herd—it could trample fields and villages with impunity. Nobody could interfere. This is what gave Cooper the idea for the climax of *Chang* (the title itself means "elephant"), when a herd of three hundred elephants destroys a village.

A pit was dug in the soft sand, and covered with logs, level with the earth. A heavy stone was placed on top. "I should have had a still of that place," said Schoedsack. "It looked like a grave. We camouflaged the pit with brush. I'm cranking away through the little hole, and the elephants are coming, and I'm hoping they'll step around the pit. Just a few of them get over, and they start kicking the camouflage all over the thing, and they cut off the view. I think they did a war dance on top. The pit only sank a couple of inches. I didn't know what I had, but it was enough. The worst part was the heat and the stench—swimming in my own sweat and smelling three hundred elephants at close range."

During this period, Schoedsack was suffering from malaria. It was the hottest part of the year, and they had a very crude, rough camp. To make things worse, a cholera epidemic broke out among seven hundred men invited to round up the elephants.

Having observed the elephant drive, they decided to use native labor to construct a kraal for the film, somewhat larger than the one they had seen, and built in the open. Schoedsack had a platform built in a high tree, and he photographed much of the scene from this vertigo-inducing height, while still suffering from malaria. (He suffered sunstroke no less than five times, and has been allergic to sun and heat ever since.)

One method of hunting elephants used in the film came from *Macbeth* (via *The Covered Wagon*), rather than reality. The Siamese concealed themselves behind bushes, and advanced like Birnam Wood. Cooper said they liked the idea so well they adopted it, and it thus became authentic.

Despite all their experiences, Cooper and Schoedsack were high in their praise for the Siamese. "The Siamese and the country Turks are my two favorite people," said Schoedsack. "It was such a calm, peaceful place in those days. What it's like now, I hate to think."

DISASTER WAS NARROWLY AVERTED during the developing of the film. In a normal climate a photographer would stop down and use the smallest diaphragm in bright sunlight. But Schoedsack found that the contrast was too high. He discovered that the best results were obtained by working wide open—overexposing the film, but using a soft developer.

An American living in Bangkok operated a local newsreel and had a small laboratory. He showed some of his work, and it seemed to be good, so Cooper and Schoedsack entrusted him with the precious negative of the elephant stampede. Their film was normally sent back, undeveloped, to Paramount, but before they themselves left for the United States, they wanted to ensure that the big scene was all right. It would have been, if they had not taken this precaution. "The newsreel man proudly sent me back in an envelope some samples," said Schoedsack. "I held them up to the sun. I could hardly see through them. I'm afraid he ran out of ice, went out for a drink, and the stuff boiled. A lot of it was so heavy that a copper sheen had developed on one side."

The chances of a successful retake were slim. Schoedsack realized he would have to take the negative back with him, and step-print it, giving a long exposure to each frame. This method saved the scene, but much of it still appears grainy.

When the material from Siam filtered through to Paramount, newsreel head Emmanuel Cohen wanted it for his department. Jesse Lasky had delegated responsibility for the project and was involved elsewhere. Sensing these warning signals, Cooper and Schoedsack quietly proceeded with the editing of the film, and as soon as they had cut it to their satisfaction they burned every foot of unused negative and positive. They remembered Paramount's infuriating habit of tampering with pictures—they had tried to inflate *Grass,* and sure enough Sidney Kent, head of the sales department, wanted to add another fifteen hundred feet.

"He nearly had a fit," said Cooper, "when I told him there was no more film to add!"

One shot—just one shot—was taken at the Central Park Zoo. The monkey dropping coconuts on the elephants during the stampede, a characteristic Cooper-Schoedsack touch, had not registered satisfactorily. "So we went out and bounced coconuts off the tame, mangy elephant they had in Central Park."

A novelist with the picturesque name of Captain Achmed Abdullah was hired to add an oriental flavor to the titles. He did an abominable job, and his cute, wisecracking titles are an affront to the picture. (Ramsaye's were not much better on *Grass.*) Yet Cooper and Schoedsack passed them, and Cooper wrote some of them himself. If the flowery style of the Victorian lecturer survived into the era of FitzPatrick Travel Talks, the comedy titles of *Grass* and *Chang* were perpetuated in scores of American documentaries—including the Disney True-Life Adventure Films.

Chang provided an opportunity for a new process called Magnascope. Lorenzo del Riccio had developed it from a Bausch and Lomb wide-angle lens for outdoor projection; the idea of using it as a dramatic device was Glendon Allvine's. The idea was simple; a second projector, with the sequence to be magnified, was equipped with the wide-angle lens. On cue, the screen cutouts pulled back, and the sequence was thrown on a new, gigantic screen. Magnascope had been introduced with the James Cruze sea epic *Old Ironsides.* Cooper and Schoedsack had experimented with anamorphic lenses, but they decided in favor of Magnascope. They secretly arranged for a special score from Dr. Hugo Riesenfeld, and a special preview for the Paramount people was held at the Criterion Theater.

"It was a terrific score," said Schoedsack, "and a great orchestra, with lots of brass—and six-foot thunderdrums back of the screen. They went into action as the screen opened up on the elephant stampede. You never heard a sound-track like it. Coop and I were waiting in the lobby as the big boys came out. Lasky was smiling from ear to ear. Walter Wanger and Adolph Zukor were smiling, too. Zukor said to Lasky: 'How much did the boys get?' Lasky said, 'Forty percent.' Zukor's smile disappeared."

The picture had been budgeted at $60,000. By the time the stampede was ready for shooting, they were down to $20,000. Prince Yugala charged them $30,000, a figure which appalled them both. They decided to take the risk and went $10,000 into the red.

Wrote Jesse Lasky: "I was delighted with the picture and impatient to congratulate them. I expected them to come right to my office as soon as they docked, but instead they disappeared for several days. When they did put in a nervous appearance, they handed me a check for $10,000, mumbling apologies for running over their budget and the delay in raising money to pay me back what they 'owed' me. They had been ashamed to face me until they could make it good. You would have thought they were confessing to embezzlement.

"I laughed with relief and tore up the check. I hadn't restricted their budget . . . they were actually working on an unlimited expense account but didn't know it."[6]

Chang received critical acclaim from all over the world and was one of the first Academy Award nominations. Richard Watts, in the New York *Herald Tribune*, wrote: "Messrs. Cooper and Schoedsack have incorporated into their work some of the most thrilling moments any dramatic form has been able to encompass. For they are, above all things, shrewd showmen, who have not been content to rely merely on the bald camera record of a journey through the Siamese jungle. *Grass*, the earlier picture made by Cooper and Schoedsack, fell, for example, considerably short of the marvelous show provided by the Siamese film, but it had a stark, heartbreaking sincerity that must of necessity be lacking from a production in which comedy and drama are mingled with a showman's conscious skill. It was a happy alliance of virtues that the producers, in addition to the ability to get out and get the sort of picture they wanted, were possessors of a high technical skill. The film has many of the admirable uses of tempo that *Potemkin* and *The Big Parade* employed to such effect. In addition, it is filled with pictorial beauty and photographed superbly."[7]

AFTER *Chang*, COOPER AND SCHOEDSACK wanted to make a picture about starvation among the American Indians—similar to *The Silent Enemy*. The project came to nothing, as did Cooper's attempt to persuade the Rockefeller Foundation to finance him at $10,000 a year to develop the story-telling teaching film.

Their next collaboration was *The Four Feathers*, which involved an expedition to Africa, where they shot spectacular location footage of bush fire, stampeding hippos, and battling tribesmen, to be intercut with the studio-shot narrative.[8] Schoedsack then went to Sumatra, with Ruth Rose, and made *Rango*, an exquisitely photographed, extremely funny picture about an orangutan.

Ruth Rose, in her script for *King Kong*, wrote Cooper into the character of Denham (Robert Armstrong) and Schoedsack into Driscoll (Bruce Cabot).

Ernest Schoedsack and Ruth Rose in Sumatra on Rango *(1931).*

King Kong *(1932–1933) was written by Ruth Rose (Mrs. Ernest Schoedsack), and parodies the Cooper-Schoedsack methods of production. Here, Robert Armstrong plays the expedition film-maker, and Fay Wray is as unlike Marguerite Harrison as possible.*

Merian C. Cooper and Bimbo on Chang.

The story is woven around a documentary film-maker and his journey to a mysterious island. He takes a young girl, Ann (Fay Wray), along, to give his film some chance at the box office. Aboard ship, he makes a test.

> DENHAM That was fine. I'm going to try a filter on this one.
> ANN Do you always take the pictures yourself?
> DENHAM Ever since a trip I made to Africa. I'd have got a swell picture of a charging rhino, but the cameraman got scared. The darned fool. I was right there with a rifle. Seemed he didn't trust me to get the rhino before it got him. I haven't fooled with cameramen since. Do the trick myself.

Cut to bridge. Captain Englehorn (Frank Reicher) and Driscoll leaning over, watching Denham and Ann.

> DRISCOLL Think he's crazy, Skipper?
> ENGLEHORN Just enthusiastic.

THE VIKING

The effect of *Chang* on the film-makers of the 1920s was almost as far-reaching as that of *Nanook.* It led directly to the production of such dramatized documentaries as *The Silent Enemy, Stampede,* and Varick Frissell's *The Viking.*

The Viking was a catastrophe, for when Frissell returned north to shoot a spectacular sequence of an iceberg overturning, the ship blew up, killing twenty-seven men, including Frissell and all but one of the film crew. The sole survivor of the film crew, Harry Sargent, saved the lives of two men, including the radio operator, Clayton King, who called him "the American hero." (King wrote a vivid account of the disaster in *The Book of Newfoundland,* edited by Joseph Smallwood, which is preserved in the Canadian Film Institute.)

Frissell had already made a rough sketch for the film with a documentary called *The Swilin' Racket* (also known as *The Great Arctic Seal Hunt*). A student at Yale University, Frissell tried to sail with Sealer 230, the *Boethic,* as a passenger, but Captain George Barbour gave him two choices—sign on, or get off. Two days out of harbor, the little ship was battered by a hurricane for forty-eight hours. When he had recovered from that, Frissell learned that as an ordinary crew member, he could use his camera only when he had discharged his duties. He succeeded in photographing a careful, graphic, and gruesome record of the *Boethic*'s activities, and the experience formed the basis for *The Viking.*

Originally entitled *Northern Knight,* then *White Thunder,* the picture was renamed to capitalize on the news value of the wreck. "Twenty-seven men died to open Hughes-Franklin's new Studio Theater" was how *The Viking* was exploited at its Hollywood premiere in 1931. The film, which was part silent, part talkie, had no financial success, and was forgotten until its 1966 discovery in a St. John's, Newfoundland, fish storehouse, where the ice had been as beneficial to the nitrate as to the fish. *Variety* and *Time* hailed this discovery, which surprised William K. Everson, who had long preserved a print in his own collection. His version was abridged; most of the staged scenes, with actors such as Charles Starrett and Louise Huntington, had been removed, and the picture's documentary value restored. The enacted scenes were stilted and highly melodramatic, but the actuality footage was impressive—some of it awesomely so.

Men are sent overboard to dynamite the wooden-hulled ship free of ice. "It is one mile to the bottom, and not one man in a hundred can swim." With this knowledge, the sight of men leaping from ice pan to ice pan is filled with suspense. If a pan is too far from its neighbor, the men remove their coats, holding them as sails to propel the ice across the water.

The most astonishing scenes depict vast icescapes, the tiny figures advancing toward the seals while the ice-covered sea beneath them rises and falls, like some monstrous attraction at a fairground.

The captain of *The Viking* was portrayed by Captain Bob Bartlett, survivor of the 1913–1914 Stefansson expedition, who skippered Peary aboard the *Roosevelt* in his successful 1909 dash to the North Pole, and who was a leading member of the Harry Whitney–Lucky Scott Arctic expedition, which produced an important 1913 documentary.

A director from Hollywood, George Melford, accompanied Frissell on the initial trip and spent three months in Newfoundland. A confident, workman-like director, responsible for *The Sheik* (1921) with Valentino and the more rugged melodramas *The Sea Wolf* (1920) and *The Flame of the Yukon* (1922), Melford did not go back with Frissell for the extra material; the cameraman who did, Alexander Penrod, had photographed the great whaling saga *Down to the Sea in Ships*

The Viking, *wooden-hulled, was built in 1881.*

(1922), and he, Harry Sargent, and Frissell were described by the *Viking*'s radio operator as sailors of the highest quality. During a severe storm, it was Frissell, Penrod, and Sargent who manned the pumps, while many of the men lay in their bunks, too seasick to care whether the ship foundered or not.

When the picture came out in 1931, it was accompanied by a prologue spoken by Sir Wilfred Grenfell, "the greatest living authority on the Labrador country." Grenfell described Frissell's enthusiasm for the lives of the people of that region, and how he set out to fulfill his ambition of creating a motion picture portraying the people and the country in truthful detail. "After previewing it, I can vouch for its authenticity. I am proud to see the lives of my friends thus depicted in this dramatic and authentic manner.

"When the *Viking,* a veteran ship of fifty years' battling with the bergs, steamed out of St. John's, Newfoundland, on that fatal voyage, she carried many of

Captain Bob Bartlett, skipper for Admiral Peary on his race to the North Pole in 1909, died making The Viking *(1931).*

The Viking, *an epic of the Newfoundland sealers.*

the men you will see in this picture, but who will be seen no more. Varick Frissell, the leader, who wrote this story, Captain Bob Bartlett, and many of the unnamed Newfoundlanders who lost their lives in the terrific explosion, or subsequent exposure on the ice. What caused the tragedy of the *Viking,* the rescue parties which rushed to the scene by ship, air and afoot over the ice, were unable to determine and it will probably remain forever a mystery. Every sealing ship carries explosives to blast the ice in which she is often jammed. You will see this done. Nevertheless, an explosion, which was heard ashore many miles away, tore this ship asunder. And while we must humbly bow our heads to the inscrutable will of Providence, which took Varick Frissell and his companions from us, we may console ourselves somewhat that they first accomplished their self-appointed task. We hope and trust that you will find this, their picture, a worthy memorial."[1]

Frissell is supposed to have worked with Robert Flaherty. I can find no evidence to support this; his mentor was Merian C. Cooper. He had asked for Cooper's help in editing the footage, before returning to shoot the additional material. When the ship blew up, Frissell's father and sister telephoned Cooper in desperation, begging him to attempt a rescue.

"I moved fast," wrote Cooper, "even for me. I called Jock (C. V.) Whitney, and borrowed his Boeing Amphibian, then telephoned Terry Fokker and borrowed his test pilot, Bernt Balchen,* and was off in a matter of hours. I had gathered supplies to drop on the broken ice packs to possible survivors while Balchen was coming from New Jersey to Long Island. Balchen was wonderful—the greatest Arctic pilot who ever lived. We flew in bad weather low among icebergs, dropped supplies blankets, food, etc., to scattered survivors, and guided them to shore—three or four days' desperate work. Balchen made incredible landings in broken ice—we should have been killed a dozen times. We saved the life of a lot of survivors, but poor Varick was killed when the ship blew up. I could write a whole book, but I don't think either Balchen or I ever wrote a word about it. Dr. Frissell, Varick's father, gave Bernt and me beautiful gold watches, mine inscribed 'To the Leader of the Viking Rescue Expedition.' I gave it to my son, Dick, who carries it in the pocket of his flying suit on all dangerous flights—he is as superstitious as I am. By the way, I've never seen *The Viking.* I remember it fell into the hands of some damned 'sharpies' for distribution—all those dreadful kind of people. Poor Varick, and poor Dr. Frissell and poor sister."[2]

THE SILENT ENEMY

My first contact with *The Silent Enemy* came in a letter from the man most responsible for it, W. Douglas Burden. "My old friend, Merian C. Cooper, has been here for a few days," he wrote, "reviving many very special memories—not the least of which concerns silent pictures, in which I gather you have a special interest.

* He was the first pilot to fly over Antarctica. He flew Byrd over the South Pole.

It is fun to recall that Coop's truly great picture *Chang* is directly responsible for two considerable efforts of my early years, *The Silent Enemy* and the Marineland project."[1]

Although ferreting out lost movies is one of my passions, I am as susceptible as anyone to prejudice. "There must be a reason why I have never heard of this," I thought, as I perused the program. "It must be a really dreary picture." The program included a few stills, but, as I afterwards learned, Burden did not take a stills man on location and the photographs were not particularly striking. But enclosed with the program were some reviews, and one of them, by Robert E. Sherwood, was impossible to dismiss. Sherwood was a perceptive critic.

"High on the list of the cinema's nobler achievements," wrote Sherwood in a column syndicated to the Toronto *Star,* "are the names of *Nanook of the North, Grass, Stark Love* and *Chang*. They were contributed to the screen by enterprising explorers who took their cameras into remote, neglected regions and recorded the drama that is life.

"By such courageous deeds has the humble movie justified its existence.

"Now there is another picture to be added to the distinguished list. It is called *The Silent Enemy,* and the quality of its reception by the great film-loving public will be extremely interesting to watch. For it is a story of primitive life among the American Indians as they were in the centuries before Columbus.

"Furthermore, it is without dialogue, although it does possess a synchronized score and sound effects (tom-toms, wailing of wolves, moose-calls etc.).

"To say that this admirable production is 'educational' is to condemn it to be shown in empty theatres. There is no more demand for education among movie fans than there is among college students. So I shall carefully avoid all use of this ugly word in writing of *The Silent Enemy,* and I urge all other reviewers to do likewise. It deserves to be seen, for it is beautiful, it is superbly acted and in many of its scenes, tremendously exciting. . . .

"Strangely enough the most important feature of *The Silent Enemy* is its silence. No one can tell until the returns are in whether it is possible at this time for a non-talking picture to gain the favor and support of the public. I hope so, for the production of pictures like *Nanook, Grass* and *The Silent Enemy* is one of the cinema's most important functions. Such pictures will continue to be of intense value long after Alice White and Buddy Rogers have been forgotten. They are permanent, eloquent records of races and customs that are vanishing from the earth."[2]

WHEN I RETURNED TO AMERICA, I asked William K. Everson if he knew anything about this film. With the panache of the dedicated collector, he produced three reels of the picture, adapted for showing in the public schools. The titles were for very young children, but even they could not destroy the overall effect of the visuals. *The Silent Enemy* looked very promising. A visit to George Eastman House produced a longer version, recut for sound, but the narration was so appalling that it robbed the visuals of all their dignity and quality.

I was now so fascinated with the picture that I was determined to track down the original nine-reel silent version. I traveled to Vermont and interviewed Douglas Burden. He could provide no clues. He had seen a version at the American Museum

The Silent Enemy (*1930*)*: Chief Chetoga instructs his son, Cheeka, in the traditions of his race.*

of Natural History, of which he has been a trustee since 1926, and was so disappointed that he never wanted to see it again. It had been adapted as an educational film and the print was scratched and of miserable quality. Evidently, this version referred to the animals as Mr. Beaver and Mr. Bruin.

That remarkable archivist David Shepard, who did so much to build up the collection of the American Film Institute, told me when I reached Hollywood that Paramount had just handed over a vault of seventy-six silent features. All of them were original, tinted prints. At the bottom of the list, to my delight, was *The Silent Enemy*. But that, he explained, had been left behind. The AFI had apparently acquired the negative from the Museum of Natural History. "That version is disastrous," I warned him. "You absolutely *must* get hold of the original silent version." David Shepard obligingly returned to the Paramount lot, to discover the staff panic-stricken. They had to pack four hundred prints of *The Godfather* that morning, and they were in such a state he could find no one to help him locate *The Silent Enemy*. It was weeks before the tinted, nitrate print was rescued.

By that time, I had returned to England. But George Stevens, Jr., asked me to recommend a silent film for the opening season at the AFI Theatre in Washington. I suggested *The Silent Enemy*. Stevens consulted with Shepard, and the idea was turned down. Neither of them had yet run the print. When he finally saw it, Shepard was so enthusiastic he telephoned me across the Atlantic. "I was absolutely knocked out by it," he said. "It is superb. We are definitely putting it into the opening season."

Douglas Burden was too ill to attend the gala occasion, but his co-producer, William Chanler, attended, and Burden's daughter read his message to the audience.

The picture received an ovation, and Burden was rewarded with this letter from Warren Iliff, executive director of the National Zoological Park in Washington: "Your film is an incredible achievement and one that you can feel very proud of. The audience of 1973 loved it and I can imagine what its impact must have been on movie-goers forty years ago. Without qualification the wildlife photography is the best I've ever seen. The wolves through the woods and the attack on the moose were remarkable sequences and the stampeding caribou was the best finale to a film that I can remember. And best of all was the fantastic use of natural lighting. To accomplish all this one would have had to have been a Douglas Burden with the determination to completely immerse oneself in a culture and an environment in preparation for shooting and we are glad that you are and you did!"[3]

ALTHOUGH A SILENT FILM, *The Silent Enemy* opened with an address by Chief Yellow Robe, who played Chetoga in the picture. It was a moving prologue to an extraordinary film, and Chief Yellow Robe wrote it himself:

"This is the story of my people. In the beginning the Great Spirit gave us land. The forests were ours and the prairies; the wild game was ours to hunt. We were happy when game was plenty; in years of famine we suffered. We loved our country and our homes. Now the White Man has come; his civilization has destroyed my people. Soon we would have been forgotten. But now this same civilization has preserved our traditions before it was too late; now you will know us as we really are. Everything that you will see here is real; everything is as it always has been; our buck-skin clothes, our birch-bark canoes, our wigwams, and our bows and arrows; all were made by my people just as they always have done. When you see my young men hunting, that is how their fathers hunted; when you see us cold and starving; when, after the great hunt you see us feasting and singing; that is how we always have lived; those are the songs our forefathers taught us.

"I thank the White Man on behalf of my people for making this picture. They studied the old records; they listened to our old men around the camp fire; we told them the stories our grandfathers taught us in our childhood; they lived with us in the Far North for nearly a year, sharing with us the hardships of a northern winter. Some of them traveled up into the Barren Lands over a thousand miles north of the railroad to record this history. That is why this picture is real.

"When you look at this picture, therefore, look not upon us as actors. We are Indians living once more our old life. Most of the Indians that you will see here do not speak English. They are in the forest now, hunting for game that is ever growing less, living even today the great drama of the North, the struggle for meat—a never-ending fight against *The Silent Enemy*."[4]

DOUGLAS BURDEN'S PARENTS had a deep affection for the north woods and, from the age of nine, Douglas was frequently taken to the forests of Quebec, where he was introduced to the Indians.

"That experience, during my early years, so gripped my imagination that I simply fell in love with the country. And I soon learned how different it is to travel in the woods with an Indian as opposed to a white man. He is silent. He speaks to you only when there is something important to say, and then he does so very quietly. He is entirely aware of the forest around him—he notices the wind, the

Chief Yellow Robe, a nephew of Sitting Bull—Chetoga in The Silent Enemy.

Several of these Ojibwa died shortly after production of the film ended. (Frame enlargement)

change of direction in the clouds moving over the forest. He is aware of every smell, every sound. By contrast, with a white man you feel like an intruder. You make your own world. The talk is loud and the forest is, so to speak, thrust back and much of its magic disappears.

"I went back again and again, and became devoted to the Indians as a people, and saw that their end was fast coming, because every time we'd go up there, we'd hear another Indian had died from the white man's diseases—tuberculosis, flu or pneumonia. Many of the Indians we used in the filming of *The Silent Enemy* were dead a few years later."[5]

A close friend of Douglas Burden was William Chanler, who shared the same upper-class background. While at Harvard, Burden had taken Chanler on his first trip to the woods, and he quickly developed an aptitude for the life. Before long, he was finding his way alone through the vast forests of Quebec.

"Then, in the year 1927, something happened that brought into being the idea of a movie depicting the struggle for existence of an Ojibwa tribe before the coming of the white man. That something was Merian Cooper's *Chang.* Somehow *Chang* electrified my mind to the possibility of an Indian picture along similar lines. To be sure, we did not have elephants or water buffalo or leopards and tigers and gibbon, but we did have wolves and bear and mountain lion and foaming rapids, and the hardness of deep frost and long, tough winters. In addition, it was all too obvious that the Indians were dying off so rapidly from the white man's diseases that if the story of their endless struggle for survival against starvation—their Silent Enemy—was ever to be captured on film, we had no time to lose."

Douglas Burden had already established a reputation as an explorer. He had sought the Dragon Lizard of Komodo, and had succeeded not only in finding and filming this legendary creature but in capturing two of them and bringing them back to New York.

"When I mentioned *The Silent Enemy* idea to Willy, he was immediately filled with enthusiasm. He was with a law firm in New York City, and this was so near to his heart that since he knew the head of the law firm, he got permission to spend time with me up north, helping in every way. Willy came into the picture more and more, until he became so indispensable that I said, 'This isn't a Burden production, it's a Burden-Chanler production.' I brought him in as complete equal. When we ran over budget, it was largely Willy Chanler's efforts that enabled us to complete the film."

Burden selected as director and script writer H. P. Carver and his son Richard —the team Cooper had chosen to exploit *Grass.* Carver had been general manager of Cosmopolitan Productions for William Randolph Hearst for five years (the reviews of the time referred to him as a Calgary banker and sportsman, which was not correct) and he had set up a studio in Florida.

"All I knew about Carver was that he had directed an Indian picture out west before,* and that he had a good feeling for the Indians. This turned out to be quite true. He was somebody you could get along with; he enjoyed being away out in the wilderness. He was very fond of these people, so he could get a lot out of them.

* No evidence survives about this film.

"We had a full script—scene by scene—which Dick Carver wrote. I went over every single word, and made lots of changes, but he rewrote them scene by scene so we had the whole thing outlined in detail. While we were shooting, we had Dick Carver right there, so he was able to make any changes on the spot. The script involved many months of research. The story-line was founded on a study of those remarkable volumes called *The Jesuit Relations,* a running record in seventy-two volumes of the travels and explorations of the Jesuit missionaries in New France (1610–1791) who lived among the Ojibwa. Not one episode was invented by us, with the exception of the bear on the cliff.

"When the script was ready, I invited Jesse Lasky for dinner at my apartment in New York City, together with H. P. Carver. I knew he had been to the north woods, and had financed *Chang,* and felt that he might lend a sympathetic ear. He was enthusiastic about the possibility of a picture on the Ojibwas, but doubted that we could record one-half of what the script called for. However, he finally agreed to give me a distribution contract, which I needed in order to do any financing at all.

"We didn't feel there was much of a chance of getting precisely the kind of character that we wanted just from the Ojibwa. We had to allow ourselves a broader scope. Actually, the old chief in the picture we ran into in the American Museum of Natural History. Here was this striking-looking man, wandering through the halls, looking at the exhibits. He could have been taken right off the buffalo coin. We just started talking to him, and he turned out to be the hereditary chief of the Sioux Indians, a nephew of Sitting Bull, Chief Yellow Robe. When we told him what we wanted to do, he fell in love with the idea. He and I occupied the same tepee all winter long. Remarkable to relate he seemed to bear no ill-will against the white man. And after the picture was over, I remember inviting him down to my family's home on Long Island. When he left, my father turned to me and said, 'You know, Douglas, I think that is the most aristocratic man that has ever dined at our house.' Which was kind of an entertaining comment, because my father had a very strong feeling for such things."

The leading man, if that term is applicable, was a highly decorated World War I veteran, Buffalo Child Long Lance, who had served in the Canadian Army as captain. A contemporary of Jim Thorpe on the football team at Carlisle, Long Lance was a chief of a branch tribe of the Blackfoot. The author of a book on General Custer, he had worked as a newspaperman, but *The Silent Enemy* was his first contact with motion pictures. When the film was released, he found himself in great demand.

"He was such a magnificent-looking figure that all the ladies went crazy for him. As a result of *The Silent Enemy* he became well known in Hollywood circles, and was invited everywhere. The immediate result was embroilment with all kinds of women, and finally he made an error. It was suppressed in the newspapers. Long Lance, in effect, vanished. There was never any search. The FBI never followed it up. It was just one of those awful things. I have always suspected that the error he made was in tangling with a lady whose husband had too much power and too much money. Now this is pure surmise, but I do know that he was shot."

A solution to the mystery was recently offered by Iron Eyes Cody, the celebrated Indian actor, who has been in Hollywood since the silent days. "Buffalo Child Long Lance liked a white woman, Anita Baldwin, of the Baldwin Estate, one of the

Buffalo Child Long Lance, decorated war veteran, played the lead in The Silent Enemy *and later lost his life under mysterious circumstances in Hollywood.*

Buffalo Child Long Lance in a publicity still from The Silent Enemy.

richest women in California. She would invite all of us Indians into her beautiful estate at Santa Anita and let us use the pool. The guards at the gate didn't like Long Lance. He'd come up drunk and push these guys around. He was a husky man. When he'd started drinking, boy—he'd try to break the gate down. So they said, 'Someday we're going to put one in you.' He always told me that they threatened to shoot him. 'Ah, they're crazy, those guys,' I'd tell him. One day a guy called up: 'Lance has been shot.' One of the guards had shot him, but they could never prove it. We gave him a good funeral, and Canada came down and draped the flag and shot guns over him."[6]

The rest of the cast was very difficult to find. Burden scoured the country, from Alberta to South Dakota. He spent six weeks traveling by canoe along the shores of Abitibi Lake, searching for photogenic Indians.

"I would stop at one tent after another, spending long hours with each family, attempting to persuade them to join us in the Temagami Forest Reserve. They were very dubious about it, but I finally selected a total of about a hundred and fifty Indians. And having gotten them there and assigned different parts to the various characters, they began to be homesick for their trapping grounds. Of course, the whole picture depended on the Indians staying with us. If one family decamped, that might start an avalanche and suddenly I'd be left with no Indians. So I would invite them to my tepee and the whole family would come. I would ask them what their problem was, and after a long silence the man would say, 'Me think we go back to our trapping grounds.' So then I would have to recite the whole situation. 'If you go back to your trapping grounds you will have to live on fish. There's very little fur to trap. Spring will come. You will have almost no money. After a dreadful winter, living on fish, you will have very little to get you through the summer.' The whole performance might last a couple of hours, requiring endless patience. And at the end of it, I would say, 'Well, how do you feel about it now?' And there would be another long, dreadful silence, at the end of which the Indian would say, 'Me think we go back to our trapping grounds.'

"Most of the Ojibwa understood English, although they frequently pretended they didn't. Some of them would come to see me with complaints of one kind or another in the evening. They would require an interpreter when they could speak English perfectly well. But it gave them a little more time to think.

"We had one particular Indian who was a master craftsman at building birchbark canoes. His name was Jean Mapechee. Apparently, he sold dear old Father Evain, the seventy-year-old Catholic priest, on the idea that he had just had to get out of the little town of Ville Marie; there was some very important business he had to do. I was very fearful that if any Indian left us and got to some town, he'd get as drunk as a skunk and that would be the end of it. We'd never see him again. But Father Evain promised me he would make sure the man came back. 'He will return in three days, but it is very important that he take this trip.' So Mapechee left. Father Evain left. A week went by. No Jean Mapechee. Ten days went by—and I got one little letter from Ville Marie. It said 'Please help' and it was signed 'Jean Mapechee in jail.' That gives the flavor of my relationship with these people. If one of them was in jail, he looked to me to get him out. I kept that letter for years.

"Father Evain was very helpful to me in persuading the Indians to stay with us, despite that example. But I was so dumb as to the workings of the Catholic

Church, I didn't realize why he favored us. It was because he figured he could get more money for the Church out of the Indians if they worked for me than if they were off on their trapping grounds. Dear old Father Evain would come to our camp every two months or so with his dog team, and $300 cash in his pocket. He would ask me for a check for $300, and he would deposit his $300 at our store. He would then circulate through the Indian encampment and tell them to come and collect their pay. So they would collect, and the $300 cash would be gone. The next day would be Sunday. He would ask for our biggest mess tent for services, and I would pass the plate for him. Next day, he would leave with his dog team and the $300 cash he'd brought, plus my check. It would then all go out to the Catholic Church. That was the deal. Oh, slick as a whistle, and he was so charming. He spoke Ojibwa fluently. He could lead them in their own songs. He gave them something. And he would sanctify any common-law marriages that had taken place while he was away. He would baptize the babies—practically every Indian child that whole winter was called William Chanler Benoit or Douglas Burden Baptiste. He would handle it all just beautifully, and go off with three hundred bucks."

As a matter of history, Burden thought it vital that the making of a birch-bark canoe be filmed.

"We had with us an old Indian, nearly a hundred years old, one of the few still left who knew how to make birch-bark canoes as the original pre-Columbus Indians used to make them. One day we set him to work before his tepee making a canoe. It was only a short take and after half an hour or so we had all we wanted for the scene. For about six weeks afterwards we were busy with many other things and, in fact, were so preoccupied that we didn't notice anything strange about the old man's actions.

"One day he came to us and surprised us greatly with a request to get a day off, explaining that he needed a day of rest. It was only then that we learned to our astonishment that during all those weeks the old fellow had been working away assiduously at birch-bark canoes. There wasn't a camera within miles of him, and not a soul was even aware of what he was doing."

Indians capable of the standard of craftsmanship of their ancestors were rare, but when they were found the results were impressive. "After a few weeks, we had wigwams, canoes, cooking utensils of bark and skins, bows, arrows and quivers, some pointed spears and axes, tomahawks, winter clothing from fur, snow shoes, sleighs, medicine bags, fire bags, bone knives, tom-toms, drums, and war bonnets. Some of the Indians brought with them their family heirlooms, while a large assortment of original clothing and other objects were loaned to us by courtesy of the American Museum of Natural History.

"Then with all the equipment and props ready, we had to teach the Indians their use. Old games, old customs, old methods of making fire and cooking, and many other customs forgotten by disuse were revived. To accomplish this, we consulted authorities on Indian lore and sought the advice of specialists on the subject."

Unusually for what was essentially a documentary, Burden assembled a crew consisting largely of experienced Hollywood technicians. The chief cameraman was Marcel le Picard, a Frenchman who had collaborated on the camera work for D. W. Griffith's *America* and had photographed the Will Rogers Western parody, *Doubling for Romeo.*

"I chose Marcel le Picard because he was not only a very sincere, devoted, totally reliable kind of a man who could take a lot of punishment in the North, but also because he was known as someone who had an extraordinary eye for the amount of light and never had to refer to anything. He knew light as very few cameramen knew light, and he could put the stop at just the right point to get a perfect exposure. He never missed.

"Le Picard's great difficulty up north was in the use of snow shoes. Oh my God, that poor man would get so angry when he had a pair of snow shoes on! He would lose his temper, and go clean out of his mind because he wasn't physically adept, and he had no sort of natural muscular coordination or finesse. He would end up in such a rage that he'd have to go back to his tent to cool off."

The second cameraman was Frank Broda, and the assistant was Otto Durholz. The assistant director, Earl Welch, was, in Burden's words, "an aggressive, dependable guy with a lot of guts and energy and enough ingenuity to overcome most problems." As a result, he was used as a second-unit director.

When Welch was away, his role as assistant director was taken over by Count Ilia Tolstoy (grandson of the Russian writer). Burden had met Tolstoy in South Carolina; he had traveled widely in Russia, and was anxious to lead a special expedition to film the caribou migration.

Animal specialists included Dr. Alan Bachrach and an old Indian hunter who had taken Douglas Burden on many trips through the north woods, Archie Miller. (A moving tribute to the skill of Archie Miller appears in Douglas Burden's *Look to the Wilderness.*[7])

In charge of the camp was Bob Hennessey, and his gang of lumberjacks, some of whom were French-Canadian, some Irish. "Hennessey was a really rough guy, only eighteen years old, who ruled that camp with an iron hand. He himself was a scoundrel, but a real rough, tough scoundrel. He made things move. For instance, we wanted to get a bear up onto the cliffs. Everybody had their ideas, but they didn't sound right to me. I wasn't about to lose that bear by having him mishandled. Bob Hennessey, this eighteen-year-old Irish kid, came up to me and said, 'Give me ten men and I can guarantee to get that bear up there by ten o'clock tomorrow morning. Will that do?' And he did it."

The Silent Enemy program pays tribute to Hennessey. At no time, it says, was the expedition without food or shelter. "His most difficult task was during the 'freeze-up' which lasted for about six weeks. The lakes were covered with a skim of ice too weak to walk on, but too strong for a canoe. There were no trails through the forest, which was already covered with a foot of snow, yet Hennessey and his loyal and hardy assistants worked literally day and night during this entire time in order that the outfit might continue to make pictures without bothering about how it would keep alive. The innumerable acts of real heroism performed by Hennessey and his gang will never be known, and can only be appreciated by those accustomed to the North."

Thanks to Hennessey, living conditions for the cast and crew were as pleasant as they could be. Burden explained: "Most of us lived in tents, and we had a cook tent that had a board floor. On certain occasions Chief Buffalo Child Long Lance would put on an Indian dance that was absolutely galvanizing. It would bring down the house—everybody was mad to watch, and it would really get to you to know he would do it so well. I occupied the same tepee as Chief Yellow Robe, and we used an open fire until well into the winter. Finally, it got to be pretty rugged, so we put in a stove in place of the open fire, and we had bunks raised slightly off the floor, so you had sitting places all round the tepee. He slept on one side of the stove, and I slept on the other. We were very comfortable."

Burden had contracted a mysterious illness in Nicaragua in 1924, which struck him severely on location, forcing him to remain in his tepee for three weeks at a stretch, surviving on tomato juice. Doctors could identify none of the symptoms, and with perverse simplicity, laid its cause entirely in Burden's mind. This did not advance his recovery. It took eighteen years before a doctor diagnosed it definitively as amoebic dysentery.

"To make a picture with a starvation theme, when you have to feed the people taking part in order to keep them there, is pretty difficult. Supplies to the camp were run in entirely by dog team. We were very lucky, except for one very unfortunate incident just after the freeze-up, when an Indian dog driver thought a certain lake was safe and he went through the ice. He was lost, and so were all his dogs."

Inevitably, there was friction between the Indians and the lumberjacks. "The lumberjack of Canada is a typically tough, arrogant white man who wants to domineer, and so he looks down upon the Indian. This is bound to precipitate an unfortunate situation, and you have to watch it all the time. I had to keep saying to Hennessey: 'If any of your gang behave badly, fire them.' And he did. He would fire anybody. Right away, he made his men toe the line.

"I don't think I can take any credit for the direction. I have no instinct for it. I have an instinct for a scene, and the feeling I'd like, and what I'd like to see translated to the screen, but I haven't got the ability to bring it about. I remember one occasion when I made a bad mistake. We were moving camp from Lake Temiskaming up to Rabbit Lake and the Temagami Forest Reserve. I had gone ahead, with le Picard and little Cheeka, the boy in the film. I started to shoot a scene with him on the river, beautiful autumn leaves floating down the river. I thought it was too good to miss. Well, H. P. Carver was furious, and I think rightly so. He was the director, or he wasn't the director. If he was the director, *he* was going to shoot the film. Not me. I recognized the mistake and I said okay, you're quite right. Because he was ready to walk off altogether. I was very careful from then on not to attempt to shoot anything. I left it right in his hands."

The program for *The Silent Enemy,* full of the inevitable hyperbole of press agentry, describes one poignant incident: "In the scene where Baluk (Long Lance) says good-bye to the boy Cheeka before ascending the funeral pyre, Cheeka actually believed Long Lance was going to be burned to death. Under these circumstances, his usual stoicism broke down with the results that are to be seen in the picture."[8] Burden cannot vouch for the accuracy of this account, but said that Carver had told him the story. Cheeka had grown very fond of Long Lance, and the scene was staged with such realism that it was hard to tell whether it was fantasy or not. "H. P. Carver had a way with both the girl, Spotted Elk, and little Cheeka. In no time at all, if he wanted crying, he could have them come right back on to camera, and they would just be screaming. I don't know what he used to say to them, but he'd get them. They both understood English. Later, when the film was shown away up in

An Ojibwa village before the white man came—from The Silent Enemy.

Temagami in a little theater, every time Cheeka appeared on the screen, he'd shout, 'That's me!' The girl was a Penobscot from Maine, and she became pregnant in the middle of the picture. We had to fire the boy responsible. But that's typical of the sort of problem you'd run into."

Burden was deeply anxious about the cost of the picture, for it was his friends' money he was spending. The technicians were another cause of anxiety. They worked hard, and devotedly, but after a certain number of weeks, the strain began to tell. "They'd get bushed—that's the term used in the north. They'd be so long away from their families, away from females, and so on, that finally they could stand it no longer. They would become edgy. Then I'd say, 'Okay. Get the hell out. Take a week. Go.' And they'd disappear for a while and come back fine.

"The scenes that were made in the most extreme cold were those in the Medicine Lodge in which the Medicine Man, Dagwan (Chief Akawansh), is seen naked, in a loincloth. We had one of those rabbit-skin robes off camera, available to him when he got too cold. Night after night, the temperature was 35 below zero; the winds were blasting, and the snow was driven right over him. But that man, who had TB, would stand out there for scene after scene. I don't know how he did it. At the end of each take, he would take a rabbit-skin robe and wrap it round himself, and be ready to begin again a few minutes later. Unbelievable, the circulatory capacity of these guys."

Louis A. Bonn, known as Charlie, was Jules Brulatour's right-hand man in the Eastman Kodak agency. He set up a laboratory in the field for *The Silent Enemy* and proved indispensable on the animal shooting. Although no rushes were viewed on the location, when he shot something unique, such as the fight between the mountain lion and the bear, he would develop it at once to ensure that the scene was caught. Otherwise, Burden relied on Marcel le Picard's reaction. He would watch a scene being shot, then ask, "Have we got it?" If le Picard replied, "Positively we have it," everyone relaxed, for he was totally trustworthy.

The fight between the mountain lion and the bear is a scene that causes a great deal of comment, even today. Burden was not present when Charlie Bonn shot the sequence, but he remembers the principle. "They found that the bear was always the attacker. Here was a dead deer; both the bear and mountain lion are damn hungry. They let the mountain lion get at the deer first, then they released the bear from another enclosure. He went at the mountain lion, and a fight broke out. The mountain lion escaped up a tree, and the bear was so damn mad he went up the tree after him, and right out on a limb. They fell off the limb, and continued fighting together on the ground. That was how the scene worked out.

"We didn't have many problems with safety, because it was too easy to protect a cameraman. As you know, Schoedsack took a real risk several times. We took an absolute minimum of risk.

"After *Chang* came out, I made it my business to get in touch with Merian Cooper. And it was fun, because he was so secretive. He wouldn't tell me how he had done anything. He would just laugh. But then, more and more I had the sense of what he *must* have done, and so gradually, by his not saying, 'No, I didn't do it that way,' I realized he had done it the way I was suggesting. Then I knew I could do the same thing."

Burden decided that Cooper's basic approach was to collect wild animals in their natural habitat, surrounded by a fence that they could neither jump over nor smash through. "So he had them, and he knew he could work with them. The chances are you might have to sit for six months to get some of their scenes of leopards charging, although Coop took all kinds of chances, and he had to shoot again and again to save his life and Schoedsack's life. And he never missed. But he had the animals under a certain, limited control. I figured we could do the same up north. We'll say a mountain lion and a bear; if they were both hungry, we knew they would fight for whatever meat there was. Which is exactly what happened. They were in a very large area. We just let them get hungry enough so that when a deer was available, they went after it and fought."

The great horned owl is a savage creature. Harry Raven, of the American Museum of Natural History, suggested operating on one of these owls to render it harmless. When the owl recovered consciousness from the operation, it was totally changed in character. It survived and stayed with the company throughout the picture. "It rode on the bow of canoes shooting rapids, it rode on a toboggan throughout the winter. It would sit comfortably on your shoulder. It was a completely tame owl, with no sense in its head. At the end, one of the Indian families liked it so much they took it away with them when they went back to their trapping grounds."

The Silent Enemy's equivalent to the elephant stampede in *Chang* is the caribou stampede, a sequence of such dimensions, emanating from the vast, empty icescape, that it stuns the audience with the force of a snowstorm.

Douglas Burden sent Ilia Tolstoy to get this sequence up in the Barren Lands. "Since there were no airplanes, you couldn't tell which way the caribou were going to migrate—and he missed them. The whole of Tolstoy's very costly expedition was a dead loss. Today, with helicopters, you could have filmed the whole thing without any difficulty, but then we had to send this expedition by canoe. They made terrific portages, and paddled over tremendous lakes, like Reindeer Lake, and missed the migration, which may have been five hundred miles this way, or two hundred miles that way. But anyway, they missed them, so we had to get busy and send a whole new expedition to Alaska. Earl Welch headed that one, and he got the pictures you see. He did damned well."

The sequence is a triumph of inventiveness, a brilliant sleight of hand which in no way detracts from the integrity of the film. Yet to this day, Douglas Burden is unhappy at this one lapse in the film's authenticity. "We got some pictures of true caribou, and we mixed them with reindeer.* The Loman brothers were the reindeer kings of Alaska. They arranged it all on that north slope area, not too far from Point Barrow."

Not knowing of the near tragedy that had befallen the *Frozen Justice* crew, Earl Welch took the same air route, and, like them, carried costumes and some members of the cast, including Cheeka. Ilia Tolstoy had brought parkas and other protective clothing from the Barren Lands. Earl Welch staged a stunt that is still hair-raising; he had Cheeka drop down behind a dead caribou and he drove the rest of the herd over him.

BURDEN EDITED THE PICTURE with Richard Carver. At the first showing of the film, William Chanler remembers sitting behind Madison Grant, president of the Zoological Society, after whom Grant's caribou are named. "He made two important comments, and was wrong both times," recalled Chanler. "His first comment was that he absolutely couldn't say that our wolf pictures were authentic. He said it would be impossible to take pictures of really wild wolves such as the picture contained, and that obviously we must have gotten some Eskimo huskies and wired their tails down to make them look like wolves. I told him that he was entirely wrong and explained how Douglas Burden had managed to get really wild wolves into enclosures so that they could be photographed, but I don't think he really believed me. Then, when the climax came, he announced that he had never seen such an obviously authentic picture of the caribou migration! I told him that he had better be careful what he wrote because he had been wrong on both counts, and he was much impressed with the true story about the caribou picture."[9]

Burden and Chanler were extremely gratified when *The Silent Enemy* opened at the Criterion, the same theater where *Chang* had had such a successful run. "After a screening for the Paramount personnel, Jesse Lasky rose and addressed his sales staff: 'A year and a half ago, these young men came to me for a distribution contract. After reading the scenario I told them that if they obtained even a portion of what the script called for, they would have a picture. Now I want you to know that not only have they secured everything the script called for, but a lot more besides. I want this film to receive the best advertising and promotion our organization can give it.' "[10]

But *The Silent Enemy* proved to be a box-office failure. The block-booking

---

* Reindeer are the domesticated version of the caribou. Neil Goodwin, a cousin of Douglas Burden, whose father worked on *The Silent Enemy,* made a television film about wolves from a light plane in 1972; *Following the Tundra Wolf* contained some remarkable footage of caribou.

system ensured this failure, forcing exhibitors to take *The Silent Enemy* as just another Paramount picture, and denying it the specialized treatment it demanded. Besides which, the talking-picture revolution had swept silent films off the world's screens. *The Silent Enemy* proved to be among the last authentic silent films to play on Broadway.

TRADER HORN

Turn the camera upon the wilderness, upon uncivilized tribes, upon rare species of jungle life, and according to the skill of the cameraman, a document of value will emerge. No matter how preposterous the story, the backgrounds will give the film an importance that grows with the years.

And so it is with *Trader Horn.* Covering four African colonies, thirty-five varieties of big game, and fifteen tribes, the documentary scenes, with their on-the-spot recordings,* are now of priceless value. The story, however, is a different matter. Its origin was a remarkable book, *The Life and Works of Alfred Aloysius Horn.*[1] An old tin and wire peddler came to sell a gridiron to South African novelist Ethelreda Lewis. Intrigued by his courtly manner and his elegant turn of phrase, she took the trouble to talk to him; impressed by his flood of memories, she paid him to write them down. She edited the result but had the sense to retain his idiosyncratic spelling and the vivid color of his language. Even more sensibly, she recorded his comments upon each chapter. The old man lived in a doss house, surrounded by abject poverty, and writing the book gave him a new lease on life. Its success brought him international fame and (one hopes) a fair share of fortune.

Miss Lewis thought it wise to change all the surnames, including that of Horn himself. Alfred Aloysius was born in Glasgow and raised in Lancashire, but he spent time in America, and throughout the book, he comments upon its effect on American readers. The narrative is engrossing, and highly colored, although as a former sailor, detective, cowpuncher, river pilot, and ivory hunter, he had experience enough to launch a flotilla of books. In this first volume, *The Ivory Coast in the Earlies,* he concentrated on his early youth in the Africa of the 1870s. "The correctful thing in all literary books," he wrote, "is to remember that even the truth may need suppressing if it appears out of tangent with the common man's notion of reality." In different words, this was the primary rule of the picture business, so it strikes a chord of delicious irony to think that MGM swallowed the story as gospel truth and sent a motion picture expedition, generators, and sun arcs into the African wilds to capture it all on film.

In charge of the expedition was W. S. Van Dyke. His own book about the experience, *Horning into Africa,*[2] contains harsh mention of Alfred Aloysius, whom he came to regard as a scandalous liar. But Africa had changed since the 1870s, and while Van Dyke and his company suffered from illness, insects, and injury,

* Some of the animal noises were synthetic.

Trader Horn himself (1929).

they suffered more than anything else from imagination. From the moment he landed at Mombasa, Van Dyke was thirsting for blood, desperate for savages. He was dismayed by the extent to which civilization had encroached upon the wilds. He was disconcerted that so many of his savages proved so servile. Under the influence of Edgar Rice Burroughs and H. Rider Haggard, he felt obliged to improve upon nature and to provide the thrills that Alfred Aloysius had promised. In doing so, he discarded the book and made up his own excitement. He provoked buffalo stampedes, rhino charges, and general zoological mayhem, abetted by a camera car built like a tank, a long-focus lens replacing the gun.

Alfred Aloysius had described a half-English, part-native girl, Lola D—, who lived in a joss house, as goddess of the Isorga; he and his friend, Little Peru (son of the Peruvian President), had rescued the girl, and Little Peru had married her. This seemed as commercial as any Tarzan story, so Van Dyke made it the basis of his film; the picture concentrated on the trek to find the lost girl and the struggle to return her to civilization. Although the book describes her with auburn hair, the film provides a stunning blonde, with the picturesque *nom d'écran* of Edwina Booth.* Her scanty costume and her sado-masochistic behavior with a whip would never have survived the censors in a less educational picture, but Van Dyke spared nothing—and certainly not the lives of animals—to produce more astonishing safari scenes than the screen had ever shown.

Before leaving Hollywood, he had had four hundred human skulls made from papier-mâché. When these were used to decorate an Isorga village, the natives vanished, assuming that the crew were indulging in wholesale slaughter. It took three weeks to coax them back. In Kikuyu country, on the other hand, the natives felt so at home in a village built for the picture that they moved in with their families and created a new community.

* Edwin Booth, the great American actor, had been Alfred Aloysius's elocution teacher, or so he claimed. Edwina Booth's real name was Constance Woodruff.

An experienced white hunter, Major W. V. D. Dickinson, was the company's closest ally. Despite his advice, his warnings, and his precautions, encounters with wild animals were often as petrifying as Van Dyke had hoped they would be. On one occasion, Dickinson and Van Dyke, doubling for the leading men, encouraged a rhino to charge. As it drew close, the action called for Van Dyke to run for safety. His gun-bearer misunderstood, assumed he was scared, and ran in to take his place, as demanded by the safari code. This heroism not only put his life in peril—it ruined the scene.

The leading man, Harry Carey, was an inspired choice.* His assurance and relaxed playing were just what the film needed to hold its fragmented structure together. Carey had risen to fame as a cowboy star, but unlike most of that breed, he had never ridden the range. Carey was the son of a judge and had graduated from New York Law School, taking to the screen rather than the bar. Devoted to the West, he became a cowboy star and his career flourished under the direction of John Ford. For a while, the two men were inseparable companions; Carey's widow, Olive Golden Carey, recalled that they, Pardner Jones, and a group of cowboys all lived together in a tiny house in Newhall. "When the house was full, we slept out in the alfalfa patch," said Mrs. Carey. "Oh, we were really Western!"[3]

Mrs. Carey played the part of a missionary. The rough locations of the Ford company had given the Careys splendid training for *Trader Horn.* "Oh, it was tough," said Olive Carey. "You had to fight bugs all the time, and wear mosquito boots. Harry was an avid reader, and he had read somewhere that every night, when you went to bed, you should put wood ashes around your tent, because of safari ants. One night we heard screams. Safari ants had gotten into Dickinson's tent. They'd eaten the butt off his gun and were starting on his sheets. There he was, stark naked and covered with these ants. Harry pushed him and rolled him in these ashes, which smothered the ants. And then he covered him in a blanket. Oh, what a mess! But I must admit that there was nothing that money could buy that MGM didn't buy to make us comfortable. They did everything that was humanly possible."

Paradoxically, the greater the comfort, the greater the risk. For trucks, burdened with supplies, are liable to break down en route and involve the company in greater discomfort than a more streamlined safari. Van Dyke was warned by African authorities to take nothing weighing more than a ton and a half into the bush. Yet his generator truck weighed nine tons on its own. MGM's was the largest safari on record; the previous holder was that of the Prince of Wales (later King Edward VII), celebrated for the fact that a dozen whites, fifty blacks, and eight tons of equipment had traversed so much of Africa without a casualty. Van Dyke's army consisted of three dozen whites, two hundred blacks, and ninety tons of equipment.

The British authorities refused permission for the company to enter tsetse-fly country. The Murchison Falls was in the affected area, together with large numbers of hippos and crocodiles; Van Dyke, although suffering from malaria, was determined to go. Some of the crew had malaria, too, and the doctor kept everyone loaded with quinine. Why Van Dyke was willing to expose them all to such danger is open

---

* MGM originally chose Tim McCoy but settled on Carey because he looked more rugged.

The Trader Horn *crew; W. S. Van Dyke, kneeling, right; Clyde de Vinna, with pipe, leaning over camera; Red Golden, assistant director, behind him; Josephine Chippo, script clerk, next to Golden.*

The Trader Horn *company set up an open-air movie show for cast and crew in the African bush.*

to question; certainly he was disappointed with the dramatic possibilities of Africa and was desperate to justify the vast expense of the expedition. Yet the tsetse fly carried the much-feared sleeping sickness, which had a delayed effect and was frequently fatal. Nevertheless, Van Dyke fought the decision, secured permission, and took his company in and out without mishap.

"Nobody got sleeping sickness," said Olive Carey. "I got blackwater fever, from swimming around in the river at the foot of the falls. The water had all sorts of germs and bugs in it, and also crocodiles." But even this cannot be blamed on the tsetse fly; blackwater fever is generally caused by a reaction against quinine.

Trader Horn was begun as a silent picture. Even as late as 1929, the front office was not convinced that the talkie revolution was irreversible. *White Shadows* had been a success as a silent with synchronized music and effects, and *Trader Horn* was seen as a logical sequel. "We were in Africa when they decided they would send over a sound truck to Mombasa," said Olive Carey. "They started to unload it from the boat and they dropped it overboard—so that was another three or four weeks' holdup. Andy Anderson was the sound recordist, but he'd been so dosed up with quinine, he was practically stone deaf." Much of the sound was done over again later in Culver City, where recording techniques had improved beyond all recognition.

When the company returned to New York, the MGM front office expressed its appreciation by firing virtually everyone. Irving Thalberg was extremely upset; despite the enormous sums invested, the rushes made no sense whatever, and no one could cut them together. The film was threatened with cancellation when Bernie Hyman persuaded Thalberg that the picture could be saved, provided he would approve further expenditure.

"They had six scripts, and they couldn't come up with any dialogue," said Olive Carey. "They had a conference and Thalberg said to Harry, 'We're not getting anywhere.' Harry said, 'Did you ever think to open the book?' I was there, and I remember Irving calling for his secretary, and do you know they didn't have a copy on the lot? They sent over to a bookshop—and the dialogue was mostly there—the old man talking."

Now MGM's well-oiled machinery enabled little miracles of administrative engineering to occur. Sam Marx, head of the story department, inserted Cyril Hume, until then a total failure as a screenwriter, into the vacant space of dialogue man until he produced connecting scenes, which fitted so well that Bernie Hyman was reduced to tears of relief.

Virtually all the dialogue scenes were shot on the back lot, but so artfully integrated that no one suspected. Van Dyke knew perfectly well that a great deal more needed to be shot; he had provided the backgrounds, and the remainder would have to be staged in the manner of Cooper and Schoedsack's *Four Feathers*. To this end, he had brought back from Africa Mutia Oomooloo of the Wagomba tribe, who played Trader Horn's gun-bearer Renchero, and as a companion, his own gun-bearer, Riano. They were booked, with some difficulty, into the Culver City Hotel, which had a rule against admitting blacks, but they preferred the back lot, where two large tents were erected and furnished, safari-style, by the prop department. Black residents of Los Angeles were made up as tribesmen for the extra shooting, but Mutia and Riano remained aristocratically aloof, regarding the locals as *shenzi,* a word the interpreter refused to translate.

Mutia and Riano, newly arrived from Africa with the Trader Horn *company, were subjected to posing for the same publicity stills as were the other actors. In their case, however, the effect was even more bizarre.*

The experience of these two Africans in Hollywood is one of film history's great untold stories. What must they have thought? Harry Carey learned a certain amount of Swahili and was able to converse with them; Mutia and Riano considered Hollywood *kufanu*—wild, crazy—which was hardly surprising, since everyone else felt much the same about the place. They thought Garbo was alarmingly thin and that her husband should feed her more. They caused much amusement with their opinion of Leo, the MGM lion: "Fur no good. Belly too fat. Too old. No good teeth. In Africa, he would die of hunger."

With all the extra shooting, rumors circulated that the African expedition was a fake. The publicity department was so alarmed that it caused footage of Marjorie Rambeau, who had replaced Olive Carey as the missionary, to be shelved. Having made much of the three intrepid women on this otherwise all-male expedition,

Edwina Booth, Olive Carey, and script clerk Josephine Chippo (actually, there was a fourth: Miss Gordon, the hairdresser) they feared press exposure and ridicule. Olive Carey returned to the role (at Miss Rambeau's highly inflated salary) and completed her dialogue scenes with the required English accent.

Under great secrecy, a second unit went below the border to Mexico, beyond the jurisdiction of the SPCA, and staged the fights with the animals. "If we'd ever been found out," said J. J. Cohn, MGM's production manager, "we could never have released the film." And yet the facts were openly admitted in a frank and accurate article in *Photoplay*.[4] The lions were kept without food for several days and then let loose upon hyenas, monkeys, and deer in a special corral. The results can be imagined. The killing of a lion with a spear, an unusually gruesome scene, was filmed here, too, for the authorities in Africa had not permitted it.

Fantastic rumors circulated around the enthralling figure of Edwina Booth. She had suffered more than most, for she could not seek protection beneath pith helmet and spine pad. Throughout the film, she wore virtually nothing. She was bitten and stung by insects, her flesh was torn by elephant grass, and she endured malaria and sunstroke. Publicity suggested that she had contracted some malignant disease, which would be fatal in a few months—a useful ploy to conceal what amounted to a nervous breakdown. After *Trader Horn* was released, she was assumed to have died from the tropical illness, but she survived into the 1970s, devoting herself to the Mormon religion.

Van Dyke made one more trip of this sort (for *Eskimo* in 1932–1933). He then abandoned such flamboyant adventuring. His handling of the picture had been triumphantly vindicated by rave reviews and a profit of almost a million dollars. *Trader Horn* took one hundred fifteen days to make—now he altered his style, streamlined his schedules, and became famous as "One-Take Woody Van Dyke."

Trader Horn WAS THE END OF AN ERA. No longer would vast expeditions from Hollywood set out like conquistadores for distant lands. The emergence of back projection permitted the actors to stay in the studio. Commercially, this was highly desirable. But it drained a certain vitality from the cinema. Backgrounds became the most artificial parts of a film, instead of the most authentic. Opportunities for the documentation of exotic locales passed to the makers of travelogues.

Fortunately, in our own day, television has given a new lease on life to the documentary. Sound, color, and lightweight equipment have enabled serious filmmakers to provide absolutely authentic records of forgotten peoples and the lands in which they live. Feature films with documentary backgrounds are again becoming accepted.

Yet the tradition that these films follow has been clouded by neglect. The men who made the early films of fact deserve to be remembered, and their work deserves to be exhumed. The visual evidence of the past is too precious to be destroyed.

D. W. Griffith defined the purpose of the moving picture, and there can be no better maxim for the documentary:

To narrate, to stimulate, to perpetuate.

Stampede (*1928*).

SOURCES OF THE FILMS

Instead of a detailed bibliography (most of the books referred to are credited in the end notes), I thought it would be helpful to provide a list of where the films can be seen. I cannot guarantee what kind of prints you'll find; remember that all silent films once looked sharp and clear, but many have been copied so often that they sometimes resemble photocopies of their former state. The "Lost?" lists are indictments of the studios and organizations that produced the films—and then let them rot. These lists are included in the hope that some collector somewhere will have preserved a title or two and will allow the rest of us the privilege of seeing it or them. Asterisks indicate non-exclusive ownership.

THE WAR

John E. Allen, Park Ridge, New Jersey
*The Battle in the Clouds**
The Spirit of '76 (fragments)

British Film Institute / National Film Archive, London
*The Battle in the Clouds**
*Civilization**
*The Four Horsemen of the Apocalypse**
*Hearts of the World**
Home Defense
The Invasion of Britain (fragments)
Mexican War Pictures (Romaine Fielding: fragments)
World War as Seen Through German Spectacles (English version of *Der Weltkrieg*)

George Eastman House, Rochester, New York
Battle Cry of Peace (fragments)
Barbed Wire
Joan the Woman
The Little American
The Love Light
Queen Kelly

Film Classic Exchange, Los Angeles
Spirit of Audubon

Films, Inc., Wilmette, Illinois
The Big Parade
Flesh and the Devil
*The Four Horsemen of the Apocalypse**
*Wings**

Glenn Photo Supply, Encino, California
Hearts of the World (censored material)
*My Four Years in Germany**

Imperial War Museum, London
The Battle of the Somme
Britain Prepared
*The Log of the U-35**
A vast amount of World War I coverage
Lowell Thomas Palestine campaign footage

Killiam Shows, New York (released by Blackhawk Films, Davenport, Iowa)
*The Birth of a Nation**

*The Bond**
*Four Sons**
*Hearts of the World**
*Intolerance**
*Isn't Life Wonderful?**
*What Price Glory?**

Library of Congress / American Film Institute, Washington, D.C.
*All Quiet on the Western Front**
Behind the Door (incomplete)
The Big Drive
*The Birth of a Nation**
*Blind Husbands**
*The Bond**
Bud's Recruit (one reel only)
*Civilization**
Enchanted Cottage
Face Value
*Hearts of the World**
*Intolerance**
*Isn't Life Wonderful?**
*Johanna Enlists**
The Lost Battalion
*Shoulder Arms**
*The Sinking of the Lusitania**
Terrible Teddy, the Grizzly King
The Unbeliever
The Wedding March
*What Price Glory?**
*Wings**

Museum of Modern Art, New York
*Blind Husbands**
*Civilization**
*Four Sons**
Havoc
Patria (some episodes)
*What Price Glory?**

National Archives, Washington, D.C.
American Expeditionary Force to Russia footage
*America's Answer**
Fit to Fight
Official War Review
Pershing's Crusaders
Under Four Flags
War as It Really Is (Donald Thompson)

Thunderbird, Los Angeles
*The Birth of a Nation**

United Artists 16, New York
The Patent Leather Kid

Universal 16, Los Angeles
*All Quiet on the Western Front**

Lost?
America Must Conquer (*King of the Huns*)
Arms and the Woman
The Battle Cry of Peace
The Battle of Przemysl
Be Neutral
The Capture of New York
Dangerous Days
Daughter of Destiny
Denver's Underworld
The Eagle's Eye
18–45 (*Every Mother's Son*)
England's Menace
An Englishman's Home
The Fall of a Nation
The Fighting Roosevelts (*Our Teddy*)
Germany and Its Armies Today
Germany in Wartime
Germany on the Firing Line
Greater Glory
The Greatest Thing in Life
The Great Victory
The Hero
Heroic France
If England Were Invaded
The Insurrection
The Invasion of England
Japanese Invasion
The Kaiser—the Beast of Berlin
The Kaiser's Finish
Lay Down Your Arms
Lest We Forget
The Life of Villa
Mexican War Pictures
The Ordeal
Over the Top
The Patriot
A Prisoner of Mexico
Private Peat
The Prussian Cur
The Romance of the Air
The Rough Riders
Serbia Victorious
Shell 43
Side Show of Life

Somewhere in France
The Spirit of '76
The Strafer Strafed
This Hero Business
To Hell with the Kaiser
Twenty Three and a Half Hours Leave
Under Fire in Mexico
Under the German Yoke
The Unpardonable Sin
War Brides
Warfare in the Skies
Womanhood, Glory of the Nation
Zeppelin's Last Raid

THE WEST

John E. Allen, Park Ridge, New Jersey
Buck Parvin: Buck's Lady Friend
Indians and Cow-Boys

American Museum of Natural History, New York
History of the American Indian (fragments)

Blackhawk, Davenport, Iowa
*The Battle at Elderbush Gulch**
Bond of Blood
Buck Parvin: Extra Man and Milkfed Lion
*The Great Train Robbery**
*Hell's Hinges**
*The Iron Horse**
Shootin' Mad
Ropin' Fool
The Testing Block
*Tumbleweeds**
Wagon Tracks
*Wild and Woolly**
Buffalo Bill actuality material

British Film Institute / National Film Archive, London
Curse of the Redman
*The Heart of Texas Ryan**
*The Winning of Barbara Worth**

George Eastman House, Rochester, New York
The Last of the Mohicans
Manhattan Madness

Film Classic Exchange, Los Angeles
Before the White Man Came

Films, Inc., Wilmette, Illinois
The Big Trail (to be released)
The Wind

Killiam Shows, New York
*Great K & A Train Robbery**
*Hell's Hinges**
The Indian Massacre (Heart of an Indian)
*The Iron Horse**
*Last Drop of Water**
*Tumbleweeds**

Library of Congress / American Film Institute, Washington, D.C.
The Bank Robbery
The Bargain
*The Covered Wagon**
*Custer's Last Fight**
The Dalton Boys
Lady of the Dugout
Last of the Line (Pride of Race)
*Life of a Cowboy**
North of 36
Oklahoma Roundup
*A Pueblo Legend**
Redskin
*The Squaw Man**
*Tumbleweeds**
*The Vanishing American**
Wolf Hunt

Teri C. McLuhan, New York
The Shadow Catcher

Milestone, New York
*The Vanishing American**

Museum of Modern Art, New York
*The Covered Wagon**
Doubling for Romeo
*Great K & A Train Robbery**
*The Iron Horse**
*Last Drop of Water**
Man from Painted Post

*The Massacre**
*Wild and Woolly**
Wild Bill Hickok

Radim Films, New York
Straight Shootin'

University of Washington
In the Land of the Headhunters

Lost?
Across Swiftcurrent Pass on Horseback
The Adventurer
Beating Back
Beyond the Law
Buck Parvin: *Man-Afraid-of-His-Wardrobe; Sandy, Reformer*
Buffalo Bill's Indian Pictures
Butterfly Range
Camping with the Blackfeet
A Cowboy Magnate
Cowboy Sports and Pastimes
A Debtor to the Law
De-Indianizing the Red Man
Dredges and Farm Implements in the West
Duhem and Harter's 1913 California Rodeo
Evening Star
The Exposition's First Romance
The Folly of a Life of Crime
The Friendless Indian
Gold from Weepah
Her Own People
The Hidden Spring
History of the American Indian
Indian Dances and Pastimes
Indian Life
The Iron Trail
The James Brothers
Jordan Is a Hard Road
Kit Carson
Land o' the Lizards
The Last Stand of the Dalton Boys
Life Among the Navajos
Life and Customs of the Winnebago Indians
Life's Whirlpool
Lone Star
The New Red Man
Nurse Among the Tepees
Opportunity and a Million Acres
The Passing of the Oklahoma Outlaws
Pendleton Round-Up
Quicksands
Ranch Life in the Great Southwest
The Red Woman
Ridin' Mad
The Secret Spring
Sundown
The Thundering Herd
Told in the Hills
The Tonopah Stampede for Gold
The War on the Plains
War Paint
War's Women
The Wild West Comes to Town

Note: Films like *The Devil Horse* and *Red Raiders* were put out in the 1920s and 30s in 16mm. and 8mm. and sometimes turn up secondhand on the open market.

THE WILDERNESS

Blackhawk, Davenport, Iowa
Congorilla (to be released?)
*Nanook of the North**
The Silent Enemy

British Film Institute / National Film Archive, London
Dassan
Manhatta
90° South
Primitive Love
Stampede
The Everest films*

Canadian Film Institute, Ottawa
The Viking

Films, Inc., Wilmette, Illinois
Trader Horn
White Shadows in the South Seas

Imperial War Museum, London
Lowell Thomas Palestine campaign footage

Library of Congress / American Film Institute, Washington, D.C.
*Chang**
*Grass**
*Nanook of the North**
Paul Rainey's African Hunt (incomplete)
Seeing Boston from a Streetcar
The Valley of 10,000 Smokes
Roosevelt material

Museum of Modern Art, New York
*Moana**
*Nanook of the North**
Stark Love
*Tabu**

Captain J. B. L. Noel, Brenzett, Kent
*Climbing Mount Everest**
*The Epic of Everest**

Swedish Television, Stockholm
Through the Death Deserts of Asia (Sven Hedin: fragments)

UCLA
*Chang**
*Grass**
Rango

Lost?
Balto's Race to Nome
Cannibals of the South Seas
Heart of Africa
Hunting Big Game in Africa
Hunting Big Game in Africa with Gun and Camera
Jack London's Adventures in the South Seas
Kivalina of the Icelands
Shipwrecked Among Cannibals
Twenty-four Dollar Island
Up the Congo
Wild Heart of Africa
The Wild Men of Malekula
Wonders of the Sea

NOTES

THE WAR

The Balkans (pages 4–5)

1 *The Bioscope,* 7 May 1914, p. 625.

Propaganda (pages 6–8)

1 R. Squires, "*British Propaganda at Home and in U.S.A. 1914–17,*" Harvard Monograph, 1935, p. 32.
2 *Moving Picture World,* 19 September 1914, p. 1617.

Belgium (pages 8–13)

1 *The Bioscope,* 20 August 1914, p. 737.
2 B. R. Brookes-Carrington to author.
3 Quoted in *Moving Picture World,* 24 October 1914, p. 499.
4 *Ibid.,* 28 November 1914, p. 218.
5 *The Bioscope,* 20 May 1915, p. 761.
6 *Pictures and Picturegoer,* 5 December 1914, p. 263.
7 *The Bioscope,* 22 October 1914, p. 299.
8 *Moving Picture World,* 3 October 1914, p. 50.

American Cameramen with the Germans (pages 13–22)

1 Francis A. Collins, *The Cameraman* (New York: Century, 1916).
2 *Moving Picture World,* 14 August 1915, p. 1175.
3 *Motion Picture Magazine,* February 1916, p. 56.
4 *Photoplay,* March 1916, p. 112.
5 *Moving Picture World,* 14 August 1915, p. 1134.
6 *Motion Picture News,* 6 May 1916, p. 2717.
7 *Moving Picture World,* 21 April 1917, p. 447.
8 *Ibid.,* 8 December 1917, p. 1503.
9 Telegrams in the possession of the Museum of Modern Art contain this information; see Eileen Bowser, *D. W. Griffith* (New York: Museum of Modern Art/Doubleday, 1965), p. 53.

Neutrality (pages 22–24)

1 William Leuchtenberg, *Perils of Prosperity* (University of Chicago Press, 1958), p. 14.
2 *The Bioscope,* 24 September 1914, p. 1153.
3 *Moving Picture World,* 15 August 1914, p. 963.
4 Jack Spears, *Films in Review,* June–July 1966, p. 274.

Terror Weapons (pages 24–30)

1 *War Illustrated,* 29 August 1914.
2 *Kinematograph Weekly,* 15 April 1915, p. 29.
3 *The Bioscope,* 14 September 1916, p. 1065.
4 *Kinematograph Weekly,* 13 May 1915, p. 13.
5 *The Bioscope,* 12 September 1918, p. 27.
6 *Ibid.*
7 *Ibid.*

8 *Moving Picture World,* 29 November 1919, p. 36.

The Battle Cry of Peace (pages 30–38)

1 J. Stuart Blackton, "Silence Was Golden" (unpublished ms., 1938), courtesy of David Shepard.
2 *The Theatre,* December 1915, p. 115.
3 *Moving Picture World,* 25 September 1915, p. 2158.
4 *The New Republic,* 9 October 1915, p. 247.
5 *Vitagraph Bulletin,* February 1916, p. 28.
6 New York *Times,* 23 April 1916.
7 *Ibid.,* 11 May 1916, p. 10.
8 *Moving Picture World,* 9 September 1916, p. 1667.
9 *The Bioscope,* 30 December 1915, p. 1409.
10 *Exhibitors' Trade Review,* 28 April 1917.

The Chaplin Craze (pages 38–43)

1 *The Bioscope,* 4 April 1918, p. 15.
2 Brophy-Partridge, *The Long Trail* (London: Deutsch, 1965), p. 34. Song published as sheet music in 1916; words by Edward Stanning and Thurland Chataway.
3 BBC Radio 4, *The First 75 Years,* 22 December 1973.
4 William Dodgson Bowman, *Charlie Chaplin, His Life and Art* (New York: John Day, 1931), p. 65.
5 *The Bioscope,* 28 June 1917, p. 1263.
6 Raoul Sobel and David Francis, "The Genesis of a Clown," *Quartet,* 1977, p. 155.
7 *Pictures and Picturegoer,* 23 February 1918, p. 207.
8 *The Bioscope,* 4 April 1918.
9 London *Times,* 16 April 1918.
10 *The Bioscope,* 18 April 1917, p. 7.
11 *Kinematograph Weekly,* 20 April 1917, p. 61.
12 *The Bioscope,* 26 August 1915, p. 15; *Pictures and Picturegoer,* 17 January 1916, p. 241.
13 *The Bioscope,* 21 November 1918, p. 75.
14 Frances Taylor Patterson, *Cinema Craftsmanship* (New York: Harcourt Brace, 1920), p. 133.
15 Charles Chaplin, *My Autobiography* (London: Penguin, 1966), p. 218.
16 *Moving Picture World,* 8 March 1919, p. 1344.

Cinemas at the Front Line (pages 43–47)

1 *The Bioscope,* 7 September 1916, p. xv.
2 *Kinematograph Weekly,* 1 April 1915, p. 2.
3 *The Bioscope,* 14 March 1918, p. 95.
4 *Moving Picture World,* 12 April 1919, p. 228.
5 *Ibid.,* 5 January 1918, p. 84.
6 *Ibid.,* 22 September 1917, p. 1838.
7 *The Bioscope,* 27 September 1917, p. 9.

***Britain Prepared* (pages 47–55)**

1 *Retch,* 24 March/6 April, quoted in Third Report, Imperial War Museum, London.
2 Quoted in Third Report.
3 New York *Times,* 4 June 1916.
4 Letter from Sir Gilbert Parker to Charles Urban, 14 October 1915, in Urban files, Science Museum, London.
5 Third Report, p. 107.
6 London *Evening News,* 17 January 1918, p. 4.

The Front-Line Cameraman (pages 55–68)

1 *Moving Picture World,* 6 November 1915, p. 1114.
2 *Ibid.,* 11 November 1916, p. 857.
3 Letter to acting High Commissioner for Canada, 30 March 1917, Beaverbrook papers, House of Lords records office, London.
4 Letter from P. J. Smith to author.
5 Homer Croy, *How Motion Pictures Are Made* (New York: Harper Brothers, 1918), p. 259.
6 Bela Belazs, *Theory of the Film* (London: Dobson, 1952), p. 169.
7 Jay Leyda, *Films Beget Films* (London: Allen & Unwin, 1964), p. 36.

8 *Kinematograph Weekly,* 13 May 1915.
9 *The Bioscope,* 10 June 1915.
10 *The Star,* 25 August 1916, quoted in *Sight and Sound,* Winter 1937–1938, p. 183.
11 *Kinematograph Weekly,* 7 September 1916, p. 869.
12 *Evening Standard,* 16 August 1916, quoted in *Sight and Sound,* Winter 1937–1938, p. 183.
13 *Pictures and Picturegoer,* 28 October 1916.
14 Geoffrey Malins, *How I Filmed the War* (London: Herbert Jenkins, 1920).
15 Letter from Brigadier General Charteris, 20 February 1917, Beaverbrook papers, House of Lords records office, London.
16 B. R. Brookes-Carrington to author.

Pacifism (pages 69–78)

1 *John Bull,* 24 October 1914.
2 *Moving Picture World,* 9 October 1915, p. 238.
3 *The Bioscope,* 14 October 1915.
4 *Ibid.,* 28 December 1916.
5 *Ibid.,* 4 January 1917.
6 *Ibid.,* 1 March 1917, p. 953.
7 Irvin Willat to author.
8 *Moving Picture World,* 24 November 1917, p. 1185.
9 Terry Ramsaye, *A Million and One Nights* (London: Frank Cass, 1964), p. 728.
10 Richard Griffith, *Film Notes,* Museum of Modern Art, New York, 1969, p. 21.
11 *Moving Picture World,* 22 July 1916, p. 605.
12 *The Bioscope,* 8 February 1917, p. 544.
13 *Ibid.,* p. 545.

The Germans in America (pages 78–82)

1 William Leuchtenberg, *Perils of Prosperity* (Chicago: University of Chicago Press, 1958), p. 16.
2 *Motion Picture News,* 19 February 1916, p. 998.
3 *Moving Picture World,* 5 June 1915, p. 1612.
4 Colin Simpson, *Lusitania* (London: Longman's, 1972), p. 62.
5 New York *Times,* 3 February 1918, p. 6.
6 *Photoplay,* October 1921, p. 94.

Germany's Side of the War (pages 82–87)

1 Terry Ramsaye, *A Million and One Nights* (London: Frank Cass, 1964), p. 686.
2 *Motion Picture News,* 3 February 1917.
3 *Kinematograph* 400, 26 August 1914.
4 Quoted in Furhammer and Sakson, *Politics and Film* (London: Studio Vista, 1971), p. 11.

Mexico (pages 87–105)

1 David A. Weiss, *Coronet,* February 1952, p. 38.
2 Winifred Johnston, *Memo on the Movies* (New York: Co-operative Books, 1939), p. 19.
3 Raymond Fielding, *American Newsreel* (Norman: University of Oklahoma Press, 1972), p. 72.
4 New York *Times,* 7 January 1914.
5 *Ibid.,* 8 January 1914, p. 2.
6 *Ibid.*
7 Charles Rosher to author, quoted in Kevin Brownlow, *The Parade's Gone By . . .* (New York: Knopf, 1968), p. 226.
8 New York *Times,* 23 January 1914, p. 2.
9 *Ibid.*
10 *Cinema,* 28 May 1914, p. 19.
11 *Moving Picture World,* 1 August 1914, p. 718.
12 Rob Wagner, *Film Folk* (New York: Century, 1918), pp. 147–8.
13 Francis A. Collins, *The Cameraman* (New York: Century, 1916).
14 *Moving Picture World,* 18 July 1914, p. 440.
15 Ronald Atkin, *Revolution* (London: Granada, 1972), p. 218.
16 Letter from Victor Milner to author.

17 Raoul Walsh to author. For a full account of his Mexican trip (highly colored, I suspect!), see Raoul Walsh, *Each Man in His Time* (New York: Farrar, Straus & Giroux, 1974).
18 Atkin, p. 305.
19 *Moving Picture World,* 13 May 1916, p. 1159.
20 *Ibid.,* 15 April 1916, p. 511.
21 Merian C. Cooper to author.
22 Collins, p. 37.
23 *Photoplay,* March 1917, p. 43.
24 *Ibid.*
25 William Leuchtenberg, *Perils of Prosperity* (Chicago: University of Chicago Press, 1958), p. 28.

The United States Declares War (pages 107–112)

1 William Leuchtenberg, *Perils of Prosperity* (Chicago: University of Chicago Press, 1958), p. 43.
2 *Moving Picture World,* 28 April 1917, p. 646.
3 *Ibid.,* 10 November 1917, p. 845.
4 *Ibid.,* 4 May 1918, p. 673.
5 *Ibid.,* 11 May 1918, p. 831.
6 *Ibid.,* 1 June 1918, p. 1311.
7 Cecil B. DeMille, *Autobiography* (London: W. H. Allen, 1960), p. 168.
8 *Moving Picture World,* 4 November 1916, p. 684.

The Creel Committee (pages 112–119)

1 George Creel, *How We Advertised America* (New York: Harper, 1920), p. 119.
2 *Moving Picture World,* 26 January 1918, p. 484.
3 Terry Ramsaye, *A Million and One Nights* (London: Frank Cass, 1964), p. 611.
4 *Moving Picture World,* 26 January 1918, p. 483.
5 *Ibid.*
6 *Ibid.,* 2 March 1918, front advertisements.
7 *Kinematograph Weekly,* 5 December 1918, p. 56.
8 New York *Tribune,* 30 October 1917, quoted in W. A. Swanberg, *Citizen Hearst* (Montreal: Bantam, 1963), p. 367.
9 *Kinematograph Weekly,* 5 December 1918, p. 56.
10 *Independent,* 18 September 1926, p. 325.
11 William Leuchtenberg, *Perils of Prosperity* (Chicago: University of Chicago Press, 1958), p. 39.
12 *Ibid.,* p. 42.
13 *The Bioscope,* 1 August 1918, p. 19.
14 Winifred Johnston, *Memo on the Movies* (New York: Co-operative Books, 1939), p. 27.

The Signal Corps (pages 119–130)

1 Ernest B. Schoedsack to author.
2 Irvin Willat to author.
3 Ernest B. Schoedsack to author.
4 *Stars and Stripes,* 11 April 1919, p. 3.
5 *Moving Picture World,* 3 August 1918, p. 694.
6 George Marshall to author.

The Propaganda Films (pages 130–135)

1 William Brady to George Creel, CPI files, manuscript division, National Archives; courtesy of Russell Merritt.
2 *The Nation,* 11 April 1918, p. 459; courtesy of Russell Merritt.
3 *Moving Picture World,* 12 January 1918, p. 243.
4 *Ibid.,* 7 September 1918, p. 1455.

My Four Years in Germany (pages 135–141)

1 *Pictures and Picturegoer,* 11 May 1918, p. 477.
2 *Moving Picture World,* 30 March 1918, p. 1862.
3 *Ibid.,* 4 May 1918, front advertisements.
4 *Ibid.,* 15 June 1918, p. 1571.
5 Colin Simpson, *Lusitania* (London: Longman's, 1972), p. 64.
6 London *Times,* 20 August 1915.
7 New York *Times,* 16 August 1915, p. 3.

Erich von Stroheim (pages 141–144)

1 Arthur Miller and Fred Balshofer,

One Reel a Week (Berkeley: University of California Press, 1967), p. 132.
2 Anita Loos, *A Girl Like I* (New York: Viking, 1966), p. 125.
3 Thomas Quinn Curtiss, *Von Stroheim* (London: Angus and Robertson, 1971).
4 *Der Monat,* February 1967, p. 65.
5 Letter from Herman Weinberg to author.

Griffith (pages 144–155)
1 New York *Times,* 17 March 1917, p. 11.
2 *The Bioscope,* 5 April 1917.
3 Billy Bitzer, *Billy Bitzer: His Story* (New York: Farrar, Straus & Giroux, 1973), p. 186.
4 Windsor Castle Program Notes; courtesy of the David Robinson collection.
5 Bitzer, p. 188.
6 *Photoplay,* March 1918, p. 23.
7 Lillian Gish, *The Movies, Mr. Griffith and Me* (Englewood Cliffs, N.J.: Prentice Hall, 1969), p. 201.
8 Telegram from Albert Bamzhaf, to D. W. Griffith, 18 December 1917, Museum of Modern Art.
9 Gish, p. 201.
10 *Moving Picture World,* 20 April 1918, p. 369.
11 Telegram from D. W. Griffith to Mrs. Woodrow Wilson, 15 June 1918; courtesy of Russell Merritt.

The British National Film (pages 156–158)
1 *Pictures and Picturegoer,* 12–19 October 1918, p. 372.
2 Quoted in George Geltzer, *Films in Review,* March 1955, pp. 66, 120.
3 *Film Technician,* September–October 1951, p. 14.

Peace (pages 158–161)
1 William Leuchtenberg, *Perils of Prosperity* (Chicago: University of Chicago Press, 1958), p. 52.
2 Blanche Sweet to author.
3 Jack Spears, *Films in Review,* June–July 1966, p. 347.

Smiles Films (pages 161–163)
1 Rowland V. Lee to author.
2 Rowland V. Lee, *Adventures of a Movie Director* (unpublished autobiography), p. 138.

The Russian Intervention (pages 164–171)
1 L. William O'Connell to author.
2 Phil Tannura to author.

The Departure of the War Film (pages 171–182)
1 George Stevens to author.
2 Lillian Gish, *Dorothy and Lillian Gish* (New York: Macmillan, 1973), p. 82.
3 *Moving Picture World,* 9 August 1919, p. 853.
4 *Photoplay,* June 1920, p. 68.
5 Erich von Stroheim on tape recorded by John Huntley in London, 1953.
6 *Photoplay,* February 1922, p. 74.
7 *Ibid.,* May 1922, p. 117.
8 New York *Times,* 7 March 1921, p. 8.

Reparation (pages 182–184)
1 Quoted in John Drinkwater, *Life and Adventures of Carl Laemmle* (London: Heinemann, 1931), p. 203.
2 *The Spectator* 11 April 1925, p. 590.
3 Quoted in Eileen Bowser, *D. W. Griffith* (New York: Museum of Modern Art/Doubleday, 1965), p. 32.
4 Letter from Erich Pommer to D. W. Griffith, 17 April 1925; courtesy of Russell Merritt.
5 Opera House, McConnelsville, Ohio, quoted in *Picture Play,* April 1927, p. 21.

King Vidor and *The Big Parade* (pages 184–194)
1 King Vidor to author.
2 King Vidor, *A Tree Is a Tree* (London: Longman's, 1954), p. 9.
3 This and subsequent quotations, King Vidor to author.
4 *Photoplay,* September 1928, p. 41.
5 Sam Marx, *Mayer and Thalberg* (London: W. H. Allen, 1975).

Appendix from Eddie Mannix's records.
6 *The Outlook,* 6 January 1926, p. 18.

***What Price Glory?* (pages 194–198)**
1 *Classic,* December 1924, p. 87.
2 Victor McLaglen, *Express to Hollywood* (London: Jarrolds, 1934), p. 266.
3 *Pictures and Picturegoer,* March 1927, p. 27.
4 Raoul Walsh to author.
5 *Motion Picture Director,* August 1926, p. 17.
6 Raoul Walsh to author.
7 *Ibid.*

The Elite Guard (pages 198–203)
1 *Photoplay,* June 1928, p. 43.
2 *Ibid.*
3 Robert Florey and Ned Lambert to author.
4 Letter from Robert Florey to author.
5 December 1924, p. 109.
6 Letter from Alfred Santell to author.

***Wings* (pages 205–211)**
1 *Moving Picture World,* 23 November 1918, p. 803.
2 *Motion Picture Magazine,* September 1927, p. 24.
3 Lucien Hubbard to author.
4 *American Cinematographer,* December 1926, p. 8.
5 Lucien Hubbard to author.
6 *Motion Picture Magazine,* September 1927, p. 99.
7 *Moving Picture World,* 20 August 1927, p. 525.

***Barbed Wire* (pages 211–213)**
1 *Motion Picture Magazine,* September 1927, p. 95.
2 *Photoplay,* February 1928, p. 53.
3 This and subsequent quotation, Rowland V. Lee, unpublished autobiography.
4 *Ibid.,* p. 116.
5 Both quoted in *Photoplay,* October 1927, p. 58.

***All Quiet* (pages 214–219)**
1 This and subsequent quotations, Lewis Milestone to author.
2 Erich Maria Remarque, *All Quiet on the Western Front* (London: Putnam, 1929), p. 320.

THE WEST

The Die Is Cast (pages 224–235)
1 Henry Nash Smith, *Virgin Land* (New York: Knopf, 1950), p. 115.
2 William Coleman, *Players,* December 1971–January 1972, p. 80.
3 *Moving Picture World,* 14 March 1914, p. 1370.
4 *Ibid.,* 25 October 1913, p. 362.
5 *Ibid.,* p. 368.
6 *Ibid.*
7 Denver *Post,* 19 October 1913, p. 11.
8 *Moving Picture World,* 22 November 1913.
9 *Ibid.,* p. 851.
10 Denver *Post,* 21 October 1913, p. 2.
11 *Ibid.,* no date.
12 *Ibid.,* 21 October 1913, p. 2.
13 *Ibid.,* 29 October 1913.
14 *Ibid.,* p. 6.
15 *Moving Picture World,* 12 September 1914, p. 1500.
16 Denver *Post,* no date.

Migration West (pages 235–249)
1 *Moving Picture World,* 18 November 1916, p. 1030.
2 Allan Dwan to author.
3 King Vidor to author.
4 *Moving Picture World,* 23 December 1916, p. 1845.
5 *Pictures and Picturegoer,* 7–14 July 1917, p. 78.
6 *Moving Picture World,* 11 December 1915, p. 2019.
7 *Motion Picture Magazine,* October 1926, p. 5.

8 *Moving Picture World,* 15 March 1913, p. 1133.
9 Sam Marx to author.

Broncho Billy Anderson (pages 249–253)

1 *Motion Picture Story Magazine,* March 1916, p. 101.
2 Broncho Billy Anderson, interviewed on film in 1957 by William K. Everson; courtesy of Paul Killiam.
3 Denver *Post,* 4 December 1909, quoted in George Pratt, *Spellbound in Darkness* (Greenwich, Connecticut: New York Graphic Society, 1973), p. 127.
4 *Moving Picture World,* 10 July 1915, p. 220.
5 *Film Culture,* Spring 1972, pp. 232–5.
6 1957 interview by Everson.
7 *Photoplay,* January 1926, p. 40.
8 Letter from Robert Florey to author.

Bison 101 and Thomas Ince (pages 253–262)

1 *Moving Picture World,* 10 March 1917, p. 1506.
2 Arthur Miller and Fred Balshofer, *One Reel a Week* (Berkeley: University of California Press 1967), p. 80.
3 *Moving Picture World,* 27 January 1912, p. 298.
4 *Ibid.,* 10 July 1915, p. 225.
5 *Film Fancies,* 24 February 1912.
6 *Ibid.*
7 Miller and Balshofer, p. 85.
8 *Moving Picture World,* 15 June 1912, p. 1014.
9 George J. Mitchell, *Films in Review,* October 1960, p. 470.
10 Bessie Love, *From Hollywood with Love* (London: Elm Tree Books, 1977), p. 52.
11 *Photoplay,* July 1928, p. 36.
12 Grant Whytock to author.
13 Enid Markey to author.
14 *Ibid.*
15 *Exhibitors' Herald,* 20 December 1924, p. 31.
16 *Ibid.*
17 *Photoplay,* October 1926, p. 54.
18 *Ibid.,* September 1928, p. 105.

William S. Hart (pages 263–274)

1 William K. Everson and George Fenin, *The Western* (New York: Orion, 1962), p. 67.
2 William S. Hart, *My Life East and West* (Boston: Houghton Mifflin, 1929).
3 Leona Kelly to author.
4 *Motion Picture Magazine,* September 1922, p. 14.
5 Hart, p. 14.
6 Quoted in Anthony Slide, *Films in Review,* June–July 1974, p. 383.
7 *Photoplay,* September 1917, p. 81.
8 *Ibid.,* p. 198.
9 *Ibid.,* p. 200.
10 *Ibid.*
11 *Moving Picture World,* 5 December 1914, p. 1390.
12 Hart, p. 225.
13 *Motion Picture Magazine,* November 1916.
14 *Ibid.,* April 1917.
15 *Pictures and Picturegoer,* 4 September 1920, p. 295.
16 *Ibid.,* February 1922, p. 16.
17 William S. Hart, *A Lighter of Flames* (New York: Thomas Crowell, 1923).
18 Washington *Post and Times Herald,* 24 June 1957, quoted in *Cinema Collector,* no. 2, 1957.
19 William S. Hart, *Told Under a White Oak Tree* (Boston: Houghton Mifflin, 1922), p, 24.
20 Richard Griffith, *Film Notes,* Museum of Modern Art, New York, 1969, p. 34.
21 James Card, *Image,* March 1956, p. 60.
22 *Photoplay,* December 1925, p. 112.
23 *Ibid.*

Lawmen and Outlaws (pages 275–280)

1 Zoe Tilghman, *Marshal of the Last Frontier* (Glendale, Calif.: Arthur H. Clark Company, 1949), p. 316; courtesy of Eldon K. Everett.
2 Glenn Shirley, *Henry Starr—Last of the Real Badmen* (New York:

McKay, 1965), p. 187; courtesy of Eldon K. Everett.

3 Tilghman, p. 319.

4 Letter from William Tilghman, 1 September 1915, quoted in Tilghman, p. 321.

5 Colonel Tim McCoy to author.

6 *Moving Picture World,* 5 April 1923, p. 483.

7 Jesse Lasky, Jr., to author.

8 *Moving Picture World,* 17 October 1914, p. 411.

9 *Motion Picture Magazine,* December 1925, p. 72.

10 Allan Dwan to author.

Al Jennings (pages 281–287)

1 For a lengthy account of the making of this film, see Eldon K. Everett, "Son of Gower Gulch," *Classic Film Collector,* no. 44, Fall 1974, p. 26.

2 *Moving Picture World,* 28 November 1914, p. 1235.

3 Kemp Niver, *The First Twenty Years* (Los Angeles: Locare Research Group, 1968), p. 134.

4 Allan Dwan to author.

5 *Pictures and Picturegoer,* February 1922, p. 59.

6 *Photoplay,* May 1919, p. 61.

7 *Ibid.*

8 Raymond Moley, *Will Hays* (Indianapolis: Bobbs-Merrill, 1945), p. 27.

Emmett Dalton (pages 287–289)

1 *Moving Picture World,* 20 July 1912, p. 277.

2 *Ibid.,* 7 December 1918, p. 1107.

3 *Ibid.,* 14 November 1914, p. 940.

The Cowboy in Hollywood (pages 290–300)

1 This and subsequent quotations, Al Hoxie to author.

2 Bob Reeves, *The Truth About the Movies* (Hollywood Publishers, 1924), p. 255.

3 Harry Carr, *Motion Picture Classic,* March 1926, p. 24.

4 Colonel Tim McCoy at Sun Valley Western Conference, 1976; courtesy of Jim Belson.

5 *Moving Picture World,* 20 March 1915, p. 1750.

6 Colonel Tim McCoy at Sun Valley Western Conference.

Tom Mix (pages 300–312)

1 Yakima Canutt to author.

2 *Photoplay,* February 1925, p. 114.

3 See Ronald Atkins, *Revolution* (London: Granada, 1972), p. 82.

4 *Those Enduring Matinee Idols,* October–November 1970, p. 85.

5 Paul Mix, *The Life and Legend of Tom Mix* (New York: A. S. Barnes, 1972).

6 Ellsworth Collings, *101 Ranch* (Norman: University of Oklahoma Press, 1938), p. 218.

7 Jack Spears, *Films in Review,* January 1970, p. 64.

8 Harvey Parry to author.

9 Allan Dwan to author.

10 *Photoplay,* July 1928, p. 112.

11 Lefty Hough to author.

Roundup (pages 314–327)

1 *Moving Picture World,* 17 June 1916, p. 2052.

2 *Photoplay,* April 1931, p. 110, Diana Cary, *Hollywood Posse* (Boston: Houghton Mifflin, 1975, p. 129), suggests it was a knife fight that killed Acord.

3 *Films in Review,* January 1968, p. 29.

4 *Photoplay,* March 1926, p. 40.

5 *Ibid.*

6 *Motion Picture Magazine,* September 1924, p. 33.

7 *Ibid.,* p. 82.

8 *Pictures and Picturegoer,* April 1922, p. 25.

9 Mrs. Buck Jones to author.

10 *Ibid.*

11 National Archives records, courtesy of Joseph Rosa.

12 Mrs. Buck Jones to author.

13 Letter from Winfield Sheehan to Buck Jones in collection of Mrs. Buck Jones.

14 Mrs. Buck Jones to author.
15 John Wayne to author, for Thames Television's *Hollywood* series.
16 Colonel Tim McCoy to author.

The American Indian (pages 327–338)

1 Ralph and Natasha Friar, *The Only Good Indian . . . The Hollywood Gospel* (New York: Drama Book Specialists, 1972).
2 *Ibid.*, p. 2.
3 New York *Times,* 3 June 1914, p. 12.
4 *Moving Picture World,* 12 July 1913, p. 232.
5 *Ibid.*, 15 August 1911, p. 271.
6 *Ibid.*, 4 June 1910, p. 942.
7 *Ibid.*, 6 January 1912, p. 21.
8 *Ibid.*, 27 April 1912, p. 320.
9 *Ibid.*, 10 August 1912, p. 520.
10 Allan Dwan to author.
11 *Moving Picture World,* 5 October 1912, p. 40.
12 *Ibid.*, 25 December 1915, p. 2373.
13 *Ibid.*, 8 May 1920, p. 861.
14 *Ibid.*, 6 October 1917, p. 81.

Edward S. Curtis (pages 338–344)

1 From the sound track of *The Shadow Catcher—Edward S. Curtis and the North American Indian,* 90-minute documentary produced and directed by Teri C. McLuhan (1974).
2 *Ibid.*
3 Teri C. McLuhan to author.
4 Sound track of *The Shadow Catcher.*
5 *Ibid.*
6 *Ibid.*
7 *Moving Picture World,* 19 December 1914, p. 1685.
8 Teri C. McLuhan to author.

***The Vanishing American* (pages 344–348)**

1 Quoted in Paramount publicity release for *The Vanishing American.*
2 *Picture Play,* January 1926, p. 91.
3 Ralph and Natasha Friar, *The Only Good Indian . . . The Hollywood Gospel* (New York: Drama Book Specialists, 1972), p. 133.
4 *Photoplay,* December 1925, p. 47.
5 *Moving Picture World,* 24 October 1925, p. 652.
6 *Picture Play,* February 1926, p. 143.
7 Iron Eyes Cody to author.

***Redskin* (pages 348–350)**

1 Henry Hathaway to author.

***The Devil Horse* (pages 350–354)**

1 George Stevens to author.
2 Hal Roach to author.
3 *Ibid.*
4 *Moving Picture World,* 25 September 1926, p. 214.

Yakima Canutt (pages 354–358)

1 *Moving Picture World,* 10 May 1924, p. 133, with additional dates from Yakima Canutt.
2 This and subsequent quotations, Yakima Canutt to author.

***Sundown* (pages 358–365)**

1 *Photoplay,* September 1924, p. 99.
2 Theodore Roosevelt, *An Autobiography* (New York: Macmillan, 1913), p. 104.
3 L. William O'Connell to author.
4 *Moving Picture World,* 25 October 1924, p. 717.
5 *Photoplay,* April 1925, p. 12.

***The Wind* (pages 365–367)**

1 *Motion Picture Magazine,* October 1927, p. 32.

***The Covered Wagon* (pages 368–381)**

1 New York *Times,* 17 March 1923.
2 *Film Notes,* Museum of Modern Art, New York, 1969, p. 49.
3 Jesse Lasky and Don Weldon, *I Blow My Own Horn* (London: Gollancz, 1957), p. 160.
4 *Motion Picture Classic,* September 1925, p. 26.
5 *Ibid.*, October 1924, p. 77.
6 This and subsequent quotations, Dorothy Arzner to author.
7 This and subsequent quotations, Karl Brown to author.
8 Lois Wilson to author.
9 *Picture Play,* November 1924, p. 28.
10 *Motion Picture Classic,* August 1924, p. 74; *Motion Picture Magazine,* March 1925, p. 113.

11 A. G. Shaw, *Motion Picture Magazine,* July 1925, p. 82.
12 Colonel Tim McCoy to author.
13 *Ibid.*
14 Quoted in *Covered Wagon* program, no date.

North of 36 (pages 381–386)

1 *American Cinematographer,* January 1925, p. 5.
2 Lois Wilson to author.
3 Irvin Willat to author.
4 *Picture Play,* March 1925, p. 58.
5 *Photoplay,* February 1925, p. 54.

The Iron Horse (pages 386–396)

1 George J. Mitchell, "Ford on Ford," *Films in Review,* June–July 1964, p. 328.
2 *Ibid.*
3 This and subsequent quotations, Lefty Hough to author.
4 *American Cinematographer,* March 1925, p. 5.
5 Letter from Harold Schuster to author.
6 Mitchell, p. 328.
7 Lefty Hough to author.
8 Mitchell, p. 328.
9 Harold Schuster to author.
10 Edward Sutherland, unpublished autobiography, transcribed by Oral History Research Office, Columbia University.
11 Martin Dickstein, *The Brooklyn Eagle,* quoted in *Photoplay,* November 1924, p. 8.

The Big Trail (page 399)

1 *Hollywood Filmograph,* 26 April 1930, p. 21.
2 *Ibid.*
3 John Wayne to author, for Thames Television's *Hollywood* series.

THE WILDERNESS

The Film of Fact (pages 403–418)

1 *Photoplay,* April 1930, p. 100.
2 *Ibid.,* March 1930, p. 101.
3 *Moving Picture World,* 22 March 1924, p. 312.
4 *Ibid.,* 29 May 1909, p. 712.
5 *Ibid.,* 18 December 1909, p. 872.
6 *Ibid.,* 29 May 1909, p. 712.
7 *Ibid.,* 14 May 1910, p. 793.
8 *Ibid.,* 30 April 1910, p. 682.
9 *Ibid.,* 16 December 1911, p. 890.
10 Leonard Donaldson, *The Cinematograph and Natural Science* (London: Ganes Ltd., 1912).
11 *Moving Picture World,* 29 May 1920, p. 122.
12 Lowell Thomas, *Sir Hubert Wilkins* (London: Arthur Barker, 1961).
13 *Moving Picture World,* 27 May 1916, p. 1499.
14 This and subsequent quotations, letter from Ernest Palmer to author.
15 *Motion Picture Magazine,* February 1929, p. 28.

Burton Holmes (pages 418–420)

1 *Moving Picture World,* 22 August 1908, p. 136.
2 *Motion Picture Magazine,* July 1920, p. 46.
3 *American Cinematographer,* April 1948, p. 124.
4 *Ibid.,* p. 126.
5 *Ibid.*
6 *Ibid.,* p. 124.
7 Captain Noel to author.

The Kolb Brothers (pages 421–425)

1 Ellsworth Kolb, *Through the Grand Canyon from Wyoming to Mexico* (New York: Macmillan, 1914, reprinted 1969), p. 147.
2 *Ibid.,* p. 184.
3 *Ibid.,* p. 232.
4 *Ibid.,* p. 234.

Herbert Ponting (pages 425–434)

1 Herbert Ponting, *The Great White South* (London: Duckworth, 1921), quotation from introduction by Lady Scott, p. ix.
2 *Ibid.,* p. 1.
3 H. J. P. Arnold, *Photographer of the World* (London: Hutchinson, 1969), p. 36.
4 Ponting, p. 27.

5 *Ibid.*, pp. 40–41.
6 Arnold, p. 52.
7 Ponting, p. 55.
8 *Ibid.*, p. 64.
9 *Ibid.*, p. 65.
10 *Ibid.*
11 *Ibid.*, p. 171
12 *Ibid.*, p. 247.
13 *Ibid.*, p. xiii.
14 *Ibid.*, p. 293.
15 *Ibid.*, p. 298.
16 Arnold, p. 108.
17 Ponting, p. 298.

Cherry Kearton (pages 434–441)

1 Cherry Kearton, *Wild Life Across the World* (London: Hodder & Stoughton, undated, c. 1913), foreword by Richard Kearton, p. ix.
2 *Ibid.*, quoted from Foreword.
3 *Ibid.*, p. 126.
4 *Ibid.*, p. 127.
5 *Ibid.*, p. 115.
6 *Ibid.*, p. 127.
7 Cherry Kearton, *Photographing Wild Life Across the World* (London: Arrowsmith, undated, c. 1924), p. 213.
8 *Wild Life Across the World,* p. 158.
9 *Ibid.*, p. 138.
10 *Ibid.*, p. 273.
11 *Ibid.*, p. 242.
12 *Photographing Wild Life Across the World,* p. 13.
13 *Wild Life Across the World,* p. 244.
14 *Ibid.*, p. 246.
15 *Moving Picture World,* 25 February 1911, p. 404.
16 *Wild Life Across the World,* pp. 191–2.
17 *Photographing Wild Life Across the World,* pp. 170–1.
18 *Moving Picture World,* 31 May 1913, p. 884.
19 *Photographing Wild Life Across the World,* p. 16.

Lowell Thomas (pages 441–451)

1 Norman Bowen, ed., *The Stranger Everyone Knows* (New York: Doubleday, 1968), p. 6.
2 Lowell Thomas to author.
3 This and preceding quotation, Lowell Thomas to author.
4 Lowell Thomas, *With Lawrence in Arabia* (New York: Century, 1924), p. 369.
5 Lowell Thomas to author.
6 Thomas, p. 348.
7 Letter from T. E. Lawrence to his mother, quoted in Brian Gardner, *Allenby* (London: Cassell, 1965), p. 206.
8 Lowell Thomas to author.
9 *Ibid.*
10 Letter from T. E. Lawrence to Rex Ingram; courtesy of Mrs. Alice Terry Ingram.

Captain Noel (pages 452–464)

1 Captain J. B. L. Noel, *Through Tibet to Everest* (London: Edward Arnold, 1927).
2 *Yesterday's Witness* (B.B.C. program), 8 June 1974.
3 Unless otherwise noted, quotations are taken from the author's interview with Captain Noel.
4 Noel, p. 77.
5 *Ibid.*, p. 208.
6 *Ibid.*, p. 211.
7 *Ibid.*, p. 212.
8 *Ibid.*, p. 263.
9 *Ibid.*, p. 213.
10 *Kinematograph Weekly,* 18 December 1924, p. 45.
11 *The Bioscope,* 18 December 1924, p. 35.

Mr. and Mrs. Martin Johnson (pages 464–471)

1 Martin Johnson, *Lion* (New York: G. P. Putnam's Sons, 1929), p. 71.
2 Osa Johnson, *I Married Adventure* (New York: Halcyon House, 1940).
3 *Ibid.*, p. 132.
4 *Ibid.*, p. 135.
5 *Moving Picture World,* 28 February 1920, p. 1419.
6 W. S. Van Dyke, *Horning into Africa* (Los Angeles: California Graphic Press, 1930), p. 182.
7 Martin Johnson, *Safari* (New York: G. P. Putnam's Sons, 1928), p. 204.

8 *Ibid.*, p. 77.
9 *Ibid.*, p. 126.
10 *Ibid.*, p. 193.
11 *Lion*, p. 36.
12 *Ibid.*, p. 38.

Robert Flaherty (pages 471–485)

1 BBC Talks, quoted in Arthur Calder-Marshall, *The Innocent Eye* (London: W. H. Allen, 1963), p. 55.
2 *Moving Picture World*, 17 April 1915, p. 426.
3 Robert Flaherty, *My Eskimo Friends* (London: Heinemann, 1924), p. 123.
4 *Ibid.*, p. 125.
5 *Ibid.*, p. 43.
6 Calder-Marshall, p. 67.
7 *Moving Picture World*, 17 April 1915, p. 426.
8 *Photoplay*, March 1928, p. 125.
9 *World's Work*, September 1922, quoted in Harry Geduld, ed., *Film Makers on Film-making* (Bloomington: Indiana University Press, 1967), p. 57.
10 Quoted in Richard Griffith, *The World of Robert Flaherty* (New York: Duell Sloane Pearce, 1953), p. 36.
11 Letter from David Shepard to author.
12 Calder-Marshall, p. 85.
13 Flaherty papers, quoted in Erik Barnouw, *Documentary* (New York: Oxford University Press, 1974), p. 45.
14 Flaherty, pp. 135–6.
15 *Photoplay*, May 1928, p. 126.
16 George Folsey to author.
17 "Robert Flaherty Talking," in Roger Manvell, ed., *Cinema* (London: Penguin, 1950), pp. 13–15.
18 "Art Advantages of the European Scene," *Theatre Magazine*, 1927, p. 24.
19 Calder-Marshall, p. 96.
20 *National Board of Review Magazine*, April 1927, quoted in George Pratt, *Spellbound in Darkness* (Greenwich, Connecticut: New York Graphic Society, 1973), p. 344.
21 *Ibid.*
22 *Asia* magazine, quoted in Griffith p. 69.
23 Calder-Marshall, p. 116.
24 New York *Sun*, 25 September 1926, quoted in Erik Barnouw, *Film Culture*, Spring 1972, pp. 164–75.
25 *Motion Picture Classic*, October 1927, p. 72.
26 David Shepard to author.

***Frozen Justice* (pages 485–490)**

1 All quotations in this chapter are from Charles Clarke's unpublished diary; courtesy of Charles Clarke.

***White Shadows in the South Seas* (pages 490–499)**

1 David O. Selznick to author.
2 Grant Whytock to author.
3 *Ibid.*
4 Quoted in Arthur Calder-Marshall, *The Innocent Eye* (London: W. H. Allen, 1963), p. 123.
5 For a full account of the making of *Tabu*, see Lotte Eisner's *Murnau* (London: Secker & Warburg, 1973).
6 Grant Whytock to author
7 *Motion Picture Magazine*, August 1928, p. 82.
8 *Ibid.*
9 Grant Whytock to author.
10 *Ibid.*
11 Robert Cannom, *Van Dyke and the Mythical City, Hollywood* (Culver City: Murray and Gee, 1948), p. 171.
12 Grant Whytock to author.
13 Bosley Crowther, *The Lion's Share* (New York: Dutton, 1957), p. 146.
14 Cannom, p. 176.

***Stark Love* (pages 499–507)**

1 This and subsequent quotations, Karl Brown to author.
2 *Photoplay*, May 1927, p. 52.
3 *Motion Picture Classic*, June 1927, p. 62.
4 Stella Court Treatt, *Sudan Sand* (London: Harrap, 1930), p. 129.

***Stampede* (pages 507–515)**

1 Stella Court Treatt, *Cape to Cairo* (London: Harrap, 1927).

2 This and subsequent quotations, letter from Errol Hinds to author.
3 Stella Court Treatt, *Sudan Sand* (London: Harrap, 1930), p. 116.

Grass (pages 515–529)

1 *Moving Picture World,* 6 March 1915, p. 1462.
2 Interviews with Merian Cooper and Ernest Schoedsack as well as tapes and letters. For greater detail on the extraordinary adventures of these men, see Orville Goldner and George E. Turner, *The Making of King Kong* (New York: A. S. Barnes, 1975).
3 Edward A. Salisbury and Merian C. Cooper, *The Sea Gipsy* (New York: G. P. Putnam's Sons, 1924).
4 Quoted in Merian C. Cooper, *Grass* (New York: G. P. Putnam's Sons, 1925), p. 151.
5 *Ibid.*, p. 211.
6 *Ibid.*, p. 219.
7 *Ibid.*, pp. 225–33.
8 *Ibid.*, p. 239.
9 *Ibid.*, p. 304.
10 *Ibid.*, p. 317.
11 *Ibid.*, p. 318.

Chang (pages 529–541)

1 Interviews conducted with Merian Cooper and Ernest Schoedsack, as well as tapes and letters.
2 *Asia* magazine, June 1927, p. 507.
3 *Ibid.*, p. 508.
4 *Ibid.*, p. 510.
5 *Ibid.*
6 Jesse Lasky and Don Weldon, *I Blow My Own Horn* (London: Gollancz, 1957), p. 189.
7 Quoted in Rudy Behlmer, "Merian C. Cooper," *Films in Review,* January 1966, p. 22.
8 For an account of the filming of *The Four Feathers,* see A. J. Siggins, *Shooting with Rifle and Camera* (London: Wright & Brown, 1929), and Orville Goldner and George E. Turner, *The Making of King Kong* (New York: A. S. Barnes, 1975).

The Viking (pages 541–545)

1 From the soundtrack of the prologue to *The Viking.*
2 Merian Cooper in letter to author.

The Silent Enemy (pages 545–560)

1 Letter from W. Douglas Burden to author.
2 Toronto *Star,* 17 May 1930.
3 Letter from Warren Iliff to Douglas Burden.
4 From the program of *The Silent Enemy,* p. 2.
5 This and subsequent quotations, Douglas Burden to author.
6 Iron Eyes Cody to author.
7 Douglas Burden, *Look to the Wilderness* (Boston: Little, Brown, 1956).
8 From the program of *The Silent Enemy,* p. 5.
9 Letter from William Chanler to author.
10 Douglas Burden to author.

Trader Horn (pages 560–566)

1 A. A. Horn, *The Life and Works of Alfred Aloysius Horn* (London: Jonathan Cape, 1927).
2 W. S. Van Dyke, *Horning into Africa* (Los Angeles: California Graphic Press, 1930).
3 This and subsequent quotations, Olive Carey to author.
4 *Photoplay,* April 1931, p. 30.

INDEX

A NOTE ON THE TYPE

The text of this book was set in Intertype Garamond, a modern rendering of the type first cut by Claude Garamond (1510–1561). Garamond was a pupil of Geoffroy Tory and is believed to have based his letters on the Venetian models, although he introduced a number of important differences, and it is to him we owe the letter we know as old-style.

Composed by American Book–Statford Press, Inc., Brattleboro, Vermont.
Printed by Halliday Lithograph Corporation, West Hanover, Massachusetts.
Bound by The Book Press, Brattleboro, Vermont.

Typography and binding design by Holly McNeely